CROYDON AND THE GREAT WAR

TOWN HALL, CROYDON
From the official Photograph, 1896, in commemoration of its opening by the Prince of Wales (King Edward VII.)

CROYDON AND THE GREAT WAR

The Official History of the War Work of the Borough
and its Citizens from 1914 to 1919

TOGETHER WITH

THE CROYDON ROLL OF HONOUR

Edited by
ALD. H. KEATLEY MOORE,
B.A., B.MUS., J.P.
Honorary Freeman of the Borough ; Mayor from 1906 to 1908

Assisted by
W. C. BERWICK SAYERS,
F.L.A. (Hons.)
Chief Librarian ; Author of "Samuel Coleridge-Taylor, Musician," etc.

WITH ILLUSTRATIONS AND PORTRAITS

Prepared under the direction
and at the cost of the Corporation
of Croydon and published at the
Central Public Library,
Town Hall, Croydon.

1920

CONTENTS.

Part One—INTRODUCTORY

		Page
Chapter I.	Introduction	13
,, II.	The Course of Events in Croydon during the War	18
,, III.	Croydon County Borough Council, 1914 to 1919	47

Part Two—THE MILITARY RECORD

Chapter I.	Before the Great War	57
,, II.	The Queen's	59
,, III.	The Fourth Queen's	61
,, IV.	The 1/4th Queen's	65
,, V.	The 2/4th Queen's	70
,, VI.	The 3/4th Queen's	79
,, VII.	The 4/4th Queen's	88
,, VIII.	The Fourth Reserve Queen's	90
,, IX.	The 69th Provisional Battalion (The 19th Queen's)	91
,, X.	The Surrey (Queen Mary's Regiment) Yeomanry (" C " Squadron)	93
,, XI.	The South Eastern Mounted Brigade ; Transport and Supply Column, A.S.C.	98
,, XII.	The National Reserve	100
,, XIII.	The Volunteers	102
,, XIV.	The Boy Scouts	116

Part Three—SEMI-MILITARY SERVICES

Chapter I.	Recruiting	121
,, II.	The Military Tribunals	125
,, III.	Munitions Work, and War Work of the Electricity Committee	133

Part Four—THE CIVILIAN FORCES

Chapter I.	The Croydon Sub-Division of the " W " Division of the Metropolitan Special Constabulary	137
,, II.	The Thornton Heath and South Norwood Sub-Division of the M.S.C.	150
,, III.	The Women Patrols	156
,, IV.	The Fire Brigade	157

Part Five—HOSPITAL, AID & RELIEF SERVICES

			Page
Chapter	I.	Medical and Hospital Services	163
,,	II.	Croydon War Hospital Supplies Depot	173
,,	III.	Croydon War Supplies Clearing House	175
,,	IV.	Mayor's Committee	180
,,	V.	War Pensions Committee	184
,,	VI.	Mayoress's Needlework Committee	191
,,	VII.	Mayoress's War Fund Committee	194
,,	VIII.	Mayoress's Flag Day Committee	195
,,	IX.	Belgian Refugees Fund	197
,,	X.	Soldiers' and Sailors' Recreation Rooms	200
,,	XI.	Croydon Local Central War Savings Committee	204
,,	XII.	Croydon District Association of Voluntary Organizations	208

Part Six—FOOD AND FUEL

Chapter	I.	The Allotments Movement	213
,,	II.	National Kitchens	217
,,	III.	The Control of Food	219
,,	IV.	Women's Land Army	227
,,	V.	The Control of Fuel and Light	228

Part Seven—VICTORY

Chapter	I.	Armistice Day	235
,,	II.	Peace Day	237

THE CROYDON ROLL OF HONOUR

The Glorious Dead	247
Military Honours	424
Returned Prisoners-of-War	434

LIST OF ILLUSTRATIONS.

(Excluding the Roll of Honour.)

Page

1.—Town Hall, Croydon; from the official photograph, 1896, in commemoration of its opening by the Prince of Wales (King Edward VII). . . . . . . *Frontispiece*
2.—Alderman FRANK DENNING, J.P., First War-Mayor (Nov., 1913, to Feb., 1916) 20
3.—Mrs. DENNING (Mayoress, Nov., 1913 to Feb., 1916) . 21
4.—Ruined Houses in Beech House Road; Zeppelin Air-raid (13th Oct., 1915) 28
5.—Ruined Houses in Edridge Road; Zeppelin Air-raid (13th Oct., 1915) 29
6.—Alderman HOWARD HOULDER, D.L., J.P., Second War-Mayor (Feb., 1916 to Nov., 1919); Hon. Freeman of the Borough, 1920 32
7.—Mrs. HOWARD HOULDER (Mayoress, Feb., 1916 to Nov., 1919); Hon. Freeman of the Borough, 1920 . . . 33
8.—Searchlights at Croydon; Winter of 1917-18 . . . 34
9.—Firing Maroons as warning for Air-raid, at Croydon Police Station 35
10.—Councillor CHARLES HEATH CLARK, J.P., " Peace " Mayor (from Nov., 1919) 46
11.—Mrs. HEATH CLARK (Mayoress from Nov., 1919) . . 47
12.—JOHN MONTAGUE NEWNHAM, O.B.E., D.L., LL.D., B.A., Town Clerk from Sept., 1913; Hon. Lt.-Colonel, 1 Vol. Bat., The Queen's 48
13.—Councillor PERCIVAL GEORGE ALLEN COSEDGE, East Surrey Regiment (died on active service in France, 16th Dec., 1914) 52
14.—Councillor Captain JOHN CYRIL CROWLEY, M.A., 1/4th Queen's (killed in action in Mesopotamia, 11th Sept., 1916) 53
15.—(1) R. VEITCH CLARK, M.A., M.B., Ch.B., B.Sc., D.P.H., Medical Officer of Health; (2) WM. GUNNER, Borough Treasurer; (3) J. H. MCCALL, F.S.A.A., Borough Accountant; (4) JAMES SMYTH, Clerk to the Education Committee 54
16.—(1) EDWARD F. MORGAN, Borough Road Surveyor; (2) THOS. BOYCE GOODYER, O.B.E., A.I.E.E., Tramways Manager; (3) SAMUEL JACOBS, Assistant-Town Clerk; (4) ALBERT C. GOWER, Chief Clerk, Town Clerk's Department. . 55
17.—Addiscombe College: Main Front (Hon. East India Company, 1809-1861) 58
18.—Addiscombe College: North Front (Hon. East India Company, 1809-1861) 59

	Page
19.—Lord ROBERTS presenting the Colours to the Fourth Queen's on Duppas Hill	60
20.—Alderman Sir FREDERICK THOMAS EDRIDGE, D.L., J.P., Hon. Colonel, Fourth Queen's ; Mayor, 1890—92, 1894—96, 1902 ; Hon. Freeman of the Borough	61
21.—Mobilisation of the Fourth Queen's, Croydon Barracks, 5th August, 1914	64
22.—Mobilisation of the Fourth Queen's, London Road, Croydon, 5th August, 1914	65
23.—Colonel NORMAN EDWARD CUTLER, 1/4th Queen's . .	68
24.—Lt.-Colonel S. D. ROPER, 1/4th Queen's and 2/4th Queen's .	69
25.—Lt.-Colonel HAROLD R. ATKINS, 1/4th Queen's . .	76
26.—Welcome Home to the 1/4th Queen's (15th Nov., 1919) .	77
27.—Lt.-Colonel UTTEN LAMONT HOOKE, 3/4th Queen's (*fell* in France, 21st June, 1917)	80
28.—Major (Acting Lt.-Colonel) KENNETH ALLAN OSWALD, D.S.O., 3/4th Queen's	81
29.—Inspection of the 4/4th Queen's at Crowborough by Col. Sir FREDERICK T. EDRIDGE, D.L., accompanied by the Mayor (Ald. HOULDER) and the Town Clerk . . .	82
30.—The 4/4th Queen's at Crowborough ; group of Officers ; left to right—Captain CHARD, the Town Clerk, the Mayor, Col. Sir FREDERICK EDRIDGE, Group-Commander Col. GLOSTER, and Major KENNETH WILLIAM ELDER, C.O.	83
31.—Major STANLEY R. DOCKING, T.D., C.O. Croydon Column S.E. Mounted Brigade, Transport and Supply Column A.S.C.	94
32.—Major JOHN EDWARD FOX, T.D., J.P. (Alderman) ; Mayor, Nov., 1908 to Nov., 1910 ; First C.O. of Croydon Column S.E. Mounted Brigade, Transport and Supply Column, A.S.C.	95
33.—Croydon National Reservists being inspected at Guildford by F.M. Lord ROBERTS (May, 1911)	100
34.—Major JAMES PETRIE, O.B.E., C.O. 1st Volunteer Battalion, The Queen's	101
35.—Bombing practice : 1st Volunteer Battalion, The Queen's .	108
36.—Machine Gun Team : 1st Volunteer Battalion, The Queen's	109
37.—Councillor Colonel JOHN FRANKLIN WORLLEDGE, District Commissioner, Croydon Boy Scouts	118
38.—Captain DAVID BARRIE, H.L.I., Recruiting Officer for Croydon	119
39.—Recruiting Procession (Derby Scheme), Croydon, 2nd October, 1915	122
40.—Colonel FRANK WILLIAM CHATTERTON, C.I.E., J.P., Military Representative for Croydon Military Tribunals . .	123
41.—ALEX. C. CRAMB, M.I.E.E., M.I.Mech.E., Borough Electrical Engineer	134
42.—Assistant Commander HENRY CRAVEN SWAINE, in command of Croydon Special Constabulary	135
43.—(1) Water Tower, Croydon, Observation-Post of Special Constabulary ; (2) Altazimuth	138

	Page
44.—Miss RHODA BRODIE, M.B.E., Patrol Leader, Croydon Women-Patrols .	139
45.—Councillor THOMAS W. WOOD ROBERTS, Chairman, Fire Brigade Sub-Committee (Auxiliary Fireman, Croydon and London ; Special Constable)	160
46.—JOHN WILLIAM DANE, Chief Officer, Croydon Fire Brigade.	160
47. Colonel H. E. DEANE, R.A.M.C., Officer Commanding, Croydon War Hospitals	160
48.—Lady EDRIDGE, Hon. Freeman of the Borough, 1920 .	161
49.—Exterior of "The Crescent" War Hospital (Borough Secondary Schools) .	164
50.—One of the wards of "The Crescent" War Hospital (Borough Secondary Schools) .	165
51.—Coffer of 17th century pattern, made for the War Supplies Clearing House Red Cross Auction by R. F. COLAM, K.C., Recorder of Croydon .	172
52.—Councillor FRANCIS ALLEN, M.B.E., J.P., War Pensions Committee .	173
53.—Mrs. REDFERN, who received from the King of the Belgians the Medaille de la Reine Elizabeth in recognition of work in Croydon for Belgian refugees ; and who was also on many War Committees .	208
54.—Mrs. COLCHESTER, M.B.E., Croydon War Savings Committee, etc. .	209
55.—MARK B. F. MAJOR, Founder of the Croydon Vacant Lands Cultivation Society .	224
56.—GEORGE FEARNLEY CARTER, M.Inst.C.E., Borough Engineer, Surveyor and Water Engineer ; Local Fuel Overseer .	225
57.—Peace Celebration Day (19th July, 1919), Street Procession. Naval Contingent, heading the Procession .	242
58.—Peace Celebration Day (19th July, 1919), Street Procession. School Girls .	243
59.—(1) The Hon. Editor : Alderman H. KEATLEY MOORE, J.P., B.A., Mus. Bac. ; Mayor, Nov., 1906 to Nov., 1908 ; Hon. Freeman of the Borough ; (2) The Assistant Editor : W.C. BERWICK SAYERS, F.L.A. (Hons.), Borough Librarian ; 1/12 Surrey Vol. Regt., and 1 Vol. Bat., The Queen's .	244

Note.—The portraits which illustrate the Roll of Honour appear on numbered plates I.—XXXVI. which are included in the Roll itself. The references at the end of some of the entries in the Roll form the index (e.g., " Plate XXIX., 5," means that the fifth portrait on plate XXIX. is that of the subject of the entry.)

The portraits also include a few of living soldiers, amongst whom are (Councillor) S.Sgt. J. A. Clarke, V., 1, and 2nd Air Mech. A. J. Clarke, R.A.F., VI., 5, and others from whose names reference is similarly made in the list of Naval and Military Honours.

Part One
INTRODUCTORY

I. Introduction

Without doubt the World War of 4th August, 1914 to 11th November, 1918, was the greatest crime in history. Look at it which way you will, the length and magnitude of Germany's preparation, the subtlety and meanness of her espionage, her colossal lying, her inhuman brutality, her callous shamelessness towards friend and foe alike, her reckless defiance of all decency, her innumerable and in many cases indescribable cruelties to old men, women and children, prisoners and wounded, her diabolical inventions of air-warfare, and of the still more infamous submarine warfare (waged not only against our naval and mercantile marine but also against peaceful fishermen, ordinary civilian crews and passengers, nay even, though it sound incredible, against hospital ships), and the wholesale use of poison-gases and well-poisonings, made up together an immense villainy too bad for adequate description, a heap of iniquity too colossal to grasp, the fierceness and especially the unexpectedness of which nearly overthrew the world. Even the failure of Germany leaves us maimed and exhausted, though our spirit is undaunted; for as the Duke of Wellington always declared, " Nothing is more horrible than a Victory, except a Defeat."

In naming 11th November, 1918, the date of the armistice, as the end of active war, we may indeed be called to account; for even when Peace with Germany was signed on 28th June, 1919, and even when, after many vicissitudes it was ratified on 10th January, 1920, war was still active in many quarters of the world, and it will be long subsequent to the publication of this book before peace with Germany's many accomplices can be achieved.

Englishmen stood shoulder to shoulder in this gigantic life-and-death struggle, and the blows England dealt were heavy with the weight of the whole nation.

Croydon sent 25,000 men to the War, and 2,500 of these, alas, never came back; 10,000 returned wounded, and they and the unwounded (the more fortunate remaining half of Croydon's fighters) received many medals and honours for their bravery, besides having acquired the esteem and admiration of their fellow citizens.

Every town has, published or unpublished, its Roll of Honour; and behind its contribution to the military, naval, or air forces engaged at the front, or supporting the actual combatants, it has a noble record of money raised and supplies sent and work done by non-combatants ; by the weak, the middle aged, the old, and above all by the women ; without which support the armies in the field could not have won through.

As regards the Roll of Honour it is more than three years ago that the Chief Librarian suggested to the Libraries Committee the necessity of compiling a record of every Croydon man and woman who had sacrificed life for King and Country in the Great War, or who had won naval or military honours. The Town Council unanimously adopted the proposal and the Roll of Honour was at once started. It is only just that I should record here the large share in this work performed so excellently by the Deputy Librarian (Mr. H. A. Sharp) ; by the former Deputy Librarian (Mr. John Warner, now the Librarian of Newport, Monmouth) ; by Miss Kathleen Snow, and especially by the Reference Librarian (Mr. L. Roy McColvin). An attempt was made to add a list of the wounded to our list of honours to the living and to our glorious melancholy list of the noble dead, but the difficulties proved altogether insurmountable, and it had to be abandoned.

At the Croydon Council Meeting on 21st July, 1919, the Chairman of the Libraries Committee (Councillor J. O. Pelton) proposed that an account of the military activities of Croydon men at home and on the various battle-fronts, and further a history of what we civilians did and suffered in Croydon, and the efforts we made to support the army and the country during the War should be added to this Roll of Honour, and that the whole should be published as the record of Croydon in the War. His proposal was unanimously adopted, and the work was entrusted to the Libraries Committee, with the Chief Librarian (Mr. W. C. Berwick Sayers) as secretary and sub-editor ; and the great honour of the editorship of the whole was placed upon my own shoulders. The Mayor (Alderman Howard Houlder), the Town Clerk (Dr. J. M. Newnham), and the Borough Accountant (Mr. J. H. McCall) kindly joined the Chairman in the small Editorial Committee then formed ; and those responsible for the several divisions of the town's war-work took much trouble to give us particulars of the activities over which they so efficiently presided. [After November, 1919, the new Mayor, Councillor C. Heath Clark, also came to our assistance.]

To keep the book within reasonable dimensions we have condensed our record to the extreme limit, but we hope we have not destroyed its interest. And those who wish for fuller details

INTRODUCTION

(especially as to the Roll of Honour) are referred to the Reference Library at the Town Hall, where the full text of the whole work as originally compiled may be inspected.

We have wished to show that Croydon had a worthy military history and that her own regiment " The Queen's " maintained in this last great test an already glorious record. The prowess of our Croydon Yeomanry and Croydon A.S.C. men must also be properly narrated with due acknowledgment. These and the Roll of Honour were to be the cardinal features of the book. But we desired to do more ; to give as faithful a picture as might be of the state of our town in war-time, and especially to show that those who stayed at home threw themselves ardently into every kind of work that would help the fighters, maintain civil order, and provide for the many needs that a war inevitably brings with it, in war-manufactures, in the provision of clothing, money, food and fuel. A glance through the list of contents will show what has been included.

There are, I fear, omissions from the work. For example, we have found it impossible to give more than a passing reference to the work of all the churches for the country in its hour of need. A volume might be written on that work alone, and all people must be grateful for it ; but such a record seemed beyond the scope of this book. Other matters of much private and public interest, such as the work of individual firms, the coming forward of the women to take the place of men in business houses, on the railways, on the trams, on the farms, in the Army as W.A.A.C.'s, in the Navy as W.R.N.S.'s, in War hospitals as V.A.D.'s, in the Police as Women Patrols, and in many ways not before generally deemed to be within the scope of women's work or possible to women's nerves or physical strength—these things receive only a brief mention.

The gathering of the material, and the collating and bringing it into a literary form has been arduous, but it has been a labour of love. We deeply regret that artistic difficulties have prevented us from reproducing all the photographs which were kindly sent us by the sorrowing relatives of those who laid down their lives for us. We can assure them, and our readers, however, that we have published the largest number possible.

There must be many shortcomings in a work of this complexity, many omissions, and many errors. For these we must throw ourselves upon the mercy of our readers, entreating them to believe that we have done our best to obtain complete records, availing ourselves of official documents wherever possible, and of the exceedingly great kindness of many qualified persons who checked the correctness of the facts we had brought together.

These good friends, who gave us so generously of their time, must not, however, be chargeable with defects in the work as produced. For the actual book as it stands I am responsible (except the Roll of Honour, for which Mr. Sayers is exclusively answerable), and I must bear the blame for all its imperfections. These would have been far greater if it had not been for the great amount of work Mr. Sayers has done, and for the fine literary sense he has brought to my assistance. So much is our work intermingled that no part can be said to be wholly his or wholly mine.

I must be permitted especially to thank, for innumerable services rendered to the book, the Town Clerk (Dr. J. M. Newnham), the Borough Engineer (Mr. G. F. Carter), the Borough Medical Officer (Dr. Veitch Clark), the Borough Accountant (Mr. J. H. McCall), the Assistant Town Clerk (Mr. S. Jacobs), the Chief Clerk in the Town Clerk's Department (Mr. A. C. Gower), and the Clerk to the Education Committee (Mr. James Smyth). And to all others of the Town Hall Staff, who were always ready to take trouble over my queries, I tender my best thanks; every one was helpful and cordial. The help received from all these gentlemen was continuous throughout the work. Assistance in procuring special facts, and in checking the following special chapters must be gratefully acknowledged to the undermentioned ladies and gentlemen in regard to the subjects following their names: The Mayor from 1916 to 1920, Alderman Howard Houlder, and the present Mayor, Councillor C. Heath Clark (Mayor's Committee, Military Tribunals, etc.); The Chairman of the Libraries Committee, Councillor J. O. Pelton (Croydon's Military Record before the Great War); Colonel Phillipps, Secretary, Surrey Territorial Force Association (The Queen's); Colonel N. E. Cutler (The Fourth Queen's); Colonel N. E. Cutler, Lt. Col. S. D. Roper, Lt. Col. H. A. Atkins (The 1/4th Battalion, The Queen's); Captain and Adjutant P. C. Duncan, M.C. (The 2/4th Battalion); Major (Acting Lieut. Col.) K. A. Oswald, D.S.O. (The 3/4th Battalion); Major K. W. Elder (The 4/4th Battalion); Lieut. Col. N. T. Rolls (Fourth Reserve Queen's); Major Stanley R. Docking, T.D., Sergeant McConnell and ex-Sergeant Latham (Croydon " C " Squadron Surrey Yeomanry); Major T. E. Fox, T.D., and Captain Brooks (Croydon Transport and Supply Column, A.S.C.); Major James Petrie, O.B.E. (Volunteers); Colonel John F. Worlledge (Boy Scouts); Assistant Commander H. C. Swaine (Special Constabulary); Miss Rhoda Brodie, M.B.E. (Women Patrols); Councillor T. W. Wood Roberts and Chief Officer John W. Dane (Fire Brigade); Dr. Edward H. Willock, Dr. J. J. Redfern, Col. H. E. Deane, R.A.M.C., Dr. J. J. Douglas, and

Miss Cooper (Medical and Hospital Services) ; Miss Edith Carr, Mr. Jones, and Miss Cooper (Soldiers' and Sailors' Recreation Rooms); Mrs. John Major (War Hospital Supply Depot); Mr. Albert G. Norris and Mr. Leonard S. Rogers (War Supplies Clearing House) ; Mr. Councillor Francis Allen, M.B.E., J.P. (War Pensions Committee) ; Lady Edridge (Mayoress's Needlework Committee) ; Mrs. Houlder (Mayoress's Committees) ; Mr. Bryan S. Harland and Mrs. Redfern (Belgian Refugees) ; Mrs. Colchester, M.B.E. (Croydon Local Central War-Savings Committee); Mr. Henry Berney (District Association of Voluntary Organizations, and many other chapters); Mr. A. C. Cramb (Munitions Committee, etc.) ; Miss E. L. Hudson (Allotments Movement) ; Councillor Arthur Peters, C.B.E., J.P., and Mrs. T. W. Wood Roberts (National Kitchens); Mr. J. T. Tompkins (Control of Food) ; and Mr. George F. Carter (Control of Fuel and Light).

Acknowledgment is also made to the various friends who have lent photographs or blocks ; and to the various photographers who have permitted the reproduction of the illustrations.

In addition to those whom I have named above, I have also to thank many other kind and helpful friends whose names I have not set down (for which they must forgive me, and must by no means think me, therefore, unrecognizing towards their services), and I beg them to believe that I am very grateful to them for their assistance.

The record closes with an account of the rejoicings of the Armistice (11th November, 1918) and the celebration of the Peace with Germany (28th June, 1919) on the day appointed for that glad ceremony (Saturday, 19th July, 1919) ; and last of all we add a reference to the beautiful thanksgiving performance of the " Messiah " at the Parish Church, on the following Tuesday (22nd July, 1919). This solemn and reverent service, deeply impressive to all who were privileged to attend it, fitly closed (as far as Croydon is concerned) the commemoration of England's escape from the greatest danger which ever beset her, and the uprising of the whole civilised world from beneath the heel of a blood-thirsty and debased tyranny.

H. KEATLEY MOORE.

CROYDON,

March, 1920.

II. The Course of Events in Croydon during the War

1914

Croydon was no more prepared for the world-calamity than any other place in England. The murders at Serajevo on that fatal Sunday, 28th June, 1914, had stirred the whole world, but few outside Germany and Austria realized that the spark had been set thereby to a train of events which were to lead to world-conflagration before the end of the next month. We knew, as July drew to a close, that intense communications of the gravest import were passing between the European Powers; but we believed that by some means or other Sir Edward Grey would accomplish the usual miracle, and keep us and Europe out of war. Then came the news that the German Armies were marching, and with the news the story of the violation of Belgium, and almost immediately Great Britain declared war.

At first the enormous character of the catastrophe did not dawn upon the average man. He knew that we were opposed by the greatest military and the second greatest naval power on earth; but the statement did not then convey the appalling facts that we now know. We knew only that the business was serious, and as tale after tale came to us of the struggle for Liege, the fall of that place, and the calculated savagery of the German advance into Belgium, an advance in hordes such as the world had never known, our people braced themselves for their greatest war effort. There was bewilderment at first, but there was no panic. Rather, in those early days, the motto was "business as usual." Nor was there any war-fever, that enthusiasm which finds expression in flag-flapping, cheering, boasting, and the singing of patriotic songs. It was, as one acute observer remarked, "a war without a cheer;" it was too serious a matter: for surely not one of us supposed that our "contemptible little army" of 170,000 men, which was on its gallant and glorious way to Mons, could be more than the mere spear-head of the great force that must follow it—from somewhere—if we were to arrest the rush of the nine million men whom the Kaiser was reputed to have set into motion. Everyone felt that sooner or later he or his would be involved in the great vortex. Lord Kitchener had been stopped on his way to Egypt, had taken

EVENTS IN CROYDON DURING THE WAR

his seat at the War Office as Secretary of State, and already had issued his appeal for "one hundred thousand men" to enlist for "three years or the duration of the War, whichever should be the longer." Three years! It seemed a life-time, an impossible period. Three months had been our hope, and for a time was our expectation, because even the German strategic optimists, such as Von Bernhardi, had declared that Germany could succeed only by a rapid overwhelming of Europe; but the great sphinx-like soldier statesman at Whitehall knew his task. We had yet to learn ours.

With the history of the War in general we are not expected to deal here, and in other pages of this work we treat of the gallant deeds of the soldiers who went from Croydon, and of the work of the many organizations which were called into being by the developing necessities of our great days. Here we are concerned only with the current of events in our own home-town; and even in that brief compass there is much that we must pass over in our endeavour to preserve a characteristic view of Croydon in war-days.

Anyone walking through Croydon streets on the day after War had been declared, would hear that in the night a military train had passed along the London, Brighton and South Coast Railway, and had dropped guards, who were men drawn from the City of London Volunteers, at bridges, signal boxes and other vulnerable points; there were sentries already in position at water reservoirs, gas and electricity works and similar places. Already, too, stories of spies were whispered, although so far as we know, none were ever detected in Croydon. All wireless systems in private hands, and there were several in and around Croydon, were dismantled. Grave-faced knots of people discussed the situation at every corner, and in every shop, office and restaurant. If we enter the swimming bath we shall see the swimmers stop to ask the new-comers if "there is anything new." Moving quietly through the streets are Volunteers of the Croydon National Reserve selecting and commandeering horses and vehicles from firms who are considered to be able to spare them. We hear, then, that the Territorials who are away on Salisbury Plain in camp have been properly mobilized, and all reserve men from the Post Office, the Gas Company, the Corporation and many a firm have been called up. Next day we learn that the train services have been severely restricted, all cheap tickets being withdrawn; a particularly hard matter for those on holidays or about to take them. Some, indeed, may have started on holidays at the fateful hour, but the holiday spirit has gone from the air entirely, and is not to return for many a weary day. We learn, too, that on the Continent all passenger railway services for civilians have been suspended to allow the free and rapid movement of troops. Several Croydon people are held up in Switzerland and elsewhere, without any provision in some cases for a long stay, and with little prospect of getting home again ; and are victims of the wildest rumours of the German advance, the fall of Paris, and the invasion of England. Their experiences fill many columns of the newspapers of the day.

Yet a few hours, and the walls of the town were plastered with the words, TO THE RECRUITING OFFICE, with huge arrows all pointing the way. It was a day of intense voluntary recruiting. Boys who left home in the morning convinced and palpable civilians returned home to their apprehensive, but still approving, families in the evening as convinced and palpable soldiers in their khaki. And not a few who were no longer boys went with them to take the " one day's pay " and sign the oath of military allegiance. Men of forty-five persuaded recruiting officers that they were " just thirty," in order " to do their bit," as the simple phrase for a great service fashioned itself in the speech of the soldiers. Khaki became familiar in our streets ; but soon even the khaki gave out, so great was the demand for it, and men paraded in make-shift uniforms—particularly a vile dark-blue uniform with a black forage cap. In fact England was not prepared for equipping a vast army, and the whole of the organization and *materiel* had to be improvised while the army was growing. In these early days the Boy Scouts did much useful work as messengers, in calling up the soldiers, etc., and two patrols of our Croydon Boy Scouts were dispatched in the course of the month to patrol the Kent coast for forty-five miles. During the first week the rifle clubs of the Croydon and District League held a meeting to consider the best means of promoting the national cause. At first the rifle ranges were thrown open for practice, and out of the meeting just mentioned sprang the volunteer movement which, so far as Croydon is concerned, eventuated in the fine Volunteer Training Corps with its successors the First and First-Twelfth battalions of the Surrey Volunteers, who were finally amalgamated into the First Volunteer battalion of the " Queen's " Royal West Surrey Regiment. We tell of their doings upon another page. Already too, the people were awake to the fact that war must bring suffering at home and in the field, and schemes for relief were soon under way.

The most prominent of such schemes was that great outpouring of private charity to which the King's son lent his name. The Prince of Wales' Fund was initiated for Croydon by the Mayor, Alderman Frank Denning, on 7th August ; and within a week £4,000 had been subscribed. It was intended to alleviate

Photo by W. F. Skewes

Alderman FRANK DENNING, J.P.
First War-Mayor (Nov., 1913 to Feb., 1916)

Photo by E. Norton Collins

Mrs. DENNING
Mayoress, Nov., 1913 to Feb., 1916

the inevitable financial hardships of war, and, from first to last Croydon raised £21,108 in this way. People gave willingly enough ; and it must not be forgotten that all the circumstances in which men went to the Front differed enormously from those prevailing in former wars. Many employers made allowances to their men. The Government gave its employees who enlisted their full pay while on service ; many banks did the same ; corporations like that of Croydon gave half-pay to married men, and third-pay to single men ; and many public and private companies made similar provision ; but, even so, there were many small employers who could not afford such assistance to their workers, and the need for help from other sources was widespread and real. There was a general determination, too, that so far as was humanly possible the hardships of previous wars should be reduced for the sailors and soldiers to the minimum ; and the minimum indeed exceeded in horror all previous human experience. The determination took practical shape almost immediately in the formation of public and private societies for making or otherwise providing comforts for the forces. Meetings of these were held in various parts of the Borough in connexion with the Churches—who worked for such objects freely and selflessly throughout—and with many other organizations. It was only August as yet, but the prevision of the people was such that they were already making warm woollen clothing, comforters, helmets, etc., against the coming winter. The sick and wounded were to be prepared for too ; this seemed a strangely serious business, but it was accepted cheerfully and willingly by hundreds here as elsewhere. There was a little overlapping, possibly a little confusion, at first, but all the work was admirably apt, and was soon directed into well-organised channels, as in turn the county, borough and village became co-ordinate units in one large system of service.

Croydon was fortunate in the men who had the control of her affairs. The Mayor, Alderman Frank Denning, was a man of great courage, industry and initiative ; a self-made, self-educated man, who had from humble beginnings built up the large business of Welford's Surrey Dairies and was a controlling force in many commercial concerns ; a man, too, who had also built up a reputation for straight speech and high character. He was the head of a Council which was of equally determined and well balanced character, and which under his guidance threw itself into all schemes of recognised value for the promotion of the purposes of the War ; and behind these was the Town Clerk, Dr. John Montague Newnham, who became chairman or honorary secretary of a hundred movements for the general good, and worked untiringly as their organiser, adviser, and executive officer. We wish to emphasise the services of Dr. Newnham, as the work of the Town Clerk is quiet and unobtrusive and is too often altogether overlooked; and in doing so we do not forget the admirable services—in, and, more often, out of office hours —of the other principal officers and staff of the Corporation. Everybody who could be spared from the staff, and that included practically every eligible man, was encouraged to enlist, and those who remained had anything but the "cushy job" with the possession of which most stay-at-home workers were credited. That the work of the town was carried on smoothly is sufficient tribute in itself to the Corporation and its officers.

Except for the extension of the activities we have mentioned there is no startling fact to record for the first two or three months of the war. An example of prevision must be mentioned on the part of Mr. Mark Major, who on 15th August wrote to *The Croydon Times* announcing that Mr. Douglas Young had placed vacant land at the disposal of Croydon people for allotments. This led to the whole allotments movement in which the borough was to win the record of having the largest number of plots under cultivation by amateurs in the country. The great civilian force, the Special Constabulary, came into being in the first month of the war, and actually held its first regular parade on 16th August, when 130 men were inspected by Captain Vincent. Our later pages tell of their invaluable work in detail; we need only say here that they were twitted frequently by the unthinking in the earliest days, but the blue and white brassard was soon accepted by the people, and when the days and nights of air-raids were upon us, there were few who did not recognise gratefully how efficient and meritorious were their services. The smart specially-designed uniform which became their regulation dress later on won a respect equal to that which the Englishman bestows involuntarily upon that of the regular constables; and, in fact, a prominent Croydon magistrate declared publicly that if he were contemplating a misdemeanour he would rather attempt it in an area guarded by the regular police than in one watched over by "Specials." Late in August arrangements were made for the reception and maintenance of numbers of Belgian refugees, who arrived in the first week of September, and who received cordial hospitality in the days of their exile here, the children being taken into many Croydon homes.

All this time Captain David Barrie, Croydon's recruiting officer, conducted a vigorous campaign from his headquarters at Mitcham Road Barracks, the home of the old Royal Foot Guards. Later this work was transferred to the Town Hall. Parties of men left Croydon every morning. Amongst the first to go were three members of the Council, Messrs. J. C. Crowley,

EVENTS IN CROYDON DURING THE WAR

P. G. A. Cosedge and John A. Clarke. Councillor Clarke, who was on a motor holiday at the declaration of war, returned immediately, and served in the Thornton Heath Special Constabulary for about a month, becoming one of the first three inspectors elected by the men, as was then the rule. In October he enlisted in the R.A.S.C. (Remounts) as Farrier Sergeant, and was promoted to Staff Sergeant later; and before the end of the month he went out to France in charge of twenty-two shoeing smiths, settled down in the danger zone, and had the unique experience of being shelled out of Poperinghe on his fiftieth birthday. He has a fine record of strenuous and responsible work, including the charge of a large forge at the base, until September, 1918, when he was returned to England and discharged as unfit. It is fair to add that he made no claim against the Government on account of unfitness.

His colleagues, Messrs. J. C. Crowley and P. G. A. Cosedge were not to return.

It was in October that the words " Roll of Honour," now so sadly familiar to us, began to appear in the local newspapers. Several Croydon men were lost when the Germans torpedoed H.M. Ships " Aboukir," Hogue," and " Cressy " in the North Sea ; and almost simultaneously the first of the Croydon schoolteachers to fall in the war gave his life on the battle-fields of France—Lieutenant T. R. Bottomley, B.A., of the 1st East Yorkshire Regiment, a fine, promising young soldier-scholar. These were the first of a very long list.

Sir Frederick Edridge had announced on August 27th that the Fourth Queen's had been selected for foreign service. It was some disappointment to them to learn that this was not to be service on the Western Front, but in India, for which country they departed on November 25th. The attitude of the home folk towards the troops deserves commemoration. Parcels were sent profusely and regularly containing things good to eat, cigarettes, pipes and tobacco, things useful, and not a few things alleged to be useful to soldiers by enterprising tradesmen. There is no doubt that all this helped to sustain the men in their long, and often wearisome and monotonous training.

One of the important social features of the later part of 1914 was remarked upon by the Borough Recorder, Mr. R. F. Colam, K.C., in his address to the Grand Jury at the Quarter Sessions in October, and that was the remarkable decrease in crime which showed itself already and which continued until the end of the war. This has been attributed to the rigorous restrictions imposed upon the drink traffic during the war, and it may be that these restrictions did have their part in maintaining the good record, but at the time the comment was made by Mr. Colam the ordinary hours of public houses were still in force. Others have ingeniously supposed that the adventurous spirits who found an outlet for their energies in burglary and other heinous offences, now found it in the struggle with the enemy. We record the fact, and do not attempt to explain it.

It will be remembered that the Germans startled the world in general and the people of Antwerp in particular by the bombing of that city from the air by means of Zeppelins as early as August, 1914. A few may have anticipated the rapid and extraordinary development both in power and in range of air-craft, but at this time the majority of us were sceptical and not at all alarmed. *The Spectator* assured us that it was hardly likely that Zeppelins would be able to find their way to London, or even to travel so far in view of the variability of weather conditions ; and Mr. Winston Churchill was no less confident in his assurances, that any Zeppelin which ventured into our skies would be attacked by a veritable " cloud of hornets " in the shape of defending aeroplanes. Still it was not long before precautions were quietly taken which showed that in high quarters this assurance was not completely shared. The middle of October, 1914, saw a very drastic reduction in our street lighting as a precautionary measure against aerial attack. It was not yet the " horror of darkness " which came a year later, but by contrast with our brilliantly illuminated streets of the immediate past, it was dismal enough. Old residents told us that it resembled the " good lighting " (by gas, of course) of fifty years before. The lighting was further reduced in November, but was still sufficient for the usual practical purposes.

Mr. Frank Denning was unanimously re-elected Mayor in November. In an inaugural speech, in which he made no rash promises, he pointed out the amount of work already done for war-purposes, in the way of relief through the Prince of Wales's Fund ; the Soldiers' and Sailors' Families Association ; the Belgian Hostels, which already contained 500 refugees ; and the Croydon General Hospital, where wounded soldiers were being treated.

In December was held the first of the many " Flag Days " which were a peculiar and picturesque feature of the whole of war-time. They were a variant of the Queen Alexandra Rose Day, initiated a few years before, on which charming ladies dressed charmingly, stood at street corners, railway station entrances and in other public places, with large trays of tiny artificial wild-roses which they sold to very willing buyers at

EVENTS IN CROYDON DURING THE WAR 25

prices ranging from a penny to several pounds, and the proceeds were devoted to the hospitals. To escape undue and irresistible importunity, and to show that they have done their duty in buying, the buyers wore their roses as a buttonhole. In similar manner, on flag days ladies sold miniature paper flags that might be worn on the lapel of the coat. Our first flag day, as was the case everywhere else, was devoted to the relief of Belgium, the land which had suffered most in the first days of the war, when the Belgian flag was sold, and the takings amounted to £400.

In our chapter on the Mayoress' Flag Day Committee (Part V., Chapter VIII.) we give a list of the many flag days and their variants, and we need say no more here than that in general they were cordially approved of by the people, and supported by them, even when they were repeated so often that they became weekly, or even half-weekly, occurrences. Through them much private generosity was tapped which otherwise might not have found so satisfactory an outlet.

Our first War Christmas was a sober one, although some of the former festival spirit survived. The war situation was not immediately menacing, but was obscure as to the future, and we heard much of the cold and privations of the opposing armies who now faced one another in the frozen trenches of Flanders and France. The Marne had been won, the German armies had been pushed back to the Aisne, but a deadlock seemed now to have set in, and the world was far too anxious to spend a "merry Christmas." On Boxing Day we learned that the war had taken its first toll of the Council and that Councillor Percival George Allen Cosedge had died on active service, at No. 8 Casualty Clearing Station, on 16th December. He was only thirty-six years of age, and had been an old Volunteer, and a member of the Croydon National Reserve. He became a Councillor in 1912 and during the two years of his service had given evidences of an able concern for the public welfare and keen well-controlled powers of debate. At the outbreak of war he joined the " B " Company of the 3rd East Surrey Regiment. " His action in putting his name down as a Volunteer," writes one of his colleagues, " was done with calm deliberation and a clear appreciation of all the risks he ran, for the one sufficient reason that he conscientiously believed it to be his duty . . . . He has died at an age when his character and talents were beginning to be at their best, and would have been, as I well know, freely and modestly placed at the service of those who were poor and oppressed."

Looking back from the present to the first year of the war it is curious to see how many prophecies were falsified by the event. A great shortage of food and money, unemployment, bankruptcy generally, and much other disaster were prophesied, but none of them came to pass. Later there were to be various shortages, but none within measurable distance of those foretold.

1915

We need not dwell at length on the events of 1915. It is a record in which a brief summary may be made to serve for intense and continuous activity. On 19th January the Special Constabulary received and responded to the first of many emergency calls. The same date was Khaki Day at Thornton Heath when presents for the troops were given by five hundred people. Large recruiting demonstrations were held from time to time, a memorable one occurring on 22nd February, when Mr. Will Crooks, M.P., made one of his characteristically vigorous appeals to the patriotism of our young men. Other happenings in Croydon make rather curious reading in the light of subsequent knowledge. For instance, the cost of living had gone up aggressively it seems, and a protest meeting on 25th March was held at the North End Hall, when Mr. W. C. Anderson, M.P., and other speakers participated. "A few days ago," declared Councillor Bradshaw, "the people of Croydon were paying 1s. 11d. a cwt. for coal," and "Shame!" cried the audience. In fact all the necessaries of life had gone up 25 per cent. and the meeting demanded that the Government should take control of transport, fix maximum prices, and control food to prevent the exploitation of the people. The advice of the meeting was good, but the British Government moved slowly ; still, it did move towards the policy which our meeting recommended, and ultimately accepted every one of these demands. It should be recorded that in the first years of the war certain articles of food became scarce and this was in no small measure due to the selfishness of people who hoarded supplies beyond their immediate needs. In ordinary circumstances it was counted a virtue in a housewife to keep a well-stocked store cupboard; but war transposes the values of things, and at a time of scarcity, the hoarding of more than the individual needed at the moment proved to be dangerously unpatriotic.

At the Council meeting a few days before, the first of the war-bonuses had been given to the Corporation workmen as a contribution towards the increased cost of living. The grant

EVENTS IN CROYDON DURING THE WAR

was 3s. weekly to men earning less than 30s. weekly, of 2s. for those earning between 30s. and 35s., and 1s. for those earning from 35s. to 40s.. The clerical and administrative staffs were not included. At that same meeting a Councillor ventured to forecast an unlikely event : " Supposing," said he, " the war lasted another six months ! " We were optimists still, it will be observed.

On 22nd April Princess Clementine Napoleon, cousin of King Albert of Belgium, visited Croydon to receive gifts, the collection of which had been organized by *The Croydon Advertiser* and *The Croydon Guardian* (then separate newspapers) to be sent to Belgian soldiers at the front. At the same time an appeal was made by these journals and supported by the Mayor for a " Croydon " ambulance for the Belgian armies, and this was provided and sent out in due course.

Recruiting for the " Queen's " and for the army generally continued for the whole first war year. It was at about May, 1915, that the traders everywhere were faced with the fact that they would have to relinquish more and more of their men for naval and military service. The voluntary system still persisted, but the demands of the armies were straining it to breaking point. Women were gradually replacing men at the railway stations, in shops, and in business houses. This was in many cases a complete innovation, but it was one forced upon the country by the exigencies of the time, and one in which the women as a whole justified themselves completely. On 17th May a Thornton Heath woman, Mrs. Florence Earle Lamont, was killed at Ramsgate in a Zeppelin raid. This was the first raid in which any Croydon civilian resident is known to have been killed. In June over 2½ tons of food, collected by the Primrose League, were sent out for the prisoners of war in Germany. The same month saw the notorious attacks on Lord Kitchener in connexion with shell shortage. There was no doubt need of more ammunition at this time ; and towards the end of the month an appeal was made for persons to come forward as voluntary munition workers, a large open air meeting being conducted by the Mayor in Katharine Street on 29th June. Money was also required for all war purposes, and it was now that the Government floated its great War Loan, to which on the following Monday, 5th July, the Council subscribed a first £50,000. August brought us news that the 2/4th Queen's, which had proceeded to the Dardanelles in July had been in action and had suffered severely. Mention must be made, too, of the curious but effective " no treating " order which was enforced in Croydon, as elsewhere, from 11th October, an order which cancelled the right of any man to offer a friend intoxicating liquor on licensed premises. It was probably the most intimate check on the individual will that the Government contrived, and it could only be justified by necessity, and by its success in achieving its object. Never was there greater sobriety; never was there less crime than in the years when it was in force.

This, in the baldest summary is an outline of the events in Croydon until October, an outline which conceals a multiplicity of good deeds, of sacrifices, of energy spent in one way or another for the public good.

On the memorable night of the 13th October, Croydon came as a town definitely into the war area. Zeppelins had reached London in the spring of this year, and during September they raided London on two consecutive nights. It was on the second of the September raid nights that the " thud-thud " of an airship's engines was first heard locally, approaching Croydon from the north-west, disappearing as the machine passed over South Norwood with engines shut off, and re-appearing in the direction of Elmer's End as the Zeppelin went on her way apparently to the mouth of the Thames. No public warning had been given, the authorities having conceived the curious notion that English people would be less liable to panic if danger came upon them suddenly than they would be if they had notice of its coming. One only gathered that " something was on " from the sudden silence and comparative darkness that fell upon the streets, and one missed the more distant sound of the trains, which stopped during raids.

On 13th October a somewhat heavy Zeppelin attack was made on London at a little before nine in the evening. Bombs had been dropped near Trafalgar Square, and the attack passed away. Soon after eleven o'clock a listener in Croydon heard what he thought was the syphoning of a street gas-lamp, then what appeared to be an exhausting of steam through a near-by factory chimney, and then it seemed that a very heavy motor-vehicle was drawing nearer up an adjacent street; only, all the time, he had an impression that the sound was from the air. A few seconds later a flash from the sky, a sudden illumination of the whole neighbourhood, a deafening explosion and violent tremors of the ground showed that the German invaders had actually reached Croydon. Explosions followed in rapid and terrifying succession as the Zeppelin crossed over Addiscombe, passed south and east of the London, Brighton, Railway line and then throbbed away towards Woolwich. It has not been discovered with certainty which way the airship approached; but

Photo by Walshams, Ltd.
RUINED HOUSES IN BEECH HOUSE ROAD
Zeppelin Air-raid (13th October, 1915)

Ruined Houses in Edridge Road: Zeppelin Air-raid (13th October, 1915)

the general impression is that she had made an expedition to attack an old powder-works near Guildford, which was marked on the maps, and a few bombs were dropped outside the county town without doing any serious damage. It is supposed that she then followed the railway line towards London. Over Croydon, the first great town on her route, her crew probably imagined that they had reached London, and began to discharge their bombs. Another theory is that the network of railway lines at East Croydon Station and the munitions factory at the corner of Cherry Orchard Road were the objects of the attack ; but, if this is so, both objectives were missed, if only by a narrow margin. To one in Addiscombe it seemed that the Zeppelin approached from Waddon, picked up the railway, and then followed it through Norwood Junction, turning south-east from that point. The first bomb fell in Edridge Road, where two houses were wrecked, and a mother and daughter who were in bed in one of them were thrown, bedstead and all, into the street. A baby boy in the other was pinned down by a falling roof but wonderfully escaped injury. The second bomb was far more disastrous in its effects. It fell on a house in Beech House Road, where the household consisted of a father and three sons, 10, 14 and 15 years of age, and a house-keeper. The bomb went through the house, completely wrecking the building and hurling *debris* long distances around. " I was fast asleep," said the house-keeper, " when I heard an awful explosion which awoke me. I seemed to spring from the top of the bed to the bottom. Then I groped my way to the door, which I found was on the floor. I stayed there because the side wall had fallen in on the stairs and landing. I called out to the father, asking if he was all right. He replied ' I'm all right, but I can't move.' The next thing I called for the boys. Only the elder one answered." The fire brigade arrived, and the unfortunate people were extricated. The youngest boy was dead when they reached him, the second was dead when he reached hospital, and the eldest died a little later from shock, while the father was injured and in mental collapse from his terrible loss.

Other bombs fell in rapid succession. Three fell in one road destroying all the windows far and near. A big splinter from the bomb which did damage in Chatsworth Road caught the main carrying the chief water supply of the town, where it crosses the Railway ; fortunately it only cracked the pipe, had it broken it Croydon would have been almost waterless, and the railway dangerously flooded. The lights at Creed and Bille's Factory had now been turned off, but the Zeppelin passed over it, and discharged what seemed to be a shower of bombs a little beyond it on Oval Road, destroying much property, shattering windows and furniture, and killing three people, a woman who had taken refuge in a cellar, and two young men who were in the street, one of them having run outdoors at the sound of the first explosion. Another missile burst through " Glendalough,' the house of Dr. J. H. Thompson, at the corner of Morland Road half demolishing it, but most fortunately not injuring anyone although Mrs. Thompson and others were in the house at the time. The last effective bomb hit the upper story of a villa in Stretton Road, with fatal results to three people, a mother, son and daughter. A sad feature of the tragedy was that the husband a sergeant-major, and another son, a lieutenant, were both away on active service. After this one more bomb was dropped in Howard Road, but this failed to explode.

The noise of the exploding bombs was something that will not easily be forgotten. We can only describe it as resembling the crack of a thousand rifles and the clashing of a myriad titanic cymbals, all heard simultaneously. It was indeed awful and terrific.

Beyond the outstanding tragedies of the raid considerable damage was done in the neighbourhood in which it occurred. Fragments of steel were found imbedded in trees, in walls, and deep in the ground, sometimes having pierced walls at some distance. Particles of wood, plaster, and brick were scattered everywhere, and minute fragments of glass seemed to have rained on the pavement. The Fire Brigade, the Special Constabulary and the R.A.M.C. section of the Volunteers rendered invaluable aid, and did much to alleviate the pain and to restrict the damage caused by the visitation.

What may be called the era of darkness now set in " Darkness and composure " had long ago been prescribed as the preventive against the Zeppelin, and this gradually became an inflexible rule, rigidly required of the people. To read the regulations of " D.O.R.A." in regard to lighting was to experience a feeling of eeriness. Street lighting was so reduced that it only made the general opacity more obvious and depressing, the street lamps being so obscured that a circle of illumination about three yards in diameter was carved out of the night upon the ground, and no rays whatever were thrown upward. Every house and other building was compelled to possess dark blinds or have its lights shaded in order that no direct ray should emerge. The results were inconvenient in the extreme. Such streets as Katharine Street were tunnels of blackness on moonless winter nights. When people were about one felt their presence very literally by bumping into them ; one apologized, and immediately

EVENTS IN CROYDON DURING THE WAR 31

bumped into someone else. On nights of fog or mist one felt one's way home rather than traced it. Later on, hand electric flash lamps of low power were allowed to be carried; these lighted the way for their possessors, but they had an extremely unpleasant effect on others; one was in momentary danger of temporary blindness by receiving the flash of one of these lamps in one's eyes, sometimes as a result of accident, often as a result of thoughtlessness or actual impertinence on the part of the person carrying it. Frequent accidents of a minor kind occurred in the darkness; people collided with trees, posts, and other street obstacles. One such accident occurred in North End when a respected Alderman collided with a young lady, and to prevent her falling backwards threw his arms around her. At that very moment a motor 'bus passed and its lights were strong enough to reveal the delicate situation. Whereupon the young lady remarked, somewhat tartly we believe, " You are old enough to know better." As no doubt the innocent well-meaning gentleman was.

To return to the chronicle of our doings. October, 1915 saw the beginning of " Derby " recruiting, and a local military tribunal was appointed on 2nd November. We deal with the energetic and very remarkable campaign elsewhere, which did not indeed save England from the necessity of imposing conscription, but which, nevertheless, almost did so, and in any case provided a sound foundation upon which the Military Service Act of 1916 could be worked.

1916

The year 1916 opened with a great loss to the town. On 7th February, the Mayor, Alderman Frank Denning, passed away without warning, at his house, The Elms, Cargreen Road, South Norwood, dying quietly in his sleep. He had attended assiduously to his public work all through the previous week, and had seemed in his normal health; although looking at the matter after the event, it seems that he taxed his strength incessantly beyond endurance. He had served the town as councillor and alderman for over thirteen years, and his broad and statesmanlike abilities, his courage, frankness, integrity and human sympathy, together with his invaluable work in the first two war-years, have given him a place which is quite his own in the history of Croydon. His death was mourned as a public bereavement, and some months later his portrait was hung in the Town Hall, and on the wall opposite was placed a bronze tablet with a simple and dignified inscription, as follows :

> To the Memory of
> FRANK DENNING
> Alderman and Justice of the Peace
> of this Borough
> who served the office of
> MAYOR
> during the first eighteen months
> (August 1914 to February 1916) of
> THE GREAT EUROPEAN WAR
> Elected Mayor 10th November 1913
> died in office 7th February 1916
> He was distinguished throughout
> his mayoralty by his assiduity and
> devotion to duty both as a
> PATRIOT AND CITIZEN

Mrs. Denning, who had shared his enthusiasms and public services in a marked degree, survived him for little more than a year, herself dying on 16th April, 1917. Not only by their life has Croydon benefited. They bequeathed the bulk of the by no means inconsiderable fortune which Alderman Denning had built up to trustees for the purposes of scientific and technical education, especially for Croydon people.

Councillor (now Alderman) Howard Houlder, then chairman of the Education Committee, was elected to the vacant office, and as our second War Mayor it may be said that he fulfilled amply the high expectations to which his election gave rise. As chief magistrate, chairman of the Military Tribunal, advocate for war-loans and for all funds for the support and comfort of sailors and soldiers and their families, as an indefatigable social worker in every field where influence was to be exercised for the public good, the new Mayor succeeded completely ; and what he began, with a thoughtful eloquent inaugural speech on the 21st February, 1916, he continued until November, 1919 ; for he was re-elected no less than three times and held the office for a longer continuous period than any of his predecessors. In all this he was seconded completely by Mrs. Houlder, to whom he has declared publicly is due the credit not only for much that he accomplished, but also for many activities in which she herself was the presiding spirit. Our ensuing pages will fully corroborate him.

Photo by Howard M. King
Alderman HOWARD HOULDER, D.L., J.P.
Second War-Mayor (Feb., 1916 to Nov., 1919)
Hon. Freeman of the Borough, 1920

Mrs. HOWARD HOULDER
Mayoress, Feb., 1916 to Nov., 1919
Hon. Freeman of the Borough, 1920

EVENTS IN CROYDON DURING THE WAR

The events of 1916 may be summarised briefly. In May the Government War Pensions Committee came into existence, having for its province the administration of national pensions for the fighters and their dependents, and much valuable ameliorating work has resulted. The Derby recruiting scheme came to an end altogether on 7th June, when there was an extraordinary rush of men who preferred (as was promised if they attested) to be regarded as volunteers and not as conscripts. The day before the whole Empire and its Allies had been shocked and saddened by the tragic death by drowning of the master-soldier Earl Kitchener, the veritable creator of the great voluntary armies. A memorial service was conducted by the Vicar of Croydon (Canon White-Thomson) on 13th June.

A word may be said about the Daylight Saving Bill, which became operative this year. Advocated long before the war by the late William Willett, the suggestion that the clock should be advanced one hour during summer months had not received the enthusiastic support of the conservative Britisher. Germany, however, being restrained by no democratic scruples, saw the advantages of the plan, and imposed daylight-saving upon her people quietly and effectively. England now followed suit, and the result was to lengthen the light evenings for work, drilling, gardening, and the other urgencies of the day. There were objections from farmers who regarded the clock as a Divine institution, and occasionally from mothers who found difficulty in getting children to bed an hour before their usual time; but they did not counterbalance the obvious advantages of the new system.

July found us with some apprehensions but with high hopes. A great allied offensive began this month on the Western Front, which we fondly believed would end the war. It led to terrible and bloody fighting, as History has already recorded; with such splendid heroism as was shown in the abortive British attack upon Gommecourt. We were concerned deeply, and yet we were proud to learn that the East Surrey Regiment had taken a prominent part in the opening of this "Great Push." The quixotic, thoroughly British heroism of the East Surreys in the attack on the Warren (near Montauban) will long be remembered. Each platoon officer threw down a football and called upon his men to play it forward, which they did through a swathe of hostile machine gun fire and the enemy's curtain of shrapnel, and shot their goals in the German line. News came to us daily of gigantic battles fought and great deeds done, and the roll of honour grew longer and longer in its melancholy splendour; so that before the year was ended there was scarcely a Croydon home which the Angel of Death had not visited.

c

In 1916 building came to a standstill everywhere. There had been much development in the few years preceding, especially in outer Addiscombe and in Norbury; but from 1916 to 1919 we believe that not a single dwellinghouse was erected. This was, of course, caused by the shortage of labour and materials, both of which were needed for sterner purposes. With the cessation of building there was also a cessation of road-making, and of road-repairing on any sufficient scale. To do either was an impossibility. Here were two of the most serious social factors of the time, and it is safe to say that one year of inaction in these things cannot be recovered in twice the time afterwards. The collection of house-refuse, and a certain amount of street-cleaning and watering were maintained, but only enough for the preserving of the public health. And now that the War is over, Government and the Municipality are making strenuous efforts to make good the alarming deficiencies in housing accommodation and in the state of the public streets; but there is still much leeway to be made up. A glance at the chapter on Food Control will show how great are the movements of a population such as that of Croydon, and the dearth of houses is seen in its really serious aspect when it is related to the figures given there. A certain drab character gradually descended upon the town; shop-fronts became dingy, houses almost dilapidated looking, paint was lacking. It was a minor, but nevertheless, a characteristic feature of war-time.

Zeppelin raids occurred several times during 1916, one of which was particularly startling, although no injury was done in Croydon itself. The darkness of which we have already made such feeling mention was our preserver, and it is said that the town lights were so well obscured that Croydon could not be seen from the sky. Even on moonlit nights, we are told, the town presented the appearance of a wood, an illusion also partly due to the leafy character of many of our streets. The raid of which we were speaking was one in which the raiders passed over Croydon, and dropped brilliant flares to illuminate their route. Several such flares were seen over the Borough, but it is said that they obscured the district immediately below while showing what was well in front. However that may be, bombs were dropped south of the town, and north also; on Streatham (where it must be said the street lighting was more generous than in Croydon), and on several other parts of the road from thence to London—Croydon escaped. On 3rd September, many Croydon people saw what seemed to be the northern sky on fire when the first Zeppelin to be destroyed in England fell at Cuffley, beneath the attack of Lieutenant W. Lief Robinson; on the 23rd of the same month the sight was repeated when two Zeppelins fell in flames, and again on 1st October. We began

SEARCHLIGHTS AT CROYDON: Winter of 1917—18

From a drawing by Elsie Gledstanes

Photo by Lewis

FIRING MAROONS, AS WARNING FOR AIR-RAID,
at Croydon Police Station

EVENTS IN CROYDON DURING THE WAR

to believe that at last the authorities had found means to engage the raiders, who hitherto had come and gone with perfect impunity.

The Military Service Act had come into full operation on 25th May, 1916, and in a very brief time all men between the ages of 18 and 41 were either in the Army or Navy, or had been exempted upon sufficient grounds. To ensure that none should evade military service occasional raids were made by the authorities upon places of amusement in search of absentees. One such was made in Croydon, on 8th September, but we are glad to record that only one man was discovered who could not then and there give a satisfactory account of himself.

We learned with deep regret that Captain John Cyril Crowley had been killed in Mesopotamia on 11th September, while covering with his machine gun company the retreat of a raiding party. He was a man greatly valued in the borough, as a member of the Town Council, on which he served from 1909 as a representative of the Central Ward to the time of the outbreak of war, as a business man (he was a member of the well-known Croydon firm of brewers), as well as for his fine personal qualities. Another Croydonian whose death in action this month was much lamented was Lieutenant H. A. Link, son of Councillor Charles Link (then Chairman of the Education Committee), in honour of whom a memorial service was held at George Street Congregational Church on 17th September. A royal visit was made to Croydon, on 26th October, when Their Majesties the King and Queen inspected the Croydon War Hospitals. On 9th November, Mr. Howard Houlder, who had been made an alderman a month earlier, was re-elected Mayor.

This review of the year omits many things; for instance, it makes no reference to the flag days, or the Y.M.C.A.'s Hut week, which towards the end of the year realized £6,200; nor have we commented upon the fact that by October twenty-eight of the panel doctors under the Croydon Insurance Committee were away with the forces; nor can we trace the innumerable war-activities that were pursued daily in public and in private. We may mention, however, that during the year much billeting was done in Croydon. A labour battalion of the Bedfordshire Regiment was sent here for training and was billeted in London Road, Park Hill and Park Lane, with headquarters in Wellesley Road; and the Army Service Corps was stationed at South Norwood and Upper Norwood. Khaki now dominated the streets everywhere; a young man in civilian clothes was rare; and men between forty and fifty who had perhaps hitherto thought themselves middle-aged found that they had become the young men of the home population.

As regards the War the year had been one of high hopes and much optimism, but had been disappointing in many ways. In it was fought the great inconclusive Battle of Jutland, which indeed proved that England still held the seas, but which was, in the first instance, reported to our people in so abrupt a manner that the impression of a defeat was given. The great offensive of July on the Western Front had not swept the German armies back across the Rhine as some had fondly hoped it would; the maximum depth of the British advance had been only three miles, won at an appalling cost. But military critics now say that in reality it was the crushing blow which really meant inevitable victory. Roumania had declared war on Germany on 27th August, and we believed that her ill-timed entry spelt the earlier attainment of victory, but by December Falkenhayn had carried the German standard to Bukarest, and had entirely routed the Roumanians. Moreover, the offensive power of Russia had gradually worn itself out, and she had been unable to aid Roumania, or indeed any of her allies. Casualties everywhere had become so heavy that several of the belligerent governments ceased to publish the casualties of their armies, and all settled down grimly to a war of attrition, in which it was believed that the side possessing the greatest staying power rather than the most dramatic military skill would emerge triumphant.

1917

These circumstances were indeed very serious, but the human mind cannot dwell for ever upon catastrophe, and, in spite of anxieties for absent ones, increasing cost of living, and nightly expectations of raids, the home population managed to keep Christmas cheerfully. The first note struck publicly in January, 1917, was by the Rt. Hon. Arthur Henderson, M.P., who prophesied "victory this year," at the anniversary meeting of the North End Brotherhood; but, it must be confessed that we had become confirmed sceptics so far as such prophecies were concerned. On 19th January, 1917, a tremendous, but distant, explosion was heard, the concussion of which shook every house in Croydon; it was the disaster of Silvertown, more than twelve miles away, where an explosives factory blew up, wrecking the district and causing much loss of life. Another great national financial effort, called the Victory Loan, was made this January, and the Croydon Town Council gave a good lead to the town by investing £250,000. A system by which the Mayor and other trustees obtained bonds and re-sold them to

EVENTS IN CROYDON DURING THE WAR 37

the public on an instalment plan, proved most successful, £94,000 being invested in this way by 2,094 subscribers. In the same month the Council took over the control of the allotments movement in the Borough. March was shadowed by the sudden death of the Deputy-Mayor, Alderman Samuel Rogers, J.P., which occurred on the 10th. He had served the South Ward as a councillor from 1902 to 1916, when he was elected an alderman, and had filled the office of Mayor with dignity and success in the year 1912-13. He had rendered great public service during the War, and he died honoured by the respect and esteem of his fellow citizens.

It will be remembered that 31st January, 1917, saw the beginning of "official" unrestricted submarine warfare by the Germans, when, to quote its author, the notorious Von Tirpitz, " it was clear from the outset that the existing rules of maritime law, which in the main dated from the days of sailing vessels, did not properly cover the circumstances of the present day." This infamous repudiation of international law had, of course, existed in actual fact for two years, as the bombardment of Scarborough, and the sinking of the passenger ships *Falaba* and *Lusitania*, and the hospital ship *Sussex*, had already demonstrated, but now Germany openly defied the law of civilised nations. In a remarkable story written before the War called *Danger*, Sir Arthur Conan Doyle had pictured an England starved into submission by a daring and unscrupulous submarine campaign. As Kipling makes his " Big Steamers " sing :—

> For the bread that you eat and the biscuits you nibble,
> The sweets that you suck and the joints that you carve,
> They are brought to you daily by all us Big Steamers—
> And if any one hinders our coming you'll starve.

Catastrophe after catastrophe followed ; long lists of lost vessels, torpedoed without warning, and often with the loss of the whole ship's company, appeared daily, ranging from great liners to small coast-wise vessels. Then the names were omitted ; and we were given only monthly lists of the total tonnage lost by enemy action ; and the huge figures covered infinite tragedy as well as heroism. We never came within measurable distance of actual starvation, but it must be remembered that the English nation was entirely unequipped for such an emergency, and with vanishing food-stocks, and this enormous interference with our sea traffic, food began to become dearer, then scarcer, and finally some foods seemed to vanish entirely. Various measures were adopted. In the first place an energetic campaign for economy in food was carried on with much success on a voluntary basis ; but under any voluntary system there may be some carelessness or greed in individual cases, and at the end of April the situation was felt so keenly in Croydon that a mass meeting was held at the Grand Theatre which passed resolutions demanding that the food supply should pass under Government control. The Government was forced by circumstances to move at last, and the Ministry of Food, itself a war institution, set up national rationing during the summer. Croydon's Food Committee was appointed by the Council to carry this out for the Borough on 28th August, 1917. The account given in chapter III of Part Five of this book is a most interesting and significant story of successful effort to maintain and equalize food supplies. An experiment which we record in a later chapter (National Kitchens) was commenced this year on 30th May, when the Mayor opened the first communal kitchen at Beulah Road Schools.

On 15th June the Mayor informed the Town Council that he had received news of the death of Lieutenant-Colonel U. L. Hooke, commanding officer of the 3/4th Queen's, who was killed by a shell at Rœux, and of the Rev. C. H. Schooling, a curate at the Parish Church, who had fallen in action.

The year 1917 will remain in the memory of the home population as a year of air-raids. By this time the Zeppelin had been superseded by the far more formidable aeroplane as a long-distance raider. During the early part of 1917 single German aeroplanes had paid lightning visits to the south-east coast towns, Dover and elsewhere, dropping bombs from great heights and darting away immediately. On 7th May one of the machines reached north-east London and dropped four bombs, which killed one man and injured two women ; on 25th May a large squadron of them attacked Folkestone and its neighbourhood, inflicting 250 casualties ; and on 13th June fifteen machines of the Gotha type raided the East End of London, killing 104 people and injuring 423. On 7th July the largest squadron yet recorded visited London, apparently approaching from the south-east. The machines, like a flock of diminutive black birds, high out of the range of the gun-fire then available, came sailing through a bright blue sky directly towards Addiscombe. The business of the Police Court here was suspended, and everybody took such shelter as was available. Fortunately, however, the squadron wheeled north before it reached Croydon, steering over the Crystal Palace and thence right over the City of London, where, as it will be remembered, it did damage, which although of no military consequence, was serious enough, and inflicted 240 casualties, according to the official record. In September a new terror was added to raiding when the enemy began to make his visits by moonlight.

Air-raids are so essentially part of our memories of the Great War, that it seems desirable to make as accurate a record

EVENTS IN CROYDON DURING THE WAR 39

as possible of the impression they made upon our people. But it must be claimed from the outset that their moral effect from the enemy's standpoint, was entirely the reverse of what they were intended to achieve. He desired primarily to destroy what he impudently called our " will to war," and by terrorising our civil population he hoped that they would compel the Government to make peace—on his terms. In the history of the world no more egregious psychological miscalculation has been made. After a raid, people looked tired, sad perhaps, but there was a general clenching of the teeth and always an increased determination to destroy the power which used these means of war. The exclamation of an elderly man listening to the defending guns during a raid, " By God, I wish I could help with that gun," was the spirit that our would-be terrifiers created. But, even so, the raids were a great strain, especially as casualties occurred in every one of them, and there was no adequate shelter in most of the areas. In a place like Croydon there were thousands of women and children as well as men in daily or nightly peril. We were all astronomers of a kind in those days, even those amongst us who had hitherto scarcely noticed the night-sky before. The Zeppelin preferred a moderately dark night as offering concealment, but the more fatal aeroplane greatly preferred a night when the moon was near to the full, as the peculiar quality of the moonlight made it practically impossible to see machines flying at great heights, except when they actually crossed the disc of the moon. The phases of the moon were therefore watched with anxiety, and the cry of Hippolyta, " I am weary of this moon ; would he would change," represented a general thought. But later the aeroplane came occasionally even on moonless nights ; only on the nights of storm, rain and fog were we reasonably sure of safety.

The defences of London were entirely inadequate for the first three war-years. There were too few guns and insufficient fighting aeroplanes, and during some Zeppelin raids not a defending gun-report had been heard. After the midsummer aeroplane raids of 1917, however, anti-aircraft guns were installed all round London, the chief Croydon guns being one in Gonville Road, Thornton Heath, a most rapid firing French gun, known quizzically as the " cough-drop," because of its dry, coughing sound, and a much heavier gun with a deeper note at Elmer's End. The searchlight service was gradually improved and extended so that at night the sky was frequently a maze of wheeling shafts of intense light, and to these were added peculiar spot-lights which threw blobs of light on the sky. As many as 100 separate searchlight beams have been counted from Croydon, seeming to converge from all sides on the sky above the town. We are fortunate in having a sketch of the effect, by Miss

Gledstanes. On 23rd July, 1917, the authorities, having reached the conclusion that to warn people of the approach of a raid was probably better than to allow them to become aware of it by bombs dropping upon their heads, ordered a warning to be given by the firing of two maroons in quick succession from every police station in the raid area. Raids that had been silent hitherto, except for the occasional exploding bomb, now became orgies of noise. We learned this to the full in September, 1917, when raids became nightly affairs.

It would happen thus. One would be walking on an early night, with that brightness of the rising moon which we always associate with September. Suddenly a " boom " would shatter the silence, and, turning, one would see the expiring red sparks of the waning rocket. A moment of tense silence, and then the sound would be repeated. The enemy had crossed the English coast-line. Then everyone quickened his steps homeward, or, if too far from home, took cover in one of the places which had been set aside as air-raid shelters. People who owned basements betook themselves to them. Others vacated top floors, turned round arm-chairs with their backs towards the windows—and waited. This was the most trying time perhaps in the raid. Would it materialize ? Usually it did, about twenty minutes later. Far off poppings began, at first in desultory fashion, then in increasing numbers and without pause. Then, with deep, deliberate reverberations, the Elmer's End gun came into action, making the ground vibrate. Immediately afterwards, the Gonville Road gun, which had the special quality of making all the windows rattle, followed on. We counted the discharges of this gun on one occasion, and found them to be twenty-one a minute. As the raid got nearer the shrapnel necessarily also fell nearer. The shells in their flight made a noise resembling the wailings of cats, and the bursting shell had a distinct whine about it. Then was heard the whirr, or drone, or hum—all these expressions have been used to describe it—of aeroplanes. Were they our own or the enemy's ? A difference between them could be detected. It was said that the British machines made a more droning sound, and one on a higher note, than the German. The latter made a noise of a more grinding type—" whirr—pause—whirr, whirr—pause—whirr." We were forbidden to look out of the windows, and had small inclination to do so ; but when we did venture to look out we could see only searchlights, wheeling faintly against a sky so bright that it cancelled the greater part of their power ; while away in the direction of Woolwich great fan-shaped bursts of white light marked the continuous guns of the barrage. Sounds of machines throbbed everywhere in the sky, and one machine at least always seemed to be immediately above one's own roof ; and now and then the

EVENTS IN CROYDON DURING THE WAR 41

snapping of a machine gun told of work a-doing overhead. Thus we sat, for one, two, and sometimes three hours, reading, smoking, or talking hard of anything but raids, but obviously thinking of nothing else, and " wondering where the next one would go," when a sudden shaking of the whole house proclaimed that somewhere a bomb had dropped. More adventurous spirits slept through raids. The late coroner, Dr. Thomas Jackson, advised people to go to bed as usual, and the present Editor considers he was right, as no bomb ever fell on Croydon after the fatal 13th October, 1915 ; but many had not the courage to do this. Gradually the firing would die away ; the sound of our own returning machines would be heard, and then would come silence. Sometimes it was broken by a return of the raiders ; sometimes also when an enemy, trying to escape from the barrage on the north, sought the way out south ; but more frequently the silence lasted, until, faint and welcome, came the thin bright notes of the buglers coming nearer with the most welcome sound we heard in that September, the " G.-C." of the " All Clear." All the locomotives on the railway also blew a " cock-a-doodle-do " note on their whistles. Then with devout thankfulness for one more escape, those who had stayed up all went to bed.

Officially the raid was more complicated. Some time before the maroons were fired, the police and special police received the call known as the " Field Marshal," telling them that the raiders were on the way. Then came the " stand-by," and all the special constables were called up. The public warning followed when the raid became practically certain ; but there were many alarms received officially of which the public heard nothing.

We have described a typical raid. There were about eight such raids in September, and they occurred at each full moon until May, 1918, when the defences became too strong for them and the conditions of the Western Front were such that machines could not be hazarded in attacks upon London. Certain places in Croydon, as we have hinted, were used as raid shelters. The principal of these was the basement of the Town Hall, which was well filled, and sometimes more than crowded, on raid nights. Churches, furniture repositories, breweries, libraries and business premises were also used in this way. Dug-outs were not constructed in many places ; we are only aware of two ; one, which a resident in Carlyle Road had made for his household, and a much larger one which several residents on the Ashburton Estate, Addiscombe, had dug out of the bank on the side of Addiscombe Road next to Sandpits Farm. It happened, rather ironically, that no real raid occurred after the latter dug-out was finished. During the raids the Special Constabulary made valuable observations from several points, which assisted the defences. The principal of these was the Water Tower, the equipment and work of which we record later. Both here and from the Town Hall tower a minute-to-minute observations-record was made, an example of which we give in Part IV., chapter I.

It is remarkable how slightly vital public business was retarded by air-raids. Naturally there was a cessation of work when they occurred, but an hour afterwards everything seemed to resume as usual. We have noted that the Police Court stopped work on 7th July, 1917. On 24th September the Education Committee adjourned, and took cover in the basement of the Town Hall. We believe one or two Committees continued their discussion in the basement during raids. On 18th February, 1918, the Town Council, while sitting, received an air-raid warning, but decided to " carry on." It may be stated that there were no unnecessary speeches, and that the business of the Council proceeded with a dispatch which was probably unique. So much so that most of the members got away before the raid materialised.

Very little damage was done by the raids. Shrapnel was picked up in many of the streets. A few windows were broken and ceilings were brought down by shrapnel, as might be expected when it is remembered that the whole district was peppered with falling pieces of metal. A few minor casualties resulted from the same cause ; but none, so far as we know, fatal or even serious.

On 18th December, 1917, the death occurred of Captain David Barrie, who from the beginning of the War had acted as recruiting officer for Croydon. His work had been strenuous, exacting and often irritating, but he combined organizing ability with excellent good temper and was universally popular. His death was much regretted.

1918

Looking over the impressions that remain of the year 1918, we see three outstanding features of that eventful time. The first was the food question ; the second the devastating outbreak of war-time influenza ; and the third the crowning of all war efforts by the signing of the Armistice. By the beginning of 1918 the food question had reached its climax. The Food Control Committee was very active at this time in its efforts to solve the problem of the queue. The streets were filled with

EVENTS IN CROYDON DURING THE WAR 43

housewives and others who were seeking for food. Fortunately, as the record in our later pages shows, there was food enough in the country, if only it were equitably distributed, and when the ration cards came into full working order, as they did before the end of February, 1918, the situation became tolerable, and considering all the circumstances most satisfactory.

On the 13th February the town sustained a loss in the death of Sir Reuben V. Barrow, who had been Mayor of the Borough in 1885-6, and had been an alderman from the year of his election in 1883 until the year 1916, when he retired from the Council. His long services to the Borough were important and far-reaching. He was elected a freeman on the 4th October, 1909, and his portrait hangs in the vestibule of the Town Hall.

The month of March was notable for a "Tank Day," when our townsfolk were invited to subscribe to the Victory Loan. It proved to be a huge success, the total sum received being £460,000. It is a sad thing to recall that the day was shadowed by the tragic death of a young airman, whose evolutions over the Town Hall had much interested the spectators. His engine failed, and he crashed to the ground, being killed instantly. It was about the 16th March that the Mayor received the news that his eldest son, Sergt. H. F. Houlder, M.M., R.A.M.C., who was serving with the Ambulance on the Western Front, was missing. He proved afterwards to have become a prisoner of war in Germany, and fortunately he returned safe and sound, after the Armistice.

The 23rd March, St. George's Day, will remain for ever in the memory of the English people because of the heroic attack on Zeebrugge by H.M.S. "Vindictive" and her companion ships. Croydon had an intimate interest in the event because Captain Alfred Francis B. Carpenter, V.C., the commander of the expedition, is the son of our neighbour, Captain Alfred Carpenter, R.N., D.S.O., of Sanderstead. Later on, in July, a "Vindictive" week on behalf of the War Loan was held in Croydon and East Surrey, at which the Officers of the "Vindictive" spoke, and in the course of which £600,000 was invested in War Loan, as the contribution of the district towards the cost of a new "Vindictive," and a picture of the famous attack was presented to the new ship, as we record elsewhere.

July, 1918, was marked by the sudden outbreak of war-time influenza. This scourge was called Spanish Influenza at first, and although it spread amongst the population like a conflagration, it was not very fatal in its results. It recurred, however, in a much more dangerous form in October, accompanied by a most deadly species of septic pneumonia; and again a third wave occurred at the beginning of 1919. In many houses whole families were down with the sickness together, and were without help. In some cases we know that families would have starved without the help of sympathetic neighbours. Doctors were given latch-keys in order to gain access to houses in which everybody was prostrate. The death rate was higher than any recorded for more than twenty years. Each wave of the epidemic lasted about five weeks, and although every precaution was taken by the authorities, and schools were shut, the doctors were so overworked and the national medical organization was so bad that proper treatment and certainly proper nursing were not available for a large part of the community. It was really out of this trouble that the Ministry of Health came into existence, and it is hoped that in any future epidemic a fuller medical and nursing service will be available for homes which at present cannot afford them.

From the national point of view 1918 was during its first half a most critical year. The great German offensive on 20th March had thrust back the whole Allied Western line, with enormous losses, almost to where it had stood in 1914. Parliament immediately extended the Military Service Acts to make men from 40 to 50 years of age liable for service. Many men who had hitherto been prevented from serving because of their age now joined up, among them Mr. Councillor James Stevenson, who subsequently became a captain in the Royal Army Service Corps. The Volunteers were called upon to furnish a garrison for the East Coast in order to release the regular troops for service in France, and a sufficient number of Volunteers for this purpose were obtained. The time was one of great strain. For three months the tension lasted; while the enemy made attack after attack in the direction of Paris, his last desperate bid for victory or for a peace satisfactory to himself. Then, in July, Marshal Foch launched his counter stroke, and the gradual rolling back of the German Armies began. From that time the issue was never in doubt, but recruiting and the work of the tribunals continued industriously. There was also recruiting for the W.A.A.C.'s, or, as the Corps was now called, Queen Mary's Auxiliary Army Corps. A demonstration was held in connexion with the last on 27th July which brought in a large number of recruits.

A feature of August, 1918, was a strike of the tramway men, the second that had occurred during the war. The first occurred from April to July, 1916, when the Council resisted and the strike failed. This second strike was to enforce the claim that women should be paid at the same rate as the men whose work they were doing; and the matter was concluded, in this instance successfully, by arbitration.

EVENTS IN CROYDON DURING THE WAR

October saw another campaign on behalf of the War Loan, a week being devoted to the purpose. Guns captured from the enemy were exhibited under the guard of Volunteers in Katharine Street, and were inspected by thousands of people. During " Gun Week," as it was called, the total investment of the Croydon people was £319,595.

By November the international atmosphere had cleared enormously. The British and French troops were advancing rapidly, Bulgaria had capitulated, Austria-Hungary was defeated, the Central Powers were on the verge of collapse ; and in Croydon as elsewhere hopes, long restrained, began to run high. On 9th November, Mr. Alderman Houlder was elected Mayor for the fourth successive time. He told the Council that they approached the new mayoral year under very different conditions from those of the last three or four years. Triumph was coming near. In his speech he made reference to the fact that the Vicar of Croydon, the Rev. Canon White-Thomson, had been elevated to the Archidiaconate of Canterbury. The Vicar had been in the forefront of every movement for the successful prosecution of the war and for the amelioration of the lot of the soldiers and their dependents. His preferment reflected honour upon the Borough. In a spirit appropriate to the hour, the Mayor invited the members to attend the Parish Church with him on the next day, Sunday. It would be fitting, he thought, that the representatives of the Borough should meet together in the Parish Church and unitedly and publicly give thanks for the mercies of the past and ask for Divine guidance in carrying out the responsible duties which would rest upon them in the coming year. The prophecies of the day were realized two days later. All Sunday there was an intense feeling in the air. Messages were passing to and from the battlefields and the homeland, showing that negotiations were in progress and that any minute might mean peace.

And at last, early on Monday, the 11th, we heard that the Armistice had been signed at 5 o'clock in the morning, and that the " cease fire " would be given at 11 o'clock. It was a drab November morning with intervals of falling rain ; but thousands of people were in the streets, and there was a quiet cheerfulness amongst them that had long been absent. At 11 o'clock the maroons, hitherto the heralds of air attack, now proclaimed the cessation of war by the signing of an armistice. The flag was hoisted upon the Town Hall, and the Croydon Parish Church bells rang gaily. Of the doings of the day we give a detailed account elsewhere. At the impromptu meeting in Katharine Street, which occurred immediately on the hoisting of the flag, the Mayor said a few words which deserve to be remembered. He said : " Fellow people of Croydon,—Events have moved at a tremendous pace in the last few days. The hour we have been waiting for has now come. We rejoice at it. The news being so sudden this is not the time for a speech. But I am sure I may, on behalf of the town, express humble and hearty thanks for the deliverance we have had from the menace which has threatened us for more than four years. Prussian militarism has received its final blow. Autocracy has disappeared from the earth. If there is one thing more true than another that result is due to the courage, steadfastness and tenacity of purpose of the British people. It is not for us to be unduly proud over what we have done, but it is right that we should recognise it. Further, it is our duty, aided by our glorious Allies, to recognise the responsibility that rests upon us concerning the days to come. We are the inheritors of a great heritage. The duty is incumbent upon us to lead the van in the reconstruction of the world. Just as it is a general duty, so, I hope and believe, and have every confidence, the people of Croydon will make it their particular duty to do whatever lies in their power to carry that principle out. We shall, no doubt, have other occasions of celebrating the joyous news of to-day. I appeal to the people of Croydon to comport themselves with restraint under the new conditions that have come ; and with that confident expectation and hope, I say, ' God bless Croydon and all the people who live in the town.' "

Thus ended the Great War ; and within a few weeks the boys began to come home again. But even now, as we write, more than a year after the event, we still are battling with the many problems which the delays and waste of the war have created. At the end of the war, Croydon, as we have hinted before, presented a strained and shabby appearance, with a crowded population, streets out of repair, shops and houses badly in need of repainting, and arrears to make up in all directions. We have much to be thankful for to those who directed the war in the Field and in the Central Government, but we have also a sense of gratitude to those who looked after the interests of our own town. Everybody worked, officially or unofficially, who remained at home ; there was a home front as well as a fighting front. Our gratitude to those who fought transcends words, and will never find adequate expression or acknowledgment. That is beyond us. They and we know that but for their efforts the heritage of freedom which our fathers gave us would have perished for ever from the earth.

Photo by Lewis

Councillor CHARLES HEATH CLARK, J.P.
Peace-Mayor (from Nov., 1919)

Photo by Lewis.

Mrs. HEATH CLARK
Mayoress from Nov., 1919

III. Croydon County Borough Council, 1914 to 1919

LIST OF WAR COMMITTEES.

[*The numbers after the names indicate the War-Committees on which the Members served, as given in the list below.*]

1. Belgian Refugees Fund. 2. Corporation Employees (Discharged Soldiers). 3. Croydon District Association of Voluntary Organisations. 4. Croydon Local Central War Savings. 5. Food Control. 6. Mayor's Committee. 7. Mayoress's Committee. 8. Mayoress's Flag Day. 9. National Kitchens. 10. National Registration. 11. National Service. 12. National Service (Corporation Employees). 13. Small Holdings and Allotments. 14. Tribunals. 15. War Charities. 16. War Pensions.

I. MAYORS.

Alderman FRANK DENNING, J.P.
    (Counc., 1903-15 ; Ald., 1915-16 ; Mayor, Nov., 1913, to Feb., 1916.) 1, 6, 10, 13, 14.
    Mayoress—Mrs. DENNING, 6, 7, 8.

Alderman HOWARD HOULDER, D.L., J.P.
    (Counc., 1906-16 ; Ald., 1916- ; Mayor, Feb., 1916, to Nov., 1919.) 1, 3, 4, 5, 6, 9, 10, 12, 14, 16
    Mayoress—Mrs. HOULDER, 3, 4, 7, 8, 9, 11, 16.
    Sons who served—Sergt. H. F. HOULDER, M.M., R.A.M.C., 1914-19 ; served in France, pris. of war in Germany, March, 1918-Nov., 1919.
    2/Lt. A. C. HOULDER, Queen's, volunteered from Ceylon.

Councillor CHARLES HEATH CLARK, J.P.
    (Counc., 1915-). 4, 5, 13, 14, 16.
    Mayoress—Mrs. HEATH CLARK, 16.

II. ALDERMEN.

ALLEN, GEORGE JOHN, J.P.
    (Counc., 1893-99 ; Ald., 1899-). 2, 6, 12, 14, 16.
    Sons who served—Lt. Col. CLARENCE ALLEN, M.C., R.A.S.C Col. Allen (then Capt.) took out the Surrey Brigade, T. & S. Company, with 27th Division to France. Many times mentioned in despatches.
    Capt. J. R. ALLEN, R.A.S.C., Surrey Brigade. Mentioned in despatches.
    Major STANLEY R. DOCKING, T.D. (*son-in-law*).

BARROW, Sir REUBEN VINCENT, J.P.
    (Counc., 1883 ; Ald., 1883-1916).

BETTERIDGE, THOMAS, J.P.
    (Counc., 1894-1910 ; Ald., 1910-). 1, 11, 13, 14, 16.

EDRIDGE, Sir FREDERICK THOMAS, D.L., J.P. ; Hon. Colonel 4th Queen's
    (Counc., 1889-91 ; Ald., 1891-). 2, 3, 6, 11, 14, 16.

Fox, Major JOHN EDWARD, T.D., J.P.
(Counc., 1906-09 ; Ald., 1909-   ).
Raised Croydon Column of South Eastern Mounted Brigade, A.S.C.

HANCOCK, JOHN APPLEBY.
(Counc., 1898-1917 ; Ald., 1917-   ).   5, 9.

HILLIER, THOMAS.
(Counc., 1883-1903 ; Ald., 1903-15).

JOSLIN PETER.
(Counc., 1887-98 ; Ald., 1898-1917).

KING, FRANCIS WILLIAM MARK, J.P.
(Counc., 1889-1905 ; Ald., 1905-   ).   14.   Chairman, Local Pensions Committee, South Norwood.

LILLICO, WILLIAM, J.P.
(Counc., 1889-1903 ; Ald., 1903-   ).   2, 6, 7, 10, 13, 15, 16.

MILLER, DAVID BUCK, J.P.
(Counc., 1883-91 ; Ald., 1891-1919).

MOORE, HENRY KEATLEY, B.A., B.Mus., J.P.
(Counc., 1893-98, 1902-08 ; Ald., 1908-   ).   1, 6.   Chairman, War Refugees' Committee.
Daughter who served—HELENA R. MOORE, W.R.N.S.

PRICE, GEORGE NICOLL.
(Counc., 1890-1906 ; Ald., 1906-   ).

ROGERS, SAMUEL, J.P.
(Counc., 1902-16 ; Ald., 1916-17).   2, 6, 10, 13, 14.

SOUTHWELL, WILLIAM BAINES.
(Counc., 1906-19 ; Ald., 1919-   ).   2, 5, 9, 11, 12, 16.
Son who served—Lt. WILLIAM BAINES SOUTHWELL, 1/4th Buffs (still serving).

TAYLOR, MARTIN.
(Counc., 1883-96 ; Ald., 1896-   ).   15.
Grandson who served—RONALD MARTIN PANNIERS, R.W. Kent Regt. Wounded in Somme Offensive, 1915. Was wounded on Somme, and lost an eye at Messines.

TRUMBLE, JAMES, J.P.,
(Counc., 1893-1905 ; Ald., 1905-   ).   4, 6, 9, 15, 16.

TRYTHALL, JOHN ANTHONY, J.P.
(Counc., 1901-17 ; Ald., 1917-   ).   9, 13.
Sons who served—Lt. HORACE JOHN TRYTHALL, 1st Queen's R.W.S. Regt. Badly wounded in France.
Gunner HAROLD GOODMAN TRYTHALL, R.H.A.

III. COUNCILLORS.

ADAMS, WILLIAM.
(1913-   ).   13.

ADDISON, GEORGE SCHOOLEY.
(1894-1900 ; 1909-   ).

ALLEN, FRANCIS, M.B.E., J.P.
(1917-   ).   4, 6, 15, 16.
Son who served—2/Lt. G. P. ALLEN, 3/4th Queen's R.W.S. Regt. Died of wounds received in bombing accident.

Photo by Lewis
JOHN MONTAGUE NEWNHAM, O.B.E., D.L., LL.D., B.A.
Town Clerk from Sept., 1913
Hon. Lieut. Colonel, 1 Vol. Bat., " The Queen's."

CROYDON COUNTY BOROUGH COUNCIL, 1914-19 49

AMBLER, WILLIAM.
  (1905-18).

BARKER, DAVID WILLIAM.
  (1906-   ).   5.
    Sons who served—EDWARD T. BARKER, 1/4th Queen's R.W.S. Regt. Died in India, May 18th, 1915.
    FREDERICK CHRISTOPHER BARKER, Vishna Rifles. Wounded at Jericho.
    LEONARD DAVID BARKER, London Rifles. Wounded and gassed in France.
    STANLEY BARKER, Middlesex Regt. Pris. of war in Germany for 2½ years.

BARNETT, EDWARD WATSON.
  (1903-18).
    Son who served—Major ERIK E. BARNETT, R.A.F., served throughout the war in various parts of the Mediterranean, etc.

BISHOP, SAMUEL WILLIAM.
  (1902-   ).   2.
    Son who served—A. W. BISHOP, R.A.F., May, 1917-Aug., 1920. Another son, H. BISHOP, having only one eye, was refused by the Army and served as Special Constable from Dec., 1917, until demobilization.

BRADSHAW, JOSEPH.
  (1913-   ).   2, 13, 16.

CHAMBERLAIN, WALTER JOHN.
  (1911-   ).

CHAPMAN, CHARLES TOBIAS.
  (1912-19).

CHOWN, FRANK HERBERT.
  (1919-   ).
    West London Mounted Rifles and Motor Volunteers (station and hospital work), 1915-19. Mr. Chown served in the Boer War in 1900.

CLARKE, JOHN ARTHUR.
  (1907-16, 1917-   ).   13.
    Served as Farrier Staff-Sergeant, Remounts, attached R.A.S.C., Sept., 1914-Jan., 1918.
    Son who served—2/A.M., A. J. CLARKE, R.A.F.

COLDREY, FRANCIS.
  (1915-   ).   6, 13,

COSEDGE, PERCIVAL GEORGE ALLEN.
  (1912-14).
    Served in E. Sur. Regt. Died of wounds at 8th C.C.S., France, 16th Dec., 1914.

CROWLEY, JOHN CYRIL, M.A.
  (1909-15).   13.
    Served as Captain in 1/4th " Queen's " R.W.S. Regt., 1906-11th Sept., 1916. Fell in Mesopotamia.

D

DOCKING, FREDERICK REYNOLDS.
    (1898-1903 ; 1918-19).
        Sons who served—Lieut. C. W. DOCKING, R.A.S.C., May, 1915-Sept., 1919, in Egypt and Palestine.
        Capt. F. L. DOCKING, joined Australians, 1914, and was in original landing at Gallipoli, and in Egypt, France and Flanders, and the Army of Occupation, Germany, till Oct., 1919.
FAGG, WILLIAM HENRY.
    (1913-16). 13.
FIELD, ALBERT JAMES CAMDEN.
    (1910-13 ; 1915-   ). 5, 15, 16.
        Son who served—ALBERT JOSEPH CAMDEN FIELD, 9th City of London Regt. (Queen Victoria's Rifles). Wounded at Hebuterne, May, 1916, and in the advance on Cambrai, Nov., 1917.
GOUGH, ERNEST WILLIAM.
    (1913-   ). 6.
        Served also on Demobilised Officers' Panel Committee, Horrex Hotel, London.
        Sons who served—Lt. EDWARD ERNEST GOUGH, R.G.A., S.R.
        2/Lt. WILLIAM ERIC GOUGH, R.M.L.I.
HAMMOND, JAMES CHARLES.
    (1919-   ).
HEIGHTON, JAMES HUGHES, M.A.
    (1917-   ).
HICKS, JOHN.
    (1918-   ). 13.
        Son who served—WILLIAM JOHN HICKS, Wireless Officer, R.N.V.R., on various ships ; last ship torpedoed.
HUSSEY, CHARLES, J.P.
    (1909-15).
JACKSON, ALBERT.
    (1918-   ).
LEWIS, THOMAS ARTHUR.
    (1911-   ). 6.
        Son who served—Lt. C. A. LEWIS, R.F.A., 1914-19.
LIGHTON, THOMAS.
    (1904-16.)
LINK, CHARLES WILLIAM.
    (1906-19). 4.
        Sons who served—2/Lt. HORACE A. LINK, H.A.C. Fell, near Bully Grenay, France, Sept., 1916.'
        Lt. CHARLES ERNEST LINK, R.N.V.R., attached R.N.A.S.
MARDELL, ROBERT WILLIAM.
    (1919-   ).
MOIR, ALFRED.
    (1919-   ). 4.
        1st Quartermaster 1/1st (Croydon) Surrey, V.T.C. Took part in Public Recruiting and War Savings campaigns. Enlisted, June, 1917, in 5th E. Surrey Regt. ; commissioned Nov., 1917, in Highland Light Inf. ; Capt., Oct., 1918. Served in France, Feb., 1918-May, 1919.
        Sons who served—Corp. A. DOUGLAS MOIR, R.F.A., Aug., 1915-Feb., 1919. Twice wounded.
        2/Lt. LESLIE J. A. MOIR, E. Surrey Regt. (formerly in Artists' Rifles), Feb., 1918.

MORLAND, HAROLD JOHN, M.A.
(1912-19). 9, 10, 12.
MOSS, HENRY VINCENT.
(1899-1918).
MUGGERIDGE, HENRY THOMAS.
(1911-). 5, 9.
Sons who served—Lt. HARRY DOUGLAS MUGGERIDGE, 1st Leicesters. 3 Times wounded in France, and is now lame. 1/A.M., STANLEY WILLIAM MUGGERIDGE, R.A.F., 2½ years in Egypt.
MUSSELWHITE, Miss CLARA.
(1919-). 6, 16.
OLIVER, DOUGLAS WILLIAM.
(1919-). 13.
Special Constable, Sanderstead and Croydon.
Son who served—2/Lt. D. C. M. OLIVER, R.W. Kent Regt. Was pris. of war for 11 months.
PECK, JOSEPH, J.P.
(1889-1916).
PECK, STANLEY.
(1916-18). 9, 13.
PEET, WILLIAM, F.C.A.
(1911-). 2, 3, 4, 11, 12, 15, 16.
PELTON, JOHN OLLIS, J.P.
(1905-). 5, 14.
1/12 Surrey Vol. Regt., and 1 Vol. Btn., The Queen's.
Daughter who served—DOROTHY G. (Mrs. S. DICKINS). Purley War Hospital 1915–1917; Canteen work, etc., with Y.M.C.A., Le Havre, May, 1917–Feb., 1919.
PETERS, ARTHUR, C.B.E., J.P.
(1916-). 5, 9, 11, 13.
Also Secretary Parliamentary Recruiting Committee, and Secretary, National War Aims Committee.
PICKFORD, WILLIAM JAMES.
(1915-18). 4.
PORRITT, THOMAS HERBERT.
(1912-). Special Constable.
READ, SIDNEY AUGUSTUS, J.P.
(1907-). 5, 9, 15.
ROBARTS, WILLIAM BROWN.
(1901-). 5, 6.
ROBERTS, THOMAS WILLIAM WOOD.
(1908-). 2, 10, 11, 16.
Hon. Naval Recruiting Officer, Croydon & District. Special Constable. Voluntary Fireman, Croydon & London.
Son who served—Lt. JOHN WOOD ROBERTS, R.M.L.I., of H.M.S. " Ajax," H.M.S. " Curlew," H.M.S. " Curacoa," H.M.S. " Canterbury," H.M.S. " Dunedin."
ROBINSON, GEORGE.
(1919-). 13.
RODEN. SAMUEL.
(1919-).

SAVORY, GUY.
    (1916-19). 14.
SKINNER, ALEXANDER BOWIE.
    (1919-).
SMITH, ARTHUR.
    (1917-).
    National Guard (London Volunteers).
        Sons who served—ARTHUR DOUGLAS SMITH, R.A.S.C.
        JAMES DONALD SMITH, local service and transport.
SMITH, WILLIAM VINCENT, J.P.
    (1903-06; 1908-). 2, 12, 14.
        Sons who served—Sergt. Maj. V. V. SMITH, R.A.M.C.;
        France, Sept., 1914-Feb., 1919.
        Sapper F. SUTTON SMITH; Egypt and Palestine (light railways), June, 1915-Feb., 1919.
SQUIRE, Mrs. MARGARET.
    (1919-). 16.
    Was temporary nurse at "Wallacefield" Convalescent Hospital, Croydon, and at Charing Cross Hospital.
STAPLETON, WILLIAM GEORGE.
    (1897-). 13.
        Sons who served—Sergt. DONALD YOUNG (Stepson), 18th Cameron Grenadiers; killed at capture of Vimy Ridge, Easter, 1917.
        Lt. MAURICE R. STAPLETON, Rifle Brigade; was wounded and gassed; also served in Army of Occupation, Germany.
STEVENS, LEONARD.
    (1909-11; 1913-15).
STEVENSON JAMES.
    (1913-). 1, 4, 6, 14, 16.
    Served as Captain, R.A.S.C.
        Daughter who served in Land Army—Marianne North Stevenson.
STUBBS, WILLIAM JOHN.
    (1914-19). 11, 16.
TAYLOR, JAMES ERNEST.
    (1919-). 5.
    Appointed, before election to Council, to Food Control Committee, Feb., 1918.
        Son who served—WALTER EDWARD TAYLOR, R.N. Wrecked in H.M.S. "Argyle," fought in Battle of Jutland in H.M.S. "Princess Royal"; served in H.M.S. "Vindictive" at Zeebrugge, and was badly wounded.
THOMSON, ALEXANDER AUGUSTUS.
    (1912-). 13, 16.
THORNBERRY, ROBERT EUSTACE CLARK.
    (1916-19). 9, 13.
TURTLE, LOUIS HENRY.
    (1913-17). 6.
        Son who served—Rifleman CLIFFORD L. TURTLE, 1st Queen's Westminster Rifles; fell on the Somme, 10th Sept., 1916.

Councillor PERCIVAL GEORGE ALLEN COSEDGE
East Surrey Regt. (Died on active service in France 16th Dec., 1914)

Photo by G. W. Lawrie & Co.
Councillor Captain JOHN CYRIL CROWLEY, M.A.
1/4th Queen's (Killed in action in Mesopotamia, 11th Sept. 1916)

UMNEY. HERBERT WILLIAMS.
  (1909-15). 2.

WAGDIN, HARRY FREDERICK.
  (1918-19).
    Son who served—Pte. S. F. WAGDIN, Queen's Westminster Rifles.

WEST, WILLIAM.
  (1899-). 5, 10.
  Special Constable.
    Sons who served—2/Lt. WILLIAM WEST, 9th Sherwood Foresters. Fell, Suvla, Gallipoli, Aug., 1915.

    Lt. CYRIL G. WEST, R.N., of H.M.S. "Princess Royal," H.M.S. "Weymouth," H.M.S. "Agamemnon," and H.M.S. "Monarch." Was in the Battle of Jutland.

WORLLEDGE, Col. JOHN FRANKLIN.
  (1916-). 3, 6, 15.
    Sons who served—Capt. F. H. WORLLEDGE, 26th Indian Cavalry (King George's Own).

    Lt. J. F. E. WORLLEDGE, Sussex Regt.

    Lt. L. H. WORLLEDGE, R.N.D., and 121st Indian Pioneers. Wounded at Gallipoli, July, 1915.

OFFICERS OF THE COUNTY BOROUGH
1. R. VEITCH CLARK, M.A., M.B., Ch.B., B.Sc., D.P.H.: Medical Officer of Health
2. WILLIAM GUNNER: Borough Treasurer
3. JAMES HAROLD McCALL, F.S.A.A.: Borough Accountant
4. JAMES SMYTH: Clerk to the Education Committee

OFFICERS OF THE COUNTY BOROUGH
1. EDWARD F. MORGAN : Borough Road Surveyor
2. THOMAS BOYCE GOODYER, O.B.E., A.I.E.E.: Tramways Manager
3. SAMUEL JACOBS: Assistant Town Clerk
4. ALBERT C. GOWER : Chief Clerk, Town Clerk's Department

Part Two

THE MILITARY RECORD

I. Before the Great War

Surrey, happily, has been spared the havoc of war more than almost any other County, and Croydon—which has only recently taken the first place in Surrey towns—may be said to have been totally immune from this scourge until our own day. Even Julius Caesar though he crossed Surrey did not come our way; and William the Conqueror also left us alone. Nevertheless there are a few introductory facts we may with advantage remember.

In 1264 a large body of Londoners forming part of the force of Earl Simon de Montfort, in arms against King Henry III, and flying from Prince Edward's attack at the Battle of Lewes, were stopped by Royalists at Croydon and severely handled. And in Elizabethan times Haling House and Haling Park formed the residence, from 1592 to his death in 1624, of the victor over the Armada, Lord Howard of Effingham, who (with the aid of the terrific tempest which followed his victory) delivered England in 1588 from the most terrible danger she ever ran until the Great War we are now dealing with.

Other men of military distinction, especially in the times of the Peninsular War, were Croydon men or lived in Croydon; men of whom an example was Sir Francis Bond Head, K.C.B., who fought not only in the Peninsular but in the Waterloo campaign, and who had the honour of quelling an insurrection in Canada in 1830. His house (Duppas Hall, Duppas Hill) still stands, much as he left it. And in Head's time the fear of an invasion by Napoleon caused Croydon to raise volunteers, horse and foot. The barracks—still existing in the Mitcham Road from the times of Revolutionary France (1794)—served as a station for cavalry during the preparation of troops for foreign service; and later became the depot and headquarters of the Royal Wagon Train (now Army Service Corps.) The band attached to this unit was a fine one; it happened to contain some negro bandsmen—a fact perpetuated in the signs of two of the neighbouring public houses, the " Black Boy " and the " Six Bells." The latter refers to a musical instrument then in military favour, and used in the band.

Fifty years later, in Crimean War times, recruits for the Grenadier, Coldstream and Fusilier Guards were drilled at Croydon Barracks.

But Croydon's chief connection with the military history of the country is derived from its possession of Addiscombe College, where officers for the Army of the East India Company were trained. A shortage of officers for the Company's service in India, who at that time were educated with the regular officers of the Crown, at Woolwich, determined the Hon. East India Company to create a Military Academy of their own. In 1808 Charles Jenkinson, Earl of Liverpool and Prime Minister of England, died at Addiscombe Place, Croydon—and in 1809 the house and park were purchased by the Company, and adapted to the uses of a Military College. The Company continued to train officers for the Indian Army till 1861 ; the Indian Empire having been taken over by Queen Victoria in 1859. Numerous pictures and accurate maps of the College and its subordinate buildings exist in the Croydon Library, as well as excellent histories of its career. It is sufficient here to mention that the house stood between Upper and Lower Addiscombe Roads, about 150 yards from the present Ashburton Road ; and that the park filled this space, the present Canning Road being a little within its western boundary. The College was pulled down in 1861.

The College had a distinguished career during its half century of existence. To its training we owe many fine men. For example General Cotton, the great master of irrigation and inland navigation in India, and the first engineer to bridge a great Indian river (the Godavery, four miles wide) was trained here. The great Sir Henry Lawrence, of the defence of Lucknow, and of greater though more silent achievements in Indian administration, was an Addiscombe man. So were Lord Napier of Magdala, and Pottinger of Herat, and Jacob of Jacob's Horse (after whom the town of Jacobabad in Scinde is named), and Patrick Stewart the pioneer of field telegraphy, etc., etc. And closest to us, because he was the first honorary freeman of the borough of Croydon, was Frederick, Lord Roberts, who won his V.C. in the Mutiny struggles, and who claims world-famous victories at Cabul and Candahar, and above all in South Africa. Lord Roberts said once of the men from his old College, " They were not only soldiers but administrators, who throughout their glorious careers did their duty with that singleness of heart and honesty of purpose for which the Anglo Indian official is so justly conspicuous, and which have gained for Englishmen the respect and confidence of the people of India."

ADDISCOMBE COLLEGE—Main Front (Hon. East India Company, 1809—1861)

ADDISCOMBE COLLEGE—North Front (Hon. East India Company, 1809—1861)

From a drawing by E. Pritchett

II. "The Queen's."

"The Queen's" is Croydon's Regiment. It has a very distinguished history, and is the oldest English Infantry Regiment of the line; ranking as "The Second of the Line" in the old numbering.

One Scottish regiment, "The Royal Scots," precedes it as "The First" of the Line, and this claims to be the oldest regiment in existence—as may well be, if its nickname has the slightest foundation, for it is called familiarly "Pontius Pilate's Body Guard," on the strength of the tradition that it was on duty at the Crucifixion!

In 1661 Charles II raised "The Queen's" in the suburbs of London (therefore, no doubt, including Croydon men from the very first), with many veterans from the armies of the Civil War; his purpose being to garrison Tangier, which was part of the dowry of his Queen, Catherine of Braganza. Hence comes the name of the regiment, and hence its "honour," the oldest battle-honour in the British Army, "Tangier 1662-1680," awarded it after many years' desultory fighting with the Moors: and hence also the Regimental Badge, the Paschal Lamb, then and now a part of the Arms of the Royal House of Portugal. Almost but not quite unique is another distinction of "The Queen's," a naval crown, borne on the colours to commemorate an engagement at sea (1794) wherein this great regiment took part.

In 1857, because of the needs of the Indian Empire, the second battalion of the Regiment, called therefore the "Second Queen's," came into existence, and in 1881 the "Third Queen's" was made out of the Surrey Militia: and the three battalions of the Second Regiment of foot ("Queen's Royals") now became "The Queen's Royal West Surrey Regiment."

The achievements of "The Queen's" in Africa, Asia and Europe would take too long to narrate here, but we cannot help recalling the fact that the great Duke of Marlborough began his career in "The Queen's."

And we must remember that many Croydon men enlisted during the Great War in the three "regular" battalions of "The Queen's," or were conscripted into its ranks. Col. Rolls has kindly told us of the many men of our town serving in "The Queen's" in the regular army in France, his own "batman" for instance being a Croydon man. And to show the prestige of this splendid regiment we may add a fact also kindly mentioned by Col. Rolls, that when he was sent to England in 1918 " for a rest," his " rest " included the training of raw levies of conscripts at Tunbridge Wells, in what was then called the " Fourth Reserve of The Queen's," and the success of their training (as well as over-pressure elsewhere) induced the War Office also to send levies from other parts of England to this centre. Amongst them came a company of recruits to the " Sherwood Foresters " (itself a very famous regiment) : and so proud were these men of their association with " The Queen's " that the whole 200 of them successfully petitioned the War Office to be transferred to " The Queen's," which was then sending out a large detachment to the 2/4th Queen's in France, saying in blunt language " We've trained together and we want to fight together." This is believed to be an almost unique incident.

What we have hitherto been speaking of (except as to the " Fourth Reserve " mentioned above) are the three regular battalions of the Queen's : known as the First Queen's, the Second Queen's, and the Third Queen's, dating respectively from 1661, 1857, and 1881, and we now pass to the Fourth Queen's, an exclusively Croydon force.

Lord Roberts Presenting the Colours to the Fourth Queen's on Duppas Hill.

Photo by Norman Stanislaus

Photo by Lewis

Alderman Sir Frederick Thomas Edridge, D.L., J.P.
Hon. Colonel, Fourth Queen's
(Mayor 1890-92, 1894-96, 1902)
Hon. Freeman of the Borough

III. The Fourth Queen's

On the re-planning of the Army in 1881 the old numbering of the regiments was abandoned : and the Second Regiment of Foot,"The Queen's," as mentioned above, became the Royal West Surrey Regiment, with head quarters at Guildford, and having as its special recruiting district all the South of Surrey, including Croydon. The rest of the county, exclusive of London, was assigned to the East Surrey Regiment, with head quarters at Kingston.

[In March, 1916, owing to the unwieldy nature of the district, it was found advisable to place Croydon for recruiting purposes under Kingston, and therefore in the East Surrey Regimental recruiting area ; other parts of Surrey being at the same time changed over to the Guildford recruiting area.]

Each regiment of the army, under this new plan, had three regular battalions exclusive of the Territorial battalions ; thus the 1st and 2nd Queen's (1st and 2nd battalions of "The Queen's") were regulars of the long familiar type, the 3rd Queen's were formed from the old Militia, at first under the name of Special Reserve, the 4th Queen's were the Territorial battalion of Croydon and the 5th Queen's were the Territorial battalion of Guildford.

These Territorial battalions originated from the Rifle Volunteers, who came into being just before the Crimean War, and enrolled themselves into a home-defence body under the well-remembered motto " Defence not Defiance." (It is whimsical now to remember that the very nation—France—a scare against whom had called these Riflemen into being, turned into our warmly welcomed ally in the Crimean War, almost as soon as the Rifle Volunteers had become an organised force). In 1871 the War Office obtained control of these Riflemen, and in 1881 added them, under the new army plan above described, to the various County Regiments as " Territorial battalions for Home Service only." The Croydon Rifle Volunteers therefore became (as above said) " The Royal West Surrey Regiment, the Fourth Queen's, (Territorial Battalion)." Similarly the Guildford Rifle Volunteers became the " Fifth Queen's, (Territorial Battalion)."

The 4th Queen's at the outbreak of war numbered about 600 men, under the Hon. Colonelcy of Sir Frederick T. Edridge, D.L., the acting commander being Lieutenant-Colonel Norman Cutler. They formed part of the Home Counties Territorial

Division, at that moment in training on Salisbury Plain, and were earning good opinions for their excellent discipline and marching powers ; moreover, they were all in the most eager anticipation of orders to mobilise, as it grew daily more evident that war was coming. At last, on Monday, 3rd August, the Camp began to break up in preparation for the expected immediate mobilisation ; and next day the 4th Queen's entrained at 4.30 a.m. and after a very uncomfortable journey reached Croydon late the same night, of course not knowing as yet, of the declaration of war which had just taken place. " The train was unlighted " says " L.G.D." in *The Braganza* (the Magazine published by the 1/4th Queen's) " and the carriage in which I travelled apparently had a wheel *with a flat side*." An official order met them in Croydon naming the morrow, Wednesday, 5th August, as the first day of mobilisation.

" That Wednesday (5th August) was a day to remember. It rained most of the morning, and wives and families were let into the barracks. I have vivid recollections of trying to take inventories of kit, fill up allotment forms, and issue identity discs, sitting on the floor of the drill hall, with a crowd of damp men, women and children all round me," continues " L.G.D." (Major Dibdin) in *The Braganza*.

Mobilisation, it should be noted, has to be organised long before any mobilisation order is received. Colonel Cutler had made his preparations two years before any war was thought of. All the principal tradesmen in Croydon therefore were prepared to supply various articles immediately they were ordered. So that when War against Germany was declared and mobilisation decreed, on that very day (5th August) Colonel Cutler was able to send round the Quarter-Master to all the tradesmen, and instantly supplies began to arrive at the Mitcham Road Barracks Head Quarters.

So that actually on the very day it was mobilised the Fourth Queen's left Croydon for Strood : certainly a smart piece of work.

" Arriving about 7.30 " (says L.G.D.) " we marched to a public recreation ground, blankets were issued, and policemen allotted to the companies as guides to the particular streets for billeting. That night was probably the first time for many years that the English householder, other than the licensed victualler, was compelled to put up troops. It was with a certain amount of doubt that I knocked at the first door. But I found that evening, and indeed throughout the whole three months that the battalion was in billets, very few people who were not prepared to put up gladly with the necessary inconvenience. On the other hand the men made themselves useful, and gave as little trouble as possible." Some days later, (we pass over some amusing contests on the part of L.G.D. to get back certain buildings suitable for military purposes from the various well meaning voluntary organisations which had already annexed them) " the regimental transport which we had left behind at Croydon arrived, having travelled by road. I did not envy the Transport Officer. He had 57 newly collected and impressed horses, and a miscellaneous collection of brewer's drays, corporation water carts and tip-wagons, driven by a variety of men *with no knowledge of horses*." To start from nothing in this way, meant, as these extracts show, the expenditure of much labour and infinite resource ; but when, after a fortnight at Maidstone, the Fourth Queen's arrived at Canterbury it was already a coherent and well organised body.

So much so, that at the end of September (training of course having vigorously proceeded all the time) Colonel Cutler received a telegram from the War Office asking if the battalion would volunteer for service abroad. Each Company officer read this telegram to his Company and invited men to give in their names if they chose. There was not the slightest compulsion, not even persuasion, used ; but the gratifying result was that, with a very few (quite legitimate) exceptions the whole battalion volunteered with cheers and much enthusiasm ; expecting of course immediately to be sent to the front to aid in demolishing the " Boches." But about a week later, with deep chagrin, the battalion received the order to proceed to *India*. No doubt this was in a military sense the proper thing to do, as the Fourth Queen's would set free in India well-seasoned troops of the line, whose presence helped to stop the first rush of the Germans on Paris, and so to save the Allies from disaster ; but the disappointment was sharply felt by the men, who had become proud of their discipline, and knew themselves fully equal to facing the enemy. That they were not far wrong is proved by the actual behaviour in the field of other Territorial battalions on the French front shortly afterwards. But while " the air went blue for miles " as the men themselves said, they " groused, and carried on," to use another of their phrases, and the unwelcome orders were loyally obeyed. All honour to them : for they had trained hard in peace time towards this very opportunity, and in their long Indian exile it must have been galling to hear of their 2nd line battalions serving on the different fronts while they had perforce to remain largely inactive. The Croydon men were reviewed by the King, at Canterbury, with the Home Counties Division (of which they formed part). His Majesty wished them " God Speed " and pointed out to them the important duty they were about to undertake in India.

The men who were unable to go to India and who remained in England came to be called the 2nd battalion of the Fourth Queen's, and received and trained the reinforcements which poured in. Those who had gone to India became known as the 1st battalion of the Fourth Queen's, or shortly the " 1/4th Queen's " ; and when the 2/4th volunteered for service abroad later on and were sent to Gallipoli, those who (for good reasons which all acknowledged as legitimate) were unable to leave England, became eventually in like manner the 3/4th Queen's. They too, all who could, presently volunteered in their turn, and were sent to France. The remainder permanently left in England, we call the 4/4th Queen's, and they served the most useful and necessary function of supplying drafts to their comrades actually in the field.

We have therefore now to consider these four battalions separately, and widely different were their destinies.

Beyond the 1/4th, 2/4th, 3/4th and 4/4th Queen's we have the 19th Queen's, at first called the 69th Provisional Battalion. And it may be as well here to mention that after the Fifth Queen's, already known in these pages as the Guildford Territorial battalion, came the Sixth, Seventh and Eighth Queen's, all three of which were battalions of " Kitchener's men."

Then, outside the organisation of the Queen's altogether, Croydon produced a corps of Volunteers, arising out of the Volunteer Training Corps, an entirely new body formed during the progress of the War : who in course of time were linked up, and then became the " 1st Volunteer Battalion of the Queen's."

And as well as the infantry forces above named, Croydon provided its quota of mounted men. We shall have chapters on the Croydon Squadron of the Surrey Yeomanry (Queen Mary's Regiment) ; and on the S.E. Mounted Brigade Transport and Supply Column, A.S.C.

Next we have the Croydon Army Veterans, a force originating from an idea of Lord Roberts' in 1910, and ultimately known as the " First Battalion, Surrey (Croydon) National Reserve."

And finally, since we must not neglect the opposite extreme, we will have some concluding notes on the Boy Scouts of Croydon.

The careers of all these we now proceed to trace, and of course begin with the 1/4th Queen's.

Mobilisation of the Fourth Queen's, Croydon Barracks, 5th August, 1914
Photo by Batchelder Bros.

Mobilisation of the Fourth Queen's, London Road, Croydon, 5th August, 1914

Photo by Batchelder Bros.

IV. The 1/4th Queen's

The 1/4th Queen's sailed from Southampton, 800 strong, on 26th October, 1914, in the " Grantully Castle." At Suez the battalion was held up for some time because trouble with the Turks was threatening, and the 1/4th Queen's fully expected to have to defend the Suez Canal. This alarm presently subsiding, the battalion proceeded, and arrived at Bombay, 2nd December, 1914.

From Bombay the Queen's went by train to Secunderabad, and when they marched into those cantonments their discipline and general bearing were held by onlookers to compare favourably with those of the regular troops, bound for France, whom they were relieving. After a month at Secunderabad they went on to Lucknow, where they stayed for twelve months almost to a day. While the battalion was at Lucknow they sent a draft to Mesopotamia (to the 2nd Norfolks); and several Croydon men in this draft served afterwards in Kut. Colonel Cutler had fallen ill on arrival at Bombay and had been sent home to England, Major Roper taking command of the 1/4th Queen's meanwhile; fortunately Colonel Cutler was able to return to the battalion and to resume command just before it left Lucknow for Peshawar early in 1916. At Peshawar the whole battalion was actually mobilised for the Mesopotamian campaign, and some officers and men had started before the order was cancelled. Between Peshawar and Nowshera and Cherat the 1/4th Queen's spent 17 months. Captain J. C. Crowley (an ex-Councillor of Croydon) left Nowshera, (and Lieut. E. L. Turner went with him) on 25th July, 1916, to join the Fifth Queen's (the Guildford battalion) at Nasariyah on the Euphrates, in the Mesopotamia campaign. Capt. Crowley took command of a Machine Gun Company with one British (Fifth Queen's), and two native, sections. For ten years Captain Crowley had refused promotion in order to remain in command of the Machine Guns of the Fourth Queen's; and at last his eager desire to take them into action was achieved. His Mesopotamian work alternated between periods of standing camp and raids on native insurgent villages. Such a raid had to be undertaken on 11th September, 1916, Captain Crowley's duty being to cover the retirement of the rear guard after the raid was over. The native method is to offer no resistance to the attack, but persistently to assail the troops on the retirement; the rear guard is therefore a post of incessant danger and responsibility. Captain Crowley, in what was admitted to be a fine covering movement, was shot and died

E

almost immediately. His loss was felt deeply. He was the first officer of the old Fourth Queen's to fall in battle. Altogether 8 officers and 65 non-commissioned officers and men went from the 1/4th Queen's to Mesopotamia.

There is always trouble in the stormy regions of extreme N.W. India, and in sending the 1/4th Queen's there the object of the authorities was to train them in hill-warfare and frontier fighting. In fact at this very time the Mohmands rose, and had to be firmly held with a line of wire entanglements and blockhouses for nine months on end; and four months of this weary work fell to the lot of the 1/4th Queen's to carry through, including the actual construction of one section of the block-houses.

Leaving Nowshera on 19th March, 1917, the battalion was ordered to Lahore for a month. The Mahsuds then rose, and the 1/4th Queen's were ordered to Waziristan in May. Here grave ill-health overtook them, especially a bad outbreak of malaria and sand-fly fever, etc., and at the worst time only 130 men out of 800 were fit for duty; so that perforce the battalion had to be sent to the hills at Jutogh and Dagshai, near Simla, to recuperate. This was in the middle of June, 1917. It ought here to be added that some of the officers had the good fortune to be accompanied by their wives; since, when it became certain that the 1/4th Queen's would be detained in India for a very long time, permission was given freely for the wives to come out. Whilst the 1/4th Queen's were in the hills Colonel Cutler's 8 years of command (the utmost limit allowed) came to an end, and he accepted an independent command at Wellington, near Ootacamund, on leaving the battalion.

On Colonel Cutler's retirement, 18th January, 1918, Major Harold R. Atkins succeeded to the command, being now the senior Major, since Major Roper and Captains Hooker, Fearon and D. R. Potter had been sent to Egypt in September, 1917, to complete the establishment of the 2/4th Queen's, then in that part of the world and finding themselves short of trained officers; they were getting ready, in fact, under their new Commander-in-Chief, General Allenby, for the splendid advance on Palestine across the desert.

In mid-January, 1918, one Company of the 1/4th Queen's was sent to garrison Fort Lahore; and towards the end of the month four drafts arrived from England, 130 men in all. In the middle of March, 1918, Headquarters and 3 companies went into camp at Lahore cantonment in bad weather (exceptional at that time of year); so bad, indeed, that they were swamped in their tents. At the end of March the battalion proceeded to Dalhousie and elsewhere in the hills, for the hot weather, and the whole battalion went under canvas at the end of October, 1918, at Ferozepore. Here, on two occasions, the camp was flooded out to a depth of six inches, and when the water had drained off, the damp ground quickly provided a plague of white ants, as usual. The depredations of these creatures are almost beyond belief: their predilection being for the destruction of leather or wood. To give an instance: the Colonel imprudently left his suit case on the ground when turning in for the night. In the morning the bottom was eaten away, and only by ingenious contrivances could the suit case be made of use.

The telegram announcing the Armistice reached the battalion about 8 p.m. (Indian time is about five hours later than Greenwich time), on the 11th November, 1918, but was not at first thoroughly realised, as many false rumours had been already circulated.

Excepting for a ten days' holiday in November, sanctioned by the Indian Government to celebrate the Armistice, the battalion was engaged at this time in intensive training ; but the questions of the rank and file as to what new war they were being so mercilessly trained for never received a satisfactory answer.

The fact remains that the training at Ferozepore, *after* the Armistice, was as severe as at any other time in the battalion's Indian sojourn. This intensive training happily came to an end in the middle of January, 1919, for the battalion was then engaged in competing in Divisional and other sports. In April, 1919, the battalion took part in quelling the Punjab disturbances which had arisen on account of the Rowlatt Bill, much disliked and feared by the native Indian peoples, although as a matter of fact the majority knew nothing of its provisions. India is much at the mercy of the half-educated agitator, and anything new, simply because it is new, often breeds trouble. The trouble in this case suddenly began in Kasur when a railway train was held up and the European passengers savagely assaulted, two being killed by stones thrown. By the time Colonel Atkins arrived from Ferozepore, at 2.30 p.m., with some Lewis guns in motor cars, Kasur had completely returned to rest. The dismantled station, however, and the dead bodies of the English soldiers (two warrant officers) and the group of frightened women and children who had taken refuge in the police station, gave proof of the severe hand-to-hand fighting which had taken place earlier in the day.

From this time onwards, Amritsar was a storm centre ; and the country all around it was very disturbed, until about the end of May. And while these lines are in press, January, 1920,

Amritsar is justifying its evil reputation for disorder. The
battalion had various parties serving on armoured trains, and
detachments in different parts of the district, keeping order. In
the middle of April, 1919, the battalion moved to the fine Wellington Barracks at Jullundur. The 1/4th Queen's hoped that now
at last they were nearing the call home, and in this belief enjoyed
their comfortable roomy barracks, a welcome change from the
incessant camps or crowded quarters. But it was not to be.
On 10th May the battalion was ordered on field service to
Peshawar, to take part in the Third Afghan War. Instead of
marching straight up the Khyber to the actual scene of the
fighting, the 1/4th Queen's had the unpleasant duty of guarding
Peshawar city itself; a seething mass of discontent, which might
result in an outbreak at any moment. Guards of the 1/4th
Queen's were placed on all the gates, and in the bazaars and other
dangerous places. The filth and discomfort of these quarters
in Peshawar city can scarcely be described; every sense was
assailed in the vilest way. Those quartered outside the walls
in barracks and cantonments were looked upon with envy by
their comrades. As usual, the arrival of the Queen's brought
order and peace (as order and peace are understood in India),
and the place quieted down so that no one would have dreamt
that serious war was in progress only 30 miles away. By the end
of May, 1919, the battalion proceeded to Chitral barracks,
Nowshera, thirty miles from Peshawar in an easterly direction,
an uninteresting hot cantonment. The Queen's were sorry to
reach it again, having had quite enough of it two years before.
One company was sent to garrison the Aerodrome at Risalpur.

Nowshera became the headquarters of the 16th (Indian)
Division, and in consequence was overcrowded, and more
uncomfortable than ever. After the close of the Afghan War the
battalion returned to Peshawar on 10th September and took over
garrison duty; remaining under canvas until October. They
then returned to Jullundur under orders to prepare for demobilisation, and an early departure for England. On 18th
October they embarked on the "Königin Luise" (one of the
German Hamburg-Amerika liners handed over after the Armistice), and arrived at Devonport on 12th November, reaching
Crowborough, 14th November. They were warmly welcomed
in Croydon on 15th November; but though the welcome was
warm, the weather was bitter, and Colonel Atkins publicly
assured the Mayor (Councillor C. Heath Clark) that he " had
never been colder in his life," by way of excuse for not making a
speech, as he followed the two colours of the battalion to their
home in the Town Hall.

The 1/4th Queen's had the reputation of being the smartest
Territorial battalion in the Northern Command of India, and

Photo by B. W. Fisk-Moore
Colonel NORMAN EDWARD CUTLER, 1/4th Queen's

Photo by Lewis
Lieut.-Colonel S. D. ROPER, 1/4th Queen's and 2/4th Queen's

THE 1/4TH QUEEN'S

the report of the Inspector-General of Infantry (of that Command) bears this out. And it must be borne in mind under what conditions this smartness was maintained. During the hot weather, which lasts from about March to October, reveillé is at 5.30 a.m., and all outdoor work ceases at 9.30 a.m. Men are not allowed out of barracks between 9.30 and 5.30. In these hours of enforced inaction the men exist as best they can ; the lazily swinging punkah, or overhead fan, merely moves to and fro the vitiated atmosphere, and the sweat pours off the bodies even of those absolutely motionless. Even at 6.30, if a game of footer or hockey is started, it has to be kept very short. At the same time during the active operations mentioned above, the heat has to be ignored : the fighting being carried out in a treeless, waterless country, surely amongst the most inhospitable regions of the world. In the cold weather (November to February) all energies are directed to collective training after reveillé (which is about 6.30 a.m.) and night operations are frequently carried out.

V. The 2/4th Queen's

This was formed as a composite battalion of 2/4th (Croydon) Queen's men with 2/5th (Guildford) Queen's men added, at Windsor, on 24th April, 1915, under General Marriott, D.S.O. The unit was entirely composed of men who had volunteered for foreign service. It was trained first at Cambridge, afterwards at Bedford ; and sailed for Gallipoli on the " Ulysses," on 17th July, 1915, about 1,000 strong, under the command of Colonel F. D. Watney, T.D., who had already been in command of the old Fourth Queen's some years before. Captain and Adjutant P. C. Duncan, M.C. (whose father, Dr. P. T. Duncan, is the *doyen* of Croydon doctors), served with the battalion from Gallipoli until it was disbanded, and was Adjutant for three years of this time ; but there were many changes in the Colonelcy, as will be seen.

At Alexandria " first reinforcements " were left behind ; which showed that the battalion was intended for immediate offensive action ; and indeed on the night of 8th August, 1915, the 2/4th Queen's landed at " C " beach, Suvla Bay, and the following morning were in the thick of things in the Gallipoli peninsula. No definite offensive action was taken by the battalion after the original attack in August, but there was much desultory fighting, and very hard work in the trenches. The battalion served throughout the campaign and evacuated the Peninsula on 13th December, 1915. But the continual wear of the war is shown in the fact that of the 1,000 men of the 2/4th Queen's who landed on 8th August at Suvla, even after reinforcements had been sent them, only about 200 re-embarked on 13th December. Wounds, heavy sick wastage, etc., unite with actual losses by death to make up the remainder.

A terrible blizzard of a duration and intensity beyond the experience of any living British soldier began on the 26th November, and lasted with increasing fury until the 28th, a time of griping cold, heavy thunder, hurricane rain and raging wind. " The water," says John Masefield, in his *Gallipoli*, one of the most vivid accounts of that expedition, " poured down into the trenches as though it were a tidal wave. It came in with a rush, with a head upon it like the tide advancing, so quickly that men were one minute dry and the next moment drowned at their posts. They were caught so suddenly that those who escaped had to leap from their trenches for dear life, leaving coats, haversacks, food, and sometimes even their rifles, behind them. The gale increased slowly all night ; at dawn it grew colder,

THE 2/4TH QUEEN'S

and the intensity of the blizzard reached its height on the 28th, which was known thereafter as 'Frozen-Foot Day.' Men were drowned, frozen, and frost-bitten ; and we lost in that one storm ten per cent. of the whole Army of Gallipoli."

General Sir Ian Hamilton had commanded the Gallipoli forces at the outset, but it was General Sir John Maxwell who commanded the expedition in chief, when he took it from Gallipoli to Egypt at the end of 1915. The 2/4th Queen's arrived at its first camp (near Wardan) in Egypt,on 21st December, and here Colonel Watney, who had been invalided, rejoined and took up the command. General training and reorganisation after the trials of Gallipoli, assimilation of large drafts to complete the full strength of the battalion, etc., took some time. The command in chief of the expedition passed now to General Sir Archibald Murray. On 14th February, 1916, a sudden order was issued to proceed to the Fayoum Oasis, where the Senussi Arabs had become active. Accordingly a camp was formed at El Azab in the Fayoum, and our men were kept on the alert night and day. In May however, it became manifest that the Turks were preparing to cross the 100 miles of desert which divides Palestine from Egypt, with a view of attacking the Suez canal ; and the 2/4th Queen's were ordered to Ismailia, the central point of the canal, to construct (and then to defend) redoubts of great strength, in order to hold or repel the enemy.

While the battalion was at Gallipoli, in 1915, the Turks had already attacked the Suez Canal, and had been beaten back. On this more important second attack it was not till August, 1916, that the Turkish army arrived at El Kañtarah, a ridge through which the canal cuts its way, and along which is the immemorial way from Egypt to Syria ; hence its name, which means " The Bridge." An actual swing-bridge now allows the ancient caravan route to pass on its old way, making the bridge or connection between Africa and Asia. In spite of the troubles of desert travelling the Turkish army was in fine condition on arrival, magnificently equipped and organized, thanks to the discipline of its German officers and commanders. On 4th August the British positions east of El Kañtarah were attacked, and the long struggle began. The 2/4th Queen's were hurried to Hill 40 (which means a hill 40 metres above the datum level, say 120 feet, and marked 40, therefore, upon the military contour maps—a convenient way of naming the nameless, always adopted by the army) ; Hill 40 covering El Kañtarah and supporting the front line at Romani. The attack was triumphantly repelled.

Sir Archibald Murray decided that a determined attack was the best defence of the Canal, and therefore ordered an advance across the Sinai desert to be attempted. The 2/4th Queen's were commanded by Colonel Watson, D.S.O., (of the King's Royal Rifles), since Colonel Watney had been ordered to England on account of ill health.

By 2nd December our battalion was at Bir el Abd (south of Lake Sirbonis, whose northern margin here forms the Mediterranean shore) and relieved the 2nd Highland Light Infantry in outpost duty ; and here Colonel Watson had to go into Hospital, and Colonel Wilkins of " The Queen's " shortly afterwards took command of the 2/4th Queen's. El Arish, which is practically the end of the desert, was reached by the beginning of February, 1917, and a welcome halt of three weeks was made. On 23rd February the 2/4th Queen's were gladdened by the sight of trees and grass once more at Sheik Zowaiid, after the manifold discomforts of the desert, and moreover they got the good news that the retiring enemy was only 15 miles further on. We advancing, and they retiring, the 2/4th Queen's reached Rafa on 8th March, and found the Turkish-German forces entrenched behind barbed wire, with many guns, some of them of heavy calibre, all along the line from Gaza to Beersheba. Elaborate preparations for attack were made, and the 2/4th Queen's had the distinguished honour of being the " spear head " of the column in the battle of 27th March. Their objective was a network of entrenchments called " The Warren " (so named by the airmen on their maps), strongly held by machine guns. This apparently impossible position was gallantly stormed and taken at the point of the bayonet by the 2/4th Queen's. In recognition of their valour the small hill from which the attack started is now marked on all military maps as " Queen's Hill." The battalion lost about 200 killed and wounded. The disappointment of the brave fellows at being ordered to retire during the night was intense. They had performed a fine action successfully, had held the positions, won at such heavy cost, against numerous and determined attacks, supported by the most deadly fire, all the long day ; and had, moreover, suffered the severity of thirst, as there was no water to be obtained. But since the whole army had to retire, of course the Queen's had to retire with it.

Gaza now became an entrenched modern fortress, and the Eastern front began to take on many of the characters of the Western. On 19th April, at the second battle of Gaza, an engagement as fierce and as disastrous as the first battle, the 2/4th Queen's were the liaison battalion between two divisions. The summer passed in the routine of constant trench warfare with periods of training in reserve ; the 2/4th Queen's still forming a liaison battalion between two divisions, but not often actively engaged, and therefore without heavy casualties.

THE 2/4TH QUEEN'S

But in August, General Sir E. H. H. Allenby took over the Command-in-Chief, and on 26th August he ordered the 2/4th Queen's into a training camp near Belah, about six miles from Gaza, where they at once entered upon a strenuous course of training in preparation for operations on a large scale in the autumn.

And accordingly on October 24th, 1917, the battalion moved forward by night to the Wadi Ghuzzee, about 12 miles S.E of Gaza, and thence on the 27th, eastwards, in support of Allenby's famous cavalry, who that morning had become heavily engaged with a strong enemy reconnaissance in force. Our advancing infantry were vigorously shelled with shrapnel, but held firm, and the reconnaissance withdrew baffled at dusk. Allenby had divided his attack. His 20th Corps (with which were the 2/4th Queen's) were directed towards Jerusalem by way of Beersheba, Hebron and Bethlehem; and consisted of three infantry divisions, with artillery and cavalry, and with a well equipped powerful Camel-Corps. His 21st Corps on the other hand, composed of four infantry divisions and a large force of cavalry, were to advance by Gaza and Jaffa along the coast and then eastwards from Jaffa, along the old Crusaders' route to Jerusalem. The battle of Beersheba was won on 31st October, 1917, by the 20th Corps, our 2/4th Queen's holding the left of the attack and not being very heavily engaged. At dawn on the 1st November they passed through Beersheba in pursuit of the enemy, and bivouacked eight miles further on. On 3rd November the Queen's again led the 53rd Division (of which they formed part) and came in touch with the enemy soon after mid-day in a very strong entrenched position on a hill at Khuweilfeh, 15 miles N.N.E. of Beersheba.

The battle of Khuweilfeh, which at once ensued, was a brilliant victory and productive of far-reaching results. Again the 2/4th Queen's were the " spear-head " of the division, but so intense was the enemy's fire, chiefly from machine guns and rifles, that it grew dark before he could be thrust out. All next day (4th November) the part of the hill eventually won by our Croydon men had to be held against incessant fierce attacks. The heat was intense, not a drop of water was to be had, and so agonizing were the conditions that several of our poor fellows lost their reason for the time—and yet they held on grimly. Under cover of the night, when darkness fell, the Royal Sussex and the Royal Welsh Fusiliers came over from our northern flank, and brilliantly rushed the remainder of the hill. For the next four days the enemy used all the strength he could gather, in incessant efforts to dislodge our 20th Corps. He even sent for the Turkish-German reserves supporting Gaza (which the

21st Corps was at this time besieging) and flung his famous *Sturm-truppen*, his specially trained, entirely German, " Storm troops," against us. His forces rose to five times our strength at one time, and still we held our own. Indeed in its way, Khuweilfeh was a Verdun, and was of equally disastrous effect to the enemy's campaign. For by causing the withdrawal of the Reserve and the Storm-troops from Gaza, and part of the two German divisions from Aleppo (where they were available as the Germans fondly thought, both for Palestine and for Mesopotamia), the men of the 20th Corps had rendered possible the fall of Gaza before the attack of the 21st Corps, and, as an immediate consequence, the rapid and picturesque advance which has made Allenby known as one of the great captains of history. The Commander-in-Chief indeed, in congratulating the 53rd Division, expressly mentioned these well known and brilliant results as due to their heroic resistance at Khuweilfeh. Croydon has good right to be proud of the 2/4th Queen's.

Finally, on 8th November, 1917, the fall of Gaza and the evident danger on his right flank made it incumbent on the enemy to retire ; and on the next day (9th November) our men could advance beyond the scene of their victory to Ras en Nagb, where they held a reserve outpost position till the end of the month.

By this time the 21st Corps had captured Jaffa, and turning eastward were aiming at Jerusalem from the west. On 4th December a force (Mott's column) consisting of the 53rd Division, (20th Corps), with special artillery and cavalry, was ordered to advance up the Beersheba-Hebron-Jerusalem road, the 2/4th Queen's forming of course part of that column. They reached Hebron by the evening, the enemy retiring. Next day they moved on in pursuit, and so on each day, until they came into touch with the enemy just outside Bethlehem on the morning of 9th December. All this march was in appalling weather, wet and bitterly cold, the more trying as following the exposure to great heat. One night (8th December) was popularly regarded as the worst time experienced by the battalion since the blizzard at Suvla ; freezing rain falling in torrents in a high wind, the men being in fighting gear without overcoats, and in their drill shorts with bare knees, and without any shelter whatever except their bivouac sheets, the water rushing down the hill in cataracts. After several days' marching in rain, without possibility of change, there is no wonder at the deep impression made on those who halted on this 8th December. The Turks at Bethlehem relying on our respect for their holy places boldly exposed their guns in the neighbourhood of Churches and Mosques. They had probably come to know of an absolute order of General

Allenby's to " avoid damaging any holy places, in order not to prejudice British interests with the natives of the country," who regard the Turks, of course, as their conquerors and oppressors. The 2/4th Queen's who had been subject to the fire of these guns during the half-day, were ordered to attack the hills to the south of Bethlehem, between them and the town, about 4 p.m. The Turks retired, and the hills were in our hands before dark ; so that from the summit our men looked down on Bethlehem and across to Jerusalem, and they were the first British forces to see their goal, the Holy City, in this war. On the next day (10th December) the column passed through Bethlehem into Jerusalem ; finding there the troops of the 21st Corps, who had attacked from the west, and had overnight received the surrender of Jerusalem by the Mayor, but without then seeing the town itself.

They had entered Jerusalem early in the day (10th December) and the 2/4th Queen's arrived in the dusk. The Turks had divided in their retirement, half going by the Nablus road, half by the Jericho road. They took up strong positions astride the Nablus road three miles north of Jerusalem, and across the Jericho road two miles east of Jerusalem. The 2/4th Queen's had the honour of guarding all the city gates of Jerusalem and other places in the town. On December 18th they took over the front position from the Cheshires before White Hill and Ras-es-Zamby, the strong positions held by the Turks across the Jericho road above referred to. On 21st December the 2/4th Queen's, in conjunction with the 2/10th Middlesex (Duke of Cambridge's Own) attacked at the point of the bayonet, and took these two hills after severe hand-to-hand fighting. They held them all the rest of the day against repeated violent counter-attacks, in which entrenching tools, and even bare fists, were freely used by those of our men who had for the moment lost their rifles. The hills therefore now became part of the British positions and were held through Christmas ; a period of further drenching rain, bitter wind, and general discomfort. A determined effort to recover Jerusalem about Christmas was confidently expected by the Staff, and at 2 a.m. on 27th December this attack came off, north of Jerusalem, on an eight-mile front, principally athwart the Nablus road. Also a specially violent attack on a smaller scale began at dawn on the positions held by the 2/4th Queen's athwart the Jericho road, and lasted all day. But in neither case did the Turks obtain more than local successes, one of which was the recapture of White Hill, by vastly superior numbers, during the afternoon. But the general failure of the battle compelled the enemy to retire at dark, so as to re-adjust his lines ; and we reoccupied our full position before midnight. In these two fights (21st December and 27th December) the 2/4th Queen's lost 14 officers and 315 men, killed and wounded, out of a fighting strength of about 700, which is regarded by military men as an exceptionally heavy loss. The battalion therefore went into reserve, occupying the Russian Hospice on the Mount of Olives until the end of the year.

On 1st January, 1918, another day of torrential rain and wind, the battalion marched to Ram-Allah on the Nablus road, about six miles from Jerusalem, the Turks having retired, and remained in this district till the middle of March, with occasional raids, much trench work, etc., but they fought no definite action with the exception of the capture of Tel-Asur, the highest hill in Palestine, and the adjoining positions. Then they proceeded through Jerusalem to Jericho, which had meanwhile fallen, and took up positions (again in the first line) in the valley of the Jordan opposite to the enemy's entrenchments.

After repulsing a considerable attack by the Turks in the beginning of April, the battalion returned to the Nablus-road position and remained there till June, 1918. During this time the Turks attacked and occupied the positions at Ide Hill held by the 2/4th Queen's, but happily were driven out later in the same day. In June the battalion was ordered to France, with many other troops, to withstand the great Hun attack which had started in the previous March.

Colonel Wilkins, who had been wounded at Khuweilfeh (4th November, 1917) and sent into Hospital, had been replaced at that time by Major Roper, who joined up from the 1/4th Queen's in India in September, 1917. Major Roper now became Colonel of the battalion and remained in command until May, when he was ordered to England, and Colonel Hill, D.S.O., of the Scots Guards, succeeded him in the command.

The 2/4th Queen's sailed on the " Malwa " from Alexandria in the middle of June, 1918, and landed at Taranto in the south of Italy, after escaping by a very narrow shave a torpedo fired from a German submarine 12 miles from port. Here they entrained into some cattle trucks, and seven days later, without change of carriage, reached Proven in the Ypres salient. The first ten days of July were passed in reorganisation, refitting kit, and generally getting efficient. From July 14th to August 3rd the 2/4th Queen's were sent with the 22nd Corps to assist the French in the Soissons area, and took part in this movement with great distinction, as is acknowledged by the congratulatory letters from the gratified French generals who were in command in the battles of Parcy, Tigny, Grand Rozoy and Beugneux. Again a heavy price had to be paid for glory, and the battalion

Photo by Fred Bremner
Lieut.-Colonel HAROLD R. ATKINS, 1/4th Queen's

Welcome Home to the "1/4th Queen's" (15th Nov., 1919)

Photo by Lewis

sustained about 300 casualties, killed and wounded. The French commanders did not confine their appreciation to dispatches, but awarded numerous " Croix de Guerre " to the 2/4th.

After 3rd August the battalion returned to the Ypres sector. Towards the end of August they again went to the front trenches facing Kemmel Hill. On the night of 27th August it became evident to our patrols that the Germans had evacuated their position, and accordingly we advanced in the early hours of the 28th. The 2/4th Queen's were the first on the hill, an achievement for which Captain Bannerman of Croydon, leading his Company, received the Military Cross. From this day to the Armistice (11th November, 1918) the battalion was in touch with the enemy, in continual pursuit, and was engaged in daily combats between Kemmel and Anseghem, the following being the principal actions :—Kemmel, the Vierstraat Switch (a line of trenches), the Wytschaete ridge (full of huge craters formed by mines blown up by ourselves in the well-known previous attack on Wytschaete and Messines), Oostaverne, Gheluweh, the Menin road, Rolleghem, Belleghem, and Anseghem.

After the Armistice the battalion marched by daily stages to Flawinne near Namur, and remained there till January, 1919. They then proceeded across the Rhine to positions of control (over civic populations) east of Siegburg, nine miles east of Bonn, and remained in Germany till they were disbanded. During this period they were employed on control posts in the following areas :—Allner, Seelscheid, Wahn, Kalk, Engelskirchen, Ehreshoven, Lindlar, Frankenfurst, Michaelsberg.

In March, 1919, Field Marshal Lord Plumer (as he is now known) presented the battalion on behalf of His Majesty with the " King's Colour "—now in our Town Hall : and in the same month Colonel Hill retired from the regiment, being succeeded in the command of the 2/4th Queen's by Colonel S. T. Watson, D.S.O., of " The Queen's."

In April, 1919, the " 53rd (Young Soldiers') Battalion " of the Queen's came out, as a battalion, 1,000 strong, to Germany, and were at once absorbed into the 2/4th Queen's as a *draft*—a remarkable case of the tail wagging the dog. The war-worn veterans of Gallipoli (of whom only about eight still remained), of Egypt and Palestine, and of Flanders and France, were not best pleased at their honoured name being assumed by these fresh English lads ; and on the other hand to go out as a battalion and find yourselves only a draft is not exactly exhilarating !

In June, 1919, Colonel Watson being ordered to India, the command of the enlarged 2/4th Queen's was given to Colonel Wauchope, D.S.O., of the York and Lancaster Regiment.

In October, 1919, in the monastery of Michaelsberg, at Siegberg, the battalion was disbanded, and all the men not demobilisable were divided as reinforcements between the 10th and 11th (Service) battalions of " The Queen's "; and at the beginning of November, Captain and Adjutant P. C. Duncan, M.C., and two sergeants, with the Colour presented from the King, as above recorded, were all that remained of the 2/4th Queen's.

Captain Duncan and his two sergeants arrived at Croydon the same day as the 1/4th Queen's (15th November, 1919) and handed over the 2/4th's King's Colour to the Mayor, by whom it was placed in the Town Hall with the colours of the 1/4th.

The 2/4th Queen's received the following decorations during the War :—Two D.S.O., sixteen M.C., seven D.C.M., and a large number of Military Medals and foreign decorations.

VI. The 3/4th Queen's

The third battalion of the Fourth Queen's began in the remainder of the battalion left at Windsor after the departure of the 2/4th Queen's in April, 1915. Colonel U. L. Hooke, of Croydon, was appointed to the command; and it was quickly filled out by recruits from Croydon to a battalion of full strength. Major L. S. de la Mare was the second in command, and Major K. A. Oswald the Adjutant, both Croydon men.

Progressive training was carried out in Windsor Great Park, and the battalion was armed with Japanese rifles, a musketry course being fired with them at the Runnymede ranges.

The only active service duty performed beyond the training was the occasional piqueting of the main roads. Upon receiving a sudden order an officer with a few men would be despatched to each road, and at once blocked the passage with waggons, etc. All persons were stopped. Even Staff Officers were held up by the awed but faithful subalterns, in spite of strong language; and the tears of ladies trying to reach town to fulfil theatrical engagements, etc., were ineffective, though the weeping was actual and not merely dramatic. The reason seems to have been to effect the capture of certain spies of high position by these sudden blockades; and rumour had it that they were not unsuccessful. Another humorous occurrence resulted in a valuable tactical exercise. With a view of testing some new overcoats the Colonel ordered his bugler to sound the " fall in." The bugler's intention was admirable, but his execution was so imperfect that the result was taken for the "alarm." The true "alarm" was at once sounded by a neighbouring unit, and the warning was of course repeated far and wide. The Guards, some of them at football, others at Windsor Races, doubled back to quarters and stood to arms. All other units in Windsor and Slough did the same. Fortunately some one telegraphed to Hounslow, or the whole of the London garrison would have turned out. All concerned looked for trouble over the unfortunate error, but it was held to be so excellent a practice alarm that the authorities took no notice.

Leaving Windsor early in June, 1915, the battalion was quartered in empty houses at Tunbridge Wells, where part of the billet area was wrecked by bombs from Zeppelins on 10th October, 1915, evidently a precursor, or trial trip of the only raid which seriously affected Croydon three days later (13th October, 1915), when the invaders, as will be remembered, arrived from this same direction.

While at Tunbridge Wells, the War Office decided that the men for home service only, should be separated from those available for service abroad ; and in June, 1915, some 400 officers and men were posted for home service duty to the 69th Provisional Battalion at Lowestoft. (The same force which afterwards was known as the 19th provisional battalion of the Queen's ; an account of whose services follows in chapter IX.) During June and July, 1915, Battalion Headquarters and about 600 N.C.O.'s and men were sent to Halling, near Chatham, to work on the system of trenches in connection with the London defences, considerable praise being earned for the work done.

While at Tunbridge Wells many recruits had been posted from Croydon and at this time the battalion marched to Maidstone, a distance of 18 miles, and on the following day were inspected on the march on the Wrotham Road by Lord Kitchener. They returned that same day to Tunbridge Wells, a distance of 23 miles in the one day ; a severe test, in which the battalion showed to great advantage.

During the period from August to November, 1915, the battalion was deprived of the services of several Croydon officers, among whom were—Major L. S. de la Mare, who proceeded to Egypt to the 2/4th Queen's ; Lieutenants P. C. Duncan, Peter Brodie (afterwards killed, the son of Mr. Robert Brodie, the former Headmaster of the Whitgift Grammar School) and R. W. Spicer (afterwards killed), who joined the 2/4th Queen's in Gallipoli ; and Lieutenant A. S. Redfern (son of Dr. Redfern, of Croydon) who transferred to the Royal Flying Corps. In December, 1915, Second Lieutenant G. P. Allen, the son of Mr. Councillor Francis Allen, of Croydon, was fatally injured in an accident, to the great sorrow of his comrades, with whom he was deservedly popular, while attending a course of bombing at Marden Park.

From October, 1915, to July, 1916, the battalion was quartered at Reigate : training was continued and the battalion was inspected on the march at Godstone by Lord French, Commander-in-Chief of the Home Forces, being singled out from the Surrey Brigade, of which it formed part, for special complimentary mention.

After a few days in camp at Windernesse Park, Sevenoaks, the battalion moved into camp at Westbere, near Sturry, with the 2/5th Queen's, where they arrived on 17th July, 1916, the remainder of the Surrey Brigade being in camp at Gore Street. Training was continued, and a musketry course fired at Sandwich.

Early in August upwards of 300 men, many of whom belonged to Croydon, were drafted overseas from the battalion, and the

Photo by H. P. Robinson & Son
Lieut.-Colonel UTTEN LAMONT HOOKE, 3/4th Queen's
(Fell in France, 21st June, 1917)

Major (Acting Lieut.-Colonel) KENNETH ALLAN OSWALD, D.S.O.
3/4th Queen's

majority were posted to the 22nd battalion County of London Regiment, thereby being fortunate in retaining the name of " The Queen's."

The battalion remained under canvas until 2nd November, 1916, when the weather conditions became impossible. It was then moved to Ramsgate in connection with the Coast Defences, and was there during the German bombardments of the town from the sea in February and April, 1917, and during the very frequent air raids.

Early in 1917 Captain W. G. Paget, who had been the Medical Officer of the battalion since its formation, was ordered overseas. In April, 1917, the 3/4th Queen's returned to Westbere camp.

On several occasions previously, preparations had been far advanced for an early departure overseas, but it was not until the end of May, 1917, that the 3/4th Queen's eventually sailed for France. They had the honour of being the battalion selected by merit from the Surrey Brigade for this purpose.

At all stations in England the battalion had won golden opinions for its behaviour and soldierly bearing. Not only was it in a high state of military efficiency but it also figured prominently in all sports organised in the Division and the Brigade. The Surrey Brigade Football Cup was won by the 3/4th Queen's in 1916-17, as well as many inter-battalion and naval cricket matches and cross-country races—in the latter the running of Private A. Marshall of Croydon, was always a feature. In the United Services Boxing Competition at Ramsgate, in February, 1917, Drummer G. Beale, a Croydon man, won the Welter Weights in a high class entry.

Prior to their leaving Westbere camp, the Mayor of Croydon (Alderman Howard Houlder) accompanied by the Vicar (Canon L. J. White-Thomson) and the Town Clerk (Dr. J. M. Newnham) visited the battalion, and the Mayor expressed the good wishes of the citizens of Croydon for the success of the 3/4th Queen's in France. This visit was much appreciated by all ranks of the battalion. The Hon. Colonel, Sir Frederick Edridge, was, much to the regret of all, unable to make the journey owing to ill-health.

The people of Croydon all along continued to take great interest in the doings of the 3/4th Queen's, and among other benefits the receipt each Christmas (in England and abroad) of puddings, tobacco, etc., was very much appreciated by the battalion, who gladly recognised the work of Mr. Henry Berney in this connection.

The battalion left Canterbury on 30th May, 1917, and proceeded to Havre via Southampton under the command of Lieutenant-Colonel U. L. Hooke ; Major K. A. Oswald being second in command, and Captain V. F. Samuelson, of Ewell, Adjutant. The Regimental Sergeant-Major, W. Johnson (The Queen's), who came of an old Croydon family, did much towards the excellent condition of the battalion.

From Havre the battalion moved to Laloge (Forêt d'Hesdins) for a short time and then joined the 9th Division at Duisans near Arras—they were attached to the South African Brigade ; and, as always, their training was continued.

The battalion was later attached to the 4th Division for training in trench warfare, and was soon sent forward to the fighting line in the sectors North and South of the River Scarpe to the east of Arras. On the 21st June, 1917, a great misfortune befell the 3/4th Queen's in the loss of their Commanding Officer, Lieutenant-Colonel U. L. Hooke, who was killed by a shell in the neighbourhood of the Chemical Works at Roeux. Lieutenant-Colonel Hooke, whose labours during the extended training in England had been unceasing, was universally popular with both officers and men. He was buried at Fampoux. The father of this gallant officer received at his home in Birdhurst Road the sympathy of the whole of Croydon when the loss of his son became known here. The command of the battalion was given to Major K. A. Oswald, who was appointed Lieutenant-Colonel.

The battalion was attached in July, 1917, to the 12th Division, for work in the front fighting line in the vicinity of Monchy, being quartered in the oil factory at Arras ; and the General Officer commanding the 12th Division has recorded his special appreciation of the work done by the 3/4th Queen's in connection with the attack he made on Long Trench, on 17th July, 1917.

Early in August, 1917, the battalion was ordered to join the 21st Division, which was at that time in the sector opposite Fontaine ; and after being for a short time the battalion in reserve at Croisilles, the 3/4th Queen's took over the left sector of the Brigade front, consisting for the main part of the old Hindenburg line with its extensive tunnel system. At this point there was a broad " No man's land," and the opportunity was seized for extensive patrol training which continued until complete mastery of " No man's land " was obtained. On 25th August a fighting patrol carried out a bold reconnaissance for machine guns, and some of the party worked right under the enemy wire and on to the parapet of his trench, locating the guns and emplacements. The patrol was unfortunately discovered before they could get

Inspection of the 4/4th Queen's at Crowborough by Colonel Sir Frederick T. Edridge, D.L., accompanied by the Mayor (Ald. Houlder) and the Town Clerk

Photo by Lankester, Tunbridge Wells

THE 4/4th QUEEN'S AT CROWBOROUGH

Group of Officers—left to right: Captain Chard, the Town Clerk, the Mayor, Col. Sir Frederick T. Edridge, Group-Commander Col. Gloster, and Major Kenneth William Elder, C.O.

Photo by Lankester, Tunbridge Wells

clear away, and two of the party being wounded, the withdrawal was only effected with great difficulty. For conspicuous gallantry on this occasion Second Lieutenant Gilliland was awarded the Military Cross and Lance-Sergeant Goatcher the Military Medal; and the Divisional Commander's Card of Honour was presented to Lance Corporal Matthews and Private Homewood.

On 28th August, 1917, the 21st Division had to be withdrawn from the fighting line lor rest and training, and was quartered at Warlus (West of Arras) where they remained and carried out intensive training in the newest forms of attack, until 16th September, when they took the first stage towards the Flanders fighting.

On 16th September, 1917, the 3/4th Queen's were at Le Peplier near Caestre, and were there transferred to the Second Army. At this time they received a welcome draft of 100 men, mainly from the East Kent Regiment (The Buffs). The 1st and 8th battalions of the Queen's (the 1st being the old battalion of the regular army, and the 8th one of the New Army battalions) were also quartered in this neighbourhood, and many friendships were renewed.

On 23rd September the 3/4th Queen's moved towards La Roukloshille, under the Mont des Cats. General Sir H. Plumer, in command of the Second Army, inspected the battalion at training while here, and expressed himself as most satisfied.

The 28th September, 1917, found the battalion at Reninghelst, and during this moonlight season much annoyance and discomfort was caused by the enemy aircraft.

On 30th September, 1917, a move was made to the dugouts in the banks of Zillebeke Lake, Ypres, where the final preparations were made for the coming offensive.

On the night of the 2nd/3rd October, the 62nd Brigade, to which the 3/4th Queen's was attached, relieved the 110th Brigade in the front line just east of Polygon Wood; the journey up being of a most difficult nature owing to the heavy shelling and to the moving troops being silhouetted against the light of burning ammunition dumps. As much reconnaissance as was possible was carried out the following day, but the enemy occupied high ground in close proximity, so that little movement was possible. The Artillery duels at this time were of the fiercest. The ground had become very muddy, and the constant shelling had churned the Polygon Beek into a broad and almost impenetrable morass; carrying parties had great difficulty in bringing up supplies or mud mats and other necessaries.

The attack of Plumer's Second Army on Broodseinde Ridge was launched at 6 a.m. on the 4th October, 1917, on a dark damp morning. The place of assembly was thirty feet below the first objective, and in full view of the enemy; scrub covered the slopes of the small spurs and this was heavily wired; powerful concrete blockhouses, some of three compartments and with garrisons of 20 to 30 men, commanded all approaches with machine guns and trench mortars; deep trenches were sited on all prominent positions; the beds of the streams were swept by machine gun fire, etc. As seen by daylight after the attack the enemy's position indeed appeared impregnable. The 7th Division in which were the 2nd (regular) battalion of The Queen's, attacked on the left of the 3/4th Queen's. The barrage was very dense and accurate, and although moving very slowly, the state of the ground made it difficult to keep up with it. The orders were to capture the first objective, and other battalions of the Brigade were then to pass through them to the second objective. After severe fighting, and with the greatest determination, the objective was captured, but not without heavy losses: of the 20 officers who went forward to the attack, all were killed or wounded by 2 o'clock in the afternoon; four however were able to remain at duty, and the battalion was at once reorganised with the help of the non-commissioned officers, who did splendid work. The Commanding Officer, Lieutenant-Colonel K. A.Oswald, was wounded while reconnoitring the front line early in the afternoon. The fighting had been fierce and hand to hand, and large numbers of the enemy were encountered chiefly owing to the fact that two fresh enemy divisions had just previously been moved into their line with a view to making an attack on a large scale. Our attack forestalled theirs by only a few minutes.

The battalion in spite of the severe test to which it had just been put, remained in the line until 7th October, when it was relieved.

Notwithstanding the losses, the scarcity of food and water (the carrying of which was almost stopped by the continuous enemy barrage), and the fatigue caused by the wet ground, the *morale* of all ranks remained extremely high. The victory had been complete and the enemy was signally defeated.

The congratulations of the General Officer Commanding the 21st Division were received on the magnificent work accomplished. In one Report it was said:—

> "The offensive spirit of the 3/4th Queen's in this their first attack was beyond all praise, and the capture of the powerful concrete shelters was only achieved by absolute determination to win and a complete disregard of self."

Brigadier-General C. G. Rawling, who commanded the 62nd Brigade of the 21st Division at that time, also wrote as follows :—

"I always knew any Queen's battalion would be good, but it was a severe trial to take a new battalion through that terrific barrage fire, then across those bogs, in the face of the concrete emplacements in each of which were three machine guns. It was a glorious feat. I am sorry to say that the losses are dreadful—you lost between three and four hundred killed, wounded and missing. The Boche lost heavily too, the place is littered with his dead. The battalion has added another laurel to the Regiment's Battle Honours."

In this battle of the 4th October, 1917, the 3/4th Queen's took 200 German prisoners and captured or destroyed—

8 heavy and 7 light machine guns.

5 trench mortars, and 5 " granatenwerfers."

The following awards were later made to the battalion for conspicuous gallantry and devotion to duty on that occasion :—

2 Distinguished Service Orders.
2 Military Crosses.
2 Distinguished Conduct Medals.
15 Military Medals.

On the 9th October the battalion was at Sercus and reorganisation was proceeded with, and a fortnight later was back in the line again near the scene of its late attack—east of Polygon Wood.

The 3/4th Queen's remained in this area, usually doing duty in the line in the neighbourhood of Reutel until 8th November, after which they were quartered for short periods in the Westoutre and Ecurie areas. At the latter place full preparations were made for their transfer to the Italian front, which, however, in view of the position which grew up near Cambrai, were subsequently cancelled. The strength of the battalion at this time was a little over 600.

On 21st November, 1917, Lieutenant-Colonel G. H. Sawyer, D.S.O., Royal Berks Regiment, relieved Major H. C. Cannon, M.C., in the command of the battalion.

On 4th December the 3/4th Queen's were at Long Avesnes and met the 6th Queen's battalion of the New Army in the neighbourhood of Lecrement, after which the 21st Division took over a sector of the front south of Gouzecourt, the battalion going into the fighting line in the vicinity of Vaucellette Farm.

While here on 14th December a fighting patrol of the 3/4th obtained valuable identifications by the capture of German prisoners of the 1st battalion 25th I.R. near Reudicourt. Sergeant W. G. Ford was in charge of this patrol, and was awarded the Military Medal for his exploit.

The battalion remained in this sector until 30th January, 1918, when they moved to Moislans, and the orders for the disbanding of the battalion owing to the reorganisation of the Infantry arm of the service followed soon afterwards.

The 3/4th Queen's was throughout the only Territorial Unit in the 21st Division.

By the 20th February, 1918, the disbanding was complete, all officers and other ranks being posted to other battalions of the Queen's Regiment.

To those who had the well-being of the 3/4th Queen's at heart, the sudden termination of its career was a great disappointment. It had earned a splendid reputation largely owing to a keen sense of esprit-de-corps, which Croydon by its interest and encouragement did much to foster, and it is satisfactory to know that the doings of the battalion were recognised by the high honour of the presentation of a King's Colour. At the time of writing the Colour has not yet reached Croydon. It will receive due recognition when it arrives ; and no doubt will either join the Colours of the 1/4th and the 2/4th Queen's in the Town Hall, or possibly may be hung in the Parish Church.

In a letter to the President of the Surrey Territorial Force Association, Lieutenant-General Macready, Adjutant-General to the forces, paid a marked tribute to the 3/4th Queen's on its being disbanded. " The recent reorganisation of infantry in France (the Adjutant-General wrote) involved the disbandment of certain battalions, amongst which is the 3/4th battalion The Queen's Royal West Surrey Regiment. This battalion was a third line Territorial battalion, formed on the 24th April, 1915, whose first and second lines were serving in India and Palestine. It was therefore raised to the status of an overseas unit, and was selected out of a second line Territorial Force Division serving at home, to go to France in May, 1917. The battalion was attached to the Twelfth Division in July, but in August was posted to the Twenty-first Division with which it served in the line near Croisilles, moving to Flanders in September, and taking part in a highly successful attack on Reutel on 4th October. Fifteen machine guns, ten trench mortars, and two hundred prisoners were taken, and the Chaplain, the Rev. M. Tron, M.C.,

THE 3/4TH QUEEN'S

was awarded the D.S.O. The commanding officer, Lieutenant-Colonel K. A. Oswald, D.S.O., was however wounded next day. The battalion was again in action near Reutel on 26th October, and 5th November, but moved south at the end of November, being in the line near Gouzeaucourt by 10th December. It continued in this area till disbanded in February, 1918. In every engagement in which this battalion took part during its short career in the field, it upheld the brilliant and glorious traditions of the Queen's Regiment, and was awarded during the period that it was in France, two Distinguished Service Orders, four Military Crosses, two Distinguished Conduct Medals and nineteen Military Medals. Although the 3/4th battalion has been disbanded, the Officers, warrant officers, non-commissioned officers, and the men have not been lost to the Queen's Regiment; they have all been drafted into other battalions of the Regiment, and will continue to uphold the name and traditions of this Regiment, with the same spirit, loyalty, and esprit-de-corps as they have done in the 3/4th battalion."

VII. The 4/4th Queen's

After the Fourth Queen's had left Croydon for Windsor Park, there to form part of the composite battalion of the Queen's, and eventually to produce first the 2/4th, and later the 3/4th Queen's, the Depot Company left behind in Poplar Walk, Croydon, became known as the 4/4th, and Captain Kenneth Wm. Elder became its Major and Commanding Officer in July, 1915. Major Elder had been forbidden foreign service when lieutenant in the 1/4th Queen's ; tried again and was again turned back as Captain in the 2/4th ; again, fighting against fate, he unsuccessfully volunteered in the 3/4th ; and finally had to give up the glory of fighting, and train soldiers for his beloved Queen's abroad, as Major Commanding the Depot battalion, the 4/4th. And who shall say that this brave spirit, so often foiled, did not perhaps do more for the Fourth Queen's by his fine patient support at home than those more fortunate in the athletic sense whose services overseas he so bitterly envied ?

The 4/4th was, then, essentially a draft-finding and training unit. Major Elder trained successfully and sent out drafts to the 1/4th in India, to the 2/4th in Egypt and Palestine and to the 3/4th in France and Flanders ; and at last when our forces in 1916 could no longer wait for strictly regimental drafting he sent out levies wherever men were most wanted, regulars, new army, or territorials. Nay, it is even asserted that some Croydon men of the 4/4th developed into Highlanders, and theoretically or actually discarded trousers for the kilt ! Whenever even so few as 10 men were fairly fit Major Elder sent them out. He rather looked to physical fitness than to smartness on parade, to training rather than to drilling. His men were always at muscular exercise, gymnastics, trench digging, bayonet exercise, etc. He acquired by hook or crook a machine gun and trained men to high efficiency as machine gunners. Major Elder's machine gun has found its way to the Cadets of the Whitgift Grammar School, although technically it is still regimental property.

The battalion went into open-air camp at Windsor in 1915; but the recruits to the 4/4th remained chiefly Croydon boys from first to last. In November, 1915, the 4/4th was sent from Windsor to Purfleet and left canvas tents for wooden huts. Accommodation was scanty because the battalion grew so fast, and they had an uncomfortable time towards Christmas. Then to their great pleasure arrived, just in time, Christmas puddings from Croydon, plenty of cigarettes, and other comforts, through Mr. Harry Berney and the Croydon District Association of Voluntary Organisations ; they felt they were remembered and thought of in Croydon, and all their troubles were at once cheerfully endured. Many kind pudding-makers had sent them friendly messages in the pudding tins, but the regimental cooks were in such haste to boil up the longed-for delicacies that they plunged the tins into the cauldrons just as they were, without taking off the lids ; and, alas, nearly all those kind affectionate messages " boiled out in the wash ! " Only so many remained legible as to intensify the Queen's regret for the loss of the others. And some one managed to get hold of the old 1/4th Queen's camp cooking stove, and fed 609 men gloriously therewith on its arrival at Purfleet.

At the new year, 1916, the 4/4th was sent to Cambridge, and in April to Crowborough. It was still housed in huts, but the Crowborough pattern was excellent, and accommodation was abundant. The " conscription " levies now began to arrive, and many of them were pale and non-muscular and generally poor in physique. Not only did the condition of the original men improve rapidly in the fine air of Crowborough and the good treatment of the camp, but the weaklings above referred to changed almost miraculously fast into happy, athletic, bronzed, capable soldiers. Everyone was astounded at the swiftness and completeness of the change. Even after the first month they would not have been known for the same men. So excellent a result was not obtained without incessant watchfulness, and Major Elder's necessary strictness was at first often resented ; but by the end of the month the resentment had all paled in the glow of health and spirits previously unknown, and these very men became in the rebound amongst the best soldiers Major Elder had commanded ; so that when Sir Frederick Edridge, from first to last the Honorary Colonel of the Fourth Queen's, came to inspect his regiment at Crowborough, accompanied by the Mayor (Alderman Howard Houlder) and the Town Clerk, he was delighted with the soldierly appearance and the perfection of their various exercises and evolutions. Fortunately we have a photographic record of the inspection and are glad to reproduce it here.

By the middle of 1916 the pressure of recruits due to " conscription " lessened, and training battalions such as this were brigaded, so that the 4/4th as a separate force came to an end. Major Elder went to the Brigade Staff of the Home Counties Reserve Brigade, and the Guildford men (Fifth Queen's) were added to the Croydon men (Fourth Queen's) to form a fresh unit in that Brigade, under the name of the " Fourth Reserve Battalion of the Queen's."

VIII. The Fourth Reserve Queen's

Lieutenant-Colonel J. Wyndham Wright was the first Commanding Officer of this Fourth Reserve Battalion of the Queen's, and he was succeeded by Lieutenant-Colonel W. R. Campion (M.P. for Lewes), D.S.O., T.D., who, returning to the front on expiry of leave, was followed in the command by Lieutenant-Colonel N. T. Rolls. Colonel Rolls came home from the front (6th Queen's, Kitchener's men) for six months' leave in April, 1918, was appointed to the Fourth Reserve Queen's, which had removed from Crowborough to Tunbridge Wells, and remained in command of it until it was disbanded a year later (29th May, 1919). When Colonel Rolls arrived he found the battalion diligently training new levies, and acting as convalescent home for the wounded continually arriving from the front : draft-finding in this way for the Territorial battalions abroad.

The Armistice was declared on 11th November, 1918, but the despatch of trained levies could not even then cease, since replacement of the forces in France and elsewhere continued to be necessary, in order that the war-worn soldiers might get home-leave. Further, no one could tell what devices the enemy might resort to, and the profound distrust of his good faith made reductions in army strength impossible during the many long weary months which had yet to run till Peace was signed with Germany (28th June, 1919).

One final victory, though a peaceful and merry one, must be set down to the credit of the Fourth Queen's in the Reserve state. The whole Brigade had six battalions, and all six engaged in a tournament of football, involving innumerable separate games. From this long contest for the Brigade Football Cup, the battalion which ultimately emerged victorious, and which of course still possesses the Cup, was the Fourth Reserve Queen's.

IX. The 69th Provisional Battalion (the 19th Queen's)

As already recorded in Chapter VI., the men destined for Home Service only were separated at Tunbridge Wells in June, 1915 from the 3/4th Queen's, in whose ranks at that time they were serving. Some men of similar category from the Fifth Queen's (Guildford) were united with them, and the joint force (16 officers and 960 men) were called for the time being the " 69th Provisional Battalion." [Finally on 1st January, 1917, they were re-baptised as the " 19th Queen's."] On 20th June, 1915, the 69th P.B. (19th Queen's) went by train to Eastbourne and Seaford and were engaged on coast defence ; and Major Perkins (afterwards K.C.B.) of the 2/5th Queen's, commanded them. But in a fortnight the pleasant south coast quarters were exchanged for Lowestoft, which Lord French always held to be a highly vulnerable spot. Trenches were formed along the Denes, with wire entanglements, and a line of strong points on the cliff above ; and the only shelter for the patrols on the shore was the highly inconvenient one of the local bathing-machines. Other regiments sent parties to join the battalion, and at one time (May, 1916) Major Perkins was in command of about 2,000 men ; guarding from four to eight miles of the coast, from Pakefield to Hopton. From first to last 140 officers and 5,000 other ranks passed through the 19th Queen's. They continued round Lowestoft till 6th November, 1916, when drafts and discharges had reduced the battalion to 450, but new arrivals quickly raised the numbers again to about 900. In August, 1918, the numbers were 1,700.

The most interesting part was the end of April, 1916. On the night of 24th April there were Zeppelins over the coast, and one Zeppelin was observed in the early dawn of the 25th by the Adjutant and the officer on duty to be hanging motionless at a great height. They thought it crippled, and were glad to see warships on the horizon, from which gun-flashes proceeded which they hoped would bring down the Zeppelin. But the explosion of heavy shells along the Lowestoft coast quickly made it known to them that these eight or ten ships were part of the *German* Navy. Lowestoft was being shelled by a number of heavy guns, firing as rapidly as they could. No retaliation was possible ; all that could be done was to put the troops into the bombardment trenches which had been specially prepared for such an event ; where, moreover, they would be available in case of an attempted landing. Casualties occurred to houses in the town and amongst the civilian population, but almost none amongst the troops ; the Huns' ranging being fortunately very defective. One shell passed through fourteen houses, coming to rest, still unexploded, in a bedroom of the last. Other houses were totally demolished. But in less than half an hour a few British ships hove in sight. They at once opened fire on the enemy. Though ours was but a light flotilla, and some of their ships were battle cruisers, yet it was enough : *the Navy* was there, and the Huns fled under full steam ! A renewal of the attack was anticipated, and the battalion was kept strictly to quarters, ready to turn out at any instant. Much relief was felt when the welcome message arrived " Resume normal conditions."

Air attacks, chiefly by Zeppelins, were frequent at Lowestoft. They made for this point both coming and going. Sometimes they arrived in a damaged condition, and the Yarmouth air-men were twice able to destroy them, driving them down in flames. Only once did serious damage to the town occur from overhead, and that was on the occasion of a visit from two bombing seaplanes. Many times vessels were submarined in sight of land ; and after storms detached mines would be driven against the groins, and their shattering explosions caused alarm. Once a storm drove the sea over the flats and swept away all the trenches and defences raised with so much toil. The battalion was frequently praised by the authorities for the excellence of these works and for their exemplary good behaviour.

The 19th Queen's underwent many changes with the passing of the Military Service Act and the introduction of medical categories. Frequent detachments were sent abroad, and officers came and went so quickly that it was at times difficult to know all the officers even by name, and impossible for company commanders to have that knowledge of their men which is so eminently desirable. It might be supposed that such frequent changes would be fatal to all esprit de corps. But the constant interchange with expeditionary forces in the various theatres of war was on the other hand of incalculable value in the maintenance of the 19th Queen's as an efficient fighting machine. Besides, when men see that every effort is being made for their comfort they quickly settle into good order. There is every reason to hope that all who passed through this unit will retain kindly memories of the East Coast work they performed when they were members of a famous regiment whose origin was by the sea. The 19th Queen's was disbanded in November, 1918.

X. Surrey Yeomanry (Queen Mary's Regiment) "C" Squadron

From 1900 there existed in Croydon the " C " squadron of the Surrey Yeomanry (" A " squadron being a Clapham force ; " B " squadron a Woking force ; and " D " squadron a Wimbledon force) ; and this " C " squadron had excellent Headquarters in Tamworth Road, and was an efficient and very smart unit. When the Lord Mayor of that day (Alderman Sir W. Treloar) visited Croydon in state in 1907, to open the new Fire Station in Park Lane, the Mayor of Croydon (Alderman H. Keatley Moore) was permitted to avail himself of a troop of this squadron as escort to his " big brother " of London, whom he met, thus accompanied, at Norbury brook, and took in procession to the Fire Station and eventually to the Town Hall. The smartness of the Yeomanry received universal commendation. [At this time the Regiment bore the title of " Princess of Wales's Own."]

Under the Territorial army arrangements in 1908, the Surrey Yeomanry were attached to the South Eastern Mounted Brigade as Divisional Cavalry. When war was declared, and the mobilisation order arrived (5th August, 1914) the " C " squadron of Surrey Yeomanry was with its regiment as part of the Home Counties Brigade engaged in manœuvres near Salisbury, and on this day was taking part in a march from Bordon to Amesbury, by Salisbury Plain. The Regiment was now called (since the Princess of Wales had become Queen Mary, in 1910) the " Surrey Yeomanry (Queen Mary's Regiment)." Taking train at Amesbury at 6 a.m. on the 5th, after waiting in a torrent of rain at the station all night (having to hold their horses, expecting the train every minute, they were unable to get either rest or shelter) they reached their Headquarters at Tamworth Road by the afternoon. Having returned the horses hired for the manœuvres, the first business was to replace them by horses purchased by the Government. The officers had to scour the country round, buying horses for the squadron as cheaply as they could, being limited to £50 for a trooper's horse and £75 for an officer's charger. Those who had horses of their own kept them in the squadron, being paid for them at these rates. There was some delay over the fact that the Army Remount officers were beforehand with our squadron and moreover claimed a preference as against them in certain districts. By the end of the week, however, the squadron was finally remounted. It may be said here that many horses proved unfit for cavalry work, breaking down after three or four months training, so that when " C " squadron went abroad at least half its horses had to be sold, and were replaced by Canadian horses imported for remount purposes by our Government.

On Saturday and Sunday (9th and 10th August), under the command of Major Barclay, the squadron marched to Maidstone as part of the S.E. Coast Defence, and on the way some of the troopers soon discovered that the horses under them had never been saddled before, so that the march was not without amusement at their expense. At Maidstone they remained for the rest of the month, training. Early in September they marched to Canterbury, to Old Park Farm near the barracks, where they went under canvas (horses picketed in the open) and remained in camp till the middle of November. The officers then vainly tried to find billets, and eventually commandeered the oast-houses in the Faversham hop-district. In January, 1915, " A " and "B " squadrons having left for France (and " D " squadron having been absorbed in " A "), our Croydon " C " squadron was left alone. They proceeded by train to Stratford-on-Avon, and remained there till the second week in March. During this sojourn they were re-equipped, receiving fresh rifles, swords, and saddles, and by this time had become a highly efficient force of about 120 strong. They now passed under the command of Major R. Bonsor, Major Barclay having been detached to train recruits at Canterbury to form drafts for abroad, and being advanced in rank to Lieutenant-Colonel. They had the honour of being inspected by H.M. the King at Warwick, and of receiving his commendation.

The " C " squadron now embarked (19th March, 1915) with the 29th Division at Avonmouth (Bristol) for Gallipoli; being instructed to save all the drinking water possible, as their destination was practically a waterless region. At Malta, however, they were sent to Alexandria, landing there 1st April, the horses being carried (with a few attendants) on a separate vessel from the troops. Not till the middle of June did they reach the island of Imbros, at that time General Sir Ian Hamilton's Headquarters; Major Bonsor and 100 officers and men were sent over as Headquarters guard, etc., from Alexandria and took with them just a few horses for orderly work on the island, leaving the rest of the men and nearly all the horses in Alexandria. From Imbros the squadron provided frequent fatigue parties for the front in Gallipoli (29th Division). After the evacuation of Gallipoli, January, 1916, the squadron re-united at Alexandria, but found

Photo by Lewis

Major STANLEY R. DOCKING, T.D.
C.O. Croydon Column, S.E. Mounted Brigade,
Transport and Supply Column, A.S.C.

Major John Edward Fox, T.D., J.P., (Alderman; Mayor, Nov., 1908–Nov., 1910) First C.O. of Croydon Column, S.E. Mounted Brigade, Transport and Supply Column, A.S.C.

SURREY YEOMANRY (C SQUADRON)   95

the men and horses left behind there had been sent to Cairo and thence westward on the expedition against the Senussi Arabs, in company with some fresh Surrey Yeomanry drafts trained and sent out by Colonel Barclay. After these had rejoined at the termination of the expedition the squadron was considerably over strength. At the beginning of March, 1916, leaving the horses behind—never to see them again—the men of the squadron re-embarked at Alexandria for Marseilles. They took their saddles with them, and on reaching Rouen were re-equipped and remounted ; and here on 19th March they celebrated the anniversary of their leaving Avonmouth in 1915, by a good sound snowstorm, just such another as that which speeded them from England, and as that which a year later overtook them on the Somme (1917). They rejoined their Division (29th Division) at Acheux on the Ancre for trench digging, etc., with the Royal Engineers, and laying telephone cables to the firing line, in furrows three feet deep, as it had been found too costly to let them be above ground. In May they went southward to Heilly, and joined the 15th Corps, forming a composite cavalry regiment with the South Irish Horse (also a yeomanry regiment) and taking the name of the " 15th Corps, Cavalry Regiment."

A little later it was found advisable for the " C " squadron to leave the 15th Corps and join up with the " Duke of Lancaster's Own Yeomanry " to make the 3rd Cavalry Regiment. On 1st July, 1916, the great Somme offensive started, and it was soon found that cavalry were useless, so about half the squadron dismounted and went forward to the trenches amongst the infantry, in the Albert district. The rest of the year the squadron supplied mounted orderlies, signal service despatch riders, etc., along tracks where motors and motor cycles were impossible. Just before Christmas the squadron was supplying one of the line regiments in the front with food and ammunition by means of troopers leading loaded packhorses, the roads being impassable for wheel traffic on account of the mud. At the beginning of 1917 the Australians took over this district, and the 3rd Corps Cavalry regiment proceeded to Amiens, just outside the city. The sight of the famous Cathedral piled with sandbags up to the roof was a piteous one. But at any rate the Germans were prevented from making Amiens another Rheims, though they tried their best. From Amiens the Regiment in March, 1917, went towards St. Quentin as far as Villers Bretonneux, where the Germans were missed. They were sent forward in search of the retreating foes, and had to ride three days before they found them ; the enemy aeroplanes watching their pursuit from above. Suddenly they ran into the enemy at Vermand (an outpost of the great Hindenburg line) and were held up two days until the infantry arrived and took over. There were of course many casualties, but on the whole the regiment was fortunate. Major Bonsor was in command of the "C" squadron in this smart little brush. Afterwards, for about three weeks, the "C" squadron remained clearing up booby traps, etc. In June the squadron, being then at Moislanes, was permanently dismounted, the horses being sent to Salonica via Marseilles, and the men to Etaples where they underwent five weeks' infantry training. Eventually they were incorporated with the 10th Queen's (a Battersea service battalion) and proceeded to Dunkerque, subsequently taking over the front line of the coastal defences at Nieuport from the Belgians at the beginning of October, 1917. The 10th Queen's formed part of the famous fighting 41st Division.

The Italian disaster at the Piave occurring at this time, it was necessary at once for us to go to the help of our allies, and the 41st Division was one of the three divisions sent forward. They entrained near St. Omer for Genoa, where the population received them at the station with fervent demonstrations of welcome, bringing them coffee, fruit, cakes and all kinds of good things ; a great relief from the everlasting bully beef and biscuits of the cantonments, especially to poor fellows packed at the moment by twenty-five or thirty in cattle-trucks. Owing to the kindness of the Commanding Officer (Colonel Bell) of the 10th Queen's, our men were now allowed, from Genoa to Mantua, to ride, as many as could find room, on the transport in the open wagons, so that they enjoyed a view of the beautiful country of the plains of Lombardy and could breathe the fresh air. At Mantua the division detrained, and our Croydon boys marched, still on foot, of course as part of the 10th Queen's, 150 miles in eight days, for no time could be lost. They marched via Verona straight to the Piave, but in the hurry and on account of the mountainous country, the rations and all the letters of the regimental mail went into Switzerland. The letters came back four months afterwards, but somebody (possibly the frugal Switzers) devoured the rations ; at all events the regiment never saw them again. Consequently, for three days on this forced march, hurrying at top speed to relieve our allies, at the very time when extra feeding would have been welcome to enable them to resist the fatigue of their exertions, our men had to go terribly short. On the day of the loss the emergency ration meagrely fed them, but on the next day there was nothing to eat. A mess-tin full of tea without milk or sugar, was all they had that day, and the day's march was twenty-two miles. The next day the Italians sent them a small supply, enough to give them four ounces of bully beef each and a small coarse brown loaf between every six men. On the third day things were a little better, but the march in general was a time of emptiness. Eventually they arrived at the Montella sector in the mountains near Belluno

SURREY YEOMANRY (C SQUADRON)

above the plain of the Piave, the Austrian invaders being across the river (which here flows east and west before turning southwards) immediately below our men, Corregliano lying behind them as their headquarters. Here they remained, of course with occasional skirmishes and raids, till February, 1918, by which time their purpose of checking the Austrian advance had been fully accomplished.

The whole 41st Division now returned to France, to Sous-St.-Leger, near Doullens in the Somme region. Their short rest here was broken in upon by the great German advance, which caused them to go forward as swiftly as possible (in order to resist the enemy's onslaught) to Bapaume (21st March). Here they held the line against the Germans for two days, but had then to retire before superior forces, always maintaining excellent order, in spite of severe casualties, to Achiet-le-Petit. They held on here for twelve hours, but had then to retire, and did not finally hold up the German advance till within ten miles of Amiens. What follows is matter of glorious history, and the subsequent triumphant advance of Haig's great army ended, as we all know, with the Armistice on 11th November. But the price paid by the 41st Division up to Amiens was so heavy that it was sent to Ypres (then a quiet part of the line) to recuperate and to await reinforcements. The merits of our Croydon " C " squadron men had shown themselves so great in the war that no less than fifty per cent. of those still surviving had received commissions, and had therefore been distributed throughout the army. By the time they reached Ypres (as part of the 10th Queen's) some were officers in that regiment and other line regiments ; others were officers in the Flying Corps, others were cavalry officers, and one Croydon man of a very well known High Street family was officer of a tank, and was soon after sent, to his great disgust, to overcome with his unwieldy machine the Sinn Feiners in Ireland. In the ranks there was always a certain nucleus of Croydon Yeomanry men who managed to hold together all the time. The 41st Division, brought up to strength once more, took part in the great final advance, and on Armistice day were at Nederbrakel near the scene of Marlborough's splendid victory of Oudenarde. Keeping always a day or two's march behind, they followed their defeated foes into Germany, passed through Cologne and took up outposts about twenty miles beyond the Cologne bridge-head. Here they began to be gradually demobilised and were sent home in order of seniority of service. Of the 120 fine young fellows who so gaily left Croydon in August, 1914, very many had found their graves abroad, and of the survivors who returned to Croydon more than half will carry honourable scars to their graves. And yet, if you speak to any of these men, they will all tell you " We were a very lucky squadron."

XI. South Eastern Mounted Brigade (Transport and Supply Column, A.S.C.)

In 1908 it was found under the new scheme then coming into being, that the South Eastern Mounted Brigade (Territorial Force) was deficient in the necessary Transport and Supply Column as far as this part of the county was concerned. The Surrey Territorial Force Association, by its president, General Sir Edmond Elles, K.C.B., etc., approached the then Mayor of Croydon, Major J. E. Fox, T.D., with a request that he should raise the unit in Croydon. Major Fox was then a Captain and Hon. Major in the Territorial Battalion of the Lincolnshire Regiment; but he undertook the new duty, and in spite of predictions that "it was a hopeless task," in six weeks he was able to obtain the War Office recognition of the new unit, the Croydon Column having enrolled a sufficient number for the purpose, and the unit was almost immediately up to full strength. Major Fox continued in command until compulsorily retired under the age limit. At the beginning, Captain Clarence G. Allen, M.C., and Lieutenant Stanley R. Docking, T.D., served in the Column, but later Captain Allen transferred to and took command of the Surrey Brigade Company A.S.C. (Woking). In 1912 Major Fox retired, having received his Brevet Major under the Territorial Force regulations "for distinguished services of an exceptional kind other than in the Field"; and Captain (afterwards Major) Docking took command of the Column.

At the outbreak of war the unit was mobilised. It was then at full war strength (120) at Mitcham Road Barracks. At the Inspection in June, 1914, at Folkestone, only two months before, the Inspecting Officer had made the very unusual observation that this column was "fit for mobilisation." No doubt this was due to the efficient training it had always undergone at the hands of Staff-Sergt. Major (now Captain) S. H. Brooks, the Instructor. Therefore, the work of mobilisation was very skilful and rapid, and the column was on a war-footing three days (72 hours) ahead of scheduled time. It left Croydon for its war station (Canterbury) on 12th August, 1914.

Early in 1915 the column was reorganised. About seventy per cent. had volunteered for service abroad, and many of these had joined with units of the R.A.S.C. in the New Armies then

SOUTH EASTERN MOUNTED BRIGADE, A.S.C. 99

being raised. Many of them attained high rank. As Major Docking was among these, the command of the unit now devolved on Captain (now Major) F. L. Hacking. A number of men of the unit were attached to various Yeomanry regiments, and to the Field Ambulance of the S.E. Mounted Brigade as first-line Transport Drivers, and went overseas with their new comrades to France, Italy, Salonica or Egypt. At least one officer has even been traced to the German East Africa campaign, so that it is true to say that our Croydon boys of the Transport and Supply Column served on every front. Major Docking was seconded to employment with the (Regular) R.A.S.C., in March, 1915, as said above, and thereafter commanded a divisional train in France ; he was not restored to the establishment of the Territorial Force in France until 1918.

On 24th September, 1915, the 1/1st South Eastern Mounted Brigade, Transport and Supply Column, under Major Hacking, sailed for Gallipoli, and shared in that arduous campaign until the evacuation of the Peninsula in January, 1916, with a splendid record of brave work done. From Gallipoli they went to Egypt, and were soon after disbanded, and distributed amongst various R.A.S.C. units on the Egyptian, Mesopotamian, and Salonica fronts.

Meanwhile recruiting had been proceeding towards a 2/1st Column at Croydon and Canterbury under Captain W. Curtis ; and, later on, even a 3/1st Column was formed, which last went to Ireland under Captain Cantley. On 1st September, 1916, all the Territorial A.S.C. units were posted to the regular army ; and although the 2/1st and 3/1st column continued as such they ceased to be Territorial units.

When the Conscription Act came into force (10th February, 1916) many of the medically fit men had already been drafted to the Gunners and Cavalry, to the Machine Guns and the Tanks, and in some cases to the Infantry. As has been said, they served in this way on every battle front during the Great War, and fourteen per cent. of them laid down their lives. Twenty per cent. of the whole number won commissions, and one Warrant Officer reached the rank of Major in the (regular) R.A.S.C., and won the D.S.O.—a splendid record. Another won seven decorations : D.C.M., M.M., Croix de Guerre, etc., etc. Moreover, twenty-five per cent. of the men attained the rank of Warrant Officer ; and, finally, there was not *one man* of them all who did not gain promotion of some kind, from corporal upwards. Of such fine quality were our brave Croydon lads of the South Eastern Mounted Brigade, Transport and Supply Column A.S.C.

XII. 1st Battalion Surrey (Croydon) National Reserve

It was always felt by Field-Marshal Lord Roberts that altogether to let slip trained time-expired men, " old soldiers," who had left the regular army, was a foolish waste of good material. In 1910, therefore, inspired by this idea of the Field-Marshal's, the War Office convened a meeting of such " old soldiers," in Queen's House, Croydon ; naming Major Junner as the first Commanding Officer and organiser. By May, 1911, Major Junner had gathered together three companies towards a battalion, and these with other Surrey National Reservists then paraded at Guildford and were inspected by Lord Roberts being entertained by Mr. St. Loe Strachey, an ardent advocate of the scheme. The Head Quarters were first at 70a, London Road, and were afterwards removed to Cherry Orchard Road in 1912, and to Poplar Walk, in 1913. At the declaration of War, 4th August, 1914, Croydon National Reservists mustered 939 men, a number which soon rose to 1,353. Many men of the National Reserve were still of fighting capacity, although no doubt home defence was more in Lord Roberts' mind ; and therefore on the 5th August, Captain Murgatroyd and 120 N.C.O.'s and men were called up for service. A large remount depot and camp was formed, and that very day 300 horses passed through the civilian purchasing-officer's hands and were standing in camp waiting to be taken over by the army. This was followed by a similar camp at Oxted. A company and a half (about 150 men) fully officered and in uniform joined the East Surrey Regiment ; and over three companies more (about 316 men) took on the important work of guarding the railways ; while 164 more rejoined their old regiments, and a large number of Warrant Officers and N.C.O.'s joined Kitchener's Army as Instructors. Two hundred further passed into various departments of war work ; so that in all the National Reserve (Croydon) supplied 1,700 men to help forward the great war. Captain Barrie, who to the regret of so many, died in harness, was originally Quarter-Master of the Croydon battalion, and when he became chief recruiting officer for the Croydon district all his staff were men who followed him from the Croydon National Reserve. Those

CROYDON NATIONAL RESERVISTS BEING INSPECTED AT GUILDFORD BY F.M. LORD ROBERTS (May, 1911)
Photo by Norman Stanislaus

Photo by Howard M. King

MAJOR JAMES PETRIE, O.B.E.,
C.O. 1st Volunteer Battalion, "The Queen's"

who rejoined the Army did splendid service : Captain Chapman fell with the Hampshires in France, Captain Ruddock with the Worcesters at Gallipoli. The battalion has been kept alive by the strenuous exertions of Colonel Wilson and Captain and Adjutant Voules and others, so that men now returning to ordinary life can still report themselves as reservists. In wartime they formed a Home Guard of 437 men, and were able to help many cases of distress and difficulty, especially in the matter of the accounts of men on leave from active service ; while Quarter-Master Sergeant Fowles was equally indefatigable in keeping the social side of the unit vigorous and cheerful to the very end of the war.

Farrier-Sergeant Harding deserves mention, as showing what these veterans can undertake. Though over 70 he did excellent service in the Remount department at Redhill as dispenser, in the intervals of going to and from the Cape, bringing over shiploads of horses for his department.

XIII. The Volunteers 1st V.B. The Queen's (Royal West Surrey Regt.)

On the 15th August, 1914, the High Sheriff of Surrey (Mr. St. Loe Strachey) convened a meeting of the Miniature Rifle Clubs of Surrey at Guildford, to discuss certain proposals put forward by the High Sheriff for the formation of village and town guards, and it was agreed by the meeting, with the concurrence of the High Sheriff, that the proposals were not applicable, at all events without a good deal of modification, to the case of thickly populated urban areas such as Croydon.

On Friday, the 21st August, 1914, a meeting was therefore convened at the Town Hall, by the Mayor of Croydon (Alderman Frank Denning), as an outcome of the above movement. There was a very large attendance, and the meeting unanimously decided—

(1). That a list be prepared of those members of miniature rifle clubs in or near Croydon, who, being unable to join any of the present official organised forces of the country, are willing to offer their services for use in any way the same may be required, so far as lies in their power.

(2). That as far as may be practicable, arrangements be made for the elementary drilling of those who are able to give the time necessary for the purpose.

(3). That a Committee of seven should be appointed to give effect to the foregoing resolutions.

The Committee appointed consisted of—
Messrs. W. T. Diplock, W. A. Hemsley, J. C. Moger, J. Petrie, F. H. Popkiss, H. C. Pressland and W. W. Topley ; and elected Mr. J. C. Moger (President of the Croydon and District League of Rifle Clubs) as Chairman, and Messrs. Diplock and Topley as Honorary Secretaries. It was decided to name the new organization " The Croydon Riflemen."

On the 7th September, 1914, drills commenced on the Sports Ground in Park Lane (by the kind permission of the L.B. & S.C. Railway Company), under Sergeant F. W. Clements, late 4th Queen's—270 members and 6 Instructors attending.

In October, 1914, the ground was found to be too small for efficient training, as the numbers had already increased to 560, and the Croydon Education Committee kindly granted the use, for two evenings weekly, of the schools at Tavistock Grove, Winterbourne Road, Davidson Road, Portland Road and Whitehorse Road. Contingents were also drilling two evenings weekly at Mitcham Road Barracks, Yeomanry Hall, Woodside Hall, Haling Road Hall, Brotherhood Institute (South Norwood), and St. Mary's Hall, Addiscombe.

Miniature Rifle ranges were kindly placed at the disposal of the "Croydon Riflemen," by their controlling authorities, together with the loan of rifles for practice. Free tuition was given by expert members of each rifle range, and a very high standard of shooting was reached.

A special badge was provided for each member, to be worn at drill and rifle range practice. The wearing of the badge was strictly insisted upon, as the unit was not yet recognized by the Government. The training was carried out on military lines and in strict accordance with "Infantry Training, 1914."

Route marching, including a number of night marches, took place nearly every week within an area of twenty miles of Croydon, as well as marching to a given spot in a prescribed time; and every man was soon found to be quite capable of marching twenty and thirty miles night or day. Men who had hitherto never walked more than a few yards at a time soon became able to march without any undue exertion or over-fatigue. The strength of "Croydon Riflemen" in February, 1915, was 1,100 members.

On the 20th February, 1915, the "Croydon Riflemen" were affiliated to the "Central Association of Volunteer Training Corps," of which the Rt. Hon. Lord Desborough, K.C.V.O., was the President, and Mr. Percy A. Harris, L.C.C., the Hon. Sec.

On the 8th March, 1915, the Lord Lieutenant approved the amalgamation of the "Croydon Riflemen" and the "South Norwood Volunteer Training Corps" under the title of the "1/1st Battalion (Croydon) Surrey Volunteer Training Corps," with Mr. James Petrie as Commandant, the remaining nine units in the Croydon Recruiting area being at the same time formed into the "2/1st Battalion, Surrey Volunteer Training Corps," with Colonel Quin as Commandant. This area was large, and always awkward to work. It extended from Norbury southwards as far as Dorman's Land, and from Caterham westwards to Oxted.

On the 15th March, 1915, Colonel Sir Frederick Edridge, D.L., J.P., accepted the position of Honorary Commandant of the battalion, Mr. A. W. Thomas became Adjutant, and Sergeant F. W. Clements battalion sergeant-major.

The 1/1st battalion was inspected on 11th April, 1915, by Colonel Cochran, C.B. ; its strength on this date being 18 officers and 645 N.C.O.'s and men—total 663. Colonel Cochran in his report of the inspection complimented the battalion very highly on the excellent attendance, steadiness on parade, and the exemplary manner in which the various movements were executed.

The battalion was again inspected on 4th July, 1915, by General Sir Josceline Wodehouse, the Commandant of the Surrey V.T.C. Regiment. This was the first occasion when the Commanding Officer of the Regiment had inspected the battalion. Field exercises were executed under Commandant James Petrie, as well as platoon, company and artillery formation exercises under the various junior officers, while large operations, in which the signalling, ambulance and cyclist sections were utilized were performed under the command of the inspecting General himself. An imaginary enemy was supposed to be entrenched near Croydon and the battalion had to drive him out of his entrenched position. The battalion received the cordial congratulations of General Wodehouse on their excellent work and good general bearing.

In July, 1915, the battalion was formed into four companies : (*a*) Parish Hall, South Norwood ; (*b*) Portland Road Schools ; (*c*) Winterbourne Road Council Schools ; and, (*d*) Tavistock Grove Council Schools.

Headquarters being at this time found necessary to carry on the work of the battalion, a small room was procured at the Headquarters of the National Reserve, 2 Poplar Walk, Croydon. The Commandant, Adjutant, Orderly Officer for the week, battalion Sergt.-Major and four Orderlies worked in the confined space three and four hours every night for several months. And not only in neglect to provide Headquarters, but in every way, as it seems to the Editor of this book, the Volunteers, far from receiving the encouragement they so well deserved at the hands of the military authorities of the country, were constantly neglected and not infrequently snubbed. The Headquarters of the V.T.C. in July, 1915, issued instructions that officers and men might wear uniform of a grey colour, providing the whole of the expense was defrayed by the officers and men, the Government having declined to make a grant for this purpose. Every officer and man consequently provided at his own cost the necessary uniform, putties, belt, haversack and water bottle ; and all were compelled by the Government to wear a red brassard with the letters G.R. (Georgius Rex) thereon, when attending Parade, with or without uniform. This brassard was the only equipment issued by the Government to the " Volunteer Training Corps " ; and on account of it all members of the V.T.C. throughout the country were very quickly " dubbed " by sarcastic members of the community the " Gorgeous Wrecks."

But the V.T.C. of Croydon were anything but " Gorgeous Wrecks " ; they were a sturdy body of men, determined to train and work hard to make themselves thoroughly proficient in the duties of soldiers in order to be ready to defend their hearths and homes against any invasion that might be attempted by the hateful Hun. Every officer and man was exceedingly keen, often at drill, and for long hours at a time : and was indeed maintaining himself in a high state of efficiency. In fact an excellent spirit and hard grit were shown by all ranks, in spite of the jeers of thoughtless sections of the public, and the frequent rebuffs of the Government, who continually hindered the Volunteers in every possible way, and never gave any proper support to the movement. Since rifles could not be obtained from the Government for training purposes, the battalion, not to be beaten, purchased 200 dummy rifles. They also raised money and bought entrenching tools, Army stretchers, bugles, fifes and drums, bayonet fighting appliances, etc., out of their battalion funds, finding their requests for these necessary appliances contemptuously ignored. Nor were any grants ever made for the payment of the rent of Headquarters, for the purchase of books, for stationery, postages, fees to caretakers, etc., and as it was decided not to appeal to the general public for assistance, the officers and men agreed to pay a weekly subscription to meet these liabilities. It must be admitted that to continue efficient amidst such an environment of obstacles and such an atmosphere of antagonism entitles our Croydon Volunteers to claim the possession of British bull-dog obstinacy in a very high degree : all honour to them.

Weekly well-attended lectures on military engineering were given by Commandant Petrie to officers and men, and practical work was carried out in the digging of firing, cover and communication trenches, traversers, shelters, loopholes, etc., machine gun emplacements, revetting, making and fixing fascines, on ground at Norwood Junction, kindly lent by the L.B. & S.C. Railway Company.

On the 20th September, 1915, the battalion was allotted by the London District Command the construction of a portion of the Outer London Defences at Willey Farm, Caterham and Aldercombe. This was completed on the 16th December, 1917, the time taken over the work being 90,000 hours.

General Sir Josceline Wodehouse, K.C.B., C.M.G., (Commanding the Surrey Volunteer Regiment) inspected the trench digging at Caterham, on 7th October, 1917, and "had the greatest pleasure in congratulating all concerned in regard to the satisfactory reports furnished him by the officer in charge of the works, as to the intelligence displayed by the working parties, and their ability in revetting and draining." [In one place a drain nine feet deep was under construction.]

The officers and men were paid by the Government, for refreshments, 5d. per six hours of work. The work was very arduous and was carried out in all kinds of weather, every day in the week; the largest attendances being on holidays, Saturday afternoons and Sundays. Great praise was gained from the General Officer Commanding London and District, Major General Sir Francis Lloyd, K.C.B., D.S.O., for the excellent work done. This was no doubt owing to the practical training the officers and men had previously received at Norwood Junction, under the direction and supervision of Commandant Petrie.

The battalion furnished the largest number of officers and men per week of any battalion engaged upon the defences. Great credit is due to Platoon Commanders Cook, Turner and Tough (the battalion entrenching officers) for the excellent manner all ranks carried out their duties, especially as numbers of the men were usually occupied in sedentary occupations, and were therefore not accustomed to wielding a pick, shovel or axe. Even the Commandant and the other officers were under the instructions of the platoon commanders, and "dug" and "delved" with the rest. A sergeant was heard on one occasion to say that it was only on these defences that the Commandant and officers did any real hard work; but that was a humorous calumny.

By the permission of the G.O.C. Eastern Command, a standing camp was formed at Aldercombe during August and September, 1916. The tents, blankets, tables, forms and cooking utensils were provided free of cost from Government Stores, the provision of water, food, etc., was made at the cost of the battalion. The camp was well attended at week ends, and during holidays. Work was carried out on the defences during the day for a period of ten to twelve hours, for which work officers and men received from the Government daily pay (1s. 8d. per day of twenty-four hours); if any man left the camp at the end of twelve hours, he received only 10d. for that day. The site of the camp, and the weather was ideal; and it was extraordinary how everyone at once settled down to camp life, seeing that for many of them it was the first experience of feeding in the open and sleeping under canvas. All worked hard, and with excellent spirit, and not a single " grouse " was heard during the whole of the time the camp was standing ; although backs often ached and hands were usually blistered. At no time, owing to the excellent discipline, was any man put in the guard-tent or paraded before the Camp Commandant. The camp was run on strict military lines. After working hours, guards were mounted and all officers and men took turns for duty. The cooking was carried out in an excellent manner by the battalion cook and his staff. Cricket and swimming matches were arranged in the evenings with other Volunteer battalions who were camping in the district, the battalion being so fortunate as to win every cricket and swimming match they contested.

Lectures on map reading and field sketching with practical work, on Riddlesdown and other places in the county, were given to the officers and N.C.O.'s by Commandant Petrie. The whole of the officers and N.C.O.'s of the battalion attended the lectures and practical work, and showed great interest in the subject. The knowledge obtained was found to be exceedingly useful at a later date to both officers and N.C.O.'s, when taking part in the numerous field operations, etc., that were carried out. Lectures on musketry were given to officers and N.C.O.'s by an officer of the Royal Naval Division, Crystal Palace. The attendance and results obtained were excellent. Good practice was carried out on the miniature Rifle Ranges, every officer, N.C.O. and man was an efficient shot, and ninety per cent. were first class shots. Classes were formed for officers for instruction in bayonet fighting, by Commandant Petrie and Adjutant Thomas. The officers all qualified as instructors. Emergency parades (the companies parading at their different drill centres and marching to a given spot in a prescribed time) were held at short notices, and the officers, N.C.O.'s and men responded readily in large numbers in spite of the inconvenience to many of them owing to business and other calls.

On Sunday the 27th February, 1916, one of the most interesting operations the battalion had been engaged upon up to this time, took place in Holmwood Park (near Keston Common), the seat of the Countess of Derby, in conjunction with the 4th West Kent Fencibles, Volunteer Training Corps. The 4th West Kent Fencibles, commanded by Commandant Dawson, represented a hostile convoy attempting to pass through the park. The 1/1st battalion Surrey V.T.C., commanded by Commandant Petrie, represented the defending force ; and after some very skilful manœuvring, the convoy was duly captured by the 1/1st battalion. Excellent work was done by all ranks, especially by the Cyclists section of the 1/1st battalion. The chief umpires were officers of the regular Army, and it was the first time they had seen V.T.C. men at work. They were very much surprised at the discipline maintained, and also at the thoroughness shown by all ranks in carrying out the operations, the scheme being admittedly a difficult one. The ambulance section of the 1/1st battalion Surrey V.T.C. dressed and bandaged the imaginary casualties from the firing line. Each casualty had a card pinned on his coat, stating the nature of his supposed injuries, and all bandages had to be improvised from any materials lying about the park grounds. After dressing and bandaging the injuries of the casualties on the spot behind the firing line, where they had been brought, the stretcher bearers carried them to the casualty station, when the work was criticised by the principal medical officer in charge of the V.A.D. The section was highly complimented by the P.M.O. on the excellent manner in which the impromptu bandaging, etc., had been carried out.

On Sunday, May 21st, 1916, field operations were carried out on Farthing Downs under the direction of General Wodehouse the Commandant of the entire Regiment, by the 1/1st and 2/1st battalions of the Surrey Volunteer Training Corps, under the command of Captain and Adjutant E. H. Ronca, and Captain Loughborough, respectively. The latter, a very keen officer, had succeeded Colonel Quin in the command of the 2/1st. The total strength, of over 600, included signallers, cyclists, and ambulance sections, and each battalion had its Bugle Band. With the day gloriously fine, and the undulating country looking its best, the Volunteers thoroughly enjoyed the operations.

The Cyclists section of the battalion was a very strong and capable one. It was commanded by Lieutenant Leleu, a very energetic and keen officer. Their knowledge of the roads, etc., of the county was excellent, and the reports and sketches of the main and secondary roads, water and gas mains, telegraph and telephone services, railway stations, goods yards, etc., were extremely well written and drawn. For some unaccountable reason, in May, 1916, when the V.T.C.'s were recognized by the Government and brought under the Volunteer Acts, it was decided that all Cyclists sections were to be disbanded, a decision which was much regretted and resented by the men. In consequence, a very large proportion of the men resigned and the excellent services of these Volunteers were lost to the movement.

The Signalling section (Buzzer, Morse and Semaphore) was an excellent one, which worked assiduously to perfect itself and master the many intricate problems of this fascinating subject. It rendered very valuable services to the battalion when on field operations, manœuvres, etc., and every credit is due to Platoon

BOMBING PRACTICE, First Volunteer Battalion, "The Queen's"

The bomb-thrower is supposed to be throwing over the parapet of a trench, represented by the framework; he cannot see his objective at the time of throwing, but knows its direction and distance. The left hand is raised to balance the body and to increase the momentum of the throw.

Machine Gun Team,
First Volunteer Battalion, "The Queen's."

THE VOLUNTEERS (1ST V.B. THE QUEEN'S) 109

Commander Player for the high state of efficiency the section attained. The men provided at their own cost the necessary equipment.

The battalion was also enabled to form a Machine Gun section, under Company Commander E. H. Ronca, and Company Sergt.-Major P. E. Walls, owing to the kind generosity of the Hon. Commandant of the battalion (Sir Frederick Edridge) who presented to the battalion an excellent model of the " Vickers " Machine Gun. Classes were formed, they were well attended, and the section quickly became efficient.

The Ambulance section was under the excellent supervision of Dr. B. T. Parsons-Smith, M.D., B.S., M.R.C.S., Medical Officer of the battalion. The whole of the section passed the St. John's Ambulance Association examination at the first sitting. Several members of the section rendered great service during the air raid over Croydon in October, 1915—attending to the injured, conveying them to the hospital, removing the dead, etc.

During 1916, 300 " Derby " recruits (not members of the battalion), as soon as they were attested, and while they were awaiting their calling-up notice, attended the drills set apart for them. They were trained gratuitously, and were extremely keen in gaining all the knowledge and drill that was possible before joining the Army. A large number after joining their units wrote to Commandant Petrie, expressing their deep appreciation of the instruction imparted to them, and of the patience exercised by the Instructors during their training with the Volunteers, which had enabled them to escape the drudgery of the recruit course on the barrack square. When joining up and going through their first recruit drill the officers would often ask them if they had not been in the army before, and were rather surprised when they replied : " No, but we did training with the 1/1st Battalion Surrey V.T.C."

On the 19th May, 1916, the Government decided that all battalions of the V.T.C. should be brought under the Volunteer Acts, 1863 to 1900 ; and should thenceforth be controlled by the County Territorial Force Associations. Therefore the 1/1st Battalion Surrey Volunteer Training Corps, with its 16 officers, 484 Warrant Officers, N.C.O.'s and men (the reduction from previous strength being due entirely to enlistment in His Majesty's Forces) became the " 1st Battalion Surrey Volunteer Regiment," and the 2/1st Battalion Surrey Volunteer Training Corps became the " 12th Battalion Surrey Volunteer Regiment." The General Headquarters of the Surrey Volunteer Regiment were at Victoria Embankment, London, the Hon. Commandant being Hon. Colonel Lord Ashcombe (Lord Lieutenant of Surrey), the County

Commandant Major-General F. C. Beatson, and the County Adjutant, Major G. A. Williams. The 1/1st Battalion of the Surrey Volunteer Regiment had its Headquarters at 2, Poplar Walk, Croydon, the Hon. Commandant being Lieutenant-Colonel J. M. Newnham, O.B.E., LL.D., D.L. (Town Clerk of Croydon), and Major James Petrie, the Commanding Officer. The 12th Battalion of the Surrey Volunteer Regiment had its Headquarters at 15, Cherry Orchard Road, Croydon, the Hon. Commandant being Lieutenant-Colonel Sir Frederick Edridge, D.L., and Major T. W. Loughborough the Commanding Officer.

On Sunday, 1st October, 1916, the entire Surrey Volunteer Regiment was inspected at Duppas Hill, Croydon, by Major General Sir F. Lloyd, whose opinion is given by General Wodehouse, the Officer Commanding the Regiment, in the following letter :—

3rd October, 1916.

To Officers Commanding all Battalions,
Surrey Volunteer Regiment.

General Sir Josceline Wodehouse wishes to convey to all ranks of the Surrey Volunteer Regiment his very sincere feelings of appreciation of their appearance on parade at Croydon on Sunday.

Major-General Sir Francis Lloyd, Commanding the London District, in the regretted absence, owing to illness, of Field Marshal Viscount French, expressed in most appropriate complimentary words his satisfaction at the appearance of the Regiment on parade, and of the inspiring sight of such numbers of men willing and eager to serve their country in its time of need.

What he said will, General Wodehouse hopes, be communicated to all ranks and be an incentive to continue with sustained zeal their efforts to attain an ever increasing efficiency.

The absence of the Lord Lieutenant under circumstances which evoke the deep sympathy of the Regiment in which he takes so deep an interest, General Wodehouse feels sure was regretted by all.

By order,

(*Signed*) G. A. WILLIAMS, Colonel.

Secretary, Surrey Territorial Force Association.

On Sunday, 27th May, 1917, the 1st, 9th and 11th battalions of the Surrey Volunteer Regiment, under the command of Brigadier General F. C. Beatson, were inspected on Duppas Hill by the Lord Lieutenant of the County—Colonel Lord Ashcombe, C.B., T.D.

THE VOLUNTEERS (1ST V.B. THE QUEEN'S)   111

In all the glory of an ideal English summer morning, 1,163 officers, N.C.O.'s and men took part in the operations, movements and march past. For over an hour the movements were carried out very smartly; the battalions then marched past in column and close column, with commendable precision, keeping a splendid line, and showing little trace of the fatiguing operations they had already accomplished, although they wore their heavy kit as ordered. The inspection was witnessed by a large assembly of interested onlookers, who cheered the men heartily. Lord Ashcombe addressing the men said that " the movements were a great credit to troops who did not live in barracks. There was swing and ease about their drill, orders were promptly and quickly carried out, and everybody seemed to be in place and to know what to do. The whole parade did great credit to everybody concerned."

Detachments of the Croydon Police, under Chief Inspector G. Lovie, and the Special Constabulary, under Chief Inspector H. C. Swaine, were on duty on the ground during the parade.

On the same date the 12th battalion under Major T. W. Loughborough were also inspected, on Farthing Downs, by Lord Ashcombe, and after the inspection the battalion carried out an attack in open formation, concluding with a charge. Lord Ashcombe congratulated Major Loughborough on the excellent work of the battalion.

On the 27th July, 1917, the 1st battalion Surrey Volunteer Regiment was allotted an area for guarding railway lines on the L.B. & S.C. railway around Croydon. 1 Captain, 2 Subalterns, 1 Warrant Officer, 15 N.C.O.'s and 93 men were detailed for this duty. They were thoroughly rehearsed in the duties of guarding and patrolling the line, and after a short time were fully competent to carry out their duties whenever required. The Royal Defence Corps subsequently took over these duties.

On the 24th April, 1917, the Signalling section of the 1st battalion was detailed to man the Buzzer telegraph station at East Croydon Railway station, and that of the 12th battalion to man the Buzzer stations at South Croydon and Oxted Railway stations, and both sections were very highly commended by the Defence Commander, Colonel R. E. Golightly, for the excellence of their work.

During March, 1917, on instructions from the War Office, grey-green uniform was issued to the battalion, free of cost to the W.O.'s, N.C.O.'s and men. In June, 1917, the Government further issued to the battalion, rifles, side arms and equipment, which enabled the men to be trained in musketry and to fire the classification courses as laid down by the War Office. The rifle was the 1914 pattern fitted with orthoptic sights, an excellent shooting weapon. Musketry classes were immediately formed; and the officers, W.O.'s, N.C.O.'s and men quickly attained a high state of efficiency. The classification courses were shot on the Marden Park range, and excellent results were obtained; a very large percentage of the men passing as 1st class shots.

The first camp under the control of the War Office was held in Richmond Park during August, 1917, under the command of Lieutenant-Colonel Heskett-Smith.

The training was varied and strenuous, it included signal, platoon, company, and battalion drill, route marching, field manœuvres, and outpost duties. Its intensity may be judged from the order of the day :—

Reveille	5.30 a.m.
First Parade	6.15 a.m.
Breakfast	7.30 a.m.
Second Parade	8.15 a.m.
Drills till	1.30 p.m.
Third Parade	2.15 p.m.
Drills till	6.0 p.m.

The good spirits of the men, their smartness on parade and at drill were the subject of much favourable comment amongst the officers of other battalions. Their esprit de corps and keenness were evinced by the cheerful way in which they carried their fully laden packs and rifles for four hours on the Saturday afternoon without a break, and still were able to swing into camp with a style which would not have discredited any battalion of Kitchener's Army. The camp was pitched in ideal surroundings, and all arrangements were adequate, but the heavy rain during the week previous to the men going into camp had converted the most frequented portions of the camp—such as the road to the cook-house and canteen—into a miniature morass. Major-General Beatson, C.B., the Surrey County Commandant, visited the camp on the Monday, and unhesitatingly awarded first place to the 1st Surreys (Croydon) for the tidiness and military neatness of their lines. During the field manœuvres it was the opinion of the instructional officers that the 1st Surreys were the best trained and most alert body of men engaged.

On the 1st March, 1918, the 1st and 12th battalions of the Surrey Volunteer Regiment were amalgamated, now becoming the " 1st V.B. The Queen's (Royal West Surrey Regiment)," Major James Petrie, O.B.E., being appointed Commanding Officer, Major T. W. Loughborough, Second in Command, and

THE VOLUNTEERS (1ST V.B. THE QUEEN'S) 113

Major F. A. Searle Hilton, Adjutant. [It must be noted that the rank of Major was the highest rank the War Office allowed to the Commanding Officer of any Volunteer battalion.]

The training was carried on with redoubled vigour, a large number of field operations, outpost schemes, etc., being carried out on Sundays under the supervision of the Headquarters London District and the Corps Commandant, Major General Beatson, and the Group Commander, Major General Tulloch.

Four detachments of officers and other ranks, and one Hotchkiss gun team, attended at Pirbright and Purfleet new field-firing ranges on Sundays, and carried out the "practice in attack" under the direct supervision of the Headquarters staff, London district. They obtained the highest percentage of points in the attack, and hits on the target, of any of the Volunteer detachments attending.

A camp at Tadworth for Volunteers under the Brigade of Guards was held from the 2nd to the 6th August, 1918 (inclusive). A large number of officers, W.O.'s, N.C.O.'s and men attended. The battalion was a composite one, formed of companies representing the 1st, 2nd and 3rd V.B.'s The Queen's, under the command of Major James Petrie, with Major F. A. Searle-Hinton as Group Adjutant. The training was arranged by the Guards Camp staff. It was arduous but thorough, and carried out under strict service conditions. The battalion greatly benefited by the excellent training laid down and carried out. The weather was not on its best behaviour, and all ranks realized to the full the difficulties the overseas troops encountered as regards muddy roads, wet clothes, etc. There were no cases of illness in camp, and the battalion left with a clean bill of health.

The battalion during their stay in camp were inspected by Major General Sir Francis Lloyd, G.O.C. London district.

A Special Service Company for defence duties on the east coast was formed of 4 officers, 3 W.O.'s, 12 N.C.O.'s and 36 men (total 55), and did duty for three months around Norwich under the command of Major Loughborough. They were highly praised by the Commanding and Inspecting Officers for their cleanliness and steadiness on parade, and attention to all duties; the training was very severe, but enjoyed by all. They were the only Volunteers on the east coast defences that had been previously instructed in anti-gas duties.

15 N.C.O.'s and men manned the Searchlight stations at Croydon during the air raids, and rendered very valuable assistance to the regular staff at the stations.

The whole of the officers and a large number of the W.O.'s and N.C.O.'s took and passed, with 1st class certificates, a six-weeks' course of thorough and practical military training in all branches at the London District School of Instruction under the supervision of the General Officer Commanding London District. Many other specialist courses were taken at the expense of much time and energy by various officers, N.C.O.'s and men, to the great benefit of the battalion.

In 1918 Hon. Lieutenant-Colonel J. M. Newnham, O.B.E., LL.D., D.L., was appointed (after Colonel Sir Frederick Edridge's retirement owing to illness) to the Hon. Command of the battalion.

Shortly after the Armistice was declared (11th November, 1918) the War Office issued instructions for all rifles, side arms, Hotchkiss machine guns, ammunition, etc., to be returned to stores, and announced that it was no longer necessary to insist upon men carrying out their obligation to drill. This order naturally broke up the Volunteer Force, except so far as it was kept together for a few months by means of physical training classes.

The Volunteer Force from its inception in 1914 until March, 1917, when the " grey-green " uniform was issued free of cost by the War Office, had, as has already been said, met with every possible official discouragement, but in spite of all the indifference and worse, of the authorities, it continued to exist in vigour and to show that it intended to carry out the patriotic principles for which it was formed, viz., to train (long and hard) in order to reach a high standard of efficiency, so as to be able to protect the country from invasion. Croydon has every reason to be proud of its Volunteers for "sticking it," and for reaching, in spite of colossal discouragements, the high standard of efficiency the local battalion obtained, as shown by the repeated opinions of competent military judges.

Until March, 1917, the battalion provided its own funds for working the battalion, no public appeal for funds being made. The only exceptions were a grant of £150 kindly given by the Croydon Corporation in 1916-17 to the 1st battalion Surrey Volunteer Regiment, and one of £100 to the 12th battalion Surrey Volunteer Regiment, and one of £400 in the year 1917-18 to the 1st Volunteer battalion The Queen's.

The battalion was pronounced by the London District command very efficient in all duties, and 90 per cent. of the men passed the "Musketry Classification" laid down by the War Office, the battalion securing the proud position of first place of all Volunteer Battalions under the London District. This position

THE VOLUNTEERS (1st V.B. THE QUEENS)

is entirely due to the whole of the members of the battalion working in union, and studying and working had to perfect themselves as soldiers.

The whole of the W.O.'s, N.C.O.'s and men had been disbanded and had received their discharge certificate by the 31st October, 1919. In January, 1920, when these lines are written, the officers are still on the Active List, awaiting their gazetting-out. On 30th September, 1919 (just prior to disbandment), the strength of the 1st V.B. The Queen's (R.W.S. Regiment) was 32 Officers and 846 W.O.'s, N.C.O.'s and men, and it was carrying on at that time no less than twelve training centres.

Few persons knew (certainly not the present Editor) the fine soldierly efficiency the Croydon Volunteers attained, except of course those either in the force or closely in touch with it. Had the disaster occurred which these men so patriotically prepared against, at such considerable cost to themselves in every way, any one reading this brief and condensed account must be convinced they would have encountered it most valiantly and successfully. We must all honour our Volunteers.

XIV. The Boy Scouts

No history of War-time England would be complete without some note of the doings of the Boy Scouts. In Croydon, as elsewhere, the most welcome sound that could be heard after long anxious waiting on many an air-raid night was their bugles blowing the two brief bright notes of the " All Clear." This picturesque and much appreciated service was only one of many performed by the Boy Scouts, and the following all too brief outline of those which were rendered under the direction of the Croydon Boy Scouts' Association, will not only be interesting, it will be a revelation to many people. There were about 1,000 Scouts at the end of the War; there are now nearer 1,500. Many of the former Scouts who joined up are returning as officers, and this excellent Boy-Scouts movement shows even greater vitality now than in the past.

COAST PATROLS.—During August, 1914, two mixed patrols of Croydon Scouts (from the 1st, 7th, 10th, 23rd and 25th Troops) assisted the military authorities by patrolling the coast of Kent from Pegwell Bay to Dungeness, a distance of about 45 miles. Some remained a week and some longer, until relieved by local Scouts. They were very favourably reported on. They started off at a very short notice, bicycling down to Hythe, where they had to report themselves for order, and bivouacking on the way.

Another party of 19 Croydon Scouts, of the 22nd Croydon Troop, under Scoutmaster Linton, were employed to assist the military transport authorities at Newhaven, from October, 1914 to January, 1915, and were reported on as having acquitted themselves most creditably.

A coast patrol of Croydon Boy Scouts under Scoutmaster Linton, was stationed at Littlehampton from January, 1915, until the beginning of 1916, when the Scoutmaster had to join the Army. The boys took their turn at coast patrolling by night under a Coastguardsman and also at look-out duty by day. They also assisted in beaching, towing, mooring and launching seaplanes. Scoutmaster Linton received a letter from Flight Commander F. J. Bailey, R.N.A.S., thanking the patrol for their invaluable service in saving his seaplane. The boys lived in a coastguard cottage, and did their own cooking and washing, taking turn and turn about.

THE BOY SCOUTS

PIQUETING RAILWAY STATIONS AND BRIDGES.—During the month of August, 1914, a piquet of 21 Senior Scouts and Scoutmasters guarded South Croydon Station and the adjacent bridges, under the supervision of the Military Officer in charge of the Croydon Section of the L.B. & S.C. Railway, and on being relieved, received a letter of thanks for their good work from the Officer in charge of the line, as follows :—

" To Scoutmaster G. A. Ogden,
    Commanding Scout Piquet,
        South Croydon Station.

I find it difficult to express my gratitude, but I hope you will give to all concerned my most sincere thanks for the work so nobly done.

(*Signed*) BOYTON,
Lieut. City of London Fusiliers."

OTHER ACTIVITIES.—From the outbreak of war Croydon Boy Scouts did good service for the Croydon War Supplies Clearing House by collecting parcels and acting as messengers.

Throughout the War the Scouts collected waste paper for the benefit of the Prince of Wales' National Relief Fund. By an arrangement with Messrs. Lloyds, Paper Manufacturers, the latter paid so much per ton of paper, sent to them by the Scouts, direct into the National Relief Fund, and from this source, during the four years, £570 was acquired. A special letter of thanks dated 11th February, 1916, was sent for this service to the Croydon Boy Scouts by the Prince of Wales.

In 1916 a letter of thanks was received from the Secretary of the Croydon Branch of the Red Cross Committee for services rendered during Red Cross week.

Letters of thanks for valuable assistance by the Croydon Boy Scouts, were received during February, 1917, from the Secretary of the Lord Mayor's Committee, Metropolitan War Loan Campaign ; from the Secretary of the Croydon Vacant Lands Cultivation Society ; and from the Secretary of the Croydon Borough Guild of Help.

Many Troops supplied Boy Scouts to assist regularly at Soldiers' Canteens and Recreation Rooms.

Many Croydon Scouts did orderly and fatigue work at War Hospitals.

Many Croydon Scouts assisted in collecting for St. Dunstan's Home for the Blind, Regent's Park, London.

In 1916 they raised by their earnings £32 14s. 4d. towards a Boy Scout Motor-Ambulance for France.

In November, 1918, the boys raised about £25, by giving an entertainment in aid of Dr. Barnado's Home for Boys, at the Boys' Garden City, Woodford, where funds were suffering owing to the War.

Boy Scout Buglers regularly turned out to sound the " All Clear " after air raids.

All the above services were done willingly and gratuitously, and in addition to those specially here mentioned hundreds of other small individual services were rendered.

There are 72 recorded cases of men, formerly Croydon Boy Scouts, who laid down their lives for their country in the Great War.

Photo by Howard M. King
Councillor Colonel JOHN FRANKLIN WORLLEDGE
District Commissioner, Croydon Boy Scouts

Captain DAVID BARRIE, H.L.I., Recruiting Officer for Croydon

Part Three

SEMI-MILITARY SERVICES

I. Recruiting

One of the first duties undertaken by the Mayor (Alderman Denning) and those who most closely associated themselves with him in his work in the early days of the War was recruiting, not only for the local regiments but for the Army generally. The Mayor himself, Mr. Ian Malcolm, M.P., Canon White-Thomson, Colonel Sir Frederick T. Edridge, Colonel F. D. Watney, the officers of the Queen's, the Town Clerk, Dr. E. H. Willock, Mr. Alfred Moir (afterwards Councillor), Councillor William Peet and Sergeant Nicholas were continually addressing meetings in the open air and at the theatres and other places of amusement throughout the town. On the 3rd November, 1914, Admiral Lord Charles Beresford addressed a mass meeting at the Central Baths Hall. The tramcars were placarded with large and effective appeals. Towards the end of 1914 the official organization got fully to work.

The division of Surrey for recruiting purposes was at first between the Queen's (Royal West Surrey Regiment), with Headquarters at Guildford, taking the Southern half of the County, and the East Surrey Regiment, with Headquarters at Kingston, taking the Northern half. This was found for many reasons inconvenient in practice, and therefore in March, 1916, it was arranged that for recruiting purposes Croydon should be under Kingston and not under Guildford, while the district containing Weybridge, Egham and Chertsey, an awkwardly placed area formerly under Kingston, should now in return be placed under Guildford. Therefore, after the date named, Colonel H. P. Treeby, D.S.O., the Commandant of the East Surrey Regiment, became the responsible officer for recruiting for Croydon; and immediately under him was Colonel F. W. Hyde Edwards, with Captain David Barrie as his chief representative in Croydon.

[A word as to the East Surrey Regiment seems to be necessary here.

The East Surrey Regiment came into being in the great rearrangement of 1881; its 1st battalion being the famous old 31st of the line (the Huntingdonshires) whose colours carry many battle honours, from Dettingen in 1743 (the last fight in which a King of England, George II., actually commanded in person), down to Suakin in 1885; and its 2nd battalion being the old 70th of the line. Two Surrey militia regiments were added to these, in order to form the new " East Surrey Regiment."]

Some of the more important of the public efforts to stimulate recruiting may now be mentioned. One of the earliest of these took place on 30th January, 1915, when a Football Match and Recruiting Rally were held at Selhurst; 19 motor cars came from Kingston Barracks in procession to take part. The band of the East Surrey Regiment played, the Mayor (Alderman Denning) and Colonel Sir Frederick Edridge and others spoke, and many recruits were obtained.

On the 18th June following (Waterloo Day) a Recruiting Processional March of 2,325 troops, with bands, passed through the principal Croydon streets, finishing at the Town Hall, where speeches were delivered. This also produced excellent results.

On 10th July, 1915, a Motor-Car Recruiting Demonstration took place (in which 54 cars took part), organised by Mr. D. R. Harvest. Captain Barrie and others engaged considered that the crowd of spectators was the greatest Croydon had known up to that time. Colonel F. W. Hyde Edwards was in the pilot car with Mr. Harvest; the first car of the 54 contained the Mayor, the Recorder, the Town Clerk, and the Vicar (Canon White-Thomson); and many well-known residents in Croydon filled the remainder. Balaclava Veterans, from both the famous charges, that of the Light Brigade and that of the Heavy Brigade, rode in the parade; and bluejackets and khaki were of course in full evidence, five lorries-full of them. The cars and lorries covered three-quarters of a mile, and the route extended over every part of the Borough. Speeches were made at many principal points, and those cars which halted for this purpose were promptly used to carry off the recruits who presented themselves straight to the Town Hall, then and there to be enrolled.

Six days after the Motor Car Parade, Corporal Edward Dwyer, V.C., of the East Surrey Regiment, was received by the Mayor at the Town Hall amidst a distinguished company. His V.C. was one of the first to be won in the War; and Corporal Dwyer earned it by his conspicuous bravery at "Hill 60." Corporal Dwyer's reception was of great use in the Recruiting Campaign. He was escorted to the Town Hall in procession, and a great recruiting meeting was held on the occasion.

Lord Derby, finding the stirring appeals of Lord Kitchener for more men were insufficiently met, and also in order to avoid the evidently threatened resort to conscription, put forward a scheme in September, 1915, to assist voluntary recruiting, which was adopted by the Government, and he himself was appointed Director of Recruiting to carry it out. All men of

Photo by C. Harrison Price

RECRUITING PROCESSION (Derby Scheme) CROYDON, 2nd OCTOBER, 1915

Photo by R. Rawlings

Col. FRANK WILLIAM CHATTERTON, C.I.E., J.P.
Military Representative for Croydon Military Tribunals

military age, already recorded on the National Register, were earnestly invited to attest their willingness to serve in the army when called upon. They were divided into 46 groups, the unmarried men forming the first 23 groups, ranked according to their ages from 18 to 40; and the married men forming the remaining 23 groups (24 to 46) similarly ranked according to age. Men attesting were not necessarily to be called up for service at once, the intention being to call up the groups in their order as they were required.

On the 2nd October, 1915, 2,800 sailors and soldiers, regulars and territorials and volunteers, escorted by 12 bands and a fleet of armoured cars, marched through Croydon to stimulate recruiting under the Derby scheme. The march ended at the Town Hall, where Capt. Sir Edward Clark, V.T.C., the famous advocate, delivered a stirring address. Captain Barrie, Croydon's Recruiting Officer, had from first to last the pleasure of enrolling 10,000 men of Croydon for the Army under the Derby voluntary enlistment scheme; largely in consequence of this demonstration, the most important of its kind in Croydon up to that time. The band of the Royal Marine Artillery played all the afternoon in front of the Town Hall, while the procession passed along the principal streets of the Borough in an imposing line of over a mile in length. At 5 o'clock the detachment of the Surrey Yeomanry reached the Town Hall, closely followed by men of the Royal Naval Division from the Crystal Palace, and Highlanders, pipes and all; then came armoured cars full of "Tommies," and after them the 24th Middlesex and the R.A.M.C. Our own 3/4th Queen's and the National Reserve and Surrey Guides were followed by the Whitgift Cadets and the Volunteer Training Corps, the long line ending with the Church Lads' Brigade, and of course the ubiquitous Boy Scouts, who always gave a bystander the impression that the War in some way existed for their especial behoof. In speaking at the Town Hall the Mayor (Alderman Denning) distinguished between the present and previous great recruiting parades. Heretofore he had been endeavouring to recruit Croydon men for Croydon's regiment (The Queen's); but now he was appealing for all fit men from 19 to 30 to join any regiment they might prefer (and not forgetting the Navy either) and to join immediately. During the week the gravity of England's need had been made clear by Lord Kitchener. So far the Mayor; and then there followed him the veteran, Captain Sir Edward Clark, K.C., whose uniform of the Volunteer Training Corps took many years from his age in appearance, and enabled him the more emphatically to urge men of his own standing to join the V.T.C. so as to set free younger men to go abroad, while, as he pointed out from his own experience, they incidentally derived great benefit to their own health and spirits. The great advocate was in his finest form, and his stirring speech had a great effect upon his hearers ; especially the fine peroration : " The man who serves his Country now, will have the right to speak with pride to his son hereafter."

Nor must we forget the efforts of a devoted band of canvassers, who delivered a continuous and organised attack on unattested men. As the men presented themselves to attest they were examined by the doctors, who were kept hard at work. It was well understood by all the men, that attestation did not invariably mean being called up for enlistment. Saturday, 11th December, 1915, closed this great effort. It ended in a terrible rush of attesters at all the recruiting stations on this closing Saturday, as many of us who took part, clerically or medically, well remember. But doctors and magistrates and their assistants stuck to their guns, and by midnight not one applicant was left without his papers.

The close of Voluntary Recruiting took place at midnight 1st March, 1916.

II. The Military Tribunals

On 2nd November, 1915, the Town Clerk read to the Corporation a letter from Mr. Walter Long, President of the Local Government Board, urging the Borough to assist the local Recruiting authorities under the " Derby Scheme " in their endeavour to obtain sufficient forces for our part in the Great War ; and especially to form a small Committee (not limited to members of the Corporation) to act as a Tribunal for attested men. Lord Kitchener's famous recruiting appeals, successful as they were, yet had failed to produce the enormous number, and indeed the rapidly increasing number, of men required for the Army ; so that the necessity for conscription daily became more obvious. To avoid this system, so hated by our country, Lord Derby undertook a final recruiting campaign, as has already been recorded (RECRUITING). In consequence, at this meeting, the Mayor (Alderman Denning), Ald. Sir Frederick Edridge, Ald. King, Ald. Betteridge, and Messrs. C. Heath Clark (afterwards Councillor ; and Mayor in 1919), Savory (afterwards Councillor) and Allison (as representing labour) were appointed.

The duty of the above (Derby) Tribunal was to assess the applications for release from active military service, of attested men, who, while having shown their willingness to help nationally, felt themselves for one reason or another unable to join the actual army. And Mr. Long, in English fashion, promised at the same time an Appeal Tribunal, covering a wider area, to which those aggrieved by the decisions of the local Tribunal might appeal.

Mr. Long referred gratefully in his letter to the loyal help received from the Corporation in the preparation of the National Register, wherein we were all classified on census principles. This National Register was instituted by an Act 15th July, 1915, and under it the Council became the local Registration Authority with the duty of compiling and maintaining and classifying the Register. The Council delegated all this work to a special Committee consisting of the Mayor (Alderman Denning), the Deputy Mayor (Councillor Rogers, ex-Mayor), Alderman Lillico (ex-Mayor), and Councillors Houlder (Mayor in 1916), Wood Roberts, and West ; Councillor (afterwards Alderman) Rogers being the Chairman. The Committee entrusted the work to the Town Clerk, who, with the assistance of Mr. W. C. Cubitt, of the Rate Office, and some 612 volunteers, ladies and gentlemen, amongst whom were a large proportion of the teachers of our Elementary Schools and many members of the Special Constabulary, completed the men's Register on the 11th September, and the women's Register on the 30th September. Apart from the work of enumeration these ladies and gentlemen put in no less than 4,059 attendances at the Town Hall. Members of the Corporation and School-attendance officers largely assisted, also quite in a voluntary capacity. The total cost of the Register, as far as the Borough was concerned, was therefore ridiculously small, being only £87 3s. 11d. (Only one Croydon man refused to register, and he was fined £5 for his recusancy.) The well-earned thanks of the Council were given to these patriotic workers on 27th September, 1915, when the completion of the National Register was reported, for Croydon.

When conscription came actually in sight the Derby Voluntary-attestation scheme was revived for one month (10th January to 10th February, 1916, the latter being the date when conscription began), so that men might be spared the shame of compulsion. Many hundreds availed themselves of this privilege.

On 2nd February, 1916, Croydon sustained the great loss of its first War Mayor, Alderman Denning; and this in itself would have necessitated a change in the local (Derby) Tribunal. Moreover the Military Service Act of 1916, imposing conscription, now came into force (10th February), with all the regulations for the work of a quite new Statutory Military Tribunal to be formed under that Act. This latter tribunal (of not less than 5 nor more than 25 members) was recommended by Government to consist as far as possible of the same members as the (Derby) Tribunal previously appointed, although the functions of the two were not the same. The Council appointed as the new Statutory Military Tribunal under the Military Service Act, the following eight gentlemen: The Mayor (Alderman Houlder), and Aldermen Betteridge and King, Councillors C. Heath Clark, Rogers, and W. V. Smith, and Messrs. Jas. Chapman (ex-Councillor) and Savory (afterwards Councillor). When the work proved to be so very heavy the Corporation later on appointed 5 extra members to the Tribunal: Ald. G. J. Allen, Councillors Pelton and Stevenson, Messrs. Dyer and Secretan. The Town Clerk was appointed the Clerk to the Tribunal, and had throughout the consistent and valuable help of Mr. A. C. Gower, the chief clerk in his department, as Assistant Clerk. Some time after the Tribunal had begun to sit the Croydon Hairdressers' Association made formal application that one of their body should be added to it on account of the importance and the

THE MILITARY TRIBUNALS

peculiar nature of their trade. A benighted public had the audacity to smile and take no further notice. At the same meeting it was reported to the Council that the Recorder of Croydon (Mr. Robt. F. Colam, K.C.), Colonel Sir Frederick Edridge, Mr. Grimwade, and Mr. Allison (as representing labour) had been appointed members on the Appeal Tribunal for Surrey and Croydon.

Taking first the original Military Tribunal of seven under the Derby scheme for voluntary enlistment, this Tribunal began its work on Monday, 10th January, 1916, starting with a list of over one hundred appeals from attested men against being called up. The military representative, Colonel F. W. Chatterton, C.I.E., of Upper Norwood, had the duty of holding the brief for the Army, and of seeing that no unfair appeals on the part of attested men passed the Tribunals. It was a great good fortune for Croydon that so scrupulously fair-minded a man as Colonel Chatterton held this post. It was an honorary post; and it is doubtful whether Colonel Chatterton ever received the official recognition of his arduous services which he so thoroughly deserved. In many towns the military representatives seemed to think that all appeals were attempts to shirk a patriotic duty; and some cruel decisions were enforced, and much needless heartburning was caused; but in Croydon no appellant failed whose case for delay or for exemption was a reasonable one, and the decisions of the Tribunals met with universal approval. As the soldier-phrase has it, appellants, if defeated, " groused, but carried on." In the early days much valuable clerical and administrative work in connection with the Tribunals was done by Mr. J. T. Tompkins. Mr. G. F. Carter, M.I.C.E. (the Borough Engineer) was afterwards appointed assistant military representative to Col. Chatterton.

Before coming up for judgment to the (Derby) Tribunal the cases of all men were examined and classed by a small body of five, selected by the Croydon Recruiting Committee, who were assisted by Colonel Chatterton, the military representative. If an unmarried man (since these alone were first called up) claimed delay, for instance, this small advisory Committee might recommend, that is, practically grant it, in conjunction with Colonel Chatterton; but if they did not think the case fit for delay they would refer it direct to the Tribunal, where Colonel Chatterton's duty was to present their reasons against the appellant's claim, and the Tribunal's to act as arbitrator, and decide. Even then, as above shown, there was an ultimate appeal to the Surrey and Croydon Appeal Tribunal, whose decision was final. But it must be noticed that none of these earlier bodies had any power altogether to excuse an attested man from service; they could only go so far as to put him down into a class which would be called up later. Power of total exemption from service lay only with the supreme National Tribunal of that time, sitting in London. Voluntary recruiting had now had a fair trial, and Croydon's 10,000 voluntaries are worthy of all honour; but too many able young men had shirked their duty, and the nation was in peril. Therefore Conscription, compulsory military service, against which we had fought to the last, abhorrent as it was to the English mind, had now to be suffered. Beyond the shirkers, and those who were honourably prevented from enlisting, there was also an exceedingly troublesome residuum, though happily not numerous, of genuine " conscientious objectors," and a few " slackers" who were mean enough to borrow their cloak.

After all men of military age had been classified, those in the lower categories, unfit men, had to find national work at home. How loyally they did this is shown in other chapters, *e.g.*, those on the 4/4th Queen's, the Volunteers, the National Reserve, and the Special Constabulary, etc.; work equally necessary, though not so glorious, as the heroic deeds of the men in the fighting line.

We pass now to the more important second Tribunal, of February, 1916. The first sitting of the Croydon Military Tribunal under the Conscription Act was held on 29th February, 1916, some cases being heard in private, others in public; the Mayor (Councillor, afterwards Alderman, Houlder) being in the chair. The generality of the appeals for delay came from men the sole supports of dependents; from men in necessary occupations (such as that of schoolmaster), especially if coupled with such feeble health as promised the army but a weakly soldier; from men claiming to be indispensable to a necessary office or business; from men in certain certified occupations; from men asking for delay to settle up their business; and from men asserting medical unfitness, who were of course referred to the Medical Board at Kingston for examination and report.

It is amusing to notice that at a meeting on 3rd March, 1916, when considering an application for exemption, or long delay, say over three months, the Town Clerk voicing the general opinion of the Tribunal, replied to Mr. R. J. Clark (solicitor for the appellant), " Well, we hope the War will be over by June," and all the Tribunal cried " Hear, hear," with hopeful unanimity.

Several conscientious objectors, after compulsory enlistment, came into the hands of the police for desertion. As a sample of the trials of patience of the magistrates who tried them we may give just one case in brief. W.O.P. deserted, was caught, and handed over by the Bench to an escort of the R.G.A., and promptly gave his escort the slip. This however, was too tame for a crank ; so he proceeded voluntarily to the Thornton Heath Police Station and demanded to be taken into custody to be tried again. " You escaped from the escort ? " he was asked ; and replied " No, I did not, because I never joined the Army, the Army joined me. Therefore, if I had an opportunity to get away, I was free to do so," etc., etc. And against another conscientious objector (probably not of the genuine type) it was objected by the authorities that at the work of national importance which he had selected, as a condition of being excused combatant service, he worked one day, but immediately thereafter rested two !

In June, 1916, working three days or more a week, and sitting in two divisions, each of which not infrequently sat for four hours at a time, the Croydon Military Tribunal swiftly reduced the list of 2,000 appeals with which it began its career. Proceedings gradually settled into a regular order, cases being dealt with as they arose, without arrears ; and they became more and more formal and almost dull (to bystanders) as the claims resolved themselves into well established categories ; but occasionally the sittings were enlivened by flashes of natural humour. Thus :—" Exempted till March," said the Chairman. " I am not satisfied with that," said the claimant. " Then we withdraw the exemption, sharp," said the Chairman. But he spoke to an empty chair ; the claimant had already fled, seeing that it was too dangerous to remain. And another time, when some members of the Tribunal themselves were in trouble through burst pipes in time of frost, it was remarkable even for people enjoying a certified occupation how rapidly plumbers appealing were dismissed satisfied, with scarcely a pause between entry and exit. On the other hand, not infrequently the Tribunal were bound to give, most unwillingly, decisions which though according to the inexorable facts were bound to cause extreme hardship. In such cases everything possible was done in mitigation. A curious and almost inexplicable experience was the number of persons passed by the military doctors as medically fit for active service who (as in the case of one applicant with severe valvular disease of the heart, and of another who not infrequently had three epileptic seizures in one week) were in daily danger of collapse in their ordinary occupations. The Croydon Military Tribunal made very short work in honourably dismissing these poor fellows ; but what can one think of the examining " medico "?

In September, 1917, we notice a case, by no means isolated, of a man rejected as unfit in 1915, passed for sedentary work in 1916, and now passed as fit. Of course, as soon as these facts appeared he was dismissed as unfit by the Tribunal. And at the next sitting a young man, suffering from hernia, who was discharged from the Army in 1915 as unfit, and had married and gone into business, was now called up again, in October, 1917. In homely language the Chairman described it as " a bit hard on a chap," and gave him some months' respite.

A touching appeal was that by a widow (2nd November, 1917) for her eleventh son; her sole support, and engaged in War-work, while all her other ten sons were then actually serving; five had been wounded, two were now prisoners in Germany, and one was prisoner in Turkey. Needless to say her application was granted, and the Mayor complimented her upon her very fine record. " Moreover," said the military representative, always ready to sympathise with genuine patriotism, " all the eleven sons are equally proud of their mother ! "

One of the cruellest hardships of this conscription time was the calling up of a man from his business, in which he had made a good start and was likely to do well; and his returning later dismissed as unfit, only to find his business dispersed and himself once more at the very foot of the ladder. The Tribunal became acquainted with many such cases.

Sometimes, though rarely, we were reminded of the old press-gang times, by organised raids; as for instance a descent upon the Hippodrome and Empire Theatres at Croydon by the recruiting authorities, when all men of military age were sent forward to the Town Hall to explain their presence. On this occasion 70 men went as requested, the requests being made with complete civility and being fulfilled cheerfully and even with jocularity, although one man at least " lost the last train." It is pleasant to add that on this occasion (8th September, 1916) only one shirker was found out of the 70 detained. And it is also pleasant to note the kindly aspect of both sides not only on this but also on all other occasions of the kind. Some curious particulars occur in their reports which are worth noting.

Of forms received from other towns relating to Croydon absentees, on the 15th August, 1915, there were over 9,000; and during six months 4,000 people came into residence at Croydon and 3,000 went away. It seems a large fluctuation of population for war-time. Even the changes of address, of persons registered in Croydon, amounted to about 250 in the six months. In the two months from March to May, 1916, there were 1,300 arrivals

THE MILITARY TRIBUNALS 131

in Croydon, and as many departures recorded in the Register. The total number on the Register was forbidden to be published, on the objection of the Registrar General.

The 11th hour of the 11th day of the 11th month of 1918 is a date no one who was then beyond infancy can forget. We wrongly supposed that the great Armistice, which at that moment took effect, meant peace ; whereas at the time of sending to press this book, at the beginning of 1920, peace has only just been ratified (10th January) with one only, the first and greatest though, of our enemies ; and with all the rest matters are still unsettled. But one effect immediately came about at the Armistice, at all events. The thirty applicants to the Tribunal on Friday, 10th November, 1918, were released without their cases being heard, " in view of the splendid position at the front," to use the Mayor's words ; and except formally, the Croydon Military Tribunal came to an end there and then.

The Surrey and Croydon Appeal Tribunal met for the last time together with the similar Surrey bodies sitting at Kingston and Guildford, at the offices of the Ecclesiastical Commissioners, Westminster. Sir Lewis Dibdin, the Chairman, reminded the meeting that the three Appeal Tribunals had settled 7,000 appeals (Croydon district 2,900, Kingston and Guildford a little over 2,000 each), and as a result had sent 5,500 men into the Army. It follows from what was said above as to the irregularity of medical examinations that out of 1,070 medical appeals not very far short of half (470) were allowed ; and of these, 65 appellants had agreed to do work of national importance, and 52 were adjudged to non-combatant services, not one being granted absolute exemption by the Appeal Tribunal. But of course many of these 52 non-combatant soldiers refused to do the work they were set ; and some preferred, indeed desired, to go to prison. It must be always a source of regret that so much valuable time was spent upon some ten or a dozen irreconcilables, for however great the outcry made by these extremely vocal persons and their friends, it boils down to that minimum after all.

The actual farewell appearance of the Croydon Local Military Tribunal took place on 7th January, 1919, at the Town Hall. They had existed for three years, had held 258 sittings, and dealt with 10,445 cases. Only 725 appeals had been made against their decisions ; and up to October, 1918, when they held their last sitting, they had granted 2,901 exemptions. Twenty-thousand Croydon men had gone to the colours, and only 12 per cent. of those eligible had been exempted from military service. A well-merited tribute of praise was paid at the final meeting to the successful manipulation of an almost countless host of details, by the Town Clerk, and Mr. Albert C. Gower (chief clerk in his department). A pleasant close to the meeting was the testimony of both Mr. H. T. Peard and Mr. R. J. Clark, who had acted as solicitors for so many of the applicants, to the remarkable fairness and patience shown by the Tribunal. They said that even when applications were refused their clients had again and again expressed the feeling that they had received absolutely fair play. Higher praise than that no Tribunal—military or civil—can ever hope for.

III.
Munitions Work, and War Work of the Electricity Committee

In the winter of 1915-16 the provision of munitions of war had become a very urgent question. Under the Ministry of Munitions a committee was formed for an area extending from the rural outskirts of Bromley to Sutton, and this committee met at Croydon. The Mayor (Alderman Denning) was the first chairman, the Town Clerk was another member, and the Borough Electrical Engineer (Mr. A. C. Cramb) the Honorary Secretary and District Manager. Mrs. Redfern acted for two years as an inspector and marker of Government material. The committee arranged for the making of munitions in numerous small factories, and also at the Corporation Waterworks Yard and the Borough Electricity Works.

The chief articles manufactured were 18-pound shells, together with fuses and other parts for shells. Mr. Cramb undertook the manufacture of 18-pound shells and 6-inch shell heads at the Borough Electricity Works, and made during 1915-18, 14,885 18-pound shells, and 4,121 6-inch shell heads. In addition to which about 10,000 shells from contractors in Surrey and Kent were finished off under his superintendence, by banding, base-making, varnishing, etc. A net profit of £1,337 was made at the Electricity Works over the maufacture of these shells.

This may be an appropriate place to mention that, in addition to lending the services of Mr. Cramb to this committee, the Borough Electricity Committee also gave free supplies of electricity to the following institutions :—

Hospitals.

H.R.H. Princess Christian Hospital ; Wallacefield, Coombe Road ; St. Dorothy's Convalescent Home ; 254, Brighton Road (Dr. Dempster) ; Norbury Hill House (Society of St. Vincent and St. Paul) ; Shirley Park Hotel (R.F.C. Hospital for Officers) ; Nielka Hospital, Jerviston, Ryecroft Road.

Recreation Rooms.

42, High Street, Croydon (Miss Carr); Canteen, 33-35, High Street, South Norwood; St. Aubyn's Church Hall; Comrades Club (N.U.W.W.), 68, Westow Street, Upper Norwood.

General.

War Hospital Supply Depot, Bedford Park; Recruiting Office, 30, London Road, Croydon; Committee Prince of Wales's Fund, Church Road, Upper Norwood; Red Cross Distress Committee, 366, London Road, Thornton Heath.

ALEXANDER C. CRAMB, M.I.E.E., M.I.Mech.E.
Borough Electrical Engineer

Photo by Howard M. King
Assistant Commander HENRY CRAVEN SWAINE,
in command of Croydon Special Constabulary

Part Four

THE CIVILIAN FORCES

I. The Special Constabulary

Croydon Sub-Division of the "W" Division of the Metropolitan Special Constabulary.

In times of civil and national crisis it has been the national custom to invite volunteers from the civilian population to supplement the regular forces responsible for law and order. Special constables have always come forward at such times. Especially were they needed, and never was their work more valuable, than during the Great War; for the strength of the regular constabulary was greatly reduced, first by patriotic volunteering, and later by the operation of the military service Acts; and moreover duties devolving upon the police forces were much more numerous and varied than ever before.

The following notes deal with the history of the Croydon Sub-division of the Metropolitan Special Constabulary from 10th August, 1914, when the first call for recruits was made, up to the 16th June, 1919, on which date the force was officially disbanded.

At the call 175 men at once came forward, were enrolled and attested, and the first duties were undertaken at 6 p.m., on Monday, 24th August, 1914.

Of these 175 men, 29 were still in the Force when it was disbanded. A maximum strength of 442 was attained on 3rd January, 1917.

The Station-numbers at disbandment ran up to 1,704; but of this total, 582 were not attested for duty with this Sub-Division; the remaining 1,122 men, belonging to this Sub-Division, are accounted for as follows :—

In the Force at disbandment 16th June, 1919 .	371
Resigned to join H.M. Forces	229
Resigned through ill-health	74
Resigned through pressure of business . .	160
Transferred to Sanderstead on formation of that Sub-Division	35
Transferred to other Sub-Divisions . . .	52
Resigned on leaving Croydon	55
Resigned to take up other Government work .	33
Resigned for various other reasons . . .	99
Died whilst members of this Force . . .	14
	— 751
	1122

Thirty-one members of this Force were specially commended by the Commissioner for various meritorious services.

The following is a chronological statement of the various duties performed by the Sub-Division :

On Monday, 24th August, 1914, duty commenced at 6 p.m., and consisted of guarding seven " Vulnerable Points," namely, five in connection with the Water works and one each, Gas and Electricity works ; and on Tuesday, 25th, a Guard on the Telephone Exchange was added.

On Monday, 7th September, seven Railway bridges were added for guard and three of the guarded " Vulnerable Points " of the Water works (outlying ones) were abandoned. Four of the seven bridges were withdrawn from guard on 21st September, and the remainder on 9th October.

Tuesday, 27th April, 1915, the number of men guarding the " Vulnerable Points " was reduced between 6 p.m. and midnight, and six double Patrol Beats were established.

Saturday, 25th September, 1915, a section was formed to deal with the " Lighting Orders," and the first patrol started that evening.

Tuesday, 12th October, 1915, the guards on the " Vulnerable Points " from 2 a.m. to 6 a.m. were withdrawn ; but they were re-established, so far as the Gas and Electricity works were concerned, on Tuesday, 30th November, 1915.

After 13th October, 1915 (following on the Air Raid on Croydon on this date) an Observation Section was started to man observation posts during air-raids. The men of this Section at first had no regular duties in connection with the observation work except at air-raids, but had frequent practices. They maintained their ordinary police duty throughout.

Monday, 27th November, 1916, the observation post on the Water Tower was manned daily from 6 p.m. to midnight in connection with the Metropolitan Observation Service: This work was undertaken voluntarily, and mainly in addition to the ordinary duties.

Saturday-Sunday, 17th-18th June, 1917. At mid-night, at the request of the Metropolitan Observation Service, continuous observation duty commenced day and night, and at the same time the guards on the " Vulnerable Points " at the Gas and Electricity works were withdrawn.

Friday, 2nd November, 1917. At 10 a.m. the guards on the Waterworks in Surrey Street and at the Telephone Exchange were withdrawn altogether, to increase the number of men

1. WATER TOWER, CROYDON
Observation Post of Special Constabulary

2. WATER TOWER, CROYDON—ALTAZIMUTH

Miss RHODA BRODIE, M.B.E.
Patrol Leader, Croydon Women-Patrols

THE SPECIAL CONSTABULARY

for Station Reserve duty, with a view to more rapid mobilisation of the force in event of air-raids.

Friday, 10th May, 1918. A special duty in connection with the lighting of vehicles regulations was started.

Friday-Saturday, 22nd-23rd November, 1918. At mid-night the Observation Post on the Water Tower and the " Vulnerable Point " Guard there, were withdrawn.

Monday-Tuesday, 16th-17th December, 1918. At mid-night the office was closed, no duty being thereafter performed between the hours of mid-night and 10 a.m.

Wednesday, 18th December, 1918. The " Lights " Section was transferred to ordinary duty.

Monday, 23rd December, 1918. The Patrol Beats were reduced to one Relief, from 7 to 10 p.m., and were abandoned on 26th January, 1919. The office was closed at night.

The Headquarters of this Sub-Division were originally at the Police Station, Fell Road, Croydon, but on the 3rd December, 1914, they were removed to 3, George Street, Croydon, and on the 30th December, 1914, a further move was made into premises at 87, High Street, Croydon. On Thursday, the 4th January, 1917, the offices were again transferred to 46, Friends Road, Croydon. and from thence to the Stables, Quarry Hill, Stanhope Road, Croydon, on the 10th February, 1919.

The following figures give the number of duties performed in the Croydon Sub-Division since its establishment :

General duties	188498
Emergency Calls and Special Parades . .	28754
Drills (= half a duty each)	2157
Ambulance Lectures and Drills (ditto) .	1917
Grand total of duties performed . . .	221326

In addition to which the drills, &c., not officially counted amounted to 18,747 ; making a total (of duties actually performed) of 240,073 ; and giving an average for S/C's past and present of 195 per man.

The average length of service was 560 days ; which is equivalent to one duty in every 2.87 days per man.

Drill Parades were held at the Barracks, Mitcham Road. When these premises were closed for Government purposes the Parades were held in the Whitgift Grammar School grounds, by kind permission of the Head Master.

AMBULANCE—The Ambulance Section was constituted on the 24th February, 1915, and consisted at first of twenty members.

Classes of Instruction were immediately started and were continued without intermission. The services of an Honorary Medical Officer were secured in June, 1915.

On 22nd February, 1919, the Section numbered 44, and 149 Certificates and Diplomas had been obtained by them.

The " Parsons " Cup was won by the Ambulance Section of this Sub-Division in October, 1917, and the " Sir Edward Ward " Cup for the " W " Division in 1918.

Records were not kept of the cases in which First Aid was given prior to September, 1917, but after that date they aggregate 223.

On sixteen occasions official commendations for good work have been recorded.

In March, 1916, by the kindness of the British Red Cross Society, the Force obtained the loan of a four-berth motor ambulance, which was brought into use on 120 occasions before it was returned to the owners in February, 1919.

In November, 1917, members of the Section undertook the voluntary duty of attending the arrival of convoys of wounded soldiers at East and West Croydon Stations, and of accompanying them to their respective Hospitals. Twenty-six convoys were attended, and 2,101 cases were dealt with.

Members of the Ambulance Section also attended over 120 convoys in connection with the South-Eastern Railway Centre of the St. John Ambulance Association, at which they dealt with upwards of 10,000 cot cases.

During the influenza epidemic of November, 1918, volunteers from this Force were called for to act as night orderlies at the various War Hospitals in the Town, and on every occasion it was possible to supply all the men needed.

LIGHTS.—In September, 1915, the Force took up, at the request of, and in co-operation with, the Regular Police, the enforcement of the Lighting Regulations. A special Section for this work was formed, the district was mapped out into areas and a systematic regular patrol (with the Card Index method of recording calls) was instituted. In all, calls were made in 22,195 cases of failure adequately to screen domestic and other lights. Tactful persuasion proved effectual in nearly every instance, and the improvement brought about was very marked, the general darkening of the town becoming distinctly noticeable. As a rule, householders were grateful for the calls made upon them, and it was rarely found necessary to report cases with a view to process.

THE SPECIAL CONSTABULARY

EMERGENCY CALLS (AIR RAIDS).—The first " Call " took place on the 19th January, 1915, and altogether the Force was mobilised on 63 occasions and, in addition, the preliminary steps necessitated by a " Stand-by " or warning order were taken fifteen times.

At first the whole Force assembled at the Croydon Police Station, but, in January, 1916, arrangements were made to establish three other centres at convenient points in the district, with the object of lessening the risk of extensive casualties and of enabling prompter attention to be given locally should necessity arise. These were at (1) Trojan Works, Vicarage Road, Waddon ; (2) Christ Church Schools, Clyde Road, and Addiscombe Railway Station ; (3) Wesleyan Hall, Bartlett Street, South Croydon.

Each of these points of assembly was provided with a fully equipped unit of the Ambulance Section, with stretchers and First Aid requisites ; and a motor ambulance and wheeled litter were in readiness at the Police Station, Fell Road.

Motor Transport was also provided at each point, in case it was necessary to convey men to a distance from that point ; and all points of assembly were either on, or in touch with, the telephone.

As members of the force arrived, they were detailed into squads, each of nine men under the command of a sergeant, in readiness should their services be required at any point. At each centre was also assembled a number of St. John and Red Cross men, V.A.D. Nurses and Motor Volunteers, to supplement the men of the Ambulance Section.

For some time men were stationed at the fire alarms to give any necessary information and to prevent any misuse through panic or otherwise. Many cases of local lights and sounds (*e.g.*, Trams, Omnibuses, Clocks, &c.) were taken up with the authorities concerned, with the result that noticeable improvements were effected. In many cases also local lights were detected from the Observation Posts (referred to later on), and these were either located at the time or subsequently investigated with a view to appropriate action being taken.

During 1917 the Force was called upon to assist in regulating crowds taking shelter in public buildings during Air-Raids. Cases of reported signalling during Raids were investigated, and generally proved to have been due to the actions of nervous householders.

Four Observation Posts, situated respectively at the Town Hall Tower, the Water Tower, Gillett and Johnston's Tower, and Nottingham Road, were specially manned. The duty of the men at these posts was to keep a sharp look-out for the approach of hostile Air Craft ; to note any fires and to report them to the Observation Room, Metropolitan Observation Service, in addition to the Regular Police and Fire Brigade ; and to detect any cases of excessive lighting and report same to be immediately dealt with .

A number of men were detailed for duty in connection with the various Air-Raid Shelters in the borough.

OBSERVATION.—The Observation Section owed its inception to the Zeppelin Air-Raid on the 13th October, 1915, after which numerous reports were received as to suspected signalling to enemy aircraft.

After this date several officers were stationed—during emergency calls—on the Clock Tower of the Town Hall, with direct telephone communication to the office of the Chief Inspector of the Regular Police, and a motor car was provided in readiness to convey members of the force to any necessary point.

As it was found impossible to overlook the whole of the district from one point, and as estimation by night of the exact location of a light or fire was difficult, other points were successively arranged—widely separated, and with telephones or other means of communication. Each was equipped with a series of boards with sighting bars and a means of indicating, on graduated semi-circles, the " true " bearing of any object seen. A six-inch ordnance map of the district was provided at the Police Station, marked with graduated circles with the Observation Posts as centres and provided with extensible cords, distinctively coloured. By this means, the bearings transmitted from two or more of the posts, could instantly be set out on the map, the intersection giving the spot required.

Many successive improvements were effected in these homemade instruments, including the provision of specially constructed illuminated sights, enabling bearings to be quickly taken in darkness to a fraction of a degree. As an instance of the working of the system, a fire, occasioned in some trucks on a railway line some four miles away by an incendiary bomb, was located to a few yards within two or three minutes of the outbreak.

The Nottingham Road station was also equipped as a listening post to detect the approach of aircraft or the sound of distant explosions, for which purpose a large trumpet, capable of being revolved, was used in connection with a stethoscope.

The co-ordinated reports of the four points, already referred to, on the various raids in or near to the district form an interesting account of the progress of the Air-Raids in the vicinity. The first Zeppelin seen to be brought down was at 2.20 a.m., on the 3rd September, 1916, and the spot where it fell was approximately determined, though twenty-three miles distant.

THE SPECIAL CONSTABULARY 143

The first " Observation Post " was brought into use on the night of the 31st January, 1916, and, in November, 1916, arrangements were made to work the highest and most fully equipped post in conjunction with the Metropolitan Observation Service, as one of their Stations, and this—the Water Tower Observation Post—was thenceforward manned with a sufficient and trained " crew " each night from 7 p.m. until dismissed (usually about mid-night), in charge of a specially trained officer.

On Sunday, the 17th June, 1917, a request was received that the work should be increased to a continuous day and night manning of the post. The same night this was done, and thereafter a continuous watch was maintained by a minimum " crew " of three men.

On the 17th September, 1917, at the request of the Meteorological Office, South Kensington, a continuous hourly record of fog and visibility, between sunrise and sunset, was commenced. This was kept by the officers—known as I/Cs (*i.e.*, " in charge ") —from time to time in command of the post and sent to London weekly. More detailed records of wind and weather conditions generally were also kept at four-hourly intervals during the day and night.

The post was provided with a specially designed and constructed azimuth and altitude recording instrument, enabling Vernier readings to be taken to within six minutes of arc.

A telescope with cross wires in the eyepiece was fitted in alignment with the sighting bar and was of great assistance to the unaided vision, especially as regards obtaining accurate sighting. Lights, &c., observed at night could, by means of this telescope, be more readily located by daylight observation on the same settings. The readings in azimuth and altitude were automatically reproduced on graduated revolving drums in two cabins, one containing an Exchange Telephone for reporting to the Metropolitan Observation Service and the other—a private telephone—to the Chief Inspector's Room (Regular Police), at the Police Station, this being principally used during Air-Raids.

Practically the whole of the designing, construction and installation of the instruments used (with the exception of an altazimuth instrument supplied by the Admiralty) was carried out by members of the Force, as was also the electric wiring for the lighting of the Water Tower.

We think our readers will be interested to read the record that was made from the Town Hall for the last air-raid on London, that on 19th May, 1918. We give it in full. The " bearing " numbers are, of course, map numbers, the district under observation having been plotted out for this purpose.

Police Station.
TOWN HALL.
Men reported for duty Sunday, 19th May, 1918.
681. 1302. 1596. 1112. 1057. 1141.

11.12 p.m. Aeroplane on bearing 102 shewing lights—Bright lights on bearing 15½—Signal Rockets seen in the South East.

11.23 ,, Gun flash on bearing 102 very distant.

11.25 ,, Heavy gun fire on bearing 65 to 80—Sounds of gun fire in the North East—Searchlights operating in the North East.

11.28 ,, Light on bearing 15½ just extinguished. Continuous gun fire in the North East district.

11.29 ,, Sounds of distant gun fire in the North East—Gun on bearing 48 operating.

11.31 ,, Glow on bearing 15¼ very distant—Gun fire now to the North bearing 3—Fire on bearing 19½ is now brighter—Gun flash on bearing 3 to 5.

11.38 ,, Aeroplane on bearing 124 to 125—Gun fire had been continuous on bearing 345 to 105.

11.40 ,, Elmer's End gun operating.

11.47 ,, Fire reported on bearing 19½ cannot now be seen.

11.48 ,, White signal light on bearing 115—Another white signal light on bearing 115—Searchlights concentrating to the West—Aurelia Road searchlight operating—Flash on bearing 19—*looks more than a gun flash*—Gun fire getting much nearer but no shrapnel seen.

11.49 ,, Big glow, as if a bomb dropped on bearing 10¼—Gonville Road gun operating.

11.50 ,, Shrapnel bursting on altitude 45—Searchlights on bearing 151 to 162.

11.51 ,, Signal lights on bearing 115.

11.52 ,, Elmer's End and Gonville Road guns in operation.

11.55 ,, Glow on bearing 9½—Shrapnel in the North East, altitude 45—Another flash, as if a bomb had fallen on bearing 10—Gonville Road gun again in operation—Sounds of Aeroplanes—Sounds of Aeroplanes getting nearer in the North East; searchlights are centred on them—Sounds of big explosion in the North East—Purley searchlight operating—Aeroplane above referred to thought to be very near to us (20/5/18).

THE SPECIAL CONSTABULARY

12.0 midn't Signal light on bearing 45 fairly near; the Aeroplane above mentioned thought to be more distant.
12. 3 a.m. Very heavy gun fire in the North East and North West.
12. 5 ,, Purley searchlight extinguished.
12. 7 ,, Aircraft hum in the North East seems to be getting nearer again.
12. 8 ,, Gonville Road gun operating again. Very heavy gun fire in the North East bearing 290.
12.10 ,, White signal light on bearing 30—Gun flash on bearing 138 very distant—Sounds of aircraft in the North—Sounds of aircraft getting much closer in the North East.
12.13 ,, Purley searchlight in operation—Shrapnel bursting on altitude 50 in the North East.
12.15 ,, Aeroplane travelling due East.
12.17 ,, Shrapnel bursting on bearing 64 altitude 30.
12.20 ,, Red signal light and white signal light on bearing 32—On bearing 32 thought to be an aeroplane *brought down on fire*—White signal light on bearing 115—Very heavy gun fire in the North East but too distant to see the flashes—Gun flashes from North East to North—Sounds of aircraft in the North East—Gun fire extending to the North West on bearing 345.
12.25 ,, Signal light on bearing 50—On bearing 27 a flash seen; looked very much like an explosion—Gonville Road and Elmer's End guns in operation.
12.27 ,, On bearing 97 lights in the sky, looks as if it was one of our aeroplanes.
12.30 ,, Half a dozen white rockets on bearing 95—Sounds of aircraft in the North and North East coming this way.
12.34 ,, Shrapnel bursting in the North, altitude 27.
12.35 ,, Another glow on bearing 10½, very distant; looked like a bomb having been dropped.
12.36 ,, Sounds of aircraft dying away—Sounds of aircraft in the East getting nearer.
12.39 ,, Gonville Road and Elmer's End guns in operation—Shrapnel bursting in the North East, altitude 45.
12.48 ,, Gun flashes very distant, North and North West of London.

J

12.55 a.m.		Signal light on bearing 110 high up—Gun fire revived distant North and North East—Signal light or Rocket on bearing 115.
12.58	,,	All quiet, but distant searchlights, North, North East.
1. 0	,,	Light on aircraft on bearing 105—Two very distant flickering lights on bearing 53½ on the horizon—Sounds of aircraft in the South East, thought to be one of our own.
1.10	,,	One of our aeroplanes travelling East shewing a light—Two signal lights on bearing 94.
1.19	,,	*All Clear.*
1.32	,,	Order to sound *Maroons.* On duty again—All the crew returned to their respective places.
1.38	,,	Gun flashes and searchlights in the South East—Red and white signal lights in the North East—Gun flashes on bearing 165—Gun fire due South.
1.41	,,	Shrapnel bursting South East bearing 165, altitude 16—Sounds of aircraft in the South—Aurelia Road searchlight operating—Purley searchlight operating—Sounds of aircraft South East, almost East—Sounds of aircraft disappearing North East.
1.45	,,	All searchlights extinguished—Bright light reported on bearing 3, back of Park Street.
1.50	,,	Distant searchlight operating between 40 and 80.
1.55	,,	Gun flash on bearing 135.
1.58	,,	Aurelia Road searchlight in operation and several others in the North—White signal light on bearing 31—Light reported in Park Street is now extinguished.
1.59	,,	Searchlights are now signalling.
2. 0	,,	*All Clear.*
2. 9	,,	*Dismiss.*

(Signed) H. E. T. WILCOX
(1596).

ORGANISATION FOR POLICE WORK—Each man, when attested, arranged his hours of duty to which, in the ordinary way, he adhered. Broadly speaking, the Force was divided into two; one half being on duty one week (" A " week) and the other half the next week (" B "). Each twenty-four hours was divided into six portions of four hours, and the Sub-Division was thus further sub-divided for work and discipline, each shift of four hours

THE SPECIAL CONSTABULARY 147

(known as Reliefs) being under a separate set of officers, a Sub-Inspector and Sergeants. The "Lights" Section worked on the "alternate week" system, as did also the Observation Section to a certain extent, and there were therefore sixteen separate units continually working in rotation. In some cases a man carried out his duties at different hours on different days or in consecutive weeks on the same relief, in which case he came under the superintendence of different sets of officers. It was, therefore, necessary for the office staff to keep constantly in touch with each man, so that in cases of sickness or leave the various officers concerned might be notified. The fact that most of the men on observation work also did general duty made this the more necessary, and accounted for much of the correspondence dealt with in the office. This system had its drawbacks and entailed a considerable amount of extra office work, but it had the advantage of getting the best work out of the individual members of the Force at the least inconvenience to them and their businesses, and also kept the members of the office staff more directly in touch with each man than would otherwise have been the case.

In addition to the ordinary duties, and to the 63 mobilisations and 15 "stand-bys" already mentioned, there were very many special parades and duties. The first ten special parades may serve as a sample of the sort of work done; but it must be noticed that after 1915 this class of work increased immensely.

SPECIAL PARADES AND DUTIES.

DATE	TIME	PRESENT	OCCASION
11.11.14		about 70	Opening of Parliament.
7. 2.15	3.30 p.m.	about 120	Church Parade, Parish Church Croydon.
7. 3.15	5. 0 p.m.	202	Inspection Parade, Police Station.
9. 5.15	3.30 p.m.	about 200	Inspection and Address by Mayor of Croydon, Park Hill Recreation Ground.
12. 5.15 to 17. 5.15	Daily average	144	"Lusitania" Emergency Musters.
16. 7.15	7. 0 p.m.	14	Recruiting Meeting, Town Hall Croydon.
21. 8.15	5. 0 p.m.	about 20	Presentation of motor ambulances by Corporation to Red Cross, Town Hall.
12. 9.15	4. 0 p.m.	about 40	Ambulance inspection, Park Hill Recreation Ground.
19. 9.15	4. 0 p.m.	172	Church Parade, Parish Church.
2.10.15	3. 0 p.m.	69	Recruiting "rally," Town Hall.

148 CROYDON AND THE GREAT WAR

DATE	TIME	PRESENT	OCCASION
14.10.15 to 17.10.15		average about 20	Special duties after Air-Raid in Croydon.

SPORTS AND ENTERTAINMENTS.—Six Cricket matches, four Billiard matches, one Football match, and several entertainments, Concerts, Whist drives, &c., were given by the Division; many of these with a view of collecting money for charitable purposes.

The following financial statement shows the money raised from members of the force, in this way:—

		£	s.	d.
Feb. 1915—Sale of tickets for entertainment at Palladium for Met. Police Orphanage		5	2	6
June 1915—Collected at Cricket match for Met. Police Orphanage		11	0	0
July 1915—Collected at Cricket match for Croydon General Hospital		23	15	1
Nov. 1915—Collection for late S/C Causebrook, of Carshalton Sub-Division		11	3	0
Jan. 1916—Purchase of Pair of S/C Boots, presented to Red Cross Sale		5	0	0
July 1916—Royal Irish Constabulary Fund		2	13	0
Sept. 1916—Entertainment to wounded sailors and soldiers at Whitgift Schools		86	0	11
1916–1917—Subscriptions for motor ambulance		128	15	0
Sept. 1917—Metropolitan Police Orphanage		16	2	0
Sept. 1917—Croydon General Hospital		16	2	0
Dec. 1917—Newport Training School		4	19	10
March 1918—Sale of matchboxes for St. Dunstan's Hostel		1	16	0
May 1918—Surrey Prisoners of War Fund		42	4	0
April 1918—M.O.S. Charing Cross Hospital Fund		157	13	8
Aug. 1918—St. Dunstan's Hostel		5	5	0
Aug. 1918—Burgos Home, Croydon		5	5	0
Oct. 1918—Football match for Metropolitan Police Orphanage		79	16	0
Dec. 1918—Entertainment to children of Croydon sailors and soldiers		1	1	0
1914–1918—Metropolitan Police Orphanage, Sale of Tickets for Police concerts		34	0	0
1917–1918—Purchase of cigarettes and tobacco for wounded sailors and soldiers		11	14	10
Jan. 1919—St. Dunstan's Hostel		7	19	11
Feb. 1919—Croydon General Hospital, endowment of beds		502	0	0
May 1919—Whist Drive and Dance for funds of Burgos Home		100	0	0
		£1,259	9	3

THE SPECIAL CONSTABULARY

COST OF THE SUB-DIVISION.—The official administrative receipts and expenditure, as audited, show that in all £750 4s. 3d. was received in money by the force for its expenses, in addition to the free supply of electricity by the Corporation, who also relieved the force from the payment of rates. The Corporation also presented £100 to the general funds and £50 towards the Ambulance Section.

The expenditure was £686 14s. 1d., leaving a balance of £65 10s. 2d., which was handed over to the Croydon General Hospital towards the endowment of a cot.

The force was indebted to the Regular Police for much assistance and friendly co-operation; to the Croydon Corporation and its officials, and to the Croydon Gas Company for help in many ways; and to individual members for a great number of special services outside the range of their ordinary constabulary duties.

An attempt to particularise the services of individuals would be invidious and necessarily incomplete, but many acknowledgments are due to those who ungrudgingly devoted their specialised abilities to the work, and supplemented the official financial allowances by money or material and thereby greatly assisted the general organisation.

Those who have been engaged in the work will recall many hours of weariness and physical discomfort, but mingled with it will be the memories they would not willingly forego of good comradeship, irrespective of class or social standing, and the gain of many valued friendships made while serving a common cause.

The great success achieved is largely due to the admirable work of Assistant Commander H. C. Swaine, of " Quarry Hill," Stanhope Road, Croydon; and the tact with which his salutary strictness was accompanied is shown by the gift of a handsome gold cigarette case, presented to him by the force he had so finely commanded throughout, at the disbandment, 16th June, 1919.

II. Thornton Heath and South Norwood Sub-Division

In August, 1914, a public appeal was made in the press, immediately after the declaration of War, by the Home Office, through the Commissioner of Police, and was at once responded to at the various Police stations.

In August, 1914, the first batch of Thornton Heath and South Norwood men were summoned to take up duty, and they were sworn-in on 17th August, 1914, before the Mayor, at the Town Hall, in company with Special Constables from all other parts of the Borough.

This first enrolment was followed by others on the 18th, 22nd, 24th and 28th with the result that at the end of August, 1914, there were 157 Special Constables on the strength at Thornton Heath, and 95 at South Norwood; and from then onwards the strength was well maintained at both Stations. The highest and lowest figures reached were at Thornton Heath 262 and 152; and at South Norwood 161 and 129. At Thornton Heath 586 men were enrolled from first to last, and at South Norwood 345.

At first the duties at both Stations consisted of guarding "Vulnerable Points," but gradually these were changed and street patrols were substituted. At Thornton Heath there were eight street patrols, and at South Norwood four. These patrols worked in sections from 2 p.m. to mid-night, and during the remainder of the twenty-four hours men were on reserve duty in the Stations, with a minimum of six in the night hours. The following table shows the various duties beyond the eight divisions of street patrols, covering the whole district at "Vulnerable Points," and the periods during which they were performed:—

Thornton Heath.—Norbury Pumping station, 25/8/14 to 19/10/17
    Sandfield Road Railway bridge, 27/8/14 to 23/2/15.
    Norbury Railway bridge, 27/8/14 to 15/10/15.
    Grange Wood reservoir, 1/9/14 to 28/10/17.

South Norwood.—Grange Wood reservoir, 24/8/14 to 31/8/14
    Love Lane subway, 27/8/14 to 2/5/15.
    Holmesdale Road subway, 27/8/14 to 9/11/15.
    Norwood Junction subway, 1/9/14 to 4/11/17.

At the later dates given above the Commissioner of Police under whose orders the Special Constabulary were placed considered that guards of Special Constabulary were no longer needed at "Vulnerable Points."

THE SPECIAL CONSTABULARY

Apart from the Police Armlet, and the Officers' Blue (Inspector), Red (Sub-Inspector), and Yellow (Sergeant) Armlets, the first official equipment consisted of caps which were issued to all Special Constables in the Borough by the Corporation of Croydon early in 1915. At the close of 1915 Headquarters (Scotland Yard, London) decided to provide overcoats and boots, and in May, 1916, full Uniform Suits.

Drill Certificates of Efficiency.—Thornton Heath obtained 160 and South Norwood 98; total 258.

Long Service Badges.—Thornton Heath obtained 190 and South Norwood 114; total 304.

Men who joined in 1914 and were still in the force 16-8-18, obtained *Stars* :—Thornton Heath receiving 51 and South Norwood 44; total 95.

There were many Special Parades. For instance, at the opening of Parliament, November 11th, 1914, there were thirty officers and men on duty from Thornton Heath, and twenty from South Norwood; total 50.

And there follows a list of subsequent parades of the Thornton Heath and South Norwood Special Constables, with the respective attendances at each :—

		Officers & men on duty.		
		T.H.	S.N.	Total
1915.	Mar. 13—T. H. and S. N. Inspection	97	100	197
,,	May 5—Inspect., Mayor of Croydon	118	99	217
,,	June 27—Church parade, St. Stephen's Norbury	125	—	125
1916.	Jan. 2—Church parade, Croydon Parish Church	49	36	85
,,	April 8—Div. Inspection, Streatham	156	67	223
,,	,, 30—Church Parade, Albert Hall	69	53	122
,,	Dec. 3—T.H. & S.N. Inspection	204	118	322
1917.	Feb. 7—Opening of Parliament	20	14	34
,,	June 9—Presentation of Long Service Badges	167	92	259
,,	Oct. 27—Presentation of ambulances	47	31	78
1918.	Jan. 6—Church parade, T.H. & S.N.	140	68	208
,,	Feb. 12—Opening of Parliament	21	13	34
,,	Apr. 14—Drill inspection, T.H.& S.N.	79	22	101
,,	May 26—Presentation of Stars	40	36	76
,,	July 11—Memorial Service, Westminster Abbey	41	27	68
,,	Aug. 4—Church parades, T.H.& S.N.	107	55	162

As well as parades, there were several important mobilisations of these forces, as follows :—

			Officers & men on duty.		
			T.H.	S.N.	Total
1915. May 12	—Keeping order in streets, protecting shops, etc. against expected Anti-German riots (which happily did not come off)		176	—	176
,, ,, 13	—Ditto do. do.		153	—	153
,, ,, 14	—Ditto do. do.		177	126	303
,, ,, 15	—Ditto do. do.		169	109	278
1917. Oct. 2	—Air-Raid duty at Tube stations in London		42	17	59
1918. July 7	—Round-up of deserters, etc., Wilford Road		32	18	50

And on alarms of Air-raids the Special Constables were called to duty eight times in 1915; thirteen times in 1916; no less than 32 times in 1917, and 13 times in 1918, mustering very strongly on each occasion, with an average of over 300 men. The highest muster on any one Air-raid alarm was reached on 1st October, 1916, when 226 men attended from Thornton Heath, and 138 from South Norwood; a total muster of no less than 364 men on that occasion.

On 13th October, 1915 (in the serious raid on Croydon itself) bombs were dropped from a Zeppelin in Lower Addiscombe Road, and in Stretton Road, doing great damage and causing loss of life and casualties in Stretton Road. (It should be mentioned that the police district of South Norwood reaches westward as far as the corner of the Cherry Orchard Road, along the Lower Addiscombe Road.) The South Norwood force were on duty here from mid-night until 3.30 a.m. on the 14th, engaged in rescue work and the protection of damaged property. For four days following they were employed in regulating traffic, etc., and during this period were assisted by contingents from Thornton Heath. Returning from duty in the early hours of the morning, 14th October, 1915, after the raid, Special Constable Roper, Howard Road, South Norwood, who desired not to disturb the family, was entering his house by the back door when he saw an explosive bomb lying on the back doorstep. Fortunately the Huns had neglected to remove the safety pin and the missile was therefore harmless. Due notice was given to the military authorities who *after two days* sent to remove the bomb. Needless to say strict guard was kept over it all the time it lay there.

THE SPECIAL CONSTABULARY

On 23rd Sept., 1916, a Zeppelin passed over Thornton Heath and Norbury. As it passed over Thornton Heath it let down two powerful magnesium lights evidently for the purpose of picking up its bearings. It then bore away towards Streatham, and dropped its first bomb on some open fields in Norbury. In response to a " phone " message from Streatham about 1 a.m., 60 officers and men were hurried off to lend help on that ground, and 40 more paraded for duty at Streatham the next morning at 8 a.m. Much damage was done and many lives lost.

On 2nd October, 1917, 59 officers and men from Thornton Heath and South Norwood paraded at Brixton at 6 p.m. for Air Raid duty on the Tube stations.

BUGLERS AND MOTOR TRANSPORT—At Thornton Heath seven buglers paraded for duty on Air Raid nights and 15 at South Norwood. Each bugler has received a photograph of the whole corps of buglers and a service bugle inscribed with his name, etc., at the cost of a fund especially raised in the spring of 1919. At Thornton Heath there were 16 motor cars and side cars available for use (11 of which were provided by residents voluntarily) and at South Norwood 4 (2 of which were provided voluntarily). These paraded at the Police stations on all occasions of air raids, and it was rare to find any absentees.

AMBULANCE AND FIRST AID WORK.—At South Norwood a special feature was made of this work. There was a very efficient squad of 18 men all holding First Aid Certificates. They furnished themselves at their own expense with two stretchers and complete ambulance outfit, bandages, etc., and distinctive uniform, haversacks, water bottles, etc. A tribute of thanks is due to Dr. Rose who was most kind in giving his services and conducting the ambulance instruction classes. At Thornton Heath there was also a small squad of proficient First Aid men; but there was not the same need for such work in this district, as it was already well supplied with hospitals, R.A.M.C. men, and ambulances.

SOCIAL WORK—At both Thornton Heath and South Norwood much was done in this direction. Perhaps the most striking success was an " Old Comrades' Fund," initiated by Section 4 at Thornton Heath, and maintained by weekly subscriptions from the men of that section for the benefit of old comrades who had been in that section, and who had joined up in the Navy or Army. About £150 was subscribed from September, 1916, onwards; and more than 600 parcels of cigarettes and other comforts were sent to men at the Front and in training, by their comrades in the Special Constabulary at Thornton Heath.

At Thornton Heath a Social Club was run from 1916 to 1918. By Whist drives, Concerts, etc., it contributed the following sums to the causes named :—

	£	s.	d.
To the Order of St. John of Jerusalem & British Red Cross	15	9	0
,, Croydon Hospital	21	0	0
,, the Metropolitan Police Orphanage	22	12	0
,, St. Dunstan's Hostel	52	10	0
	£111	11	0

At South Norwood various amounts were also raised in the same way for various funds. Amongst the special collections were the *Causbrook Fund*, raised for the widow of a man killed by Air-raid while on duty, and amounting to £23 9s. 0d. ; and the *Baker Fund* (another similar case), amounting to £4 13s. 6d.

Also two motor ambulances complete for the front were provided by these forces, at a cost of £723 5s. 1d., of which Thornton Heath contributed £468 8s. 7d. ; and South Norwood £254 16s. 6d.

A large number of the men at both stations subscribed weekly to the Police Orphanage fund. Many other collections were made at both stations for comrades in trouble and need, which resulted in substantial sums being raised. At South Norwood Section IV. had a flourishing War Savings Certificate Fund.

A FEW PERSONALITIES.—(Thornton Heath). Sub-Inspector Pearson (101), in command of a ship which was torpedoed off the coast of Spain by an Austrian submarine, was taken as a prisoner to Austria. S/C Richardson (176) was taken prisoner at Kut. S/C Walker (363) was awarded the Military Medal, and **Inspector Williams was awarded the Military Cross.** S/C Doubell (148) was commended for stopping a run-away horse in London, and S/C Wetherell for valuable assistance to the Regular Police.

(South Norwood). S/C Cutress (49) was commended in Police Orders for arrest of a suspected burglar in May, 1916. S/C C. Norman (20) was awarded the Military Medal. Inspector Mugford (5) was commended in Police Orders for stopping a run-away horse in July, 1916 ; and S/C Thompson (263) saved two boys from drowning at Brighton, 16th August, 1918.

In this Sub-Division there was one member of the force (Inspector Gale, of Thornton Heath) who, it is believed, held the record for the number of duties done by him during the four

THE SPECIAL CONSTABULARY 155

years ending 16th August, 1918, which total altogether 1,513½ (a drill being equal to half a " duty " which accounts for the fraction).

Obituary.

T.H.—S/C Barrow (441), killed in France	14/4/18
S/C Coombs (46), killed in France	10/3/18
S/C Clark (273), died of wounds in Grantham Military Hospital	27/7/18
Inspector Crittenden (77), Headmaster of Beulah Road Council School, died in Denmark Hill Military Hospital	7/9/17
S/C Franklin (312), killed in France	24/6/17
Inspector Leete (51), died	21/4/17
S/C Battley (353), died	7/2/18
S/C Harris (74), died	30/3/18
S/C Hatt (109), died	4/7/18
S/C Howell (245), died	23/6/18
S/C Jones (495), died from wounds in hospital in France	5/1/18
S.N.—S/C Evans (112), killed in France.	8/3/17
S/C Goodman (162), died from wounds in hospital in France	10/5/18
Inspector Laker (28), died in Salisbury Hosp.	15/1/18
S/C Shackell (43), drowned in SS. " India "	12/4/16
S/C Stupart (172), killed in France	5/3/17

III. Croydon Women Patrols

Voluntary Women-Patrols were started in 1915 by the National Union of Women Workers (now the National Council of Women) with the sanction of Sir Edward Henry (Commissioner of police). A card of authorisation bearing his signature was carried by each patrol. Women-patrols were also backed by the authority of the Admiralty and of the War Office. The Croydon Women-patrols received much help and encouragement from Chief Inspector Lovie, of the Metropolitan Police, who gave them a good deal of interesting and responsible work to do; from the then Mayor and Mayoress (Mr. and Mrs. Howard Houlder) who took a keen interest in them throughout; and from a specially organised committee of ladies in Croydon, of which the Hon. Secretary was Miss Glazier.

The work was started as a War measure to help in raising the tone of the behaviour of young people in the streets and open spaces; and the preventive welfare work of the women-patrols carried out tactfully, and by trained women, did much to achieve this object.

During the War there were about forty Croydon women-patrols under the Patrol Leader, Miss Brodie, M.B.E. They patrolled in couples for two hours in the evening. Their uniform was a heavy blue coat and skirt, black hat with the badge N.U.W.W., and a distinctive armlet bearing their registered number under the Metropolitan Police. They carried a police whistle and a lantern. Their work was purely voluntary and unpaid with the following few exceptions :—

From January, 1917 to September, 1918, some of the women-patrols worked for three hours at night instead of two, and were paid at the police rate. In June, 1918, four of them were specially trained to do whole time police work of seven hours a day, and were paid by the Metropolitan Police. They continued this work till the Metropolitan Women-Police were started early in 1919.

The voluntary women-patrols continued work till 30th September, 1919, when the Commissioner of Police (General Macready) replaced them by Women-Police, although the work of the latter force hardly covers the same ground as that done by the women-patrols as indicated above.

IV. Fire Brigade

Even as early as 3rd August, 1914, Retained Fireman Carter, who was a reservist of the Royal Marine Light Infantry, was called up because of the rapidly growing certainty of war; and on 5th August when general mobilisation was ordered three more reservists were taken from our Croydon Fire Brigade, as well as the fireman on duty at the Mental Hospital, to replace whom the Croydon Brigade had to send a fourth man from their depleted staff.

Beyond these losses of staff there was the probability of actually increased activity for the brigade. The Chairman of the Fire Brigade Sub-Committee (Councillor T. W. Wood Roberts) therefore took steps to replenish the ranks by voluntary help. Messrs. Grant, Kennard and Allder, all of them, patriotically assisted, by allowing thirteen of their assistants to volunteer; and they served in turn by four men each night, from 7 p.m. to 7 a.m. Presently the demands of military needs, business, and health ate into the number of voluntary members; and the ever-active Chairman (who himself attended throughout the war) had to canvass amongst his personal friends for volunteers. By one way or another the four volunteers every night were kept up for all the earlier years of the war; from first to last 48 volunteers in all served the fire brigade, and seven were serving at the time of the Armistice. The average length of service was $13\frac{1}{2}$ months, but one volunteer served 54 months, and another 45. They wore as nearly as possible the uniform of the brigade, and slept on their duty-nights at the fire station.

Air-raids caused 68 mobilisations of the brigade, and the volunteers served in 65 of them; an average of seven volunteers turning out at each mobilisation. It was the seventh of these air-raids (13th October, 1915, warning received at 8.23 p.m.) which was that which Croydon so fatally remembers. About 9 p.m. an airship was visible over London, but everything quieted; then, suddenly, without any preliminary warning, bombs began to fall in Croydon at 11.20 p.m., and eighteen bombs fell on the town, seventeen of which exploded. The first call was for Edridge Road, and the brigade were fortunate to rescue a sufferer from the ruins there; then they were sent to Oval Road to assist the injured and search the damaged houses. In Beech House Road, where the motor escape was sent, four persons were imprisoned in the debris on the second floor of one house, which was so badly damaged as to be in danger of collapse. A woman was released, and recovered from her injuries; but the lad who was released at the same time, and who was sent with her to the Hospital, succumbed to his injuries. The bodies of two other lads were uncovered, but the falling masses had already killed them. The prompt and excellent work of the fire brigade was commended by the Council at the meeting on 23rd October, 1916. At Stretton Road the rescue work was performed by R.A.M.C. men, from Davidson Road War Hospital, by police officers and civilians. The fire alarms were disabled in that district by the explosions, so that warning only reached the brigade very late. Eleven persons were killed and seventeen injured in this raid; and the places damaged were in Mason's Avenue, Edridge Road, Park Lane, Beech House Road, Woodstock Road, Friends Road, and Chatsworth Road, the Railway line, Fairfield Road, Cherry Orchard Road, Oval Road, Lebanon Road, Leslie Park Road, Leslie Grove, Lower Addiscombe Road, Albert Road, Alexandra Road, Morland Road, Stretton Road, Exeter Road, Leicester Road, Rymer Road, Edward Road, and Freemason's Road, according to the report of the Chief Officer of the fire brigade (J. W. Dane). In all about 800 buildings were damaged and it was estimated that the money loss was £20,000; fortunately no fires resulted, although a gas main was broken. The large water main crossing the railway was cracked, but happily no great waste occurred. If that had gone, and fires had broken out, the position would have been a serious one. By one of the usual ironies of fate one of the Volunteer firemen on arriving at one of the calls during the night's work of helping others found that it was at his own house, and, moreover, unfortunately it was badly shattered. But this was happily the only occasion when bombs fell in Croydon, though warnings were frequent (as has been said) and the brigade was kept constantly on the alert. It may be conjectured that the stringent way in which lighting was controlled contributed to the immunity of the town. It will be remembered that in the raid on 2nd September, 1916, the attacking Zeppelin dropped bombs both at Kenley and at Streatham, but passed over Croydon, sheltered in its darkness.

On 28th September, 1916, the brigade undertook observation work in conjunction with the London fire brigade at the request of the Admiralty; and continued until this work was undertaken by the Special Constables.

In September, 1917, the Croydon brigade was joined (under D.O.R.A.) with the other fire brigades in the Metropolitan Police district, to act as one large force during air raids, under a

FIRE BRIGADE

mobilising officer ; and many joint drills were held with the London fire brigade and with neighbouring brigades. Sometimes these mobilisations were far from pleasant ; for nothing was moved until the " Take cover " order was issued, and consequently machines and other appliances had to proceed along roads after the guns were already in action, and were exposed to the falling shrapnel, etc. On 30th September the brigade had rather a lively time. They were engaged in the ordinary way at a fire in Wickham Road when an air-raid warning was received. All who could be spared at once took up their air-raid stations—but those still at work on the fire had to continue their work unsheltered, while air fighting was going on above them and shrapnel from our own guns was falling.

The fire brigade also undertook the ambulance service of the borough on 18th September, 1915 ; and in order that the town might be in a position to render " first aid " to any sufferers, lectures were delivered to the men at Headquarters by Dr. McIntyre. All who attended his classes (including the Chairman) sat for, and obtained, the certificate of the St. John Ambulance Association. Further, the Chief Officer advised the Military Hospitals in the borough, munition works, stores, etc., etc., as to protection from fire ; and held several fire drills of squads of soldiers, etc. The brigade was constantly at work, regulars and volunteers ; most fortunately the elaborate precautions undertaken and maintained were rarely wanted ; but had a disaster occurred, as was only too likely, the borough in war time would have blessed the sleepless vigilance of its Fire Brigade.

Photo by Lewis
Councillor THOMAS W. WOOD ROBERTS
Chairman, Fire Brigade Sub-Committee (Auxiliary Fireman, Croydon and London ; Special Constable)

Photo by Lewis

JOHN WILLIAM DANE
(Medal of the Order of the British Empire)
Chief Officer, Croydon Fire Brigade

Photo by F. W. Berry
Colonel H. E. DEANE, R.A.M.C.
Officer Commanding, Croydon War Hospitals

LADY EDRIDGE
Hon. Freeman of the Borough, 1920

Part Five

HOSPITAL AID & RELIEF SERVICES

I. The Medical and Hospital Services

Early in the progress of the war it became clear that an extraordinary strain would be placed upon the medical resources of the country, owing to the unprecedentedly large forces engaged and the innumerable casualties involved, as well as because of the sickness which is an unavoidable accompaniment (however careful may be the sanitary precautions) of the massing of enormous bodies of men. Never in any previous war had the arrangements for the care of the health of the troops been made with such prevision and success ; never was the rate of sickness so small in relation to the numbers of men engaged ; but, even so, it was so great that every iota of medical power in the country had to be organized so as to procure a sufficient service for the fighters. Moreover, there was the civilian population needing the usual medical care—in some cases, indeed, needing it more, as the strain of the war, the rationing of food (experts notwithstanding), and, later, the epidemic influenza, all tended to lower the vitality of the people at home ; or, at any rate, did not make for an increased standard of general health.

At the beginning of the war the War Office called for medical recruits, and got them in generous numbers ; the medical profession proved itself worthy of its traditions. With the expansion of the armies, and the passing of the Military Service Act, something more drastic than a volunteer measure became necessary, in order to distribute the growing medical burden more evenly and equitably over the country. Doctors, it will be remembered, were exempted from the operations of the Military Service Act, but they instituted a form of self-conscription (if we may use the expression) to meet the situation described. They produced a series of " Tribunals " of their own. At the head of these in London and in close touch with the War Office was the Central Medical War Committee, whose business it was to procure doctors for the Services in the numbers demanded by the Government. The Central Committee in turn made demands upon the local areas, and for this purpose the country was divided up into local units and in each of these a Local Medical War Committee was formed. So far as Croydon was concerned the area included Leatherhead, Epsom, Sutton, Wallington and Croydon itself ; and the committee was presided over by Dr. C. O. Fowler, with Dr. E. H. Willock as Honorary Secretary, and Dr. C. G. C. Scudamore as Hon. Assistant Secretary.

The Committee was both a committee of selection and a tribunal. The whole area was carefully considered, and the needs of the people steadily borne in mind. The simple principles which governed the selection of doctors for the forces were to take those who were fit in age and physique, those who were unmarried, and those with partners or whose practices could be worked by neighbouring doctors. The decision of the committee was usually acted upon, but the recruits had a right of appeal to the Central Medical War Committee. As concerns the Borough of Croydon it was further necessary to have regard to the medical side of the National Health Insurance Act, both as regards doctors and chemists. Fortunately for us the Insurance Panel contains almost all of them, and excellent relations have always prevailed between them and the Insurance Committee; so that gradually the War Office tended more and more to accept the Insurance Committee's lists of doctors and chemists who could be spared for the army without running unfair risk to the civilian population. It may be said authoritatively that every doctor and every chemist served who could. The doctors in the early part of the war entered as lieutenants, and were then promoted to the rank of captain; but later they assumed the latter rank at the beginning of their military service. Not only were doctors sent into the army, the needs of the navy were also served, and at least one gentleman, Dr. Horsley, served first in the army and then in the navy, while Dr. Thompson began with the navy and went later to the army. All enlisted for a certain period—one year was a common period, though many served longer: and some served a second period. The honours won while on service by our doctors were as follows :—

Distinguished Service Order	Dr. E. Marshall Cowell.
Military Cross	Dr. P. W. James.
,, ,,	Dr. J. L. Menzies.
,, ,,	Dr. John McIntyre.
,, ,,	Dr. J. W. Wayte.
Distinguished Service Cross	Dr. R. G. Elwell.

The medical men who remained at home shouldered the several tasks that the profession has been called upon to bear; and we should fail signally in our duty if we did not record with gratitude the unflagging service they gave day and night, not only amongst their own and their absent colleagues' patients, but also in War Hospitals, and after Air Raids. The doctor who did less than the work of two men at least was unknown during these critical years.

Of the work which may especially be called War work, most was perhaps done in connection with the War Hospitals. These, as will be remembered, were established in the Council Schools

Exterior of "The Crescent" War Hospital (Borough Secondary Schools)

Photo by C. Harrison Price

One of the wards of "The Crescent" War Hospital (Borough Secondary Schools)

Photo by C. Harrison Price

as a rule. For this purpose, the Davidson Road, Ecclesbourne Road, Ingram Road, and Stanford Road council schools were converted into Military Hospitals, as also were the Boys' and the Girls' secondary schools in the Crescent ; and the children normally to be found in these schools were distributed amongst other schools and buildings of the town. The total number of beds thus provided was one thousand. The Medical Officer Commanding was Colonel Morris, who after about a year of service was succeeded by Colonel H. E. Deane, R.A.M.C. These had, of course, a staff of R.A.M.C. doctors, but these were far too few for the heavy work which fell upon the hospitals. It was arranged therefore that much of the work should be done by the Croydon practitioners, who became a civil medical staff taking regular duty in turn.

The Croydon General Hospital served as an auxiliary hospital, and played a most valuable part in the treatment of the wounded. Watchers in Croydon will long remember the convoys of war ambulances looming up in the darkness in their impressive progress along the London Road. They brought the wounded straight from the Western Front to our Hospital. Two wards were exclusively War Wards, where the soldiers were received ; they contained about fifty beds, and they were rarely unoccupied. This meant a considerable addition to the labours of the staff, but the work was done cheerfully and with remarkable success ; and, moreover, without other recompense than the gratitude of the soldiers and their friends. Especially arduous were the labours of the General Hospital during times of air raids. When the police gave the " stand-by " warning (usually some time before the explosion of the official maroons) the whole resident staff of the Croydon General Hospital was mobilised ; the nurses were all up ; a surgeon was always present. There were, as a matter of fact, few air-raid casualties in the borough of Croydon except those during the fatal Zeppelin attack in October, 1915 ; but the Hospital served a wider area, and patients came from Streatham and Purley, as well as Croydon during the raids ; mostly, we understand, people who were caught in the streets by the barrage (sometimes, we fear, through their own fault), who sustained shrapnel wounds, and although these were generally slight, they required skilled and immediate attention. When it is remembered that most of the staff of the Hospital are the general practitioners of the town, and that these were depleted to the lowest possible number, as mentioned above, it will be realized how much the air-raids must have added to their work. In addition to the 50 beds at the Croydon General Hospital there were provided 80 beds at the Reigate Infirmary, and 20 at Oxted.

These hospitals were originally distributed to provide treatment for the following special classes of cases occurring in the Eastern Command : injuries to nerves and to jaws, diseases of the ear, and cases requiring physical treatment ; and to provide for the sick of any troops in the neighbourhood. As time progressed, and service exigencies became accentuated, it was decided to transfer ear and nerve cases to other centres, and to use the accommodation thus set free for the reception of cases from overseas, which were distributed among the various hospitals.

The first patients were admitted on the 30th June, 1915, and the hospitals were finally closed on the 9th May, 1919. The total number of patients admitted was 19,182, of whom 4,153 were discharged as invalids. The number of deaths was 196, and of these 79 occurred during the influenza epidemics of 1918. Thus, excluding the influenza epidemics, the mortality was under 1 per cent.

At the Stanford Road Hospital, devoted to injuries of the jaw, Mr. J. F. Colyer, F.R.C.S., was Consulting Dental Surgeon, and for his brilliant work was awarded the K.C.B.E. Mr. F. Newby, F.R.C.S., who was senior Surgeon, was awarded the O.B.E., as was also Dr. R. G. Davidson, who was anæsthetist to the Stanford Road Hospital ; and the services of Dr. G. Genge, anæsthetist to the Crescent Hospital, were commended to the Secretary of State. The services of Lieutenent E. Stafford, Durham Light Infantry, who also was selected by Colonel Deane to carry out the details of his applications of ordinary gymnastic apparatus to the treatment of wound disabilities, were rewarded by the M.B.E. And Lieutenant Colonel Deane himself received his brevet as full Colonel.

A word must be added in recognition of the admirable services of the 80 nurses on the staff, many of whom were V.A.D.'s. At one time the whole of the nursing staff consisted of nurses from the other extremity of our Empire, being members of the Australian nursing services.

Only one death occurred amongst the doctors during the whole of these war years, but that was a sufficiently lamentable one. Dr. Hy. Hetley, J.P., who was sent to the Davidson Road school-hospital at the very first, and who served there until he entered a nursing home in London, may almost be said to have died at his post. He threw himself into the work of the hospital with characteristic energy, studying every case with a minute care and attention to detail that was the envy of his colleagues. One of them sums up a sketch of our lamented friend in words which are fitter than any this Editor could devise, and he makes no apology for quoting them here, therefore, just as they reached him.

" His notes were a model of concise and lucid expression of what he saw ; his inferences were the fruit of sound judgment and experience, and his operative skill was excellent. He combined in his views an up-to-date knowledge of recent medical and surgical progress and a true conservative instinct in treatment. By the soldiers he was beloved and respected for his frank manly generosity and openness of mind, and for his sterling personal qualities. To his colleagues his ripe judgment and courteous assistance at all times were invaluable. Though obviously in failing health, he stuck to his work up to the last moment, and when on his death bed did not fail to send a most pathetic and touching message to the soldiers he served so well, and to his professional colleagues. The public and the medical profession alike sustained a severe loss in his untimely and lamented death."

When the six Croydon schools were taken over, there were few amenities for the men. The Mayoress (Mrs. Denning) and Lady Edridge found them quite unsupplied with books or games of any kind. They applied to Mr. Henry Berney, who was Secretary of the Fourth Queen's Equipment and Comforts Fund (see the chapter on the Fourth Queen's) for assistance. The fund he administered was, of course, not available for this purpose ; but he and these ladies just mentioned threw themselves into the promotion of another fund which was known as the War Hospitals Comforts Fund, and Mr. Berney served this, too, as Secretary. Subsequently the Committee of three was enlarged, and the Mayor and Mayoress, Sir Frederick and Lady Edridge, the Colonel in command, and the Town Clerk all served upon it. Public sympathy in very practical form was forthcoming from the first in a remarkable degree ; no less than five full-sized billiard tables (besides many not of full size and a score of bagatelle boards) were offered privately and placed in the school-hospitals. The Christmas of 1915 was observed with all the good cheer of the season : turkeys, Christmas puddings, cakes, apples, nuts, and the various other delights of the season were provided, and were then added to by the Mayor and Mayoress ; and each succeeding Christmas told a similar story, except that after the death of Mayor Denning, in February, 1916, his high privileges and responsibilities were passed on to his successor, Mayor Houlder. But Christmas was only an annual climax, as it were, in the good work. Daily " comforts " in the form of cake, eggs and jam were sent to the Croydon General Hospital. In all £3,100 in money, as well as gifts of the approximate value of £1,500, were provided for the hospitals through the energies of the committee ; and furniture and other effects were lent, up to the value of £1,000.

It is difficult to give more than an indication of the way in which help was given to the wounded and sick. Owners of motor cars came forward to take the patients for drives, or lent their cars for the purpose. For four years this was continuously done by Mrs. G. M. Worsley ; and for the same period Mr. A. H. Allen, Mr. E. Stanley Walters, and Mr. C. S. Thorne used their private cars every day in connection with work at the hospitals. Others gave valuable nursing assistance. Mrs. X. M. Edgelow served for three and a half years at the Crescent Hospitals in the role of hairdresser, and in that period shaved and cut the hair of over 42,000 cases, using 20 ordinary (not safety) razors, for which good work she was known first as the "Lady Barber," and later as the "Beauty Specialist"—" which name," writes Mrs. Edgelow, "I think I deserved after removing from a patient a week's growth of beard, and in some cases even a fortnight's growth." When it is remembered that at the beginning Mrs. Edgelow had had no experience with a razor, and that she was also frequently called upon to shave limbs in preparation for operations, something of her courage and endurance will be recognized. "The most difficult part I had to play," she says, "was to explain to the patients that I loved to make them comfortable and clean, and that there was no charge, as my services were entirely voluntary." Reference must also be made to the really splendid work done by Miss Purdy and Miss Feetum at, and in connection with, Davidson Road hospital. For four years these ladies placed themselves at the disposal of the matron and nurses every day, and provided comforts and sick diet whenever they were required to do so. Without their generous help the hospital would often have been in difficulties. Another example of great and sustained help was shown by Mrs. A. E. Bidmead, who arranged, at no little sacrifice, no less than one hundred dramatic entertainments for the men in hospital. From the outset a small committee of ladies busied themselves with providing amenities of various kinds at the hospitals : Mrs. Chamberlain undertaking Davidson Road school-hospital ; Mrs. Scudamore, the Crescent ; Mrs. Hetley, Ingram Road ; Mrs. Trumble and Mrs. Warren, Ecclesbourne Road ; while the similar arrangements for Stanford Road school-hospital were in the very capable hands of the Manager of the L.C.W. & Parr's Bank, Norbury, Mr. E. R. Horne. There were many other cases that deserve to be chronicled, and if we have omitted to name them here, it is not because our sense of their value is not real, but owing to considerations of space. So many were the acts of kindness that it is actually impossible to record them all.

MEDICAL AND HOSPITAL SERVICES 169

H.R.H. Princess Christian's Hospital.

In 1914, No. 82 London (St. John) V.A.D., assisted by No. 118 London (St. John) V.A.D., feeling the need of a local hospital for the wounded, secured and equipped with willing assistance from the neighbourhood, the house known as "Whitehall," on South Norwood Hill. H.R.H. Princess Christian graciously accorded her patronage.

From March 24th, 1915, when the first convoy of patients was admitted, till March 24th, 1919, the good work went on uninterruptedly.

A representative committee of management from the neighbourhood was formed; with first the late Sir Ernest Tritton, Bart., as chairman, and after his death, Colonel F. Campbell, C.B.

The hospital was affiliated to the 4th London General Hospital at Denmark Hill, and provided for the first two years 52 beds, afterwards increasing that number to 60. The total number of patients was 1,823. There were no deaths.

From March, 1915, till early in the following year, No. 118 London (St. John) V.A.D., with Lady Falkland as its Commandant, helped in the nursing. After that the entire work of the hospital was carried on by members of No. 82 London V.A.D., with occasional help from members of the Croydon Detachment. The V.A.D.'s worked under a staff of trained nurses consisting of a Matron and three Sisters.

The hospital was delightfully situated, and its beautiful garden, furnished with an open-air shelter, helped largely in the recovery of the patients. It had its own operating theatre, excellently fitted up, x-ray, massage and electricity rooms, and its own well-appointed little chapel. The Rev. J. Sutherland Gill acted as Honorary Chaplain. The work of the wards, the Quartermaster's office, the kitchen, the linen room, the pantries, the house and the garden, was undertaken with untiring devotion by the voluntary workers.

A feature of the hospital was the annual sale of work (in part the work of the patients themselves) held in the hospital grounds in 1916, 1917 and 1918, bringing in for the hospital funds such helpful sums as £129, £150 and £195 respectively.

The inevitable weariness of hospital routine and discipline was alleviated by the kindness of the neighbourhood. The patients were taken for drives, invited out to teas, fêtes, pic-nics, and provided with theatre tickets, etc. They had a splendid selection of books in their library at the hospital and outdoor games for the garden. Frequently the patients were given a party for their relatives and friends, and were provided with tea and a concert, garden fete, or Christmas tree, according to the season of the year. Considerably over 100 concerts for the nurses and patients were arranged and provided for by Mr. Leigh Bennett and his friends.

The financial situation was always satisfactory. The hospital committee published four reports, one for each year's work, shewing clearly all the accounts. For the careful presentation of the latter the hospital is very deeply indebted to Mr. H. Gaster, the Honorary Secretary.

Dr. J. J. Douglas acted as Commandant of the V.A.D. Detachment, and Mrs. Colegrave, M.B.E., as its Lady Superintendent.

In consequence of its excellent work the hospital received the following generous share of honours :—

Royal Red Cross 2nd Class.—Miss S. T. Biddulph Pinchard, Matron for three years ; Miss Foreman, Sister for three years and afterwards Matron ; Mrs. J. J. Douglas, V.A.D.

M.B.E.—Mrs. Colegrave, Lady Superintendent.

Specially " Mentioned."—Mrs. Colegrave, Lady Superintendent ; Miss Benbow, Head Cook ; Miss E. Cooper, Masseuse; Miss E. Dentith, Quartermaster and Masseuse ; Mrs. Douglas, Miss Foreman, Mrs. Le May, Miss McNaughtan, Miss Williams, and Mr. H. Gaster, Honorary Secretary.

At the end the hospital was able to hand over the following sums to local charities : £1,200 to the Norwood Cottage Hospital; £100 to King's College Hospital ; and £100 to the Royal Normal College for the Blind.

Convalescent Homes.

A delightful remembrance amid all the suffering caused by the War is the way in which Croydon endeavoured to alleviate the weariness and pain of convalescence. We give examples.

Mr. George Goodsir, J.P., gave up his beautiful home, " Wallacefield," Coombe Road, entirely to convalescents from the army. At first Miss Ethel Link, M.B.E., took charge, and as soon as Mrs. Goodsir was ready she herself succeeded Miss Link, and remained in charge till the close. Miss May Goodsir was on duty as Honorary Secretary and Q.M. from first to last. The rest of the family lived elsewhere. The first arrivals were fifteen Belgians from Antwerp via Aberdeen, headed by two Englishmen, who arrived on 23rd October, 1914, and who for twenty-four hours luxuriated in the possession of a private house,

MEDICAL AND HOSPITAL SERVICES

with a large staff of lady nurses and helpers all to themselves. From that time forward, however, the staff was fully employed day and night, and from first to last 1,152 wounded soldiers regained health under their care. It is very gratifying to learn that although most of the men were happy-go-lucky private soldiers, and some wear and tear might reasonably been expected, one broken lamp glass was all the injury that the house suffered at the hands of these " Tommies " over the period of $4\frac{1}{2}$ years. [For it is a curious fact that " Wallacefield " served its benevolent purpose for exactly the same number of days that the War lasted, being opened in September, 1914, a few weeks after the War began and outlasting the Armistice by just the same number of days to December, 1918.] Defaulters were punished with the threat of instant return to the military hospital, which proved quite efficacious—a fact which speaks well for the men's appreciation of the house.

In " An Unspoken Speech on Demobilisation " (which may be seen in the Reference Library at the Town Hall)Mr. Goodsir gives an interesting history of the house. All the helpers were voluntary, and one of the boys, comparing notes with another boy from a neighbouring hospital, boasted that he had " real ladies to wait upon him," and clenched the argument by asserting that " even the kitchen maids at Wallacefield drove up in their own cars."

Friends were always forthcoming with concerts and other amusements to keep up the spirits of the sufferers. The Christmas days were real home festivals ; and on bright summer days, croquet, bowls, and tennis were played, or the men lounged in the shade with books, or hung over the garden wall to chaff the passers by. One or two incidents occurred which have a somewhat regrettable, if also a humorous side. We quote Mr. Goodsir :—

" Do you remember that other Belgian—I forget his name —who made a pretty speech in Belgian-French, translated by Miss Link, about having lost his home, his friends and all his possessions except his uniform, but, out of gratitude for his treatment here, would present Mrs. Goodsir with two buttons from his tunic ? (This at a time when collecting soldiers' buttons was all the rage). How Mrs. Goodsir had the buttons gilded and made into a brooch, which was worn in triumph : until she discovered that the donor had cut them from the tunic of another man of the same regiment whilst he lay helplessly ill in Ward F., and also that the generous Belgian was an old jailbird with no reputation worth preserving ? "

Miss Ethel Link continued her fine national service. Through the great kindness of many friends she was enabled to start a Convalescent Home called " St. Dorothy's," in connexion with the 4th London General Hospital, first in Castlemaine Avenue, and afterwards in Croham Manor Road. The Home was opened and consecrated to its gracious and merciful object on 15th January, 1916, and was closed on 1st June, 1919. During that period 470 men passed through its doors; they never had to be closed either from lack of guests or the means of supplying their needs. The men belonged to all departments of voluntary service, as well as to the " Old Contemptibles," and all the colonies had their representatives as well. The evening re-laxations which had formed so pleasant a feature at "Wallace-field " were continued as well at " St. Dorothy's " by the willing help of Miss Link's numerous musical and artistic friends.

Other Hospitals.

Other hospitals for wounded and convalescent sailors and soldiers deserve mention, in order that this record may be complete, although a detailed account of them cannot be included. A small, but most effective and beneficent hospital was that conducted by Dr. W. Dempster at 254, Brighton Road, which was known as the Brighton-road Hospital. On the north-western edge of the Borough, two hospitals, Norbury Hill House (under the care of the Society of St. Vincent and St. Paul), and Nielka Hospital, " Jerviston," Ryecroft-road, did noble work. On our eastern side, Shirley Park Hotel, of recent years an hotel and the centre of a fine golfing course with beautiful scenery, was a hospital for officers of the Royal Flying Corps and Royal Air Force. It is interesting to recall that at one time the building was known as Shirley House (built 1720), aud was the residence of Lord Chancellor Eldon and the place where he died. Another house with historical associations and beautiful surroundings which was turned to war-hospital uses was Addington Palace, for a century the country residence of the Archbishops of Canterbury, which although just outside the Borough is closely affiliated with it in our minds. Here thousands of wounded troops from France were restored to health, but later on it was devoted to troops from India, Mesopotamia and the East generally, as a special centre for the treatment of malaria, dysentery, and other eastern and tropical diseases.

Coffer of 17th Century Pattern
Made for the War Supplies Clearing House Red Cross Auction by R. F. Colam, K.C., Recorder of Croydon

Councillor FRANCIS ALLEN, M.B.E., J.P.
War Pensions Committee

II. The Croydon War Hospital Supply Depot

On 19th July, 1915, in consequence of the clamant demand for hospital requisites for the British and Allied Armies, this association began work at 44, Park Lane, in a house kindly lent by the Croydon Gas Company. The Mayoress (Mrs. Denning) was President, and Lady Edridge Vice-President ; the organisers and managers throughout were Mrs. P. B. Beddow and Mrs. John Major. For the first month the buyer was Mrs. W. W. K. Robinson (at whose house the preparatory meetings had been held), and afterwards the buying was undertaken by the organisers. An influential Executive Committee was secured. The organisers were fortunate in obtaining generous loans of sewing machines, work tables and furniture. By the end of July there were 300 working members, each contributing one shilling per week, and the house could no longer hold them all ; so that " next door," No. 42, was most kindly added by the Gas Company. Even these two houses soon proved insufficient, and in September the Depot accepted the generous offer of " The Homestead," Bedford Park, from Mrs. Walton, and there remained for the rest of its existence. By the end of August 7,000 articles had been made and despatched, and the demand ever grew. Mr. R. F. Colam, K.C. (Recorder of Croydon), and the late Mr. Wm. Harris now became joint Treasurers.

At " The Homestead " the work was organised into departments. One of the most interesting rooms was the Shirt-room, where busy sewing machines turned out shirts with such unusual success that " Croydon shirts " became famous in their own way, and were often specifically demanded by officers zealous for the comfort of their men. Then there were the Slipper-room, the Swab-room, and the Cutting-out-room ; and other departments dealt with Bandages, Rollers, Needlework, Knitting, Splints, Carpentry and Wood-work. There was a large Store Room for materials and for finished goods, though the latter were never long before they were packed up and despatched to Military Hospitals, not only in England, but all over the world. The " Colam " gaiter was a speciality always in request and largely made. In November the Depot was recognised by the War Office, and after the Directorate-General of Voluntary Organizations was formed (which co-ordinated all such efforts) the Depot received requisitions from that source.

In February, 1916, the Mayor's death caused Mrs. Denning's resignation, and the incoming Mayoress (Mrs. Houlder) became President. At this time the membership had risen to 800, who were formed into rotas so that the work might be continuous. On 19th July, 1916, an " At Home " was held by the Mayoress (Mrs. Houlder) in celebration of one year's work ; a year later a Garden Fête, opened by Lady Haig, commemorated the second year's work ; and at the close of the third year Lady Beatty presided over the festivities.

These anniversary fêtes were utilised also to supplement the large funds which were necessary to finance so extensive a work, and brought in £442. A Christmas Fair in 1918 added £280. Two Flag Days provided £842, and Thés Chantants, Concerts, etc., added £364. The backbone financially was, however, the weekly contributions of all the members, and from first to last these amounted to £4,731. The total receipts were £8,660, and the expenditure for materials was £7,545. The running expenses were rigidly kept down, and only rose to six per cent. of the whole. When the Depot was closed the Treasurer had £485 in hand, and this was presented to the Croydon General Hospital.

The measure of the comfort and healing imparted to our troops all over the world by means of the many hundred of thousands of articles produced at the Depot—from dressing gowns to tiny surgical swabs—will never be fully known. But appreciation of all that was done was touchingly manifested, and many a letter from many a hospital, both British and Allied, testified to their gratitude for the extraordinary variety, novelty, and ingenuity of the supports, splints, etc., in metal and in wood, invented and made by the Recorder in his workshop at the top of " The Homestead," astonishing and delighting the puzzled hospital surgeons whose difficulties they so wonderfully surmounted. Enthusiastic volunteers assisted the Recorder in this beneficent work.

One of Mr. Colam's appliances (for drop foot) made by the Depot workers at a cost of only about 1s. 6d., produced such numbers of applications from all parts of the country that it was difficult to keep pace with them. It had the advantage of being invisible, and at the same time was more comfortable and efficient than appliances costing several guineas.

Early in 1919 the need for the Depot happily ceased, and it was closed in February. Its hard, close and happy and successful work had lasted more than three and a half years, and its memory must ever be held in honour in our town.

III. Croydon War Supplies Clearing House

At the beginning of September, 1914, gifts were being sent with indiscriminate generosity by Croydon people direct to the fighters, and there was no co-ordination whatever. It occurred to Mr. Albert G. Norris, the Croydon district manager of the Sun Life Assurance Society, that some organization was needed which would first find out where things were really required, and then collect those things and send them there; in order that gifts should be placed to the best advantage for the sailors and soldiers. He found willing colleagues, and the Croydon War Supplies Clearing House came into being; with the Lord Mayor of London (Sir T. Vansittart Bowater) as patron, and Georgina, Countess of Dudley, as patroness; Mr. Norris acting as secretary, Mr. Leonard S. Rogers as publicity secretary, and Mr. Henry Terrell Peard as chairman, while Mr. Henry Berney, who was " in " almost every movement for the good of the soldiers, gave constant helpful support. A year later Sir Frederick Edridge became President and Lady Edridge a patroness; and in February, 1916, the new Mayor and Mayoress (Alderman and Mrs. Houlder) became respectively patron and patroness. Sixteen receiving depots were established in Croydon and the neighbourhood, where goods, clothing and any useful gifts whatever might be deposited, with a motor transport service to collect from them twice weekly. The scheme was submitted to the War Office, and received not merely its approval but also its warm commendation. It is interesting to note that when the national body under the Director-General of Voluntary Organisations was begun two years later it was almost on exactly similar lines, and was most probably a result of the Croydon suggestion. The central office was opened on 2nd November, 1914, at a shop in George Street; and here the committee were inundated with gifts of clothing, food, games, comforts, and all kinds of things useful for the troops. Cordial support was forthcoming immediately from prominent Croydon people, including many members of the Corporation, although at this time the Corporation itself was not identified with the movement. In the strenuous work of the Clearing House, which drew to it a large staff of unselfish assiduous helpers, the continuous invaluable work of Mrs. S. J. E. Iredell, who became lady superintendent of the staff and depot at the beginning and remained at her post until the end, must receive special mention.

She worked daily throughout the whole war without intermission, often into the small hours of the morning. Her assistant, Miss Enid Colam (now Mrs. Colam), supported her enthusiastically and competently. Another worker whose unremitting help covered the whole of the war was Mrs. C. J. Gladwell, who as chief assistant to Mr. Leonard Rogers, as distributing secretary and, later, as chief clerk, did work of inestimable value. Other helpers are gratefully remembered, though their names are too numerous for inclusion here.

Apart from general collecting for the forces, the purpose of the Clearing House was to supply occasional special demands as they arose, either from the war hospitals or from the forces. For example, it furnished more than one of the houses which were set aside in Croydon as hostels for the accommodation of the Belgian Refugees. Again, the military forwarding officers in France on one occasion made a special request for condensed milk. The committee at once formed ten district committees of ladies to decentralize this work, and within a fortnight 63,492 tins of condensed milk, weighing 17 tons, and valued at £925, were delivered at the Small Public Hall, where they were taken over by Lady Malcolm. On another occasion an appeal for help towards the Comforts Fund was met by a " Union Jack " flag day, in July, 1915, when collecting was confined to the centre of the town, and £330 was raised.

At another time the committee was asked to raise funds for the Red Cross, and this led to the formation of a special committee, over which Lady Malcolm presided as chairman, to collect materials and saleable objects of all kinds and to arrange for their sale by public auction. Six months were devoted to preparation, the ambition of the committee being to raise £3,000. On 20th January, 1916, Princess Christian opened the auction sale at the Public Hall, and for a week articles of all sorts, useful, beautiful and curious, which had been contributed by well-wishers, were sold. Amongst them was a beautiful coffer of 17th century pattern, designed by the Borough Recorder, Mr. R. F. Colam, K.C., and also carved by himself from cedarwood grown in his garden. The auctioneers of the town and their assistants kindly gave their services, and that these were somewhat arduous may be deduced from the fact that the biddings did not cease until midnight on some occasions. The traders of the town gave signal help by the selling of Red Cross stamps which had been specially designed in competition for the occasion—one of the approved designs, it is interesting to know, being by a boy in the Borough Secondary School. The total takings for this object were no less than £8,746, far surpassing the original hope of the committee. A letter of " congratulation upon the

WAR SUPPLIES CLEARING HOUSE

splendid success" of the auction was received from Queen Alexandra, which is one of the treasured mementoes of the committee's work.

In September, 1916, a collection for Y.M.C.A. Huts, intended to be made during one day, developed into a "Hut Week" under the stimulus of the Mayor's energy, and no less a sum was raised than £6,458, with which several " Croydonia " huts were equipped and endowed, as well as a " Croydonia " Travelling Cinema. It is interesting to record that Lady Malcolm when in France helping the Y.M.C.A. had some of the " Croydonia " huts under her charge. " Croydonia Hut " No. 1 was a personal gift previously made to the Y.M.C.A. by Mr. Hector Morison, M.P., then resident in Croydon.

In the autumn of 1917, footballs and boxing gloves were sent out, and in 1918 the Comforts Fund benefited to the extent of £309 by a matinee arranged at the Hippodrome. The same year the Clearing House carried through Croydon's Record Flag Day, in which £1,273 14s. 9d. was raised for St. Dunstan's foundation for the Blind, Regents Park. (This total sum was run very close by the Mayoress's Flag Day for the Red Cross, " Our Day," which followed shortly after (24th October, 1918), and realised £1,269.)

When the Clearing House closed, 17th April, 1919, and the Secretaries drew up a summary of the work done since the opening on the 2nd November, 1914—nearly four and a half years of strenuous work—some very remarkable figures were obtained. From a certified account we extract the following few particulars.

The Clearing House itself collected and despatched 2,373 cases, containing 260,170 separate items, to the forces; and beyond this, despatched 786 other cases, containing 176,823 items, on behalf of the Croydon Association of Voluntary Organizations, which had collected them. In actual money the Clearing House raised £20,500.

In its own 260,170 items are 4,771 tins of tea, coffee, cocoa, and preserved milk (in addition to the special milk collection previously referred to, of 63,492 tins); 684 packets of chocolate, and 1,121 of other sweets; 10 boxes of cigars and 702 lbs. of tobacco, with 606 pipes to smoke it in, and 476 packets of boxes of matches to light up with. Amongst the much appreciated clothing gifts we see 1,686 handkerchiefs, 3,277 scarves, 1,286 woollen mufflers, as well as a large number of these things forwarded on behalf of the C.D.A. Voluntary Organizations. Nearly 1,000 shirts, and a third of that number of nightshirts, 1,500 pairs of gloves, and 5,500 pairs of mittens, and not far short of 4,000 pairs of socks we observe, while presently the compiler, growing weary of enumerating, lumps a lot together as "Sundry garments, mostly second-hand," running up to 6,000 —all but 15. Passing over great quantities of blankets and bedding we find 864 sets of splints, knee-pads, etc. ; 1,304 sticks and crutches ; 1,362 tins or boxes of disinfectants, etc. ; 3,819 bandages, 670 rolls of lint, 926 respirators, etc., for the hospitals : 1,161 sandbags to help the trenches as well as 926 respirators for those using the sandbags ; and to make them feel less neglected, 303 razors and strops were supplied, with 1,105 boxes of stationery and writing pads to keep the boys in touch with home. Games to the number of 1,690, over and above 1,000 packs of cards, kept the minds of our boys alert, while 7,294 packets and tins of food, 375 tins of jam, and 267 tins of biscuits helped their bodies. One hopes the 500 eggs reached France unbroken ; and we know of the joy with which the 6,105 Christmas puddings were received. We see, with a certain amount of pleasure, that the moderate number of 42 bottles of wines and spirits figures in this most interesting list, and with even more pleasure we note the stupendous number of 112,150 books, etc. Musical instruments are lumped with " soap, brushes, etc." in a total of 14,500, so that it is impossible to gather either the nature or the quantity of the supply available for the service of the Queen of all the Fine Arts. Cigarettes were collected for the benefit of the men in hospital, under the attractive name of the " Farthing Fag Fund," and we note that in one of the yearly reports of the Clearing House the number of cigarettes distributed is apologetically named as only 81,545, as it " has fallen off a great deal."

It must be always remembered that the British prisoners in Germany would have starved, but for the parcels of food sent to them ; and therefore the War Supplies Clearing House very wisely abandoned, towards the last, this part of their work, forwarding their parcels through the Government in the names of the donors, rather than sending them direct as before, the Government cases having an infinitely better chance of reaching the sufferers than any private packages could have.

Another branch of activity was the maintenance of a cinema at Addington Park Hospital ; and so popular did this become, and so incessantly was it worked, that the machine wore out, and began to dazzle the eyes of the patients and rouse the ire of the doctors. So a new and steady machine had to be got, and the report, with a sort of smothered groan, admits that it cost nearly £90. However, it was procured, and the " pictures " continued to delight the patients.

The collection of waste paper and other waste materials largely by the willing help of the Boy Scouts, realised £354—

quite a welcome addition to the funds of the Clearing House, upon which there was incessant demand. Looking through the minutes we often come upon phrases such as " Loan from the Chairman," " Overdraft at the Bank," etc., at seasons when it was necessary upon some urgent call to run clean beyond the funds in hand, and trust to the future for reimbursement. We are glad to be able to say that this trust was never in vain.

The balance in hand—£317 12s. 1d., on 17th April, 1919, when the Clearing House was closed—was used to endow a bed in the Children's Ward at the Croydon General Hospital, to be known as " The War Supplies Clearing House Cot," and to carry a preference in favour of the children of those who had served in the War.

IV. The Mayor's Committee.

For the Prevention and Relief of Distress arising out of the War, and for other purposes incidental to the War.

(NATIONAL RELIEF FUND.)

The Mayor (Alderman Frank Denning) was not in Croydon when War was declared in the evening of 4th August, 1914; but needless to say he arrived the next day, and at once began vigorous measures to prepare Croydon for its formidable task of coping with the emergencies of war.

On 7th of August the Mayor summoned a public meeting of the Council, the Magistrates, the Guardians, the Clergy and Ministers,the Trades Councils, and all Philanthropic Committees; and the Mayor's Committee with the title at the head of this chapter was immediately formed. There were at the beginning 81 members, and more joined later. A small Advisory Committee of 8 members was appointed, and this sat daily at the Town Hall for several weeks. Sub-Committees were also appointed for employment, finance and relief; and Ward Committees were also set on foot.

The Prince of Wales issued an appeal for funds, which was supported by the Queen, and the collection of money for the " Prince of Wales's Fund " became at once a chief duty of the Mayor's Committee, and of the Ward Committees. £11,000 was paid in a week or two towards this Fund. The plan adopted was to send all money to Buckingham Palace (or, later, to the offices of the Prince of Wales's Fund) and to ask for such sums to be sent to Croydon as the needs of the town demanded from time to time. Later in the War this great fund changed its name to the National Relief Fund, and may therefore in future bear that name in this chapter.

Recruiting was also a primary duty, and was assisted by the Mayor's Committee, who urged it upon the separate Wards as a pressing need. Elsewhere we show the vigour with which volunteer recruiting was pursued.

The medical profession nobly responded, as always, to the call upon them, and all the doctors in Croydon at once offered to attend gratuitously the dependents of soldiers or sailors on active service, when requested through the Ward Committees or

THE MAYOR'S COMMITTEE

the Central Committee. And the Pharmacists of the Borough, not to be behindhand, similarly declared themselves willing (on proper notification made, as above) not only to make up all prescriptions for such dependents, but also to provide the drugs needed at their own cost. The last part of their generous offer was, however, not accepted, the National Relief Fund paying for the drugs.

Many other citizens helped in their various capacities as the doctors and chemists had done, and we all became conscious of a spirit of unity pervading the whole Borough—a shoulder-to-shoulder feeling ; a sentiment of brotherhood hitherto unknown shared by all ranks and classes in the face of our common danger.

The feeding of children was one of the special needs of the families whose fathers had enlisted ; and this was easily arranged through the School Canteen Committees, not only for school children, but for all young persons up to 16, the permits being issued by the Ward Committees, and the Central Committee providing the necessary funds. And to cope with a kindred necessity a committee of ladies undertook in October, 1914, to maintain 10 centres, in various parts of the Borough, for the provision of good mid-day meals for nursing and expectant mothers, and their children ; a constructive work designed for the benefit of the next generation, so likely to be hard hit by the war, but in practice proving to be a welcome relief for a very special type of distress which soon became apparent, since the mothers' love often led them to deny themselves, for the sake of their children, things they specially needed at such times. These dinners were continued till 30th April, 1916.

As the winter drew on arrangements were made for the distribution of tickets, especially to families of sailors and soldiers on active service, entitling the holder to buy two cwt. of coal on each ticket at 1s. 3d. a cwt. At the time of writing (January, 1920) this price has become incredible, and we must be grateful that in the winter of 1914-15 coal was still procurable at a reasonable price. There were 369 tons of coal thus supplied to the poor that winter.

On 17th February, 1915, the Town Clerk reported the gift of 200 bags of flour, each bag containing 7 stone (98 lbs.), from Canada, British Columbia, and New Brunswick ; and the patriotic offer of the Croydon bakers to convert this fine gift into loaves. And on 24th September the same year 2,000 lbs. of tea was received from Ceylon Tea-planters, which was held over a little and distributed at Christmas. Mr. W. E. Wilson kindly made up the whole gift, for convenience, into half-pound packets.

For a considerable period during this winter (1914-15) workshops to provide for women were carried on at the Adult School, Croydon, and the Polytechnic, South Norwood, but the increasing demands for war work of all kinds eventually rendered these unnecessary.

The National Relief Fund gave £400 towards relief of the damage in the Oval Road district by the air-raid of 13th October, to replace furniture and the daily utensils of about 150 houses, and Mr. Harry Sidey, to whom this work was entrusted, had every claim adjusted and satisfied within twenty-one days of the raid. In many instances the Mayor's Committee had to find housing accommodation for the sufferers, as their houses were uninhabitable. Many allowances were also made to wives whose husbands were injured, to parents whose wage-earning sons were killed, etc.

The Mayor's Committee also accepted responsibility for, and indeed entered largely into the work of the Soldiers' and Sailors' Families Association and the Soldiers' and Sailors' Help Society in the Borough. These Societies became as it were a special division of the Mayor's Committee and one of the utmost importance. It has been found necessary to devote a special chapter to it.

The total amount collected for the Mayor's Fund established by this Committee was £21,108 12s. 4d., of which £16,008 6s. 4d. was paid into the National Relief Fund, the greater part of which came back to Croydon in the following form :—

		£	s.	d.
For	Soldiers' and Sailors' Families Association..	11,600	0	0
,,	Soldiers' & Sailors' Help society..	600	0	0
,,	Women's workroom	475	0	0
,,	Air Raid	449	9	6
,,	Civilian distress	2,527	0	0
		£15,651	9	6

In 1915, a special account was opened by Mayor Denning for the relief of persons suffering from the air-raids, which was administered by this Committee. £779 5s. 7d. was raised (of which £449 9s. 6d. was contributed by the National Relief Fund) and fortunately only £619 9s. 6d. was required, as Croydon, except for one serious attack, was mercifully spared any great air-raid disaster. The balance of this air-raid fund was transferred by consent of the subscribers to the Croydon Civic Service League, under Mayor Houlder, in 1919.

Mrs. Summers, of Upper Norwood, whose son was killed in London, in an air-raid, received £51 Treasury award, and the Treasury also sent £70 to be divided between two other sufferers.

Civilian cases of distress caused by the war, such for example as a lady of some position left absolutely penniless because all her income was derived from remittances from Turkey, and many similar distressful cases, were sent up when ascertained by the Ward Secretaries, to the Town Hall, and referred by the Town Clerk and Mr. A. E. Welstead to the weekly, and subsequently monthly, Relief Sub-Committee. The total number of such cases assisted by weekly grants was 532, and the cost was £3,026 16s. 10d. On the 15th September, 1919, the then outstanding cases were taken over by the War Relief Trustees, and the Committee ceased to exist.

It is interesting to place on record that the great monument of public beneficence called the National Relief Fund, translated into actual figures, meant no less than £6,437,733 ; the largest sum of the kind ever raised in the history of the World.

Mayor's Account.
NATIONAL RELIEF FUND.

Financial Statement to 30th June, 1919.

RECEIPTS.

	£	s.	d.
Subscriptions Received	20,522	7	11
Interest on Deposit Account	419	4	5
Interest on £4,000 four per cent. National War Loan	167	0	0
	£21,108	12	4

PAYMENTS.

	£	s.	d.
Amount paid over to the Prince of Wales Fund (National Relief Fund)	16,008	6	4
Registration Fee	0	5	0
BALANCE—			
Cash at Bank £1,100 1 0			
£4,000 four per cent. National War Loan 4,000 0 0			
	5,100	1	0
	£21,108	12	4

WM. PEET, F.C.A., J. H. McCALL,
   Hon. Auditor.   *Borough Accountant.*

V. War Pensions Committee

The alleviation of the difficulties necessarily arising in the families of working folk where the breadwinner has gone to fight for his country, and rent, clothes and food are suddenly all to seek, had for many years been the task of the Soldiers' and Sailors' Families' Association, and the care of the men disabled by war was in like manner the task of the Soldiers' and Sailors' Help Society. The Croydon Branch of the Soldiers' and Sailors' Families' Association when it resumed active work in August, 1914, on the outbreak of war, found a home at the Guild of Help Offices in Park Street, whence it was soon forced (for lack of accommodation) to remove to the Head Quarters of the Fourth Queen's in Poplar Walk.

At this time the Croydon Branches of these two societies covered a wide area, extending from Mitcham to Caterham. When the Fourth Queen's were mobilised (5th August, 1914), and recruiting at once began for the regular army, the civilian distresses above referred to instantly made themselves manifest. Fortunately the two Associations had a small sum (about £150) unspent after the Boer War, and this gave them a day or two's start. No arrangements had been made for the prompt issue of separation allowances, payment of rent, etc., and, further, the Mayor was being pressed, as were all Mayors, to take these matters into his own care, since the all-important recruiting was being interfered with by these rapidly accumulating cases of hardship. Too many men being warned by the troubles their neighbours had incurred, answered the appeal of the earnest recruiters, official or voluntary, with the incontrovertible " I don't mind goin', Gov'nor ; but what about the Missus and the Kids ? " It was also evident that in the interest of efficiency the Borough must be separated from the rural areas ; and very soon, therefore, the Soldiers' and Sailors' Association work in the Borough was taken over by a newly formed " Croydon Borough Division " of the Association, the Mayor (Alderman Denning) being its President, and Sir Frederick Edridge its Vice-President, the Town Clerk (Dr. Newnham) its Honorary Secretary and Honorary Solicitor, and the Borough Treasurer (Mr. Gunner) its Honorary Treasurer. And at the same time the whole of the (Borough) Association was moved from Poplar Walk to the Town Hall, and Ward Committees were set up in each Ward, with the proper machinery of chairmen, secretaries, etc., for the discovery and investigation of cases needing assistance. In this way the organisations and power of the Town Hall authorities could be fully applied to the work, which was immediately set on foot, the Mayor devoting himself to it with all his well-known vigour. With the Town Clerk were associated Miss May Donaldson and Mr. Francis Allen (now Mr. Councillor Allen, M.B.E.) as acting Secretaries. After a time Miss Donaldson retired and the enormous amount of daily work was shouldered by Mr. Francis Allen, with whom Sir Frederick Edridge was ever in co-operation. The original Croydon Branch of the Soldiers' and Sailors' Families Association (rural area) still continued its beneficial work with Mr. William Ashcroft as its Honorary Secretary.

The "Croydon Borough Division of the Soldiers' and Sailors' Families Association" (as its official title ran) worked in close co-operation with the "Mayor's Committee for the prevention and relief of distress arising out of the war," and in fact was run almost as a special division of the Mayor's Committee. The funds which became immediately necessary in considerable amounts for this and other forms of War distress, were provided through the Prince of Wales's Fund; a little later on they were drawn from the Statutory Committee presently to be described; and finally they were provided by the Ministry of Pensions when that Ministry was set up in 1916; and remittances for treatment of disabled men, &c , are still (January, 1920) provided by that Ministry, and continue to require as much as £10,000 a month.

We have indicated the organisation for 1914 and 1915. But during 1915 the Naval and Military Pensions Act made certain provisions relating " to pensions, grants and allowances made in respect of the present war," and the care of officers and men disabled in consequence of the war; that is, it proceeded to take over the work of the two societies already named. It went on to order the Royal Patriotic Fund Corporation to set up a Statutory Committee to administer the Act, and the Government of the day financed this Statutory Committee with a million pounds, the Prince of Wales becoming its Chairman. An early movement of this body was on 21st February, 1916, to instruct the new Mayor of Croydon (Alderman Houlder) to form at once a "War Pensions Committee," which was done, and which took up its work on 15th May, 1916. The plan followed under the Mayor's Committee, and now agreed still to be continued, was to refer the cases, which were pouring in, to their own Wards for investigation. As has already been stated, Ward Committees had been set up for this purpose at the beginning of the war, and many of the principal inhabitants of Croydon were members of such Committees. The Ward

Secretaries, after investigation, applied to the Town Hall for the necessary grants in approved cases, and prompt relief was forthcoming. It is difficult, when all worked so hard and for so long a time, to give names without running the risk of leaving out the names of others equally deserving of mention; but the Editor has had the following list given him, by fellow-workers on the War Pensions Committee, of those who, amongst others, devoted much time to this service, both during the first two years of the war under the Mayor's Committee and subsequently, in many cases in similar capacities, under the War Pensions Committee itself: Aldermen Allen, Betteridge, King, Lillico, and Trumble; Councillors Allen, Heath Clark, Camden Field, Muggeridge, Peet, Stubbs, and Thomson; Canon White-Thomson; Major Hubbard; Messrs R. Andress, W. Ashcroft, J. R. Browning, F. H. Carey, Bryan Harland, Henry Lee, L. A. Marshall, and F. Theobalds; Mesdames Brain, Hetley, de Layen, Douglas Moore, Nealon, Newnham, and Squire; Sister Olive; and the Misses Benbow, Berney, Collyer, Donaldson, Wilson, and Duncan. It must be understood that these are only a few of the names of the more devoted workers, as supplied by their appreciative colleagues.

The success of the whole organisation, which was very great, in preventing distress, and in coping with it when it had in some cases already arisen without the knowledge of the Committee, and in administering to the comfort of the families whose bread-winners were serving their country, was largely due to the quiet, patient and incessant work of these Ward Committees and their helpers.

And we must not forget also to add an expression of our sense of the willing labours of the Medical Officer of Health (Dr. R. Veitch Clark) and his staff; the Tuberculosis Officer, (Dr. Agnes Bernfeld), the Inspectors of Licences (Mr. Harry Sidey, formerly a Councillor, and Mr. H. Jenkins, formerly Chief Inspector of Police at Croydon), who did an immense amount of valuable work as investigators of special cases; and Mr. A. E. Welstead of the Town Clerk's Office, who was really the Town Clerk's private secretary through these trying years, and whose activity, willingness and courtesy every one connected with the work gratefully acknowledged. The staff in the office of the Borough Accountant (Mr. McCall), beyond Messrs. Sidey and Jenkins above-mentioned, also need a word of thanks, if only because their labours are known to so very few. In November, 1918, all the Civil-liabilities grants were transferred from the Post Offices to the Borough Accountant's Office, and at the same time the system of payment of rent-grants to the landlords against the vouchers previously issued to the tenants

WAR PENSIONS COMMITTEE

by the Committee, was stopped. This involved payment to each one of a very large number of tenants, instead of to a comparatively few landlords, or landlords' agents. When about 3,000 persons arrived, on the first pay-day under the new system, consternation reigned ; and arrangements were swiftly made to divide this large transaction amongst the separate Wards by means of pay-stations. Even then the counting out and preparation of so large a number of money-parcels kept a large staff many extra hours at work every month, and this was voluntary labour, cheerfully undertaken. The arrangements for distribution at the pay-stations kept twelve members of the staff at work for three days every month. As with the counting of the money on Flag Days, referred to elsewhere, these many hours of unpaid extra service on the part of the Borough Accountant's Staff call for our grateful recognition.

Beside the two parent Soldiers' and Sailors' Associations, who continued the chief administration of the work in their Town Hall guise as described above, many other public bodies had representatives upon the War Pensions Committee, such as the Territorial Force Association for Surrey, the Croydon Chamber of Commerce, the Croydon Trades and Labour Council and the Women's Co-Operative Guild, with the addition of certain prominent citizens ; so that every organisation was in touch with the War Pensions Committee that had any claim so to be.

From first to last the Croydon Borough Division of the Soldiers' and Sailors' Families Association received £13,133, out of which a balance of £91 remained at 30th June, 1919, and this was paid over to the Association. Our division of the Soldiers' and Sailors' Help Society received £639, and had in hand at the close a balance of £7, which was paid over to the parent Society.

A Sub-Committee dealing with both branches of the work sat weekly at the Town Hall, its chairman being at first Alderman Sir Frederick Edridge, and afterwards Mr. Alderman Trumble ; and under its authority the actual day-to-day labour was undertaken by a special executive sub-committee, an exceptionally hardworking body. This daily executive varied a little as time went on, but the more permanent of its members were Councillor Francis Allen, Miss E. Berney, Miss Mary Collyer, and Mrs. Newnham.

All allowances were at the discretion of the War Pensions Committee, whether the Government or the Committee provided the money for them ; and they could be withdrawn in cases of misconduct. Exceedingly few of such cases arose. As examples of the work of the Committee may be mentioned : Advances made to wives until their separation allowance arrived, and similar advances to dependents ; grants towards rent ; additional grants, usually of 2/6 per week, to wives unable for valid reasons to work ; and grants to widowed mothers and their children or other dependents, to sisters of a soldier at the front who were looking after his motherless children, etc. These allowances were of course exclusive of the regulation separation allowances, grants to motherless children, etc. In the emergency of sickness 5/- extra per week was allowed, and if the illness resulted in death a funeral grant of £4 (or for children £2) was given, so that such charges might be prevented from falling upon the poor-rate. Further, if a child of a soldier had been admitted to any institution, an outfit was provided up to a cost of £2. In placing such children the late Miss Nash (Lady Probation Officer to the Magistrates) was at once invaluable and indefatigable. War-widows awaiting their pensions received advances, and the Committee also defrayed urgent or necessary expenses resulting from the death of their husband, such as removal of the home, illness from shock, etc., up to £3. As for disabled men, they received an allowance until the Government allowance arrived ; and partly disabled men received a temporary allowance while under training for such work as they could attempt, or while in a convalescent home, to make up for the loss of earnings they would have gained had they not been disabled ; and when trained and waiting for an artificial limb, or for tools, or for a chance of employment, such men received appropriate grants up to a limit of £5.

Eventually, in November, 1916, the War Pensions Committee in conjunction with the Labour Exchange issued a labour-scheme, so well planned, thanks to the energy and ability of the Town Clerk, that it was circulated widely by the Employment Department of the Board of Trade as a model of what such a scheme should be. Other efforts were constantly made to help our war-worn defenders to make a fresh start in life. The Tramways Committee gave the convalescents free rides daily in the less crowded hours of the day ; and for many months the children and other dependents of men on service were medically treated without charge. When this last privilege was disallowed by the Government the Committee arranged for all such persons to be treated at the Croydon Dispensary, and contrived to pay their fees for them.

In February, 1918, at the suggestion of the Ministry of Pensions, two disabled discharged soldiers and one war-widow were added to the Committee ; these were ex-Sergeant Major Hill, ex-Sergeant Osmond, and Mrs. Cosedge, the widow of the late Councillor Cosedge.

WAR PENSIONS COMMITTEE

A special Croydon Committee was formed to assist discharged, and especially disabled, men to become fit for work and to find work for them, and the Town Clerk and Mr. Councillor Stubbs were sent as Croydon delegates to advise a similar Committee formed by the Counties of Surrey, Kent and Sussex. Classes in commercial subjects, in electrical engineering, and other suitable subjects were established for the benefit of these men by the Croydon Education Committee. The Minister of Pensions appointed Doctors Newby, Redfern and Willock Medical Referees for the examination and certification of disabled men ; and these Doctors with the addition of Doctors Genge and Veitch Clark were also made members of the " Disablement Sub-Committee," a new name for the " Discharged Soldiers Sub-Committee."

The Borough Accountant has with great courtesy prepared a general statement for this book of the expenditure of the War Pensions Committee (using this term to cover all the changes of designation of the same work done by the same people) for the years 1917, 1918 and 1919. And as regards the Administrative Expenses of the Committee (which in the year 1919, for example, amounted to over £2,500) it may be said that they were borne on the Corporation Accounts, but by a provision of 1917 the Corporation afterwards received from the Government two-thirds of this expenditure.

	1917.	1918.	1919.	Number of cases in 1919 only.
	£ s. d.	£ s. d.	£ s. d.	
Advances	2,246 6 9	2,243 3 10	6,161 3 4	1,298
Separation Allowances	14,981 4 3	22,628 15 10	23,965 3 3	7,000
Temporary Grants	344 17 1	9 18 6	— — —	—
Emergency Grants	1,467 7 7	2,159 12 8	1,924 18 1	1,061
Gratuities	243 15 4	750 14 8	— — —	—
Royal Warrant Orders, etc.	433 2 7	14,116 18 5	69,109 15 3	4,596
	19,716 13 7	41,909 3 11	101,160 19 11	13,955

It will be observed how rapidly the distress increased as the war went on. In 1917 relief to about £20,000 was needed, but this was doubled in 1918, and quintupled in 1919 ! Better administration soon wiped out the temporary grants and emergency gratuities needed in the first years of the war, but the emergency grants (mostly in respect of rent) always remained a substantial sum. There were 3,000 wives and dependents in receipt of weekly rent allowances on 31st December, 1918, their total weekly drawings being £770. In the whole of 1919, 1,061 persons received emergency grants of every kind, funerals (£209), assistance to disabled men (£400) and other allowances.

The payments under Royal Warrant are observed to grow rapidly, because these include treatment of disabled men, £51,012 in 1919, their training for employment, £9,456, and pensions to widows of soldiers dying after their discharge £1,674.

As the war progressed, more and more men were disabled, and the need for their treatment and training grew very rapidly, as the table shows. Other divisions had to be formed, until, as the War Pensions Committee reported to the Council on 28th October, 1918, there were already at that time 23 separate branches of the Ministry of Pensions, each dealing with a distinct sphere of work, and this number continued to increase!

Much of this vast amount of voluntary work was brought to an end by the Ministry of Pensions in August, 1919, taking a house at Katharine Street and carrying on the main administration with a paid official staff. The War Pensions Committee still, however, exists; its Disablements Sub-Committee meets weekly, and other Sub-Committees at wider intervals. The work tends more and more to become centralised. The Soldiers' and Sailors' Families Association, and the Soldiers' and Sailors' Help Society found congenial new quarters under the wing of the Croydon Civic Service League, which now undertakes the whole administration of their Croydon Borough Division.

Of all the chapters in this book the present one is perhaps that which has given the Editor the greatest pleasure to prepare, in spite of its complexity; for it deals with the Borough's genuine endeavour to make the best return it could, however inadequate that return may appear, for the sacrifices of those brave men who laid down their lives for us and ours in the great war, and of those who at the price of their own disablement maintained us and ours unharmed. At the time of writing this, a further expression of the Borough's gratitude is on its way to fulfilment, a monument or cenotaph in front of the Town Hall to the memory of those who fell; and indeed, this book is itself such a monument of another kind, perpetuating their very names in its Roll of Honour. But also it has been with pride that this record has been written of matters known very little beyond the Committee itself, a narrative of strenuous, long continued and unwearied efforts on the part of so many of our fellow citizens to carry into effect these poor expressions of our gratitude through the medium of the War Pensions Committee.

VI. The Mayoress's Needlework Committee.

(Queen Mary's Needlework Guild)

Simultaneously with the establishment of the "Mayor's Committee for the prevention and relief, etc.," in August, 1914, the Mayoress, Mrs. Denning, called together an Advisory Committee, and organized subsidiary Ward Committees, in connection with Queen Mary's Needlework Guild. These Needlework Committees were to be considered as sub-committees of the Ward Committees under the Mayor's scheme; but in reality they were independent in their action, and were highly industrious and useful bodies, providing a very large quantity of garments for the public need. All garments were sent to the Town Hall, and day after day the Mayoress and Lady Edridge and others were examining and classifying them, their willing helpers distributing certain garments for relief in Croydon according to the grants made by the Central Committee, and in these local relief cases the garments were stamped with the initials of the Mayoress's Committee to secure them against being sold or pawned. Many wives and families were of course left in some distress in Croydon by the going away to the war of the husband and bread winner. Queen Mary, in her practical way, sent a caution to the Mayoress (and other ladies in similar positions) warning them that care should be taken not to injure the employment of sempstresses and others, and also that only such garments should be made for soldiers and sailors as the War Office and Admiralty would be unlikely to buy, a list of Government issues being appended to the circular as things to be avoided. "All kinds of garments will be needed for distribution in the winter," the Queen's circular concluded, "if there is exceptional distress." Obediently to the Queen's command, sempstresses in need of work were commissioned to make garments by their Ward Committees and were given material and paid for their work at the cost of the Central Committee, but most of the work was from first to last unpaid.

The old Minute-book makes an interesting reading, and gives fragmentary peeps into this strenuous time. Mayoress Denning reports to her Advisory Committee one day (24th September) that she has about £40 in hand, and it is agreed to buy socks for the Croydon Territorials with it ; but she points out that more shirts still are needed for the Fourth Queen's. Yet at the same time she is authorised to send 100 shirts to the Y.M.C.A. depots at Newhaven and Shorncliffe, with socks to match. Someone sends her a bale of cloth, someone else offers to get it made into boys' suits in London at her own expense. On 12th October, 1914, we find her reporting that she has received over 13,500 garments and other articles, and has distributed (under proper precautions) 11,595 ; not bad work for two months. And at the same time she reports that every man in the Fourth Queen's and the S.E. Mounted Brigade Transport and Supply Column has now a good flannel shirt, socks, and a blanket ; and that large numbers of these and other stores have been sent to Army stations and to the Red Cross and St. John Ambulance Societies. Then in December Mayoress Denning tells her committee how a letter of hers in the Croydon Press has brought her 1,541 Christmas puddings for the troops at the front, and how the Croydon and District War Supplies Clearing House has been of great assistance to her in collecting and despatching this gift.

On 3rd March Mayoress Denning reports to her Committee that a Military Hospital is to be established in Croydon, and that forthwith they must set to work on 2,000 bed jackets, 2,000 nightshirts, 2,000 draw-sheets, 500 pillow-slips, as well as bed socks, handkerchiefs, hot water bottle covers, etc., etc., and (typical of her worship's warm heart) a warm shirt for every man when his turn came to be discharged from the Hospital. Promptly orders were sent to the Ward Committees, dividing out the work amongst them ; and suggestions that " Comforts-funds " for the sufferers should be started. The Wards responded nobly with 15,000 garments and the Matron of the Military Hospital found herself well supplied by the time her 1,000 wounded arrived. About this time it was found possible to cease the distribution of clothing to military, naval and civilian cases in the Borough ; and that was opportune, for the Matron of the Military Hospital, not content with her 15,000 garments, found she needed 200 dressing gowns, 100 pyjamas, 60 screen covers, and more day shirts. At the same time Col. Watney wanted 500 more respirators. So the 100 pyjamas were struck out as luxuries in favour of the so necessary soldiers' respirators. Col. Watney was just taking out the 2/4th Queen's to Gallipoli, and besides the respirators he desired 1,000 pairs of socks. Says the Mayoress on 8th July, 1915, " I have sent him the whole of the stock I had in hand and all I have been able to get at short notice —altogether some 800 pairs "—which was a fine response. She goes on to add " There is a constant demand for extra socks for men on active service and for men in training, and I shall always

MAYORESS'S NEEDLEWORK COMMITTEE

be glad to receive and send to the regiments requiring them as many socks as possible." She notes that her total of garments up to date is 27,000 for the eleven months of the War !

Then comes the Hospital Matron again in early October with a requisition for scarves, woollen gloves, Cardigan jackets, and coloured blankets ; and the harassed Mayoress puts aside an appeal for comforts made by Queen Mary (as winter is now drawing on) in order to make a desperate attempt to satisfy the exigeant Matron. Presently Col. Deane (Commandant of the War Hospitals) applies in December for the assistance of ladies in hospital service and in the recreation rooms, and the Mayoress forms a rota for each hospital. The work of these ladies is briefly recorded in the chapter on the Medical and Hospital Services. As 20 ladies were present at the committee when this matter was so efficiently organised, the Mayoress had the happy idea to bind them all to send 12 mince pies each to the hospitals for Christmas ; but many more than 240 were actually contributed.

In February, 1916, the Mayor (Ald. Frank Denning) died suddenly, and Mrs. Denning ceased to be Mayoress ; and the (Needlework) Mayoress's Committee, which she had conducted so efficiently and which had provided so generously for the needs of the soldiers and sailors, the hospitals and the poor, as far as clothing was concerned now came to an end. The Council recorded " their sincere appreciation of her devoted work for so many months," and to Lady Edridge also was given, as the last act of the Mayoress's Committee, a hearty vote of thanks for her great and long-continued assistance in collecting and sorting the garments given to the Fund. And though Mayoress Denning did not long survive her husband, her memory is yet with us, as that of one who gave her whole energy to the fulfilment of her high office, and these notes on her especial committee show how well she accomplished her work, and with what affectionate and loyal support she was assisted by the ladies of the Borough. It has been Croydon's great good fortune to have capable Mayoresses, but none have had quite such strenuous times thrust upon them as Mrs. Denning and her admirable successor Mrs. Houlder. Many garments still remained when the Needlework Fund was closed, and these were distributed, as suitable occasions presented themselves, by the new Mayoress. The Mayoress's War Fund Committee established by Mayoress Houlder in 1916 is the subject of the following chapter.

VII. Mayoress's War Fund Committee

This committee was formed by the Mayoress (Mrs. Houlder) in May, 1916, to aid the District Association of Voluntary Organisations, and to provide comforts and clothing for sailors and soldiers and their wives and families, and for the relief of prisoners of war and like objects.

Funds were raised by subscriptions, by a Flag Day, and by the collection and sale of waste paper, etc. The total amount raised and distributed was £3,527 5s. 8d.

As examples of the way in which the funds were distributed we may mention a few characteristic items : " Daily Telegraph " Christmas Pudding Fund (1916), £187 17s. 1d.; Prisoners of War Fund, £135 19s. 4d.; Grants to Voluntary Working Organisations, £137 1s. 7d.; Road Construction Battalion in France, £26 5s. 0d.; Hospital Supply Depot, £50 0s. 0d.; Serbian Help Society, £100 0s. 0d.; Fourth Queen's Funds, £50 0s. 0d.; Grants to Croydon District Association of Voluntary Organisations, £1,221 3s. 3d., etc.

The balance (£160) was paid to the Croydon Borough Division of the Soldiers' and Sailors' Families Association and the Croydon Borough Division of the Soldiers' and Sailors' Help society in equal amounts of £173 10s. 0d. each, and the remainder (£263 10s. 0d.) went towards paying the cost of the maintenance and training, in the Croydon Training-home for Young Servants, Morland Road, of six daughters of men who had served in the Navy or Army or Air-force during the war.

VIII. Mayoress's Flag Day Committee

The Mayoress's Flag Day Committee was founded by Mrs. Denning (Mayoress from the outbreak of War in 1914, to February, 1916), and was continued by Mrs. Houlder, who succeeded her as Mayoress. Between December, 1914, and June, 1919, the Committee organised twenty-eight Flag Days—including five Alexandra-Rose-Day Collections and one special collection for the Surrey Prisoners of War Fund—amounting in the aggregate to £18,160 9s. 0d., and benefiting over sixty societies and organisations.

The following ladies constituted the later committee, covering the greater part of the period from February, 1916, onwards ; that is, after the lamented death of Mayor Denning : the Mayoress (Mrs. Howard Houlder), Lady Edridge, Miss Betteridge, Mrs. Douglas, Mrs. Feaver, Mrs. Hetley, Mrs. Lillico, Mrs. Martin, Mrs. Newnham, Mrs. Redfern, Councillor Mrs. Roberts, Mrs. Rogers, Mrs. Stapleton, Mrs. Trumble (ex-Mayoress), Mrs. Warren, Mrs. Welman, Mrs. Wright ; and they were assisted by 450 collectors who sold emblems in the streets, whatever the weather might be. In fine weather perhaps it was not so very trying, but in cold wintry weather a certain heroic endurance had to be summoned forth.

The details are so interesting that we have considered it advisable to give the entire list of the twenty-nine appeals with their results, as audited by the Borough Accountant, Mr. J. H. McCall. This seems a fitting opportunity to recognise the enormous amount of work thrown upon the Borough Treasurer (Mr. W. Gunner) and subsequently on the Borough Accountant and their staff (amongst whom Mr. Harland rendered special assistance) in connection with these numerous funds, with their many unavoidable complexities, all of it being cheerfully undertaken and most successfully carried out. We should also acknowledge the valuable assistance rendered by the Manager of the Union Bank (Mr. Worman) and his staff, particularly by Mr. Roffey ; and the valuable help rendered by the Assistant Town Clerk, Mr. Samuel Jacobs.

	Amount collected.
1914. (Mrs. Denning).	£ s. d.
Dec. 19—Belgian Flag-Day	394 9 5
1915.	
June 23—Alexandra-Rose-Day	550 18 3
Oct. 16—Serbian Flag-Day	480 5 11
Nov. 18—Russian Flag-Day	430 10 10
Dec. 18—Belgian Flag-Day	328 3 6
1916.	
Jan. 20—" Our Day " (Red Cross Flag-Day) .. (Mrs. Houlder).	475 1 5
Mar. 17—Irish Soldiers'-Day	311 2 6
May 13—Mayoress's Flag-Day	444 8 5
June 21—Alexandra-Rose-Day	577 6 6
July 14—French Flag-Day	640 8 7
Sep. 30—Russian Flag-Day	454 4 2
Oct. 19—" Our Day " (Red Cross Flag-Day) ..	738 18 5
Nov. 18—Kitchener Day (Roll of Honour) . ..	208 4 10
1917.	
Mar. 1—Welsh Flag-Day	298 18 11
May 9—R.S.P.C.A. (Wounded Horses)	238 4 8
June 20—Alexandra-Rose-Day	417 7 10
July 6—" Silent Tribute Day " (Lord Roberts Memorial Workshops)	276 10 8
July 14—French Flag-Day	351 14 6
Aug. 1—Lord Roberts Memorial Fund	414 0 0
Oct. 18—" Our Day " (British Red Cross Flag-Day)	697 9 10
Dec. 1—Life-Boat-Day	283 12 5
1918.	
Mar. 22—" Y.W.C.A." (Women's Day)	334 2 5
May 11—Surrey Prisoners of War Fund	706 10 3
May 11—Do. Special Collection	5003 15 6
June 4—Church Army Hut Day	324 12 10
June 19—Alexandra-Rose-Day	539 17 10
July 12—French Flag-Day	366 12 1
Oct. 24—" Our Day " (British Red Cross Flag Day)	1269 5 5
1919.	
May 15—Lord Roberts Memorial Workshop Fund	129 17 1
June 26—Alexandra-Rose-Day	491 14 0
	£18,160 9 0

IX. Belgian Refugees Fund
(Croydon War Refugees Committee)

In the Autumn of 1914 the then Mayor—the late Mr. Alderman Frank Denning—opened a fund to be used for the benefit of Belgian Refugees who were at that time arriving in Croydon (August, 1914). Many private houses ("hostels") were at once generously devoted to their reception; whilst other refugees were cared for by a small self-appointed committee which took the name of the "Belgian Refugees Committee." Between 800 and 900 Belgians found shelter in the Borough during the earlier months of the Great War.

As soon as possible a representative committee covering the whole Borough was formed, and took the name of the Croydon War Refugees Committee (to distinguish it from the small "Belgian Refugees Committee" above referred to), Mr. Alderman H. Keatley Moore being Chairman, Miss Scarff, Hon. Secretary, and Mr. Bryan Harland, Hon. Treasurer. Two sub-committees dealing with questions of housing, and of furniture and clothing, were appointed; their Secretaries being Miss Rhoda Brodie, M.B.E., and Mrs. Douglas, respectively; and through the excellent work of these ladies and their many helpers, comparative comfort and adequate housing were assured to many Belgians during their term of exile. During the whole time of the activity of the Croydon War Refugees Committee it was generously granted the use of the offices of the Croydon Guild of Help, and in many other ways was assisted by that Guild.

Grants were made to refugees from the Mayor's Fund, through the Borough War Refugees Committee, and also through the "Belgian Refugees Committee"; and the managers of the hostels, a number of which had been opened in various parts of the town, were also helped, through the War Refugees Committee, to carry on their beneficent work. The generosity of owners of empty houses, who lent them to be used as hostels, in most cases rent-free, deserves recognition. Furniture and clothing were contributed in considerable quantities, and their distribution was made possible through the kindness of Alderman Major Fox, T.D., who lent his large hall in Park Street to be used as a store. A quantity of meat, sent weekly from the central War-refugees association, was distributed to refugees by the friendly aid of Miss West, North End, who kindly also organised the cutting-up and weighing. The costs of administration were chiefly met by the Mayor's Fund ; at the same time it must be added that other sums, of which we have been unable to learn the details or even the gross amount, were locally raised by the " Belgian Refugees Committee " above named, and by many of the local managers of numerous hostels, especially those at Thornton Heath and South Norwood. Schools opened their doors to Belgian pupils at reduced fees, or, in necessitous cases, without any fees at all ; medical and dental practitioners placed their services gratuitously at the disposal of the refugees ; and other similar kind offices were rendered to them on all sides.

The Belgians themselves were not slow to recognise the fact that they were very well cared for in our town ; and it is gratifying to find, in many a letter received since their return to Belgium, the wish expressed that they " might be in Croydon once again."

One of the most serious problems that had to be faced in connection with the Belgian Refugees was the question of their employment. In many towns workshops were opened where various articles, such as saddlery for Service use, furniture, etc., might be manufactured. The Belgian Government undertook to supply raw material and tools, if the other organisation could be undertaken locally. Such an employment scheme was explained to Croydon at a meeting at the Town Hall in March, 1915, by Sir Ernest Hatch and Count Goblet d'Alviella, and a committee to deal with the employment of Belgian refugees in Croydon was appointed, with the Mayor (the late Mr. Alderman Denning) as Chairman, and the Town Clerk (Dr. Newnham) and Mrs. Redfern as Hon. Secretaries. A workshop was opened in premises belonging to the Corporation in High Street ; various builders kindly lent carpenters' benches, and wood and tools were sent by the Belgian Government. In this little workshop about a dozen Belgians were employed for a year in making excellent household furniture, under the able supervision of Mr. Maylam, of George Street, who gave much valuable time and attention to the work. The furniture was ultimately shipped to the Headquarters of the Belgian Government at Havre. As all these Belgian workmen were receiving hospitality in hostels, they were only paid a small weekly sum by way of pocket money—the Mayor's Fund providing this payment.

Similarly several Belgian women were employed in the making of plain garments for women and children, under the auspices of Queen Mary's Needlework Guild, at the Adult School Hall, Park Lane. Miss Allport kindly superintended this work and arranged for the Belgians to join the meals of the

Croydon workers. Altogether some 350 useful garments were made, these also being sent to Havre for the use of Belgian refugees in France.

Gradually, as enlistment proceeded and Croydon was drained of its workmen by the Army, general work became available, and Belgians were absorbed into various occupations, many of them being placed through the direct instrumentality of the Employment Committee; till finally, when conscription became law, every Belgian who had not already been enrolled in the ranks of the army of his own country, easily found work; and the Employment Committee came automatically to an end.

The Croydon War Refugees Committee, in case any emergency should arise, remained in being, though its work in the last years of the war gradually decreased to a minimum, until 11th April, 1919, when it held its last meeting and was formally dissolved.

The Committee, with the approval of the Charity Commissioners, paid the balance to Cardinal Mercier's Fund for Destitute Belgians.

The Belgian Refugees Fund received in the aggregate £1,147 14s. 6d., of which £722 was provided by the proceeds of the two December Flag-Days in 1914 and 1915, £44 was collected by some of the churches in the borough, and £27 by the schools.

X. Sailors' and Soldiers' Recreation Rooms

In September, 1915, Miss Edith Carr and Miss Kathleen Taylor, as a personal enterprise of their own, opened rooms at 42, High-street, Croydon, for the benefit of soldiers billeted in the town and the men in the six large military hospitals. The rooms were from the first well patronised, and the numbers steadily increased until towards the end fully 5,000 men came in each week in winter.

From ten in the morning till half-past nine at night, light refreshments were served at a very cheap rate (2 cups of tea, coffee or cocoa for 1d., cake 1d., eggs at cost price, and so on). Large quantities of stewed fruit and custard also were consumed. Although everything was so cheap the work was practically self-supporting after the initial expense. No cards were allowed, but billiards, chess and draughts were all free, and there was always plenty of music. The men always seemed thoroughly happy, and often said what a great boon the place was to them. They came not only for food, but stayed on to rest and read and write—notepaper being provided free.

Sunday was usually an especially happy and busy day. At 5.15 p.m. there was a service taken by Miss Taylor, which was always well attended ; and later in the evening, before prayers at nine o'clock, hymns with an occasional sacred solo were sung for nearly an hour, the men choosing what they wished. There was also a short service on Friday evenings, and prayers every evening at 8.45. The men were most responsive to these services, and many have written grateful letters saying how they had been blessed and helped.

The daily work was arranged in two shifts, seven helpers in each. All the help was voluntary. About 180 ladies took part during the $3\frac{3}{4}$ years, three of whom, Miss Cutler, Miss Kathleen Humble and Miss May Taylor were regular helpers the whole time. During the last two years Miss Wightman and Miss Marshall rendered excellent service.

At the closing of the room the helpers gave some handsome silver presents to Miss Carr and Miss Taylor to show their appreciation.

SERVICES RECREATION ROOMS

The weekly takings were for some time about £50, but for several weeks over £80 was taken, the highest being £91 10s. in one week. No public subscription was raised, but during the time the rooms were opened friends subscribed £120. After all accounts were settled £22 of the surplus money was given to Reedham Orphanage, Purley, and the remaining balance (£32) was used for sending working women and others for short much-needed holidays. The rooms were closed on Sunday, 1st June, 1919.

"Popular Canteen" for Sailors and Soldiers, High Street, South Norwood

It was in November, 1916, that the Military Authorities decided to billet soldiers in vacant premises in South Norwood. The Vicar, the Rev. John Warner, invited representatives from the Established and Free Churches in the district to join him in inaugurating a place of recreation and refreshment for the soldiers. It was felt that such an institution was absolutely necessary for the well-being of the men. Fifty pounds was subscribed to finance the undertaking, premises in High Street, South Norwood, were secured, and the Canteen opened its doors on 4th December, 1916.

The General Committee consisted of the Minister and two members of each congregation. Miss A. F. Carter was Lady Superintendent (afterwards assisted by Miss F. Verner), Mrs. Long was Secretary, Mrs. Sumpter, Assistant Secretary, and Mr. W. F. Castle, Hon. Treasurer. In September, 1917, Mr. E. P. Jones took over the arduous duties of Mrs. Long and Miss Sumpter, and worked till the close. The following ladies took charge of the cooking arrangements: Mrs. Trezise, Miss Emblem, Mrs. Leggett, Mrs. Stringer, Miss Gattrell, Miss Morton, Miss Wildish, Mrs. Groves, Mrs. Nickerson and Mrs. Godsmark. Each of these ladies was assisted by a willing band of about a dozen helpers each evening, comprising both ladies and gentlemen, so that in all there were over one hundred workers. The canteen was greatly appreciated as the numerous letters since received from all parts of the globe help to prove. The following gentlemen on their respective evenings assisted in the amusement of the men: Rev. W. Trezise (who had been Mayor Denning's Chaplain), Messrs. Groves, Bailey, Moore, Albert Nickerson, Tennent, Robinson, Leggett, Baumer, Davis, Hacker, Jones and Vale. A special word is due to Mr. Vale, who was in attendance at the door for three nights every week for 2½ years, from 5 to 9.30 p.m.

Three billiard tables and other games were provided for the entertainment of the men, and rooms for reading and writing.

There was also a bath-room, the use of which was a great boon, as proved by its often being booked up several nights beforehand.

During the winter months a concert was held every Monday evening. Amongst the concert givers were Mr. and Mrs. Edward A. Martin, Mr. Back, " The 'Owlers Concert Party," and the A1 Pierrot Troupe. Whist drives were held once a month, the helpers kindly providing the prizes.

Miss A. F. Carter, the Lady Superintendent, catered for the men most admirably, notwithstanding the stress of short rations. The average attendance was 250 men nightly, and the amount of work entailed will be evidenced by the fact that about 200,000 meals were served, which produced, in small amounts, the gross total of £3,600 during the period of 2½ years that the canteen remained open.

The canteen closed on 7th March, 1919, with a Whist Drive, and free refreshments were on this occasion served to all the men as a parting send-off.

The Canteen was registered as a charity, and the balance at the wind-up (£525) was allocated as follows :—

	£	s.	d.
Waifs & Strays Society, South Norwood .	25	0	0
St. Dunstan's Home for Blinded Soldiers	150	0	0
Croydon General Hospital	150	0	0
National Children's Home & Orphanage..	200	0	0

The above donations to be used exclusively for the benefit of disabled sailors, soldiers, or their dependents, or for the benefit of dependents of deceased sailors or soldiers.

Canteen Clubs

In the autumn of 1916 two Canteen Clubs in connexion with All Saints' Church, Upper Norwood, were opened at the instigation of Miss Cutler, for the use of the men of the R.A.S.C., and other units, which had been billeted in large numbers at about this time in Church Road, Auckland Road, South Norwood Hill, and elsewhere in the district. Numerous members of the congregation were responsible for running these, amongst whom may be specially mentioned Mr. Skyrme, Mrs. Aste, and Mrs. Cartwright, who undertook the difficult task of catering. The men showed their deep appreciation of the trouble taken on their behalf by presenting the Parish with a framed address and photograph, which has been placed on the wall in the porch of All Saints' Church as a souvenir of the Great War.

SERVICES RECREATION ROOMS

Mrs. Sutherland Gill with an influential Committee opened a Canteen Club in St. John's Hall, Sylvan Road, on the arrival of the R.A.S.C. in Upper Norwood. She was at once surrounded by ready helpers. Those men who required a quiet room in which to read and write much enjoyed the opportunity afforded them. A liberal supply of refreshments was provided, for which the men paid a nominal sum, writing materials were given, and cigarettes and even matches could be obtained without difficulty. The large number of men who visited the Club daily proved the success of the undertaking.

Other canteens and recreation rooms which did similar excellent work were established in other parts of Upper Norwood, as that at St. Aubyn's Hall, and that conducted by the National Union of Women Workers Club under the name of the Comrades Club, at Westow Street, Upper Norwood, where a specially large amount of work was done amongst the men of the Navy, R.N.V.R., etc., stationed at what will long be known as H.M.S. Crystal Palace.

In addition, at each of the Croydon Public Libraries special writing tables with writing materials were provided, which were in continuous use, and special arrangements were made whereby men in hospital or billeted in the town could borrow books without any intervening " red tape."

XI. Croydon Local Central War Savings Committee

This Committee was formed in March, 1916, at the invitation of the National War Savings Committee (set up in the preceding month by the Chancellor of the Exchequer) under the presidency of the Mayor and Mayoress (Mr. and Mrs. Houlder); Mr. Councillor Stevenson being Chairman, and Mr. Councillor C. Heath Clark (Mayor in 1919) Vice-Chairman. The Town Clerk was Chairman of the Organising Committee, the Borough Treasurer and Borough Accountant were Honorary Treasurers, Mr. Councillor Peet and Mr. Baster, Honorary Auditors, and Mrs. Colchester, M.B.E., Honorary Secretary.

The Committee's aim was the formation of Associations for War Saving ; and as a result of a vigorous propaganda, no less than 101 such Associations, with a gross membership of about 8,500, were in operation within six months. Subsidiary committees were formed in connection with the various " weeks " and other special efforts, including Food Economy, War Loan of 1917, War Bonds Campaigns, Victory Loan Campaign, etc.; and 118 of the leading ladies and gentlemen of Croydon served upon them.

The following remarkable money-results, amongst others, were obtained :—

Tank Day (16th March, 1917) realised	£462,170
" Vindictive " Week (July, 1918) ,,	£323,658
Gun Week (October, 1918) ,,	£319,595
Victory Loan (July, 1919) ,,	£908,087

Tank-Day.—As a " business-man's week " (March 4th to 9th inclusive, 1917) was arranged in the War Savings Campaign throughout greater London, by the National Committee, and as the visit of a Tank had been promised, the Croydon Committee resolved to combine the two efforts, with the gratifying result shown above ; the strenuous fortnight's work culminating on 16th March, when the Tank duly arrived and took up its position outside the Town Hall, and was busy all day stamping war bonds and war savings certificates for eager purchasers. Letters in the press, pictures on the Cinemas, speeches in the open air, posters on the trams, banners stretched across the streets, all means were utilised in a united effort at publicity. On the day

CENTRAL WAR SAVING COMMITTEE

itself relays of bands performed continuously. One picturesque feature was a march of all the work-people from Gillett and Johnston's factory (transferred from peaceful clock-making to the production of war-appliances), when Lieut. Cyril Johnston handed in at the Town Hall their collective Tank-contribution of £5,500. Other large engineering works collected handsome sums. And it was very remarkable to many of us, familiar with the stately ways of the " Old Lady of Threadneedle Street," to find a duly accredited temporary branch of the Bank of England installed at the Town Hall in our Rate Office, issuing bonds and certificates against money, and relays of clerks from the Post Office issuing War Bonds and War Savings Certificates along the corridors. The amount of £170,131 19s. 6d. was received during this day.

"*Vindictive*" *Week* (15—20th July, 1918) was held in honour of the famous ship which destroyed Zeebrugge and then blocked up the Ostend Channel, being part of a " War-Weapons " campaign promoted by the National Committee. It was specialised on the " Vindictive " because of the close associations of her Captain (Captain A. Francis Carpenter, V.C.) and his father (Captain Alfred Carpenter, D.S.O.), with our Borough. The money was permitted to be utilised towards helping to pay for the cost of the new ship " Vindictive," which had to be added to the Navy to replace her heroic battered sunken namesake. On 20th July, Katharine Street was decorated with captured German guns, and smaller captured weapons were exhibited in the Town Hall. Again the Gillett and Johnston war-workers were to the fore, this time with more than £10,000 ; and bands and concerts enlivened the day. The total " Vindictive " collection was £323,658, and if we add to that the collections made at the same time, and with the same object, by the surrounding districts (£239,217), we arrive at a gross amount raised in Croydon and neighbourhood towards the new ship, of £562,875. A picture of the storming of Zeebrugge mole was commissioned from the naval artist, Charles de Lacey (who was instructed by Admiral Sir Roger Keyes, K.C.B., and Captain A. Francis Carpenter, V.C.), and when complete was purchased by private subscription, headed by the Mayor (Alderman Howard Houlder), and presented, on behalf of the Borough, to the Captain of the new ship " Vindictive " (Captain Edgar Grace, R.N.), in the Council Chamber of the Town Hall, by the Mayor, on 19th March, 1919. It now hangs in the Ward Room of the new " Vindictive," *in perpetuam memoriam.*

Gun Week.—On Saturday, 12 October, 1918, a week of similarly strenuous work culminated in the arrival of an actual 6-in. howitzer before the Town Hall, in its full war paint, camouflaged with wavy coloured lines and ready for action ; but fitted in the open breech with a stamp for War Bonds receipts and certificates. Munition Store No. 10 brought, in a procession of their workers, a shell filled with their collective subscription. During the day itself £226,801 was received; and during the whole week £319,595.

The efforts of the Croydon War Savings Committee towards the purpose for which it was created—the sale of War Savings Certificates and the promotion of War Savings Associations—resulted in the formation of 158 such associations in all ; and about 190,000 War Savings Certificates of 15/6 each were purchased in this way. At the time of writing one of these associations (St. Matthew's and the East Ward) has collected no less than £22,000.

In January, 1917, another scheme was inaugurated, with the Mayor, Alderman Sir F. T. Edridge, and the Borough Treasurer as Stockholders, for the purchase of £5 per cent. War Loan by instalments spread over a period of two years. As a result of strenuous effort and of an arduous and ingenious publicity campaign in all £80,025 War Loan at 95 was allocated to subscribers. The profit balance of £252 16s. 3d. arising out of the whole transaction was given to the Croydon General Hospital.

Victory Loan.—In June, 1919, a further scheme was established for the purchase of 4 per cent. Victory Bonds, and 4 per cent. Funding Loan, by instalments ; the Stockholders being the Mayor, Mr. Councillor C. Heath Clark (Mayor in the following November), and the Town Clerk. The total amount of Bonds and Stock taken up under this scheme was approximately £30,000. This was part of the Victory Loan Campaign, which covered in all four weeks, ending 12th July, 1919. There were conversions from other loans into Victory Loan also, to the amount of £36,020 ; and the total amount of Victory Loan subscribed in the borough, after sustained effort on the part of the Committee and their friends, was no less than £908,087.

The out-of-pocket expenses and costs of printing and advertising, etc., connected with this Committee were met by Government grants, but all clerical and administrative work from first to last, and the amount of it seems almost incredible to look back upon, was carried out by the honorary officers and some other members of the Committee entirely without payment.

Food Economy.—A very important subsidiary effort of this Committee in April, 1917 and onwards should be mentioned. At the request of Lord Devonport, then Food Controller,

CENTRAL WAR SAVING COMMITTEE

alarmed at the shortage of food which we all so well remember, War Savings Committees, and amongst them Croydon, took up an earnest campaign in favour of food economy. At Croydon we formed a special advisory committee of clergy of all denominations, doctors, school teachers, cookery lecturers, electrical and gas engineers, and chairmen or secretaries of friendly societies, trades unions and similar bodies. An executive was appointed, and an information bureau opened at the Town Hall. Frequent conferences were held, and many demonstrations and lectures given. In this respect the town was greatly indebted to the Croydon Gas Company, who provided gas stoves (and supplied the gas, moreover) whenever the cookery lectures required them. Forty-four such practical lectures were given all over the borough, not to speak of countless less formal talks and practical addresses. In many of our schools economical and tasteful dishes of cereal foods other than wheaten flour (which was growing very difficult to obtain) were systematically exhibited. At the Public Hall a considerable exhibition of Food-economy devices was held, from 30th May to 7th June; and many lectures and demonstrations were given on the bottling, for preservation, of fruit and vegetables, on the value of gas and electricity in cooking, and on economical cookery recipes, etc. In all, no less than 3,574 cheap cookery pamphlets were sold. Lantern lectures were given under the auspices of the Public Library on kindred subjects. And on Empire Day the Mayor read publicly the King's Proclamation (enjoining on all his subjects the necessity for stringent economy in food) from the Town Hall steps, and at Thornton Heath and at South Norwood. An amusing incident (though of serious import in itself) may be mentioned in conclusion. The Board of Agriculture offered to supply the bottles for the preservation of fresh fruit, which were referred to above, at about half the retail cost (namely, 4/6 a dozen) if large quantities were ordered. Mrs. Colchester, the Honorary Secretary, a living impersonation of energy, searched out and found nearly 250 fruit-bottlers, and coaxed the authorities at our Education Offices in a weak moment to agree to receive the bottles. One can faintly imagine the astonishment of the Clerk when 7,200 bottles descended from the blue sky upon him. But when the 250 " bottlers " presently arrived, all clamouring for their respective dozens or scores, it seemed as if pandemonium reigned in the " groves of Academe." This Editor did not see it with his own eyes, but he has it on the highest authority that a notice, " Bottle Department," was actually, and of necessity, posted to direct the " bottlers " to their prey.

XII. Croydon District Association of Voluntary Organisations

This was a district association in connection with the work of the Director-General of Voluntary Organisations (Sir Edward Ward) which began operations in November, 1915, and closed on 31st March, 1919. It consisted of 15 branches, sub-divided into 54 groups, with a total number of members of 2,511. The Mayor and Mayoress (Mr. and Mrs. Howard Houlder) were Presidents of the Association, and the Town Clerk was Chairman of the Executive and Finance Committees. Mr. A. G. Norris was Honorary Secretary till May, 1916, and Miss Rhoda Brodie, M.B.E., from that date to the close. Assistant Hon. Secretaries were, in succession, Miss Roper, Miss King, Mrs. E. Colam, and Miss Haward. Other enthusiastic ladies helped throughout. The Borough Treasurer and Borough Accountant were Joint Treasurers. The total number of articles despatched was 584,013, and in addition the association procured and forwarded £30 worth of games; the total value of the whole of the contributions being £27,740.

The "comforts" collected were despatched to France, Egypt, Mesopotamia, Russia, Italy, Serbia, Rumania, etc.; to the French Red Cross and the French Wounded Emergency-Fund; to Lady Smith-Dorrien's Bag Fund; to mine-sweepers, prisoners of war, clearing stations, ambulance trains, ambulance flotillas, field ambulances, military V.A.D., and auxiliary hospitals; to the military wards of Croydon General Hospital, Croydon military hospitals, Wallacefield and St. Dorothy's convalescent-hospitals, and to Addington Palace, Shirley Park, Purley, and Brighton Road auxiliary hospitals.

All articles were collected by Miss Haward in her own car and were packed at the office of the War-Supplies Clearing House. The Supply Committee (Mrs. Newnham, Chairman, Mrs. Hetley, and Mrs. Lillico) kept a stock of materials which they either sold in the office of the Association (at a price slightly exceeding the cost, so that the loss in cutting up might be covered, or distributed as free material to be worked up by the members. The stock finally remaining unsold was given to the Croydon Mothers' and Infants' Welfare Association; and the small balance of £37 cash was paid over to the Mayoress's War-Fund.

Mrs. REDFERN
Who received from the King of the Belgians the Medaille de la Reine Elizabeth, in recognition of work in Croydon for the Belgian Refugees; and who was also on many War Committees

Photo by Florence Baxter

Mrs. COLCHESTER, M.B.E.
Croydon War Savings Committee, etc.

VOLUNTARY ORGANISATIONS

The amount dealt with by this Association was £3,661.
The list of branches (with Secretaries) is as follows:—

1. War Hospital Supply Depot . Mrs. Major & Mrs. Beddow.
2. War Supplies Clearing House. Mrs. Iredell.
3. Central Ward Branch . . Mrs. Lillico.
4. East Ward   ,,   . . Mrs. Trubshawe.
5. West Ward   ,,   . . The Mayoress, Mrs. Houlder.
6. South Ward   ,,   . . Lady Edridge.
7. Norbury . . . . Mrs. Allen.
8. Upper Norwood . . . Mrs. Hetley & Miss Thur-
9. South Norwood . . . Miss Weise.   [burn.
10. Purley . . . . Miss Brailsford.
11. Broad Green . . . Mrs. Trumble.
12. St. Stephen's, Norbury . Miss Lawrence.
13. Mitcham . . . . Mrs. Cato Worsfold.
14. Coulsdon . . . . Miss Lintott.
15. Thornton Heath . . . Mrs. Owen Fowler.

The following list of articles despatched through the War Supplies Clearing House, is taken from the record of the latter, and serves to show the general trend of the work of the Association. It pretends only to be a complete account of the 176,823 articles in the 786 cases which the Clearing House handled.

Handkerchiefs	3627
Scarves and mufflers	9539
Woollen helmets, caps	6404
Vests	1975
Jerseys, etc.	191
Pants	139
Shirts	2723
Nightshirts	3272
Bedgowns	2329
Pairs of gloves	494
Pairs of mittens	17909
Pairs of socks	7816
Pairs of hospital socks	10354
Rugs	66
Blankets	96
Mattresses and pillows	1658
Towels	386
Bed-rests	150
Splints	70
Bandages	54649
Lint	8180
Sunshields, pads, etc.	7012
Mossbags	11000
Miscellaneous, including musical instr.	26779

Part Six
FOOD AND FUEL

I. The Allotments Movement
Food Production : War Allotments
(Croydon Vacant Lands Cultivation Society)

The beginning of the War found towns such as ours with a large number of houses and small gardens, a certain number of allotments belonging to the Corporation (in Croydon 104 acres divided into 1694 plots), and a percentage of idle land, held over for building, but unused except perhaps for a little grazing, and in private ownership.

It was not at first realised, but soon became of course self-evident, that as much food as possible must be raised in England for use during the War, and a fine example was at once set in 1914 by Mr. Douglas Young, a respected member of the Croydon Borough Guild of Help, who offered his building land in South Croydon for cultivation by those who were ready to work. Mr. Mark Major, the originator of the Guild (which is now merged in the Croydon Civic Service League), had made one or two attempts through that body to deal with vacant lands in the borough, and he with Miss E. L. Hudson and others called a conference at the offices of the Guild, out of which sprang the Croydon Vacant Lands Cultivation Society (23rd September, 1914) ; the Guild of Help providing office room. Mr. Mark Major became its Chairman, Miss Hudson its Secretary, Mr. Geo. Reader very kindly supplying the necessary legal knowledge for the simple agreements, etc. Alderman Rogers became President. The practical gardening side was provided by members of the Croydon Horticultural Associations, and much voluntary valuable work of instruction was given to the cause by their members, especially by Messrs. Bignell (Chairman of the Garden Committee), Boshier and Dingwall. The newspapers were also very helpful in affording space for reports as to what was going on.

Mr. Douglas Young most generously offered to compensate cultivators for loss of their crops should he be compelled to take over his land again at short notice ; and 20 applications were quickly filled, though the soil was in parts rather rough. Other land owners followed suit, some of their own accord, but most in response to the efforts of the Croydon Vacant Lands Society, so that by December, 1915, about a year after the beginning of the movement, the society had 20 acres in working belonging to 22 owners, and cultivated in plots of 10 rods, by 260 cultivators. There was also a waiting list of 150 would-be cultivators. As a guarantee against loss the cultivators paid 4/- a year each (raised later to 5/-) towards a compensation fund for loss of crops should unexpected disturbance occur.

The Water Committee of the Corporation, by supplying water without charge, provided the cultivators adopted waste-preventing methods, and made their own connection to the mains, set an example which was in advance of many other Corporations, and the Council also was liberal in the matter of rates. At this time the journal of the Board of Agriculture, which took much interest in this vigorous experiment, published a careful calculation showing that from May, 1915, to March, 1916, the value of the crops on a certain plot of 9 rods came to £6. During the first 15 months the total expenses of the Society, owing to the generous work voluntarily contributed, only reached £9.

During 1916 the land cultivated under the society rose from 20 acres to 68, lent by 81 owners, and cultivated by 1,000 plotholders, branches having arisen at Purley and Wallington. The arrangements were so skilfully drawn as not to be liable to stamp-duty, a clever saving of not inconsiderable value on so large a number.

Croydon's effort had, as said above, aroused much interest, and inquiries poured in from all parts of the country, and at least one investigation was made on the part of Johannisburg, while *The Daily Mail* sent down a special commissioner to report on the movement in its columns. Speakers from the society were asked to attend other communities to explain Croydon methods, which were enthusiastically adopted here and there.

In December, 1916, the Government issued an Order under "D.O.R.A." (as the "Defence of the Realm Act" provisions were familiarly called), which was the most socialistic measure ever known in England ; nothing less than granting powers to Corporations forcibly to take possession of idle land and to have it cultivated for the benefit of the community. Hitherto the Croydon Vacant Lands Cultivation Society had been entirely dependent for obtaining land upon persuasion and goodwill. The Corporation appointed an Allotments and Small-Holdings Committee (whose chairman was Mr. Councillor Adams) and entered at once upon 61 acres of land, which they divided into 790 plots, and leased at an annual charge of 5/- for 10 rods, and in the first rush 100 acres were dealt with in one week. Later in the year the Council took further powers to enter occupied land, and through the Vacant Lands Society added another 65

THE ALLOTMENTS MOVEMENT

acres, in 850 plots, paying various rents for this land, up to £3 an acre ; and all this land was also quickly taken up by cultivators. By the end of the year 1917 the Croydon Vacant Lands Cultivation Society was responsible for 176 acres, secured by voluntary agreement and let in 2,377 plots, including the Purley and Wallington branches ; beyond this there were about 1,700 plots acquired compulsorily by the Corporation as above decided. Decentralization was now encouraged, and six registered societies and eight unregistered came into being, each looking after the interests of the cultivators in its own neighbourhood.

Early in January, 1918, the Corporation resumed possession of the land already entered upon by them and passed over to the Vacant Lands Society, and also took possession, under the increased powers above referred to, of land let to the Vacant Lands Society by the owners, in order to let the whole to the various plot-holders' associations. Isolated plots or small groupings, not large enough for a society to be required, still remained in the hands of the Vacant Lands Society, and these amounted to 630 plots on 70 different holdings, which increased by the autumn of 1918 to 745 plots, adding 20 more acres to the land already under the Society earlier in the year. The compensation fund had grown (as no serious charges had been made upon it) to nearly £500, when the separate plot-holders' associations were set up ; and this sum was therefore equitably divided between the parent society, the branches, and these separate associations.

As to compulsorily taking over that land which had so patriotically been lent by the owners there were differences of opinion, but the associations of plot-holders pressed this course upon the Corporation as making them surer of being undisturbed in their allotments than they would be if their plots were upon a voluntary tenure. The Vacant Lands Society protested, but in vain. " Dora " took little account of fine feelings under the necessities of the time.

The excellence of the crops raised was manifested in many vegetable shows in the borough, both those promoted by the great horticultural societies and many others arranged by the plot-holders' associations. Great industry and no little skill were shown on all sides by the cultivators ; lectures and practical demonstrations were frequently given and well attended. Further, much good-will and many kindly offices existed amongst the plot-holders. When the local sweep went abroad to fight, his wife's allotment was kept going at full strength by her neighbours. There will be heartburnings when the owners of the " valuable building-sites," which have for these last years been feeding us with potatoes and cabbages, desire to replace those crops with indigestible bricks and mortar. But it is ill to talk about crossing the bridge before you come to the stream, and we must hope for the best. What remains always to the good is the love of work on the land the War-allotments have engendered among our people. " i am Riten for a peace of Lotment," an actual application, duly put into shape and dealt with by the Vacant Lands Society, represents in its rude speech a very earnest longing for land, which once roused, as our French peasant neighbours show us, brings a great steadiness amongst the people, and moreover never dies out. Thus, in the present case, not only the Vacant Lands Society itself but also all the larger plot-holders' associations above referred to, have obtained regular leases of several large pieces of land, originally taken over in the temporary manner already described ; and these more permanent arrangements cover about 100 acres already. At the time of completing this book (January, 1920) there are (including all varieties of allotments in occupation of land, as above named) 640 acres, divided into 8,500 plots.

There was, in fact, very little available ground in the borough, during the war, which escaped the eagle eyes of the ardent cultivators.

One day, and this seems to be regarded as the Secretary's (Miss Hudson's) finest achievement, her attention was drawn by a disappointed applicant, to a piece of land in his neighbourhood often resorted to by bad characters (as it lay out of the way), containing moreover an evil smelling pond full of carcases of dead dogs and other refuse. He pleaded that some of this might be given to him as an allotment, since no other was available. The place was found to bear out his description, the owners proved amenable to the wiles of the Society, and in the end the Corporation took it over, and created 100 permanent allotments there ; so that now, after so long a time of unsavoury wastefulness, " the desert shall rejoice and blossom as the rose."

II. National Kitchens Committee

The feeding of the people of course caused much anxiety during war-time, and the Croydon Council finally determined on 23rd April, 1917, to allow an experiment of two Communal Kitchens (as they were at first called), one on the Beulah Road Council School premises, and one at Princess Road Council school, and provided £150 for working capital and preliminary expenses. These kitchens were administered by a committee, which elected Mr. Councillor Peters as its chairman, and (a little later) Mrs. T. Wood Roberts as its honorary executive officer. School attendance officers, teachers, and other people gave valuable assistance, especially during the earlier times.

The kitchens were opened on 30th May and 6th June, 1917, respectively, and continued working till the end of September, 1919. The kitchen at Beulah Road paid its way well, and at the end of the $2\frac{1}{4}$ years of its existence showed a profit of £94 12s. 6d. on the working; but that at Princess Road was conducted at a steady loss. At September, 1919, the total loss on working was £150 17s. 10d. A third kitchen ran for nine months at Selhurst Road, South Norwood, from 5th December, 1918, onwards; and a fourth at Upper Norwood was also sanctioned, but was never actually opened. The loss on the working at South Norwood in the nine months of its existence was £62 13s. 4d. If to the losses at Princess Road and Selhurst Road be added the cost of equipment (less sales of material on closing), which was net £185 9s. 6d., and if the Beulah Road profit be set off on the other side, the total cost of the venture was £304 8s. 2d.

It is probable that the financial failure—or rather non-success—of the experiment was due in a large measure to the fact that there was a tendency to the mistaken view that the "national kitchen" had some affinity with the charitable soup-kitchen; people of all classes did not realize that this was a public service as free from such associations as is the public light or water supply. In any case they did not appreciate the benefits offered them so fully as was anticipated. It was however an experiment well worth trying, and much thought and energy were spent upon it, especially by the honorary executive officer. It undoubtedly gave the public an excellent opportunity of testing a form of communal service which seemed to be especially necessary in view of the fact that the times demanded the utmost economy of fuel and food. It is not too much to say that from this point of view the kitchens proved a distinct success and were of decided advantage to the general community. Such practical object-lessons often have a far-reaching effect, producing good results long after they have themselves ceased. Further, the amount of business actually done was considerable. From first to last 184,305 portions were sold at Beulah Road, and 161,714 at Princess Road.

III. The Control of Food

The historian of the future, seeking for material for his work, will perchance find garishly-coloured postcards obviously of early twentieth century production, showing a man, with guilt depicted on every feature, stealthily secreting pots of jam in a strong safe ; or showing a solitary piece of sugar scintillating in lonely splendour upon a plate, and labelled " priceless " ; or he will find a reference in a newspaper to a single potato which had been displayed in a Croydon greengrocer's window with the legend : " A rare tuber, once a common British food ; now nearly extinct." Turning to the immortal *Punch*, he will come upon a picture of a burning mansion, in front of which is the distracted owner dancing frantically about the fireman with the hose, beseeching him to " concentrate on the coal-house." These are the lighter expressions, which most fortunately the British can utter, of one of the most difficult times in the history of the world, and few things in our record will have more interest for the coming social historian than the ways in which we met the almost universal shortage of food and fuel which resulted from the war. We deal first with food. For the nation as a whole the Ministry of Food was established, and to carry out the work of that department local committees were formed. We are concerned here only with the Croydon Food Control Committee.

This important committee, praised by the discerning few who admired the large amount of good work it accomplished, severely condemned by the unthinking, and grumbled at by nearly all of us (for we were necessarily all sufferers at its hands), was set up on 28th August, 1917, to regulate supplies on account of the serious shortage.

The then Mayor (Ald. Howard Houlder) was its first Chairman and remained throughout in the chair, and was always one of the most active members. Councillor Peters was (and is still, at the time of writing) Deputy-Chairman, and Chairman of the Executive Sub-Committee and of the Sugar Sub-Committee. Mr. Councillor Camden Field was Chairman of the Supplementary Rations Sub-Committee, and of the Meat Sub-Committee ; and Mr. Councillor Muggeridge of the Milk Sub-Committee. The Town Clerk was and is Honorary Executive Officer, and Mr. J. T. Tompkins was and is Deputy-Executive Officer, responsible for all executive duties under the Town Clerk.

In all, the Committee numbered 15, of whom 8 were members of the Town Council, and 3 were ladies. Objection was taken to a few of the original members : Councillors Pelton, West and Southwell (now Alderman); because of their connection with the grocery and meat trades, although the Corporation had expressly appointed them in order to derive assistance from their expert knowledge of those trades ; but feeling was stirred up over the matter, and the situation promised to become unpleasant, so that these three members retired (25th February, 1918), and the town was deprived of their valuable services. Other persons were elected in their places.

Immediate necessity for action on the part of the Committee arose because of the serious sugar-shortage, which rapidly became so acute that in September, 1917, rationing of sugar was set up. Sugar-retailers were registered on 15th September, and sugar-cards issued to purchasers, the issue being made with the kindly voluntary help of the school-teachers of the borough, and being completed by 26th October, 1917. No praise can be too great for the patriotic efforts of the teachers referred to ; they worked late at night, and cheerfully, on a special emergency, gave up Sunday also. We might refer especially to the valuable services of Mr. Edgar H. Fowles (Chairman of the Croydon Head Teachers Association), who supervised this special work.

Few persons beyond those who were actually engaged in the work know the great amount of local labour involved in Food-Control, and when we add to this the governmental and official work, the total operations take on a colossal aspect. Here in Croydon, under the Rationing Scheme begun in February 1918, 626,000 letters were received and 356,000 replies posted ; and 15,000 of these were directly dealt with by the Deputy-Executive Officer himself. The telephone calls reached 7,000.

Directly the Sugar-Control was set up in September, 1917 (and this was the first department started), caterers, institutions, manufacturers, etc., had to apply for authority to purchase wholesale, and to use, sugar. The retailers, distributing to the public, had received the well known ration-cards from their customers by November, and the wholesale suppliers could then be authorised to supply the amount of sugar needed.

Almost immediately after the sugar-control came the fixing of the retail prices of meat, and all purchases and sales of meat were then checked every fortnight ; and it was not long before the butchers were registered.

In October wholesale and retail prices for milk were fixed ; and powers of control, and of securing priority of supply to children and invalids, were given to our local committee, followed by the registration of potato dealers and constant examination of their stocks.

In November came the scarcity of tea; the quantity received in England for some months about that time only amounting to a third of the ordinary consumption; and provisional prices were fixed. At this juncture it was evident that a campaign of education in food economy was necessary; and the committee loyally endeavoured, and with most gratifying success, to carry out the suggestions of the Government in this regard. To the honour of the inhabitants of the borough it must be stated that they all reduced their consumption not only of the rationed, but also of the unrationed foods to the narrowest limit. We all remember how our weight was reduced, and how every morsel of food was gauged and all superfluity rigidly cut off; nay, in cases, danger to health was patriotically faced. This campaign lasted through parts of November and December, but the effect in the homes of the people continued for many months.

In December the bacon-retailers had to be registered; and the supplies of margarine ran ominously short.

Then came the day of the queue, which few of us who have lived through it will ever forget; a day of rumour of plenty here, there, and everywhere, except the shop at which one dealt ordinarily. People were out with daylight, and much before, on the food quest; and at 6 a.m., on those cold December mornings, long queues of people would line up before the barred premises of provision dealers to wait their turn in the hope—too often a vain hope—of getting a quarter-pound of butter or margarine; and, if they were disappointed at one shop, they would trudge to the next, and so on, often during the whole day. We did not love margarine over-much in pre-war days; some of us even dared to despise it, but in these days it assumed immense importance, seeing that animal fat had also become scarce.

The Town Clerk and Mr. Tompkins, seeing what was coming, prepared a scheme for requisitioning supplies, distributing them, and rationing the retail purchases of margarine. On December 22nd, 1917, things became so serious that immediate action became necessary; and the Committee was summoned by telegram, so that the prepared scheme might be put into action that very day. Meanwhile people, especially large numbers of working people, on reaching their retailers on this day heard that all margarine had been requisitioned, and somehow inferred that unheard of stocks were held up in the Food Control Offices under the Reference Library at the Town Hall. They became alarmed, angry and expectant all at once, and crowds surged into the Library at 8 p.m., completely blocking up the entrance for the users of the Library, and all demanding margarine. Of course there was actually none at the Town Hall, and by this hour the Food Office staff had all gone home. The Library officials, who endeavoured vainly to persuade the people to disperse, were roundly informed that *they* had taken good care to get margarine for themselves, and were forced to listen to many stories of homes where there was none. At last the locked, darkened doors of the Food Office—together with the gentle explanations of the police who now came and regulated the crowd with great tact—impressed the truth upon the people, and they went off gradually in deep disappointment. By Monday, however, the scheme had saved the situation. It worked admirably, and though the citizens freely availed themselves of the Englishman's privilege of grumbling before he obeys the order given him, the distressing queues which caused so much anxiety and inconvenience during the closing months of 1917 gradually lessened, and in time disappeared.

By Christmas, meat was dangerously scarce, and the supply of meat to Croydon was on the point of stopping altogether. Retail maximum meat prices had been fixed as against the butchers, but the cost to the butchers was not fixed; so that as meat became exceedingly dear by reason of the scarcity, butchers had to pay very high prices, while on the other hand they were limited to a moderate selling price. Of course the butchers could not face this great loss, and ceased for the moment their strenuous efforts to obtain meat.

Meat-queues then began. Special and drastic action was taken by the Committee on 18th December to cope with this rather alarming situation, and by means known only to a few persons and the Committee, and indeed before the inhabitants of the borough had appreciated the danger they stood in, a supply of meat for Christmas was happily secured.

On 27th December a full rationing-scheme for butter, margarine, lard, meat, bacon and tea, with power to extend to other articles, was framed by the Town Clerk and adopted by the Committee, and sent up to the Minister for approval. Other local bodies of course, all pressed by their acute needs in the same way as Croydon was, also evolved and sent up similar schemes. The hand of the Ministry was forced, and a general governmental official Rationing Scheme for London and the Home Counties was promulgated, and the Croydon committee at once set to work upon it.

The first general scheme of rationing began in February, 1918, and from first to last no less than one million food and

THE CONTROL OF FOOD

meat cards and books were provided, in addition to the already rationed sugar. Emergency rations for visitors to the town and other temporary inhabitants were issued to the number of 27,811; and special rations for invalids and certain classes of manual workers to the number of 8,387. Sailors and soldiers on leave were rationed, and a grateful country gave them much more liberal rations than we civilians received—and 30,369 availed themselves of this provision, while 10,142 ration books were issued to demobilised men. Much work was caused by removals and changes of residence, amounting to 33,000 cases in all; a figure throwing strong light on the remarkable amount of movement during the war amongst our Croydon population. Persons from overseas, or discharged from institutions, etc., accounted for 35,000 extra books; and 2,312 children were born during the rationing period and demanded ration books before they could speak (or at all events, their mothers did for them); and further, 1,166 foolish persons lost their ration-cards, and had to pay amongst them £26 13s. 6d. for their carelessness. At one time the corridors of the Town Hall were filled for several weeks with 164 temporary clerks at long tables, issuing supplementary ration cards (13,162 cards in all) to certain grades of manual workers and adolescents, allowing them an extra amount of a half-pound of bacon weekly.

There were three issues of ration-cards, each issue needing its own index, so that the 275,000 applications received and dealt with involved an equal number of index cards, all necessarily continually to be sorted and kept up to date; and, moreover, constantly interfered with by additions of new cards and subtractions of cards belonging to persons removing out of Croydon or ceasing to be rationable in the borough for any other reason. Finally, the Food Ministry realized that it had forgotten to provide for an index of ration-card holders and the retailers with whom they were registered. As a step towards supplying this omission, and in order to ascertain the best method of doing it, the Ministry selected certain well-organized places and requested them to do the work experimentally. Croydon received the somewhat onerous compliment of being one of the towns selected. It involved the collection of all the counterfoils of the ration-books from the retailers, and these counterfoils numbered a million and a quarter. All this mass of 1,250,000 counterfoils had to be sorted into streets and houses, indexed, etc., etc., so that at least 12,500,000 handlings were involved in all. And with the national carelessness, 750,000 of these counterfoils had arrived without the name of the retailer being written on them, and the work of supplying this information also fell upon the staff. The interference of all this with the ordinary routine of the Town Hall is one of those minor worries of the war which every one had cheerfully to encounter, but it was, nevertheless, considerable. Rooms were annexed; for instance, the Library's Newspaper-room, and its Magazine-room, the Grand Jury-room, Magistrates'-room, and even the committee-rooms of the Town Hall (to say nothing of the occupation at various times of the Council Chamber, the three branch Libraries, and the South Norwood Polytechnic), and the borough work done in those rooms had to be crowded into other places, until eventually the control clerks overflowed even all these rooms, and had to fill the corridors as above described.

Margarine and Butter.—The committee dealt during the 49 weeks of rationing with 673 tons of margarine (£65,500 in value), receiving 13 tons a week; and with 3 tons of butter (£788) during the time that butter was separately rationed.

Sugar.—1,140 Certificates of Registration (Sugar) were issued in September and October, 1917, to retailers, manufacturers and caterers; and 131 such applicants were refused. To the purchasers 175,000 cards were issued. When the system was changed in December, 1917, 200,000 sugar-tickets were issued, superseding the above mentioned cards, to over 46,000 householders. In all, the committee dealt with 3,200 tons of sugar; and received twelve million sugar coupons, of which 600,000 were sent to the Ministry for purposes of checking. It will be remembered that those persons who possessed fruit trees were allowed to obtain extra sugar for preserving, both in 1918 and 1919, which involved considerable work in sorting or allotting the sugar, and issuing special authorities to the retailers; 23,000 such applications were received and 200 tons of preserving-sugar issued amongst them.

Meat.—The fortnightly returns of sales and purchases of butchers, which had to be checked, amounted to 6,000; and the weight of meat dealt with, 508 tons. From February to June, 1918, 12 million meat-coupons were received, counted and dealt with in Croydon; on June 18th, 1918, the Central Clearing House was set up, and since that time 34 millions more coupons have been received and 1¼ million of these sent to the Clearing House to be checked, as a sample, against the fortnightly returns of the retailers. Actual purchases and distributions of meat by the Committee amounted to £296.

Tea.—5,884 Applications were dealt with in connection with the rationing of tea; and 175,000 counterfoils were received, counted, examined, sorted, etc.

Milk.—119 Retailers were registered; 1,624 priority milk-certificates were issued and 253 special permits for cream (babies

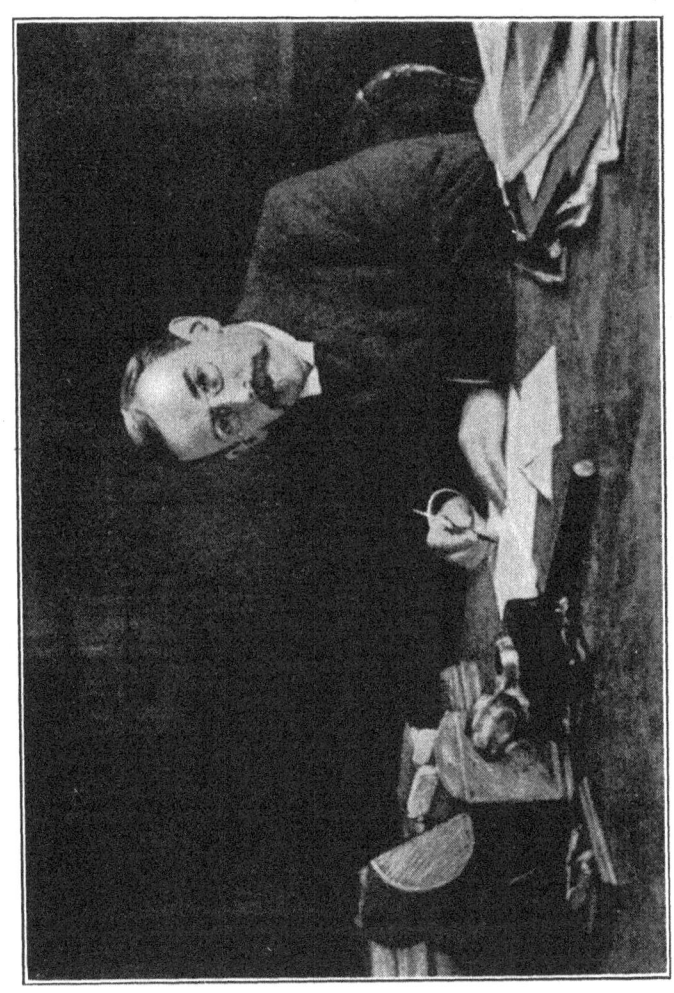

Mark B. F. Major, Founder of the Croydon Vacant Lands Cultivation Society

Photo by Macbeth-Raeburn

Photo by Skewes

GEORGE FEARNLEY CARTER, M.Inst.C.E.
Borough Engineer, Surveyor and Water Engineer;
Local Fuel Overseer

and invalids); 1,300 weekly returns had to be dealt with; and of condensed milk very nearly two million tins were distributed on the order of the committee.

Bread.—204 Tons of potatoes were sold by the committee to bakers, to assist them in the production of bread, at a loss of £3 a ton; the Croydon bakers paid £822, and it cost the Ministry £612 more than this. Of course, a good deal of careful book-keeping was involved to adjust the payments and losses as they occurred in this account.

Fish.—There are 69 retailers of fish in the borough, and each of these had to send in weekly returns of prices.

Bacon.—A return of bacon, ham, and lard, sold in Croydon in the year 1916, was demanded by the Ministry, and this showed the year's consumption for 1916 to have been 33,267 cwt. of bacon, 3,506 of ham, 6,831 of lard. Upon this return, which was made in December, 1917, bacon was registered, and 200,000 forms were issued to and received back from the retailers of bacon. Cheese and lard had, of course, also to be dealt with, but not to such large numbers.

The cash handled by the committee was £5,667 apart from the expenses paid through the Borough Accountant. Eighty-nine serious cases arose in which the committee had to prosecute and the fines and costs received amounted to £790.

Since 3rd May, 1919, the work has in every way materially lessened. Two articles of food (sugar and butter) still remain rationed (December, 1919), and therefore ration-cards must still be maintained, but a staff of 22 now suffices for the work of the committee. But the end is not yet in sight, for it is only a short time since that the Ministry of Food sent Croydon an intimation that Food Control would be extended to June, 1920, and that the Committee must remain in charge until at least that date.

The general correspondence is still considerable. People continue to write somewhat as follows :—(Report of the Committee, 21st July, 1919).

" The enclosed rubbish " (in fact a fair sample of Demerara sugar) " was sold to me by Mr.——— for sugar, will you please prosecute him, or order him to supply me with loaf sugar."

Another correspondent intimates that she " has been charged 1d. too much for an unnamed quantity of an undescribed joint on a date she regrets she does not remember, by an assistant of her butcher whom she cannot identify. She desires him to be

o

prosecuted, but intimates that whatever happens her name is not to be mentioned, as she declines to be mixed up with any Police Court and does not desire any unpleasantness. It is the duty, she presumes, of the committee to prosecute in all such cases on the evidence contained in her letter."

It is pleasant to be able to finish the account of such serious and long continued effort upon this note of gaiety. While not exaggerating, but erring (if at all) rather in the opposite direction, it is to be hoped that this chapter may have, in spite of its multitude of dry statistics, reminded those who read it of a very critical time in our national history, when wholesale shortage of food from time to time came within measurable distance, and when the nation was saved from this awful disaster by the patriotic labours of such Committees as this of Croydon, backed by the indomitable courage and willing sacrifice of the inhabitants of the borough. Nor shall we be doing mere justice if we fail to acknowledge the unprecedented and entirely gratuitous work of the Town Clerk, Dr. J. M. Newnham, in producing this result; his organisation, fertility in expedients for meeting difficult situations, and long self-denying labours were as evident here as they were in every work with which he was associated during the War—and he seems to have been associated with everything.

IV. Women's Land Army

So many agricultural labourers were drawn from the fields to serve in the trenches that farmers found themselves increasingly less able to produce food for the people as the War proceeded. Eventually it became manifest that we must take a leaf from Continental books and utilise the strongest of our girls on the farms, or let the farms go out of cultivation. This eventually shaped into the formation of a " Women's Land Army," and early in 1917 the W.L.A. Organizing Secretary for Surrey approached the Mayoress of Croydon (Mrs. Howard Houlder) on the subject of forming a recruiting centre for this new movement. The Mayoress at once called a meeting to consider the scheme, and a Selection Board was appointed, with Mrs. Redfern as Chairman and District Representative, and Miss Hodges as Honorary Secretary. Later, Miss Hodges, on leaving Croydon, was succeeded by Miss Barbara J. Carpenter. The present Mayoress (Mrs. C. Heath Clark), as a farmer's daughter, was a most valuable member of the Selection Board, and worked diligently and with full *connaissance de cause*. Recruiting began in Croydon in April, 1917, and ended in the summer of 1919, and during that period 719 women were interviewed by the Board. Of these only 304 were accepted for service, mainly because of the very high physical standard which was a necessary qualification for the arduous work to be undertaken. Many Croydonians will remember the successful recruiting rally in the spring of 1918, when some 70 Land Army girls in their picturesque uniforms marched through the streets accompanied by decorated farm wagons kindly lent by the Croydon Borough Farm.

Though the Women's Land Army ended its official existence in November, 1919, the call of the land has been so strong that many a Croydon girl has elected to continue her occupation as " farmer's boy," her interests now being guarded by the " National Association of Landswomen."

V. The Control of Fuel and Light

With the great coal-fields of Northern France in the hands of the enemy, and with the submarine aggression hampering the passage of coal across the Atlantic, the fuel resources of Great Britain were strained to the uttermost in the third year of the war. Not only were there the great demands for coal of the home country with all its war-industries running at high pressure; there was the demand from France and our other Allies, who were unable to supply themselves from their own mines in enemy occupation, and, of course, could not get their usual supplies from Germany.

Economy had been necessary for more than a year, but at the end of 1917 a coal-famine, together with its natural corollary, a failure of gas and electricity, was well within sight. Rationing was determined upon by the Government early in 1918, a Coal Controller was appointed, and the Household Fuel and Lighting Order was put into operation. The local administration of the Order was carried out by local fuel overseers, and for Croydon the Borough Engineer, Mr. G. F. Carter, undertook this onerous work.

The Order provided that the Local Fuel Overseer, in addition to the work of rationing consumers, should :—

(*a*) Report to the Controller upon the requirements for storing, handling, delivering, and retailing coal, and make recommendations, as well as suggestions for other means than those ordinarily provided by persons engaged in the coal trade.

(*b*) Report to the Controller any failure, and the proper provision for the supply of coal to the merchants within the district.

(*c*) Deal with all questions of complaints of consumers or merchants relating to the supply, sale, or delivery of coal, gas and electricity.

(*d*) Keep records and make reports and returns from time to time as the Controller might require.

(*e*) Carry out the instructions of the Controller.

CONTROL OF FUEL AND LIGHT

During the period June, 1918, to November, 1919, a total of 43,867 persons were registered as consumers of fuel and lighting. Of these 9,277 were "small consumers," or persons who obtained their coal supply from trolley men and did not require more than one cwt. each per week, excepting during the months of January, February, and March, when the supply was not more than one and a half cwt. each. Small consumers were also restricted to not more than 24,000 cubic feet of gas and 400 units of electricity during the year.

Claims for additional allowances, numbering 2,147 in all, were received. These entailed a considerable amount of enquiry work, and, as far as the acute shortage of coal permitted, each claim was assessed as accurately as possible.

The number of requisitions completed accurately by the inhabitants of Croydon was small, due no doubt to the complicated nature of the form F.H.F. (3). It was therefore found necessary by the Borough Engineer to re-allocate the coal, coke, gas, and electricity, on the requisitions, as nearly as possible in accordance with the implied wishes of the consumers, before certificates of supply could be issued.

Eventually 80,553 certificates of supply were issued to the various merchants, dealers, and undertakings concerned. Then there arose 3,000 consumers who requested a variation of their allocations, these consumers having saved on one class of fuel (say "gas") and desiring to increase in the consumption of another (say "coal"). Where possible these requests were acceded to, but the work entailed the cancellation and re-issue of approximately 7,000 certificates.

One hundred and twenty-eight merchants and dealers were registered for the sale of coal, and, in accordance with the provisions of the Order, weekly returns showing particulars of trade transacted were received from all these. The returns were collated and a return, together with a report on the coal situation was forwarded to the Controller each week throughout the year.

Considerable difficulty was experienced during the winter of 1918-19 in endeavouring to prevent hardship to consumers owing to certain merchants and dealers failing to obtain adequate supplies of coal to meet the certificates of consumers registered with them. Arrangements were made from time to time to transfer coal from one merchant to another, and it was also found necessary to impose restrictions in delivery during certain periods. Several trucks of coal ordered for the Corporation were disposed of to merchants to help the public supply.

On the 4th October, 1918, an Order was issued preventing the supply of more than one ton at a time to householders without the permission of the Local Fuel-Overseer, and no deliveries were to be made where more than one-third of the annual supply was in hand.

On the 17th December, 1918, an Order was issued that from the 19th December to the 4th January *no coal* was to be delivered to private dwelling houses where the stock was more than sufficient to meet current requirements, the object being to ensure supplies to meet the needs of small consumers.

On the 31st January, 1919, an Order was issued that coal merchants must give preference to the supplies to small consumers and one ton lots were not to be delivered excepting under special circumstances of need until the requirements of dealers, shops, etc., were made in full.

On the 12th February, 1919, the position had become serious and the Borough Engineer was notified that the reserve stocks in the whole of the Metropolitan area was only equal to four days' deliveries at the then rate of consumption. A circular was issued that no delivery of coal, coke, or other solid fuel to a dwelling-house must exceed half-a-ton until the 1st March.

On the 25th March, 1919, an Order was issued that owing to the strike of miners in the Notts and Derby coalfields not more than two cwts. of coal might be supplied to any private dwelling house till 3rd April, and that *no coal* might be supplied where the stock in hand was greater than ten cwts.

At this time the population of Croydon was 186,917; and the number of houses 43,399. The number of applications under F.H.F. (2) received during the year June, 1918-19 was 34,590; and the number of applications for registration as "small consumer" 9,277. In all 43,867, or practically the same as the total number of houses.

The additional allowances granted may be classified as under :—

(a) Aged persons, invalids, etc. . . . 770
(b) Use of extra fires for lodgers . . . 181
(c) Use of rooms for profession, etc. . . 184
(d) Upkeep of fires for nightwork . . . 20
(e) Temporary illness 318
(f) Use of rooms for industrial purposes . . 674

2,147

The total number of certificates for supply of coal issued during this year was 33,803 ; coke 7,071 ; gas 32,924 ; electricity 4,608 ; and additional allowances (as above) 2,147 ; making a total of 80,553 certificates.

141,113 Tons of coal were consumed during the year June, 1918-19, as follows : tonnage of coal required to meet certificates of supply in respect of F.H.F. (*a*) requisitions, 93,985 ; F.H.F. (4) special assessments, 16,791 ; F.H.F. (63) small consumers obtaining supplies weekly, 27,000 ; and for additional allowances 3,337.

The tonnage of coal required for additional allowances may be classified as under :—

(*a*) Aged persons, invalids, etc. . . 862 tons.
(*b*) Use of extra fires for lodgers . . 228 ,,
(*c*) Use of rooms for profession, etc. . . 404 ,,
(*d*) Upkeep of fires for nightwork . . 19 ,,
(*e*) Temporary illness . . . . 253 ,,
(*f*) Use of rooms for industrial purposes . 1571 ,,

and beyond this coal 16,991 tons of coke were required for household and quasi-domestic industries.

The rationing of fuel still continued with certain modifications after the expiration of the 1918 Order.

On the 14th July the Board of Trade made an order increasing the maximum prices of coal and coke by six shillings per ton or $3\frac{1}{2}d$. per cwt. for small quantities. These increases came into force on the 21st July, 1919, and were not removed till November, although it had been fully shown that the advance had never been necessary. Indeed the Government reduced the price for domestic consumption not by 6s. only, but by 10s., in November, 1919.

On the 26th September, 1919, owing to the emergency caused by the strike of railway employees, the Board of Trade, under the powers conferred on them by the Defence of the Realm Regulations, issued various orders.

(*a*) Requiring gas undertakings to manufacture gas in such a way as will enable them to spread the consumption of their supplies of coal over as long a period as possible.

(*b*) Requiring the discontinuance of all outside advertisement or display lighting on any premises.

(*c*) Limiting purchases or deliveries for household consumption to one cwt. of coal per week, prohibiting purchases by or deliveries to persons who have more than 10 cwt. of coal in stock, and giving power to local fuel overseers to cut off supplies of gas or electricity where there is waste.

Instructions were issued to the merchants and dealers concerned, and a statement of stocks of coal in hand was obtained from all industrial premises within the Borough. An embargo to the extent of 25 per cent. of all stocks held by industrial establishments was placed, in order that, if necessary, the requirements of essential food industries could be maintained. Constant inspection was maintained throughout the period of the strike in order that the provisions of the orders should be observed.

But eventually, on the 11th October, the provisions of these Emergency Orders were considerably modified ; and an instruction was issued that deliveries of not more than one ton of coal might be made, in rotation, to private consumers.

All this extremely complicated business devolved upon the Borough Engineer, Mr. Carter, and was carried through by him with extraordinary smoothness and success. It is the more fitting that public acknowledgment of these great services should be here made, since the Borough Engineer himself is so modest and unobtrusive in all his public duties that only those engaged with him, or in the inner circle of the Corporation activities, know what whole-hearted devotion and skill he brings to anything he undertakes. And as far as the present Editor is aware, the knowledge of difficult work well done is the only reward he has received for all this extra work. Perhaps to a man of his temperament, that, after all, suffices.

Part Seven
VICTORY

I. Armistice Day
(11th November, 1918)

At 11 o'clock on the 11th day of the 11th month of 1918 news was officially promulgated that at 5 o'clock (French time) that morning the armistice had been signed, at Versailles, and that at the moment of the announcement, on the very stroke of 11, hostilities with Germany had ceased on the French front. The Kaiser had already fled to Holland in the craven way invariably attaching to a defeated braggart and bully, and the bubble of German domination was pricked at last. The King led the cheers with waving cap from the balcony of Buckingham Palace, the Queen waved the Union Jack, and others of the Royal Family joined in the enthusiasm of the crowd beneath, when the Prime Minister's official announcement was displayed upon the railings; and London hung out its flags. The fighting had begun on the 4th August $4\frac{1}{4}$ years before, and had lasted just 1,561 days.

It was already known by a few in Croydon that the signature had been obtained; but there had been many disappointments, and all waited for authority to indulge in the heartfelt relief brought by the cessation of the long anxiety in which for so many years we had been plunged. Therefore, as it were in a solemn hush of the mind, we waited. At 11 o'clock the maroons went off, not to proclaim danger as of old, but the abolition of danger; and after their long silence the Church bells once more pealed out in a full chorus; the Town Hall Union Jack and the flag on the Church tower were run up—all at the same moment. The official 15 seconds elapsed and the maroon signal was repeated, a memory of so many air-raid warnings, now no more to be feared; and thereupon the Mayor, from the Town Hall steps led the cheers which acknowledged the glad tidings. A happy idea struck the Deputy Mayor (Alderman Trumble) and the boy scouts were summoned to parade the Borough for the last time sounding their bugle-call "All clear," that call which on so many occasions they had blown with all the breath of their body along the streets at night, happy boys, encouraged (wonder of wonders) to ride at topmost speed, making as much noise as they could! It was a kind thought of the Alderman's to give them this one last chance. Then the

National Anthem was sung with fervour, the Mayor's fine voice distinctly leading ; and " Praise God from whom all blessings flow." Finally the simple little ceremony closed with a stirring speech from Mayor Houlder, acknowledging the thankfulness of the inhabitants for their deliverance from the menace that had threatened them for more than four years," asserting that " Prussian Militarism had received its death blow " and that " Autocracy had disappeared from the Earth." Wherefore, said the Mayor, " it is our bounden duty to lead the race in the reconstruction of the world after the terrible war which we can now reasonably say has come to an end. God bless Croydon ! " Needless to say the Mayor's happy speech was greeted with three times three, followed by three for himself, who had borne so brave a part throughout, and then very appropriately by three for the brave boys at the front who had won for us this most glorious of all victories, ending the greatest and most ferocious of wars.

Croydon noisily manifested its joy while aeroplanes flew gaily overhead, but there was no real disorder. Flags quickly appeared on shops and houses, and in smaller editions were waved in a hundred hands. Big crowds assembled here and there and tramcars and omnibuses were occasionally held up in North End and High Street ; there was on all sides much shaking of hands, and bursts of cheering continually arose.

Then as the darkness came on a significant thing happened. The plague of darkness had been one of the greatest discomforts of Croydon by night during the long years of great discomforts ; and here suddenly arose a moon over the centre of Croydon, not a cause of anxiety and a prelude to air-raids, but gradually revealing itself to the astonished eyes of the happy crowds as the once familiar face of the illuminated Town Hall Clock. A drizzle was falling, though the joyous throngs disregarded it ; for every eye was gladly raised to the Town Hall tower ; flagrantly disobeying the now useless law prohibiting lights at night. In a few minutes many of the principal shopkeepers illuminated, and quite a number of private residents followed the suggestion of the Town Hall Clock ; though it was not till the next evening that the inhabitants in general lit up our roads at night all over the Borough. The Armistice Day was fitly wound up by a special evening commemoration service hurriedly arranged for and attended by a large and thankful congregation at the Parish Church.

II. Peace Day
(19th July, 1919)

Unlike Armistice Day, which came somewhat suddenly upon us, on Monday, 11th November, 1918, Peace Day was a fixed National Festival. We all knew that the peace with Germany which had been signed at Paris, on Monday, the 28th June, 1919, was to be celebrated on Saturday, 19th July; consequently Croydon had time wherein to make due preparations. The Borough rose to its opportunity.

The Corporation voted £2,000 in order to have a celebration worthy of the town, and began by supplying the necessary background of colour. All Katharine Street, and the long central line of High Street and North End to West Croydon Bridge, and beyond as far as Broad Green, were hung with flags of every colour on great loops of cord suspended from crimson "Venetian masts" (as decorators call them), and amid the clash of the joyful church bells, these fluttered and waved and filled the streets with gladness. The weather was propitious in the morning, and with unusual mercifulness did not turn to rain until after the procession had passed, so that the large crowds could enjoy the long perspectives of the streets to their heart's content, and could appreciate the success with which the Town Hall as the vital centre of Croydon had put on festival attire. Great sweeps of flags were stretched from the balcony of the tower to the roofs of the Reference Library on the one side and the main building on the other; vertical streams of colour, mainly royal blue and gold, marked the principal lines of the structure, while a great splash of colour spread horizontally across above at the balcony height, carrying on its breast the word "Victory," surmounted in the centre with the flags of our allies: France, Belgium, Italy, the United States, Serbia and Japan at the sides, and the Union Jack floating above them all. On the opposite side of the street stretched a huge "God Save the King." At the corner of High Street with Katharine Street rose a four-square arch on columns dedicated respectively to our greater "dominions," Canada, Australia, New Zealand and South Africa.

Then the burgesses added to this already splendid decoration many flags, along the houses of the procession route, and those who had "tin hats," or German field-caps, or bits of shells, or any other keepsakes, proudly displayed them. Nor was humour wanting even on the house-fronts; as witness the announcement on an empty shopfront in the London Road : " Having finished my holiday in France, 1914-1919, I am shortly opening this shop as a greengrocer," a gay prophecy of that rebuilding of the national prosperity which was to be our chief task from that time onwards. Soon after noon it really seemed as if no more people could be crowded into the centre of the town.

Ex-Service men and women assembled in the Park Hill recreation ground at 2 p.m., and disabled men shortly afterwards in Lansdowne Road, and thereafter the carefully arranged programme planned by the Town Clerk was punctually carried out. The school children of the borough lined the streets by schools at 2.45, boys here, girls there; each school vying with the rest in some characteristic touch. A bevy of happy schoolgirls in white, holding a woven rope of leaves and flowers would be seen along one section, a long line of boys with smart bouquets of flowers along another; and so on in charming variety. With 5,500 school children to work upon (as representing Croydon's 25,000 scholars) and teachers of fine fancy and good taste, it was not difficult to reach a beautiful living decoration in this way, and at the same time to give the children a good view of the proceedings which it was so desirable to fix upon their memory. Many schools sang merrily while they waited, and the shrill childish voices rose gaily above the murmur of the crowd. Volunteers in a long line protected the rows of children.

All the bands in Croydon were enrolled for the procession, and beyond their music and the children's, a quite novel and highly successful musical contribution was made by the Croydon Musical League in the shape of what one might call a perambulating concert of national melodies. This league had come into being in response to the widespread feeling that England should be prepared to celebrate great occasions in some more worthy manner than by the " mafficking " of our fathers. A League of Arts formed in London summoned Croydon to join it; but a few of our leading musicians, with Alderman H. Keatley Moore as Chairman, Mr. Alan J. Kirby as conductor, and under the presidency of Mayor Houlder, preferred to form a Croydon league, aiming not quite so high as the London body, but confining itself to simple music in which all bystanders might easily join. All choirmasters in Croydon were communicated with. The league's ambition was to get together a thousand voices as a festival choir, and though their ambitions were not fully satisfied, they got together a large body of good voices. To this considerable vocal contingent they joined what was

PEACE DAY

considered the best band in Croydon, the Silver Temperance Band, detaching it from the procession for that purpose. Rehearsals were held in the hall of the large bath, Scarbrook Hill, the only room big enough for the purpose, which had most fortunately remained floored-over for military uses, and was most obligingly lent by the officers commanding in the town.

When the Borough School Cadets and the Girl Guides had made a line on the pavement edge opposite to the Town Hall, the Mayor and Council and the Magistrates took up their position on the platform in front of the Town Hall steps at 3 o'clock. The band and the League Choir filtered with difficulty through the dense throng and formed up in the remains of the vacant space which should have been reserved for them, and which the irresistible crowd had considerably narrowed. After the Mayor had distributed many war medals and decorations to gallant fellows who had won them, he gave the signal, and " God Save the King " was played and sung. The streets resounded with that noble tune so dear to Englishmen all over the world, while the Town Hall flung back sonorous echoes. Then the band and choir did their best with the not very fine tune which does duty for " God Bless the Prince of Wales." Then followed the grandest of all choruses, the " Hallelujah Chorus," which the Mayor had especially desired. Those in charge had doubted if it would be effective in the open air, but were glad to be proved to be wrong and to own that His Worship had been right.

As the last " Hallelujah " resounded, distant cheers announced the arrival of the procession, and all Katharine Street shouted itself hoarse as Col. Roper brought his war-veterans to the salute in a long column of fours, interspersed with bands. Fourth Queen's, Fifth Queen's, Royal Engineers, Royal Artillery, Naval men, Air Force men, Royal Army Medical Corps, Royal Defence Corps, the Army Service Corps (led by Councillor Capt. Stevenson), the Labour Corps, and even a small body of warmly welcomed Colonials, headed by the Whitgift Cadets and their band, and followed by the girls of the W.A.A.C. and W.R.A.F., passed the Mayor, who took the salute which each component part gave him ; and mixed with them were machine-guns, military motor cars, war lorries, and many carriage loads of the wounded. All were heartily greeted along the far stretching line, but the loudest cheers of all were " Bravo, the Queen's." Last of all came the fine body of Special Constables, led by their energetic chief, Commander Swaine. Then the Mayor and his company having entered their carriages, brought up the rear of the procession. Impeded by the closely packed crowds the long line proceeded with difficulty by the High Street and North End to Broad Green, thence by Handcroft Road, Pitlake, and the Old Town to Duppas Hill, so far as the Mayor's division was concerned; while the Deputy Mayor with the remainder of the procession went straight on to Brigstock Road and so to Grange Wood. As the procession drew clear the streets filled up, and whenever room could be found there were couples singing and dancing; plenty of rough merriment and noise, but never any real disorder.

In mid-career, at 4 o'clock, upon a pre-arranged signal given by maroons the whole procession stopped, the bands ceased playing, the cheers and the joyful talk of the crowds were hushed, the church bells were silent, men stood bareheaded and still, not only along the line of route but all over the borough. In memory of the great dead all Croydon solemnly struck two minutes from its life and remained everywhere motionless and soundless until a bugler sounded "The Last Post" from the Town Hall. He was followed by other buglers along the line, the tension ceased, and the festival spirit reassumed sway. But no one who experienced it will ever forget that two minutes' silence; the thoughts that filled it remain part of the mind for ever; it was the culminating moment of the day. As a mere "effect" it was overwhelming, beyond the power of words to convey.

On Duppas Hill a cricket match "between Old and New Croydon," *i.e.*, between men over 40 and men under 40, had been arranged, the difficulty being not to find players, but to select two elevens from the large number of cricketers presenting themselves, and this was proceeding vigorously when the Mayor and his company reached Duppas Hill. A portable platform being provided, the Mayor spoke from it to the large crowd—cricketers and all—which gathered round him, expressing the Borough's glad welcome of peace, and at the same time recalling the great price that Croydon had paid for it, since few of those around him had not lost someone near and dear to them. Then he ended on a note of praise and gratitude for the bravery of the fine men who had achieved this greatest of all victories.

At 5 o'clock in a little drizzle, entirely disregarded, the cricketers began again, and the Mayor's portable platform having been conveyed down one of the Duppas Hill slopes, a charming open-air concert of national melodies was given by the massed choirs of the League in the natural amphitheatre provided. In addition to the music sung at the Town Hall and now repeated, "Rule Britannia," "Annie Laurie," "The Minstrel Boy," and the "March of the Men of Harlech," were heard as representing

respectively England, Scotland, Ireland and Wales; while the
" Land of Hope and Glory," as the best national song of our
own times, and " Auld Lang Syne " for friendship's sake, were
performed also by this fine body of voices and their accompanying
band. It is to be hoped that the stimulus thus given in the
name of Peace to collective musical production in Croydon will
never again die out. Then came country dances by school
children; and soon a general dancing of old and young was set
up all over the summit of the hill, to the music of some of the
bands from the procession.

At Grange Wood 8,000 to 10,000 people assembled, and
as soon as the northern part of the procession had arrived, bands
took it in turn to play, and Winterbourne Road school girls and
Ecclesbourne Road school girls took turns in a most delightful
succession of part singing, games, and country dances on the
lawn until the rain drove the dancers indoors and the spectators
under the shelter of the trees. At 8 o'clock the massed choirs
of the League, having been conveyed across the borough in
special tram-cars, sang the same programme as at Duppas Hill;
and the Mayor who had also arrived, with Mrs. Houlder, spoke
pithily and well upon the lesson of the day, between two of the
pieces, he and the large crowd and the choir and band quite
disregarding the rain, which now began to fall heavily. The
Mayor in full robes and chain, with the Macebearer accompanying him, loyally stood out the concert; which indeed was well
worth getting a wetting for. (At the Council Meeting, on the
following Monday, the Mayor expressed his thankfulness for
the Peace and his gratitude to all who had helped to celebrate
it, and crowned the edifice of the celebration by a gift of £500
for beds at the Croydon Hospital, with preference to wounded
soldiers.)

At many other points in the borough, besides these two
chief gatherings, local celebrations were held. The Mayor went
from Grange Wood to South Norwood to attend one of these,
at which the school children danced morris dances to the band's
playing. Another was organised at Woodside; 2,000 people
assembled at Pollard's Hill to make merry in the daylight and
to burn mighty flares at night; at Wandle Park the Boy Scouts
gave a display; and at Addiscombe a lordly bonfire twenty feet
high, was lit at 8.30, accompanied by fireworks and by a distribution of sweets and biscuits to the many thronging, shouting
children.

This last was the more welcome since Addiscombe and
other distant-living children were unable to get to Duppas Hill
to see the fireworks once more, after so many years (but at

P

treble or quadruple the cost of heretofore), provided, in his magnificent way, by Alderman Sir Frederick Edridge. Huge crowds thronged the slopes in thousands. Even the rain paused as if to look at splendours impossible during the war, but now for more than an hour delighting massed Croydon, and forming a magnificent ending to Peace Day. " Victory " sang the fireworks in blazing tones, " Keep the home fires burning," and finally " Thanks to the Boys," while the school children burst spontaneously into the strains of " Rule Britannia," taught them by their teachers so that they might join in with the massed League choir. (And that is one of the tiny touches of national unity which throughout the war-period constantly thrilled us in Croydon, every one being on the watch to join fraternally in everything going on in the borough.) At 11 o'clock the fireworks had ceased, and so (nearly) had the rain, and on the stroke of the hour a gorgeous ring of fire illuminated the whole sky, great flares arising from the Water Tower, Croham Hurst, Addington Hills, Beulah Hill, Pollard's Hill, and Russell Hill ; and on the further clouds reflected lights showed that beyond Croydon's blazing ring the country on every side was celebrating the great Victory in fire. Some illuminations brightened the night also, the most prominent being the electric lights above the Town Hall tower, and the very effective lighting of the tower at Gillett and Johnston's works. Then, on the road home, every street was filled with dancing crowds, the wonder being how they found room to dance. Again we must say, plenty of merriment and noise but not the slightest disorder.

In a day so full and so varied it was inevitable that small contretemps would occur. The line of the procession could not be kept always intact because of the immense pressure of the crowds ; but wherever it broke it quickly reunited ; and so with other things arranged for, which became momentarily disarranged, and rearranged themselves as quickly. The whole programme was not only carried out, but was to time, and the celebration from first to last was worthy of the town. Probably never before were so many people packed into North End.

And closing these great rejoicings on a deeper and more solemn note, *The Messiah* was performed in the Parish Church on the following Tuesday by a large choir and as large an orchestra as could be accommodated, conducted in a most finished manner by Mr. Alan Kirby, the additional organ accompaniments being performed by Mr. Leslie Smith. The mass of sound was ample when grand effects were wanted, while the solo voices could add the beauty of the softest tones whenever they were appropriate, since the church is admirable for sound. Many competent musicians present amongst the

PEACE CELEBRATION DAY (19th July, 1919). Street Procession.
Naval Contingent, heading the Procession

Photo by C. Harrison Price

PEACE CELEBRATION DAY (19th July, 1919): Street Procession. School Girls

Photo by C. Harrison Price

crowded audience were at one in saying that they had never so fully realised the grandeur of Handel's masterpiece as on that occasion ; forming as it then did part of a service, not interrupted by the usual display and applause, but running its splendid course in perfect freedom, and enhanced by surroundings of the highest beauty and impressiveness such as our noble church provides.

Of such a kind was Croydon's memorable Celebration of Peace Day, 1919.

1. The Hon. Editor :
Alderman H. KEATLEY MOORE, J.P.,
B.A., Mus. Bac.
Mayor, Nov., 1906 to Nov., 1908)
Hon. Freeman of the Borough

2. The Assistant Editor :
C. BERWICK SAYERS, F.L.A. (Hons.),
Borough Librarian
2 Surrey Vol. Regt., and 1 Vol. Bat.,
" The Queen's."

THE CROYDON ROLL OF HONOUR

PREFATORY NOTE

In compiling the Roll cordial help has been received from many people and institutions, including the clergy and ministers of religion, schoolmasters, secretaries of societies, and others too numerous to name individually. Some of these were good enough to gather much information and to provide long lists of the men known to them. To all grateful thanks are due. Every method that suggested itself has been employed to secure completeness and accuracy; such as posters displayed on church notice boards, in public buildings and on hoardings; advertisements in the local press, and letters kindly inserted by the Editors; public exhibitions at the Branch Libraries, and the publication of " Provisional Lists "; while the entire list of the fallen and of the Military Honours, as it presented itself at that date, was published in the " Peace " souvenir issue of *The Croydon Times*, on 26th July, 1919. Many names have been obtained from announcements in the official lists and in the newspapers; but in some cases it has been impossible to discover the addresses of next-of-kin in order to check the information. It is hoped, however, that the lists are reasonably complete and free from serious error, but it is not to be hoped that they are perfect, although no energy has been stinted in the attempt to make them so. The Roll contains the names of

    2506 of the Fallen
    499 of those who have won Military Honours
    207 Returned Prisoners-of-War.

In order to bring the lists within manageable compass, abbreviations have been used freely. It is believed that most of these are clear, and the following is a list of those likely to be unfamiliar.

A.B.	Able-bodied Seaman.	prep.	preparatory.
A.M.	Air Mechanic.	prev.	previous-ly.
act.-	acting.	ret.	returned.
b.	born.	*s.*	son of.
bdr.	bombardier.	sec.	secondary.
C.C.S.	Casualty Clearing Station.	secty.	secretary.
D.	Died.	stat.	stationary.
D.T.M.O.	Divisional Trench Mortar Officer.	stn.	station.
e.s.	elder, eldest son of.	trans.	transferred.
G.S.O.	General Staff Officer.	U.	Upper.
M.	Middle.	*w.*	wounded.
M.T.	Mechanical Transport.	*y.s.*	younger, youngest son of.
P.O.	Petty Officer.		
par.	parish.		

Hyphened names are entered under the last part of the name. In one or two places the strict alphabetical arrangement of names has been very slightly varied in order that the names of brothers might be entered together.

The plates bearing the portraits are numbered throughout in Roman figures and the portraits on each plate in Arabic figures. The Roll serves as a key, a reference being given at the end of each entry in connexion with which there is a portrait; thus " (Plate X., 3) " indicates that the third portrait on plate ten is that of the man.

I. The Glorious Dead

"Their name liveth for evermore."—
Ecclesiasticus, XLIV., 14.

ABBOTT, ALFRED, Cpl., E. Sur. Regt.
b., '80; married. *Res.*, S. Norwood. Member of Nat. Res. *D.*, of pneumonia, 18 Oct., '14; *buried*, St. James' Cem., Dover.

ABDEE, CHARLES, 3318, Pte., 2/4 R.W.S. Regt.
b., Bandon Hill, 14 May, '94. *Educ.*, Beddington Cent. Sch. and St. James' Sch., Croydon. Single. Shop Asst. *Enl.*, Nov., '15. *Fell*, Suvla Bay, 9 Aug., '16. (Plate III., 1).

ABDEE, GEORGE, Pte., R.W.S. Regt.
b., '79; married. *Fell*, France, 1 Jul., '16.

ABEL, HENRY THOMAS, Pte., R.W.S. Regt.
b., Finsbury, 21 Aug., '75; married. Government Packer. *Res.*, 29 Stroud Rd., Woodside. *Enl.*, 8 May, '17. *Fell*, nr. St. Quentin, 21 Mar., '18.

ABNETT, FRANK, Cpl., W. Yorks. Regt.
b., '87; married; 1 child. Empl. by L.B. & S.C.R. *Res.*, 16 U. Drayton Place, Croydon. *Enl.*, in R.E., Sept., '14; *w.*, 1 Nov., '17. *Fell*, 24 Mar., '18.

ACOCK, S. W., Pte.
Educ., Abp. Tenison's Sch., Croydon. Nurseryman. *Enl.*, Aug., '14. *Fell*, France, 6 Feb., '16.

ADAMS, C. A. G., Rflmn., R. Irish Rif.
b., '98; *e.s.*, Mr. & Mrs. C. P. Adams, 14 Dennett Rd., Croydon. *Educ.*, Brit. Sch., Croydon. Empl. by Welldon Engine Works. *Enl.*, Apr., '16. *D.*, 15 Apr., '18, while a pris. of war, from wounds recd. 21 Mar., '18.

ADAMS, C. H., 2/Lt., R.W.S. Regt.
b., '90; 3rd *s.*, Mr. & Mrs. John Adams, 21 Addis. Grove, Croydon. *Educ.*, Surrey House, Margate, and Dulwich Coll. *W.*, '15. *Fell*, 20 Sept., '17.

ADAMS, EDGAR, Pte., Artists Rif., 28 Lond. Regt.
b., '97; *y.s.*, Mr. & Mrs. John Adams, 21 Addis. Grove, Croydon. *Fell*, 27 Sept., '18.

ADAMS, F. M., Sgt., 2 Btn., 1 Can. Contingent.
b., Croydon, 24 Jan., '93; *s.*, Mr. & Mrs. Henry Adams, 94 Selsdon Rd., Croydon. *Educ.*, Dering Pl. Sch., Croydon. *Enl.*, Sept., '14, at Cobourg, Ontario. *Fell*, nr. Zillebeke, 3 Jun., '16.

ADAMS, H. N., Sgt., 19 R. Fus.
b., 11 Nov., '96. *Educ.*, Whitgift G. Sch. *Enl.*, '14. Ment. in despatches, '16. *Fell*, France, 2 Jan., '16.

ADAMS, JAMES RAYMOND, 1381, Rflmn., Q.W.Rif. (1/16 Lond. Regt.).
b., Acton Green Lodge, Middlesex, 26 Apr., '93; *s.*, George G. & Ada J Adams, 16 Elmwood Rd., Croydon. *Educ.*, Colet Court, W. Kensington, Pembroke Sch., Bruges, and Whitgift G. Sch. Single. Clerk in Surveyor's Off. *Enl.*, 20 Nov., '11; *w.*, Ypres, 28 Oct., '15. *D.*, Nervi, nr. Genoa, 19 Jul., '17. (Plate III., 2).

ADAMS, JOHN RODWAY, Pte., R.N.V.R.
b., 27 Aug., '89; *s.*, Mr. & Mrs. Edward Butler Adams, Park Rd., Wallington. *Educ.*, Whitgift G. Sch., '00-02. Ment. in despatches. *Killed* while engaged on anti-submarine work.

THE CROYDON ROLL OF HONOUR

ADAMS, R., 7101, Pte., Lond. Regt:
Fell, '17.

ADAMS, T. G., R.N.
b., '84; married; 2 children. *Res.*, 13 Laurier Rd., Addis. *Lost*, with H.M.S. "Aboukir," torpedoed by German submarine U9 in North Sea, 22 Sept., '14.

ADDERLEY, EDWARD JOHN, Pte., Can. Inf.
b., Terozepore, 12 Nov., '89; *e.s.*, E. J. & A. Adderley, 35 Beulah Rd., T. Heath. *Fell*, 15 Aug., '17.

ADDISON, GEOFFREY, Pte., 5 Can. E.F.
b., '84; *e.s.*, Dr. & Mrs. W. B. Addison, formerly of T. Heath. *Fell*, 26 Sept., '16.

ADDY, KENNETH JAMES BALGNY, 2/Lt., K.R.R.C.
b., 12 Apr., '92; *s.*, Mr. & Mrs. George Henry Addy, Ightham, Kent. *Educ.*, Whitgift G. Sch., '04-08. *Enl.* in Artists Rif., Aug., '14. *Fell*, France, 3 Oct., '15.

ADNITT, ERNEST EDWARD, 8469, Pte., R.B.
b., 18 Frith Rd., Croydon, 13 Jul., —. *Educ.*, Par. Ch. Sch., Croydon. Married. Labourer. *Res.*, 9 Southsea Rd., Croydon. *Enl.*, 9 Feb., '15. *Fell*, Ypres, 30 Jul., '15.

AGATE, SYDNEY HERBERT, 2/Lt., 4 Beds. Regt.
b., Croydon, 11 Jul., '84; 2nd *s.*, Mr. & Mrs. W. G. Agate Headcorn, Kent. *Educ.*, M. Whitgift Sch. Single. *Res.*, Forest Hill. *Enl.*, in Lond. Scottish, Nov., '14; commis., Aug., '16. *Fell*, nr. River Ancre, Nov., '16.

AHERNE, R. H., Trooper, — Yeom.
Educ., Whitgift G. Sch. *Fell*, '18.

AINSWORTH, CHARLES JOSEPH, Pte., R.W.S. Regt.
b., 17 Grove Rd., Redhill, 27 Apr., '17. *Educ.*, Redhill. Married. Coal porter. *Res.*, 20 Dickenson's Lane, Woodside. *Enl.*, 9 Jan., '15; *w.*, Festubert, 16 May, '15, Mametz, 2 Jul., '16. *W. and missing*, presumed fallen, Vimy, 23 Apr., '17.

AIREY, W. H., 82933, Bdr., R.G.A.
b., '89; married. *Res.*, 19 Hartley Rd., Croydon. Empl. at Croydon Electricity Works. *Enl.*, 19 May, '16. *Fell*, France, 10 Jul., '17.

AIRRISS, GEORGE FREDERICK, Pte., 22 Manchr. Regt.
b., 19 Jul., '84. *Educ.*, T.C.T., Goldsmiths' Coll., Lond. Univ. Teacher, Croydon Council Sch. *Enl.* in 24 Middlesex Regt. about Dec., '15; went to France, Jun., '16. *Fell*, nr. Bucquoy, France, 14 Mar., '17.

ALDOUS, ALFRED E., Pte., R.A.S.C,
b., '89; *e.s.*, Mr. & Mrs. Aldous, 19 Queen St., Croydon; married; 2 children. *D.*, of influenza, at Calais, 20 Feb., '19.

ALDOUS, HORACE J., Pte., 2/4 R.W.S. Regt.
b., '98; *y.s.*, Mr. & Mrs. Aldous, 19 Queen St., Croydon. *Educ.*, Abp. Tenison's Sch., Croydon. Empl. by Croydon Gas Coy. *D.* of wounds, Palestine, 26 Apr., '18.

ALEXANDRE, JOHN WILLIAM, Middlesex Regt.
s., Capt. & Mrs. Alexandre, St. Brelade's Bay, Jersey. *Res.*, 27 Hawke Rd., U. Norwood. *Fell*, '17.

ALLAWAY, WILLIAM THOMAS WALTER, Pte., 1 E. Kent Regt.
b., Camberwell, 5 May, '79; *s.*, Mr. & Mrs. Allaway, Herne Bay, Kent. *Educ.*, Bryers Sch., Forest Hill. Married. Insurance Clerk. *Enl.*, 30 Nov., '15. *D.*, 20 May, '16, at 8 Stat. Hosp., Wimereux, of wounds recd., 16 May, '16.

ALLEN, A., 41133, Pte., R. Innis. Fus.
Res., T. Heath. *Fell*, Jul., '17.

ALLEN, E. W., 201732, Pte., R.W.S. Regt.
Res., T. Heath. *D.,* of wounds, 30 Jun., '17.
ALLEN, F. BLAIR-, L/Cpl., D.L.I.
b., 7 Sept., '88 ; *s.,* Rev. & Mrs. Edward Blair-Allen. *Educ.,* Whitgift G. Sch.
ALLEN, FREDERICK THOMAS, Pte., Border Regt.
Res., 49a Beulah Grove, Croydon. Empl. by Messrs. Sainsbury, Purley. *Enl.,* May, '15 ; *w.,* '16. *D.* of wounds, 6 May, '18.
ALLEN, G. P., 2/Lt., 3/4 R.W.S. Regt.
b., Limpsfield, Surrey, 1 Dec., '96 ; *s.,* Mr. & Mrs. Francis Allen, 21 Duppas Hill Terrace, Croydon. *Educ.,* Tonbridge Sch Single. Gazetted, 3 Jun., '15. *D.,* at Caterham Cott. Hosp., 21 Dec., '15, of wounds recd. in bombing accident at Godstone, 19 Dec., '15. (Plate XXXVI., 6).
ALLEN H. J., Pte., Northd. Fus.
b., '84. *Educ.,* Whitehorse Rd. Sch., T. Heath. Married ; 2 children. *Res.,* 130 Burlington Rd., T. Heath. Empl. by Messrs. J. Grundy. *Enl.,* in R.W.S. Regt., '16. *D.,* at King George Hosp., 17 Apr., '18, of wounds recd. in France, 15 Apr., '18 ; *buried,* Queen's Rd. Cem., Croydon.
ALLEN, HARRY, 225524, Pte., 2/2 Lond. Regt.
Married ; 1 son. *Res.,* 271 Bensham Lane, T. Heath. Empl. by Croydon Corp. Tramways. Taken pris., 21 Mar., '18. *D.,* of pneumonia while pris. of war, at Wass Elnheim Elsass War Hosp., 29 Jun., '18.
ALLEN, JOHN SYDNEY, Cpl., Q.V. Rif. (9 Lond. Regt.).
b., '95 ; *y.s.,* Mr. & Mrs. F. J. Allen, T. Heath. *Educ.,* M. Whitgift Sch. Empl. at Lloyds Bank. *Enl.,* '14. *Fell,* 1 Jul., '16.
ALLEN, JOHN T. N., Pte., R.W. Kent Regt.
b., 4 Sylverdale Rd., Croydon, 31 Mar., '92. *Educ.,* Par. Ch. Sch., Croydon. Married. Baker. *Enl.,* 4 Feb., '17. *Fell,* Dickebusch, nr. Ypres, 17 Jul., '17.
ALLEN, ROBERT WILLIAM BOLTON, Lond. Regt.
b., '92 ; *s.,* Mr. & Mrs. Robert L. Allen, Dale Rd., Purley. *Fell,* '17.
ALLPORT, FRANK, Pte., 25 Aust. I.F.
b., S. Afr. ; *s.,* Mr. & Mrs. Allport, Fountains Creek, Miles, Queensland, Aust. *Educ.,* Boro. Sec. Sch., Croydon. Single. Farmer. *Res.,* Queensland. *Enl.,* Sept., '15. *D.* of wounds at 47 C.C.S., France, Jul, '18.
AMOS, EDWIN ALFRED, 61827, Pte., 13 R. Fus.
b., Fulham, 26 Oct., '97. *Educ.,* Brit. and M. Whitgift Schs., Croydon. Single. Insurance clerk. *Res.,* 13 Royal Mans., Lond.Rd., Croydon. *Enl.,* 12 May, '16. *Fell,* Monchy-le-Preux, 10 Apr., '17
ANDERSON, ALFRED, Sgt., Lond. Irish Rif. (18 Lond. Regt.)
Educ., High Sch., Croydon. *Enl.,* '14. *Fell,* 28 May, '17.
ANDERSON, BASIL, Capt.
Educ., High Sch., Croydon. M.C. *Fell,* '18.
ANDERSON, ERIC.
Educ., High Sch., Croydon. *Fell,* Nyassaland, '18.
ANDERSON, F., 48601, Pte., Welsh Regt.
Res., S. Croydon.
ANDERSON, FRANK, L/Cpl., R. Suss. Regt.
b., '86 ; married : 4 children. Empl. by Croydon Corp. Tramways. *Res.,* 4 Crunden Road, Croydon. *Enl.,* Aug., '14 ; *w.,* 11 Nov., '14. *D.,* of heart stroke, 15 Jul., '17.
ANDREW, A. R., Lt., M.G.C.
Educ., Whitgift G. Sch. *Missing.*

ANNAN, ROBERT P., L/Cpl., R.E. (T.)
    s., Mr. & Mrs. James Annan. *Res.*, Croydon. *Fell*, 30 Nov.,'17.

ANSCOMB, WILLIAM, L/Cpl., 7 R.W.S. Regt.
    b., Shirley, 1 Apr.,. '95 ; *s.*, F. & M. Anscomb, 45 Gillett Rd , T. Heath. *Educ.*, Shirley Ch. Sch. Single. *Res.*, 12 Elm Rd. T. Heath. *Enl.*, Nov., '13 ; *w.*, 4 times. Taken pris., 23 Mar., '18. *D.* at Lamsdorf pris. of war camp, Germany, 9 Aug., '18.

ANSCOMB, WILLIAM ANDREW, 1st Class Stoker, R.N.
    b., Horsham. *Educ.*, Christ Ch. Sch, Croydon. Married ; 3 daughters. *Res.*, Bute Rd., Croydon. Served 14 years in R.N. *Lost* with H.M.S. " Genista," 23 Oct., '16.

APPLEBY, CHARLES FREDERICK, 3670, Pte., R.W.S. Regt.
    b., Beddington, 24 Mar., '93 ; *s.*, F. W. & C. G. Appleby, 4 Farm Cott., Beddington Lane, Croydon. *Educ.*, Beddington Cent. Sch. Single. Farm labourer. *Enl.*, 1 Dec., '14 ; *w.*, '15. *Fell*, Mametz, 1 Jul., '16.

APPLETON, DAVID HOPKINS, 31223, Rflmn., R.B.
    b., Croydon, '88 ; removed to North Camp, Aldershot, '90, returning to Croydon, '00. *Educ.*, Redan Hill Sch., Aldershot. Single. Joiner and carpenter. *Res.*, 20 Wandle Rd., Croydon. *Enl.*, 11 Oct., '16. *D.*, of wounds recd. at Ypres, 14 Oct., '17.

ASHBY, ALBERT CYRIL, 533039, Pte., Lond. Regt.
    b., '96 ; *s.*, Mr. & Mrs. A. Ashby, 37 George St., Croydon. *Fell*, France, 25 Jun., '17.

ASHBY, ARTHUR, Cpl., R.W.S. Regt.
    b., 80 Whitehorse Rd., Croydon, 12 Nov., '94 ; *s.*, B. G. & Caroline Ashby, 47 Neville Rd., Croydon. *Educ.*, St. James' Sch., Croydon. Single. Labourer in flour mills. *Enl.*, Jan., '15. *D.*, 9 Aug., '17, of wounds recd. on Somme, 1 Jul., '16.

ASHBY, HARRY ERNEST, Rflmn., 6 Lond. Regt.
    b., Clapham, 23 Sept., '95 ; *s.*, late Mr. & Mrs. Ashby, 29 Wiltshire Rd., Croydon. *Educ.*, St. Andrew's Sch., Stockwell. Single. Checker, empl. by Tower Margarine Coy., Mitcham Common. *Enl.*, in 3/4 R.W.S. Regt., '15. *D.*, 26 May, '17, at St. Omer, of wounds recd. accidentally while engaged in rifle-grenade practice.

ASHBY, HERBERT WILLIAM, Rflmn., 13 K.R.R.C.
    b., 11 Queen St., Croydon, 8 Feb., '91 ; *y.s.*, John & Fanny Ashby, 10 Fawcett Rd., Croydon. *Educ.*, Par. Ch. Sch., Croydon. Married. *Res.*, Forest Hill. *Enl.*, 10 Sept., '14. *Fell*, Wytschaete, 3 Jul., '17.

ASHBY, S., 1316, Pte., Middlesex Regt.
    Fell, Jul., '16.

ASHCROFT, WILLIAM WORSLEY, Maj., R. Irish Rif. (attd. M.G.C.)
    b., '79 ; *e.s.*, Mr. & Mrs. W. Ashcroft, 13 The Waldrons, Croydon *Educ.*, Aldenham. Married ; 2 children. Partner of Messrs. Fuller, Moon & Fuller. Hon. Sec., E. Sur. Agricultural Assn. *Gazetted*, 2/Lt., Jun., '15. *Fell*, France, 16 Apr., '18.

ASHLIN, WILLIAM H., Pte., 1 R.W.S. Regt.
    b., '89 ; *e.s.*, Mr. & Mrs. Ashlin, 142 Stanley Rd., Croydon. Married. Empl. by Messrs. Fremlin. *Enl.*, Apr., '16 ; *w.*, '16. *Fell*, 25 Sept., '17.

ASKEW, CYRIL HORACE, 2/Lt., 8 Middlesex Regt.
    b., '93 ; 2nd *s.*, Mr. & Mrs. J. W. Askew, 19 Belvedere Rd., U. Norwood. *Educ.*, Acton County Sch. Clerk, Lond., City and Midland Bank. *Enl.*, in Q.V. Rif., '14. Commis., '17. *Fell*, Arras, 9 Apr., '17.

THE GLORIOUS DEAD 251

ASTON, GEORGE, C.Q.M.S., 3 E. Sur. Regt.
  b., Croydon, 3 May, '79 ; *s.*, George & Emily Aston, 17 Warwick Rd., T. Heath. *Educ.*, St. Saviour's Ch. Sch., Croydon. Married; 2 children. *Enl.*, 3 Dec., '97 ; served in S.A. War (med., 6 bars) *Fell*, nr. Hangard Wood, 4 Apr., '18.

ATHA, LEONARD EDWARD, 2/Lt., R.F.C.
  b., Dulwich, 19 May, '99 ; *s.*, H. M. & G. Atha, 69 Northampton Rd., Croydon. *Educ.*, Whitgift G. Sch. Single. Bank clerk. *Enl.*, as cadet, May, '17. *Fell* on his first war flight, nr. St. Quentin, 5 Mar., '18. *Buried*, Mil. Cem., Ham, France. (Plate V., 5).

ATKINS, ARTHUR CHARLES, 2/Lt., 3 Lond. Regt.
  b., Nunhead, 20 Apr., '97 ; *e.s.*, Charles W. & S. Selina Atkins, 68 Norbury Crescent, S.W. *Educ.*, M. Whitgift Sch., and City of Lond. Sch. Single. Empl. by Phœnix Insur. Coy. *Enl.*, in Inns of Court O.T.C., 10 Jul., '15. *Fell*, nr. Ginchy, 9 Sept., '16.

ATKINS, E. R. J., 238863, Sapper, R.E.
  Res., S. Norwood. *Fell*, '17.

ATKINSON, JAMES PERCY, Pte., 6 R.W.S. Regt.
  b., Wilford Rd., Croydon, 26 Apr., '95. *Educ.*, Princess Rd. Sch., Croydon. Single. Shop asst. *Res.*, 24 Beulah Grove, Croydon. *Enl.*, 26 Aug., '14. *Fell*, France, 14 Oct., '15.

ATKINSON, LEWIS DE BURGH, Capt., R. Suss. Regt.
  b., 26 Aug., '79 ; *s.*, Mr. & Mrs. Alexander Humphry Atkinson, King's Rd., Cheltenham. *Educ.*, Whitgift G. Sch., '91-94. Married. *Res.*, " Birchgrove," E. Croydon. Mentioned in despatches, Jan., '17. *Fell*, France, 16 Aug., '16.

ATKINSON, SIDNEY WILLIAM, Pte., 2/4 R.W.S. Regt.
  b., Smith's Yard, High St., Croydon. *Educ.*, Princess Rd. Sch., Croydon. Single. Carman. *Enl.*, 14 Jun., '15. *D.*, Alexandria, 25 Dec., '17, of wounds recd. in Egypt 2 days prev.

ATTEWELL, ALFRED WILLIAM, Pte., M.G.C.
  b., Wandsworth, 10 Jul., '97 ; *s.*, Mr. & Mrs. Alfred William Attewell, 26 Leslie Pk. Rd., Croydon. *Educ.*, Sevenoaks Counc. Sch., and Oval Rd. Sch., Croydon. Single. Printer. *Enl.*, in 2/4 R.W.S. Regt., 19 Oct., '14. *Fell*, France, 29 Aug., '16.

ATTWELL, FRANCIS.
  Res., Addison Rd., S. Norwood. *Fell*, in retreat from Mons, '14.

AUSTIN, THOMAS CARNELLEY MACDONALD, Capt., 4 S.W.B.
  b., Leytonstone, 27 Aug., '91 ; *s.*, Rev. George Beesley & Mrs. Elen Austin, 7 Mowbray Rd., U. Norwood. *Educ.*, City of Lond Sch., & Oriel Coll., Oxford. Single. Undergraduate. *Joined*, 2/Lt., Aug., '14 ; ment. in despatches for services at Gallipoli, Dec., '15. *Fell*, on second attempt to relieve Kut, 9 Apr., '16.

AVELINE, A. H., Sgt., R.W.S. Regt.
  b., Elgin Rd., Paddington, '89. *Educ.*, Abp. Tenison's Sch., Croydon. Single. Chauffeur. *Res.*, 26 Oval Rd., Croydon. *Enl.*, 31 Aug., '14. *Fell*, 9 Mar., '16.

AYLEN, F. E., 59421, Pte., Lab. Corps.
  Res., S. Norwood. *D.*, of wounds, Oct., '17.

BABER, KEMBLE FREDERICK, 201853, Pte., 2/4 R.W.S. Regt.
  b., Croydon, 27 May, '82 ; *s.*, Johnson & Mary Charlotte Baber, late of 114 Dennett Rd., Croydon. *Educ.*, Christ Ch. Sch., Croydon. Married ; 2 sons. Decorator's foreman. *Res.*, 20 Cecil Rd., T. Heath. *Enl.*, 29 Jul., '15 ; served in Egypt and Palestine. *Fell*, France, Jul., '18. (Plate IV., 6).

THE CROYDON ROLL OF HONOUR

BADCOCK, EDWARD S., 200042, Sgt., R.W.S. Regt.
  b., '88 ; s., George Edward & Annie Badcock, 184 Holmesdale Rd., S. Norwood. *Educ.*, Whitehorse Rd. Sch., T. Heath. Married. Empl. by L.B.& S.C.R. *Res.*, Wallington. *Fell*, Albert, 16 Jun., '18.

BADCOCK, HENRY ALBERT, Cpl., 1 Can. Inf.
  b., Southwark, 29 Apr., '90 ; s., George Edward & Annie Badcock, 184 Holmesdale Rd., S. Norwood. *Educ.*, Whitehorse Rd. Sch., T. Heath. Single. Farmer. *Res.*, Ontario, Can. Previously booking clerk, Norwood Junc. Stn., L.B. & S.C.R. *Enl.*, Jan., '15. *Fell*, Courcelette, 21 Sept., '16.

BADHAM, W. E., 1183, Sgt., R.F.A.
  Res., S. Norwood. *Fell*, Jun., '16.

BAGWELL, E. J., Pte., Middlesex Regt.
  b., '94 ; y.s., Mr. & Mrs. Arthur Bagwell, 353 Brighton Rd., Croydon. *Enl.*, May, '15. *Fell*, France, 26 Mar., '18.

BAILEY, EDWARD HENRY, Pte., R.W.S. Regt.
  b., 43 Russell Rd., Croydon, 3 Sept., '94. *Educ.*, Sydenham Rd. Sch., Croydon. Single. Labourer. *Enl.*, Mar., '11. *Fell*, Zonnebeke, 21 Oct., '14.

BAILEY, F. G., Pte., R. Suss. Regt.
  Empl. by Croydon Corp. Tramways. *Fell*, '17.

BAILEY, JAMES, Pte., 6 R.W.S. Regt.
  b., '94 ; s., Mr. & Mrs. Bailey, 16 Bruce Rd., S. Norwood. *Educ.*, Ecclesbourne Rd. Sch., T. Heath. Telegraph messenger. *Fell*, 11 Oct., '15.

BAILEY, JAMES ALFRED, Sgt., 11 R. Fus.
  b., Harlow, Essex, 19 Aug., '86 ; s., Mr. & Mrs. J. Bailey, Harlow, Essex. *Educ.*, Harlow. Married ; 3 children. Butchers' Canvasser. *Res.*, 17 Newark Rd., Croydon. *Enl.*, 9 Sept., '14. M.M., Theipval, 26 Sept., '16 (medal presented to widow by Duke of Connaught at Wellington Barracks, 31 Aug., '17). *Fell*, France, 17 Feb., '17.

BAILEY, LIONEL KEITH H., 1st A.M., R.F.C.
  b., Aylesford, Kent, 6 Nov., '92 ; s., Mr. & Mrs. W. S. J. Bailey, 263 Whitehorse Lane, S. Norwood. *Educ.*, Portland Rd. Sch., S. Norwood, and Lond. Polyt. Single. Clerk at Lloyd's. *Res.*, Addis. *Enl.*, 19 Jan., '15. *Killed* in accident, Auchy-au-Bois, 18 Sept., '17. *Buried*, Lillers Communal Cem. (Plate V., 6).

BAILEY, LOUIS JOHN, 2/Lt., R.F.C.
  b., T. Heath, 25 Jul., '93 ; s., W. & Ellen Bailey, 369 Bensham Lane, T. Heath. *Educ.*, Mackenzie Sch., Slough. Single. Commercial clerk. *Enl.*, in Artists Rif., 8 Dec., '15. *Fell*, Poperinghe, 17 Jun., '17.

BAINES, ARTHUR, 3481, Pte., R. Fus.
  b., Tooting, '88 ; e.s., Mr. & Mrs. S. G. Baines, 57 Lr. Addis. Rd., Croydon. *Educ.*, Oval Rd. Sch., Croydon. *Enl.*, 3 Apr., '16 ; w., 13 Nov., '16. *D.*, France, 2 Aug., '17, of wounds recd., 31 Jul., '17.

BAKER, A. E., 5226, Trooper, Hussars.
  Res., T. Heath.

BAKER, A. W., Cpl., R.F.A.
  Res., Croydon.

THE GLORIOUS DEAD

BAKER, ALBERT GEORGE, 9927, L/Cpl., Lond. Regt. (attd. M.G.C.)
   b., 11 Jul., '96 ; *s.*, Mr. & Mrs. G. Baker, 17 Leander Rd., T. Heath. *Educ.*, Winterbourne Rd. Sch., T. Heath, and St. Olave's Sch. Empl. by Lond. & River Plate Bank. *Enl.*, '14 ; *w.*, Jan., '15. *D.*, of wounds at C.C.S., Maricourt, 14 Sept., '16. *Buried*, Corbie sur Somme.

BAKER, ALFRED, Pte., R.W.S. Regt.
   s., Mr. & Mrs. W. Baker, 51 Newark Rd., Croydon. *Educ.*, Abp. Tenison's Sch., Croydon. *D.*, Birmingham, Mar., '16.

BAKER, ARTHUR, 4874, Gnr., R.F.A.
   b., '89 ; *s.*, Mr. & Mrs. W. Baker, 51 Newark Rd., Croydon. *Educ.*, Abp. Tenison's Sch., Croydon. *Enl.*, Mar., '16. *D.*, of wounds recd. 9 Aug., '17.

BAKER, E., Sgt., Manchr. Regt.
   s., Mr. & Mrs. W. Baker, 51 Newark Rd., Croydon. *Educ.*, Abp. Tenison's Sch., Croydon. Married. *D.*, 6 Sept., '18, of wounds recd. 21 Aug.. '18.

BAKER, ERNEST, Pte., Essex Regt.
   b., Croydon, 13 Jul., '89. *Educ.*, Mitcham Rd. Sch., Croydon. Married. Laundry engineer. *Res.*, 5 Lambeth Rd., Croydon. *Enl.*, 10 Jun., '16. *Fell*, France, 5 Apr., '18.

BAKER, FREDERICK EDWARD, R.N.
   b., '00. *Educ.*, Par. Ch. Sch., Croydon. *Joined*, '14. *Lost* with H.M.S. " Warrior," Battle of Jutland, 1 Jun., '16.

BAKER, GEORGE, L/Cpl., Essex Regt.
   b., Edenbridge, 30 Sept., '98. *Educ.*, Four Elms. Married. Labourer. *Res.*, 25 Tait Rd., Croydon. *Enl.*, 24 Jun., '16. *Fell*, France, 13 Apr., '17.

BAKER, HAROLD WILLIAM, Pte., R. Fus.
   Fell, 16 Apr., '17.

BAKER, HARRY E. R., L/Cpl., R.W. Kent Regt.
   b., '75 ; married. *Fell*, 27 Mar., '16.

BAKER, HENRY JAMES, Pte.
   Educ., M. Whitgift Sch. *Fell*, 25 Sept., '17.

BALDING, REGINALD NORMAN, 2/Lt., 3/5 Beds. Regt. (attd. M.G.C.)
   b., Colombo, Ceylon, 5 Apr., '95 ; *y.s.*, Rev. & Mrs. J. W. Balding, 21 Chatsworth Road, Croydon. *Educ.*, St. Michael's, Limpsfield, and King's Sch., Ely. Single. Bank clerk. *Enl.* in H.A.C., Feb., '15 ; commis., Sept., '15. *Fell*, Jebel Hamrin, Mesopotamia, 30 Mar., '17. (Plate III., 6).

BALDWIN, WILLIAM CHARLES, Pte., 1/23 Lond. Regt.
   b., '94. *Enl.*, 4 Jan., '16. *D.*, of wounds, Somme. *Buried*, Albert.

BALLOT, J., Pte., 1 Ox. & Bucks. L. I.
   b., Lr. Church St., Croydon. *Res.*, 14 Frith Rd., Croydon. *Fell*, Marne, '14.

BANCE, A. F., 73503, Pte., Sher. For.
   s., Mr. & Mrs. Bance, 74 Cherry Orchard Rd., Croydon. *Fell*, Mar., '18.

BANKS, FRED LAKEMAN, L/Cpl., L.R.B. (5 Lond. Regt.)
   b., 19 Jan., '74 ; *s.*, Mr. & Mrs. Fredk. Seymour Banks, 4 John St., Lond., W.C. *Educ.*, Whitgift G. Sch, '87-91. R. Humane Soc. Med. ; winner of Spencer Cup, Bisley ; served in S.A. War. Twice *w*. *Fell*, Ypres, 13 May, '15.

BANKS, HENRY BELLWOOD.
   s., late H. B. Banks, S. Norwood. *D.*, of wounds, France, 22 May, '18.

THE CROYDON ROLL OF HONOUR

BANYARD, FREDERICK WILLIAM, Cpl., 11 R.W.S. Regt.
    b., Sydenham, 24 Jul., '94 ; *s.*, Mr. & Mrs. R. Banyard, 50 Addison Rd., S. Norwood. *Educ.*, Portland Rd. Sch., S. Norwood. Married. Clerk. *Res.*, 21 Harrington Rd., S. Norwood. *Enl.*, 6 Nov., '15. *Fell*, Flers, France, 16 Sept., '16.

BARBER, FREDERICK WILLIAM, C.Q.M.S., 2 R.B.
    b., St. Pancras, 7 Mar., '77 ; *s.*, Mr. & Mrs. T. D. Barber, 43 George St., Croydon. *Educ.*, Oval Rd. Sch., Croydon. Married. Empl. in ham & beef trade. *Enl.*, 18 Jan., '97. *Fell*, Neuve Chapelle, 10 Mar., '15.

BARBER, H., Pte., 5518, Leinster Regt. (attd. R.E.)
    b., '82. Married ; 4 children. Empl. by Croydon Corp. *Res.*, 20 High St., T. Heath. *Enl.* in R.F.A., 6 May, '16. *D.*, 15 Aug., '17, of wounds recd. at Ypres, 5 Aug., '17.

BARKER, EDWARD THOMAS, Pte., 1/4 R.W.S. Regt.
    b., 8 Dec., '91 ; *s.*, Mr. & Mrs. David William Barker, 4 Beech House Rd., Croydon. *Educ.*, M. Whitgift Sch., and Whitgift G. Sch, '04-08. *D.*, of sunstroke, Lucknow, '15.

BARKER, H., 243158, Pte., E. Kent Regt.
    Res., Croydon. *Fell*, '17.

BARKER, L. H., 49864, Pte., D.L.I.
    Res., Croydon. *D.*, of wounds, '17.

BARKER, WILLIAM, Stoker, R.N.
    b., '88 ; *s.*, Mr. & Mrs. Frederick Barker, 55 Cobden Rd., S. Norwood. Married. Gardener. Killed on H.M.S. " Hawke," when torpedoed by enemy submarine, Oct., '14.

BARKHAM, CYRIL NORMAN, 4150, Rflmn., L.R.B. (5 Lond. Regt.)
    b., '93 ; *s.*, Mr. & Mrs. H. B. Barkham, 10 Cameron Rd., Croydon. Single. *D.*, at 34 C.C.S., nr. Albert, 27 Oct., '16, of wounds recd. nr. Combles, 8 Oct., '16.

BARKHAM, HERBERT THOMAS CLIFFORD, 5391, Pte., H.A.C.
    s., Mr. & Mrs. H. B. Barkham, 10 Cameron Rd., Croydon. Single. *D.* of broncho-pneumonia, Wimereux, 15 Aug.,'17. (Plate III., 5).

BARLEY, ARTHUR CECIL, Rflmn., Q.W.Rif. (16 Lond. Regt.)
    b., Croydon, 15 Dec., '92 ; *s.*, late Fredk. Barley, 36 Leander Rd., T. Heath. *Educ.*, High Sch., Croydon. Single. Clerk, Stock Exc. *Res.*, 338 Lond. Rd., Croydon. *Enl.*, Aug., '14. *Fell*, Ypres, 4 Oct., '15.

BARNES, A., 5329, Pte., R. Suss. Regt.
    Res., Croydon. *Fell*, '17.

BARNES, C. E., L/Cpl., Lancs. Fus.
    e.s., Mr. & Mrs. Chas. H. Barnes, 44 Ederline Av., Norbury. *D.*, of heart failure, 22 May, '18, while pris. of war at Brussels.

BARNES, HERBERT, 111040, Gnr., R.G.A.
    b., '86. Married ; 1 child. Empl. at Rates Dept., Croydon Corp. *Enl.*, 27 Jul., '16. *Fell*, 3 Oct., '17.

BARNES, J. C., 32087, Cpl., R.F.A.
    Res., Norbury. *Fell*, '16.

BARNES, W. J., 683068, Pte., Lond. Regt.
    Res., W. Croydon. *Fell*, '17.

BARNES, WILLIAM ALFRED, 1048, Cpl., 6 R.W.S. Regt.
    b., '96 ; *s.*, Mr. & Mrs. C. Barnes, 13 Dundee Rd., S. Norwood. Empl. by Messrs. W. H. Smith & Sons. *Enl.*, 2 Sept., '14. *Fell*, Vermelles, 4 Apr., '16.

BARNETT, ALBERT, Pte., Can. Scottish.
    Educ., Ecclesbourne Rd. Sch., T. Heath. Farmer. *Res.*, Can. *Fell*, Sept., '16.

I.

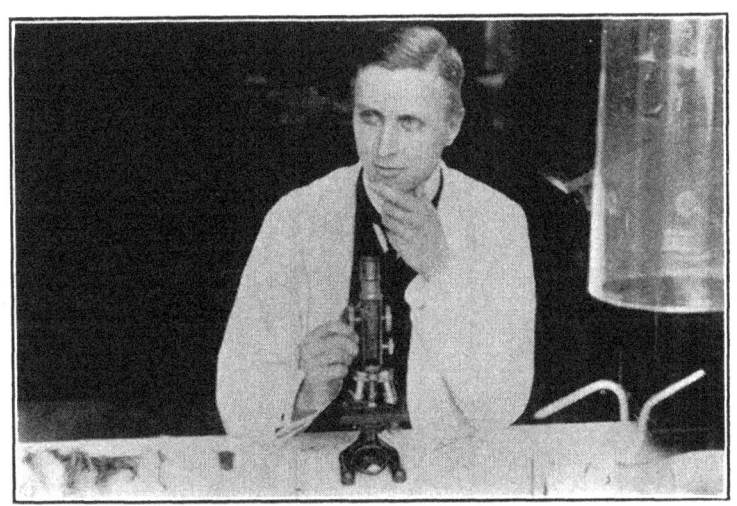

1. Pte. N. McColvin, 8 Border Regt.
2. 2/Lt. A. West, M.C., 2 R.W.S. Regt.
3. 2/Lt. W. West, 9 Sherw. For.
4. Dr. E. D. Parsons

II.

1. S/Sgt. J. A. Clarke, R.A.S.C. (Remounts)
2. Bdr. F. C. Walter, R.F.A.
3. Gnr. E. W. Jex, R.F.A.
4. Sgt. A. E. Bridges, R.F.A.

THE GLORIOUS DEAD

BARNETT, H. W., 2/Lt., 26 R. Fus.
b., '93 ; *s.*, Mr. & Mrs. K. Barnett, Pampisford Rd., Croydon. Married. Empl. by Messrs. Hammond & Hussey, Croydon. *Fell*, 20 Sept., '17. (Plate XIV., 1).

BARNEVELD, ROBERT WILLIAM, Rflmn., L.R.B. (5 Lond. Regt.)
b., Croydon, 20 Sept., '99 ; *s.*, Mr. & Mrs. T. A. Barneveld, 19 Norman Rd., T. Heath. *Educ.*, Ecclesbourne Rd., and Boro. Schs., Croydon. Single. Training for articles in accountancy. *Enl.*, Oct., '17. *Fell*, Berry-au-Bac, Aisne, 27 May, '18.

BARNHAM, JOHN WILLIAM JAMES, Sgt., 14 R.W. Kent Regt.
b., Clifton Rd., S. Norwood, 10 Mar., '95 ; *s.*, James & Rosina Selina Barnham, 243 Whitehorse Rd., Croydon. *Educ.*, Portland Rd. Sch., S. Norwood. Empl. by Croydon Electricity Works. *Res.*, 17 Manor Rd., S. Norwood. *Enl.*, 29 Nov , '15 ; M.M., 7 Jun., '17 ; *bar*, 20 Sept., '17. *Fell*, Grossett, Italy, 1 Dec., '17.

BARRAT, WILLIAM T., Lt., Manchr. Regt.
b., '77. Married. Empl. by Croydon Gas Coy. *Enl.*, in Lond. Regt., '15 ; commis., '16. *D.*, 25 Apr., '17, of wounds recd. 24 Apr., '17.

BARRETT, SIDNEY, 37033, Pte., R.W.S. Regt.
Married. *Res.*, 132 Lebanon Rd., Croydon. *Fell*, 21 Sept., '18.

BARRIE, DAVID, Capt., H.L.I.
b., Dundee, '64. Married. *Res.*, Lynton Rd., Croydon. *Enl.*, in Black Watch, '80 ; served in Egypt, '80-82 ; N.W. Frontier, etc., '84-00. Commis. as Lt. & Q.M., '00. Ret. to England on res. of officers, 12 Dec., '06. Commander, Croydon recruiting sub-area, '14-17. *D.*, of internal hæmorrhage, 18 Dec., '17.

BARRIE, WILLIAM ANDREW, Pte., Lond. Scottish (14 Lond. Regt.)
b., 8 Jan., '97 ; *s.*, Mr. & Mrs. Andrew Barrie, Purley Knoll, Purley. *Educ.*, Whitgift G. Sch., '06-13. *Fell*, 6 Sept., '16.

BARROW, GEORGE, Cpl., Glo'ster Regt.
b., 20 Jun., '80. Married. *Res.*, T. Heath. *Enl.*, 30 Apr., '17. *Fell*, nr. St. Quentin, 23 Mar., '18.

BARRY, GEORGE, 3143, Pte., R.W.S. Regt.
Res., 25 Strathmore Rd., Croydon. *Enl.*, 27 Oct., '14 ; served in France. *D.*, Netley Hosp. while undergoing operation, Aug., '17. *Buried*, Queen's Rd. Cem., Croydon.

BARTLETT, GEORGE RICHARDSON, Despatch Rider, R.E.
b., Lond.. 6 Mar., '00 (?) ; *s.*, Mr. & Mrs. Bartlett, 9 Lincoln Rd., S. Norwood. *Educ.*, Enfield G. Sch. Single. Marine insurance clerk in connection with Lloyd's. *Enl.*, 2 Apr., '15 ; *w.*, Ypres, Sept., '17 ; ret. to France, Jan., '17. *Fell*, France, Nov.,'18.

BARTLETT, H. J., 4390, Pte., R.W.S. Regt.
Res., 2 Haslemere Rd., T. Heath. *Fell*, 14 Jul., '16.

BARTLETT, WILLIAM STANLEY, L/Cpl. 1/4 R.W.S. Regt.
b., Harvey Rd., Camberwell, 2 Nov., '89 ; *s.*, James William & Emily Bartlett, 21 Southwell Rd., Croydon. *Educ.*, Boston Rd. Sch., Croydon. Single. Wood machinist. *Enl.*, in Terr., 8 years before war ; mobilised, 5 Aug., '14 ; went to India, Oct., '14 ; *served* at Persian Gulf, Baghdad, Kut-el-Amara ; *w.*, Ctesiphon, 21 Dec., '15 ; taken pris. at Kut. *D.* at Entilli, Turkey, as a result of his wounds, ill-treatment, and starvation, Sept., '16.

BARTON, W. S., Gnr., R.F.A.
s., late Simon, & Mrs. Barton, Wisbeach Rd., Croydon. Married ; 3 children. *Res.*, 48 Zion Rd., T. Heath. *Enl.*, Jul., '15 ; *served* in Salonica and France. *D.* of gas poisoning, France, '17.

BASE, SAMUEL DAVIS, Rflmn., K.R.R.C.
  b., 11 Sept., '82; *s.*, Mr. & Mrs. Edward William Base, 24 Birdhurst Rd., Croydon. *Educ.*, Whitgift G. Sch., '94-98. *Fell*, '16 (?).
BASHFORD, A., Sgt., H.L.I.
  Married. *Res.*, Croydon. *W.*, 13 Nov., '14. *Fell*, France, 4 Sept., '15.
BASHFORD, D., 8459, Pte., E. Sur. Regt.
  b., Croydon, 29 Sept., –. *Educ.*, Dunstan Rd., Hammersmith. Married. Decorator. *Res.*, 123 Harrington Rd., S. Norwood. *Enl.*, Jan., '15. *D.* of fever, Salonica, 25 Jul., '16.
BASSETT, GEOFFREY E., Lt., R.A.S.C. (attd. Ox. & Bucks. L.I.).
  b., '94; *e.s.*, John Dollin & Edith Bassett, "Littledene," S. Croydon. *Fell*, 21 Mar., '18.
BATCHELAR, ROBERT THOMAS, 2/Lt., 7 R.W.S. Regt.
  b., '86; *e.s.*, late Thomas G., & Mrs. Batchelar, Chatsworth Rd., Croydon. *Fell*, 23 Mar., '18.
BATCHELOR, THOMAS, Pte., 1 R.W.S. Regt.
  Educ., Mitcham Rd. Sch., Croydon. Empl. by Messrs. Packham, Croydon. *Res.*, 77 Priory Rd., Croydon. *Enl.*, 6 Aug., '14. *Fell*, 21 Sept., '18.
BATEMAN, EDWARD CHARLES, L/Cpl., Essex Regt.
  b., 2 Mar., '97; *s.*, Jacob & Emily Bateman, 21 Charnwood Rd., S. Norwood. *Educ.*, Whitehorse Rd. Sch., T. Heath, and Stanley Tech. Sch., S. Norwood Single. Stockbrokers' clerk. *Enl.*, 13 Apr., '16. *Fell*, France, 13 Nov., '16.
BATEMAN, J., 5789, Pte., R. Berks. Regt.
  Res., T. Heath. *Fell*, '16.
BATEMAN, JACK, Pte., R. Fus.
  b., '89; *e.s.*, Mr. & Mrs. Bateman, 2 Bridge Place, Croydon. Greengrocer. *Fell*, 23 Aug., '18
BATEMAN, S. JACOB, 2219, L/Cpl., 3 R. Fus.
  Empl. by Messrs. Carter, Paterson. *D.*, Etaples, 10 Oct., '15, of wounds recd. at Loos, 28 Sept., '15.
BATESON, FREDERICK CHARLES.
  b., '90. *Fell*, France, 21 Aug., '17.
BATSON, HENRY THOMAS, 2/Lt., R.W.S. Regt. (attd. R.F.C.)
  b., '89; *e.s.*, Mr. & Mrs. T. Batson, 32 Broadway Av., Croydon. Empl. by Croydon Board of Guardians and Paddington Board of Guardians. *Enl.* in H.A.C., Nov., '15; commis., Feb., '17; *w.*, Beaumont Hamel, Jun., '16. *Fell*, 11 Sept., '17.
BATT, P., 10156, Pte., R. Fus.
  Res., U. Norwood. *Fell*, '17.
BAYES, A. V., Rflmn.
  Married. Empl. by Messrs. C. Brown & Co., Waddon. *Res.*, Neville Rd., Croydon. *D.*, 26 Sept., '16, of wounds recd. 15 Sept., '16.
BAYLISS, ARTHUR WENTWORTH, L/Cpl., L.R.B. (5 Lond. Regt.)
  b., E. Dulwich, 20 Jul., '93; *s.*, Edward Swayn & Sophie Alice Bayliss, Pollards Hill E., S.W. *Educ.*, M. Whitgift Sch. Single. Bank clerk. *Enl.*, 5 Aug., '14. *D.*, 2 Northern Mil. Hosp., Leeds, 16 Nov., '16, of wounds recd. Ypres, 28 Jan., '16.
BEADELL, H., 21868, Pte., R.W.S. Regt.
  Res., Addis. *Fell*, '17.
BEADLE, EDWARD JOHN, L/Cpl., S.W.B.
  b., Banstead, 22 Oct., '84; *s.*, Edward Henry & Laura Sarah Beadle. *Educ.*, Par. Ch. Sch., Croydon. Married. Storekeeper. *Res.*, 28 Bourne St., Croydon. *Enl.* in R.W. Fus., 17 Nov., '15. *Fell*, Monchy, 23 Apr., '17. (Plate III., 4).

III.

1. Pte. C. AEDEE, 2/4 R.W.S. Regt.
2. Rflmn. J. R. ADAMS, Queen's Westm. Rif. (16 Lond. Regt.)
3. Cpl. A. G. GREENHEAD, 1 Duke of Cornwall's L.I.
4. L/Cpl. E. J. BEADLE, S.Wales Borderers.
5. Pte. H. T. C. BARKHAM, H.A.C.
6. 2/Lt. R. N. BALDING, Beds. Regt. (attd. Machine Gun Corps)

IV

1. Rflmn. F. J. BOXALL, Lond. Rif. B.
2. Pte. H. W. BLUNDELL, 11 R.W.S. Regt.
3. L/Cpl. W. G. BRADLEY, 1 Oxf. & Bucks. L.I.
4. Lt. T. R. BOTTOMLEY, 1 E. Yorks. Regt.
5. 2/Lt. B. BONCKER, E. Yorks. Regt.
6. Pte. K. F. BABER, 2/4 R.W.S. Regt.

THE GLORIOUS DEAD

BEAGLEY, A. E., L/Cpl., Lond. Regt.
b., '94. Married. *Res.*, 31 Southbridge Rd., Croydon. *Enl.* in R.W.S. Regt., May, '15. *Fell*, Cambrai, 30 Nov., '17.

BEAGLEY, FRANK, Pte., Lond. Regt.
b., '91 ; *e.s.*, Mr. & Mrs. Beagley, 2 Lancing Rd., Croydon. *Educ.*, Boston Rd. Sch., Croydon. *Fell*, High Wood, Somme, Sept., '16.

BEALE, G. H., 19832, Pte., R. Suss. Regt.
Res., Croydon. *Fell*, '17.

BEALL, ALFRED, 235048, Pte., Middlesex Regt.
b., '98 ; *s.*, Mr. & Mrs. Alfred E. Beall, 32 Pitlake, Croydon. *Enl.*, Mar., '17. *Fell*, France, 3 Aug., '17.

BEARD, FREDERICK GERALD VESEY, Lt., Worcester Regt.
b., 17 Dec., '89 ; *s.*, Dr. & Mrs. F. Beard, " The Crossways," S. Croydon. *Educ.*, Epsom Coll., and Trinity Coll., Dublin (B.A.) Single. Schoolmaster. Commis., 17 Sept., '14 ; served in Gallipoli, Egypt, France. *Fell*, Beaumont Hamel, 4 Jul., '16.

BEARMAN, CECIL LAWRENCE, 2/Lt., R.W.S. Regt.
b., '97 ; *s.*, Mr. & Mrs. C. E. Bearman, 228 Melfort Rd., T. Heath. *Educ.*, Boro. Sec. Sch., Croydon. *Enl.*, in 16 Middlesex Regt. (Publ. Sch. Btn.), '15 ; *w.*, Oct., '17 ; commis., 30 Apr., '17. *Fell*, France, 23 Aug., '17.

BEART, THOMAS FITT, Pte., C Squadron, 6 Mounted Bde., S.A.Forces.
b., Croydon, 7 Feb., '80 ; *s.*, Henry John & Susan Beart, 26 St. Peter's Rd., Croydon. *Educ.*, M. Whitgift Sch. Married. Stud groom. *Res.*, Bloemfontein, since '98. *Enl.*, '15 ; served in German S.W. Africa ; discharged owing to ill health, '16. *D.* of kidney disease at Bloemfontein, Jul., '16.

BEAUCHAMP, ARTHUR WILLIAM, 326, Pte., 10 R. Fus.
b., '95 ; *s.*, Mr. & Mrs. A. R. Beauchamp, 23 Richmond Rd., T. Heath. *Res.*, 231 Melfort Rd., T. Heath. *Fell*, Pozieres, 15 Jul., '16.

BEAUMONT, SIDNEY, 2/Lt., E. Lancs. Regt.
b., '79. Married. Headmaster, Oval Rd. Sch., Croydon ; formerly Hon. Secty., Croydon Liberal Assoc. *Enl.*, in R. Suss. Regt., May, '16. M.C. *D.*, of wounds, France, 28 Mar., '18.

BECHLEY, ERIC WHITE, 2/Lt., D.L.I.
b., Waddon, 19 Dec., '94 ; *s.*, Mr. & Mrs. K. M. Bechley, 12 Clifford St., Glasgow. *Educ.*, Commercial Travellers Schs., Pinner. Single. Engineer. *Res.*, 79 Nova Rd., Croydon. *Enl.* as pte., Aug., '14. *D.*, 9 Jun., '18, at 4 Can. Gen. Hosp., of wounds recd. nr. Pernes, 4 Jun., '18.

BECK, E. R., Sgt.
b., '92 ; *s.*, Mr. & Mrs. Beck, 22 Birchanger Rd., S. Norwood. *D.*, 9 Sept., '18, at Le Tréport, of wounds recd. 28 Aug., '18.

BECKETT, H. G., 1127, Pte., R.W.S. Regt.
Fell, '16.

BECKFORD, C., 14365, Rflmn., K.R.R.C.
Res., S. Norwood. *D.*, of wounds, '16.

BEDFORD, WILLIAM EDWIN HENRY, Pte., R. Suss. Regt.
b., Chelsea, 24 Dec., '99 ; *s.*, Mr. & Mrs. W. J. Bedford, 139 Moffatt Rd., T. Heath. *Educ.*, Beulah Rd. Sch., T. Heath. Single. Plumbers' mate. *Enl.*, 18 Jan., '18. *D.*, France, 10 Aug., '18, of wounds recd. 8 Aug., '18.

BEEBY, WILLIAM SINCLAIR, L/Cpl., 6 Middlesex Regt.
 b., Sanderstead, 21 Apr., '85 ; s., W. & E. Beeby, 31 Pemdevon Rd., Croydon. *Educ.*, Par. Ch. Sch., Croydon. Married. Fishmonger. *Res.*, 88 Lakehall Rd., T. Heath. *Enl.*, Jun., '16. *Drowned*, whilst on way to Palestine, through transport being torpedoed, 30 Dec., '17.

BEENHAM, WILLIAM ERNEST, Pte., Middlesex Regt.
 b., 15 Bolton Gardens, Lond., W., 23 Aug., '86 ; *s.*, Charles & Elizabeth Beenham, 47 Grasmere Rd., S. Norwood. *Educ.*, St. Mark's Coll., Chelsea. Married. Solicitor's clerk. *Res.*, 46 Grasmere Rd., S. Norwood. *Enl.*, Sept., '14. *Fell*, Somme, 21 Jul., '16.

BEER, WALTER G., M/4112408, Pte., R.A.S.C.
 b., Croydon, 22 Aug., '76 ; *e.s.*, Alfred George & Martha Ann Beer, 4 Latimer Rd., Croydon. *Educ.*, Par. Ch. Sch., Croydon. Married. Carpet planner. *Res.*, 191 Whitehorse Rd., Croydon. *Enl.*, 10 Jul., '15. *Fell*, Salonica, 12 Nov., '16.

BEHM, ERNEST EMIL JOHN ALFRED, Chief P.O., R.N.
 b., 11 Apr., '87 ; *s.*, Mr. & Mrs. Ernest John Behm, Selbourne Cott., Sanderstead. *Educ.*, Whitgift. G. Sch. *Enl.*, in R.N.V.R. before war. *Fell*, on H.M.S. "Queen Mary," during Battle of Jutland, 31 May, '16.

BELCHAMBER, ERIC HAROLD, Pte., R. Fus.
 s., Mr. & Mrs. H. C. Belchamber, Lond. County & Westminster Bank House, Addis. *Fell*, 22 Mar., '18.

BELCHER, ALBERT, Pte.
 Fell, France, Oct., '16.

BELCHER, BERTRAM THOMAS, 6888, Pte., K.O.Y.L.I.
 b., Stoke Newington, 19 Jul., '97 ; *s.*, Mr. & Mrs. Belcher, 24 Spring Lane, Woodside. *Educ.*, Woodside Sch., S. Norwood. Single. Ironmonger's asst. *Enl.*, in R.W.S. Regt., 24 Aug., '14 ; twice *w*. *Fell*, nr. Arras, 10 Apr., '17. *Buried*, Boyelles.

BELL, ANDREW, Ordinary Seaman, Merchant Service.
 b., Newcastle, 19 Aug., '99 ; *y.s.*, John Joseph & Elizabeth Bell, 18 Brocklesby Rd., S. Norwood. *Educ.*, Jesmond, and Portland Rd. Sch., S. Norwood. Single. Entered Mercantile Marine, Feb., '15. *Drowned* on S.S. "Cairnstrath," torpedoed in Bay of Biscay, 4 Aug., '17.

BELL, HENRY, 2/Lt., 8 Yorks. Regt.
 b., Newcastle, 27 Nov., '92 ; *s.*, John Joseph & Elizabeth Bell, 18 Brocklesby Rd., S. Norwood. *Educ.*, Jesmond. Single. Clerk. *Enl.*, Jun., '10 ; served in France, Oct., '14-16 ; permanent commis., 20 Jun., '16 ; *w.*, France, Jul., '16. *D.* at Rouen, 17 Oct., '17, of wounds recd. at Inverness Copse, Ypres, 20 Sept., '17. *Buried*, St. Denis Cem., Rouen.

BELL, JOHN JOSEPH, Sgt., 13 Cheshire Regt.
 b., Newcastle-on-Tyne, 30 Apr., '89 ; *e.s.*, John Joseph & Elizabeth Bell, 18 Brocklesby Rd., S. Norwood. *Educ.*, Newcastle. Married, '15 ; 1 daughter. Served as 2nd mate in Mercantile Marine for 10 years. *Enl.*, early in '15. D.C.M., 4 Oct., '15, bestowed on his widow by Mayor of Wallasey, Feb., '17. *Fell*, France, 6 Jul., '16.

BELL, WILLIAM, A B. Seaman, R.N.
 b., Newcastle, 31 May, '98 ; *s.*, John Joseph & Elizabeth Bell, 18 Brocklesby Rd., S. Norwood. *Educ.*, Jesmond. Single. Hotel servant. *Enl.*, Apr., '15. *Lost*, on H.M.S. "Indefatigable," sunk in Battle of Jutland, 31 May, '16.

THE GLORIOUS DEAD

BELL, HENRY, Pte., Middlesex Regt.
b., 15 Feb., '96. *Educ.*, Princess Rd. Sch., Croydon. Married. Carman. *Res.*, 13 Union Rd., Croydon. *Enl.*, 8 Jun., '15. *Fell*, France, 2 Mar., '17.

BELL, WILLIAM ERNEST COLYER, Pte., 11 E. Yorks. Regt.
b., W. Croydon, 21 Feb., '95. *Educ.*, Christ Ch. Schs., Croydon. Single. Model aeroplane maker. *Res.*, 99 Tamworth Rd., Croydon. *Enl.*, 6 Aug., '15. *Fell*, Arras, 5 May, '17.

BELLAMY, GEORGE WARRINGTON, Pte., R.W.S. Regt.
b., '94 ; *s.*, Mr. & Mrs. Bellamy, 11 Hamilton Rd., T. Heath. *Enl.*, 5 Sept., '14 ; *w.*, 26 Sept., '15. *Fell*, 1 Jul., '16.

BENGER, ALFRED HORACE, Maj., Leicester Regt.
b., '78 ; *y.s.*, Mr. & Mrs. Alfred Benger, 10 Park Hill Rise, Croydon. *Fell*, '17.

BENHAM, ALFRED GORDON, 23 Lond. Regt.
b., Croydon, 30 Jan., '98 ; *s.*, James Henry & Charlotte Amelia Benham, 46 Sundridge Rd., Addis. *Educ.*, Boro. Sec. Sch., Croydon. Single. Clerk, L.B. & S.C.R. *Enl.*, 7 Sept., '14. *Fell*, Somme, 16 Sept., '16.

BENHAM, HERBERT LOUIS, Gnr., R.G.A.
e.s., Mr. & Mrs. Herbert Benham, 8 Waldegrave Rd., U. Norwood. *Drowned*, 17 Jun., '18.

BENNEFIELD, ALBERT, Pte., M.G.C.
b., 3 Mayo Rd., Croydon, 30 Sept., '97 ; *s.*, Mr. & Mrs. A. Bennefield, 14 Northbrook Rd., Croydon. *Educ.*, Princess Rd. Sch., Croydon. Single. Empl. at poultry farm. *Enl.*, 3 Oct., '14. *Fell*, France, 29 Aug., '16.

BENNETT, H., 35212, Pte., R. Fus.
Res., T. Heath. *Fell*, '16.

BENNETT, L. E., 2/Lt., R.W.S. Regt.
Fell, '16.

BENNETT, S. F., 4542, Pte., Lond. Regt.
Fell, '16

BENTHAM, THOMAS, Lt., R.A.M.C.
b., Croydon, '85 ; *s.*, Rev. Thomas & Maud Bentham, " St. Mildred's," Addis. Rd., Croydon. *Educ.*, Whitgift G. Sch., & Queen's Coll., Oxford. Single. Lecturer on zoology, Armstrong Coll., Newcastle-on-Tyne. *Joined* R.A.M.C. as Lt., in '17, being employed as Protozoologist & Bacteriologist ; 2 yrs. at Mil. Hosp., Malta ; in 1919 he was appointed to Addington Mil. Hosp., but died before he could take up his work there. Mentioned in despatches for valuable services in the diagnosis of dysentery. *D.*, of pneumonia, at " St. Mildred's," Addis. Rd., Croydon, 12 Mar., '19.

BENTLEY, A. G., Gnr., R.G.A.
b., '85 ; *s.*, Mr. & Mrs. W. Bentley, 48 Eridge Rd., T. Heath. Married. *Res.*, 1 Portland Cott., Beddington. *Enl.*, 17 May, '17. *Fell*, 26 Sept., '17.

BENTLEY, FREDERICK ARTHUR, Pte., 2/4 R.W.S. Regt.
b., Croydon, 7 Mar., '94 ; *s.*, Mr. & Mrs. Eliza Bentley, 296 Brighton Rd., Croydon. *Educ.*, Sydenham Rd. Sch., Croydon. Single. Clerk. *Enl.*, Nov., '14. *Fell*, Jerusalem, Dec., '17. *Buried*, N.E. slope of Mt. of Olives.

BENTON, FRANK, 2/Lt., K.R.R.C.
b., Aveley, Essex, 30 Mar., '81 ; *s.*, Mr. & Mrs. John Benton, Birdhurst Gardens, Croydon. *Educ.*, Whitgift G. Sch, '93-97. Single. Insurance broker. Played Rugby football for Essex & Surrey. *Enl.*, in R. Fus., '15 ; commis., Jun., '16. *Fell.*, Flers, Somme, Sept., '16.

BERG, LESLIE CYRIL VON, Pte., Can. Inf.
   b., '90 ; *e.s.*, Mr. & Mrs. Clement von Berg, St. Augustine's Av., Croydon. *Fell*, 27 Sept., '18.
BERRY, ALGERNON LAURENCE, 2/Lt., 14 (attd. 8) R. Fus.
   b., 15 Abbey Gardens, St. John's Wood, N.W., 17 Dec., '79 ; *s.*, late Henry Berry, & Caroline Elizabeth Berry, " Rutherford.' Pampisford Rd., Croydon. *Educ.*, Whitgift G. Sch. & private sch. at Cambridge. Married. Land & estate agent. *Res.*, 28 Herondale Av., Wandsworth Common, S.W. *Enl.*, as pte., Aug. or Sept., '14. *Fell*, Ovillers, 7 Jul., '16. (Plate VI., 1).
BERRY, LEONARD HUGH, Pte., 13 Essex Regt.
   b., Ilford, 20 Dec., '79 ; *s.*, Theophilus & Rosetta Berry, Wimbledon. *Educ.*, St. Mark's Coll., Fulham. Married. Accountant (A.L.A.A.). *Res.*, 38 Nutfield Rd., T. Heath. *Enl.*, 22 Sept., '16. *Fell*, nr. Cambrai, 3 Feb., '18.
BERRY, PERCY HAMILTON, Pte., Artists Rif. (28 Lond. Regt.)
   b., 9 Feb., '98 ; *s.*, Mr. & Mrs. B. Alfred Berry, Croham Park Av., Croydon. *Educ.*, Whitgift G. Sch., '07-13. *D.* of fever, at St. Omer, 30 Apr., '15.
BEVAN, ERNEST VICTOR, Pte., Aust. I.F.
   b., 18 Dec., '91 ; *s.*, Mr. & Mrs. H. Bevan, Teddington. *Educ.*, High Sch., Croydon. Single. Farmer. *Res.*, Melbourne, Australia. *Enl.*, Sept., '14. *Fell*, Gallipoli, 8 May, '15.
BEVAN, GORDON FREDERICK, Pte.
   b., Stanwell, Middlesex, 3 Aug., '88 ; *s.*, Mr. & Mrs. H. Bevan, Teddington. *Educ.*, High Sch., Croydon. Horticulturist. *Res.*, Seattle, U.S. *Enl.*, Sept., '14. *Fell*, 16 Mar., '15. Buried, Abbaye des Chartreux, La Boutillerie, Flanders.
BEVEN, GEORGE, Pte., Dorset Regt.
   Fell, 3 Oct., '18.
BICKERSTAFF, W. E., 99922, R.E.
   Fell, '16.
BICKMORE, ARTHUR, Pte., 1/23 Lond. Regt.
   b., '87 ; *s.*, Mr. & Mrs. W. Bickmore, 5 Clarence Rd., Croydon. *Fell*, Givenchy, 26 May, '15.
BIGG, G. A., 168937, Gnr., R.F.A.
   Res., Croydon. *D.*, of wounds, '17.
BIGNELL, ERNEST VICTOR, Cpl., R.W.S. Regt.
   b., Croydon, '92 ; *s.*, Mr. & Mrs. A. Bignell. *Educ.*, Oval Rd. Sch., Croydon. Married. Gardener. *Res.*, 1 St. John's Rd., Croydon. Served in Gallipoli, Palestine, France, & Army of Occ., Germany. *D.*, at Crescent Hosp., Croydon, 18 Feb., '19. Buried, Queen's Rd. Cem., Croydon.
BIGNELL, WILLIAM, L/Cpl., Lond. Regt.
   b., '97 ; *e.s.*, David Bignell, hon. superintendent, Croydon Vacant Lands Cultivation Soc., & Mrs. Bignell. *Enl.*, in R.W.S. Regt., Aug., '14 ; discharged owing to ill-health, 26 Mar., '15 ; re-enlisted in Lond. Regt. ; *w.*, Sept., '15 and Jun., '16. *Fell*, 22 Aug., '18.
BILTON, A. E., 25269, Rflmn., R.B.
   Res., T. Heath. *D.*, of wounds, Jul., '17.
BINNS, JOHN ERIC, 2/Lt., Wilts. Regt.
   b., Horwich, Lancs., 7 Jan., '94 ; *s.*, Mr. & Mrs. John D. Binns, 18 Morland Rd., Croydon. *Educ.*, Bedford G. Sch. Single. Student at Inst. of Civil Engineers. *Enl.*, 2 Sept., '14 ; commis., Jun., '15. *Fell*, Sanna-i-Yat, Mesopotamia, 9 Apr., '16. (Plate VIII., 3).

THE GLORIOUS DEAD

BINSTEAD, CHARLES HENRY, A.B. Seaman, Torpedoman, R.N.
b., Croydon, 23 Aug., '77 ; *s.*, Mr. & Mrs. C. Binstead, Parson's Mead, Croydon. *Educ.*, Brit. Sch., Croydon. Married. Decorator. *Fell*, on H.M.S. " Barham," Battle of Jutland, 31 May, '16.

BIRMINGHAM, EDWARD BRICE, Pte., 7 R.W.S. Regt.
b., '90. Married. *Res.*, 27 St. John's Grove, Croydon. *D.*, of wounds, 2 Jul., '16.

BISHOP, F. J., 293404, Gnr., R.G.A.
Fell, '17.

BLACKIE, CHARLES DOUGLAS, Pte., R. Fus.
b., '89 ; *s.*, Mr. & Mrs. W. M. Blackie, 5 St. George's Court, S. Kensington, formerly of 10 Beech House Rd., Croydon. *Fell*, Somme, 15 Sept., '16 ; *buried*, Les Boeufs.

BLACKMAN, GEORGE DULLAM, Sgt., 1 Sur. Rif. (21 Lond. Regt.)
b., Beverley, Yorks., 9 Jul., '83 ; *s.*, Mr. & Mrs. Blackman, Greenside Rd., Croydon. *Educ.*, Harlesden Coll., Harlesden. Married. Authorized clerk, Stock Exc. *Res.*, Wallington. *Enl.*, 4 Aug., '14. *Fell*, Vimy Ridge, 23 May, '16.

BLACKMAN, GEORGE HERBERT, Pte., Aust. Inf.
b., 41 Sussex Rd., Croydon, 22 Aug., '95 ; *s.*, Albert & Elizabeth Blackman, 41 Sussex Rd., Croydon. *Educ.*, Brighton Rd. Sch., Croydon. Single. Gardener. *Res.*, Batlow, Australia. *Enl.*, 11 Aug., '15. *Fell*, nr. Moquet Farm, France, 17 Aug., '16.

BLACKMAN, WILFRED ERNEST ARTHUR, Capt., M.G.C.
b., S. Bermondsey, 21 Mar., '93 ; *s.*, Henry C. & Amy Blackman, 21 Apsley Rd., S. Norwood. *Educ.*, Portland Rd. Sch., S. Norwood, Boro. Sec. Sch., Croydon, and King's Coll., Lond. Single. Schoolmaster. *Enl.* in Lond. Scottish, Sept., '14 ; *w.*, Loos, 25 Sept., '15 ; commis., '16 ; ment. in despatches. *D.* from pneumonia, Royal Herbert Hosp., Woolwich, 14 Oct., '18.

BLAKE, CHARLES, Pte., 2 Middlesex Regt.
b., Chadwell Heath, Essex, 25 Dec., '82 ; *s.*, Daniel & Martha Blake, 13 Lambeth Rd., Croydon. *Educ.*, Christ Ch. Sch., Croydon. Married. Grocer's asst. *Res.*, 41 Richmond Gardens, Shepherd's Bush. *Enl.*, Sept., '15. *Fell*, France, 1 Jul., '16.

BLAKE, JOHN JACOB, Pte., 2/4 R.W.S. Regt.
b., '97 ; *s.*, Mr. & Mrs. W. A. Blake, 44 Johnson Rd., Croydon. *Enl.*, 19 Jul., '15 ; served in Egypt and France. *Fell*, 29 Jul., '18.

BLAKE, ROYDON GEORGE, Pte., M.G.C.
b., Croydon, 15 Jul., '97 ; *s.*, James William & Emily Edith Blake, 24 Alpha Rd., Croydon. *Educ.*, Oval Rd. Sch., Croydon. Single. Machinist. *Enl.*, in R.W.S. Regt., May, '15. *Fell*, France, 28 Aug., '16.

BLAND, LESLIE, 510019, Cpl., 5 Can. Div. Arty., Heavy Trench Mort. Bty.
b., T. Heath, 31 Mar., '97 ; *s.*, Mr. & Mrs. James E. Bland, 39 Beauchamp Rd., U. Norwood. *Educ.*, Beulah Rd. Sch., T. Heath, & Stanley Tech. Sch., S. Norwood. Single. Mechanical engineer. *Res.*, Lowell, Mass., U.S.A. *Enl.*, Jul., '15. *Fell*, France, 28 Apr., '18.

BLOOMFIELD, CHARLES WILLIAM, Wireless Operator.
b., '95 ; *s.*, Mr. & Mrs. Bloomfield, 31 Howley Rd., Croydon. *Killed* on mine-sweeper through its striking an enemy mine, 18 Jan., '18.

BLOOMFIELD, ERIC, Rflmn., Q.W. Rif. (16 Lond. Regt.)
b., '92 ; *s.*, Mr. & Mrs. F. G. Bloomfield, 48 Beulah Rd., T. Heath. *Fell*, 19 Sept., '16.

BLOWER, FREDERICK, L/Cpl., 8 E. Sur. Regt.
   y.s., Mr. & Mrs. Blower, 21 Haling Rd., Croydon. Married
   Fell, 23 Oct., '18.
BLOWER, JOSEPH, Pte., Seaforth H.
   e.s., Mr. & Mrs. Blower, 21 Haling Rd., Croydon. Married.
   Empl. by Croydon Corp. *Res.*, 36 Helder St., Croydon. *D.*,
   of wounds, 25 Sept., '18.
BLUNDELL, CHARLES A., Pte., 8 R.W. Kent Regt.
   b., 7 Feb., '96 ; *s.*, Mr. & Mrs. Blundell, 1 Wood Cottages, Shirley.
   Enl., '14. *Fell*, Loos, 26 Sept., '15.
BLUNDELL, HERBERT WILLIAM, Pte., 11 R.W.S. Regt.
   b., Northampton, 8 May, '97 ; *s.*, Charles & Elizabeth Alice
   Blundell, 105 Pemdevon Rd., Croydon. *Educ.*, Ecclesbourne
   Rd. Sch., T. Heath. Single. Control cleaner. *Enl.*, 29 Nov.,
   '15. *Fell*, Le Bizet, nr. Armentières, 8 Jul., '16. *Buried* opposite
   Gunner's Farm. (Plate IV., 2).
BOAKES, WILLIAM EDWARD, Pte., R. Fus.
   b., Birling, Kent, 23 Jun., '91. *Educ.*, Goodrich Rd. Sch., E.
   Dulwich. Single. Salesman. *Res.*, 64 Parchmore Rd., T.
   Heath. *Enl.*, 13 Nov., '15. *D.*, from cerebro-spinal meningitis,
   Dover, 6 Mar., '16.
BOATWRIGHT, HERBERT, 589 Lab. Coy.
   b., '90. *Res.*, Shirley Church Rd., Croydon. *Enl.*, in 4 R.W.S.
   Regt. Served in India, '14-16. *D.* of pneumonia, at Neville
   Park (V.A.D.) Hosp., Tunbridge Wells, 3 Nov., '18.
BODLEY, ERIC ERNEST, Pte., R. Fus.
   b., '98. *Fell*, France, 7 Oct., '16.
BOGDEN, W. G., 1697, Pte., R. Fus.
   Res., U. Norwood. *Fell*, '17.
BOGUE, PATRICK YULE, 2/Lt., E. Sur. Regt.
   b., '96 ; 2nd *s.*, late Patrick Yule Bogue, of Dublin, & Mrs.
   Bogue, 29 Central Hill, U. Norwood. *Fell*, 24 Jul., '17.
BONCKER, BARRY, 2/Lt., E. Yorks. Regt.
   b., 23 Farquhar Rd., U. Norwood, 26 Aug., '97 ; *s.*, Fred. &
   Violet Boncker, 70 Auckland Rd., U. Norwood. *Educ.*, Ardingly
   Coll., Hayward's Heath. Single. Clerk, Nat. Bank of S. Africa.
   Res., 12 Upper Grove, S. Norwood. *Enl.*, in 4 R.W.S. Regt,
   1 Sept., '14. *Fell*, Fricourt, 1 Jul., '16. (Plate IV., 5).
BOND, ALBERT GEORGE, Pte., 4 R.W.S. Regt.
   b., 2 Albion Mews, S. Norwood, 7 Jan., '98 ; *s.*, Albert George
   & Amy Louisa Bond, 3 South Vale, U. Norwood. *Educ.*,
   Rockmount Rd. Sch., U. Norwood. Single. Fishmonger's asst.
   Enl., 14 Aug., '14. *Fell*, Dardanelles, 9 Aug., '15.
BOND, CHARLES NESBITT, Lt. & Adjt., 1/4 Lincoln. Regt.
   b., Hull, 14 Jun., '97 ; *s.*, late Francis, & Mrs. Bond, 26 Ashburton
   Rd., Croydon. *Educ.*, Whitgift G. Sch. Single. Empl. by
   Messrs. Edward Lloyd, Salisbury Court, E.C. *Enl.*, in L.R.B.,
   Aug., '13. *Fell*, Gommecourt, France, 30 Jun., '16. (Plate VI., 2).
BONEY, E., 18947, L/Cpl., Cameronians.
   Res., Croydon. *Fell*, '16.
BONNELL, HENRY, Pte., R.A.S.C.
   s., Mr. & Mrs. Bonnell, 26 Apsley Rd., S. Norwood. *D.*, of
   pneumonia, '18.
BONYUN, VERNON, R.F.C.
   Educ., High Sch., Croydon, and Lond. Univ. *Fell*, '18.
BOOTH, ALFRED HAROLD, Pte., Beds. Regt.
   b., '82 ; *y.s.*, Mr. & Mrs. F. W. Booth, 18a Lr. Addis. Rd., Croydon. Married. *D.*, of wounds recd. 12 May, '18.

THE GLORIOUS DEAD

BOOTH, T., R.N.
    Educ., Beulah Rd. Sch., T. Heath. *Lost* with H.M.S. " Good Hope," sunk off Coronel, Chili, 1 Nov., '14.
BORTHWICK, DONALD WALKER, 2/Lt., R.W.S. Regt. (attd. M.G.C.)
    b., Blackford, Perthshire, 5 Nov., '98 ; *s.*, Mr. & Mrs. John J. Borthwick, 48 Chatsworth Rd., Croydon. *Educ.*, Whitgift G. Sch. Single. *Enl.*, as Trooper in Sur. Yeom., 19 Dec., '14 ; commis. Nov., '15. *Fell*, Lake Doiran, 28 Dec., '16.
BOSWORTH, AUBREY CECIL, Pte., 2/4 R.W.S. Regt.
    b., U. Mitcham, '98 ; *s.*, Mr. & Mrs. E. Bosworth, 19 Lucerne Rd., T. Heath. *Educ.*, Beddington Ch. Sch. & Ecclesbourne Rd. Sch., T. Heath. Single. Empl. by Francis' Stores, Streatham. *Enl.*, 9 Nov., '14. *Fell*, Suvla Bay, 9 Aug., '15.
BOTTERILL, S., Rflmn., L.R.B.
    Educ., Whitgift G. Sch., '02-11. *Fell*, '17.
BOTTING, W. H., 12964, Pte., Coldstream Gds.
    Res., Croydon. *Fell*, '16.
BOTTOMLEY, THOMAS REGINALD, Lt., 1 E. Yorks. Regt.
    b., Rippenden, nr. Halifax, Yorks., 17 Oct., '87 ; *s.*, Thomas & Ellen Bottomley, 25 Norman Rd., T. Heath. *Educ.*, Rishworth G. Sch., nr. Halifax, St. John's Coll., Battersea, and Birkbeck Coll., Lond. Univ. Married, 29 Aug., '14. Teacher, Oval Rd. Sch., Croydon, prev. to Apr., '14 ; graduated, Lond. Univ., '13 ; B.A. *Joined* Lond. Univ. O.T.C., Apr., '11 ; commis., Apr. '14. *Fell*, Chemin des Dames, Aisne, 23 Sept., '14. (Plate IV., 4).
BOUGHTON, SYDNEY HERBERT, Pte., 17 R. Fus.
    b., 20 Gibson's Hill, U. Norwood, 16 Aug., '99 ; *s.*, Thomas & Harriet Boughton. *Educ.*, Rockmount Rd. Sch., U. Norwood. Single. Steward. *Enl.*, 15 Sept., '17. *Fell*, nr. Arras, 6 Jun., '18.
BOURKE, WALTER, 18840, Pte., Gren. Gds.
    Fell, '17.
BOURNE, HORACE DUNCOMBE, Pte., E. Sur. Regt.
    y.s., A. D. & M. Bourne, 10 Bedford Pl., Bedford Park, Croydon. *D.*, from heat stroke, Agra, India, 3 Aug., '18.
BOWERS, ALAN RICHARD, Gnr., R.G.A.
    b., 62 Wandle Rd., Croydon, 9 Nov., '95 ; *s.*, Robert & Elizabeth Bowers, Pumping Stn., Manor Farm Rd., Norbury. *Educ.*, Winterbourne Rd. Sch., T. Heath. Single. Apprenticed to organ-building trade. *Enl.*, May, '15 ; *w.*, '16 ; taken pris., 27 May, '18 ; last heard of 18 Aug., '18. *Presumed fallen.*
BOXALL, FREDERICK JAMES, Rflmn., L.R.B. (5 Lond. Regt.)
    b., Brassey Sq., Lavender Hill, 25 Feb., '99 ; *s.*, Mr. & Mrs. James Boxall, 27 Maplethorpe Rd., T. Heath. *Educ.*, Ecclesbourne Rd., & Winterbourne Rd. Schs., T. Heath. Single. Junior asst., Croydon Publ. Libraries, '13-15 ; asst., Sion Coll. Library, '15. *Fell*, France, 7 Nov., '18. (Plate IV., 1).
BOYCE, ALFRED JOHN, 1st Class Boy, R.N.
    b., '99 ; *s.*, Mr. & Mrs. Boyce, 17 Lahore Rd., Croydon. *Educ.*, Sydenham Rd. Sch., Croydon. *Lost* with H.M.S. " Indefatigable," sunk in Battle of Jutland, 31 May, '16.
BOYD, A., 7684, Cpl., K.R.R.C.
    Fell, '16.
BOYKETT, ROBERT EVELYN, 5290, Rflmn., Q.W. Rif. (16 Lond. Regt.)
    b., Croydon, 6 Jan., '74 ; *s.*, late Mr. & Mrs. Francis Boykett, Park Hill Rd., Croydon. *Educ.*, Brighton, & Whitgift G. Sch., '87-91. *Enl.*, in R.E., Dec., '15. *Fell*, France, 18 Oct., '16.
BRABNER, H. S., Midshipman, R.N.
    Educ., Whitgift G. Sch. *Lost* on the Transport " Don Arturo," torpedoed in Bay of Biscay, '17.

THE CROYDON ROLL OF HONOUR

BRADDON, OTTO JAMES, Rflmn., L.R.B. (5 Lond. Regt.)
b., Montana, Coolgardie, W. Australia, 4 Oct., '99 ; *s.*, Frank W. & Edith H. Braddon, 6 Tylecroft Rd., Norbury. *Educ.*, Winterbourne Rd. Sch., T. Heath, & Boro. Sec. Sch., Croydon; matriculated, Lond. Univ., Jun., '16. Empl. by Messrs. Annan, Dexter and Co., chartered accountants. *Enl.*, 4 Oct., '17. *Fell*, 8 Aug., '18.

BRADFORD, J., 26508, Pte., K.O.R.L. Regt.
Fell, '17.

BRADFORD, WILLIAM THOMAS, Pte., 12 Middlesex Regt.
b., Bermondsey, S.E., 4 Aug., '86 ; *s.*, Mr. & Mrs. John S. Bradford, 71 Tunstall Rd., Addis. *Educ.*, Birchanger Rd. Sch., S. Norwood. Single. Railway clerk. *Enl.*, 4 May, '16. *Missing*, Bullecourt, 3 May, '17.

BRADLEY, ERNEST, Pte., 3 R. Fus.
Educ., Abp. Tenison's Sch., Croydon. Empl. by Messrs. Hammond & Hussey, High St., Croydon. *Fell*, nr. Zonnebeke, '15.

BRADLEY, FREDERICK CHARLES SIDNEY, 1237, Pte., R.W.S. Regt.
b., 6 Nov., '85 ; *e.s.*, Mr. & Mrs. C. W. Bradley, 86 Gloucester Rd., Croydon. *Educ.*, St. James' Sch., Croydon. Single. Slater. *Enl.*, 3 Sept., '14. *Fell*, Somme, 1 Jul., '16.

BRADLEY, WILLIAM GEORGE, L/Cpl., 1 Ox. & Bucks. L.I.
b., 27 Aug., '87 ; 2nd *s.*, Mr. & Mrs. C. W. Bradley, 86 Gloucester Rd., Croydon. *Educ.*, St. James' Sch., Croydon. Single. *Enl.*, 14 Feb., '07 ; served in India, Persian Gulf, and retreat from Baghdad to Kut. *D.*, of malarial fever, 7 Oct., '16, while pris. of war with Turks in Asia Minor. (Plate IV., 3).

BRADMAN, WALTER ROBERT, Pte., 17 R. Fus.
b., Stockwell, 13 Mar., '95. *Educ.*, Adys Rd. Sch., E. Dulwich. Single. Clerk. *Res.*, 41 Ferndale Rd., S. Norwood. *Enl.*, 10 Sept., '14. *Fell*, Delville Wood, Somme, 27 Jul., '16.

BRADSHAW, ALFRED, Pte.
Fell, 26 Aug., '15.

BRADSHAW, W., Sgt.-Bugler, E. Sur. Regt.
b., '71 . Married ; 9 children. Served in France ; invalided home with shell shock. *D.*, at 49 Macclesfield Rd., S. Norwood, 16 Nov., '17, of consumption contracted on active service.

BRAGG, ERIC WENSLEY, Lt., R.A.F.
b., Manchester, '95 ; *s.*, Mr. & Mrs. H. Bragg, 64 Auckland Rd., U. Norwood. *Educ.*, Whitgift G. Sch., where he won House Cup in Sen. Sch., and got his colours for Rugby Football. Left sch. to enl. in 3 Lond. Scottish, Dec., '14 ; cpl. ; commis. in 10 Essex Regt. ; transf. as Lt. to M.G.C. ; twice *w.* ; invalided out of Army as result of wounds ; *re-joined* in R.A.F. *Killed*, Oct., '18, at E. Fortune Airship Stn., Edinburgh, crashing while setting out on bombing raid over German Fleet.

BRAITHWAITE, MICHAEL LLOYD, Lt., R.F.C.
Res., Croydon. *D.*, France, '15, of injuries recd. in an accident while landing.

BRAITHWAITE, RICHARD WILFRED, Capt., 10 D.L.I.
Educ., Marlborough. Married. Member of Lond. Stock Exc. *Served* in S.A. War. Commis., '14. *Fell*, 31 Jul., '15.

BRAMMER, H. B., Pte., 4 Middlesex Regt.
s., Mr. & Mrs. Brammer, 80 Morland Rd., Croydon. *Fell*, Monchy, 10 Apr., '17.

BRANCH, ROBERT DOUGLAS, P.O., R.N.
b., '93 ; *e.s.*, Mr. & Mrs. Branch, Merstham. *Educ.*, Par. Ch. Sch., Croydon. *Fell*, 19 Jan., '17.

THE GLORIOUS DEAD

BRAND, H. J., Pte., Coldstream Gds.
  b., '90. *Educ.*, Sydenham Rd. Sch., Croydon. *Res.*, 54 Milton Rd., Croydon. *Fell*, '16.

BRAND, L. N., 632836, Lond. Regt.
  Res., S. Norwood. *Fell*, '17.

BRANDY, ERNEST H., 1314, Sgt., Lond. Regt.
  Married. *Res.*, S. Norwood. *Fell*, Flers, France, 15 Sept., '16.

BRAY, L/Cpl.
  Educ., Whitehorse Rd. Sch., T. Heath. *Res.*, Lucerne Rd., T. Heath. *Fell*, 16 Sept., '16.

BRAY, ERNEST A., Pte., K.O.S.B.
  b., Croydon, 11 Apr., '78. Married. *Res.*, 4 Oakwood Rd., Croydon. *Enl.*, '14. *D.*, Hawick Mil. Hosp., Scotland, 28 Oct., '18.

BRAY, HERBERT A., 201135, Pte., Cameron H.
  b., '83. Married ; 1 child. Insurance agent. *Res.*, 55 St. Saviour's Rd., Croydon. *Enl.*, 18 May, '16 ; *w.*, Apr., '17. *Fell*, 28 Jul., '17.

BRAY, J., 57305, Northd. Fus.
  Res., W. Croydon. *Fell*, '17.

BRAZIER, GEORGE, Pte., 20 Can. Inf.
  b., Croydon, 5 May, '83 ; *s.*, John & Emma Brazier. *Educ.*, Mitcham Rd. Sch., Croydon. Single. Labourer. *Res.*, Toronto, Canada. *Enl.*, 10 Jun., '15. *D.*, of wounds, 17 C.C.S., France, 27 Apr., '16.

BRESSEY, SYDNEY HERBERT, 2/Lt., R.E.
  b., 1 Reynold's Rd., Peckham, 13 Jan., '93 ; *s.*, Mr. & Mrs. Bressey, 48 Kynaston Rd., T. Heath. *Educ.*, M. Whitgift Sch. Single. 2nd Class clerk, H.M. India Office. *Enl.*, in Civil Service Rif., Nov., '12 ; mobilised, 5 Aug., '14 ; *w.*, Vimy, 22 May, '16 ; commis. in R.E., 25 May, '18. M.M. awarded 31 May, '16, for repairing telephone wires under heavy fire, and bestowed at Winchester, May, '17. *Fell*, Templeux le Guerard, 10 miles E. of Peronne, 21 Sept., '18. (Plate XI., 2).

BRETT, E. H. W., 2/Lt., D.C.L.I.
  Fell, 2 Aug., '16.

BRETT, J. H., 43418, Pte., Dev. Regt.
  Res., Croydon. *D.*, of wounds, '17.

BRIAN, HERBERT CECIL, Act.-Cpl., 8 R.B.
  b., Penge, 16 Jan., '16 ; *e.s.*, Mr. & Mrs. Eugene Owen Brian. *Educ.*, Brit. Sch., Croydon. Single. Clerk. *Res.*, 16 Cairo Rd., Croydon. *Enl.*, 31 Aug., '14. *Fell*, Hooge, Ypres, 30 Jul., '15.

BRIAN, R., 42063, Pte., M.G.C.
  Res., S. Norwood. *Fell*, '17.

BRICE, C., 24018, Gnr., R.G.A.
  Res., S. Croydon. *D.*, of wounds, '17.

BRIDGES, ALFRED EDWARD, Sgt., R.F.A.
  b., Harvey Rd., Camberwell, 12 Dec., '88 ; *s.*, Mr. & Mrs. Bridges, 38, Daneville Rd., Camberwell. *Educ.*, George St., Camberwell. Married. Monotype operator. *Res.*, 70 Tylecroft Rd., Norbury. *Enl.*, 24 Sept., '14. *Fell*, nr. Arras, 17 Jul., '16. (Plate II., 4).

BRIDGES, HENRY ARTHUR, Pte., 2/4 R.W.S. Regt.
  b., Ratcliff, 6 May, '85 ; *s.*, Mr. & Mrs. Bridges, 34 Ferndale Rd., S. Norwood. *Educ.*, Woodside Sch., Croydon. Single. Window cleaner. *Enl.*, 16 Jun., '15 ; served in Gallipoli and Egypt. *Fell*, nr. Longpont, France, 26 Jul., '18. (Plate IX., 2).

BRIDGLAND, JOHN WILLIAM, 17398, Pte., 8 E. Sur. Regt.
b., Brockley, 13 Oct., '94 ; *y.s.*, Francis A. & Martha Bridgland 3 Sangley Rd., S. Norwood. *Educ.*, by Mr. Everest,"Valentia House," S. Norwood, and at Clark's Coll., Croydon. Single. Clerk, Port of Lond. *Enl.*, Feb., '16. *Missing*, nr. Cherisey, S.E. of Arras since 3 May, '17.

BRIDLE, WALTER, 203432, Pte., Duke of Wellington's (W. Riding) Regt. *Educ.*, Mitcham Rd. Sch., Croydon. *Res.*, 35 Lambeth Rd., Croydon. *Fell*, 9 Oct., '17.

BRISTOW, JOHN, Pte., 2 R.W.S. Regt.
b., '95. *Res.*, St. James' Rd., Croydon. *D.*, of wounds recd. at Ypres, 29 Oct., '15.

BRISTOW, WALTER EDWIN, Pte., R.W.S. Regt.
Res., 250 Bensham Lane, T. Heath. *Enl.*, Oct., '15. *Fell*, Jerusalem, 21 Dec., '17. (Plate VI., 4).

BRITTAIN, FRANK MORRIS, Brit. Red Cross.
b., '72. *Res.*, Croydon. *D.*, of cholera, '16.

BRITTON, EDWARD W., 2/Lt., D.L.I.

BROADHURST, A. V., 17744, Pte., R. Fus.
Res., S. Norwood. *Fell*, '16.

BROCK, E. G., Lt., King's L'pool. Regt.

BROCK, FRANK A., Act.-Wing Comdr., R.N.A.S.
e.s., Mr. & Mrs. A. Brock, Cheam. *Educ.*, Dulwich Coll. *Res.*, formerly at Selhurst Rd., S. Norwood. *Enl.*, in R.H.A. ; transf. to R.N.A.S. ; worked for some time with Inventions Board. O.B.E., Jan., '18. *Fell*, Zeebrugge Mole, 22 Apr., '18.

BROCKETT, HENRY CHARLES, Cpl., 1/23 Lond. Regt.
b., Croydon, 12 Jun., '83 ; *s.*, Mr. & Mrs. Charles Brockett, 134 Windmill Rd., Croydon. *Educ.*, Princess Rd. Sch., Croydon. Married. Decorator. *Enl.*, Mar., '15. *Fell*, France, 15 Oct., '18.

BROCKETT, HERBERT JAMES, 53518, Act.-Bdr., R.H.A.
b., Croydon, 18 Feb., '90 ; *s.*, Mr. & Mrs. Charles Brockett, 134 Windmill Rd., Croydon. *Educ.*, Princess Rd. Sch., Croydon. Single. Telegraph messenger. *Enl.*, 14 Nov., '08. *Fell*, France, 1 Jul., '16.

BRODIE, PETER BELLINGER, 2/Lt., 2/4 R.W.S. Regt. (attd. Imp. Camel C.).
b., Croydon, 19 Jul., '81 ; *s.*, Robert & Emma Betsy Brodie, 20 St. Peter's Rd., Croydon. *Educ.*, Whitgift G. Sch. Single. Clerk, Lond. & Westminster Bank. *Enl.*, in R. Fus., Oct., '14 ; served at Gallipoli. *Accidentally killed*, Wadi en Natrum, Egypt. 12 Aug., '16.

BROMLEY, WILLIAM COLLINGHAM, L/Cpl., R. Fus.
b., New Town, U. Norwood, 12 Dec., '86. *Educ.*, Rockmount Rd. Sch., U. Norwood. Married. Policeman. *Enl.*, 18 Feb., '04. *Fell*, Somme, 1 Jul., '16.

BROOKES, PERCY JOHN.
b., '94. *Res.*, 62 Oval Rd., Croydon. *Killed*, during Zeppelin raid, Oct., '15.

BROOKS, ALBERT ALEXANDER, Sgt., R.E.
b., Westminster, 17 Jan., '78. *Educ.*, Addington Street Sch., Westminster. Married. Engineer, empl. by G.P.O. *Res.*, 20 Ashburton Av., Addis. *Served* in S.A. War. *D.*, Netley Hosp., 14 Nov., '16. (Plate XIII., 4).

BROOKS, PHILIP HOWARD, A.B. Seaman, Gnr., R.N.
b., Croydon, 1 Apr., '00 ; *s.*, Mr. & Mrs. S. Brooks, 43 Tamworth Rd., Croydon. *Educ.*, British Sch., Croydon. Single. Engineer. *Res.*, W. Hartlepool. *Enl.*, 19 Jul., '15. *Lost*, with H.M.S. "Defence," sunk during Battle of Jutland, 31 May, '16. (Plate VI., 3).

THE GLORIOUS DEAD

BROTHERWOOD, LEONARD, Pte., Middlesex Regt.
  b., '84. Married. Res., 18 Gloucester Rd., Croydon. Fell, 5 Oct., '17.

BROUGHTON, ARTHUR WILLIAM, Gnr., R.F.A.
  b., 18 Sept., '97 ; 3rd s., John & Emily Broughton, 136 Gloucester Rd., Croydon. Educ., St. James' Sch., Croydon. Single. Empl. by Messrs. Still & Son, dairymen. Enl., 4 Sept., '16. Fell, Salonica, 16 Sept., '18.

BROWN, A. F., Pte., Sher. For.
  3rd s., Mr. & Mrs. F. Brown, "The Joiners' Arms," Woodside. Enl., Oct., '15 ; served in R.A.O.C. D., of wounds, 18 Nov., '17.

BROWN, ALFRED JOSEPH, Pte., 20 R. Fus.
  b., Peckham, 12 Sept., '95 ; s., Mr. & Mrs. Joseph R. W. Brown, Sefton Rd., Addis. Educ., St. Dunstan's Coll., Catford. Single. Bank Clerk. Enl., 1 Jul., '15. Fell, 15 Apr., '17. Buried, S.E. of Heninel, nr. Arras.

BROWN, CHARLES ROYDON, Capt., Essex Regt.
  b., Lewisham, 3 Apr., '92 ; s., Mr. & Mrs. Charles F. Brown, 120 Brigstock Rd., T. Heath. Educ., Beulah Rd. Sch., T. Heath, St. Andrew's Coll., Dublin, Boro. Sec. Sch., Croydon, and Lond. Sch. of Economics. Single. Empl. by Law Fire Insurance Soc.; Associate, Chartered Insur. Inst. Joined Lond. Univ. O.T.C. as cadet, 12 Aug., '14 ; commis. and posted to 9 Essex Regt., 26 Aug., '14 ; w., Hulluch, France, Oct., '16. Ret. to France with 13 Essex Regt., '16 ; invalided home with typhoid, contracted on Somme, '16 ; posted to 1 Essex Regt., and promoted Capt., 16 Mar., '17 ; ment. in despatches, Jan., '16 ; M.C. for general good service rendered in the field, Jan., '16. Fell, Infantry Hill, Monchy-le-Preux, on or after 14 Apr., '17.

BROWN, CLIVE ANDREWS, Capt. & Adjt., R.E.
  b., '90 ; e.s., Mr. & Mrs. George Andrews Brown, Melville Av., Croydon. Educ., Dulwich Coll., King's & Univ. Coll., Lond. Empl. in Croydon Boro. Engineers' Office ; A.M.I.C.E. Enl., in Lond. Scottish ; commis., Sept., '15 ; Capt., Jun., '17. D., from influenza, at Mil. Hosp., Shorncliffe, 7 Nov.,'18. Buried, Bandon Hill Cem.

BROWN, ERNEST RICHARD, R.E.
  b., Reigate, 11 Dec., '95 ; s., Ernest & Florence Brown, 78 Frith Rd., Croydon. Educ., Par. Ch. Sch., Croydon. Married. Horsekeeper. Enl., 28 Nov., '15. Fell, France, 5 Oct., '16.

BROWN, F. E., Cpl., R.A.F.
  b., '82. Married ; 3 children. Res., 24 Manor Rd., S. Norwood. Enl., '16. D., of wounds, 17 Sept., '18.

BROWN, F. J., Pte., H.A.C.
  b., '99 ; s., Mr. & Mrs. Brown, 19 Ingram Rd., T. Heath. Educ., Ingram Rd. Sch., T. Heath, and Clark's Coll. Single. Empl. by Board of Trade. Enl., '17. D., from pneumonia, Cologne, 11 Feb., '19.

BROWN, FRANCIS CLEMENT, Lt., Lond. Regt.
  b., Blackheath, '92 ; e.s., Mr. & Mrs. R. L. Brown, 26 Stafford Rd., Croydon. Educ., Whitgift G. Sch. Hon. Sec. of Croydon Swimming Club. Enl., Nov., '14 ; commis., Jul., '15 ; served in France, Salonica, Egypt, Palestine. Ment. in despatches, '17. Fell, in sight of Jerusalem, 8 Dec., '17.

BROWN, FRANK EDMUND, L/Cpl., R. Fus.
  b., '87 ; 4th s., late Peter S. & Mrs. Brown, Pollard's Hill N., Norbury. Married Muriel Quiney. Fell, 22 Aug., '18.

BROWN, JOHN BROOK, Rflmn., 12 Lond. Regt.
b., 139 Lond. Rd., Croydon, 1 Sept., '80 ; *s.*, Mr. & Mrs. William Brown, Hastings, Sussex. *Educ.*, Christ Church Sch., Croydon, and M. Whitgift Sch. Single. Engineer ; M.I.H.V.E. *Res.*, 62 Southbridge Rd., Croydon. *Enl.*, Oct., '14. *D.*, 5 Northern Gen. Hosp., Leicester, 21 May, '15, of wounds recd. at Hill 60, Ypres, 3 May, '15.

BROWN, JOHN GORDON, Capt., D.T.M.O., 47 Div.
b., Croydon, 13 Feb., '94 ; 2nd *s.*, Sir Herbert & Lady Brown, Coombe Lodge, Addington Hills. *Educ.*, Limes Sch., Croydon, "Yardley Court," Tonbridge, and Tonbridge Sch., '07-13, where he became head of his House and Sch. Praeposter, '12, and won middle weight boxing, '12 ; studied milling at Sheffield, '13-14. Single. Miller. *Res.*, Croydon. *Enl.*, in 10 R. Fus., Aug., '14 ; commis., Sept., '14 ; Lt., May, '15 ; went to France, Sept., '15 ; Capt., Jul., '16 ; M.C., Jul., '16 ; D.T.M.O., Sept., '16–Oct., '18 ; ment. in despatches. *Missing*, Radinghem, nr. Lille, 5 Oct., '18.

BROWN, KEITH ANDREWS, Capt., 1 R.W.S. Regt.
b., '96 ; *y.s.*, Mr. & Mrs. George Andrews Brown, Melville Av., Croydon. *Educ.*, Dulwich Coll. Farmer. *Enl.*, 1 Nov., '14, in Q.W.R. ; went to Sandhurst, May, '15 ; commis., Nov., '15 ; *w.*, High Wood, Somme, 15 Jul., '16. *D.*, 22 Sept., '18, of wounds recd. prev. day. *Buried*, nr. Epehy, France.

BROWN, T. E., Cpl., R.A.F.
b., '82. Married ; 3 children. *Res.*, Manor Rd., Croydon. *Killed*, in accident whilst flying, France, '18.

BROWN, W. S., Cpl., Civ. Serv. Rif. (15 Lond. Regt.)
b., '88 ; *s.*, Mr. & Mrs. Brown, 67 Elmwood Rd., Croydon. *Fell*, 7 Oct., '17.

BROWN, WILLIAM BERT, Pte., 16 R. Fus.
b., Bexley Heath, 9 Apr., '93 ; *s.*, Mr. & Mrs. A. J. Brown, 115 Selhurst Rd., S. Norwood. *Educ.*, Church Rd. Sch., Bexley Heath. Married. Slater. *Res.*, 1 Spring Lane, Woodside. *Enl.*, 11 Feb., '16. *Fell*, Guillemont, 23 Jul., '16.

BROWN, WILLIAM WALL, 608406, Rflmn., L.R.B. (5 Lond. Regt.)
s., Mr. & Mrs. G. Wall Brown, 18 Ion Rd., T. Heath. *Educ.*, Boro. Sec. Sch., Croydon. Empl. in Accountant's Office, L.B. & S.C.R. *Enl.*, Dec., '14. *D.*, of wounds in Notre Dame Hosp., Cambrai, 25 Mar., '18. (Plate VII., 5).

BROWNE, CHARLES EDWARD, Pte., R.W.S.Regt.
b., '95 ; *y.s.*, late Edwin, & Mrs. Browne, 28 Vicarage Rd., Croydon. *Educ.*, Parish Ch. Sch., Croydon. Sign-writer. *Enl.*, in Sur. Yeom., 2 Nov., '15. *Fell*, 9 Mar., '18.

BROWNE, JOHN, Coy.Sgt.Maj., K.R.R.C.
b., Queen St. Barracks, Belfast, 21 Jan., '81 ; *s.*, late James, & Mrs. Browne, Winchester. *Educ.*, St. Peter's (R.C.) Sch., Winchester. Married. Police Constable, City of Lond. *Res.*, Walworth, and 218 Northborough Rd., Norbury. *Enl.*, in R. Mun. Fus., '93 ; Queen's S.A. Med., 3 bars ; King George Coronation Med. (Police). Rejoined as Sgt., in K.R.R.C., 10 Sept., '14. *Fell*, Delville Wood, Somme, 6 Oct., '16.

BRYAN, EDWIN, Pte., 2 Can. Inf.
b., Croydon, 1 Jul., '84 ; *s.*, Mr. & Mrs. Frank Bryan, Croham Rd., Croydon. *Educ.*, Surrey House Sch., Margate. Single. Farmer. *Res.*, Edmonton, Canada. *Enl.*, Jan., '16. *D.*, at Poperinghe, 16 Jun., '16, of wounds recd. at Ypres, 14 Jun., '16.

THE GLORIOUS DEAD

BRYANT, SIDNEY ARTHUR, L/Cpl., 1 R.W.S. Regt.
b., Croydon, 26 Jun., '85 ; *s.*, John & Fanny Bryant, 68 Waddon Marsh Lane, Croydon. *Educ.*, Brighton Rd. Sch., Croydon. Married. Postman. *Res.*, 34 Purley Rd., S. Croydon. Served in S.A. War (King's & Queen's Meds.). *Enl.*, 26 Mar., '01. *Rejoined*, 5 Aug., '14. *Fell*, Ypres, 21 Oct., '14.

BRYANT, WALTER THEODORE GRAHAME, A.B. Seaman, "Hawke" Btn., R.N.D.
b., 179 Westcombe Hill, S.E., 23 Aug., '97 ; *s.*, Walter William & Marian Bryant, 1 Biddulph Rd., Croydon. *Educ.*, Stratheden House, Blackheath, and St. Bees, Cumberland. Single. Clerk, Cape Government Office. *Res.*, 21 Charlton Rd., S.E. *Enl.*, 16 Nov., '14. *Fell*, Cape Helles, Gallipoli, 10 Jun., '15.

BUCK, CYRIL ALFRED SPENCER, 2/Lt., Lond. Regt.
b., Southsea, Hants., 8 Jul., '95 ; *s.*, Mr. & Mrs. Janet Buck, "Cranleigh," Fairview Rd., Norbury. *Educ.*, Portsmouth G. Sch. Single. Bank clerk. *Enl.*, as Rflmn. in 1/18 Lond. Regt., 3 Sept., '14 ; went to France, Aug., '15 ; M.M., for work done as Bde. Observer, Somme, 2 Sept., '16 ; gazetted, Jun., '17. *Missing*, Poelcapelle, Passchendaele Ridge, 26 Oct., '17.

BUCKERIDGE, H. S., Pte., M.G.C.
b., '90. Empl. by "Croydon Advertiser." *D.*, of wounds, France, 21 Oct., '16.

BUCKLAND, JOHN MARTIN, Pte., 1 Norfolk Regt.
b., Earlsfield, S.W., 22 Jan., '98 ; *s.*, Mr. & Mrs. Buckland, 73 Lebanon Rd., Croydon. *Educ.*, St. Andrew's Sch., Croydon, and Reedham, Purley. Single. Clerk. *Enl.*, 9 Mar., '14. *D.*, 27 Apr., '16, at Lond. Hosp., Whitechapel Rd., E.C., of wounds recd. at Arras, 4 Nov., '15.

BUCKLAND, JOHN RICHARD THOMAS, L/Cpl., R.W.S. Regt.
b., '91. *Educ.*, Beulah Rd. Sch., T. Heath. Golf caddy. *Res.*, 32 Nursery Rd., T. Heath. *Enl.*, '14. *Fell*, France, 5 Dec.,'16.

BUCKWORTH, ALAN B., 2/Lt., R. Innis. Fus.
b., '98 ; *s.*, Mr. & Mrs. Ernest Benjamin Buckworth, 25 North End, Croydon. *Fell*, 16 Aug., '17.

BUCKWORTH, HERBERT THOMPSON, 2/Lt., R. Fus.
b., 16 Dec., '80 ; *s.*, Mr. & Mrs. Ernest Benjamin Buckworth, 25 North End, Croydon. *Educ.*, Whitgift G. Sch.

BUCKWORTH, WALLACE ALFRED, Lt., R. Innis. Fus.
b., 25 May, '82 ; *s.*, Mr. & Mrs. Ernest Benjamin Buckworth, 25 North End, Croydon. *Educ.*, Whitgift G. Sch., '93-97. *Fell*, Gallipoli.

BUCKWORTH, WILLIAM, Lt., R.B.
b., '77 ; *s.*, Mr. & Mrs. Ernest Benjamin Buckworth, 25 North End, Croydon. *Fell*, 14 Aug., '17.

BUDD, FREDERICK CHARLES, 2/1 Lond. Regt.
b., '83 ; *s.*, Mr. & Mrs. Budd, 7 Lansdowne Rd., Croydon. *Fell*, 1 Jul., '16.

BUDD, WRINCH JOSEPH CHARLES, Lt., 2 S.W.B.
b., Clapham, 23 Sept., '75 ; *s.*, Mr. & Mrs. Budd, 84 Melrose Av., Norbury. *Educ.*, Westminster Sch. Single. Chief clerk, Municipal Council, Shanghai. Served in S.A. War. Commis., Feb., '15. *Fell*, Gallipoli, 28 Jun., '15.

BUDDS, CECIL, Pte., R.A.M.C.
s., Mr. & Mrs. Thomas Budds, 48 Melfort Rd., T. Heath. *D.*, of dysentery on H.M. Hosp. Ship, "Nevasa," 27 Jun., '16.

BUDGEN, G. H., 10043, R.W.S. Regt.
b., Croydon, '94. *Res.*, 2 Railway Cottages, Sydenham Rd. W. Croydon. *Fell*, Jul., '16.

BUDGEN, SIDNEY NORMAN, Lt.
b., '86; e.s., Sidney & Fanny Budgen, Croham Rd., Croydon.
Fell, Ypres, 4 Oct., '17.

BULLER, HENRY GEORGE ROBERT, Pte., 2/4 R.W.S. Regt.
b., Croydon, 11 Aug., '94; s., Mr. & Mrs. Henry William Buller, 4 Portland Rd., S. Norwood. Educ., Sydenham Rd. Sch., Croydon. Single. Tea-packer. Res., 32 Union Rd., Croydon. Enl., 10 Aug., '15; served in Egypt, Feb., '16-Jul., '18; w., Gaza, Mar., '17, and White Hill, nr. Jerusalem, 26 Dec., '17. Fell, nr. Soissons, 29 Jul., '18.

BULLMANN, HADDON R. H., 2/Lt., M.G.C.
Educ., Whitgift G. Sch. Enl., in Artists Rif., Aug., '15. Fell, '18 (?)

BUNDLE, HARRY NORMAN, 2/Lt., Lond. Regt.
b., '96; s., Mr. & Mrs. Bundle, Whitehorse Rd., Croydon. Empl. by Croydon Corp., Boro. Electrical Engineers' Dept. Enl., '14; w., Loos, Sept., '15; commis., Apr., '17. Fell, France, 20 Sept., '17.

BUNKELL, F. J., 30104, Pte., R.W. Fus.
Fell, '16.

BUNN, GEORGE BERTIE, Sgt., 7 R. Fus.
Married. Lithographic artist. Res., Selhurst. Enl., 9 Sept., '14. Fell, Aveluy Wood, France, 5 Apr., '18.

BURBAGE, EDWIN JOSEPH, Lt., Middlesex Regt.
b., '88; s., Mr. & Mrs. J. P. Burbage, 44 Surrey St., Croydon. Black and white artist. Enl., in R. Fus., Sept., '14; commis., Jun., '15; passed through Higher Mil. Sch., Cairo, Sept., '16. Fell, '17.

BURBERRY, THOMAS WILLIAM, 2 S. Lancs. Regt.
s., Mr. & Mrs. Burberry, 5 Troy Rd., U. Norwood. Single. Fell, Vailly, 20 Sept., '14.

BURCH, HERBERT CHARLES, 20635, Cpl., 1 Essex Regt.
b., '91; s., Mr. & Mrs. John Burch, 14 Inglis Rd., Addis. Chief steward on "Medway." Enl. in Norf. Regt., 10 Dec., '14; Cpl., '14; stationed at Felixstowe; trans. to Essex Regt. and drafted to Gallipoli, Jul., '15; on "Royal Edward," torpedoed in Aegian Sea. Fell, Gallipoli, 10 Oct., '15.

BURDEN, L. G., Rflmn., L.R B. (5 Lond. Regt.)
Res., 13 Blenheim Pk. Rd., Croydon. Fell, '16.

BURGESS, ERIC A., 2/Lt., R. Fus.
b., 28 Feb., '98; s., Mr. & Mrs. Sydney H. Burgess, Malacca and Littlehampton. Educ., Whitgift G. Sch., '12-13. Single. Enl., '15. Fell, France, '17.

BURGESS, L., 24749, E. Sur. Regt.
Res., T. Heath. D., of wounds, '17.

BURLACE, HENRY EDWARD I., Trooper, Indian Camel C.
s., Mr. & Mrs. Sarah Burlace, 34 Greenside Rd., Croydon. Educ., Hornsey G. Sch., and High Sch., Sutton. Enl., in 3 County of Lond. Yeom. (York Hussars); served in Egypt for 2 years. Fell, Gaza, Palestine, 21 Apr., '17.

BURN, ROBERT, Pte., 4 R.W.S. Regt.
b., Kensington, 3 Apr., '85; s., Mr. & Mrs. Wm. Burn, 46 Elgin Rd., Croydon. Educ., M. Whitgift Sch. Married. Designer. Enl., Aug., '14; taken pris. at Kut. D., in Hosp. at Yarbachi, Oct., '16.

BURNETT, WILLIAM THOMAS, Pte., 7 R.W.S. Regt.
b., 83 Frant Rd., T. Heath, 10 Jan., '96; s., Mr. & Mrs. W. Burnett, T. Heath. Educ., Ecclesbourne Rd. Sch., T. Heath. Single. Shopman. Enl., 9 Sept., '14. Fell, France, 1 Jul., '16.

THE GLORIOUS DEAD 271

BURR, BENJAMIN WILLIAM, Pte., 12 Suff. Regt.
b., Croydon, 16 Sept., '89. *Educ.*, Whitehorse Rd. Sch., T.Heath. Married; 1 child. Labourer, empl. at Messrs. Crowley's Brewery. *Res.*, 31 Wisbeach Rd., Croydon. *Enl.*, Sept., '15. *Fell*, France, 31 Jul., '16.

BURREE, STANLEY ARTHUR, 2/Lt., R.A.F.
b., '93. Married. Empl. by Messrs. Teetgen & Co., tea merchants. *Res.*, 15 Beulah Rd. E., T. Heath. *Enl.*, in Gren. Gds., Sept., '15; *served* in France; commis., Mar., '18. *Accidentally killed* while flying in England, 5 Jul., '18. *Buried*, Mitcham Rd. Cem., Croydon.

BURRY, C. H., Cpl., 22 Lond. Regt.
Enl., in R.W.S. Regt., Nov., '14; trans. later to Lond. Regt.; served in France, Jun.,-Dec., '16; went to Salonica, Dec., '16; M.M. *Fell*, 30 Mar., '18.

BURSNOLL, WILLIAM, 21 Lond. Regt.
b., Tring, Herts., 28 Dec., '88; *s.*, Mr. & Mrs. W. Bursnoll, St. James' Rd., Croydon. *Educ.*, Christ Church Sch., Croydon. Married; 2 children. Shop assistant. *Res.*, 11 St. James' Rd., Croydon. *Enl.*, 21 Mar., '16. *Fell*, France, 15 Sept., '16.

BURT, CECIL WALTER, Cpl., R.E.
b., Weymouth, 22 Aug., '87; *s.*, Walter & Jessie Burt, Weymouth. *Educ.*, High Sch., Croydon. Single. Engineer. *Enl.*, Sept., '14. *Fell*, Loos, 26 Sept., '15.

BURTENSHAW, W. J., R.F.C.
Res., T. Heath. *Fell*, '17.

BURTON, ALFRED WALTER, L/Cpl., Q.W. Rif. (16 Lond. Regt.)
b., 35 St. John's Grove, Croydon, 13 May, '92; *s.*, late John L. Burton, & Mrs. Dunham, 1 St. John's Grove, Croydon. *Educ.*, Whitgift G. Sch. Single. Builder's clerk. *Enl.*, 5 Sept., '14; went to France, Aug., '15; taken pris., 28 Mar., '18. *D.*, of pneumonia and heart failure while pris. of war at Le Quesnoy, 26 Jul., '18.

BURTON, ROBERT STEPHEN, Shoeing Smith, R.F.A.
b., India, 16 Oct., '95; *s.*, Mr. & Mrs. Alfred Burton, 29 Lynton Rd., Croydon. *Educ.*, St. Mary's Sch., Croydon. Single. Blacksmith. *D.*, of appendicitis, France, 4 Mar., '16.

BUSBY, DONALD ARTHUR, 2/Lt., R.A.F.
b., Fulham, 6 Mar., '00; *s.*, Mr. & Mrs. A. C. Busby, 34 Temple Rd., Croydon. *Educ.*, Whitgift G. Sch. Single. Insurance clerk. *Joined*, R.N.A.S. as 2/Lt. (Pilot), 10 Mar., '18. *Killed* in accident at Stockbridge, Hants., 3 Sept., '18.

BUSSEY, FRANK, Capt., R.E.

BUSTIN, WALTER JOSEPH, L/Cpl., 7 R.W.S. Regt.
b., Peckham, 7 Sept., '96; *s.*, Mr. & Mrs. W. Bustin, 31 Alderton Rd., Addis. *Educ.*, Woodside Sch., Croydon. Single. Electrician. *Enl.*, 13 Aug., '14. *Fell*, Somme, 1 Jul., '16.

BUTCHER, HAROLD THOMAS, 2/Lt., 11 R.B.
b., Bermondsey, 20 May, '90; *s.*, Mr. & Mrs. Henry William Butcher, " Coxley Plane," Purley. *Educ.*, Whitgift G. Sch. Single. In business with his father, corn merchant, Mark Lane, Lond. *Enl.*, in L.R.B., Aug.,'14; was one of 7 ptes. under Sgt. Belcher who held the line after troops on either side had retired, against repeated German attacks, 13 May, '15, at Ypres, and for which Sgt. Belcher was awarded V.C. *Fell*, Ypres, 18 Feb., '16.

BUTLER, W., 7976, Coy.Sgt.Maj., E. Sur. Regt.
Res., Croydon. *Fell*, '17.

BUTLER, WILLIAM, Pte., 26 R. Fus.
Educ., M. Whitgift Sch. *Fell*, Oct., '16.

THE CROYDON ROLL OF HONOUR

BYFIELD, HAROLD, Pte., 1 R.W.S. Regt.
 b., 29 Mar., '96 ; s., Mr. & Mrs. H. H. Byfield, 18 Park Lane, Croydon. *Educ.*, St. Peter's and Parish Church Schs., Croydon. Single. Grocer's asst. Asst. Scout Master. *Enl.*, '13. *Fell*, Aisne, 16 Sept., '14.

BYFORD, J. W., 511869, Lond. Regt.
 Res., S. Croydon. *D.*, of wounds, '17.

BYRNE, EDWARD, 2/Lt., 9 D.C.L.I.
 b., 16 Dec., '86. Teacher. *Fell*, Aug., '17.

BYRNE, R., Pte., Wilts. Regt.
 e.s., Mr. & Mrs. Byrne, 69 Exeter Rd., Croydon. *Enl.*, Apr., '17. *Fell*, 4 Oct., '18.

CAGE, SAMUEL, 29526, Driver, R.F.A.
 Married. *Res.*, 10 Strathmore Rd., Croydon. Served in S.A. War. *Fell*, Vimy Ridge, 22 Apr., '17.

CAHILL, ALBERT GILBERT, Lond. Regt.
 b., '92. *Fell*, 8 Oct., '16.

CAHILL, EDWARD JAMES, Pte., 2/4 R.W.S. Regt.
 b., Croydon, 4 Mar., '97 ; s., James George & Annie Cahill, 12 Laurier Rd., Addis. *Educ.*, Woodside Sch., Croydon. Single. Shop asst. *Enl.*, Oct., '14. *Fell*, Palestine, 21 Dec., '17.

CAMPBELL, J. D., 2/Lt., R.W.S. Regt.
 Fell, '16.

CANDY, H. J., 121029, Driver, R.F.A.
 Res., S. Norwood. *Fell*, '16.

CANNON, ARTHUR, Pte., R.W.S. Regt.
 s., Mr. & Mrs. Cannon, 10 Princess Rd., Croydon. *Enl.*, Aug., '14. *Fell*, France, 7 Mar., '16.

CANNON, FRANK, Pte., R. Suss. Regt.
 s., Mr. & Mrs. Cannon, 10 Princess Rd., Croydon. *Enl.*, Oct., '14. *Fell*, France, 13 Feb., '16.

CANNON, WILLIAM, Pte., Ox. & Bucks. L.I.
 s., Mr. & Mrs. Cannon, 10 Princess Rd., Croydon. Served 8 yrs. in India. *D.*, of wounds, Mesopotamia, 26 Dec., '15.

CANNON, EDWIN HERBERT, Pte., 2 Lond. Regt.
 b., Stratford, Essex. *Educ.*, at a private sch., St. Saviour's Rd., Croydon. Single. Shipping clerk. *Res.*, 156 Melfort Rd., T. Heath. *Enl.*, Sept., '14. *Fell*, Hebuterne, 20 Jun., '16.

CANTWELL, P., Pte., S. Lancs. Regt.
 b., '77 ; *y.s.*, late Mr. & Mrs. P. Cantwell, Brook Rd., Waddon. *Res.*, Croydon. *Enl.*, Aug., '14 ; served 18 months in France with R.A.S.C. *D.*, of wounds, 7 Aug., '17.

CAPERN, CHARLES EDWARD, Bdr., 236 Bde. (T.) R.F.A.
 b., S. Lambeth, 20 Nov., '94 ; s., Mr. & Mrs. W. H. Capern, 216 Portland Rd., S.Norwood. *Educ.*, Church Street Sch., Kennington, S.E. Married. Inland Revenue clerk. *Res.*, 2 Claylands Rd., Clapham, S.W. *Enl.*, Feb., '13. *D.*, nr. Albert, 23 Aug., '14, of wounds recd. same day.

CARD, A., 30900, Pte., E. Sur. Regt.
 Res., Croydon. *D.*, of wounds, '17.

CARD, HARRY C., Pte., R.W.S. Regt.
 b., '97 ; *y.s.*, Mr. & Mrs. J. Card, 67 St. Saviour's Rd., Croydon. *Fell*, France, 1 Jul., '16.

CARE, EDWARD JAMES, Pte., R.W.S. Regt.
 b., 20 Sept., '90. *Educ.*, Bynes Rd. Sch., Croydon. Married ; 1 child. Gardener. *Res.*, 12 Kemble Rd., Croydon. *Enl.*, 12 Oct., '16. *Fell*, France, 7 Oct., '17.

V.

1. S/Sgt. J. A. CLARKE, R.A.S.C.
2. Pte. C. DAWSON, 1 E. Kent Regt.
3. Bdr. F. P. CLARKE, R.F.A.
4. Pte. E. J. COLLINS, 2/5 Lincoln Regt.
5. 2/Lt. L. E. ATHA, R.F.C.

VI.

1. 2/Lt. A. L. Berry, 14 (attd. 8) R.Fus.
2. Lt. & Adjt. C. N. Bond, 1/4 Lincoln. Regt.
3. Seaman Gnr. P. H. Brooks, R.N.
4. Pte. W. E. Bristow, R.W.S. Regt.
5. 2nd Air Mech. A. J. Clarke. R.A.F.

THE GLORIOUS DEAD 273

CARE, ROBERT GEORGE EDWARD, 683076, L/Cpl., 1/22 Lond. Regt.
b., Croydon; 2 Aug., '96 ; *y.s.*, Mr. & Mrs. Elizabeth Care, 2 Rolleston Rd., Croydon. *Educ.*, Bynes Rd. Sch., Croydon. Single. Empl. at Streatham Motor 'Bus Garage. *Enl.*, 21 May, '15 ; twice *w*. *Fell*, France, 22 Aug., '18.

CAREY, FRANCIS AMBROSE, 2/Lt., 32 R. Fus.
b., 82 Boswell Rd., T. Heath, 11 Aug., '96 ; *s.*, Francis Harwood & Edith Leonora Carey, " Whitlev Lodge," Beulah Rd., T. Heath. *Educ.*, Davies' Sch., Whitgift G. Sch., and St. Dunstan's Coll., Catford. Single. Engineer. *Res.*, 40 Beulah Rd., T Heath. *Enl.*, as pte., 6 Aug., '14. *Fell*, Flers, Somme, 15 Sept., '16.

CAREY, H., 26946, Pte., Northd. Fus.
Res, W. Croydon. *Drowned*, '17.

CARLEY, H. V., 2/Lt., 7 Norf. Regt.
D., of wounds recd. in France, '15.

CARLEY, HENRY JOHN, Pte., R. Fus.
b., Westminster. *Educ.*, Regents (L.C.C.) Sch. Married. Gardener. *Res.*, 26 Howard Rd., S. Norwood. *Enl.*, 10 May,'15. *D.* at Winchester Hosp., 13 Mar., '17, of neuritis and dysentery, contracted in France, Jan.-Mar., '17.

CARLTON, CLAUDE GRAY, 2/Lt., 9 Dev. Regt
b., '87 ; 5*th s.*, J. Crichton & Mary Carlton, 7 Spencer Rd., Croydon. *Fell*, Gheluvelt, 26 Oct., '17.

CAROLIN, J. J., 201916, Pte., Manchr. Regt.
Res., T. Heath. *Fell*, '17.

CARPENTER, CECIL HENRY, Pte., H.A.C.
b., Carshalton, 19 May, '93 ; *s.*, Henry William & Emelie Carpenter," St. Heliers," Carshalton. *Educ.*, Homefield Prep. Sch., Sutton, and Whitgift G. Sch. Single. Bank clerk. *Enl.*, 3 Nov., '15. *Fell*, Beaucourt, France, 14 Nov., '16.

CARPENTER, D. T., 1381, Pte., R. Fus.
Res., S. Norwood. *Fell*, '16.

CARPENTER, ROBERT LESLIE, Lt., 1/17 Lond. Regt.
b., Margate, 17 Apr., '95 ; *s.*, Mr. & Mrs. Robert Carpenter, 69 Barrowgate Rd., Chiswick. *Educ.*, Reigate G. Sch., and Whitgift G. Sch. Single. Clerk in Lond. County & Westminster Bank. *Res.*, 52 Friends' Rd., Croydon. *Joined* as 2/Lt., 6 May, '14. *Fell*, Loos, 26 Oct., '15. *Buried*, Loos.

CARR, FRANK SEPTIMUS, Pte., 1 Lond. Scottish (14 Lond. Regt.)
b., Walthamstow, Essex, 12 Mar., '81 ; *s.*, Mr. & Mrs. Carr, 45 Gonville Rd., T. Heath. *Educ.*, Wilson's G. Sch., Camberwell. Single. Chartered accountant's managing clerk. *Res.*, 45 Gonville Rd., T. Heath. *Enl.*, 21 Feb., '16. *Fell*, Ginchy, 9 Sept., '16 ; *buried*, Guillemont Rd. Mil. Cem.

CARRACK, CHARLES J., Pte., R. Fus.
b., 19 Feb., '94 ; *s.*, Rev. & Mrs. T. M. Carrack, Middleton Vicarage, Godalming. *Educ.*, Whitgift G. Sch., '07-14. Single. *Enl.*, '14. *Fell*, '17.

CARRELL, GEORGE, Pte., 6 R.W.S. Regt.
b., Beckenham, 5 May, '95 ; *s.*, George Henry & Ellen Carrell, 55 Beulah Gr., Croydon. *Educ.*, Bromley Rd. Sch., Beckenham, and Sydenham Rd. Sch., Croydon. Single. Porter. *Enl.*, 7 Sept., '14. *Fell*, Armentières, 26 Jun., '15.

CARSON, ALBERT, Seaman, R.N.
b., '99 ; *s.*, Mr. & Mrs. Albert E. Carson. *Res.*, 14 Albion St., Croydon. *Enl.*, Dec., '14 ; took part in Dardanelles operations, Nov., '15. *Reported missing*, 13 Jul., '16.

R

CARTER, A. W., 2558, Pte., R.W.S. Regt.
    Res., S. Norwood. *Fell*, '16.
CARTER, CHARLES STANLEY, Leading Seaman, R.N.V.R.
    Took part in defence of Antwerp. *Fell*, Dardanelles, 30 Jun., '15.
CARTER, E.
    Married. Empl. by Croydon Corp. Rds. Dept. *Res.*, 18 Ellara Rd., Streatham. *Enl.*, 12 Oct., '14. *Fell*, Gallipoli, 8 Aug., '15.
CARTER, FREDERICK JOHN, R.M.L.I.
    b., '94; *s.*, Mr. & Mrs. Carter, Lansdowne Rd., Purley. *Educ.*, Purley Nat. Sch. Milkman. *Enl.*, Aug., '14. *Fell*, Dardanelles, '15.
CARTER, G., 12284, Pte., R. Fus.
    Res., W. Croydon. *Fell*, '17.
CARTER, J. A., Lt., D.C.L.I.
    b., '93; *s.*, Mr. & Mrs. H. Carter, "Steep," Beech Av., Sanderstead. *Educ.*, Whitgift G. Sch., and Queen's Coll., Oxford. *Joined*, as 2/Lt., '14; twice *w. D.*, of wounds, 4 Apr., '17, while pris. of war.
CARTER, M. R., Capt., R.W.S. Regt.
    Educ., Whitgift G. Sch. *Fell*, '18.
CARTER, P., 1399, Pte., R.W.S. Regt.
    Fell, '16.
CARTER, WILFRED ARTHUR DOUGLAS, 2/Lt., Dorset Regt. (attd. R.F.C.)
    b., '97; *s.*, Mr. & Mrs. Henry Carter, S. Norwood. *Killed*, while flying, 23 May, '17.
CARTWRIGHT, E., 13713, Pte., R.W.S. Regt.
    Res., T. Heath. *D.*, of wounds, '17.
CASEY, J. W., Pte., M.G.C.
    Married; 1 daughter. Empl. by Croydon Electricity Works. *Enl.*, 20 Jun., '15; *w.*, '16. *D.*, 11 Sept., '18, at Poole Military Hosp., of wounds recd. in France, 21 Apr., '18. *Buried*, Queen's Rd. Cem., Croydon.
CASON, J., Pte., Lab. Coy. (R.E.)
    b., '73. Married; 3 children. Empl. at Norwood Junc. Stn., L.B. &. S.C.R. *Res.*, 44 Cresswell Rd., S. Norwood. *Served* 2 yrs. in France. *Fell*, 2 Sept., '17.
CASSIDY, ALBERT VICTOR, Pte., 7 R. Suss. Regt.
    b., '87. Married; 1 daughter. *Res.*, 6 Kingswood Rd., Penge. *D.*, 29 Nov., '17, at 5 C.C.S., France, of wounds recd. 20 Nov., '17.
CASSWELL, F. C., Lt., Beds. Regt.
    s., Mr. & Mrs. F. H. Casswell, Pollards Hill N., Norbury. *Lost*, on H.M. Transport, "Royal Edward," 13 Aug., '15.
CASTLE, EWART WILLIAM KING, Rflmn., Q.W. Rif. (16 Lond. Regt.)
    b., Beckenham, 5 Mar., '99; *s.*, Mr. & Mrs. William F. Castle, 24 Upper Grove, S. Norwood. *Educ.*, St. Olave's G. Sch., Southwark. Single. Shipping clerk. *Enl.*, 5 Mar., '17. *Fell*, nr. Bullecourt, 28 Aug., '18.
CATCHPOLE, DAVID, L/Cpl., R.W.S. Regt.
    b., '80. Married; 3 children. Policeman. *Res.*, Handcroft Rd., Croydon. Served in S.A. War with Som. Yeom. *Enl.*, Jun., '15. *Fell*, France, 4 Oct., '17.
CATCHPOLE, H., 18001, L/Cpl., Som. L.I.
    b., '89; *s.*, Mr. & Mrs. Catchpole, Queen's Rd., Croydon. Married; 3 children. *Res.*, 80 Thornton Rd., Croydon. *Enl*, Apr., '15; *w.*, Aug., '16. *Fell*, '17.
CATES, JAMES, 8191, Sgt., R.W.S. Regt.
    Married. *Res.*, Rymer Rd., Addis. *Fell*, 25 Sept., '17.
CATHIE, SYDNEY, Pte.
    Married. *Fell*, 21 Oct., '16.

THE GLORIOUS DEAD

CATO, CHARLES FRANCIS, 2nd A.M., R.A.F.
b., 15 May, '84 ; *s.*, late Mr. & Mrs. Cato, 140 Richmond Rd., Leytonstone. *Educ.*, at a private sch. Married ; 2 children. Journalist. *Res.*, 45 Sherwood Rd., Addis. *Enl.*, Jul., '17. *D.*, of pneumonia at Aire, France, 9 Apr., '18.

CAWSON, G. A., 2/Lt., R.F.C.
Educ., Whitgift G. Sch. *Fell*, Cambrai, '17.

CAWSTON, R., 1st A.M., R.A.F.
b., '83. Married ; 2 children. Goal-keeper, Addis. Football Club. Served in France 2½ yrs. *D.*, of bronchial pneumonia, France, '18.

CHADBOND, JOHN WILLIAM, Pte., R. Fus.
b., 3 Feb., '90 ; *s.*, Mr. & Mrs. Frank Charles Chadbond, Lenham Church Street, Epsom. *Educ.*, Whitgift G. Sch. *D.*, of wounds, France, 31 Dec., '15.

CHAFF, E., Pte., 7 R.W.S. Regt.
b., '84 ; *s.*, Mr. & Mrs. Chaff, 115 High St., Croydon. *D.*, of enteric fever at R. Victoria Hosp., Netley, Oct., '15.

CHALK, DUDLEY, Pte., R.M.L.I.
b., '91 ; *s.*, Mr. & Mrs. Chalk, Penge. *W.*, at Antwerp, '14. *Fell*, Dardanelles, '15.

CHALLEN, H. J., 6589, Bty. Sgt. Maj., R.G A.
Res., S. Norwood. *Fell*, '16.

CHALMERS, HARRY FRANK, R.N.V.R.
b., '89 ; *s.*, Mr. & Mrs. Chalmers, 65 Winterbourne Rd., T. Heath. *Fell*, Gallipoli, 4 Jun., '15.

CHAMBERLAIN, CYRIL JOHN, Lt., 1 R.B.
b., Hammersmith, '92 ; *s.*, Mr. & Mrs. Chamberlain, 457 Lond. Rd., T. Heath. *Educ.*, Latymer Upper Sch., Hammersmith, and Emanuel Sch., Wandsworth Common. Single. Schoolmaster (L.C.C.). *Enl.*, 4 Sept., '14 ; commis., Aug., '15 ; *w.*, Delville Wood, Sept., '16. *Fell*, nr. Poelcappelle, 7 Oct., '17.

CHAMBERS, H. C., Pte., Welsh Regt.
Married ; 1 child. *Res.*, 83 St. Saviour's Rd., Croydon. *Enl.*, in R.A.S.C. (M.T.), '16. *Fell*, 1 Aug., '17.

CHAMPION, GEORGE, Rflmn., K.R.R.C.
b., 55 Marville Rd., Fulham, 12 Jun., '87 ; *s.*, Mr. & Mrs. Champion, Rochester. *Educ.*, Boro. Sec. Sch., Croydon. Single. Clerk. *Res.*, 312 Lr. Addis. Rd., Croydon. *Enl.*, 17 May, '15. *Fell*, nr. Ypres, 10 Apr., '16.

CHANDLER, JAMES EDWARD, 42086, Cpl., 4 Bty., 1 Div. Can. Fld. Arty.
b., 8 Southbridge Place, Croydon, '85; *y.s.*, Mr. & Mrs. Chandler, 35 Waddon New Rd., Croydon. Single. *Res.* in Croydon previous to '06, being empl. by Messrs. Hammond & Hussey ; emigrated to Canada, Feb., '06. *Res.*, Peterboro', Ontario. Memb. of Volunteers until '06. *Enl.*, '14. *Fell*, Flanders, 10 Jun., '16.

CHAPLIN, W. A., 2473, L/Cpl., Lond. Regt.
Fell, '16.

CHAPMAN, ARTHUR THOMAS, Capt., 3 E. Sur. Regt.
b., '73. Married. Chairman of Messrs. Chapman & Sons, Croydon. *Res.*, Coulsdon. Helped to form 1st Croydon Btn. of Nat. Res. ; *served* in S.A. War. *Joined* as Lt. *Fell*, 26 Apr., '15.

CHAPMAN, CHARLES LESLIE, Pte., 1/7 Lond. Regt.
b., Croydon, 13 Feb., '95 ; *s.*, Mr. & Mrs. Edmund Chapman, 186 Canterbury Rd., Croydon. *Educ.*, Christ Ch. Sch., Croydon. Single. Ironmonger's asst. *Enl.*, Nov., '15. *Fell*, Cambrai, 1 Dec., '17.

CHAPMAN, EDWARD THOMAS, L/Cpl., R. Fus.
b., 22 Purley Rd., Croydon, 31 Jan., '96 ; *s.*, Henry William & Mary Ellen Chapman. *Educ.*, Bynes Rd. Sch., Croydon. Married. Grocer's asst. *Enl.*, 8 Sept., '14. *Fell*, Somme, 7 Oct.,'16.

CHAPMAN, HAROLD BYRON JAMES, Pte., R.A.M.C.
b., Croydon, '88 ; *s.*, Mr. & Mrs. Chapman, " Eversholt," Stanton Rd., Croydon. *Educ.*, Mod. Sch., Croydon. Married. Clerk. *Res.*, Stanton Rd., Croydon. *Enl.*, Sept., '14. *Fell*, Cambrai, 26 Nov., '17.

CHAPMAN, JOHN EDWARD, R.A.M.C.
b., '80. *Res.*, 12 Kidderminster Rd., Croydon. *D.*, at R. Victoria Hosp., Netley, 20 Aug., '17 ; *buried*, Mitcham Rd. Cem., Croydon.

CHAPPELL, 2/Lt., R.E.
Educ., High Sch., Croydon. *Fell*, '16.

CHARLICK, E. H. R., 62920, Pte., 7 R. Fus.
b., Croydon, '82; *s.*, R. Charlick, ex-station master, Selhurst Stn., & Mrs. Charlick. Married. Empl. by Messrs. Matthews & Wilson, Portland Rd., S. Norwood. *Res.*, 25 Cresswell Rd., S. Norwood. *Enl.*, in 3 R.W.S. Regt., 4 Jan., '17. *W.,& missing*, Bailleul, 23 Apr., '17.

CHARMAN, ALBERT, Pte., K.O.Y.L.I.
b., '96. *Res.*, 81 Mitcham Rd., Croydon. *Enl.*, Sept., '14. *D.*, Boulogne, 29 Dec., '14, of wounds recd., 20 Dec., '14.

CHART, GEOFFREY, Pte., S.A.F.
b., '81 ; *s.*, Ald. R. M. Chart, J.P., & Mrs. Chart. *Educ.*, Whitgift G. Sch. Married ; 2 children. *Res.*, S. Africa. *Enl.*, in R.A.S.C., '14 *D.*, 23 Sept., '17, France, of wounds recd. 2 days prev.

CHATTEN, WALTER FRANCIS, Pte., 2 S. Lancs. Regt.
b., Dartnell Rd., Croydon, 11 Jun., '96 ; *s.*, Mr. & Mrs. G. E. Chatten, 21 Laurier Rd., Croydon. *Educ.*, St. Mary's (R.C.) Sch., Croydon. Single. Dock labourer at Lond. *Enl.*, 25 Jan., '15. *Fell*, Loos, 25 Sept., '15.

CHATTERTON, HAROLD M. N., 2/Lt., 9 R.W.S. Regt.
D., 18 Jun., '16, France, of gas poisoning, contracted 2 days prev.

CHECKER, JOHN, Pte., Lond. Regt.
Fell, '16.

CHEQUER, HERBERT HENRY, Drummer, 1 Beds. Regt.
b., 75 The Drive, T. Heath, 10 Jul., '88 ; *s.*, George & Sophia Chequer, 75 The Drive, T. Heath. *Educ.*, Whitehorse Rd. Sch., T. Heath. Single. *Enl.*, 16 Nov., '03. Ment. in despatches. *D.*, 28 Sept., '14, at 4 Gen. Hosp., Versailles, of wounds recd. in retreat from Mons, 25 Sept., '14.

CHERRY, ALFRED JOHN, W.O., R.N.
b., 13 Parker Rd., Croydon, 11 Oct., '85 ; *3rd s.*, late George and Mary Rebecca Cherry, 55 Tunstall Rd., Croydon. *Educ.*, St. Andrew's Sch., Croydon. Single. *Res.*, 82 Southbridge Rd., Croydon. *Joined* R.N., 11 May, '01. *Lost* with H.M.S. "Defence," Battle of Jutland, 31 May, '16. (Plate IX., 5).

CHESHIRE, EDGAR MURRAY, 2/Lt., R.F.C.
b., T. Heath, 21 Apr., '93 ; *s.*, Mr. & Mrs. M. E. Cheshire, 9 Raymead Av., T. Heath. *Educ.*, M. Whitgift Sch. Single. Bank clerk. *Joined*, 6 Jun., '17. *D.*, as result of accident while flying, Shoreham, 6 Mar., '18; *buried*, Mitcham Rd. Cem., Croydon.

CHESTER, D., Sgt., R. Fus.
Educ., Shoreham G. Sch. Clerk, Croydon Branch, Nat. Provincial Bank. *Res.*, 42 Hathaway Rd., Croydon. *Enl.*, '14. *Fell*, 24 Apr., '17.

THE GLORIOUS DEAD

CHEVINS, WALTER, Pte., 1 Lond. Regt.
   b., '99 ; s., Mr. & Mrs. Chevins, 3 Edward Rd., Addis. *Educ.*, Davidson Rd. Sch., Croydon. *Enl.*, Sept., '15. *Fell*, France, 15 Sept., '16.
CHILD, A. G., Staff Sgt. Maj., 4 R.W.S. Regt.
   Enl., '95 ; went to India, Oct., '14. *D.*, from an abscess on the liver, Poona, Aug., '15.
CHILMAID, F. A., 14788, Pte., E. Sur. Regt.
   Res., T. Heath. *Fell*, '17.
CHILTON, ERNEST, Bdr., R.F.A.
   s., Mr. & Mrs. Chilton, 6 Penrith Rd., T. Heath. *Accidentally killed*, France, 4 Jan., '16.
CHILVER, S. G., 608039, Pte., R. Irish Fus.
   Res., Croydon. *Fell*, '17.
CHITTELL, STANLEY S., 10 R. Fus.
   s., Mr. & Mrs. J. Chittell, 74 Westow St., U. Norwood.
CHITTENDEN, ALBERT EDWARD, 99058, L/Cpl., 245 Coy., M.G.C.
   b., Peckham. *Educ.*, Dulwich. Married. Shipping manager. *Res.*, 34 Beechwood Av., T. Heath. *Enl.*, Aug., '15. *D.*, 15 Jan., '17, of wounds recd. in Mesopotamia.
CHITTENDEN, LEONARD LLOYD.
   b., '95 ; s., Mr. & Mrs. H. Chittenden, Addis. *D.*, in Switzerland, 15 Oct., '18, having been released from Austria six days before.
CHITTENDEN, WALTER, Pte., 12 Suff. Regt.
   b., Whyteleafe, 16 May, '80 ; s., John & Ellen Chittenden, Welcome Terr., Kenley. *Educ.*, Kenley Sch. Married. Painter. *Res.*, 30 Purley Rd., Croydon. *Enl.*, 2 Oct., '15. *Fell*, 7 Sept., '18.
CHURCH, W., Pte., R. Fus.
   b., '92 ; y.s., Mr. & Mrs. J. Church, 49 Saxon Rd., S. Norwood. *Educ.*, Woodside Sch., Croydon. Married. *Enl.*, Apr., '16. *Fell*, Givenchy, 9 Apr., '17.
CHURCHER, F., Gnr., R.F.A.
   y.s., Mr. & Mrs. H. Churcher, 10 Cobden Rd., S. Norwood. *D.*, 24 Nov., '17, of wounds recd. in France 2 days prev.
CHURCHER, HENRY WILLIAM, Sapper, R.E.
   b., Carmichael Rd., S. Norwood, 29 Oct., '81 ; s., Mr. & Mrs. Churcher, 10 Cobden Rd., S. Norwood. *Educ.*, Birchanger Rd. Sch., S. Norwood. Married. Bricklayer. *Res.*, Apsley Rd., S. Norwood. *Enl.*, '99 ; S.A. Med. & Bars ; called up on Res., '14. *Fell*, nr. Armentières, 24 Jul., '15.
CHUTTER, GEORGE PHILIP, Lt., Glo'ster. Regt.
   b., '98 ; 3rd s., Mr. & Mrs. Chutter, Brighton Rd., Croydon. *Fell*, 15 Jun., '18.
CLACK, J., 55882, Pte., M.G.C.
   Res., Croydon. *Fell*, '17.
CLARICOAT, ARTHUR JOHN, Rflmn., Lond. Regt.
   b., Sutton, 7 Sept., '96 ; s., Mr. & Mrs. Claricoat, 7 Tait Rd., Croydon. *Educ.*, Tavistock Grove Sch., Croydon Single. Grocer's asst. *Enl.*, in 3/4 R.W.S. Regt., 17 Sept., '14. *Fell*, Belgium, 7 Jun.,' 17.
CLARIDGE, LAWRENCE BRAHAM, Pte., 2/4 Lond. Regt. (R.Fus.)
   b., S. Norwood, 22 Jun., '81 ; s., George Frederick & Frances Claridge, 28 Morland Rd., and 59 George Street, Croydon ; now of Leighton Buzzard. *Educ.*, Whitgift G. Sch. Bank clerk, Anglo S. American Bank, Chili. *Enl.*, Nov., '14 ; *served* in Egypt, Dardanelles, France. *D.*, 31 May, '16, in France, of wounds recd. the prev. day.

CLARK, ALBERT, 1880, Pte., R.A.S.C. (M.T.)
  b., Caller St., King's Cross, 5 Dec., '85 ; *s.*, Mr. & Mrs. Thomas Clark, 52 Gloucester Rd., Croydon. *Educ.*, Sydenham Rd. Sch., Croydon. Single. Fitter. *Res.*, Liverpool. *Enl.*, 10 Aug., '14. *D.*, of enteric fever, 21 Jan., '15.

CLARK, ARTHUR GEORGE, 27042, Cpl., R. Scots.
  b., Croydon, 8 Aug., '95 ; *s.*, Mr. & Mrs. Thomas Clark, 52 Gloucester Rd., Croydon. *Educ.*, Sydenham Rd. Sch., Croydon. Single. Empl. as ticket collector by L.B. & S.C.R. *Enl.*, 9 Nov., '15. *Fell,* France, 27 Aug., '18.

CLARK, BERT, Pte., Lond. Regt.
  2nd *s.*, Mr. & Mrs. Clark, Tamworth Pl., Croydon. Married. *Res.*, Croydon. *Enl.*, in Middlesex Regt. *D.*, of wounds, '18.

CLARK, EDWARD, R.B.
  Educ., Shirley Sch., Wickham Rd., Croydon. *Fell*, '15.

CLARK, F., 810444, R.F.A.
  Res., S. Norwood. *Fell*, '17.

CLARK, J. F., L/Cpl., H.A.C.
  b., '87 ; *s.*, Mr. & Mrs. Harry M. Clark. *D.*, of pneumonia, Italy, '17.

CLARK, JOE, Pte., R.W.S. Regt.
  b., '96 ; 3rd *s.*, Mr. & Mrs. Clark, 28 Tamworth Pl., Croydon *Fell*, 6 Apr., '18.

CLARK, THOMAS HENRY, Seaman, R.N.
  b., Croydon, '96 ; *s.*, Mr. & Mrs. T. Clark, Redhill. *Joined*, '12 ; served on H.M. Ships " Ganges," " Magnificent," & " Donegal." *Lost*, with H.M.S. " Amphion," Aug., '14.

CLARKE, ALFRED WILLIAM, Pte., 2/4 R.W.S. Regt.
  b., Croydon, 22 Nov., '74. *Educ.*, St. Andrew's Sch., Croydon. Married. Bricklayer. *Res.*, 40 Bredon Rd., Addis. *Enl.*, 23 Nov., '14. *D.*, 27 Mar., '17, Khanyunas, Palestine, of wounds recd. prev. day.

CLARKE, FRANK PERCY, Bdr., R.F.A
  b., S. Norwood, 19 Oct., '88 ; *s.*, Samuel & Sarah Clarke, 5 Sydney Rd., S. Norwood. *Educ.*, Birchanger Rd. Sch., S. Norwood. Married ; 1 child. Labourer empl. by L.B. & S.C.R. Served for 6 yrs. in R.W.S. Regt. before the war. Re-*enl.*, 3 Nov., '14. *Fell*, St. Quentin, 5 Jul., '17. (Plate V., 3).

CLARKE, H. B., Pte., R.W.S. Regt.
  s., Mr. & Mrs. W. A. Clarke, 39 Tamworth Rd., Croydon. Married, Parish Ch., Croydon, 16 Jun., '17. *Enl.*, Oct., '16. *Fell*, 31 Jul., '17.

CLARKE, H. J., Pte., R.W.S. Regt
  Postman. *Enl.*, Aug., '14. *Fell*, Jun., '15.

CLARKE, HUGH MARTIN, Lt., Lond. Regt.
  b., 25 Feb., '89 ; *s.*, George William Clarke (Town Clerk, Stepney). *Educ.*, Whitgift G. Sch., '01-07 : took his degree at Clare Coll., Camb., '11 ; called to the bar (Middle Temple), '12. Married. Commis., Jun., '13. *Fell*, France, 27 Sept., '15.

CLARKE, JOHN GAY, Capt., 9 R. Suss. Regt.
  s., Mr. & Mrs. Stephenson Clarke, West Hoathly, Sussex, formerly of Croydon. *Fell*, France, Sept., '15.

CLAYDON, ERNEST DIGBY, Signaller, 1/17 Lond. Regt.
  b., Camberwell, 9 Nov., '98. *Educ.*, Mina Rd. Schs., Old Kent Rd., Lond. Single. Clerk (Civ. Serv.). *Enl.*, 17 Jan., '17.

CLAYDON, S., 2114, Pte., E. Sur. Regt.
  Fell, '16.

THE GLORIOUS DEAD

CLAYTON, KEITH HERBERT, Lt., 1 Camb. Regt.
s., Mr. & Mrs. T. G. Clayton, 2 Bedford Pl., Croydon. *Res.*, Newlands Lodge, Caterham. *Fell*, 22 Aug., '18.

CLEAVER, G. J., 7792, Pte., K.R.R.C.
Res., Croydon. *Fell*, '16.

CLEMENT, FREDERICK, Pte., Aust. I.F.
b., '83; *y.s.*, John & Mary Clement, 4 Sumner Rd., Croydon. *Res.*, New S. Wales. *Served* through S.A. War with King's Liverpool Regt. *Fell*, Passchendaele, 12 Oct., '17.

CLEVERLY, FRANK, Pte., 1 R.W.S. Regt.
b., Stoke Newington, 4 Nov., '84; *s.*, Mr. & Mrs. Cleverly, 24 Howley Rd., Croydon. *Educ.* at Croydon. Single. *Res.*, Croydon. *Enl.*, about Mar., '01; *served* 8 yrs. in India. *Fell* in the retreat from Mons, 31 Oct., '14.

CLIFF, F., 41683, Pte., R. Irish Fus.
Res., T. Heath. *D.*, of wounds, '17.

CLIFTON, WILLIAM STREDDER, Gnr., M.G.C.
b., '97. *Res.*, 37 Parson's Mead, Croydon. *Enl.*, in 3/4 R.W.S. Regt., 17 May, '15. *Fell*, Jun., '17.

CLIVE, ROBERT, Special Signal Boy, R.N.
At one time chargeable to the Croydon Union; sent to Training Ship "Exmouth." *Lost* with H.M.S. "Columbia," sunk by torpedo while engaged on mine sinking operations, 1 May,—

COATMAN, STANLEY WILLIAM, L/Cpl., Kensington Rif. (13 Lond. Regt.)
b., '96; *s.*, Mr. & Mrs. William Coatman, 23 Windmill Rd., Croydon. *Enl.*, '15. *D.* of pneumonia, at St. Pol Hosp., 8 Nov., '18.

COBB, H. J., Coldstream Gds.
Fell, '16.

COCKRAM, ARTHUR HERBERT, Pte., 1 Sur. Rif. (21 Lond. Regt.)
b., Tooting, 13 Dec., '96; *s.*, Arthur Edward & Fanny Cockram, 66 Queen's Rd., U. Norwood. *Educ.*, Rockmount Rd. and Woodland Rd. Schs., U. Norwood. Single. Telegraph messenger. *Enl.*, Jan., '14. *D.*, 22 Sept., '16, at 36 C C.S., of wounds recd. at High Wood, Somme, 15 Sept., '16. *Buried*, Mericourt.

COE, HERBERT J., Lt., Tank C.
b., Lond., S.E., 4 Oct., '93; *s.*, Mr. & Mrs. J. Coe, 39 The Avenue, Kenley, Surrey. *Educ.*, Abp. Tenison's Sch., Croydon, where he distinguished himself as a swimmer. *Enl.* in Middlesex Yeom., '13; *served* with M.G.C. in Egypt, Dardanelles, and Salonica. Returned to Eng. and recd. commis. in Tank C., '17; went to France, Nov., '17. *Fell*, nr. Lamotte-en-Santerre, Somme, 8 Aug., '18.

COLDHAM, J., Cpl., R.E.
b., Woodbury Cottage, Addis. Rd., Croydon. Married. Empl. as fitter at Croydon Gas Works. *Res.*, 6 Enville Terrace, Carew Rd., T. Heath. *Enl.*, Jun., '15.; M.M., '18. *Fell*, 9 Jun., '18.

COLDWELLS, CHARLES ALBERT, 2/Lt., 108 Bde., R.F.A.
b., 15 Jun., '95; *s.*, Mr. & Mrs. Joseph George Coldwells, Wallington *Educ.*, M. Whitgift Sch., & Whitgift G. Sch., '07-11. *Enl.*, in Sur. Yeom.; gazetted to R.F.A., Nov., '14. *Fell*, nr. Loos, 28 Sept., '15.

COLDWELLS, FRANCIS BAKER.
b., 25 Nov., '91; *s.*, Mr. & Mrs. Joseph George Coldwells, Wallington. *Educ.*, Whitgift G. Sch.; senior scholar, Wadham Coll., Oxford; instructor, Oxford O.T.C. *Joined*, Aug., '14. *Fell*, 1 Jul., '16.

THE CROYDON ROLL OF HONOUR

COLDWELLS, LEONARD GEORGE, Pte., Lond. Scottish (14 Lond. Regt.)
  b., 2 Nov., '93 ; s., Mr. & Mrs. Joseph George Coldwells, Wallington. *Educ.*, Whitgift G. Sch., '04-09. *Enl.*, 1 Apr., '14. *Fell*, France.

COLE, A. F., 202086, Pte., R.W. Kent Regt.
  Res., Croydon. *Fell*, '17.

COLE, CHARLES STANLEY GEORGE, Pte., Lond. Regt.
  b., '99. *Res.*, 9 Amersham Rd., Croydon. *Enl.*, Aug., '14. *D.*, 13 Oct., '16, of wounds recd. 9 Oct., '16.]

COLE, G., 474095, Pte., Lond. Regt.
  Res., W. Croydon. *Fell*, '17.

COLE, J., 12824, Pte., Yorks. Regt. (?)
  Fell, '16.

COLE, W. S.
  D. of wounds, 23 Nov., '15.

COLEBROOK, ALBERT CHARLES, Gnr., R.F.A.
  b., '95 ; s., Mr. & Mrs. Colebrook, 8 Haling Rd., Croydon. *Educ.*, Dering Pl. Sch., Croydon. *Enl.*, Aug., '14 ; *served* 2½ yrs. in France. *D.* of wounds recd., 1 Dec., '17, at Cambrai.

COLEMAN, EDWIN ARTHUR, Sapper, R.E.
  b., Croydon, 15 Aug., '95 ; s., late Mr., & Mrs. Coleman, 2 Longley Rd., Croydon. *Educ.*, Woodside Sch., Croydon. Single. *Enl.*, 19 Nov., '14. *D.* at his res., 2 Longley Rd., Croydon, 26 Aug., '19.

COLEMAN, WILLIAM, Rflmn., R.B.
  b., Woodside, S. Norwood, 30 Aug., '92 ; s., Tom & Elizabeth Ellen Coleman, 48 Stanger Rd., S. Norwood. *Educ.*, Woodside and Portland Rd. Schs., S. Norwood. Married. Butcher. *Res.*, 9 Morland Bldgs., Earl St., Westminster. *Enl.*, 23 Jan., '17. *D.*, 26 Aug., '17, in 17 C.C.S., of wounds recd., Menin Rd., Ypres, two days prev. *Buried*, nr. Poperinghe.

COLLETT, P. F., 16220, Pte., E. Sur. Regt.
  Res., Addis. *Fell*, '16.

COLLINGS, E. D. A., 2/Lt., R.W.S. Regt.
  Fell, '16.

COLLINS, DENNIS, Bdr., R.F.A.
  b., 51 Leighton St., Croydon, 27 Sept., '90 ; s., Thomas & Laura M. Collins, 28 Napier Rd., Croydon. *Educ.*, St. Mary's (R.C.) Sch., Croydon. Single. Labourer, empl. on railway work. *Enl.*, 10 Apr., '12 ; M.M., '16. *Fell*, nr. Arras, 14 May, '17. *Buried*, Arras.

COLLINS, EDWIN JAMES, Pte., 2/5 Lincoln. Regt.
  b., 9 Keen's Rd., Croydon, 26 Oct., '98 ; s., D. G. & E. C. Collins, 16 Edridge Rd., Croydon. *Educ.*, St. Andrew's Sch., Croydon. Single. Porter. *Enl.*, 4 Sept., '16. *D.*, 27 Sept., '17, at 47 C.C.S., France, of wounds recd. at Messines prev. day. *Buried*, Oost Vleteren, N. of Poperinghe. (Plate V., 4).

COLLINS, FRANK A., Pte., M.G.C.
  b., '83. Married. Clerk, Croydon Gas Co., since '99. *Enl.* in E. Sur. Regt., '16. *Fell*, 24 Apr., '17.

COLLINS, HAROLD GEORGE, Lt., R.F.C.
  b., '95 ; s., Mr. & Mrs. D. George Collins, Shirley Park, Croydon. *Educ.*, Wellingborough Coll. *Enl.*, as pte. in E. Kent Regt., '14 ; commis. in R.A.S.C. ; transf. to R.F.C., '16. *Fell*, 9 Apr., '17.

COLLINS, L., 27321, Pte., Suff. Regt.
  Fell, '16.

THE GLORIOUS DEAD

COLLYER, WILLIAM JOHN, Pte., 1/6 Black Watch.
 b., S. Norwood, 15 Sept., '87. Educ., Birchanger Rd. Sch., S. Norwood. Married. Compositor. Res., 20 Park Rd., S. Norwood. Enl., '16. Fell, 26 Oct., '18.

COLTMAN, VICTOR JOSEPH, Pte., R. Suss. Regt.
 s., Mr. & Mrs. James Coltman, 20 West St., Croydon. Married ; 3 children. Res., 39 Wandle Rd., Croydon. Enl., 16 Aug., '16. Fell, France, 3 May, '17.

COMBER, JOHN, 1907, Pte., 1/15 Lond. Regt.
 b., Sydney, N.S.W., 10 Aug., '94 ; e.s., William J. B. & Clara L. Comber, 44 Cotford Rd., T. Heath. Educ., privately. Single. Civil servant. Enl. in Terrs. before war. Missing, 20 Dec., '15, after enemy raid on Hohenzollern Redoubt ; presumed killed.

COMBER, WILLIAM, Pte., 15 Lond. Regt.
 b., Sydney, N.S.W., 23 Apr., '97 ; y.s., William J. B. & Clara L. Comber, 44 Cotford Rd., T. Heath. Educ., Winterbourne Rd. Sch., T. Heath, & Whitgift G. Sch. (scholarship). Single. Clerk at Lloyd's. Enl., Oct., '15. D., 10 Apr., '17, at 3 Can. C.C.S., Belgium, of wounds recd. prev. day. Buried, Lipsenthoek.

COMLEY, EDGAR C., Lt., R. Mun. Fus.
 s., Mr. & Mrs. Comley, Croydon. Awarded M.C., Oct., '17. D. as result of an accident, 27 Sept., '18.

COMPTON, NEVILLE GEORGE, 2/Lt., 13 Worcester Regt.
 b., 22 Dec., '93 ; s., Mr. & Mrs. Richard Webb Compton, Warwick Lodge, Redhill, formerly of 37 Ashburton Rd., Addis. Dental student.

CONSTABLE, LEONARD ALBERT LONGMAN, Seaman, R.N.
 b., Farnborough, 8 Jan., '98 ; s., John & Georgina Constable, 66 Saxon Rd., S. Norwood. Educ., Whitehorse Rd. Sch., T. Heath. Single. Grocers' boy. Joined, 2 Mar., '14. Lost, with H.M.S. " Hampshire," sunk nr. Orkney Islands, 5 Jun., '16.

CONWAY, GUY, 2/Lt., 11 R.W.S. Regt.
 b., '97 ; s., Mr. & Mrs. C. Conway, 344 Lr. Addis. Rd., Croydon. Educ., Bedford House Sch., Croydon. Single. Res., 46 Inglis Rd., Croydon. Enl., as trooper in Sur. Yeom., 23 Oct., '14 ; trained with O.T.C., at Corpus Christi Coll., Camb. Fell, Belgium, 29 Sept., '18.

COOK, ARTHUR B., Pte., Hants. Regt.
 b., Brighton, 21 Sept., '81 ; s., William Richard & Frances L. Cook, 4 Alexandra Pl., S. Norwood. Educ., Brighton. Single. Enl., Mar., '15. D. of wounds, 19 C.C.S., France, 28 May, '17.

COOK, FRANCIS JOHN RICHARD, Pte., Lond. Scottish (14 Lond. Regt.)
 b., Yorks., '97. Educ., Whitgift G. Sch. Res. with his guardians, William Buttle, & Rev. W. F. Buttle, 3 Upper Grove, S. Norwood. Bank clerk. Enl., '16. Fell, France, Nov., '16.

COOK, GEORGE, L/Cpl., Seaforth H.
 b., '95 ; y.s., Mr. & Mrs. S. Cook, 25 Birchanger Rd., S. Norwood. Enl., Sept., '14. D. of wounds, 21 Nov., '16.

COOK, JAMES, Lond. Scottish (14 Lond. Regt.)
 b., Herne Hill, '81 ; s., Mr. & Mrs. James Cook, " Woodvale," Beddington Gdns. Educ., City of Lond. Sch., & King's Coll. Enl., '14. D. of wounds, Oct., '15.

COOK, LESLIE GEORGE, Pte., 3 Middlesex Regt.
 b., Clapham, 20 Jun., '95 ; s., William & Susannah Cook, 71 Hampton Rd., Croydon. Educ., Sydenham Rd. Sch., Croydon. Single. Butcher. Enl., Jan., '15. Fell, Loos, 25 Sept., '15.

COOKE, EDWARD RALPH, Pte., H A.C.
 b., 16 Mar., '79 ; s., Mr. & Mrs. Alfred E. Cooke, Carshalton. Educ., Whitgift G. Sch., '92-94. Married. Res., Reading. Fell,'17.

COOKE, HAROLD GEORGE, L/Cpl., 1 R.W.S. Regt.
s., Mr. & Mrs. Cooke, 50 Rymer Rd., Addis. *Enl.*, '11. *Fell*, 31 Oct., '14.

COOMBER, W. A., Pte., E. Sur. Regt.
Res., 26 Lancing Rd., Croydon. *Fell*, 25 Jul., '16.

COOMBS, WILLIAM HENRY, Sgt., R.A.S.C. (M.T.)
b., Brixton, 8 May, '82 ; s., Mr. & Mrs. Coombs, 13 Howberry Rd., T. Heath. *Educ.*, Beulah Rd. Sch., T. Heath. Married ; 2 sons. Furniture salesman. *Res.*, Sandfield Rd., T. Heath. Acted as Spec. Const. before enlisting. *Enl.*, 7 Jun., '15. *D.*, 29 Mar.,'18, at 8 Stat. Hosp., Wimereux, of wounds recd.prev.day.

COOPER, C., Pte., 3/4 R.W.S. Regt.
Fell, '16.

COOPER, CHARLES GEORGE DANIEL, 12231, Pte., 9 Dev. Regt.
b., Caterham, 25 Aug., '88 ; s., George Charles F. & Elizabeth A. Cooper, 11 Southsea Rd., Croydon. *Educ.*, Mitcham Rd. Sch., Croydon. Single. Railway shunter. *Res.*, Nuneaton, Warwickshire. *Enl.*, 1 Sept., '14. *Fell*, Ypres, 26 Oct., '17.

COOPER, CLARENCE E. NOOTH, Lt., Lincoln. Regt. (attd. R.F.C.)
b., Putney, 7 May, '91 ; e.s., Mr. & Mrs. George C. Nooth Cooper, 107 S. Norwood Hill. *Educ.*, Whitgift G. Sch. Single. Traveller for firm of wire rope makers. *Enl.*, in 9 Lond Regt. (Q.V.Rif.), Oct., '14 ; commis., Feb., '15. Killed by fall from a kite balloon through parachute failing to open, nr. Montauban, Somme, 16 Sept., '16.

COOPER, F. C., Cpl., L.R.B. (5 Lond. Regt.)
b., '87. Manager of Messrs. Price & Sons, wine merchants. *Fell*, France, 1 Jul., '16.

COOPER, FRANCIS MORDAUNT (FRANK M.), Sgt., Lond. Regt.
b., Croydon, '97 ; y.s., Mr. & Mrs. Dunham Cooper, " Campbell," Blenheim Cres., S. Croydon. *Educ.*, T. Heath Sch., & Elmhurst Coll. Served in France, Mar. '15 to Jan., '17. *Fell*, Ypres, 18 Jan., '17.

COOPER, FRANCIS NICHOLAS NOOTH, Lt., R.A.S.C. (attd. S.W.B.)
b., Sudbury, nr. Harrow, 22 Oct., '96 ; s., Mr. & Mrs. George Nooth Cooper, 107 S. Norwood Hill. *Educ.*, Whitgift G. Sch. Single. *Enl.*, as pte., in L.R.B., Sept.,'14 ; served at Dardanelles, on Suez Canal defences, & in Mesopotamia. *Fell*, nr. Cambrai, France, 21 Nov., '17.

COOPER, FREDERICK WILLIAM AUGUSTUS, Pte., Gren. Gds.
s., late Mr. William Cooper, & Mrs. King, Selhurst Rd., S. Norwood. Married ; 1 child. Solicitor. *Enl.*, Dec., '14. *Fell*, 27 Aug., '18.

COOPER, HARRY, Driver, R.W.S. Regt.
b.,'96. *Educ.*, Whitehorse Rd. Sch., T. Heath. *Res.*, 72 Pawson's Rd., Croydon. *Enl.*, Sept., '14. *D.*, 14 Jul., '16, at Cannes, of wounds recd. in France, 1 Jul., '16.

COOTE, GEORGE H., Pte., R. Suss. Regt.
b., '98. *Res.*, 28 Sandown Rd., S. Norwood. *Enl.*, 30 Aug., '16. *Fell*, '17.

COPPIN, RICHARD A., Capt., R.W.S. Regt.
b., 14 Apr., '97 ; s., Mr. & Mrs. Richard Henry Coppin, Addington. *Educ.*, Whitgift G. Sch., '10-14. Single. *Enl.*, as pte., in Artists Rif., Jan., '15 ; commis., Dec., '15 ; Capt., Nov., '16. *Fell*, France, 12 Apr., '17.

CORBETT, J. A., 81037, R.F.A.
Res., Addis. *D.* of wounds, '17.

CORDOCK, F. G., Pte., E. Sur. Regt.
b., '93. *Educ.*, Abp. Tenison's Sch., Croydon. Married, Mar., '18, Miss A. Grantham, of Selhurst New Rd., S. Norwood. *Enl.*, Sept., '14; *w.*, Ypres, Apr., '15, & Loos, Sept., '15. *Fell*, France, 20 May, '18.

CORDREY, HAROLD COURTNEY, Cpl., 10 R. Fus.
b., Southwark, 7 Feb., '94; *s.*, Arthur & Virginia Cordrey, " Ravenswood," Oakfield Rd., Croydon. *Educ.*, Whitgift G. Sch. Single. Traveller. *Enl.*, Aug., '14. *Fell*, Pozieres, 15 Jul., '16.

CORKE, GUY HAROLD, 2/Lt., Northd. Fus.
b., 23 Nov., '90; *s.*, Mr. & Mrs. Benjamin Corke, Wimborne Rd., Bournemouth. *Educ.*, Aberdeen G. Sch., & Whitgift G. Sch., '02-09; open Science Scholarship, Camb., '08; B.A., Camb., '11. Ment. in despatches, 13 Jul., '16.

CORNHILL, GEORGE HENRY LEWIS.
b., '94; *y.s.*, Mr. & Mrs. Cornhill, " Lyndale," Tamworth Rd., Croydon. Aero employment in France. *D.* from pneumonia and septic poisoning, 21 Oct., '18.

CORNISH, ROBERT FENTON, Pte., Middlesex Regt.
b., Earlswood, 4 Mar., '82. Married. Sign writer. *Res.*, 6 Naseby Rd., U. Norwood. *Enl.*, 14 Aug., '16. *Fell*, Monchy le Preux, 23 Apr., '17. *Buried* in Mil. Cem., between Heninel and Croisilles.

CORRY, JOHN BEAUMONT, Major, R.E.
b., '75; 2nd *s.*, late Mr. John Corry, of Park Hill Rd., Croydon, a member of Croydon County Bench, and Mrs. Corry. *Joined* army, '04; served in N.W. Frontier, India, '97-98, Tirah campaigns, Waran Valley, etc.; awarded D.S.O. and ment. in despatches for service at capture of Fort Nodiz, Meckran, '01. *Fell*, 5 Nov., '14.

COSEDGE, PERCIVAL GEORGE ALLEN, E. Sur. Regt.
b., '78. Twice married; 1 son & 1 daughter. Managing clerk to firm of Lond. solicitors. *Res.*, Estcourt Rd., Woodside. Memb. of Croydon Nat. Res. and 1 Sur. Rif; has won many prizes for shooting. Elected to Croydon Boro. Council, '12. *D* at 8 C.C.S., of wounds recd. 16 Dec., '14. (For portrait see list of Illustrations).

COTHILL, C., 2080, L/Cpl., R.W.S. Regt.
Taken pris., believed dead.

COTTLE, STEPHEN JOHN, A.B. Seaman, R.N
Married. *Res.*, 2 Priory Rd., W. Croydon. Served on H.M.S. " Jason " (mine-sweeper). *Killed*, 3 Apr., '17.

COTTON, WILLIAM FRANK, 8 R.W.S. Regt.
b., 19 Oct., '87; *s.*, Mr. & Mrs. Charles Cotton, 57 Sangley Rd., S. Norwood. *Educ.*, Abp. Tenison's Sch., Croydon. Single. Horticultural builder. *Res.*, 240 S. Norwood Hill. *Enl.*, Sept., '14. *Fell*, Delville Wood, Somme, 2 Sept., '16.

COULDREY, DOUGLAS JOHN, 2/Lt., 24 Lond. Regt.
b., Lewisham, 5 May, '94; *y.s.*, Mr. & Mrs. Couldrey, " Holm Croft," Lansdowne Rd., Croydon. *Educ.*, Sevenoaks G. Sch., and Denstone Coll., Staffordshire. Single. Commercial trav. *Enl.*, Sept., '14, in W. Kent Yeom. *D.* of wounds, Beersheba, 31 Oct., '17. (Plate VIII., 5).

COVILL, G., Pte., Middlesex Regt.
Fell, 31 Aug., '16.

COWLIN, H., Cpl., L.R.B. (5 Lond. Regt.)
Educ., Whitgift G. Sch., '96-02. *Fell*, France, 1 Jul., '16.

Cox, Albert Edward, Pte., 14 R. Irish Rif.
 b., Croydon, 1 Feb., '98 ; y.s., Fred. & Annie Cox, 118 Whitehorse Rd., Croydon. *Educ.*, Sydenham Rd. Sch., Croydon, and Boro. Sec. Sch., Croydon. Single. Empl. in accountant's office, L.B. & S.C.R. *Enl.* in 23 Lond. Regt., Sept., '14. *D.* of wounds, 53 C.C.S., France, 21 Apr., '17. (Plate VII., 4).

Cox, G. H., Pte., R.W.S. Regt.
 Res., T. Heath. *Fell*, '16.

Cox, William, K.R.R.C.
 Enl., Sept., '14. *Fell*, '15.

Cozens, Cyril Percy, Rflmn., L.R.B. (5 Lond. Regt.)
 b., '99 ; s., Mr. & Mrs. P. J. Cozens, 4 Carew Rd., T. Heath. *Educ.*, Westminster Sch. Single. Clerk, County & Westminster Bank. *Enl.*, Jul., '17. *Fell*, 11 Oct., '18.

Cozier, A., 22619, Pte., E. Sur. Regt.
 Res., S. Norwood. *Fell*, '17.

Crabb, Norman Frank, Pte., L.R.B. (5 Lond. Regt.)
 b., W. Norwood, 18 Feb., '90 ; s., Thomas & Martha Crabb, 72 Parchmore Rd., T. Heath. *Educ.*, Beulah Rd. Sch., T. Heath, and Battersea Polytechnic. Single. Clerk. *Enl.*, 1 Oct., '15. *Fell*, Gommecourt, 1 Jul., '16.

Craig, Joseph Kerr, Rflmn., Civil Serv. Rif. (15 Lond. Regt.)

Crane, Frank, Cpl., R.W.S. Regt.
 b., Deptford, 17 Jun., '95 ; s , Mr. & Mrs. Crane, 17 Alpha Rd., Croydon. *Educ.*, Scarbrook Rd. Sch., Croydon. Single. Empl. by L.B. & S.C.R. *Enl.*, 23 Nov., '14. *Fell*, between Monchy and Chinery, France, 3 May, '17.

Cranston, Henry James, Rflmn., K.R.R.C.
 b., 1 St. John's Rd., Croydon, 24 Jun., '92 ; s., Harry & Harriet Alice Cranston, St. John's Rd., Croydon. *Educ.*, Par. Ch. Sch., Croydon. Married. Empl. as roundsman by Messrs. Sainsbury. *Enl.*, 25 Apr., '16 ; w., France, Sept., '16. *Fell*, 17 Feb., '17.

Craven, Brian Thornthwaite, 2/Lt., R.F.A. (Trench Mortar Bty.)
 b., '86. Empl. by Messrs. Robert Schwarzenbach, of Aldermanbury, E.C. *Enl.* as pte. in Lond. Scott. ; commis., Aug., '15. *Fell*, 1 Jul., '16.

Creek, Stanley Alister, Act.-Coy.Sgt.Maj., 1/20 Lond. Regt.
 b., Croydon, 29 Mar., '91 ; s., late J. H. & Catharine Creek, 48 Clyde Rd., Croydon. *Educ.*, Boro. Sec. Sch., Croydon, and Goldsmith's Coll., Univ. of Lond. Single. Schoolmaster. *Enl.*, 23 Aug., '14. *Fell*, High Wood, Somme, 15 Sept., '16. (Plate VII., 6).

Crisp, F., Pte.
 Married ; 2 children. Greengrocer. *Res.*, Queen's Rd., Croydon. *D.* from bronchitis, '17.

Crittenden, Frederick, 2/Lt., R.G.A.
 b., '80. Married, Lily Thornton ; 2 sons. Headmaster of Ingram Rd. Sch., T. Heath ; prev. asst. mast. Beulah Rd. Sch., T. Heath. Connected with Elem. Sch. Athletic Assoc., and George St. Cong. Sunday Sch. ; first head of Evening Inst. at Whitgift G. Sch. ; was an Inspector in Special Constabulary. *Enl.*, in Inns of Court O.T.C., Nov., '15 ; gazetted to R.G.A., Sept., '16. *D.* at King's Coll. Hosp. from illness contracted on active service, 7 Sept., '17.

Croft, W., 18938, Pte., K.R.R.C.
 Fell, '16.

Crofts, Eric.
 b., '97 ; y.s., Mr. & Mrs. Crofts, 6 The Exchange, Lond. Rd., T. Heath. *Fell*, 27 Mar., '18.

THE GLORIOUS DEAD 285

CROPLEY, T. R., Sgt., Q.W. Rif. (16 Lond. Regt.).
Educ., M. Whitgift Sch. *Fell*, 27 Nov., '17.

CROPP, JOHN, Pte., A.C.C.
Married ; 1 child. Empl. by Messrs. Hardy, bookbinders, Lond. Rd., Croydon. *Res.*, 19 Pawson's Rd., Croydon. *Enl.*, Jul., '15 ; served 2 yrs. in Salonica. *D.*from pneumonia, Salonica, 28 Nov.'18.

CROSS, SAMUEL GEORGE, Driver, 36 Div. R.F.A.
b., Bowbrickle, 6 Sept., '75. *Educ.*, Brighton Rd. Sch., Croydon. Married. Labourer. *Res.*, Beulah Rd., T. Heath. *Enl.*, 26 Apr., '15. *Fell*, France, 24 Apr., '17.

CROUCH, LEONARD ALBERT, Pte., 8 E. Sur. Regt.
b., 30 Eland Rd., Croydon, 4 Jul., '86 ; *e.s.*, Mr. & Mrs. Crouch, 64 Lr. Addis. Rd., Croydon. *Educ.*, Par. Ch. Sch., Croydon. Married ; 1 child. Baker's journeyman. *Res.*, 205 Gloucester Rd., Croydon. *Enl.*, 3 Jun., '16. *Fell*, Belgium, 12 Oct., '17.

CROWHURST, JOHN MOSES, Coy.Sgt.Maj., R.W.S. Regt.
b., '80. Married. Empl. by L.B. & S.C.R. *Res.*, 64 Tamworth Rd., Croydon. Served in S.A. War with E. Sur. Regt ; went to France, '14, fighting in battles of Aisne, Marne and Mons. *Fell*, 21 Aug., '16.

CROWLEY, JOHN CYRIL, Capt., 4 R.W.S. Regt.
b., Croydon, 2 Dec., '77 ; *s.*, A. Charles & Florence Mary Crowley, "Woodlands," Coombe Rd., Croydon. *Educ.*, Wimborne, and Keble Coll., Oxford ; M.A., '99. Single. Member of firm of A. C. S. & H. Crowley, brewers ; represented the Central Ward on Croydon Boro. Council from Jan., '09 to Oct., '15. *Joined*, 4 R.W.S. Regt., '06, as 2/Lt. ; served in India and Mesopotamia. *Fell*, Nasiriyeh, 11 Sept., '16. (Plate VIII., 4).

CROWLIN, HORACE, Rflmn., L.R.B. (5 Lond. Regt.)
b., 13 Dec., '83 ; *s.*, Mr. & Mrs. Crowlin, "Elmwood," Mitcham. *Educ.*, Whitgift G. Sch., '96-02. Fell on live bomb to save his fellows, and was *killed*.

CROZIER, ERNEST JOHN, Pte., 8 R. Berks. Regt.
b., Anerley, 5 Aug., '97 ; *s.*, John William & Louisa Crozier, 61 Denmark Rd., S. Norwood. *Educ.*, Portland Rd. Sch., S. Norwood. Single. Printer. *Enl.*, 15 Sept., '14. *Fell*, between Vermelles & La Bassée, 25 Sept., '15.

CUDMORE, W., Pte.
b., '96. *Res.*, 114 Wellesley Rd., Croydon. Served at Dardanelles, Egypt, and Palestine. *Fell*, Jerusalem, 28 Dec., '17.

CULLIS, ALFRED, 41667, Rflmn., R. Irish Rif.
Empl. at one time by Messrs. Nalder & Collyer, brewers, Croydon. Member of St. Mark's, S. Norwood, C.L.B. *Fell*, France, 16 Aug., '17.

CULVER, JOHN HAROLD, Pte., Gordon H.
b., Croydon, 21 Feb., '84 ; *s.*, Mr. & Mrs. J. Culver, 285 Lond. Rd., Croydon. *Educ.*, Brit. Sch., Croydon, & M. Whitgift Sch. Married. Engineer. *Res.*, Toronto, Canada. *Fell*, 26 Sept., '16.

CUMMINGS, HENRY GEORGE ALBERT, Cpl., 8 R.W.S. Regt.
b., 23 Senegal Rd., S.E., 19 Nov., '92 ; *s.*, James Henry & Emma Harriet Cummings, 19 Kynaston Rd., T. Heath. *Educ.*, Ecclesbourne Rd. Sch., T. Heath, & Boro. Sec. Sch., Croydon. Single. School teacher. *Enl.*, 12 Oct., '14. *Fell*, Loos, 25 Sept., '15.

CURRIE, BRIAN.
b., '05. *Res.*, 12 Beech House Rd., Croydon. *Killed*, during Zeppelin raid, Oct., '15.

CURRIE, GORDON.
    b., '00. *Res.*, 12 Beech House Rd., Croydon. *Killed*, during Zeppelin raid, Oct., '15.

CURRIE, ROY.
    b., '01. *Res.*, 12 Beech House Rd., Croydon. *Killed*, during Zeppelin raid, Oct., '15.

CURTIES, D. T. LEES.
    s., Mr. & Mrs. Lees Curties, "Glenesk," Brigstock Rd., T. Heath. *D.*, on active service, 24 Oct., '18.

CURTIS, A., 1427, Pte., R.W.S. Regt.
    Fell, '16.

CURTIS, ROBERT, Pte., R.W.S. Regt.
    b., Bourne St., Croydon ; *s.*, William & Elizabeth Curtis, 39 Old Town, Croydon. *Educ.*, Par. Ch. Sch., Croydon (?). Married. House decorator. *Res.*, 69 Boro. Hill, Croydon. *Enl.*, 3 Dec., '14. *Fell*, Loos, 25 Sept., '16.

CUTHBERT, A. E., Pte., 1 R.W. Kent Regt.
    s., Mr. & Mrs. Cuthbert, 11 Percy Rd., S. Norwood. *Enl.*, Jan., '15. *Missing*, believed *killed*, Somme, 22 Jul., '16.

CUTLER, H. A., Lt., M.G.C.
    Educ., Whitgift G. Sch. *Missing*, '18.

DADY, J. A., 392878, Pte., Lond. Regt.
    Res., Norwood. *Fell*, '17.

DAISLEY, A., 1232, Pte., R. Fus.
    Res., Croydon. *Fell*, '17.

DALE, E. H., Gnr., R.G.A.
    b., '91 ; *s.*, Mr. & Mrs. E. H. Dale, 17 Henderson Rd., Croydon. *Enl.*, '09 ; was serving in China at outbreak of war. *Fell*, France, 28 Mar., '18.

DALZIEL, TOM, Sgt., Artists Rif. (28 Lond. Regt.)
    b., '78 ; 2nd *s.*, Mr. & Mrs. J. R. Dalziel, 12 Bramley Hill, Croydon. *Enl.*, Sept., '14. *Fell*, 29 Oct., '17.

DANIEL, A., Essex Regt.
    Educ., High Sch., Croydon. *Fell*, France, 4 Oct., '17.

DANIELS, J., 550, Pte., R. Suss. Regt.
    Res., Addis. *Fell*, '16.

DARAGON, W., 20328, Pte., R. Suss. Regt.
    Res., W. Croydon. *Fell*, '17.

DARG, DAVID BRUCE, 24305, Pte., Gren. Gds.
    b., Jarvis Rd., Croydon, 21 Aug., '81 ; *s.*, late Mark James & Harriott Darg. *Educ.*, Brighton Rd. Sch., Croydon. Single. Milkman. *Enl.*, '15. *Fell*, Somme, 25 Sept., '16.

DAVIES, E. T., Yeoman of Signals, R.N.
    Married. *Fell*, on H.M.S. "Formidable," '15.

DAVIES, HAROLD HARPER, Pte.
    b., Stockwell, 29 Sept., '90. *Educ.*, M. Whitgift Sch. Married. Clerk. *Res.*, "St. Omer," Norman Av., Sanderstead. *Enl.*, Apr., '16. *Fell*, Ypres, 23 Jul., '17.

DAVIES, J. J., Pte., 17 Scott. Rif.
    b., Gloucester Rd., Croydon, '94. Married ; 1 child. Labourer, empl. by L.B. & S.C.R. *D.* from influenza in Oakbank War Hosp., Glasgow, Feb., '19.

DAVIES, JAMES GORDON, Capt., 10 Welsh Regt.
    b., 29 Mar., '91 ; *s.*, Mr. & Mrs. James John Davies. *Educ.*, Whitgift G. Sch. & Camb. Univ., which he represented in boxing and gymnastics. *D.* of wounds, France, 10 Feb., '16.

DAVIS, ALBERT CHARLES, Lt., R.A.F.
b., Dulwich, 11 Jun., '92; s., Mr. & Mrs. C. H. Davis, 73 Limes Rd., Croydon. *Educ.*, St. Xavier's Coll., Calcutta. Single. Traveller. Mobilised with R.N.V.R. as seaman, 4 Aug., '14; served at Antwerp; transf. to R.N.A.S., in which he obtained commis., becoming flight instructor. *Killed*, while flying at Cranwell Aerodrome, Lincolnshire, 28 Jun., '18. *Buried*, Queen's Rd. Cem., Croydon. (Plate XI., 4).

DAVIS, EDWARD JAMES, 4193, Pte., 1 R.W.S. Regt.
b., 31 Bynes Rd., Croydon, 16 Jun., '95; s., Mr. & Mrs. Daniel Davis, Bynes Rd., Croydon. *Educ.*, Bynes Rd. Sch., Croydon. Single. Electrician. *Enl.*, 13 Jan., '15. *Fell*, nr. Bethune, 1 Nov., '15.

DAVIS, F., 4754, Pte., R.W.S. Regt.
Fell, '16.

DAVIS, HERBERT CHOPE, Act.-Squadron Q.M.Sgt., M.G.C. (Cavalry)
b., Croydon, 11 Aug., '88; s., Herbert & Eliza Leah Davis, 86 Oakfield Rd., Croydon. *Educ.*, High Sch., Croydon. Single. Empl. on Post Office Engrs. Staff. *Enl.*, as trooper in 3 Lond. Yeom., Mar., '14; M.M. for services at fall of Beersheba. *Fell*, Moalsaka, Syria, 28 Oct., '18.

DAVIS, HUBERT EDWARD.
Educ., M. Whitgift Sch.

DAVIS, LEOPOLD, Cpl., R.E.
b., 11 Jul., '89; s., Mr. & Mrs. Leopold Frederick Davis, 312 Lond. Rd., Croydon. *Educ.*, Whitgift G. Sch., '02-08; B.Sc., Lond.

DAVIS, LEWIS HENSHELL, Pte., 1 E. Sur. Regt.
b., Croydon, 20 May, '78. *Educ.*, M. Whitgift Sch. Married. Clerk. Terr. Force Efficiency Med. *Enl.*, 11 Sept., '14. *D.*, 26 Mar., '15, at Bailleul, of wounds recd. at Wulverghem.

DAVIS, MAURICE OLIVER ARTHUR (GUY), 2/Lt., Lond. Regt.
b., Birchanger Rd., S. Norwood, 28 Sept., '94; s., Mr. & Mrs. Davis, "Teighmore," Grange Rd., Sutton. *Educ.*, Albert Rd., S. Norwood, & Asher Sch., Hatcham. Single. Civil Service clerk. *Enl.*, as pte., '16. *D.*, 28 Feb., '18, of wounds recd. at Ypres, 23 Feb., '18.

DAVISON, ROBERT ARTHUR POOLE, Pte., 1/7 Lond. Regt.
b., 31 May, '88; s., Mr. & Mrs. Robert Arthur Poole Davison, 28 Balfour Rd., S. Norwood. *Educ.*, Whitgift G. Sch., '01-05. *Fell*, France, 25 Sept., '15.

DAW, R. W., Pte., 1 R. Fus.
Educ., Whitgift G. Sch., '03-07. *Missing*, '16.

DAWSON, CLAUDE, Pte., 1 E. Kent Regt.
b., Teddington, 8 Aug., '97; 2nd s., Mr. & Mrs. Charles William Dawson, 32 Avondale Rd., Croydon. *Educ.*, Caterham Sch. Single. Audit clerk, S.E. & C.R. *Enl.* in R.G.A., 23 May, '16. *Fell*, France, 4 Mar., '17. (Plate V., 2).

DAWSON, WILFRED LEEDHAM, 2/Lt., R. Warwick. Regt.
e.s., Mr. & Mrs. William Alfred Dawson, 6 Birdhurst Rise, Croydon. *Fell*, '17.

DAY, GEORGE WILLIAM, Pte., 194 Coy., M.G.C.
b., S. Norwood, 9 Sept., '97; s., George & Ellen Day, 32 Percy Rd., S. Norwood. *Educ.*, Birchanger Rd. Sch., S. Norwood. Single. Butcher's roundsman. *Enl.*, Jun., '16. *Fell*, France, 5 Aug., '17.

288   THE CROYDON ROLL OF HONOUR

DAY, HAROLD, Cpl.
b., '95 ; *s.*, Mr. & Mrs. E. Day, 9 Ringwood Rd., Croydon. *Educ.*, Abp. Tenison's Sch., Croydon. Awarded Belgian Croix de Guerre for gallantry and devotion to duty at Ypres, 31 Jul.,-1 Aug., '17.

DAY, HORACE ERNEST, Rflmn., K.R.R.C.
b., 23 Edward Rd., Croydon, 20 May, '98 ; *s.*, Herbert & Nellie Day, 98 Cherry Orchard Rd., Croydon. *Educ.*, Oval Rd. Sch., Croydon. Single. Clerk. *Res.*, 15 Leslie Park Rd., Croydon. *Enl.*, 6 Sept., '14. *D.*, 15 Apr., '17, at 48 C.C.S., Bray, of wounds recd. nr. Peronne, 4 Apr., '17.

DAY, WALTER DANIEL, 44720, Rflmn., R.Irish Rif.
b., 25 Mar., '90. *Educ.*, S. Norwood. Married. Clerk. *Res.*, 147 Portland Rd., S. Norwood. Served 8 yrs. as Terr. in R.W.S. Regt. ; transf. first to Lond. Regt., then to R.E. ; served at Gallipoli, '15-16 ; ret. home, time-expired, Mar., '16 ; rejoined R. Irish Rif., 10 Jun., '16. *Fell*, 27 Mar., '18.

DEACON, WALTER, L/Cpl., R.W.S. Regt.
b., '93 ; *e.s.*, Mr. & Mrs. Deacon, 27 Newark Rd., Croydon. *Enl.*, 4 Sept., '14. Taken pris., 16 Nov., '16. *D.*, Cambrai, 28 Feb., '17. *Buried*, Notre Dame Cem., Cambrai.

DEAN, CYRIL, R.F.A.
b., '99. *Educ.*, High Sch., Croydon. *D.* of pneumonia, France. '17.

DEAN, FREDERICK THOMAS, Pte., 1/6 Lond. Regt.
b., 27 Dec., '95 ; *s.*, Mr. & Mrs. G. H. Dean, 11 Sissinghurst Rd., Addis. *Educ.*, Holbeach Rd. Sch., Catford, & St. Dunstan's Coll., Catford. Single. Insurance clerk. *Enl.*, 24 May, '15, in 4 R.W.S. Regt. *Fell*, Cambrai, 30 Nov., '17.

DEAN, H. F., 32140, Pte., 9 E. Sur. Regt.
b., 24 Gilbert Rd., Kensington, 21 Nov., 96 ; *s.*, Henry George & Emily Ann Dean, 40 Windsor Rd., T. Heath. *Educ.*, St. Philip's, Kensington, Christ Ch. Sch., Croydon, & Ecclesbourne Rd. Sch., T. Heath. Single. Electrician. *Enl.*, Aug., '17. *W. & Missing*, 21 Mar., '18.

DEAN, J. N., 81373, Pte., M.G.C.
Res., E. Croydon. *D.* of wounds, '17.

DEAN, R., 24368, Pte., R.W.S. Regt.
Res., Croydon. *D.* of wounds, '17.

DEE, H. W., Pte., R.W.S. Regt.
Res., S. Norwood. *Fell*, '16.

DEELEY, J., 30300, Gnr., R.F.A.
Res., Croydon. *Fell*, '17.

DELLAWAY, A., 12139, Pte., E. Kent Regt.
Res., T. Heath. *Fell*, '17.

DE LUC., ARTHUR BERNARD, 4261, Rflmn., K.R.R.C.
b., 44 Millman St., Lond., W.C. ; *s.*, Mr. & Mrs. De Luc, 5 Elmers Rd., Woodside. *Educ.*, Woodside Sch., Croydon. Single. Butcher's asst. *Enl.*, 22 Jul., '15. *Fell*, Thiepval, 3 Sept., '16.

DELVAILLE, ERNEST HENRY, Sgt., R.A.S.C. (M.T.), attd. R.F.A.
b., Stratford, E., 7 Dec., '94 ; *s.*, late Daniel Alfred & Henrietta Delvaille, 13 Nicholson Rd., Croydon. *Educ.*, Beulah Hill, U. Norwood. Single. Chaffeur. *Enl.*, Feb., '15 ; *w.*, nr. Ypres, Jul., '16. *D.* of consumption due to exposure while on active service in Italy, 5 Aug., '19.

THE GLORIOUS DEAD

DELVAILLE, STANLEY HILTON, L/Cpl., 2 R.W.S. Regt.
  b., Stratford, E., 2 Mar., '96 ; *s.*, late Daniel Alfred & Henrietta Delvaille, 13 Nicholson Rd., Croydon. *Educ.*, Beulah Hill, U. Norwood. Single. Chauffeur. *Enl.*, Aug., '14 ; discharged with pneumonia, Feb., '15. *D.* of heart failure, at 13 Nicholson Rd., Croydon, 14 May, '16.

DENHAM, DOUGLAS HAROLD, L/Cpl., 6 Lond. Regt.
  b., Ramsgate, 28 Jan., '92 ; *s.*, Mr. & Mrs. George Denham, 41 Avondale Rd., Croydon. *Educ.*, M. Whitgift Sch. Single. Clerk. *Enl.*, Aug., '14. *Fell*, Loos, 25 Sept., '15.

DENMAN, WILLIAM, Pte., R. Defence Corps.
  b., S. Croydon, 7 Feb., '68. Married. Labourer. *Res.*, 87 Sutherland Rd., Croydon. Served 12 yrs. in R B. *Re-enl.*, May, '15. *D.*, Salisbury, 22 Jul., '17.

DENNETT, T. F. P. T., 2/Lt., R.W.S. Regt. (attd. R.F.C.)
  b., '95 ; *s.*, Mr. & Mrs. Frank Dennett, Croydon, & Pett, Hastings. *Educ.*, Whitgift G. Sch. Med. Student, Guy's Hosp., Lond. *Enl.*, as trooper in Sur. Yeom., '14 ; served with 29 Div. at Dardanelles and France ; commis., 19 Dec., '16. *D.* of wounds recd. in France, while engaged as observer, 4 Aug., '17.

DENNING, ALBERT S., Pte., W. Yorks. Regt.
  b., '99 ; *s.*, Mr. & Mrs. Denning, 10 Sutherland Rd., Croydon. *Educ.*, Tavistock Grove Sch., Croydon. Single. Empl. in machine dept., " Croydon Advertiser." *Enl.*, 3 Oct., '17. *Fell*, France, 13 Oct., '18.

DENNIS, F., 7091, Pte., Ox. & Bucks. L.I.
  Res., T. Heath. *Fell*, '17.

DENNIS, FREDERICK WILLIAM, Lond. Irish Rif. (2/18 Lond. Regt.)
  b., 109 Queen's Rd., U. Norwood, 14 Sept., '96. *Educ.*, Rockmount Rd., U. Norwood. Married. Glass stainer. *Enl.*, 20 Oct., '15. *D.*, 9 Apr., '18, of wounds recd. at Palestine, 30 Mar.,'18.

DENNIS, G., 68552, Cpl., R.F.A.
  Res., T. Heath. *Fell*, '17.

DENNIS, PERCY GEORGE Cpl. 1 Northd. Fus.
  b., Barnard Castle, Co. Durham, 28 Jul., '96 ; *s.*, Mr. & Mrs. Dennis, 8 Lucerne Rd., T. Heath. *Educ.*, Barnard Castle. Single. *Enl.*, 1 Jul., '14. *Fell*, 31 Dec., '17.

DENNIS, RUSSELL, Cpl., R.M.L.I.
  b., Cornwall, 5 Sept., '89. *Educ.*, Walmer, Kent. Married. *Lost* with H.M.S. " Hogue," 22 Sept., '14.

DENSHAM, STEPHEN HUGH, Rflmn., L.R.B. (5 Lond. Regt.)
  b., " Waldronhyrst," Croydon, '96 ; *y.s.*, late John L., & Mrs. Densham, " Waldronhyrst," Croydon. *Educ.*, Limes Sch., Croydon, & Dulwich Coll. Single. 'Cellist. *Enl.*, '16. *D.*, 10 Dec., '17, at 56 Gen. Hosp., Etaples, of wounds recd. nr. Arras, 2 Dec., '17. (Plate VI., 6).

DENYER, —, Chief P.O., R.N.
  Educ., Ecclesbourne Rd. Sch., T. Heath. *Fell*, on H.M.S. " Arethusa," Heligoland, '14.

DICKER, A. S., Pte., R. Fus.
  s., Mr. & Mrs. Dicker, 76 Pawson's Rd., Croydon. *Fell*, 31 Mar., '18.

DICKER, JAMES HORACE STANLEY, Trooper, 21 Lancers.
  b., 15 Jan., '92 ; *s.*, Mr. & Mrs. J. Dicker, 6 Queen's Rd., Croydon. *Educ.*, Mitcham Rd. Sch., Croydon. Single. Labourer. *Res.*, 184 Mitcham Rd., Croydon. *Enl.*, 23 Jan., '12. *D.*, 9 Sept., '15, at Peshawar Hosp., India, of wounds recd. at Shabkdar, N.W. Frontier of India, 5 Sept., '15. (Plate X., 6).

DICKSON, CYRIL GARLIES, L.N.Lancs. Regt.
  b., 17 Apr., '90 ; s., Mr. & Mrs. James John Garlies Couper Dickson, " Nuthurst," Avondale Rd., Croydon. *Educ.*, Whitgift G. Sch., '01-05, & Blundell's Sch., Tiverton. *Fell*, E. Africa, '14.
DIGHTON, J., 43634, Pte., Lincoln. Regt.
  Res., Croydon. *Fell*, '17.
DILLOWAY, ALBERT, Pte., 29 Middlesex Regt.
  b., '81. Married. Cabman. *Res.*, St. James' Rd., Croydon. D. of throat disease, '16.
DILMOT, FREDERICK J., Rflmn., K.R.R.C.
  Married. Empl. at " Penge & Anerley Press " Offices. *Fell*, 18 Sept., '18.
DINNIE, DIGBY, Pte., R. Scots.
DIPPLE, WILLIAM JOHN, Rflmn., 1/6 Lond. Regt.
  b., Lond., 29 May, '95 ; s., Mr. & Mrs. Dipple, 17 Drummond Rd., Croydon. *Educ.*, Dering Pl. Sch., Croydon. Single. Butcher. *Enl.* in 3/4 R.W.S. Regt., 31 May, '15. *Fell*, Bourlon Wood, 30 Nov., '17
DIVES, ROBERT BRAMMELL, Gnr., R.G.A.
  b., 28 Feb., '83. Married. Foreman printer. *Res.*, 29 Luna Rd., T. Heath. *Enl.*, 24 May, '16. *Fell*, France, 18 Sept., '17.
DIXON, HENRY PHILIP NORMAN, 2/Lt., Northd. Fus.
  b., Croydon, '92 ; *y.s.*, Mr. & Mrs. Henry Dixon, " Ebenezer," Whitehorse Lane, S. Norwood. Single. Asst., Croydon Public Libraries, '06-13 ; and Asst. Librn., St. Bride Tech. Lib., Lond. D. of wounds at Dettinglis, 4 Sept., '17, while a pris. of war. (Plate XXXVI., 4).
DOBLE, LESLIE STEPHEN NEWTON, 301397, Rflmn., L.R.B. (5 Lond. Rgt.)
  b., 21 Oct., '92 ; s., William & Annie Doble, 38 Elgin Rd., Croydon. *Educ.*, M. Whitgift Sch. Single. Bank clerk. *Enl.*, Apr., '15 ; w., 16 Jun., '17. *Fell*, Glencorse Wood, 16 Aug., '17.
DODD, ARTHUR CUBITT, Sgt., Sur. Yeom.
  b., Rotherhithe, 21 Aug., '78 ; s., Peter D. & M. A. Dodd, " The Poplars," Rolleston Rd., Croydon. *Educ.*, M. Whitgift Sch. Single. Clerk empl. by Messrs. Hooker & Webb. *Enl.*, '00 ; Terr. Force Efficiency Med. D., 26 Oct., '15, at University Mil. Hosp., Southampton, of enteric fever contracted at Gallipoli.
DODDRELL, WILLIAM THOMAS, L/Cpl., 1 City of Lond. Rif.
  b., Brafferton Rd., Croydon, '97 ; s., Mr. & Mrs. A. M. Doddrell, 6 Mead Place, Croydon. *Enl.*, Oct., '14. *Fell*, 23 Jul., '17. (Plate IX., 6).
DODDS, HERBERT ALEXANDER CHRISTOPHER, 2/Lt., 3/5 York & Lancs.Rgt.
  b., Chili, 10 Apr., '83. *Educ.*, Royal Masonic Sch., Wood Green. Married. Clerk in empl. of Middlesex County Council. *Enl.* in an O.T.C., 28 May, '15. D. of pneumonia, 13 Jun., '16, at Northern Gen. Hosp., Sheffield. (Plate IX., 1).
DOE, ROBERT, Pte., R.W.S. Regt.
  b., '81. *Fell*, 1 Jul., '16.
DOODY, MAURICE EDGAR, L/Cpl., 1 R.W.S. Regt.
  b., Hornsey, 15 Sept., '94 ; s., W. H. & H. L. Doody, 45 Elgin Rd., Croydon. *Educ.*, M. Whitgift Sch. Single. Clerk. *Enl.*, 1 Sept., '14. *Fell*, Mametz, 16 Jul., '16.
DOODY, WILFRED GEORGE, Bdr., 156 Bde., R.F.A.
  b., Croydon ; s., W. H. & H. L. Doody, 45 Elgin Rd., Croydon. *Educ.*, M. Whitgift Sch. Married. Clerk. *Enl.*, Feb., '15. *Fell*, Mametz, 22 Jul., '16.

THE GLORIOUS DEAD

DORÉ, D., Cpl., M.G.C.
  b., '97; s., Mr. & Mrs. Doré, "Belmont," St. Paul's Rd., T. Heath. *Educ.*, Beulah Rd. Sch., T. Heath. Empl. by an engineering firm at Mitcham. *Enl.*, '16; M.M. for bravery, 23 May, '18. *Fell*, 23 Oct., '18.

DOUGLASS, ARTHUR WILLIAM, Pte., R.A.S.C. (M.T.).
  b., Caterham, 2 Oct., '96. *Educ.*, Caterham. Single. Chauffeur. *Res.*, 55 Sussex Rd., Croydon. *Enl.*, Oct., '15. *D.* of blackwater fever, Brit. E. Afr., 29 Nov., '16.

DOUTHWAITE, A. G., Signaller, R.G.A.
  Res., 74 Pemdevon Rd., Croydon. Served with Brit. Red Cross for 2½ yrs. *Enl.*, 3 Apr., '17. *Fell*, France, 20 Mar., '18.

DOULTON, ALBERT EDWARD JOHN, 22281, Pte., 12 E. Sur. Regt.
  b., Croydon, 16 Jan., '84; s., Albert & Kate Doulton, 3 Coldharbour Lane, Croydon. *Educ.*, Par. Ch. Sch., Croydon. Married. Carman. *Res.*, 10 Queen St., Croydon *Enl.*, 10 Jun., '16. *Fell*, Ypres, 21 Sept., '17.

DOVE, SIDNEY HERBERT, A.B. Seaman, R.N.
  Educ., Bynes Rd. Sch., Croydon. Single. *Res.*, 19 Bynes Rd., Croydon. *Joined* R.N., 3 Aug., '01. *Lost* with H.M.S."Goliath," sunk at Dardanelles, 13 May, '15. (Plate VII., 3).

DOVEY, THOMAS DANIEL, Pte.
  Married; 2 children. Empl. by Messrs. Nalder & Collyer, brewers, and L.B. & S.C.R. *Res.*, 66 Old Town, Croydon. *Enl.*, Oct., '14; *w.*, Loos, Sept., '15, and Somme, '16. *Fell*, France, 21 Mar., '18.

DOWDEN, ALBERT SIDNEY, Pte., 7 K.O.Y.L.I.
  b., Eland Rd., Croydon, 14 Dec., '94; *y.s.*, Frederic Felix and Sarah Dowden, 93 Waddon Rd., Croydon. *Educ.*, Par. Ch. Sch., Croydon. Single. Collier. *Res.*, Wales. *Enl.*, 4 Jun., '17. *D.* 29 Nov., '17, at Rouen, of wounds recd. nr. Cambrai, 21 Nov., '17.

DOWDEN, GEORGE FRANK, Pte., M.G.C.
  b., Eland Rd., Croydon, 10 Mar., '92; s., Frederic Felix & Sarah Dowden, 93 Waddon Rd., Croydon. *Educ.*, Par. Ch. Sch., Croydon. Single. Metal casement maker. *Res.*, Wolverhampton. *Enl.*, Aug., '15. *Fell*, Somme, 20 Sept., '16.

DOWDEN, WILLIAM HERBERT JOHN, Pte., 28 Can. Inf.
  b., Addington Rd., Croydon, 21 Dec., '84. s., Frederic Felix and Sarah Dowden, 93 Waddon Rd., Croydon. *Educ.*, Par. Ch. Sch., Croydon. Single. Gas & hot-water fitter. *Res.*, Moose Jaw, Canada. *Enl.*, Apr., '15. *Fell*, Somme, 17 Sept., '16.

DOWLEY, ARTHUR WILLIAM, Seaman, R.N.
  b., '80. Painter & sign writer. *Res.*, 7 Helder St., Croydon. *Enl.*, '14. *Lost* with H.M.S. "Vanguard," destroyed by internal explosion, 9 Jul., '17.

DOWN, LIONEL WYNDHAM, 21 Div. Sig. Coy., R.E.
  s., Mr. & Mrs. H. W. Down, 67 Coombe Rd., Croydon. *Res.*, Croydon. *Fell*, France, 8 Dec., '18.

DRAY, H. W., 301602, Pte., Lond. Regt.
  Res., S. Norwood. *D.*, '17.

DREW, G. A., 2/Lt., Dev Regt.
  Educ., Whitgift G. Sch. *Missing*, '17.

DRIVER, F., 201154, L/Cpl., W. Yorks. Regt.
  Res., S. Norwood. *Fell*, '17.

DRYSDALE, ADRIAN CASTLELAW, Pte., H.A.C.
  b., Apr., '93; s., Mr. & Mrs. John William Drysdale, "Hurstleigh," Howard Rd., S. Norwood. *Educ.*, Whitgift G. Sch. *Fell*, France, 30 Jan., '15.

DUDLEY, WILLIAM A. DEVALL, Pte., 2 N.Z. (Wellington) Regt.
  3rd s., Mr. & Mrs. Dudley, 76 Sumner Rd., Croydon. *Educ.*,
  Christ Ch. Sch., Croydon. *Enl.*, Dec., '17 ; *w.* & gassed, 25
  Aug., '18. *D.* at Brockenhurst Mil. Hosp., 9 Nov., '18. *Buried*,
  Mitcham Rd. Cem., Croydon.

DUFF, HARLEY NORMAN, Pte., Lond. Scottish (14 Lond. Regt.)
  b., 9 Jun., '16 ; *s.*, Mr. & Mrs. Norman Duff, " Bellfield," Purley.
  Educ., Whitgift G. Sch., '09-12. *Fell*, Messines, 1 Nov., '14.

DUNCAN, EDWARD WALLACE BRUCE, Driver, R.F.A.
  b., Fulham, 10 Feb., '94. *Educ.*, Sydenham Rd. & Whitehorse
  Rd. Schs., T. Heath. Single. Fruiterer's asst. *Res.*, 27 Arundle
  Rd., Croydon. *Enl.*, '13. *D.*, 8 Apr., '17, at 3 Gen. Hosp., Le
  Tréport, of wounds recd. 1 Apr., '17.

DUNFORD, ARTHUR CHARLES, E. Sur. Regt.
  b., '96 ; *4th s.*, Mr. & Mrs. Dunford, 47 Parchmore Rd., T.Heath.
  D., 18 Sept., '16, of wounds recd. 3 days prev.

DUNHAM, HENRY GEORGE, Sgt., 7 E. Sur. Regt.
  b., Bridport, Devon, 2 Feb.,'74 ; *s.*, Mr. & Mrs. Henry S. Dunham,
  Tonbridge. Married. Ironmonger. *Res.*, Grove Cott., St.
  John's Grove, Croydon. *Enl.*, 11 Sept., '16. *Fell*, Vermelles,
  12 Mar., '16. *Buried*, Hulloch. (Plate X., 5).

DUNN, S. E., L/Cpl., R. Suss. Regt.
  b., '94 ; *y.s.*, Mr. & Mrs. Dunn, 47 Northbrook Rd., Croydon.
  Enl., Jan., '12; *w.*, France, 26 Sept.,'14. *D.* of wounds, 25 Jul.,'17.

DUNN, W., Pte., R.W.S.Regt.
  e.s., Mr. & Mrs. Dunn, 45 Sumner Rd., Croydon. *Fell*, 15
  Sept., '16.

DUNN, W. J., 16497, Pte., Dev. Regt.
  Fell, '16.

DUNN, WALTER STANLEY, Pte., 10 R.W.S. Regt.
  b., Croydon, 10 Nov., '96 ; *s.*, Mr. & Mrs. Mary E. Dunn, 45
  Sumner Rd., Croydon. *Educ.*, Boston Rd. Sch., Croydon. Single.
  Welder. *Enl.*, 24 Jan., '15. *Fell*, Somme, 15 or 16 Sept., '16.

DUNNETT, LEONARD HUGH, Sgt., K.R.R.C.
  b., Walworth, 25 Mar., '95 ; *s.*, Mr. & Mrs. Dunnett, 53 Beulah
  Gr., W. Croydon. *Educ.*, Kenley. Single. Printer & comp.
  Enl., 24 Sept., '14. *Fell*, Beaumont Hamel, 13 Nov., '16.

DUPLOCK, HARRY LEWIS, Pte., 6 D.C.L.I.
  b., Cripplegate, E.C., 6 Feb., '82 ; *s.*, Mr. & Mrs. Duplock, 60
  Hathaway Rd., Croydon. *Educ.*, Anglo-French High Sch.,
  Stroud Green, & Hornsey G. Sch. Single. Silk warehouseman.
  Enl., 31 Aug., '14. *Fell*, Weiltje, nr. Ypres, 8 Dec., '15. *Buried*,
  St. Jean. (Plate IX., 4).

DURANCE, B., 2114, Pte., Lond. Regt.
  Res., T. Heath. *Fell*, '16.

DURLING, GEORGE JOSHUA, 291976, Pte., 2/10 Middlesex Regt.
  s., Mr. & Mrs. G. W. Durling, 10 Colson Rd., Croydon. *Fell*,
  Jerusalem, 21 Dec., '17.

DYE, H. L., Pte., R.W.S. Regt.
  Empl. by Messrs. Chapman, builders. *Res.*, 18 Bourne St.,
  Croydon. *Enl.*, '14. *Fell*, 23 Apr., '17.

VII.

1. Lt. C. S. CALVER, M.C., 7 E. Sur. Regt.
2. Pte. G. R. HAMMOND, H.A.C.
3. A.B. Seaman S. H. DOVE, R.N.
4. Pte. A. E. COX, R. Irish Rif.
5. Rflmn. W. W. BROWN, Lond. Rif. B.
6. Act.-Coy. Sgt.Maj. S. A. CREEK, 1/20 Lond. Regt.

VIII.

1. Capt. J. M. Donaldson, M.C., 16 King's R.R.C.
2. 2/Lt. J. W. Everitt, King's R.R.C.
3. 2/Lt. J. E. Binns, Wilts. Regt.
4. Capt. J. C. Crowley, 4 R.W.S. Regt.
5. 2/Lt. D. J. Couldrey, 24 Lond. Regt.
6. Capt. C. N. Dyer, H.A.C.

THE GLORIOUS DEAD

DYER, CHARLES NETTLETON, Capt., H.A.C.;
  b., King William's Town, Cape Colony, '78 ; *2nd s.*, Frederick Dyer, J.P., & late Frances Dyer, 45 Park Hill Rd., Croydon. *Educ.*, Clifton Coll., & Balliol, Oxford ; 1st Mod. Hist. & B.A., '01 ; Univ. Trial & Coll. Eights, '98-00. Married, '14, Maud Hamilton, daughter of Mr. Fredk. Link, C.C., J.P. ; 1 son. Became a solicitor, '04 ; director & later partner, Messrs. Dyer and Dyer, Ltd., Lond. *Joined* H.A.C. as a Gnr., '05 ; commis., '10 ; Lt., '11 ; Capt., May, '14. Served on Suez Canal from Apr., '15, and through N.W. Frontier Campaign. *D.*, 14 Jul., '16, at 18 Stat. Hosp.,Suez, of enteric fever, contracted at Ayum Musa. (Plate VIII., 6).

DYER, E., 77486, Gnr., R.G.A.
  Res., Croydon. *Fell*, '17.

DYER, F., 201094, Pte., R.W.S. Regt.
  Res., Croydon. *Fell*, '17.

DYNE, G., 34989, Pte., R. Fus.
  Res., Croydon. *Fell*, '17.

EADE, H., 12103, Pte., E. Kent Regt.
  Res., Croydon. *D.* of wounds, '17.

EARL, PERCY LIONEL, P.O., R.N.
  b., Acton, 27 Oct., '71 ; *s.*, late Mr., & Mrs. Bessie Earl, 78 Barrow Rd., Streatham Common. *Educ.*, N. Lond. Collegiate Sch. Married. Mercantile marine. *Res.*, 5 Francis Terrace, Eridge Rd., T. Heath. *Joined*, Sept., '14. *Lost*, with H.M. Hosp. Ship, "Llandovery Castle," torpedoed between Valentia and Fastnet, 27 Jun., '18.

EASTER, WILLIAM ARTHUR CHARLES, Pte., R.F.C.
  b., '96 ; *s.*, Mr. & Mrs. H. W. Easter, Oxted, & 54 Norbury Rd., T. Heath. *Educ.*, Boro. Sec. Sch., Croydon. *Accidentally killed*, 22 Apr., '18. *Buried*, Oxted Church.

EASTON, SIDNEY JAMES, Cpl., 7 R.W.S. Regt.
  b., 82 Waddon New Rd., Croydon, 6 Sept., '94 ; *s.*, Mr. & Mrs. Easton, 11 Old Palace Rd., Croydon. *Educ.*, Par. Ch. Sch., Croydon. Single. Empl. by Croydon Corp. Roads Dept. *Enl.*, 4 Sept., '14. *Fell*, 16 Oct., '15.

EBBUTT, JOHN STREETER, Signaller, 1/4 R.W.S. Regt.
  b., Croydon, 10 Nov., '86 ; *s.*, Thomas Henry & Anne Ebbutt, 91 High St., Croydon. *Educ.*, Whitgift G. Sch., Croydon. Single. Bank clerk. *Enl.*, Sept., '14. *D.* of pneumonia, Brit. Hosp., Nowshera, 2 Oct., '19.

EDBROOK, E. C., 25003, Pte., R.W.S. Regt.
  Res., T. Heath. *D.* of wounds, '17.

EDMONDS, FRANCIS D., 2/Lt., R.A.S.C.
  Res., Croydon. *D.* of wounds recd. in Palestine, 1 Dec., '17.

EDWARDS, A., 5272, Pte., Lond. Regt.
  Res., S. Norwood. *Fell*, '16.

EDWARDS, ALBERT J., Lt., R. Fus.

EDWARDS, CHARLES, Cpl., 1 R.B.
  Educ., Shirley Sch., Wickham Rd., Croydon. *Enl.*, Nov., '06 ; studied at Kneller Hall Mil. Sch. of Music. *Fell*, Ypres, '15.

EDWARDS, F. W., 207869, Pte., R.W.S. Regt.
  Missing, Mar., '18.

EDWARDS, G., 10490, Rflmn., R. Irish Rif.
  Res., E. Croydon. *Fell*, '17.

EDWARDS, HENRY, Pte., 11 R.W.S. Regt.
  b., '83 ; *2nd s.*, Mr. & Mrs. J. Edwards. *Educ.*, St. James' Sch., Croydon. Married. Labourer. *Res.*, 200 Gloucester Rd., Croydon. *Enl.*, 10 Nov., '15. *Fell*, Ypres, 7 Jun., '17.

THE CROYDON ROLL OF HONOUR

EDWARDS, HUBERT PERCY, Pte., R.M.L.I.
　　b., '93 ; *s.*, Mr. & Mrs. H. G. E. Edwards, 113 Albert Rd., Addis Single. *D.*, 27 Jun., '15, at 21 Gen. Hosp., Alexandria, of wounds recd., 22 Jun., '15.

EDWARDS, S. C., 207905, Pte., R.W.S. Regt.
　　Missing, 1 Aug., '18.

EDWARDS, WILLIAM, Pioneer, R.E. (Lab. Coy.)
　　b., '70. Married. *Res.*, 84 Princess Rd., Croydon. *Enl.*, '15. *D.*, 5 Jun., '18, of wounds recd. nr. St. Quentin.

EGERTON, CHARLES ALFRED, 16008, Cpl., 1 R. Fus.
　　b., '97. *Res.*, 93 Crowther Rd., S. Norwood. Memb. of St. Mark's, S. Norwood, C.L.B. *D.* of wounds, France, 23 Apr., '16.

EGGLESTON, RICHARD JAMES.
　　b., '83. Labourer. *Res.*, Selhurst Rd., S. Norwood. *Enl.*, Sept., '14. *D.* of meningitis & pneumonia, '17.

ELGER, M. E., Rflmn., Lond. Regt.
　　b., '98. Empl. by " Croydon Advertiser." *Fell*, France, 23 May, '17.

ELLIFF, ARTHUR GEORGE, Pioneer, 317 Road Construction Coy., R.E.
　　b., 42 Whitehorse Lane, S. Norwood, 9 Mar., '90 ; *s.*, Mr. & Mrs. Elliff, 51 Broadway Av., Whitehorse Rd., Croydon. *Educ.*, Princess Rd. Sch., Croydon. Married. Furniture porter. *Enl.*, 15 Apr., '16. *Fell*, Cambrai. 19 Sept., '18.

ELLIFF, ERNEST FRANK, 23024, Pte., 1 Border Regt.
　　b., S. Norwood, 31 Dec., '89 ; *s.*, William & Alice Elliff, 42 Whitehorse Lane, S. Norwood. *Educ.*, Whitehorse Rd. Sch., T. Heath. Single. Gardener. *Enl.*, 15 Jan., '15. *Fell*, France, 19 May, '17.

ELLIFF, FREDERICK, 37114, Pte., R. Irish Rif.
　　b., S. Norwood, 1 May, '83 ; *s.*, William & Alice Elliff, 42 Whitehorse Lane, S. Norwood. *Educ.*, Whitehorse Rd. Sch., T. Heath. Married ; 2 children. Gardener. *Res.*, 45 Lenham Rd., T. Heath. *Enl.* in Beds. Regt., 16 Jun., '16. *D.* of wounds, St. Omer, 7 Aug., '17.

ELLIFF, THOMAS EDWARD, 32577, Pte., 1/4 Norf. Regt.
　　b., S. Norwood, 5 Aug., '99 ; *y.s.*, William & Alice Elliff, 42 Whitehorse Lane, S. Norwood. *Educ.*, Whitehorse Rd. Sch., T. Heath. Single. Chauffeur. *Enl.*, 12 Mar., '17. *D* of wounds, Alexandria, 12 Dec., '17.

ELLIFFE, —, L/Cpl., Middlesex Regt.
　　Pawnbroker's asst. *Res.*, 12 Keen's Rd., Croydon. *Enl.*, 3 Mar., '15 ; *w.*, in France. *Fell*, '17.

ELLIOTT, A., 47048, Rflmn., R. Irish Rif.
　　Res., S. Norwood. *Fell*, '17.

ELLIOTT, FRANCIS EDWIN, Pte., 33 Aust. I.F.
　　b., Brixton, 21 Jun., '95 ; *s.*, Mr. & Mrs. Elliott, 1 Southcote Rd., Woodside. *Educ.*, Portland Rd. Sch., S. Norwood. Single. Farmer. *Res.*, Australia. *Enl.*, Nov., '16 ; *w.*, Messines, Jun., '17. *Fell*, nr. Peronne, 30 Aug., '18.

ELLIOTT, S., Gnr., R.F.A.
　　b., '97 ; 2nd *s.*, late Mr., & Mrs. Elliott, 50 Cross Rd., Croydon. Empl. by Home and Colonial Stores, Cherry Orchard Rd., Croydon. *Fell*, 8 Jun., '17.

ELLIOTT, S. F., 38435, Driver, R.F.A.
　　Res., E. Croydon. *Fell*, '17.

ELLIS, ARTHUR SYDNEY, Rflmn., 1 Sur. Rif. (21 Lond. Regt.)
　　b., Leander Rd., Brixton Hill, 24 Oct., '95 ; *s.*, Arthur William & Clara Ellis, " Carn Brae," Kilmartin Av., Norbury. *Educ.*, Nevill House, Eastbourne, Strand Sch., & King's Coll., Lond. Single. Clerk. *Enl.*, 2 Sept., '14. *Fell*, Festubert, 25 May, '15.

THE GLORIOUS DEAD

ELLIS, CHARLES JOHN, Pte., 26 R. Fus.
 b., 1a York Villas, Alexandra Rd., Croydon, 27 Jul., '96 ; *s.*, Charles William & Gertrude Emma Ellis, 15 Alton Rd., Waddon, Croydon. *Educ.*, M. Whitgift Sch. Single. Bank clerk, Lloyd's, Lombard St., E.C. *Enl.*, 20 Nov., '15. *Fell*, nr. Flers, Somme, 15 Sept., '16.

ELLIS, MONTAGUE ARTHUR, Pte., 6 Northants. Regt. (Lab. Btn.)
 b., 29 Jan., '97 ; *s.*, Mr. & Mrs. Arthur John Clement Ellis, 70 Holmesdale Rd., S. Norwood. *Educ.*, Brit. Sch., Croydon. Single. Newsagent. *Enl.*, 17 Jul., '17. *Fell*, France, 22 Mar., '18.

ELLIS, OLIVER, attd. E. Kent Regt.
 b., '92 ; *y.s.*, Mr. & Mrs. J. W. Ellis, W. Runton, Norfolk, formerly of Addis. *Fell*, 16 Jul., '18.

ELLIS, PHILLIP HENRY, Pte., 10 R. Fus.
 b., 20 Mar., '94 ; *s.*, Mr. & Mrs. James Ellis, 220 Melfort Rd., T. Heath. *Educ.*, Whitgift G. Sch., '06-09. Clerk, City and Midland Bank.

ELSEY, ALFRED SIDNEY.
 b., '85. Married. *Res.*, 11 Maplethorpe Rd., T. Heath. *Fell*, 27 Aug., '18.

ELSEY, ARTHUR, Pte., Gren. Gds.
 Educ., Ingram Rd. Sch., Croydon. *Fell*, 27 Sept., '15.

ELSEY, W., 1084, Pte., E. Sur. Regt.
 Res., T. Heath. *Fell*, '16.

ELTON, ARTHUR, L/Cpl., R.W.S. Regt.
 s., Mr. & Mrs. Charles Elton, 12 Grace Rd., Croydon. Empl. by Brit. Wood Heel Co. *Res.*, 26 Queen's Rd., Croydon. *Enl.*, 12 Nov., '15 ; *w.*, May, '16 and May, '17. *Fell*, 30 Jun., '18.

ELY, DENNIS JAMES, Capt., D.L.I.
 b., 27 Feb., '96 ; *s.*, Mr. & Mrs. George Herbert Ely, Haling Park Rd., Croydon. *Educ.*, Ayr Academy & Whitgift G. Sch. *Enl.* as pte. in R. Fus., Aug., '14.

EMERY, E. W., Cpl., Lond. Regt.
 Res., T. Heath. *Fell*, '16.

EMERY, HERBERT J., Pte.
 Educ., Abp. Tenison's Sch., Croydon. *Res.*, 49 Selsdon Rd., Croydon. *Fell*, Somme, 24 Sept., '16.

EMMENS, GEORGE HAROLD, Sgt., 10 W. Yorks. Regt.
 b., Milton Rd., Croydon, 12 Mar., '89 ; *s.*, late Thomas Emmens, & Mrs. White, 186a Oval Rd., Croydon. *Educ.*, Oval Rd. Sch., Croydon. Married. Clerk. *Res.*, Bradford, Yorkshire. *Enl.*, 14 Sept., '14. *Fell*, France, 19 Sept., '18.

EMY, ERNEST LUDOVIC, Pte., 2 Wilts. Regt.
 b., Croydon, 21 Sept., '88 ; *s.*, Charles & Ellen Emy, 1 St. James' Park, Croydon. *Educ.*, Brit. Sch., Croydon. Single. Clerk. *Enl.*, 31 Aug., '14. *Fell*, Neuve Chapelle, 12 Mar., '15.

ENDEAN, FREDERICK JAMES HENRY, Pte., Lab. Corps.
 b., Dean St., Lond., 23 Apr., '98 ; *s.*, Mr. & Mrs. Endean, 36 Notson Rd., S. Norwood. *Educ.*, Portland Rd. Sch., S. Norwood. Single. Munition worker. *Enl.*, 1 Mar., '15. *D.* of wounds and acute bronchitis, Boulogne, 11 Jun., '18.

ENDERBY, ARTHUR A., Lt., 4 R. Fus.
 b., Canterbury, 17 Nov., '95 ; *s.*, Major & Mrs. H. H. Enderby, 63 Birchanger Rd., S. Norwood. *Educ.*, Retford G. Sch., Notts. Single. *Enl.*, as pte. in 3 Beds. Regt., Aug., '14 ; commis. as 2/Lt. in 23 R. Fus., Nov., '14 ; Lt., Jan., '15 ; Double Distinguished at Hythe School of Musketry, Jan., '17. *D.*, 2 Aug., '17, at 3 C.C.S., France, of wounds recd. 25 Jul., '17.

EPPS, PERCY EDWARD, 1511, Pte., R.W.S. Regt.
b., Croydon, 11 Mar.,—. *Educ.*, Sydenham Rd. Sch., Croydon. Single. Warehouseman. *Res.*, 65 Union Rd., Croydon. *Enl.*, 8 Sept., '14. *D.*, 9 May, '16, of wounds recd. in France 3 days prev.

EUSTACE, WILLIAM WILLIAMSON, Trooper, 10 Aust. Light Horse.
b., 29 Oct., '90 ; *s.*, Mr. & Mrs. Fred Owen Eustace, " Makado," Harewood Rd., Croydon. *Educ.*, Bedford Mod. Sch. & Whitgift G. Sch., '02-06. *Fell*, Russell Top, Walker's Ridge, Gallipoli, 7 Aug., '15.

EVANS, DOUGLAS LANE, Capt., Northants. Regt.
b., T. Heath, 15 Jul., '95 ; *s.*, Mr. & Mrs. F. C. Evans, 369 Lond. Rd., T. Heath. *Educ.*, T. Heath Sch., St. Paul's Sch., and King's Coll., Camb. Served 3 yrs. in O.T.C. ; gaz., 2/Lt., Nov., '14 ; Capt. & Adj., 22 May, '16. *D.* of wounds, 26 Sept., '16.

EVANS, LESLIE FURMSTON, Cpl., Can. Inf.
Educ., Elmhurst Sch., Croydon, & Brighton Coll. *D.* of wounds, 16 Mar., '16.

EVANS, NORMAN REGINALD, Cpl., R.E.
b., 24 Bynes Rd., Croydon, 15 Nov., '95 ; *s.*, Mr. & Mrs. Evans, 8 Helder St., Croydon. *Educ.*, Bynes Rd. Sch., Croydon, and Tolworth Council Sch. Single. Motor engineer. *Res.*, 191 Ellerton Rd., Tolworth. *Enl.*, in R.N.A.S., Dec., '14 ; 8 months as P.O. with armoured car squadron in France ; transf. to R.E. as desp. rider. *D.*, 25 Aug., '16, at Ipswich Hosp., of injuries recd. in accident prev. day, while carrying despatches at Ipswich.

EVANS, FRANCIS EDWARD, Sgt., 11 R.B.
b., Clapham, 3 Apr., '95 ; *s.*, Mr. & Mrs. Evans, 39 Balfour Rd., S. Norwood. *Educ.*, Woodside & M. Whitgift Schs., Croydon. Single. Stockbroker's clerk. *Enl.*, 10 Sept., '14. *Fell*, France, 24 Aug., '16.

EVANS, PERCY JOHN, Pte., 22 R. Fus.
b., Clapham, 27 Oct., '92 ; *e.s.*, Mr. & Mrs. Evans, 39 Balfour Rd., S. Norwood. *Educ.*, Woodside & M. Whitgift Schs., Croydon. Single. Bank clerk. *Enl.*, 10 Feb., '16. *D.*, 18 Mar., '17, at Rouen, of wounds recd. in France, 10 Mar., '17.

EVE, EVELYN CHARLES J., E. Afr. Force.
Educ., M. Whitgift Sch. *D.* of dysentery, Mombasa, Apr., '16.

EVE, FRANK A., Lt., Can. Inf.
e.s., Mr. & Mrs. Arthur G. Eve. *Educ.*, Whitgift G. Sch. Engaged in telephone construction work. *Res.*, Canada. *Fell*, 15 Sept., '16.

EVELEIGH, ERNEST H., 37072, Pte., 8 R.W.S. Regt.
Missing, 31 Mar., '18.

EVERITT, JOHN WILSON, 2/Lt., K.R.R.C.
b., Camberwell, 6 Oct., '94 ; *s.*, John William & Matilda Everitt, 17 Edridge Rd., Croydon. *Educ.*, Whitgift G. Sch. Single. Empl. in Accountant's Dept., Royal Exchange Assurance Co. *Enl.*, as pte. in Inns of Court O.T.C., Jan., '16. *D.*, 12 Apr., '18, at Reserve Gen. Hosp., Beaufort, of wounds recd. at Mézières, 29 Mar., '18. (Plate VIII., 2).

EVEZARD, GEORGE, Capt., Leicester Regt.
b., 24 Jul., '93 ; *s.*, Mr. & Mrs. Evezard, " Reedhamcote," Purley. *Educ.*, Whitgift G. Sch., '07-08. *Fell*, '17.

EWALD, FRITZ EDWARD HENRY, Pte., R.A.M.C.
b., 7 Aug., '97 ; *s.*, Mr. & Mrs. Henry Ewald, " Shunnerfell," Foxley Rd., Kenley. *Educ.*, Whitgift G. Sch., '12-14.

EXELBY, CHARLES R., Pte., Q.W. Rif. (16 Lond. Regt.)
  b., 16 Jan., '93 ; s., Mr. & Mrs. William Exelby, " Haroldene," Cedar Rd., Croydon. *Educ.*, Whitgift G. Sch., '08-10 *Fell*, '17.
FAIRBAIRN, EDGAR, Pte., Aust. Inf.
  b., '94; s., Mr. & Mrs. James Fairbairn, 1 Outram Rd., Croydon. *D.* of wounds, 15 Oct., '17.
FAIRBAIRNS, JOSEPH M., 2/Lt., R.F.A.
FAIRMAN, F., 13126, Rflmn., R.B.
  Res., T. Heath. *D.*, '16.
FAIRS, ERNEST WILLIAM, Pte., L.R.B. (5 Lond. Regt.)
  b., Banstead, Surrey, 15 Dec., '95 ; s., William & Ellen Sarah Fairs, 32 Beaconsfield Rd., Croydon. *Educ.*, Sydenham Rd. Sch., Croydon. Single. Auctioneer & estate agent's clerk. *Mobilised*, 4 Aug., '14. *Fell*, Ypres, 3 May, '15.
FALCON, GEOFFREY WILLIAM LOCKHART, Lt., 11 E. Sur. Regt. (attd. 2 Hants. Regt.)
  b., Punjab, India, 28 Sept., '93 ; s., Lt.-Col. & Mrs. Robert Morgan Falcon. *Educ.*, Repton, '07-12, & Balliol Coll., Oxford, '12-14. Single. Undergraduate. Gazetted, 2/Lt., Oct., '14. *Fell*, Gallipoli, 6 Aug., '15.
FARMER, G., Driver, R.F.A.
  b., '84 ; e.s., Mr. & Mrs. J. Farmer, 42 Coventry Rd., S. Norwood. Empl. by Messrs. Foster Biggs, contractors, S. Norwood. *Enl.*, Mar., '16 ; trench fever, Feb., '17. *Fell*, 3 Sept., '18.
FARMER, J., 959, Pte., R.W.S. Regt.
  Res., W. Croydon. *Fell*, '17.
FARNCOMBE, JOSEPH C., Pte., 8 Leicester Regt.
  b., Croydon ; s., Mr. & Mrs. C. J. Farncombe, Southbridge Rd., Croydon. *Educ.*, M. Whitgift Sch. Married ; 3 sons. Empl. in his father's business as printer & publisher. *Enl.*, Jun., '16. *D.*, while pris. of war in Germany, 14 Aug., '18.
FAUCHERRE, FREDERICK T., Pte., L.R.B. (5 Lond. Regt.)
  Educ., Gordon Boys' Home, 24 Morland Rd., Croydon. *D.*, Le Tréport, 1 Apr., '16.
FEAST, F. W., 45017, L/Cpl., Lond. Regt.
  Res., T. Heath. *Fell*, '17.
FELTS, H., 22512, Pte., E. Kent Regt.
  Res., Croydon. *Fell*, '17.
FENN, R. P., Q.M.S., Sur. Yeom.
  Educ., Whitgift G. Sch. *Missing*, '18.
FENTON, ALFRED EDWARD, Pte., E. Kent Regt.
  b., S. Bermondsey, 5 Mar., '82 ; s., late J. & Annie Fenton, Melbourne, Australia. *Educ.*, Gallywell Rd. Sch., S. Bermondsey. Married. House decorator. *Res.*, 56 Oakley Rd., S. Norwood. *Enl.*, 7 Sept., '14. *D.*, Oct., '15, while pris. of war in Germany, of wounds recd. at Loos, 25 Sept., '15.
FENTON, FRANK MERRIFIELD, L/Cpl., Lond. Scottish (14 Lond. Regt.)
  b., Rotherhithe, 14 Oct., '94 ; s., Mr. & Mrs. Fenton, 76 Parchmore Rd., T. Heath. *Educ.*, Whitehorse Rd. Sch., T. Heath, and Stanley Tech. Sch., S. Norwood. Single. Cinematograph film printer. *Enl.*, 29 Nov., '15. *Fell*, Wancourt, nr. Arras, 2 Jul., '17.
FENTON, R. G., 11221, Pte., R.W.S. Regt.
  Res., Norwood. *Fell*, '17.
FERGUSON, THOMAS RICHARD AUGUSTUS, L/Cpl., 24 Lond. Regt.
  b., Croydon, 19 Oct., '97 ; s., Richard & Bertha Augusta Ferguson, 27 Waddon Pk. Av., Croydon. *Educ.*, Old Palace Sch., Croydon, M. Whitgift Sch. & Christ's Hosp. Single. Clerk. *Enl.*, 7 Sept., '14. *Fell*, Givenchy, nr. La Bassée, 25 May, '15.

THE CROYDON ROLL OF HONOUR

FEWTRELL, FRANK E., Rflmn., 2 R. Irish Rif.
    b., 21 Sept., '81. *Educ.*, Alton, Hants. Married. Salesman (Wholesale millinery). *Res.*, 15 Blackhorse Lane, Addis. *Enl.*, 8 Mar., '17. *Missing*, presumed *fallen*, nr. St. Quentin, 24 Mar., '18.

FIELD, H., Pte., R. Fus.
    b., '95. Empl. at Cement Works, Beddington. *Res.*, 112 Wentworth Rd., Croydon. *Enl.*, 26 Oct., '15. *Fell*, '17.

FIELD, HASSELL D., Capt., R.A.M.C.
    y.s., Mr. & Mrs. Walter Field, "Thirlmere," Norbury. *Educ.*, Uppingham. Married Olive, daughter of Mrs. Locke, Weston-super-Mare; 1 son. Resident house-surgeon, Royal Victoria Hosp., Bournemouth; M.R.C.S., '14; L.R.C.P., '14.; commis., Apr., '15. *D.*, of wounds, 28 Sept., '17.

FIELD, LESLIE GEORGE, Pte., Q.V. Rif. (9 Lond. Regt.)
    b., Fernhead Rd., Maida Vale, 14 May, '89; *s.*, Mr. & Mrs. Chesher Field, 20 St. James' Pk., Croydon. *Educ.*, St. Saviour's Sch., Croydon. Single. Clerk. *Enl.*, 17 Nov., '15. *D.*, 8 Sept., '18, at 48 C.C.S., France, of wounds recd. prev. day. (Plate X., 2).

FILLINGHAM, REGINALD JOHN, Maj., R.G.A.
    b., Aldershot, 14 Jul., '90; *s.*, Mr. & Mrs. Fillingham, 7 Albert Rd., Hibernia Rd., Hounslow. *Educ.*, St. Mary's Sch., Croydon. Married Alice Maud, *y.* daughter of Mr. & Mrs. Wiebkin, 5 Eldon Pk., S. Norwood, 13 Mar., '15. *Res.*, The Barracks, Mitcham Rd., Croydon, & 77 Greenside Rd., Croydon. *Enl.*, in R.W.S. Regt., 14 Jul., '04; transf. to R.G.A., 2 Sept., '08; commis., 6 Mar., '15; M.C., for conspicuous gallantry & good work, 4 Jul., '16, & bar to M.C., 16 Sept., '16. *D.*, 29 Sept., '18, of wounds recd. nr. Peronne, 2 days prev. (Plate XII., 2).

FINDLAY, CYRIL OLNEY, 2/Lt., 4/8 Somerset L.I.
    b., Reading, 4 Oct., '93; *s.*, Rev. W. Alexander & Lillian S. Findlay, "The Manse," Wallingford, Berks. *Educ.*, Croydon & Taunton. Single. Medical student. When medically unfit served for nearly a year at the Red Cross Hosp., "Star & Garter," Richmond. *Entered*, Inns of Court O.T.C., 17 Oct., '16; commis., 26 Apr., '17; bombing officer, 63 Bde., 37 Div. *D.*, 17 Oct., '17, in Australian Hosp., nr. Bailleul, of wounds recd. Passchendaele Ridge, 14 Oct., '17. (Plate X., 4).

FINN, DANIEL, 22576, Pte., 6 Border Regt.
    b., N. Shields, '80; *s.*, late Mr., & Mrs. Finn, 35 Boston Rd., Croydon. *Educ.*, St. Mary's Sch., Croydon. Single. Labourer empl. by Croydon Gas Coy. *Enl.*, Feb., '15. *Fell*, France, 23 Jul., '17.

FINN, JOHN, 238848, Gnr., R.F.A.
    b., Croydon, '96; *s.*, late Mr., & Mrs. Finn, 35 Boston Rd., Croydon. *Educ.*, St. Mary's Sch., Croydon. Single. Labourer empl. by Croydon Gas Coy. *Enl.*, May, '17. *Fell*, Passchendaele, 3 Dec., '17.

FINN, JOHN WALLACE, L/Cpl., 6 E. Kent Regt.
    b., Bexley Heath, Kent; *s.*, Herbert Arthur & Flora Adelaide Finn, 20 Amhurst Rd., Hackney. *Educ.*, M. Whitgift Sch., Croydon. Single. Empl. in wholesale provision trade. *Res.*, 34 Clyde Rd., Addis. *Enl.*, 7 Sept., '14. *Fell*, Mametz, 3 Jul., '16.

FINN, W. J., 68808, R.F.A.
    Res., Croydon.

FINN, WILLIAM, 54516, Sapper, R.E.
  b., Croydon, '89 ; *s.*, late Mr., & Mrs. Finn, 35 Boston Rd., Croydon. *Educ.*, St. Mary's Sch., Croydon. Single. Labourer empl. at Cement Factory, Mitcham Rd., Croydon. *Enl.*, Oct., '14. *Drowned* at Dunkirk, France, 19 May, '18.
FIRTH, F. W., 3192, Lond. Regt.
  Fell, '16.
FISHER, FRANCIS J., Gnr., R.F.A.
  b., '96 ; *s.*, Mr. & Mrs. Garnham Fisher, 11 Burdett Rd., Croydon. *Enl.*, Apr., '15. *Fell*, 19 Sept., '17.
FISHER, FRANK, Maj., 470 Coy., R E.
  b., Brighton, 18 Jul., '75. *Educ.*, Brighton G. Sch. & R. Coll. of Science, Lond. Married. Civil servant. *Res.*, Oxted, Surrey. *Joined*, as 2/Lt., Jan., '15. *Fell*, nr. Ypres, 26 Sept., '17.
FISK, ALFRED, Sapper, R.E.
  b., '78. Married ; children. Decorator. *Res.*, Thirsk Rd., S. Norwood. *D.*, after operation, Jul., '18.
FITSALL, J., Pte., R.W.S. Regt.
  b., '99 ; *s.*, late Mr. & Mrs. Fitsall, 85 Sutherland Rd., Croydon. *Educ.*, Boston Rd. Sch., Croydon. Empl. by Messrs. Holloway & Smyth, Church St., Croydon. *Enl.*, '15. *Fell*, Mar. or Apr., '18.
FITZGERALD, ALFRED.
  b., '79 ; *s.*, Mr & Mrs. Fitzgerald, Old Town, Croydon. *Fell*, 29 Sept., '18.
FITZGERALD, LAWRENCE GEORGE, L/Cpl., R.W.S. Regt.
  b., Peckham, 9 Nov., '96 ; *s.*, George & Alice Fitzgerald, 53, Dundee Rd., S. Norwood. *Educ.*, Lyndhurst Grove Sch., Peckham, Grove Vale Sch., Dulwich, & Portland Rd. Sch., S. Norwood. Single. Shipping clerk. *Enl.*, 9 Nov., '14. Twice wounded & once gassed. *Fell*, Monchy, 1 Aug., '17.
FLACK, WILFRED G., Capt., Coldstream Gds.
  Empl. as policeman at E. Croydon Stn., '12-13, & later as waiter at Union Jack Club. *Called up* on reserve as pte., Aug., '14 ; promoted sgt. & later given commis. on field ; *w.*, 4 times. M.C. and bar. *D.*, of wounds.
FLAY, A. C., 13984, L/Cpl., R. Fus.
  Res., S. Norwood. *Fell*, '16.
FLECKER, H., Pte., R. Fus.
  Educ., High Sch., Croydon. *D.*, of pneumonia, '15.
FLETCHER, F. W., 57327, R. Fus.
  Res., T. Heath. *Fell*, '17.
FLOWER, ALBERT CHARLES, Pte., 5 Seaforth H.
  b., 11 Oct., '96 ; *s.*, Mr. & Mrs. Albert E. Flower, 12 Clyde Rd., Addis. *Educ.*, Whitgift G. Sch., '08. *Fell*, France, 11 Mar., '16.
FLUCK, A. S., 110793, Gnr., R.F.A.
  Res., T. Heath. *Fell*, '16.
FOGDEN, GEOFFREY, L. A., Gnr., H.A.C.
FOLEY, JOHN PATRICK, Pte., E. Sur. Regt.
  b., Croydon, 14 Oct., '97. *Educ.*, Brighton Rd. Sch. & Bynes Rd. Sch., Croydon. Single. Porter, empl. by Messrs. Sainsbury. *Res.*, 2 Napier Rd., Croydon. *Enl.*, 25 Oct., '15. *Fell*, 15 Apr.,'16.
FOOTNER, ARTHUR HENRY, 2/Lt., 1 Essex Regt.
  b., 14 Oct., '87 ; *s.*, Mr. & Mrs. Henry Footner, 35 Croham Rd., Croydon. *Educ.*, Whitgift G. Sch., '01-05. *Res.*, Ceylon. Served with Ceylon Overseas Contingent ; attd. to Staff, N.Z. Contingent : took part in landing at Gaba Tepe. *Fell*, Dardanelles, 6 Aug., '15.

THE CROYDON ROLL OF HONOUR

FORD, C., Cpl., Lond. Irish Rif. (1/18 Lond. Regt.)
 Educ., British Sch., Croydon. Member of Croydon Wanderers Football Club. *Fell*, nr. Loos, 25 Sept., '15.

FORD, F. H., Pte., R.W.S. Regt.
 Married ; 1 child. Empl. as driver by Amer. Steam Laundry. *Res.*, 16 Addison Rd., S. Norwood. *D.*, of malarial fever, India,'17.

FORD, GEORGE HENRY, Barrack Warden, R.A.S.C.
 b., '69. Married. Formerly empl. as railway signalman. *Res.*, Lower Coombe St., Croydon. *D.*, of chronic heart disease while home on leave, Apr., '17.

FORD, R. E., Rflmn.
 Res., Colwyn Rd., T. Heath. Member of Croydon Wanderers Football Club. *Fell*, 2 Sept., '16.

FOREMAN, ALFRED, 9497, Drummer, R.Scots. Fus.
 s., Mr. & Mrs. Foreman, Brisbane. *Res.*, 73 Cecil Rd., T. Heath. *Fell*, 28 Jul., '17.

FORREST, J. R., 15020, Gordon H.
 Res., Woodside. *Fell*, '17.

FORRESTER, FRANK OLIVER, Lt., R.N.V.R.
 b., '92 ; 6*th s.*, Mr. & Mrs. John Forrester, 16 Addis. Rd., Croydon. *Educ.*, High Sch., Croydon. *Res.*, "Brenchley," Fairfield Rd., Croydon. M.C. *Fell*, 25 Mar., '18.

FORSDICK, HORACE REGINALD, Sgt., R.A.F.
 b., Dover, 19 Sept., '99 ; *s.*, Mr. & Mrs. Charles Forsdick, 27 Bensham Manor Rd., T. Heath. *Educ.*, Boro. Sec. Sch., Croydon. Single. Shipping clerk. *Enl.*, in Cadet C. of R.F.C., 19 Sept., '17 ; held 1st class flying certif. *Killed*, while flying at Wye, Kent, 6 May, '18.

FORSTER, WILLIAM EDWARD BLAKE, 2/Lt., R.F.A.
 b., 20 Mar., '82 ; *s.*, Mr. & Mrs. William George Forster, South Parade, Southend. *Educ.*, Whitgift G. Sch., '99-00. *Accidentally killed.*

FORSYTH, WILLIAM IRVING, Can. Mounted Rif.
 Res., formerly at T. Heath. *Fell*, 27 Aug., '18.

FOSBURY, W. A., 7484, Cpl., R. Fus.
 Res., W. Croydon. *Fell*, '16.

FOSTER, GEOFFREY CHARLES, Pte., M.G.C. (Cavalry).
 Enl., in Essex Yeom., Sept., '14. *Fell*, Monchy, 11 Apr., '17.

FOSTER, GEORGE, Bdr., R.F.A.
 b., '94 ; 2nd *s.*, Mr. & Mrs. Foster, 65 Addison Rd., S. Norwood. Single. *D.*, of pneumonia, 15 Feb., '17.

FOSTER, GORDON, Welsh Regt.
 b., '89 ; *y.s.*, Mr. & Mrs. Foster, "The Uplands," Whitehorse Lane, S. Norwood. *Fell*, 31 Jul., '17.

FOSTER, GRAHAM EDWIN, 301666, Sgt., L.R.B. (2/5 Lond. Regt.)
 b., 426 Whitehorse Rd., T. Heath, 3 Oct., '94 ; *s.*, Edwin & Eliza Foster, 13 Quadrant Rd., T. Heath. *Educ.*, Whitehorse Rd. Sch., T. Heath. Single. Bank clerk. *Enl.*, Jul., '15 ; M.M., for gallantry at Bullecourt, 20 May, '17, bestowed at Town Hall, Croydon, 13 May, '18. *Fell*, N.E. of St. Julien, Ypres, 20 Sept.,'17. (Plate XIII., 5).

FOWLER, EDWARD ALBERT, Pte., E. Lancs. Regt.
 b., Epsom, '89. Married ; 1 child. Compositor. *Res.*, 36 Sheldon St., Croydon. *Enl.*, in E. Kent Regt. *Fell*, 4 Oct., '17.

FOWLER, WILLIAM, Pte., R.W.S. Regt.
 b., '95 ; *s.*, Mr. & Mrs. Fowler, 18 Crescent Mews, Lancaster Rd., S. Norwood. *Fell*, Somme, 1 Jul., '16.

IX.

1. 2/Lt. H. A. C. DODDS, 3/5 York & Lancs. Regt.
2. Pte. H. A. BRIDGES, 2/4 R.W.S. Regt.
3. Sgt. W. D. EDWARDS, M.M., 12 R.B
4. Pte. H. L. DUPLOCK, Duke of Cornwall's L.I.
5. Warrant Officer A. J. CHERRY, R.N.
6. L/Cpl. W. T. DODDRELL, 1 City of Lond. Rif.

X.

1. 2/Lt. B. HAIZELDEN, 2/10 Lond. Reg^t.
2. Pte. L. G. FIELD, Q.Vict. Rif.
3. Cpl. J. JOHNSON, Aust. Field Engineers
4. 2/Lt. C. O. FINDLAY, 4/8 Somerset L.I.
5. Sgt. H. G. DUNHAM, 7 E. Sur. Regt.
6. Trooper J. H. S. DICKER, 21 Lancers

THE GLORIOUS DEAD

Fox, A., 97229, Gnr., R.G.A.
  Res., S. Croydon. *Fell*, '17.
Fox, C., 16003, Pte., Norf. Regt.
  Res., T. Heath. *Fell*, '17.
Fox, RICHARD PAGET, Pte., R.A.M.C.
  b., '87 ; *s.*, Mr. & Mrs. A. S. Fox, " The Limes," Francis Rd., Croydon. *D.*, 12 Jun., '15, at E. Suff. Hosp., Ipswich, of wounds recd. in France, 16 May, '15.
FRANCIS, ALAN BULLER, 2/Lt., D.C.L.I.
  b., Harlesden, 28 Feb., '96 ; 2nd *s.*, Mr. & Mrs. E. W. Francis, 31 Broughton Rd., T. Heath. *Educ.*, M. Whitgift Sch. Single. Insurance official. *Enl.* in A.P.C., Sept., '14 ; commis., Mar., '15. *Fell*, Montauban, 24 Aug., '16.
FRANCIS, EDWARD DAVID, Cpl., E. Sur. Regt.
  b., Brighton, 23 Dec., '75. Married. Gardener, empl. by Miss Watney, Haling Pk., Croydon. *Res.*, 148 Selsdon Rd., Croydon. Served in S.A. War. *Re-enlisted*, 28 Sept., '14. *Fell*, Hill 60, Ypres, 20 Apr., '15.
FRANCIS, LEONARD, 6 Lond. Regt.
  b., Kenley, 16 Sept., '98 ; *s.*, Henry James & Clara Francis, Whyteleafe. *Educ.*, Whyteleafe. Single. Motor mechanic. *Enl.*, 15 Jul., '15. *Fell*, France, 16 Apr., '16.
FRANCIS, SYDNEY HERBERT, Driver, R.A.S.C.
  b., Croydon, 9 Jan., '93 ; *s.*, F. W. & A. J. Francis, 32 Laud St., Croydon. *Educ.*, St. Andrew's Sch., Croydon. Single. Milk carrier. *Enl.*, 20 Feb., '15. *D.* of heat apoplexy, St. Andrew's Hosp., Malta, 11 Aug., '15.
FRANKLIN, FREDERICK CHARLES, Pte., 3/4 R.W.S. Regt.
  b., Watford, 10 Jun., '80 ; *s.*, Mr. & Mrs. Franklin, St. Alban's Rd., Watford. *Educ.*, Watford Nat. Sch. Married ; 4 children. Commercial traveller. *Res.*, 30 Hunter Rd., T. Heath. Member of Spec. Constab., May, '15-Feb., '17. *Enl.*, 1 Mar., '17. *Fell*, Arras, 24 Jun., '17.
FRANKLIN, FREDERICK CHARLES, 2/9 Middlesex Regt.
  b., '93 ; *y.s.*, Mr. & Mrs. F. C. Franklin, 161 Melfort Rd., T. Heath. *D.*, 18 Aug., '15, of wounds recd. at Dardanelles, 10 Aug., '15.
FRANKLIN, HENRY H., L/Cpl., R.W.S. Regt.
  b., '95 ; 2nd *s.*, Mr. & Mrs. Franklin, formerly of Belmont Rd., S. Norwood. *Fell*, 1 Jul., '16.
FRANKLIN, WILLIAM HYSLOP, Capt., K.O.S.B.
  b., '88 : *s.*, Mr. & Mrs. James Franklin, " Craigmillar," Norman-ton Rd., Croydon. *Educ.*, Bradfield Coll. *Fell*, France, '15.
FREEMAN, J. W., R.E. Signal Serv.
  Educ., Whitgift G. Sch. *Enl.*, Oct., '14. *Fell*, nr. Ypres, '17.
FREEMAN, WILLIAM THOMAS, Pte., Can. Inf.
  b., Feb., '88 ; 3rd *s.*, Mr. & Mrs. Frederick Thomas Freeman, 116 Melfort Rd., T. Heath. *Educ.*, M. Whitgift Sch., Croydon. Single. Farmer. *Enl.*, Nov., '14. *D.* of wounds, France, 10 Apr., '17.
FREIGHT, STANLEY, Pte., 4 R.W.S. Regt.
  b., '85 ; *s.*, Mr. & Mrs. Freight, " Holly Lodge," Windmill Rd., Croydon. *D.* of enteric fever at Lucknow, '15.
FRENCH, ALBERT, Pte., 19 Can. Inf.
  b., 11 Bourne St., Croydon, 20 Jan., '90 ; *s.*, Mr. & Mrs. French, 11 Bourne St., Croydon. *Educ.*, Mitcham Rd. Sch., Croydon. Single. *Res.*, Canada, '07-14. *Enl.*, 9 Oct., '14. *Fell*, St. Eloi, 10 Apr., '16.

FRENCH, CHARLES ERNEST, L/Cpl., 7 R.W.S. Regt.
b., 11 Bourne St., Croydon, 28 Dec., '96 ; *s.*, Elijah & Mary Ann French, 11 Bourne St., Croydon. *Educ.*, Mitcham Rd. Sch., Croydon. Single. Bricklayer. *Enl.*, 5 Sept., '14. *Fell*, Irles, Arras, 24-27 Feb., '17.

FRENCH, FRANK GEOFFREY, Pte., 3 R. Fus.
b., 11 Bourne St., Croydon, 20 Feb., '98 ; *s.*, Elijah & Mary Ann French, 11 Bourne St., Croydon. *Educ.*, Mitcham Rd. Sch., Croydon. Single. Shop asst. *Enl.*, 31 Aug., '16. *Fell*, France, 4 Oct., '18.

FRENCH, STEPHEN THOMAS, Pte., Can. Inf.
b., 11 Bourne St., Croydon ; *s.*, Elijah & Mary Ann French, 11 Bourne St., Croydon. *Educ.*, Mitcham Rd. Sch., Croydon. Married. Glazier & painter. *Res.*, Hamilton, Ontario. *Enl.*, May, '16. *D.*, 13 Apr., '17, of wounds recd. at Vimy Ridge, 10 Apr., '17.

FRENCH, EDWARD JAMES, Rflmn., L.R.B. (2/5 Lond. Regt.)
b., Alderney, Channel Islands, 7 Jan., '92 ; *s.*, Elijah & Mary Ann French, 32 Greenwood Rd., Croydon. *Educ.*, M. Whitgift Sch. Single. Civil servant. *Res.*, 72 St. Saviour's Rd., Croydon. *Enl.*, Dec., '15. *Fell*, Flanders, 20 Sept., '17.

FRENCH, W., 10455, L/Cpl., E. Sur. Regt.
Res., S. Norwood. *Fell*, '17.

FRENCH, W. J. H., Sgt., R.W.S. Regt.
b., '89. *Res.*, 22 Crunden Rd., Croydon. *Enl.*, 18 Aug., '14 ; trench fever, Apr., '17. *Fell*, 20-22 Sept., '17.

FRIEND, CHARLES DAVID, Pte., R.W.S. Regt.
b., S. Croydon, 28 Mar., '95. *Educ.*, Bynes Rd. Sch., Croydon. Married. Labourer. *Res.*, 21 Strathmore Rd., Croydon. *Enl.*, 4 Aug., '14. *D.* of wounds at 3 Can. C.C.S., Belgium, 4 Jan., '17. *Buried*, Poperinghe.

FRISCH, CHARLES, 2/Lt., 9 Ghurkas (Indian Army).
b., Croydon, 28 Mar., '87 ; *s.*, Mr. & Mrs. George Joseph Frisch, Littlehampton. *Educ.*, Whitgift G. Sch., '97-01. Tea planter. *Res.*, Darjeeling, India. Served in Indian Army Res. prev. to war. *Believed killed*, before Kut, '16.

FRISCH, GEOFFREY, L/Cpl., 3 R. Suss. Regt.
b., Croydon, 5 Nov., '89 ; *s.*, Mr. & Mrs. George Joseph Frisch, Littlehampton. *Educ.*, Whitgift G. Sch., '99-01. *Missing*, 15 Jan., '15.

FRISCH, MAURICE, 2/Lt., 2 R.B.
b., Croydon, 21 Dec., '93 ; *s.*, Mr. & Mrs. George Joseph Frisch, Littlehampton. *Educ.*, Littlehampton, & Brighton Coll. *Missing*, 25 Oct., '16.

FRITH, F. W., 3192, Lond. Regt.
Fell, '16.

FRITH, WILLIAM, L/Cpl., K.O.R.L. Regt.
b., '95 ; *y.s.*, Mr. & Mrs. Frith, 6 Union St., Croydon. Greengrocer. *Res.*, Croydon. *Enl.*, Feb., '16. *D.* of wounds, 22 Jun., '18.

FROHOCK, W. E., Pte., R.W.S. Regt.
b., '98 ; *s.*, Ernest & Alice Frohock, 6 Crouch Villas, Cedar Rd., Croydon. *Enl.*, Sept., '14 ; gassed ; trench fever, Oct., '17. *Fell*, France, 23 Aug., '18.

FROST, ARTHUR BYFIELD, Lt., R.W.S. Regt.
y.s., Mr. & Mrs. William Frost, " Sywell House," Warlingham *Educ.*, St. Winifred's, Kenley, & Whitgift G. Schs., where he was Capt. of Sch, '14-15, and Cadet Officer. *Commis.*, 23 Jun., '15 ; M.C., Oct., '17. *Fell*, France, 23 Mar., '18.

THE GLORIOUS DEAD

FRY, F. C., R.W.S. Regt.
    b., '92. Empl. at rubber works. *Res.*, 7 Elliott House, Elliott Rd., T. Heath. *Enl.*, 11 Aug., '14. *D.* of wounds, 3 Jul., '16.

FRYER, SYDNEY, R. Suss. Regt.
    b., '84; *s.*, Mr. & Mrs. Fryer, Graffham, Sussex; formerly of Heath Rd., T. Heath. *Educ.*, Beulah Rd. Sch., T. Heath. *Enl.*, Sept., '14. *Fell*, 15 Aug., '16.

FULCHER, WILLIAM E., 57920, Pte., 17 King's L'pool. Regt.
    Clerk, Croydon Gas Co. *Enl.*, in R.F.C., '15. *D.*, 3 Aug., '17, of wounds recd. 31 Jul., '17. *Buried*, nr. Zillebeke, Ypres.

FULLALOVE, G. Y., 2/Lt., R.F.C.
    Fell, 13 Aug., '17.

FULLER, A., 1628, Cpl., R.W.S. Regt.
    Taken pris. Believed dead.

FULLER, COLIN MELVILLE, 4 Seaforth H.
    b., 10 Epsom Rd., Croydon, 13 Sept., '94: *s.*, Mr. & Mrs. R. H. Fuller, "Saxon Villa," 10 Epsom Rd., Croydon. *Educ.*, Boro. Sec. Sch., Croydon. Single. Empl. in motor car trade. *Enl.*, Sept., '14. *Fell*, Neuve Chapelle, 11 Mar., '15.

FULLER, E. P., 2/Lt., 10 R.W.S. Regt.
    b., Croydon, '92. *Educ.*, Whitgift G. Sch. *Enl.* as pte. in Artists Rif., '15; commis. in R.W.S. Regt., '16. *Missing*, Menin Rd., 20 Sept., '17.

FULLER, LEONARD A., Lt., R.F.C.
    b., 3 Jan., '92; *y.s.*, Mr. & Mrs. Edward Fuller, "Walton House," Chepstow Rise, Croydon. *Educ.*, Whitgift G. Sch., '04-10, Imp. Coll. of Science, & Royal Sch. of Mines. *Joined* Lond. Univ. O.T.C., '14; commis. in 17 D.L.I.; transf. to R.F.C. *Fell*, 17 May, '17.

FULLER, MORRIS R., 2/Lt., 10 R. Fus.
    b., 29 Jan., '97; *y.s.*, Mr. & Mrs. Ernest Fuller, "Lydford," Croham Rd., Croydon. *Educ.*, Whitgift G. Sch., '10-13. Single. *Enl.*, in a Publ. Sch. Btn., Oct., '14; commis., '16. *Fell*, Arras, 11 Apr., '17.

FULLER, WALTER, Lt. & Quartermaster, Somerset L.I.
    b., Greenham, Berkshire, 24 Dec., '73. *Educ.*, Sonning, nr. Reading. Married. *Res.*, Woodley. *Enl.*, 17 Oct., '89; S.A. Med.; King George V. Coronation Med.; from '08, R.Sgt.Maj., 4 R.W.S. Regt., going to India in '14; *commis.*, and transf. to Som. L.I., '18; served in Mesopotamia. *D.*, Malta, 3 Jan., '20, of injuries recd. in action, and of malarial fever.

FUNNELL, W. H., Sgt., R.F.A.
    Res., T. Heath. *Fell*, '17.

FURNELL, W., Pte., 6 R.W.S. Regt.
    Fell, France, 12 Nov., '15.

FYFE, JOHN CHARLES, Civ. Serv. Rif. (1/15 Lond. Regt.).
    b., 7 Dec., '98; *s.*, Mr. & Mrs. Fyfe, 28 Albert Rd., Croydon. *Educ.*, Woodside & Boro. Sec. Schs., Croydon. Single. Clerk (Inland Revenue). *Enl.*, 16 Feb., '17. *Fell*, France, 23 Mar., '18.

GADD, FREDERICK GEORGE, Rflmn., R.B.
    b., Paxton Yard, W. Norwood; *s.*, Mr. & Mrs. Gadd, 17 Upton Rd., T. Heath. *Educ.*, Ingram Rd. Sch., T. Heath. Single. Golf caddie. *Res.*, 105 Northwood Rd., T. Heath. *Enl.*, 12 Feb., '12. *Fell*, France, 9 May, '15.

GAGE, GEORGE JOWAKI INKERMAN, J20419, A.B. Seaman, R.N.
    b., King's Rd., S. Norwood, '96; *s.*, Wm. & Elizabeth Gage, 25 Harrington Rd., S. Norwood. *Educ.*, Birchanger Rd. Sch., S. Norwood. Single. Butcher's asst. *Res.*, 50 Westgate Rd., S. Norwood. *Joined* training ship, "Impregnable," Sept., '12. *Lost*, with "Queen Mary," sunk during battle of Jutland, 31 May, '16.

GAMBLING, W., Sgt., K.R.R.C.
 s., Mr. & late Mrs. Gambling, 9 Cuthbert Rd., Croydon. Empl.
 at Beddington Cement Works. *Enl.*, Jan., '15. M.M. *Fell*, 16
 Oct., '17.
GAMMON, F., 34256, Gnr., R.G.A.
 Res., S. Norwood. *Fell*, '17.
GAMMON, THOMAS, Pte., 7 Border Regt.
 b., Penge. *Educ.*, Melvin Rd. Sch., Penge. Married. Plate-
 layer. *Res.*, 41 Russell Rd., Croydon. *Enl.*, 1 Jun., '15. *Fell*,
 Loos, 23 Apr., '17.
GANDEY, WILLIAM ALFRED, 31626, Pte., E. Sur. Regt.
 b., 21 Bute St., Brighton, 15 Mar., '82. *Educ.*, Queen's Pk. Sch.,
 Brighton. Married. Motor upholsterer. *Res.*, 204 Albert Rd.,
 Croydon, & later, 4 Freemason's Rd., Croydon. *Enl.*, 27 Feb., '17.
 Fell, nr. Vimy Ridge, 18 Jul., '17.
GARDINER, JOSHUA (JOHN), L/Cpl., E. Sur. Regt.
 Tobacconist. *Res.*, T. Heath. *Enl.*, '16. *D.* of wounds, 6 Nov., '17.
GARDNER, FRANK ROBERT, Pte., Duchess of Connaught's Own I.C.
 Rangers (?).
 b., Willesden Lane, Kilburn ; *s.*, Mr. & Mrs. Gardner, 137a
 Ecclesbourne Rd., T. Heath. *Educ.*, Ecclesbourne Rd. Sch.,
 T. Heath. Single. Ship's steward. *Enl.*, 13 May, '15.
 D., 7 Nov., '17, of wounds recd. at Cambrai.
GARDNER, STANLEY DOUGLAS, Lt.-Col.
 2nd *s.*, Mr. & Mrs. Gardner, " Homewood," Croydon. *Fell*,
 France, 29 Sept., '18.
GARDNER, SYDNEY, Driver, R.F.
 b., '82. Married : 1 child. *Res.*, 156 Albert Rd., S. Norwood.
 Fell, France, 9 Jun., '18.
GARNELL, J., 1063, L/Cpl., R.W.S. Regt.
 Res., W. Croydon. *Fell*, '16.
GARNETT, GEORGE HERBERT, Pte., 13 Lond. Regt.
 b., London, 4 Apr., '87. *Educ.*, John Ruskin's Sch., Croydon.
 Married. *Res.*, 1a Clifton Rd., S. Norwood. *Enl.*, 29 May, '16.
 Fell, France, 9 Oct., '16.
GARRARD, FREDERIC GEORGE, 2/Lt., Gordon H.
 b., '98 ; *e.s.*, Mr. & Mrs. F. W. Garrard, " Brambledene," Downs
 Rd., Purley. *Educ.*, Whitgift G. Sch, where he was Sgt. in O.T.C.
 Joined Inns of Court, O.T.C. ; commis., '16. *D.*, 22 May, '18,
 of wounds recd. 16 May, '18.
GARRARD, FREDERICK GABRIEL, Pte., R.W.S. Regt.
 b., '98 ; *s.*, late Mr. & Mrs. Garrard, 72 Bynes Rd., Croydon.
 Educ., Bynes Rd. Sch., Croydon. Empl. by Messrs. Frost,
 dairymen. *Enl.*, '16 ; *w.*, Messines, Jun., '17. *Fell*, 24 Mar., '18.
GARRATT, J., Lt., R.F.C.
 Educ., High Sch., Croydon. Missing, '17.
GATHERCOLE, HENRY JAMES, Pte., 2/4 R.W.S. Regt.
 b., 7 Longley Rd., Croydon, 24 Sept., '96 ; *s.*, Mr. & Mrs. Gather-
 cole, 12 Kemble Rd., Croydon. *Educ.*, Par. Ch. Sch. & Welcome
 Hall, Croydon. Single. Sanitary asst., Town Hall, Croydon.
 Enl., 19 Apr., '15 ; served in Suvla Bay, Egypt, Palestine, France.
 Fell, France, 29 Jul., '19.
GATLAND, ERNEST GEORGE, Pte., 2/4 R.W.S. Regt.
 b., Croydon, 24 Sept., '95 : *s.*, Frederick & Alice Gatland, 7 Rol-
 leston Rd., Croydon. *Educ.*, Bynes Rd. Sch., Croydon. Single.
 Gardener. *Enl.*, 20 Oct., '14 ; *w.*, Dardanelles, Aug., '15, and
 Egypt, '17. *Fell*, Palestine, 3 Nov., '17. (Plate XV., 3).

THE GLORIOUS DEAD

GATLAND, G., 9167, Coy.Sgt.Maj., Scot. Rif.
  Res., S. Croydon. *Fell*, '17.
GATLAND, WILLIAM, Trooper, R. Horse Gds.
  b., Queenstown, Ireland, 6 Aug., '86. Married. *Res.*, E. Croydon. *Enl.*, '04. *D.*, 8 Jun., '15, at 7 Cairo Rd., Croydon, of wounds recd., France, Apr., '15.
GEERTS, FERDINAND LOUIS, Pte., 12 Suff. Regt.
  b., Croydon, '93 ; *s.*, Louis A. & E. A. Geerts, 65 Albert Rd., Addis. *Educ.*, Oval Rd. Sch., Croydon, & Boro. Sec. Sch., Croydon. Single. Clerk. *Enl.*, 24 Feb., '17. *Fell*, France, 24 Nov., '17. (Plate XI., 3).
GEORGE, DAVID VICTOR, Pte., R.W.S. Regt.
  b., '95 ; *s.*, Mr. & Mrs. George, 280 Bensham Lane, T. Heath. *Enl.*, 3 Sept., '14 ; *w.*, Jul., '16 ; M.M., Feb., '17. *Fell*, 7 Jun., '17.
GEORGE, WALTER REGINALD, L/Cpl., 1 Artists Rif. (28 Lond. Regt.)
  b., Dunmon, Essex, 12 Sept., '98 ; *s.*, Mr. & Mrs. L. George, 81 Tamworth Rd., Croydon. *Educ.*, Brit. Sch., Croydon. Single. Clerk. *Res.*, Ilford. *Enl.*, Feb., '17. *D.*, from the effects of gas and shell shock, at Amer. Hosp., Rouen, 29 Mar., '18. (Plate XV., 4).
GIBBONS, W., L/Cpl., Middlesex Regt.
  Res., W. Croydon. *Fell*, '16.
GIBBS, ALBERT, Pte., 1 R.W.S. Regt.
  b., Croydon, 15 Jun., '86 ; *s.*, Charles Henry & Emma Gibbs, 6 Sumner Rd., Croydon. *Educ.*, Mitcham Rd. Sch., Croydon. Single. Carman. *Enl.*, Aug., '14. *Fell*, France, 18 Dec., '14. (Plate XV., 6).
GIBBS, CHARLES T., Pte., 2 R. Suss. Regt.
  b., '90 ; *s.*, Mr. & Mrs. Gibbs, 113 Lakehall Rd., T. Heath. *Fell*, 25 Sept., '15.
GIBBS, G. A., R. Fus.
  Res., W. Croydon. *Fell*, '17.
GIBBS, GEORGE ALBERT, Pte., R.W.S. Regt.
  b., Croydon, 13 Nov., '79 ; *s.*, Peter & Esther Gibbs, 110 Sutherland Rd., Croydon. *Educ.*, Beulah Rd. Sch., T. Heath. Married. Labourer. *Res.*, Spa Rd., T. Heath. *Enl.*, 19 Aug., '14. *Fell*, Givenchy, 2 Jan., '16.
GIBBS, SIDNEY JAMES, Pte., 6 R.W.S. Regt.
  b., Croydon, 8 Sept., '84 ; *s.*, Peter & Esther Gibbs, 110 Sutherland Rd., Croydon. *Educ.*, Boston Rd. Sch., Croydon. Single. Labourer. *Res.*, 99 Boston Rd., Croydon. *Enl.*, 12 Aug., '14 ; *w.*, France, 31 Dec., '15. *Fell*, Somme, 3 Jul., '16.
GIBBS, WILLIAM JAMES, L/Cpl., R.W.S. Regt.
  b., '98. *Res.*, 190 Livingstone Rd., T. Heath. *Fell*, 25 Sept., '17.
GIBSON, ALAN, Pte., 1 L.R.B. (5 Lond. Regt.)
  b., Croydon, 15 Dec., '98 ; *s.*, Mr. & Mrs. T. H. Gibson, 14 Dingwall Rd., Croydon. *Educ.*, High Sch., Croydon. Single. Bank clerk. *Res.*, 25 Broughton Rd., T. Heath. *Enl.*, Sept., '16. *Fell*, Hooge, nr. Ypres, 14 Aug., '17.
GIDDINGS, G., Gnr., R.F.A.
  Res., 21 Grace Rd., Croydon. *Fell*, 30 Jul., '16.
GIDDINGS, MARK WILLIAM, 12 Lancers.
  s., Mr. & Mrs. A Giddings, 21 Grace Rd., Croydon. *Enl.*, '99. *D.*, of wounds, France, '14.
GILBERT, CHARLES A., Pte., R. Fus.
  b., '96 ; *s.*, Mr. & Mrs. Gilbert, 26 Tankerton Terrace, Mitcham Rd., Croydon. *Fell*, 27 Apr., '17.

T

GILBERT, JOB, Sergt., R.F.A.
  b., 3 Godstone Cott., Coulsdon ; s., Mr. & Mrs. Gilbert, 69 Milton Rd., Croydon. *Educ.*, St. James' Sch., Croydon. Married. Metal worker. *Res.*, 8 Tait Rd., Croydon. *Enl.*, 16 Jan., '15 ; ment. in despatches, 9 Apr., '17. *D.* of gas poisoning, Nottingham Hosp., 25 Dec., '17.

GILBERT, REGINALD, Cpl., 11 Field Amb., R.A.M.C.
  b., Stockwell, S.W., 21 May, '92 ; s., William Richard & Emily Alice Gilbert, 22 Princess Rd., S. Norwood. *Educ.* at Croydon and London. Single. Clerk. *Res.*, 56 Dagnall Pk., S. Norwood. *Enl.*, Jan., '15. *D.* of wounds recd. at Gonnehem, nr. Bethune, 10 May, '18.

GILES, ARTHUR FREDERICK STEWART, Pte., 17 Middlesex Regt.
  b., Hawkstone Rd., Southwark, 11 Jan., '96 ; s., Lewis Sidney and Susan Elizabeth Giles, 52 Norton Gardens, Norbury. *Educ.*, Emmanuel Sch., Streatham, & Winterbourne Rd. Sch., T. Heath. Single. Helmet maker. *Enl.*, Feb., '15. *Fell*, Delville Wood, Somme, 27 Jul., '16.

GILES, ERNEST WILLIAM, Pte., M.G.C.
  b., 130 Church Rd., Croydon, 18 Feb., '99 ; s., James & Annie Giles, 130 Church Rd., Croydon. *Educ.*, St. Andrew's Sch., Croydon. Single. Cycle warehouseman. *Enl.*, 20 Mar., '17. *D.*, 30 Apr., '18, at Boulogne, of wounds recd. 2 days prev.

GILL, WILLIAM GERALD OLIVER, 2/Lt., Essex Regt.
  b., '96. *Educ.*, Dulwich Coll. *Res.*, S. Norwood. Played for Young Amateurs of Surrey, at Oval, '13. *Joined*, '14. *Fell*, '17.

GILLIAM, WILLIAM HENRY, Cpl., 1/22 Lond. Regt.
  b., Alton, Hants, 30 May, '99 ; s., W. & E. Gilliam, 73 Waddon New Rd., Croydon. *Educ.*, Par. Ch. Sch., Croydon. Single. Shop asst. Member of Croydon Parish Ch. C.L.B. *Enl.*, in 3/4 R.W.S. Regt. Nov., '14. *Fell*, France, 3 Jan., '17. (Plate XIV., 6).

GILLIE, A. J., L/Cpl., Lond. Regt.
  b., '93 ; e.s., J. & A. Gillie, 180 Mitcham Rd., Croydon. Married. *Enl.*, in R.W.S. Regt ; w., 8 Oct., '16. *Fell*, 2 Sept., '18.

GILLIE, WALLACE JOHN, Sgt., 1 K.R.R.C.
  b., Montreal, Canada, 20 Jul., '95 ; s., J. & A. Gillie, 180 Mitcham Rd., Croydon. *Educ.*, Boston Rd. Sch., Croydon. Single. Clerk. *Enl.*, 22 Jan., '14. *Fell*, Hooge, nr. Ypres, 30 Jul., '15.

GILSON, E. H., Pte., R. Fus.
  b., '78 ; s., late Mr. & Mrs. R. A. Gilson, Addis. *Res.*, 33 Grove Pk. Rd., Chiswick. *Fell*, 30 Oct., '17.

GILTRAP, G. H.
  Schoolmaster, High Sch., Croydon. *Fell*, '18.

GLANDFIELD, ALBERT VICTOR, Pte., 1 R.W.S. Regt.
  b., 135 Bensham Grove, T. Heath, 28 Dec., '93 ; s., Thomas William & Rebecca Glandfield. *Educ.*, Beulah Rd. Sch., T.Heath. Single. Labourer. *Enl.*, 26 Aug., '12. *Fell*, Somme, 1 Jul., '16.

GLASS, ALFRED, 1 R.B.
  Educ., Shirley Sch., Wickham Rd. *Enl.*, Oct., '07. *Fell*, '15.

GLAZE, ALFRED G., L/Cpl., R. Fus.
  Res., 11 St. John's Rd., Croydon. Empl. by Messrs. Hope Bros. *Enl.*, Feb., '15. *Fell*, France, '17.

GLAZE, WALTER EDWARD, Pte., R.Fus.
  s., Mr. & Mrs. Glaze, 11 St. John's Rd., Croydon. Married. Railway porter. *Res.*, 61 Derby Rd., Croydon. *Enl.*, Mar., '15 ; w., Somme, June, '16. *D.*, 4 Jun., '19, at Croydon Hosp., of heart trouble resulting from gas-poisoning.

THE GLORIOUS DEAD

GLIDDON, MAURICE, Lt., R.F.A.
Educ., Whitgift G. Sch. Married ; 1 son. *Joined* as 2/Lt., Nov., '14 ; M.C. *Fell*, '17.

GLOVER, B. H., 2/Lt., R.W.Kent Regt.

GOBLE, R. E., Pte., R.A.S.C.
Married ; 2 children. Empl. by Croydon Corp. Tramways. *Res.*, 65 Churchill Rd., Croydon. *Enl.*, Jan., '16. *Fell*, France, 9 Sept., '17.

GODDARD, A. E., Pte., E. Sur. Regt.
Memb. of Ancient Order of Foresters. *D.*, France, 15 Jul., '18.

GODFREY, STEPHEN MERVYN, Lt., Artists Rif. (28 Lond. Regt.)
b., Forest Hill, 26 Jul., '92 ; *s.*, Mr. & Mrs. Godfrey, 159 Melfort Rd., T. Heath. *Educ.*, Whitgift G. Sch. Single. Chartered accountant's clerk. *Enl.*, as pte., '10 ; mobilised 6 Aug., '14. *Fell*, France, 30 Dec., '17.

GOLD, A. E., Pte., Can. Mounted Rif.
b., '94 ; *s.*, Mr. & Mrs. W. H. Gold, " Weybourne," Foxley Lane, Purley. *D.* of wounds, '17.

GOLD, PERCY, 2/Lt., Scots Gds.
b., '83 ; *e.s.*, Mr. & Mrs. W. H. Gold, " Waldronhyrst," Croydon. Partner in the firm of Evatt & Co. *Fell*, 1 Jul., '16.

GOLDING, F. E., Pte., Dorset Regt.
b., '93. *Educ.*, Mitcham Rd. Sch., Croydon. Married ; 1 child. Footman to Lord Michelham, Princes' Gate. *Res.*, 69 Derby Rd., Croydon. *Enl.*, '14. *Fell*, 5 Apr., '18.

GOLDS, FRANK, 2/Lt., E. Sur. Regt.
b., '80 ; *y.s.*, late Hugh, & Mrs. Golds, Croydon. *Fell*, 5 Oct., '16.

GOOCH, KENNETH, Lond. Regt.
Fell, France, 1 Jul., '16.

GOODING, FREDERICK BERTIE, Pte., 1 Middlesex Regt.
b., Oxford Coffee Tavern, T. Heath, 11 Sept., '85 ; *s.*, Mr. & Mrs. Gooding, 117 Frant Rd., T. Heath. *Educ.*, Boston Rd. Sch., Croydon. Married. Decorator *Res.*, 27 Cross Rd., Croydon. *Enl.*, 14 Aug., '16. *Fell*, Clapham Junc., Polygon Wood, nr. Ypres, 26 Sept., '17.

GOODMAN, RALPH THOMAS, Pte., 10 Essex Regt.
b., Cherry Orch. Rd., Croydon, 14 Jul., '98 ; *s.*, Mr. & Mrs. A. W. Goodman, 24 Clarence Rd., Croydon. *Educ.*, Croydon. Single. Asst. clerk to accountants. *Enl.*, Aug., '16. *Reported missing*, presumed fallen, Crassiere Wood, France.

GOODMAN, REGINALD ARTHUR, Band-Sgt., K.O.R.L. Regt.
b., '89 ; *s.*, Mr. & Mrs. Goodman, Clarence Rd., Croydon. Married, Ethel née Keywood ; 1 child. *Res.*, Sangley Rd., S. Norwood. Founder & conductor, Orpheus Orchestra. *Enl.*, in Middlesex Regt., Mar., '16. *D.*, 9 May, '18, of wounds recd. nr. Bethune the prev. day.

GOODWIN, HENRY, Tank C.
b., '98 ; *s.*, Mr. & Mrs. Thomas H. Goodwin, Norbury. *Fell*, 24 Mar., '18.

GOODWIN, T. J., 8747, Pte., D.L.I.
Fell, '16.

GORDON, ELIZABETH MARJORIE, Nurse, V.A.D.
e. daughter of late Gen. William Gordon, C.I.E., & Mrs. Gordon, " Arradoul," Tavistock Rd., Croydon. *D.* of malaria at Salonica, 11 Sept., '17.

GORRINGE, C. H., 683099, Pte., Lond. Regt.
b., '98. *Res.*, Norbury. *Fell*, 7 Jun., '17.

THE CROYDON ROLL OF HONOUR

GOSLING, JAMES THOMAS, Pte., R.M.L.I.
    b., 18 Dec., '74 ; *s.*, James & Sarah Gosling, 71 Union Rd., Croydon. *Educ.*, Sydenham Rd. Sch., Croydon. Married. Baker. *Res.*, Whitehorse Rd., Croydon. *Enl.*, 4 Aug., '92 ; Long Serv. Med. & Benin Exped. Med. *Lost* with H.M.S. " Defence," sunk during battle of Jutland, 31 May, '16.

GOSLING, JOHN, A.B. Seaman, R.N.
    Educ., Ashford Schs. Married. Postman. *Res.*, 22 Sheldon St., Croydon. *Lost* with H.M.S. " Good Hope," sunk off Coronel, Chili, 1 Nov., '14.

GOSS, HERBERT, Bugler, 21 Can. Inf.
    b., '87 ; *s.*, Mr. & Mrs. George Goss, 83 Mitcham Rd., Croydon. Married. *Fell*, 24 Jun., '16.

GOSTLING, HERBERT, Sgt. (Observer), R.A.F.
    b., Streatham, 20 Feb., '91 ; *s.*, Mr. & Mrs. Gostling, 220 Selsdon Rd., S. Croydon. *Educ.*, Dering Pl. & Abp. Tenison's Schs., Croydon. Single. *Enl.* in 7 Dragoon Gds., 29 Mar., '08 ; transf. to 6 Inniskilling Dragoons, M.G.C., and R.A.F. *Fell*, over German lines while on bombing raid. *D.*, Heitern, nr. Neu Breisach.

GOULD, E., 15556, L/Cpl., North'd. Fus.
    Res., Croydon. *Fell*, '16.

GOULD, JOSEPH STEPHEN, Pte., R.A.S.C.
    b., Ducklington, Oxon., 11 Nov., '59. *Educ.*, Ducklington, nr. Witney, Oxon. Married. Greengrocer. *Res.*, 4 Thornton Rd., T. Heath. *Enl.*, 16 Oct., '14 ; served 1 yr. in France. *D.* of pneumonia, Woolwich, 3 Aug., '16.

GOWARD, PATRICK LINDSAY, Cpl., Black Watch.
    s., Mr. & Mrs. Goward, 39 Dominion Rd., Addis. *Fell*, 8 May,'16.

GOY, G., 17808, Cpl., Essex Regt.
    Res., S. Norwood. *D.* of wounds, 17.

GRABHAM, EDWARD WILLIAM, Pte., 8 R.W.S. Regt.
    b., Croydon, 19 Oct., '96 ; *s.*, Harry & Harriet Jane Grabham, 24 Wandle Rd., Croydon. *Educ.*, Welcome Hall, Croydon. Single. Shop asst. (wine & spirit trade). *Enl.*, 9 Sept., '14. *Fell*, Tower Bridge, Hulloch, Loos, 25 Sept., '15.

GRAND, ARTHUR LEONARD, 1576, Pte., 7 R.W.S. Regt.
    b., 29 Surrey St., Croydon, 21 May, '95 ; *s.*, Mr. & Mrs. Harry Grand, 1 Upper Drayton Pl., Croydon. *Educ.*, Parish Ch. Sch., Croydon. Single. Hairdresser. *Enl.*, Sept., '15. *D.*, 10 Jul., '16, at 2 Stat. Hosp., Abbeville, of wounds recd., Somme, 1 Jul.,'16.

GRAND, FREDERICK, 18946, Cpl., 6 E. Kent Regt.
    b., Croydon, 12 Jun., '90 ; *s.*, Mr. & Mrs. Harry Grand, 1 Upper Drayton Pl., Croydon. *Educ.*, British Sch., Croydon. Married. Hairdresser. *Res.*, Wellesley Rd., Croydon. *Enl.*, 17 Jun., '16. *Fell*, France, 3 May, '17.

GRANT, J. P., 510056, Lond. Regt.
    Res., Croydon. *D.* of wounds, '17.

GRANT, JOHN ANDERTON, 2/Lt., 3 R. Suss. Regt.
    b., 39 Clyde Rd., Croydon, 4 Jul., '98 ; *s.*, Francis Octavius & Annie Edith Grant, 48 Birdhurst Rd., Croydon. *Educ.*, " The Limes," Croydon, & Eastbourne Coll., Eastbourne, where he was head of his House and sen. Sgt. in O.T.C.; passed prelim. exam. of Inst. of Chartered Accountants. *Joined* Inns of Court O.T.C., as pte., 2 Sept., '15, becoming Sgt. ; commis. (in Spec. Res. of Officers), 28 Mar., '17 ; went to France with 11 R. Suss. Regt., 10 Aug., '17 ; *w.*, 27 Sept., '17 ; ret. to France with 8 R. Suss. Regt., 18 Apr., '18. *Fell*, nr. Amiens, 14 May, '18. Buried, Henencourt Communal Cem. Extension, W. of Albert. (Plate XI., 5).

XII.

1. Pte. A. H. HEARTFIELD, 6 Duke of Cornwall's L.I.
2. Maj. R. J. FILLINGHAM, M.C., R.G.A.
3. L/Cpl. H. E. GUNN, 1 Lond. Scottish
4. L/Cpl. H. HOWARD, 10 R. Fus.
5. Gnr. H. L. GUILLON, R.F.A.
6. Lt. D. GUNN, Seaforth H.

XI.

1. Pte. S. Harris, R.M.L.I.
2. 2/Lt. S. H. Bressey, R.E.
3. Pte. F. L. Geerts, 12 Suff. Regt.
4. Lt. A. C. Davis, R.A.F.
5. 2/Lt. J. A. Grant, 3 R. Suss. Regt.
6. Pte. J. W. Gray, Machine Gun Corps.

THE GLORIOUS DEAD

GRANTHAM, JOHN DAVID, R.N.
  b., '88. Educ., Oval Rd. Sch., Croydon. Married. Page boy. Res., Albert Rd., Addis. Joined, '02. Lost on H.M.S. "Formidable," torpedoed in English Channel, 1 Jan., '15.

GRAVESTOCK, W., 37085, Pte., R.W.S. Regt.
  Res , S. Norwood. Fell, '17.

GRAY, ARTHUR STANLEY.
  s., Mr. & Mrs. Gray, 22 Barclay Rd., Croydon. Fell, 14 Sept., '16.

GRAY, JOSEPH WALTER, Pte., M.G.C.
  b., Croydon, 8 Nov., '97 ; y.s., George & Harriet Gray, 10 Nicholson Rd., Addis. Educ., Woodside Sch., Croydon. Single. Shop asst. Res., 10 Nicholson Rd., Croydon. Enl., 2 Oct., '14. Fell, France, 2 Dec., '16. (Plate XI., 6).

GRAY, OLIVER JOHN, 60272, Pte., R.A.M.C.
  b., Castlemarton, Worcestershire ; s., William Valentine & Emmeline Ruth Gray, 92 Bingham Rd., Addis. Educ., London. Single. Civil service clerk. Res., S. Norwood. Enl., 19 Jun., '15 ; ment. in despatches, 30 May, '17. D., 8 May, '17, at 15 Stat. Hosp., German E. Africa, of black water fever.

GRAY, ROBERT GEORGE, L.R.B. (1/5 Lond. Regt.)
  b., 24 May, '90 ; s., John Andrew & Emma Gray, 58 Hartley Rd., Croydon. Educ., Reading. Single. Architect's asst. Enl., 19 Nov., '15. Fell, Ypres, 25 Aug., '16.

GRAYSMARK, JOHN WILLIAM BLAKE, Rflmn., L.R.B. (5 Lond. Regt.)
  b., 14 Junction Cottages, Gloucester Rd., Croydon, '96 ; s., Mr. & Mrs. Graysmark, 85 The Crescent, Croydon. Single. Grocer's asst. Enl., Apr., '15. Fell, France, 9 Oct., '16.

GRAYSON, —.
  Empl. as conductor by Croydon Corp. Tramways.

GREEN, ALFRED HENRY, Seaman, R.N.
  s., Mr. & Mrs. Green, 15 Selsdon Rd., Croydon. Served on H.M. Ships "Ganges," "Albemarle," "Bulwark," "Zealandia," "Vernon," & "Tipperary," during the war. Fell, Battle of Jutland, 31 May, '16. (Plate XIII., 6).

GREEN, C., 511280, Lond. Regt.
  Res., S, Norwood. Fell, '17.

GREEN, CHARLES LAYTON, 2/Lt., Essex Regt. (attd. R.F.C.)
  b., '93 ; e.s., Dr. & Mrs. Green, Woodside. Educ., Durlston Court, Swanage, & St. Bees Sch., Cumberland ; matriculated, Lond. Univ. ; entered Guy's as med. student, '13 ; went to Edin. Univ. Joined, Edin. Univ. O.T.C., Sept., '14 ; enl., in 1st Sportsman's Btn. ; commis., Dec., '14 ; w., '16 ; transf. to R.F.C. '16 ; injured in flying accident, 7 Jan., '17. Killed in flying accident, 9 Jun., '17.

GREEN, LEONARD A., Pte., Lancs. Fus.
  b., '99 ; y.s., Mr. & Mrs. Green, 6 Chelsham Grove, Croydon. Educ., Abp. Tenison's Sch., Croydon. Fell, 9 Sept., '18.

GREEN, LESLIE ALAN, 2/Lt., 6 (attd. 23) R. Fus.
  b., E. Dulwich, 27 Jul., '94 ; s., Mr. & Mrs. James Green, 17 Warminster Rd., S. Norwood. Educ., Sutton County Sch. Single. Bank clerk. Enl., as pte. in H.A.C., May, '15. Fell, Beaumont Hamel, 14 Nov., '16.

GREEN, R. C., Sgt., R.G.A.

GREEN, W. E., Gnr., R.G.A.
  Fell, '17.

GREEN, WALTER CHARLES, 200601, Sgt., Tank C.
  b., Brighton, 8 Nov., '15 ; e.s., Mr. & Mrs. Charles Green, 12 Alpha Rd., Addis. Educ., Oval Rd. Sch., Croydon. Asstd. with his father's business as nurseryman & landscape gardener. Enl., in K.R.R.C. ; transf. to M.G.C., & later to Tank C., Nov., '15. Awarded D.C.M. for "the courageous manner in which he brought his tank out of action" at Cambrai, Nov., '17 ; Croix de Guerre, May, '18. Fell, nr. Morlancourt, 8 Aug., '18.

GREENHEAD, ALFRED GEORGE, Cpl., 1 D.C.L.I.
    b., Croydon, 6 Mar., '94 ; *s*., Alfred George & Alice Maud Greenhead, 71 Dennett Rd., Croydon. *Educ*., Mitcham Rd. Sch., Croydon. Single. Mineral water worker. *Res*., 54 Wentworth Rd., Croydon. *Enl*., 17 Apr., '12 ; *w*., France, Oct., '14. *Fell*, Delville Wood, 16 Aug., '16. (Plate III., 3).

GREENHEAD, LEONARD BERTRAM, L/Cpl., 12 R. Irish Rif.
    b., 3 Fisherman Cottages, Windmill Rd., Croydon ; *s*., Charles E. & Alice Greenhead, 24 Bishop's Rd., Croydon. *Educ*., Sydenham Rd. Sch., Croydon. Single. Fitter's mate. *Enl*., in 16 R. Suss. Regt., 11 Oct., '15. *Fell*, 16 Aug., '17. (Plate XIV., 2).

GREENWAY, KENNETH, Lt., 13 Worcester Regt.
    b., 18 Feb., '97 ; *s*., Mr. & Mrs. Greenway, 28 Highland Rd., U. Norwood. *Educ*., Whitgift G. Sch., '10-14, & Bootle Boro. Tech. Sch. Was Sgt. in Whitgift O.T.C. *Enl*., in Univ. & Pub. Sch. Bde., '14 ; commis., Oct., '14. *Fell*, Gallipoli, 27 Nov., '15.

GREET, N., 36590, Pte., M.G.C.
    Res., Croydon. *Fell*, '17.

GREGORY, GEORGE, Sgt., 8 R.B.
    b., '77. Married. *Res*., S. Norwood. Served in India with R.B. prev. to '07 ; memb. of Nat. Res. *Fell*, Hooge, '15.

GREGORY, HENRY.
    b., '74. *Res*., 32 Waddon Marsh Lane, Croydon. *D*. of dysentery, 16 Jul., '16, at 15 Stat. Hosp., Mbuyuni, E. Africa.

GREGORY, LAURIE LESLIE, Bdr., 34 Bty., R.F.A.
    b., 60 Canterbury Rd., Croydon, 13 Sept., '96 ; *s*., Mr. & Mrs. Gregory, 60 Canterbury Rd., Croydon. *Educ*., Christ Ch. Sch., Croydon. Single. Plumber's mate. *Enl*., 16 Jul., '15. *D*., of meningitis, Croydon Infirmary, 28 Dec., '19.

GRIFFIN, A. R., 25930, Pte., 9 M.G.C.
    s., Mr. & Mrs. Griffin, 21 Derby Rd., Croydon. *Missing* since 25 Apr., '18.

GRIFFITHS, ALFRED JAMES, Pte., 3/4 R.W.S. Regt.
    b., Bermondsey, 5 Jun., '91 ; *s*., Mr. & Mrs. A. J. Griffiths, 148 Dalmally Rd., Addis. *Educ*., Portland Rd. Sch., S. Norwood. Married. Clerk. *Res*., 150 Dalmally Rd., Addis. *Enl*., 27 May, '15. *Fell*, Somme, 6 Feb., '17. *Buried*, Peronne.

GRIGG, FRANCIS, 2/Lt., 10 E. Lancs. Regt.
    b., 21 Apr., '95 ; *s*., Mr. & Mrs. Frank Charles Grigg, "Yvetot," Foxley Hill Rd., Purley. *Educ*., Whitgift G. Sch., '09-10.

GRIGGS, WILFRED LEONARD, Rflmn., L.R.B. (5 Lond. Regt.)
    b., '99 ; *s*., William & Ethel Griggs, 31 St. John's Grove, Croydon. *Educ*., Brit. Sch., Croydon. Manager in boot warehouse. *Enl*., in Civil Serv. Rif., Jul., '17. *D*., 20 Nov., '18, of wounds recd., France, 7 Nov., '18.

GRINHAM, G. S., 2621, Pte., Middlesex Regt.
    Fell, '16.

GRINHAM, GEORGE ROWLAND, Seaman Torpedo-man, R.N.
    Res., 115 St. James' Rd., Croydon. *Accidentally drowned*, while serving on Submarine B1, '16.

GRINHAM, TOM H., Cpl., R.W.S. Regt.
    b., '81. *Fell*, 30 Jan., '17.

GROOM, A., Pte.
    b., '89 ; *s*., Mr. & Mrs. Walter Henry Groom, 107 Milton Rd., Croydon. *Educ*., Whitehorse Rd. Sch., T. Heath. Married ; 2 children. Empl. by Messrs. Richards & Son, sheet metal workers, Wellesley Rd., Croydon. *Fell*, 10 Nov., '17.

THE GLORIOUS DEAD

GROOM, F. C., Cpl., A.P.C.
  b., '79. Married, E. A , daughter of Mr. W. J. Clark, 6 Ullswater Rd., W. Norwood. *Res.*, " Novello," Saxon Rd., Selhurst. *D.*, 5 Dec., '18, at Wimereux, of heart failure, following influenza.

GROVER, PERCY, Cpl., L.R.B. (5 Lond. Regt.)
  b., Croydon, 19 Feb., '95 ; *s.*, Mr. & Mrs. H. J. Grover, 33 Elgin Rd., Croydon. *Educ.*, Abp. Tenison's Sch., Croydon. Single. Stockbroker's clerk. *Enl.*, Aug., '15. *Fell*, Les Bouefs, Somme, Aug., '15.

GRUBB, PERCY GEORGE, Sapper, R.E.
  b., Wimbledon, 12 Apr., '86. *Educ.*, Oval Rd. Sch., Croydon. Married. Plumber. *Res.*, 61 Fairholme Rd., Croydon. *Enl.*, 10 Apr., '16. *Fell*, Arras, 13 Apr., '17.

GRUMBRIDGE, H., Sgt., 3 R. Fus.
  b., '90 ; *s.*, Mr. & Mrs. Grumbridge, 72 Church St., Croydon. *Served* 8 yrs. in India. *Fell*, France, 9 Feb., '15.

GUBBY, A. R., Gnr., R.G.A.
  b., '83 ; *e.s.*, Mr. & Mrs. Gubby, 17 Hampton Rd., Croydon. *Educ.*, Sydenham Rd. Sch., Croydon. Married ; 4 children. *Enl.*, 18 Oct., '15. *Fell*, France, 10 Jul., '17.

GUBBY, ALBERT EDWIN, Cpl., 21 Siege Bty., R.G.A.
  b., 21 Union Rd., Croydon ; *s.*, Mr. & Mrs. William Gubby, 8, Westbury Rd., Croydon. *Educ.*, Sydenham Rd. Sch., Croydon. Married. Porter, empl. by L.B. & S.C.R. *Res.*, 8 Westbury Rd., Croydon. *Enl.*, May, '05. *Fell*, nr. Reninghelst, Belgium, 22 Aug., '18.

GUBBY, R., 5433, Pte., Leinster Regt.
  Res., W. Croydon. *D.* of wounds, '17.

GUBBY, WALTER C., Sgt.Maj., R.G.A.
  b., '82 ; *e.s.*, Mr. & Mrs. Gubby, 8 Westbury Rd., Croydon. *Educ.*, Sydenham Rd. Sch., Croydon. Married ; 4 children. *Enl.*, when 17 yrs. old ; served in France from 8 Aug., '14. *Fell*, 13 Dec., '17.

GUDGIN, LEONARD A., Cpl., 3 N.Z.R.B.
  s., Mr. & Mrs. F. Gudgin, Sydenham Rd. Schs., Croydon. *D.*, 1 Dec., '17, of wounds recd. at Passchendaele, Nov., '17.

GUILLON, HENRI L. M., Gnr., R.F.A.
  b., '82 ; *s.*, Mr. & Mrs. Guillon, 2 Broughton Rd., T. Heath. *Educ.*, Beulah Rd. Sch., T. Heath. Married ; 1 son. *Enl.*, '16. *Fell*, 10 Jun., '18. (Plate XII., 5).

GUNN, DAVID, Lt., Seaforth H.
  2nd *s.*, Mr. & Mrs. John Gunn, " The Birches," Howard Rd., S. Norwood. *Enl.*, as pte. in Cameron H., '14 ; invalided home from France with frozen feet, Apr., '15 ; commis. in Seaforth H., '15 ; Lt., 1 Jul., '17. *Fell*, 13 Oct., '17. (Plate XII., 6).

GUNN, HERBERT ERNEST, L/Cpl., 1 Lond. Scottish (14 Lond. Regt.)
  b., London, 18 May, '94 ; *s.*, Mr. & Mrs. John Gunn, 1 Balfour Rd., S. Norwood. *Educ.*, Portland Rd. Sch., S Norwood. Single. Stockbroker's clerk. *Res.*, 26 Woodside Rd., S. Norwood. *Enl.*, 28 Aug., '11. *Fell*, Hebuterne, 19 Aug., '16. (Plate XII., 3).

GURNELL, JOHN, L/Cpl., R.W.S. Regt.
  b., '87. Married. *Res.*, 2 Derby Grove, Croydon. *Fell*, 18 Apr., '16.

GUTTERIDGE, HENRY J. M., Pte., Australian I.F.
  e.s., Mr. & Mrs. H. Gutteridge, 20 Brigstock Rd., T. Heath. Married ; 1 son. *Res.*, Toowong, Queensland, Australia. Served with 11th Hussars during S.A. War. *Fell*, 12 Oct., '17.

HADFIELD, W. J. M., Lt., S. Lancs. Regt.
  s., Maj.-Gen. C. A. & Mrs. Hadfield, "Kintaugh," Ashburton Rd., Addis. *D.* of wounds, '14.
HADDOW, A. J., 34169, Hants. Regt.
  Res., W. Croydon. *Fell*, '17.
HAILL, STANLEY VICTOR, Pte., R. Fus.
  b., '94 ; *s.*, Mr. & Mrs. Haill, 37 Northcote Rd., Croydon. Baker, empl. by Messrs. Wilson, Brigstock Rd., T. Heath. *Enl.* in R.A.S.C., '14. *Fell*, '17.
HAINES, CHARLES STEWART, A.M., R.F.C.
  b., '97 ; *y.s.*, Mr. & Mrs. J. G. Haines, Edridge Rd., Croydon. *Educ.*, M. Whitgift Sch. Empl. in Rental Dept., Croydon Gas Co. *Enl.*, Nov., '15. *D.* of wounds, France, 10 Apr., '18.
HAIRBY, FRANK, 3844, Rflmn., Q.V.R. (1/9 Lond. Regt.).
  s., Mr. & Mrs. Alfred Hairby, 115 Dalmally Rd., Croydon. *Missing*, Gommecourt Wood, 1 Jul., '16.
HAIRBY, LESLIE, Pte., 1/20 Lond. Regt.
  s., Mr. & Mrs. Alfred Hairby, 115 Dalmally Rd., Croydon. *D.* of wounds at Gosforth War Hosp., Newcastle, 4 Oct., '16.
HAIZELDEN, BENJAMIN, 2/Lt., 2/10 Lond. Regt.
  b., Balham, 20 Nov., '98 ; *s.*, John & Elizabeth Haizelden, 35 Abbey Rd., Croydon. *Educ.*, Boro. Sec. Sch., Croydon. Single. Bank clerk. *Gazetted*, 2/Lt., 5 Oct., '16. *D.*, 30 Aug., '18, of wounds recd. in France the prev. day. (Plate X., 1).
HALE, LEONARD, Lincoln Regt.
  Married ; children. *Res.*, 10 Cecil Rd., Croydon. *D.*, 9 Dec., '14, of wounds recd. at Ypres, a few days prev.
HALEY, HENRY WILLIAM, Coy.Sgt.Maj., 4 R.W.S. Regt.
  b., Waltham Abbey, Essex, 15 Jul., '69. *Educ.*, Princess Rd. Sch., Croydon, and London, E. Married. Vellum binder's finisher. *Res.*, 87 Queen's Rd., Croydon. *Enl.*, 19 Apr., '87. *Mobilised*, 4 Aug., '14. *D.* of cancer on liver, Crescent War Hosp., Croydon, 11 Nov., '18.
HALL, CECIL ADRIAN, 22504, Pte., 1 R.W.S. Regt.
  b., Battersea, 11 Oct., '96 ; *s.*, Mr. & late Mrs. Hall, 30 Carmichael Rd., S. Norwood. *Educ.*, Birchanger Rd. Sch., S. Norwood. Single. Clerk. *Enl.*, 22 Sept., '14 ; *w.* at Suvla Bay, '15 ; twice in hosp. in England with Bright's disease ; sent to France, Jan., '17 ; awarded M.M. for work as company runner, Meteren, 12-14 Apr., '18. *D.* of wounds recd. at Erie Camp, Poperinghe, 29 May, '18.
HALL, F., 1492, L/Cpl., R.W.S. Regt.
  Res., T. Heath. *Fell*, '17.
HALL FREDERICK, Pte., 6 R.W.S. Regt.
  b., Croydon, 22 Jul., '96 ; *e.s.*, Edward & Emily Hall, 51 Church Rd., Croydon. *Educ.*, Par. Ch. Sch., Croydon. Single. Apprentice to boot maker. *Enl.*, 28 Aug., '14. *D.* 28 Jan., '16, at St. Omer, of wounds recd. at Ploegsteert, 16 Jun., '15.
HALL, H., Pte., R. Fus.
  b., '96. *Res.*, 16 Charnwood Rd., S. Norwood. *Fell*, 18 Sept., '16.
HALL, HARRY, Pte., 1 Northd. Fus.
  b., 26 Nov., '87 ; *s.*, Mr. & Mrs. Hall, 23 Grange Rd., T. Heath. *Educ.*, Whitehorse Rd. Sch., T. Heath. *Fell*, Neuve Chapelle, 5 Mar., '16.
HALL, JACK, Pte., 6 R.W.S. Regt.
  b., 16 Jul., '96 ; *s.*, Mr. & Mrs. F. J. Hall, 32 Sydenham Park, Sydenham. *Educ.*, Boro. Sec. Sch., Croydon. Single. *Res.*, Saxon Rd., Selhurst. *Enl.*, 28 Aug., '14. *Fell*, Fricourt, Somme, Jul., '16. (Plate XVIII., 4).

THE GLORIOUS DEAD

HALL, P., 14731, Pte., E. Sur. Regt.
  Res., Croydon. *Fell*, '17.
HALLETT, FREDERICK PERCY, Pte., 2 R.W.S. Regt.
  b., Croydon, 11 Oct., '97 ; *s.*, Mr. & Mrs. Hallett, 11 Cambridge Rd., T. Heath. *Enl.*, 27 Feb., '15. *Fell*, France, 5 Sept., '16, *killed* by German bomb, on which he threw himself, thus saving lives of 7 comrades.
HALLIDAY, FRANCIS, 2487, Cpl., 9 E. Sur. Regt.
  b., Nutcroft Rd., Peckham, 4 Feb., '94 ; *s.*, Mr. & Mrs. George Henry Halliday, 12 Selhurst Rd., S. Norwood. *Educ.*, Sydenham Rd. Sch., Croydon. Single. Hairdresser. *Enl.*, Sept., '14. M.M., 21 Jun., '16. *D.* of wounds, 16 Aug., '16. (Plate XXXII., 4).
HALSEY, DOUGLAS, Rflmn., L.R.B. (5 Lond. Regt.)
  b., '98 ; *s.*, Mr. & Mrs. W. H. Halsey, Dulwich. *Fell*, 16 Apr., '18.
HAMILTON, ALBERT CHARLES, Pte., 2 R. Berks. Regt.
  b., Sumner Rd., Croydon. 25 Nov., – ; *s.*, Mr. & Mrs. Hamilton, 28 Cuthbert Rd., Croydon. *Educ.*, Mitcham Rd. Sch., Croydon. Single. Labourer. *Enl.*, 15 Mar., '06 ; King George's Durbar Med. *Fell*, France, 9 May, '15.
HAMILTON, S. J., 5650, Pte., Lond. Regt.
  Res., Croydon. *Fell*, '16.
HAMMOND, F., Pte., M.G.C.
  y.s., Mr. & Mrs. Hammond, 8 Surrey St., Croydon. *Enl.*, in R.W.S. Regt., '14 ; transf. to Lond. Regt. and served in France, '16-17 ; sent home as under age, and drafted to Camb. Regt. ; ret. to France with M.G.C. *Fell*, nr. Rheims, 21 Jul., '18.
HAMMOND, GEORGE RATHBONE, Pte., H.A.C.
  b., Croydon, 3 Jun., '87 ; *s.*, Mr. & Mrs. R. M. Hammond, 20 Addis. Grove, Croydon. *Educ.*, High Sch., Croydon, & Wellingborough Pub. Sch. Single. Ironmonger. *Enl.*, 19 Apr., '15. *D.*, 14 Nov., '16, of wounds recd. at Beaumont Hamel the prev. day. *Buried*, Mesnil, nr. Albert. (Plate VII., 2).
HAMMOND, HARRY CECIL, 62221, 8 R. Fus.
  s., Mr. & Mrs. Hammond, 24 Edith Rd., S. Norwood. *Educ.*, M. Whitgift Sch. *Missing*, Cambrai, 30 Nov., '17.
HAMMOND, JOHN MARTIN RICHARD, Lt., 11 Essex Regt.
  b., Croydon, 15 Oct.,'96 ; *s.*, Mr. & Mrs. Harold Martin Hammond, 35 Heathfield Rd., Croydon. *Educ.*, Whitgift G. Sch. Single. *Res.*, Westcliff-on-Sea. *Joined* as 2/Lt., 22 Sept., '14. *Missing*, Loos, 26 Sept., '15.
HAMPTON, J. L., L/Cpl., L.R.B. (5 Lond. Regt.)
  b., 28 Jun., '77 ; *s.*, Mr. & Mrs. C. A. Hampton, Selling House, Ewell. *Educ.*, Whitgift G. Sch., '89-96. Member of L.R.B., '97-03 ; served in C.I.V. Mounted Inf. during S.A. War. *Re-enlisted*, '14 ; served in France, Nov., '14—May, '15. *Fell*, nr. Ypres, 3 May, '15.
HAMPTON, W., Pte., L.R.B. (5 Lond. Regt.)
  s., Mr. & Mrs. C. A. Hampton, Selling House, Ewell. *Fell*, '15.
HAMSHAR, V., Act.-Sgt., R.A.S.C.
  Fell, '17.
HANCOCK, C., 11566, Pte., E. Sur. Regt. (attd. R.E.)
  Res., S. Norwood. *Fell*, '16.
HANCOCK, FREDERICK, Pte., 44 Can. Inf.
  b., '87 ; *y.s.*, George & Minnie Hancock, 42 Lr. Coombe St., Croydon. *Accidentally drowned* at Allanburg Post, Ontario, 6 Jun., '16.

HANDSCROFT, –., Sgt., R.E.
  Married; 1 son. *Res.*, 106 Northwood Rd., T. Heath. *Enl.*, Apr., '16; D.C.M., bestowed by Mayor of Croydon and Col. Thompson. *D.* of gas poisoning, Apr., '18.

HANDS, FREDERIC, Capt., R.E.
  b., '87; *s.*, Mr. & Mrs. Hands, Haling Pk. Rd., Croydon. *Fell*,'17.

HARBER, S. G., 15841, Pte., 12 E. Sur. Regt.
  Res., S. Croydon. *Enl.*, Nov., '15. *D.* of wounds, 19 Jun., '17. *Buried*, Lyssenthoek Mil. Cem., Belgium.

HARDING, B., 13696, Pte., Scots Gds.
  Res., S. Norwood. *Fell*, '16.

HARDING, GEORGE HENRY, L/Cpl., 3/4 R.W.S. Regt.
  b., 32 Leslie Grove, Croydon, 15 Feb., '96; *s.*, Mr. & Mrs. Harding, 41 Northcote Rd., Croydon. *Educ.*, Davidson Rd. Sch., Croydon. Single. Cellarman, Messrs. Price, wine and spirit merchants. *Enl.*, 8 Nov., '14. *Fell*, France, 9 Oct., '16.

HARDING, W. J., Pte., R. Fus.
  Res., 51 Windsor Rd., T. Heath. *Enl.*, Apr., '16. *Fell*, France, 4 Oct., '16.

HARDINGHAM, E., 703265, Pte., Lond. Regt.
  Res., Tooting. *Fell*, '17.

HARDY, ALFRED JOHN, Pte., 11 Middlesex Regt.
  s., Mr. & Mrs. Hardy, 17 Kimberley Rd., Croydon. *Fell*, 20 Nov., '17.

HARMAN, WILLIAM, Pte., 6 R.W.S. Regt.
  b., T. Heath, 30 Mar., '86; *s.*, Mr. & Mrs. Harman, 91 Northwood Rd., T. Heath. *Educ.*, Whitehorse Rd. Sch., T. Heath. Single. Labourer. *Enl.*, Aug., '14. *D.*, 15 Mar., '16, at 3 Gen. Hosp., Sheffield, of wounds recd. in France.

HARMAN, WILLIAM, R.F.A.
  Educ., Whitgift G. Sch., where he was Capt. of Mason's House. *Enl.*, Aug., '14; served in Egypt and Gallipoli. *Fell*, France, 27 Mar., '18.

HARMER, E., Pte., 6 R.W.S. Regt.
  Fell, '14.

HARMER, S. H. H., 147412, Gnr., R.G.A.
  Res., W. Croydon. *Fell*, '17.

HARMSWORTH, ERNEST, Pte., K.O.R.L. Regt.
  b., '94; *e.s.*, Mr. & Mrs. Harmsworth, 7 Henderson Rd., Croydon. Empl. by Messrs. Still, Norbury. *Fell*, 13 Nov., '16.

HARPER, C., 89609, Pte., R.W.S. Regt.
  Res., W. Croydon. *Fell*, '17.

HARRINGTON, WALTER, Pte., 2 R.W.S. Regt.
  b., Belchamp St. Paul's, Essex, 6 Apr., '77; *s.*, William & Mary Ann Harrington, Belchamp St. Paul's. Married. Labourer. *Res.*, 1 Old Palace Rd., Croydon. *Enl.*, 1 Dec., '14. *Fell*, France, 9 Apr., '15.

HARRIS, ALMA, Pte., 2 R.W.S. Regt.
  Married. *Res.*, 21 Sussex Rd., Croydon. *Fell*, Festubert, '15.

HARRIS, DICK, Driver, R.E.
  b., '93. *Educ.*, Beulah Rd. Sch., T. Heath. *Res.*, 72 Moffatt Rd., T. Heath. Member of Elmhurst (T. Heath) Football Club. *Enl.*, 10 Aug., '14. *D.*, in France, of pneumonia, '18.

HARRIS, FREDERICK ALBERT, Pte., 2 Australian I.F.
  b., Westminster, 26 May, '95. *Educ.*, Portland Rd. Sch., S. Norwood. Single. Labourer. *Res.*, Newcastle, New S. Wales. *Enl.*, 20 Aug., '14. *D.*, 15 May, '17, of wounds recd. at Bullecourt, 6 May, '17.

THE GLORIOUS DEAD

HARRIS, FREDERICK JOHN, Pte., R. Fus.
 b., Brixton, 10 Nov., '93 ; *s.*, Mr. & Mrs. Harris, 169 Norbury Crescent, Norbury. *Educ.*, M. Whitgift Sch. Single. Clerk. *Enl.*, Sept., '14 ; served in Egypt, Dardanelles, France. *D.*, 9 Jul., '16, at Le Tréport, of wounds recd. at Gommecourt, 2 Jul., '16.

HARRIS, G. H. C., 67571, Cpl., R.G.A.
 Res., W. Croydon. *Fell*, '17.

HARRIS, HERBERT, 34816, Pte., 7 R. Fus.
 b., '89 ; *s.*, Mr. & Mrs. M. Harris, 16 Devonshire Rd., Croydon. Empl. by Messrs. Nalder & Collyer, brewers. *Enl.*, 16 Dec., '15. *Fell*, France, 30 Dec., '17.

HARRIS, RICHARD, Pte., E. Kent Regt.
 b., 14 Mar., '87. Married ; 5 children. Builder. *Res.*, 44 Addington Rd., Croydon. *Enl.*, Aug., '16. *Fell*, 18 Mar., '18.

HARRIS, STEPHEN, Pte., R.M.L.I.
 b., 112 Queen's Rd., Crown Hill, U. Norwood. *Educ.*, Eden Rd. Sch., W. Norwood. Single. Gardener. *Enl.*, 6 Aug., '14. *Lost* on H.M.S. " Indefatigable," Jutland, 31 Aug., '16. (Plate XI., 1).

HARRIS, SYDNEY FRANCIS, P.O., "Anson" Btn., R.N.D.
 Educ., M. Whitgift Sch. *Fell*, 20 Feb., '17.

HART, CLEMENT ALBERT, Pte., R.W.S. Regt.
 b., Redhill, 14 Apr., '78 ; *s.*, Mr. & Mrs. Hart, 36 Leslie Pk. Rd., Croydon. *Educ.*, Par. Ch. Sch., Croydon. Single. Ship's steward, P. & O. Line. *Res.*, 118 Miles Rd., Epsom. *Enl.*, 6 May, '16. *Fell*, Ypres, 24 Feb., '17.

HART, CONWAY JOHN, Lt., Notts. & Derby. Regt.
 Fell, '16.

HART, HENRY REGINALD ESSEX, Sgt., 2/4 R.W.S. Regt.
 b., 63 Gowrie Rd., Clapham Junction, 20 Feb., '86 ; *s.*, Mr. & Mrs. Hart, 97 Melfort Rd., T. Heath. *Educ.*, St. Peter's Sch., Eaton Sq., London, S.W. Single. Clerk. *Res.*, Clapham Junction. *Enl.*, Aug., '14. *Fell*, Suvla Bay, 9 Aug., '15.

HARTFIELD, F. G., 17407, L/Sgt., Gren. Gds.
 Res., T. Heath. *Fell*, '16.

HARVEST, GORDON LINDSAY, Lt., L.R.B. (5 Lond. Regt.)
 b., Sept., '95 ; *e.s.*, D. Richard & Mabel Harvest, " Glengarry," Campden Rd., Croydon. *Educ.*, St. Anselm's, Croydon, Repton, and Jesus Coll., Camb. *Enl.* as pte. in Lond. Regt., Aug., '14 ; went to France, winter of '14 ; commis., '15 ; M.C., '17. *Fell*, Croisilles, France, 20 Jun., '17.

HARVEY, HERBERT HENRY, L/Cpl., R.W.S. Regt.
 b., '85. *Educ.*, M. Whitgift Sch. Married. *Res.*, Stanley Rd., Croydon. *Fell*, 1 Oct., '18.

HARVEY, JOHN, Pte., R.E.
 b., Southwark, 26 Dec., '75. *Educ.*, Southwark. Married. Master builder. *Res.*, 77 Denmark Rd., S. Norwood. *D.*, 13 Oct., '15, of wounds recd. at Loos, 10 Oct., '15.

HASELDEN, A. C. G., 650430, Sgt., Lond. Regt.
 Res., Croydon. *Fell*, '17.

HATT, FREDERICK, Driver, R.F.A.
 b., '95 ; *s.*, Mr. & Mrs. R. J. Hatt. Single. Operator at Electric Palace, T. Heath. *Enl.*, Aug., '14. *D.*, 12 Aug., '17, of wounds recd. in France the prev. day.

HATTEN, —, R.N.
 b., Croydon. *Educ.*, Dering Place Sch., Croydon. *Joined*, '15. *Killed* on H.M.S. " Defence," '16.

HATTEN, WILLIAM, Sgt., R.F.A.
e.s., Mr. & Mrs. W. Hatten, 9 Southbridge Place, Croydon. Married ; 2 children. Empl. by Messrs. Crowley. *Res.*, 17 Southbridge Place, Croydon. *Enl.*, '14. *Fell*, 24 Sept., '18.

HAWKEN, HEDLEY, Cpl., Australian M.-G.Btn.
b., '95 ; *s.*, Squadron Sgt.Maj. & Mrs. Hawken, 107 Richmond Rd., T. Heath. *Educ.*, Winterbourne Rd. Sch., T. Heath. *Res.*, Australia. *Enl.* at Melbourne, Aug., '14 ; served in Egypt, Gallipoli, France ; *w.*, once at Gallipoli, twice in France. *D.*, 12 Aug., '18, of wounds recd. in France 2 days prev.

HAWKINS, KENNETH EDWARDS, Capt., R. Fus.
b., '93 ; 3rd *s.*, late Mr. & Mrs. H. J. Hawkins, " Beaumont," Stanton Rd., Croydon. *Educ.*, King's Sch., Canterbury. Went to France as rflmn. in Q.W. Rif., Nov., '14 ; commis. early in '15. M.C. *D.* of gas poisoning, 21 Mar., '18.

HAWXWELL, CHARLES BAKER, Pte., 12 Middlesex Regt.
b., Battersea, 23 Dec., '80 ; *s.*, late Philip James, & Sarah Jane Hawxwell, 12 Dagmar Rd., S. Norwood. *Educ.*, Whitehorse Rd. Sch., T. Heath. Single. Gardener, Hyde Park. *Enl.*, 18 May, '16. *Fell*, Cherisy, 3 May, '17.

HAYES, ALFRED CHARLES, Pte., 7 E. Sur. Regt.
b., Waddon, '97 ; *e.s.*, Mr. & Mrs. Alfred Charles Hayes, formerly res. Gloucester Rd., Croydon, and Woodside, and now of 32 Malyon's Rd., Ladywell. *Educ.*, Woodside Sch., Croydon ; *w.*, at Philsophe, France, 11 Nov., '16. *Fell*, France, 4 Aug., '17.

HAYTER, C. F., Pte., R.W.S. Regt.
b., '98 ; *s.*, Ex Police-Constable & Mrs. Hayter, Clifton Rd., S. Norwood. *Enl.*, Aug., '14. *Fell*, France, May, '15.

HAYWARD, A., 19242, R.B.
Fell, '16.

HAYWARD, EDWARD JOHN, 2/Lt., 5 R. Fus.
b., 15 Jun., '92 ; *s.*, Mr. & Mrs. John Neal Hayward, Shanghai, China. *Educ.*, Whitgift G. Sch., '07-10. *Fell*, Gallipoli, 15 Nov., '15.

HAZELL, FREDERICK GEORGE, Sapper, R.E.
b., 29 Carmichael Rd., S. Norwood, 12 Feb., '97 ; *s.*, Mr. & Mrs. Frederick George Hazell, 37 Carmichael Rd., S. Norwood. *Educ.*, Birchanger Rd. Sch., and Stanley Tech. Sch., S. Norwood. Single. Electrical engineer. Memb. of St. Mark's C.L.B. *Enl.*, 24 Nov., '14. *Fell*, Ypres, 19 Jan., '16.

HEAD, A. G., 7547, Pte., Lond. Regt.
Res., T. Heath. *Fell*, '16.

HEARTFIELD, A. H., 10900, Pte., 6 D.C.L.I.
s., Mr. & Mrs. Heartfield, 6 Station Rd., S. Norwood. *Enl.*, 28 Aug., '14. *Fell*, 23 Sept., '15. (Plate XII., 1).

HEASMAN, HORACE JAMES, Pte., 6 Lond. Regt. (Rifles.)
b., Dolgelly, N. Wales, 19 Oct., '93 ; *s.* Edgar & Alice H. Heasman, 8 Palmerston Rd., Croydon. *Educ.*, Whitehorse Rd. Sch., T. Heath. Single. Clerk at Army & Navy Stores. *Enl.*, 6 Sept., '14. *Fell*, Loos, 25 Sept., '15.

HEDGES, G., Pte., M.G.C.
b., '82. Married ; 2 children. *Res.*, 64 Farnley Rd., S. Norwood. *Fell*, 24 Jul., '17.

HEGARTY, JOSEPH HAROLD, Pte., M.G.C.
b., Hethpool St., Paddington, '99 ; *s.*, Mr. & Mrs. Hegarty, 62 Saxon Rd., S. Norwood. *Educ.*, Whitehorse Rd. Sch., T. Heath. Single. Apprentice engineer, empl. by Messrs. Turner & Co., Park St., Croydon. *Enl.*, Mar., '17. *D.*, 1 Nov., '18, at 5 Northern Gen. Hosp., Leicester, of wounds recd. at Cambrai, 11 Oct., '18. *Buried*, Queen's Rd. Cem., Croydon, 5 Nov., '18. (Plate XVII., 1).

XIII.

1. Capt. R. B. HERBERT, 13 Lond. Regt. (attd. R.E. Sigs.)
2. Capt. A. L. JAMES, 7 Suff. Regt.
3. Lt. R. Y. HERBERT, 235 Bde., R.F.A.
4. Sgt. A. A. BROOKS, R.E.
5. Sgt. G. E. FOSTER, M.M., Lond. Rif. B.
6. Seaman A. H. GREEN, R.N.

XIV.

1. 2/Lt. H. W. BARNETT, 26 R. Fus.
2. L/Cpl. L. B. GREENHEAD, 12 R. Irish Rif.
3. Rflmn. H. R. JAMESON, 21 Lond. Regt.
4. Sgt. F. W. J. HULETT, M.M., Machine Gun Corps
5. Pte. W. A. HURSEY, R.W.S. Regt.
6. Cpl. W. H. GILLIAM. 1/22 Lond. Regt.

THE GLORIOUS DEAD

HEMMANS, WILLIAM JOHN WEATHERALL, Pte., 10 R. Fus.
  b., '81 ; s., late Maj. S. E. W., & Mrs. Hemmans, Waddon. *Educ.*, Bancroft Sch., Woodford, Essex. Married. Empl. on Stock Exc. *Res.*, 64 Waddon Rd., Croydon. *Enl.*, Aug., '14. *D.*, 5 May, '16, at 19 C.C.S., Doullens, of wounds recd. at Monchy, nr. Arras.
HENDERSON, H. W., Lt., 3 (attd. 24) Manchr. Regt.
  Res., 23 Beatrice Av., Norbury. *D.* of pneumonia, in Italy, 13 Nov., '18.
HENDERSON, PATRICK GORDON, 2/Lt., 2 Duke of Well. (W. Riding) Regt.
  b., Aberdeen, 28 Nov., '98 ; s., Mr. & Mrs. A. Duff Henderson, " Fernwood," Lawrie Pk. Av., Sydenham. *Educ.*, " The Limes," Croydon, " The Hall," Sydenham, & Cheltenham Coll. Single. Student. *Res.*, Sydenham. *Joined*, Oct., '17. *D.*, 2 May, '18, at Netley Hosp., Hants., of wounds recd. in France, 15 Apr., '18.
HENMAN, CHARLES HENRY ROWED, Q.M.Sgt., 1 Field Coy., R.N.D.
  b., '79 : s., Mr. & Mrs. Charles Henman (Architect of Croydon Town Hall), 12 Northcourt Rd., Worthing, and formerly of Croydon. *Educ.*, Whitgift G. Sch. Married. *Fell*, Dardanelles, 29 Jul., '15.
HENRY, CYRIL LLOYD, L/Cpl., 1 H.A.C.
  b., '87. *Fell*, Flanders, 16 Jun., '15.
HENSMAN, E. H., Sgt., 16 Middlesex Regt.
  Asst. Master, Abp. Tenison's Sch., Croydon, since Nov., '04 *Enl.*, Nov., '14. *Fell*, France, 29 Jan., '16.
HENWOOD, JOHN EDWIN, 2/Lt., R.W.S. Regt.
  b., '96 ; 2nd s., Mr. & Mrs. H. J. Henwood, " Ivydene," Bensham Manor Rd., T. Heath. *Enl.*, Aug., '14 ; w., Ypres, Jul., '15. *Accidentally killed*, Egypt, 1 Jul., '16.
HERBERT, ROBERT BINGLEY, Capt., 13 Lond. Regt. (Kensingtons), attd. R.E. Signal Serv.
  b., Park Lane, Croydon, 25 Nov., '82 ; s., Edward & Helen Frances Mather Herbert, Ludford House, Duppas Hill, Croydon. *Educ.*, Bradfield Coll., Berks. Married, Margery, y. daughter of Richard Joseph Grant, of Croydon. Stockbroker. *Res.*, " The Corner House," Links Rd., Epsom. *Enl.* in Kensingtons 5 or 6 yrs. before war ; signals officer, 142 Inf. Bde. *Fell*, nr. " The Tower Bridge," Loos, 30 Sept., '15. (Plate XIII., 1).
HERBERT, RONALD YOUNG, Lt., 235 Bde., R.F.A. (5 Lond. Bde.)
  b., Oakfield Rd., Croydon, 9 Apr. '78 ; s., Edward & Helen Frances Mather Herbert, Ludford House, Duppas Hill, Croydon. *Educ.* by Rev. W. J. Bomford, " Homefield," Sutton, at Bradfield Coll., Berks., & Balliol Coll., Oxford ; 2nd class Hon. in Mod. History, '01 ; M.A. Single. Solicitor. *Joined* as 2/Lt., Aug., '15 ; ment. in despatches, '16. *Fell*, Wytschaete Wood, Flanders, 23 Sept., '17. (Plate XIII., 3).
HEROD, LEONARD WILLIAM, Cpl. (Act.-Sgt.), 7 Northants. Regt.
  b., 107 Cherry Orch. Rd., Croydon, 17 Mar., '94 ; s., Mr. & Mrs. Herod, 109 Cherry Orch. Rd., Croydon. *Educ.*, Oval Rd. Sch., Croydon. Single. Railway clerk. *Res.*, 109 Cherry Orch. Rd., Croydon. *Enl.*, Oct., '14. *Fell*, 17 or 18 Aug., '17.
HERRINGTON, WILLIAM JAMES, Pte., R.W.S. Regt.
  b., '94 ; s., Mr. & Mrs. Herrington, 31 Derby Rd., W. Croydon. *Fell*, 22 Apr., '16.
HERSEY, H., 10938, Pte., R.W.S. Regt.
  Res., W. Croydon. *Fell*, '17.
HERSEY, W., 1 R.W.S. Regt.
  Fell, '15.

HESKETH, JOHN JAMES, Bandsman, 2 R.W.S. Regt.
    b., Caterham, 23 Aug., '97 ; *s.*, John & Ellen Hesketh, 36 Bynes Rd., Croydon. *Educ.*, Caterham. Single. *Res.*, Caterham. *D.* of wounds, 4 Oct., '17.

HEWENS, RONALD C., Pte., Glo'ster Regt.
    s., Mr. & Mrs. Hewens, 56 Buxton Rd., T. Heath. *Educ.*, Boro Sec. Sch., Croydon. Empl. by Messrs. J. & J. Colman, Ltd., of Cannon St., E.C. *Fell*, 31 May, '18.

HEWETT, EDMUND GEOFFREY, Capt., 4 R.W.S. Regt.
    b., 18 Nov., '95 ; *s.*, Mr. & Mrs. Percival William Hewett, Waterfield, Wallington, Surrey. *Educ.*, Whitgift G. Sch., '07-13. *Fell*, Gallipoli, 2 Dec., '15.

HEWITSON, JACK, Pte., Middlesex Regt.
    b., '84. Married. *Res.*, 50 Galpin's Rd., T. Heath. *Fell*, '17.

HEWITT, G., Pte., 11 Essex Regt.
    b., '83 ; *s.*, Mr. & Mrs. Hewitt, 180 Moffatt Rd., T. Heath. *Educ.*, Beulah Rd. Sch., T. Heath. *Enl.* in Middlesex Yeom., Aug., '15 ; proceeded to France, 29 May, '17 ; awarded M.M. and French Croix de Guerre for gallant conduct nr. Dickebush, Ypres, 28 May, '18. *D.* of wounds recd. in France, 2 Jun., '18. *Buried*, Esquelbecq.

HEWITT, J., 6710, R.W.S Regt.
    Res., Croydon. *D.*, while pris. of war in German hands, '17.

HEXTALL, LEONARD JOHN, Lt., Can. Inf.
    b., 6 Nov., '90 ; *s.*, Mr. & Mrs. John Hextall, Canada. *Educ.*, Whitgift G. Sch., '05-06. Ment. in despatches.

HEYWARD, HARRY NEALE, 2/Lt., 2 D.L.I.
    b., Dulwich, '89 ; *3rd s.*, Dr. & Mrs. Heyward, 11 Dornton Rd., Croydon. *Educ.*, Farnham G. Sch., and Durham Univ.; studying for Holy Orders. *Res.*, Castlemaine Av., Norbury. *Joined*, Durham Univ. O.T.C., '14. *Fell*, Somme, 10 Oct., '16.

HEYWARD, MAURICE, Act.-Capt., 8 Dev. Regt.
    b., Dulwich, '91 ; *s.*, Dr. & Mrs. H. Heyward, 11 Dornton Rd., Croydon. *Educ.*, Farnham G. Sch., and King's Coll., London ; B.A., with Hon.; studying for Holy Orders. *Joined* Lond. Univ. O.T.C., '14 ; commis. in Dorset Regt. *Fell*, Somme, 20 Jul., '16.

HICKS, FRANK HAROLD, Cpl., 1 Lond. Regt.
    Educ., M. Whitgift Sch. *Fell*, 30 Oct., '17.

HIDER, HENRY, Pte.
    b., '97 ; *s.*, Mr. & Mrs. Hider, 10 Bensham Lane, T. Heath. *Enl.*, 20 Jan., '15 ; *w.*, early in '17. *Fell*, 20 Sept., '17.

HIERONS, JOHN HENRY, Pte., 13 Glo'ster Regt.
    b., T. Heath, 5 Jan., '81 ; *s.*, Charles & Eliza Hierons. *Educ.*, Beulah Rd. Sch., T. Heath. Married. Bricklayer. *Res.*, 11 Crowland Rd., T. Heath. *Enl.*, 20 Jan.,'17. *Fell*, France, 30 Mar., '18.

HILL, H., Pte., E. Kent Regt.
    b., '80. Married ; 1 child. Groundsman at Purley Downs Golf Links. *Res.*, 84 Bynes Rd., Croydon. *Enl.*, Jun., '16. *Fell*, 3 May, '17.

HILL, REGINALD GORDON, Lt., R.A.M.C.
    b., '87 ; *s.*, Mr. & Mrs. George W. Hill, Highgate. *Educ.*, Chigwell Sch., Whitgift G. Sch., Lond. Univ.& St. Bartholomew's, Hosp., where he graduated M.B., & B.Sc. Married Ivy Elizabeth, daughter of Mr. & Mrs. W. G. Rayner, of " Armaside," Purley. For some time House-surgeon, St. Batholomew's Hosp., House-surgeon, Great Northern Hosp., and first Surgeon to the Ottoman Forces in Tripoli during war between Italy and Turkey. Commis. in R.F.A., '14 ; served in France and Egypt ; later transf. to R.A.M.C. and attd. to Coldstream Gds. ; M.C., '17. *Fell*, 11 Oct., '17.

THE GLORIOUS DEAD 319

HILL, S. G., 48949, Gnr., R.G.A.
 Res., T. Heath. *Fell*, '17.
HILLMAN, HAROLD ALEXANDER MOORE, Lt., 11 Yorks. Regt.
 b., Wallington, Surrey, 1 Feb., '85 ; *s.*, Mr. & Mrs. A. S. Hillman, 12 Quadrant Rd., T. Heath. *Educ.*, High Sch., Croydon. Single. Empl. by Law Guarantee and Trust Soc. Society entertainer. *Enl.* in R. Fus. as pte., Sept., '14. *Fell*, Fricourt, 1 Jul., '16.
HILLS, R., 31052, Pte., S. Lancs. Regt.
 Res., S. Norwood. *Fell*, '17.
HILLYARD, HARRY THOMAS, Act.-Cpl., 1 R.B.
 b., Wandsworth Common, 23 Jul., '99 ; *s.*, Thomas William & Eva Emily Hillyard, 88 St. James' Rd., Croydon. *Educ.*, M. Whitgift & Whitgift G. Schs. Single. Chartered accountant's clerk. *Enl.*, 23 Aug., '17. *Fell*, nr. Drocourt-Queant Switch (Hindenburg line), 1 Sept., '18.
HILTON, ALFRED W., E. Sur. Regt.
 Ex-Croydon Volunteer Fireman.
HINRICH, WALTER, L/Cpl., 9 R.W.S. Regt.
 b., Croydon, 5 Sept., '91 ; *s.*, late Mr. & Mrs. Hinrich, 89 Edward Rd., Croydon. *Educ.*, Woodside Sch., Croydon. Single. Slater and tiler. *Enl.*, Oct., '15. *D.* 1 Jul., '16, of wounds recd. prev. day. *Buried*, Corbie, Somme.
HINTON, A. E., 11048, Pte., D.C.L.I.
 Res., Croydon. *Fell*, '16.
HINTON, W., 6282, Pte., Middlesex Regt.
 Res., Croydon. *Fell*, '17.
HOBBS, ALFRED HERBERT, Leading Signalman, R.N.
 b., Upper Holloway, 20 Nov., '77. *Educ.* Nat., Sch., Brighton. Married. Caretaker, Croydon Gas Coy's Offices. *Joined*, '95 ; served on H.M.S. " Impregnable " ; Somaliland Med.; left the service in '07, and *re-joined* as reservist, Aug., '14, *Lost* with H.M.S. " Cressy," torpedoed in N. Sea, 22 Sept., '14.
HOCKHAM, STEPHEN, Pte., 10 R.B.
 b., Newtown, U. Norwood, 29 Dec., '84 ; *s.*, Mr. & Mrs. Hockham, 22 Eagle Hill, U. Norwood. *Educ.*, Rockmount Rd. Sch., U. Norwood. Married. Labourer. *Res.*, 3 Eagle Hill, U. Norwood. *Enl.*, Sept., '14. *D.*, 25 Aug., '16, at his residence, from the effects of gas poisoning.
HOCKLFY, JESSE, Pte., Duke of Wellington's (W. Riding) Regt.
 Married ; 3 children. Empl. as motor van driver by Whitehorse Laundry. *Res.*, 135 Ecclesbourne Rd., T. Heath. *Enl.*, 16 Feb., '16. *Fell*, Cambrai, 27 Nov., '17.
HODDER, GEORGE JOSEPH, L/Cpl., Northants. Regt.
 b., Penge, 1 Aug., '99 ; *s.*, George Joseph William & Martha Jane Hodder, 57 Wortley Rd., Croydon. *Educ.*, Boston Rd. Sch., Croydon. Single. Asst. druggist. *Enl.*, 9 Oct., '17. *D.*, 27 Sept., '18, at 6 Gen. Hosp., Rouen, of wounds recd. 18 Sept., '18.
HODGE, JOHN PERCIVAL HERMON, 2/Lt., 1/4 Ox. & Bucks. L.I.
 Educ., Summerfield Sch. & Radley Coll. *Joined*, Sept., '14. *Fell*, 28 May, '15.
HODGES, ARTHUR BERKELEY, Pte., 8 Leicester Regt.
 b., Wimbledon, 22 Mar., '99 ; *s.*, Mr. & Mrs. F. Hodges, 92 St. James' Rd., Croydon. *Educ.* by Miss Harlands, at Brit. Sch., Croydon and Clark's Coll. Single. Civil Service clerk. *Res.*, 92 St. James' Rd., Croydon. *Enl.*, Mar., '17. *Killed* by enemy bomb while in Epernay Mil. Hosp., France, where he was recovering from wounds.

THE CROYDON ROLL OF HONOUR

HODGSON, C. M., Lt., R.F.A.
    2nd s., Rev. & Mrs. H. A. Hodgson, Beddington Rectory. *Educ.*, Whitgift G. Sch., '92-01. *D.,* of wounds recd. 17 Jun., '17.

HODGSON, W., 20994, Pte., E. Yorks. Regt.
    Res., Croydon. *Fell,* '16.

HOGG, ERNEST, Pte., R. Fus.
    Fell, '15.

HOGG, H. W., 9673, Driver, R.F.A.
    Res., Mitcham. *Fell,* '17.

HOLDSWORTH, W. H., 8 Manchr. Regt.
    s., Mr. & Mrs. Holdsworth, " Black Boy," Pitlake, Croydon. *Enl.* about '00. *Fell,* Dardanelles, 1 Jun., '15.

HOLLAND, ARTHUR JAMES, Pte., 6 E. Kent Regt.
    b., 42 Waddon New Rd., Croydon, '91 ; *s.*, Arthur James & Annie Holland, 4 Derby Grove, Croydon. *Educ.,* Par. Ch. Sch., Croydon. Single. Undertaker's coachman. *Enl.,* 9 Aug., '17. *Fell,* Epehy, 18 Sept., '18.

HOLLAND, FRANK, Trooper, 3 Bde., 1 Can. Contingent.
    b., 28 Nov., '83 ; *s.*, Mr. & Mrs. Walter Holland. *Educ.,* Whitgift G. Sch., '99-02. *Fell,* Flanders, 17 Jun., '15.

HOLLANDS, ALBERT EDWARD, Pte., 4 King's L/pool Regt.
    b., 74 Addison Rd., S. Norwood, 9 Nov., '95 ; *s.*, Charles & Annie Hollands, 57 Addison Rd., S. Norwood. *Educ.,* Birchanger Rd. Sch., S. Norwood. Single. Asst. pastry cook. *Enl.,* 9 Jan., '16. *Fell,* France, 22 Apr., '17.

HOLMAN, GEORGE, Cpl., R.W.S. Regt.
    W., Nov., '14. *Fell,* France, 22 Aug., '15.

HOLMES, C., Sgt.
    Married ; 3 children. *Res.*, 135 Southbridge Rd., Croydon. *Fell,* 9 Aug., '18.

HOLMES, EDWARD MARMADUKE, L/Cpl., Middlesex Regt.
    b., 41 Fontarabia Rd., Clapham, 23 Apr., '93 ; *s.*, Mr. & Mrs. Edward Holmes, 46 Selhurst Rd., S. Norwood. *Educ.,* T. Heath Sch. (Mr. Davies). Single. Corn dealer. *Enl.,* 18 May, '16. *Fell,* Geauzecourt, nr. Peronne, 9 Apr., '17.

HOLMES, HAROLD RALPH, Rflmn., Lond. Regt.
    b., '97 ; *s.*, Mr. & Mrs. E. A. Hardy, Sunbury House, Mitcham Rd., Croydon. *Educ.,* Boro. Sec. Sch., Croydon. Bank clerk, Lond. City & Mid. Bank. *Enl.,* '16. *Fell,* France, 16 Aug., '17.

HOLMES, HUBERT HAROLD, Pte., 22 R. Fus.
    b., St. Paul's, Deptford, 23 Feb., '89 ; *s.*, Mr. & late Mrs. George Holmes. 24 Bredon Rd., Croydon. *Educ.,* Birchanger Rd. Sch., S. Norwood. Single. Clerk at E. Croydon Stn. *Enl.,* 2 Jun.,'16. *Fell,* Petit Miraumont, 17 Feb., '17.

HOLMES, SYDNEY EWART, Pte., 7 R. Fus.
    b., Leicester, 18 Nov., '91 ; *s.*, Mr. & Mrs. Frances Holmes, 59 Collier's Water Lane, T. Heath. *Educ.,* Whitehorse Rd. Sch., T. Heath & Boro. Sec. Sch., Croydon. Single. Clerk. *Enl.,* 3 Apr., '16. *Fell,* France, 13 Nov., '16.

HOLYMAN, C. W.
    b., '77. *Educ.,* Whitgift G. Sch. *Fell,* '17.

HOLYMAN, LESLIE EBENEZER, 2/Lt., 1/5 R.W. Kent Regt.
    b., 23 Jun., '93 ; *s.*, Mr. & Mrs. Ebenezer Holyman, "Glendower," Woodcote Rd., Wallington. *Educ.,* Whitgift G. Sch., '03-06.

HONE, GILBERT BENTOIT, 2/Lt., R.F.A.
    s., Mr. & Mrs. Daniel Hone, S. Norwood. *Fell,* 18 Aug., '17.

HOOK, FREDERICK GEORGE, Pte., Manchr. Regt.
    b., 33 Basing Rd., Peckham. Married. *Res.,* 3 Sunny Croft Rd., S. Norwood. *Enl.,* in R.W.S. Regt. *Fell,* France, 23 Apr., '17.

XV.

1. Gnr. J. H. Mugford, R.G.A.
2. Pte. J. A. Mitchell, 1/5 Seaforth H.
3. Pte. E. G. Gatland, 2/4 R.W.S. Regt.
4. L/Cpl. W. R. George, Artists Rif.
5. A.B. Seaman S. H. Letts, R.N.
6. Pte. A. Gibbs, 1 R.W.S. Regt.

XVI.

1. Pte. E. W. H. KNELL, Civ. Serv. Rif. (15 Lond. Regt.)
2. Signaller P. KENT, R.W.S. Regt.
3. 2/Lt. J. J. LANGFORD, 18 King's R.R.C.
4. Pte. C. F. KIRSCH, Lancs. Fus.
5. Trooper E. S. JONES, 20 Hussars
6. 2/Lt. W. G. LANGFORD, 18 King's R.R.C

THE GLORIOUS DEAD

HOOK, J., 4821, R.W.S. Regt.
Res., W. Croydon. *D.*, while prisoner in German hands, '17.

HOOKE, JOHN CLEMENT, Pte., 14 Aust. I.F.
b., 14 May, '79; *s.*, John & Avis Hooke, 23 Birdhurst Rise, Croydon. *Educ.*, Whitgift G. Sch., '89-94. *Served* in S.A War with C.I.V.; S.A. Med., 2 clasps for Modder River & Paardeburg. *D.* of pneumonia, Egypt, 7 Mar., '15.

HOOKE, UTTEN LAMONT, Lt.-Col., 3/4 R.W.S. Regt.
y.s., John & Avis Hooke, 23 Birdhurst Rise, Croydon. Married, Enid Ayesha, daughter of Mr. & Mrs. Wyndham Brodie, of Wylde Green, Birmingham : 1 son. Director of Teetgen & Coy., Ltd. *Res.*, 68 Park Lane, Croydon. *Enrolled* in the 2nd Volunteer Btn. of R. Suss. Regt., '99-00 ; served with a commis. in 1st Volunteer Btn., R.W.S. Regt., '05-07 ; transf. to Terr ; Capt., 7 Jan., '07 ; Maj., 7 Mar., '10 ; Lt.-Col., 5 May, '15 ; posted to 2/4 R.W.S. Regt., 17 Nov., '14. and to 3/4 R.W.S. Regt. 17 Apr., '15. *Fell*, Roeux, France, 21 Jun., '17.

HOOKER, E. D., 19738, Pte., Border Regt.
Res., Croydon. *Fell*, '17.

HOOLE, R. H., 2/Lt., R.W.S. Regt.
Fell, '16.

HOOPER, J., 47833, Pte., Northd. Fus
Res., T. Heath. *Fell*, '17.

HOOTON, EDWARD CEDRIC, Lt., R. Warwick. Regt
b., '91 : *y.s.*, late Mr., & Mrs. Edward Charles Hooton, 1 Chepstow Rise, Croydon. *Fell*, 26 or 27 Jun., '16. (Plate XXXII., 2).

HOPE, BERTIE FREDERICK, 7155, Pte., 1 R.W.S. Regt.
b., W. Firle, Suss., 28 Jun., '85. Married. Labourer. *Res.*, 192 Gloucester Rd., E. Croydon. Called up on res., 5 Aug., '14. *Fell*, Ypres, 6 Nov., '14.

HOPKINS, ERNEST, Sapper, R.E.
b., Brighton Rd., Croydon, 22 Jun., '91 ; *s.*, Robert Walter & Elizabeth Hopkins, 10 Beaconsfield Rd., Croydon. *Educ.*, Brighton Rd. Sch., Croydon, & Hook Rd. Sch., Epsom. Single. Carpenter. *Enl.*, 6 Apr., '15. *D.* of dysentery, 31 Gen. Hosp., Port Said, 17 May, '16.

HOPKINS, LAURENCE HILTON, Capt., 1/1 Huntingdonshire Regt., attd. 1 Cambs. Regt.
b., "The Rectory," Chigwell Row, Essex, 30 Jan., '92 ; *s.*, Mr. and Mrs. Hopkins, Woodmansterne Rd., Purley. *Educ.*, St. John's Sch., Leatherhead. Single. Engineer. *Res.*, Peterborough and Purley (from '16). *Enl.*, as pte., 3 Sept., '14. *Fell*, Dublain St. Nazair, France, 7 Oct., '18.

HORN, G. A., 17337, Pte., R. Berks. Regt.
Res., Croydon. *Fell*, '17.

HORNBY, E. R.

HORNETT, MICHAEL JAMES, Pte., 3/4 R.W.S. Regt.
b., Croydon, 1 Apr., '83 ; 2nd *s.*, late Mr. & Mrs. John Hornett, Keeley Rd., Croydon. *Educ.*, St. Mary's Sch., Wellesley Rd., Croydon. Married. Dairyman. *Res.*, 5 Tamworth Rd., W. Croydon. *Enl.*, 7 Jun., '16. *Fell*, France, 22 Oct., '17.

HORNETT, WILLIAM ROBERT, Pte., 9 E. Sur. Regt.
b., London, 9 Dec., '87 ; *s.*, Mr. & Mrs. William Hornett, 112 Old Town, Croydon. *Educ.*, St. Mary's Sch., Croydon. Married. Decorator. *Res.*, Percy Rd., S. Norwood. *Enl.*, Oct., '14 : *w.*, 28 Feb., '16. *Fell*, Delville Wood, 3 Sept., '16.

HORNEY, GORDON ARTHUR, Pte., Lond. Regt.
  b., Croydon, 13 Nov., '98 ; s., Arthur & Decima Horney, "Knapdale," St. James' Rd., Croydon. Educ., Par. Ch. Sch., Croydon. Single. Sign writer. Enl., Feb., '17 ; w., Egypt, '18. D. of wounds recd. in France, 28 Jul., '18 ; buried, Mont Noir Cem., St. Jans Cappel, nr. Poperinghe.

HORNSBY, ERNEST RICHARD.
  y.s., Mr. & Mrs. W. E. Hornsby, London Rd., Croydon. M.M. D. of wounds at 55 C.C.S., France, 14 Nov., '18.

HORTON, CYRIL AUBREY, Pte., Aust. I.F.
  b., 20 Apr., '96 ; s., Mr. & Mrs. Emmanuel William Horton, "Sunnylands," Hinton Rd., Wallington. Educ., Whitgift G. Sch. Fell, Gallipoli.

HOSKINS, S., Sgt., R.F.C.
  Empl. by Croydon Corp. Roads Dept. D. of bronchial pneumonia, '18.

HOWARD, ALBERT EDWARD, Pte., M.G.C.
  Educ., Par. Ch. Sch., Croydon. Married. Carman. Res., Adelaide Cottage, Adelaide St., Croydon. Enl., 16 Aug., '17. D., 26 Mar., '18, at 41 Stat. Hosp., of wounds recd. on Somme prev. day.

HOWARD, CHARLES EDWIN, Sgt., 2 Border Regt.
  b., Brockley, 14 Feb., '87 ; s., Mr. & Mrs. Howard, 124 Foxbury Rd., Brockley. Educ., Brockley Rd. Sch. Married. Motorman. Res., 29 Guildford Rd., Croydon. Enl., 3 Aug., '14. Fell, France, 28 Feb., '17.

HOWARD, HENRY VINCENT, Sub-Lt., R.N.V.R.
  b., Bethnal Green, 17 Oct., '90 ; s., Mr. & Mrs. Howard, "Moineau Lodge," Longstock, Stockbridge, Hants. Educ., Salway Coll., Leytonstone, Essex. Single. Audit clerk. Res., 20 St. John's Gr., Croydon. Enl., as seaman, 8 Sept., '14. Fell, Ancre, 13 Nov., '16.

HOWARD, HERBERT, L/Cpl., 10 R.Fus.
  Married. Head gardener, "Belmont," Radcliffe Rd., Croydon. Res., 17 Northway Rd., Croydon. Enl., 29 Jul., '16. Fell, Frampaux, nr. Arras, 23 Apr., '17. (Plate XII., 4).

HOWARD, L. B., 9529, Pte., R.W.S. Regt.
  Res., S. Norwood. Fell, '16.

HOWELL, PERCY VICTOR GEORGE, Pte., Can. A.M.C.
  b., Croydon, 24 Oct., '83 ; s., Mr. & Mrs. G. F. Howell, 66 Limes Rd., Croydon. Educ., Brit. Sch., Croydon. Married. Empl. on hosp. staff. Res., London, Ontario. Enl., Sept., '15. D., 12 Mar., '18, at St. Pol Mil. Hosp., France, of wounds recd. at Passchendaele Ridge, 9 Mar., '18.

HOWLETT, ARTHUR ALFRED, L/Cpl., E. Sur. Regt.
  b., Southbridge Rd., Croydon, 31 Oct., – ; s., Mr. & Mrs. Howlett, 44 Priory Rd., Croydon. Educ., Mitcham Rd. Sch., Croydon. Single. Carman. Res., 113 Wentworth Rd., Croydon. Enl., 8 Jan., '11. Fell, France, 25 Apr., '15.

HOWLETT, ERNEST GEORGE, Pte., 7 R.W.S. Regt.
  b., S. Croydon ; s., Mr. & Mrs. R. Howlett, 44 Priory Rd., Croydon. Educ., Mitcham Rd. Sch., Croydon. Single. Syphonfiller. Enl., 27 Feb., '15. Fell, France, 1 Jul., '16.

HOWLETT, GEORGE CHARLES, Sapper, R.E.
  b., Kennington, 20 Feb., '96 ; s., Mr. & Mrs. Howlett, 33 Ion Rd., T. Heath. Educ., Whitehorse Rd. Sch., T. Heath. Single. Gas fitter. Enl., 5 Sept., '13. Discharged, unfit for further service, 20 Jan., '16. D. at his home, 23 Oct., '16.

THE GLORIOUS DEAD

HOY, JOB (JOE), Cpl., 1 R.W.S. Regt.
 b., '94 ; *s.*, Mr. & Mrs. Hoy, 30 Holmesdale Rd., S. Norwood. Married. *Enl.*, '14 ; served in France, '14 (Mons)-'18 ; twice *w.* and gassed. *Fell,* France, 21 Sept., '18.

HUBBARD, CHARLIE F., Pte., Dev. Regt.
 b., '95 ; *y.s.*, Mr. & Mrs. G. Hubbard, late of 21 Derby Rd., Croydon. Empl. by Croydon Co-Operative Soc. *Enl.*, '14 ; *w.*, Oct., '15. *Fell,* 1 Aug., '17.

HUBBLE, FREDERICK RICHARD, 2/Lt., R.Å.S.C. (M.T.)
 b., Hunton, nr. Maidstone, Kent, 11 Feb., '80 ; *s.*, Mr. & Mrs. W. W. Hubble, " The Elms," Hunton, nr. Maidstone. *Educ.,* Chatham House, Ramsgate. Married. Hop factor. *Res.*, 46 Chisholm Rd., Croydon. *Enl.* as pte., 30 Nov., '15. *D.*, 2 Aug., '18, at 10 Stat. Hosp., St. Omer, of concussion, incurred nr. St. Omer, 24 Jul., '18.

HUGGETT, HAROLD CHARLES, Rflmn., K.R.R.C.
 b., Deptford, 2 Feb., '99 ; *s.*, Mr. & Mrs. E. A. Huggett, 4 Meadvale Rd., Croydon. *Educ.,* Mantle Rd. Sch., Brockley, & Clark's Coll., New Cross. Single. Clerk. *Enl.*, 15 Mar., '17. *Fell,* Flavey le Martel, France, 21 Mar., '18.

HUGGETT, W., 1252, Pte., R. Fus.
 Res., Croydon. *Fell,* '16.

HUGHES, E., 88415, Pte., Lab. Corps.
 Res., S. Norwood. *Fell,* '17.

HUGHES, GORDON MCGREGOR, 2/Lt., R. Berks. Regt.
 b., 22 Dec., '94 ; *s.*, Mr. & Mrs. Alfred McGregor Hughes, Newlands Pk., Sydenham. *Educ.,* " The Hall," Sydenham, and Whitgift G. Sch., '09-11. *Enl.* in L.R.B., '14 ; trench feet, '14 ; commis., '15. *Fell,* 8 Aug., '16.

HULETT, EZRA JAMES STANNELL, Signaller, 67 Coy., M.G.C.
 b., Eversley, Hants, 18 Jul., '97 ; *s.*, Frederick & Emily Hulett, 14 Grasmere Rd., Woodside. *Educ.,* Birchanger Rd. Sch., S. Norwood, and Skerry's Coll., Croydon. Single. Solicitor's clerk. *Enl.* in 24 Middlesex, Nov., '15. *D.* of malarial fever, at 29 Gen. Hosp., Salonica, 22 Oct., '16. ■(Plate XVII., 3).

HULFORD, GEORGE ERVIN, Gnr., R.F.A.
 b., '93 ; *e.s.*, Mr. & Mrs. Hulford, 88 Waddon New Rd., Croydon. Seaman, empl. by Shaw, Saville & Albion Line. *Enl.*, Feb., '15 ; *w.*, twice in '17. *Fell,* 9 Dec., '17.

HUMPHREY, H. E., 61897, Pte., R. Fus.
 Res., T. Heath. *Fell,* '17.

HUMPHREY, W. J., E. Sur. Regt.
 b., '86. Married. *Res.*, Sussex Rd., Croydon. *D.* of wounds recd., France, 10 Jan., '16.

HUMPHREYS, PERCY G., Cpl., 6 R.W.S. Regt.
 Empl. by Croydon Gas Coy. *Res.*, Caterham. *Enl.*, in Territorials prev. to war ; served in India 22 months. *Fell,* Arras, 9 Apr., '17.

HUMPHREYS, STANLEY HOWARD, 2/Lt., E. Sur. Regt.
 Fell, Cambrai, 20 Nov., '17.

HUMPHRIES, WALTER WILLIAM, Pte., 7 E. Kent Regt.
 b., 5 Mitcham Rd., Croydon, 1 L Jan., '98 ; *2nd s.*, late Mr. & Mrs. John Humphries, 5 Mitcham Rd., Croydon. *Educ.,* Christ Ch. Sch., Croydon, and Sir John Cass Tech. Inst. Empl. as metal refiner by Messrs. Johnson, Matthey & Co., assayers. *Enl.*, 12 Jan., '17. *Fell,* Poelcapelle, 12 Oct., '17.

324   THE CROYDON ROLL OF HONOUR

HUNT, ALFRED JOHN, Gnr., R.F.A.
b., Barking, 17 Apr., '97 ; s., Mr. & Mrs. A. J. Hunt, 18 Jesmond Rd., Croydon. Single. Enl., Aug., '15. Fell, France, 7 May, '17.

HUNT, ARTHUR WILLIAM, Sgt., 8. R.W.S. Regt.
b., 12 Apr., '94 ; y.s., Mr. & Mrs. Hunt, 22 St. John's Rd., Croydon. Educ., Par. Ch. Sch., Croydon. Single. Clerk, empl. by Messrs. Rickett Smith. Enl., in Terr., '08 ; awarded certificate for distinguished conduct in the field, 22-31 Oct., '17. D. of wounds recd. in France, 6 Nov., '18.

HUNT, CYRIL GLADSTONE, Sapper, 4 Field Survey Coy. R.E.
b., Grayshott, Hants., 10 May, '98 ; 2nd s., Mr. & Mrs. William Charles Hunt, 154 Frant Rd., T. Heath. Educ., Boro. Sec. Sch., Croydon. Civil Service clerk (Inland Rev.). Enl., Feb., '17, in Civil Service Rif. (15 Lond. Regt.) ; transf. to K.R.R.C. ; w., 27 Aug., '17 ; transf. to R.E. Fell, Broodseinde, Ypres, 9 Apr., '18. Buried, Potizge Chateau Cem., Ypres.

HUNT, ERNEST JOHN, Torpedo Instructor, R.N.
b., '85 ; e.s., Mr. & Mrs. John Hunt, 58 Love Lane, S. Norwood. Educ., Birchanger Rd. Sch., S. Norwood. Married ; 2 children. Joined when 16 years old. Fell, Jan., '18.

HUNT, G. VICTOR, 1 E. Sur. Regt.
b., '98. D. of wounds recd. at Hill 60, 22 May, '15.

HUNT, HAROLD ARTHUR, Sgt., 10 Can. Cont.
s., Mr. & Mrs. Edward Allen Hunt, 17 Eileen Rd., S. Norwood. D., 1 Jun., '15, at Boulogne, of wounds recd., France, 22 May, '15.

HUNT, HARRY WILLIAM KINGSWELL, Trooper, 2 King Edward's Horse.
b., 21 Nov., '82 ; s., Mr. & Mrs. George Henry Hunt, " Leecroft," St. Peter's Rd., Croydon. Educ., Whitgift G. Sch., '96-00. Married. Served in S.A. War. Fell, Flanders.

HUNT, J., 6744, Middlesex Regt.
Res., Croydon. Fell. '17.

HUNT, LESLIE ERNEST, Pte., R. Fus.
b., '87 ; 2nd s., Mr. & Mrs. G. H. Hunt, 70 Bedford Court Mans., London, W.C., and formerly of Croydon. Married. Res., 20 Wydehurst Rd., Croydon. D., 24 Oct., '17, of wounds recd. prev. day.

HUNT, LOUIS GORDON, 2/Lt., Q.V. Rif. (9 Lond. Regt.)
b., Streatham, 7 Nov., '98 ; y.s., F. A. & E. A. Hunt, 112 Brighton Rd., Croydon. Educ., Boro. Sec. Sch., Croydon. Single. Clerk. Enl., as rflmn. in 5 Lond. Regt., 8 May, '16. Fell, Epehy, 22 Sept., '18.

HUNT, T. R., 1563, Pte., R.W.S. Regt.
Fell, '16.

HUNTER, ALEXANDER F., 2/Lt.
Res., S. Norwood. Fell, 23 May, '16.

HURSEY, WILLIAM AUGUSTUS, Pte., R.W.S Regt.
b., Oak Cottage, Caterham, 20 Jul., '97 ; s., late Mr. & Mrs. Hursey, Court Rd., Caterham. Educ., Caterham Counc. Sch. Single. Under-gardener. Enl., 3 Sept., '13. Fell, France, 18 Jan., '15. (Plate XIV., 5).

HYDE, P. C., 65052, Pte., Lab. Corps.
Res., S. Croydon. D. of wounds, '17.

IDLE, ARTHUR WILBERFORCE, L/Cpl., 5 Lond. Regt. (L.R.B.)
b., Clapham, 14 Oct., '90 ; e.s., Mr. & Mrs. Idle, 42 Dagnall Pk., Croydon. Educ., Sydenham Rd. Sch., & Boro. Sec. Sch., Croydon. Single. Traveller. Enl., 5 Aug., '14 ; served in France, Nov., '14-Mar., '18. Missing, France, Mar., '18.

THE GLORIOUS DEAD

IDLE, GEORGE STEPHEN, Rflmn., Civil Serv. Rif. (15 Lond. Regt.)
 b., Clapham, 12 Mar., '92 ; 2nd s., Mr. & Mrs. Idle, 42 Dagnall Pk., Croydon. *Educ.*, Sydenham Rd. Sch., & Boro. Sec. Sch., Croydon. Single. Insurance clerk. *Enl.*, 31 Aug., '14. *D.*, 4 Jul., '16, at Newport, Mons., of wounds recd. nr. Bethune, Nov., '15.

IGOEA, W. E., 20808. Gnr., R.F.A.
 b., '98. *Res.*, 58 Croydon Gr., Croydon. *D.* of wounds, France, 5 Apr., '16.

ILES, H., 25529, Pte., E. Sur. Regt.
 b., Croydon, '85. *Educ.*, Oval Rd. Sch., Croydon. Married. *Fell*, 12 Oct., '17.

ILLOTT, F. H., 71373, Sgt., R.F.A.
 Res., Croydon. *Fell*, '17.

IMISON, ARTHUR ERNEST, Sapper, R.E. Sig. Coy.
 b., St. Andrew's St., Wandsworth Rd., Clapham, 19 Sept., '98 ; s., Richard George & Rosa Maria Imison, 26 Notson Rd., S. Norwood. *Educ.*, Woodside, Bynes Rd., & Sydenham Rd. Schs., Croydon, & Tennyson St. Sch., Battersea. Single. Booking clerk, L.B.& S.C.R. *Enl.*, 26 Apr., '15. *Fell*, N. of Ypres, 12 Jun., '17. Buried in cem. on banks of Yser Canal.

INGHAM, J., 94792, Gnr., R.F.A.
 b., '94 ; s., Mr. & Mrs. Ingham, 107 Sutherland Rd., Croydon. *Enl.*, '14 ; w., Loos, '15. *D.*, of fever contracted in Mesopotamia, '17.

INGRAM, FREDERICK, Sgt., Middlesex Regt.
 b., '81. Married. *Fell*, 3 Jan., '18.

INGRAMS, FRANK RIDLEY, Capt., 9 E. Sur. Regt.
 b., 8 Dec., '97 ; s., Mr. & Mrs. Frank Charles Ingrams, 7 Birdhurst Rd., Croydon. *Educ.*, M. Whitgift Sch., & Whitgift G. Sch., Croydon,'12-14. Ment. in despat., '16 ; M.C., Sept., '16. *Fell*, Delville Wood, Somme, 3 Sept., '16.

INKERMAN, GEORGE J., A.B. Seaman, R.N.

INMAN, T., Gnr., R.F.A.
 b., '89 ; 2nd s., Mr. & Mrs. Inman, 87 Waddon New Rd., Croydon. Married. Hairdresser. *Enl.*, '17. *Fell*, 2 Oct., '18.

INNES, J. S. D'A., Lt., R.F.A.
 b., '87 ; y.s., Mr. & Mrs. C. E. S. Innes, 5 Bingham Rd., Addis. Married. *Res.*, 20 Grasmere Rd., S. Norwood. M.C. *Fell*, 5 Aug., '17.

INNOCENT, E. J., Lt., R.W. Kent Regt.
 Fell, '16.

ISAACS, HENRY ROLAND, 2/Lt., Suff. Regt.
 b., 20 Feb., '97 ; s., Mr. & Mrs. Joseph A. Isaacs, 140 Lr. Addis. Rd., Croydon. *Educ.*, Whitgift G. Sch., '12-13. *Enl.* in Artists Rif. *Fell*, France, '17.

IVESON, EDWIN, Pte., R.W.S. Regt.
 b., Hackney, 9 Oct., '93 ; s., William James & Frances Iveson, 111 Woodville Rd., T. Heath. *Educ.*, Ecclesbourne Rd. Sch., T. Heath. Single. Photo process photographer. *Enl.*, in Sur. Yeom., 18 Oct., '14 ; served in Italy, France, & Dardanelles. *Fell*, Achiet-le-Grand, 22 Mar., '18.

IVISON, EDGAR SYDNEY, Gnr., R.F.A.
 Educ., M. Whitgift Sch. Drowned, 23 Oct., '15.

IVORY, JOHN ARTHUR, Lt., M.G.C. (attd. R.N.D.)
 b., '95 ; s., Mr. & Mrs. A. J. Ivory, Coulsdon. *Educ.*, Whitgift G. Sch. Served in France, '16-18 ; w., Ypres, May, '17 ; shell shock, '18. *Fell*, 27 Sept., '18

JACKSON, A. E., Pte., 3 R. Fus.
  b., S. Norwood, 22 Jan., '95 ; s., David & Sarah Jackson, 29 Kynaston Rd., T. Heath. *Educ.*, Birchanger Rd. Sch., S. Norwood. Single. Apprentice compositor. *Res.*, 29 Kynaston Rd., T. Heath. *Enl.*, 7 Sept., '14 ; trained at Falmouth ; went to France, 27 Feb., '15. *Fell*, Ypres, 24 May, '15.

JACKSON, E. R., Pte., R.W.S. Regt.
  Empl. by Messrs. Page & Overton, Croydon. *Res.*, 102 Mitcham Rd., Croydon. *Enl.*, 1 Nov., '14. *Fell*, 25 Sept., '15.

JACKSON, F., Cpl., R. Fus.
  Educ., Par. Ch. Sch., Croydon. Married. *Res.*, 58 Church St., Croydon. *Fell*, 14 Mar., '17.

JACKSON, HENRY STEWARD, Lt., K.O.Y.L.I.
  b., 23 Aug., '95 ; s., Rev. & Mrs. Sydney Jackson, 12 Graham Rd., Mitcham. *Educ.*, St. John's Sch., Leatherhead, & Whitgift G. Sch., '08-11. Medical student at Lond. Univ.

JACKSON, STEPHEN, Pte., Essex Regt.
  2nd s., Mr. & Mrs. Jackson, 33 Lodge Rd., Croydon. Married ; 1 child. *Enl.*, '15. *Fell*, 11 Jul., '17.

JACKSON, WALTER JAMES, Pte., 2 R.W.S. Regt.
  b., Croydon, 5 Apr., '93 ; s., Mr. & Mrs. Jackson, 57 Exeter Rd., Croydon. *Educ.*, Woodside Sch., Croydon. Single. Labourer. *Enl.*, 6 May, '15. *Fell*, Delville Wood, Somme, 1 Sept., '16.

JACOBS, A. J.
  Res., Surrey St., Croydon. *D.* in Italy, 29 Oct., '18.

JAMES, ARTHUR LING, Capt., 7 Suff. Regt.
  b., Bury St. Edmunds, 15 Aug., '84 ; s., A. & H. E. James, "Newbury," Quadrant Rd., T. Heath. *Educ.*, Soham G. Sch. Single. Civil Service clerk (India Office). Served in Territorials for 6 years prior to war ; mobilised with Civil Service Btn., as signal sgt., 12 Aug., '14 ; commis, 9 Sept., '14. *Fell*, Mouquet Farm, France, 8 Aug., '16. (Plate XIII., 2).

JAMES, THOMAS, Cpl., Demonstration Coy.
  Married. *Res.*, 4 Theobald Rd., Croydon. *Fell*, 30 Mar., '18.

JAMES, THOMAS SPENCER, Rflmn., 12 Lond. Regt.
  b., Ely, Cambs., 30 Oct., '91 ; s., A. & H. C. James, "Newbury," Quadrant Rd., T. Heath. *Educ.*, M. Whitgift Sch. Single. Insurance clerk. Member of Norwood Cricket Club, & Addis. Park Football Club. *Enl.*, 14 Aug., '14 ; served in France, 25 Dec., '14-May, '15. *D.*, 8 May, '15, of wounds recd. at Fortuen, Ypres, 2 days prev. Buried, Hazebrouck.

JAMES, WILLIAM, Gnr., R.F.A.
  b., '86. Married ; 1 child. Empl. by Croydon Gas Coy., as lamplighter. *Enl.*, May, '16. *D.* of gas poisoning, France, 21 Oct., '18.

JAMESON, HAROLD RISBOROUGH, Rflmn., 1 Sur. Rif. (21 Lond. Regt.)
  b., W. Norwood, 16 Jun., '92 ; s., William Alexander & Emma Risborough Jameson, "Hill View," Godstone Rd., Kenley. *Educ.*, M. Whitgift Sch., Croydon. Single. Bank clerk, Anglo S. Amer. Bank. *Enl.*, 10 Aug., '14. *D.*, 4 Apr., '15, at Bethune, of wounds recd. at Richebourg, prev. day. (Plate XIV., 3).

JAMIESON, C., 24128, Pte., S.W.B.
  Res., S. Norwood. *Fell*, '17.

JARMAN, A. W., 1845, Pte., R. Suss. Regt.
  Fell, '16.

JARRETT, THOMAS, Cpl.

THE GLORIOUS DEAD. 327

JASTRZEBSKI, HUBERT STEPHEN SLEPOWRON DE, 2/Lt., 24 Lond. Regt.
b., Harringay, 25 Mar., '95 ; *s.*, Thaddeus Theodore Slepowron de Jastrzebski & Frances Elizabeth Slepowron de Jastrzebska, 102 Avondale Rd., S. Croydon. *Educ.*, Whitgift G. Sch. Single. Empl. by Central Insurance Coy., Cornhill, E.C. *Enl.*, in 5 Lond. Regt. (L.R.B.), Sept., '13 ; *w.*, Ypres, May, '15, & Feb., '16 ; commis., Aug., '15. *D.*, 5 Apr., '17, at 5 C.C.S., of wounds recd. at Havrincourt Wood prev. day. (Plate XVII., 6).

JAY, CECIL A., N. Staff. Regt.
Res., Hillcrest, St. Mary's Rd., S. Norwood. *Fell*, 23 Jan., '18.

JEAL, A. E., 47934, Pte., R. Fus.
Res., Croydon. *D.* of wounds, '17.

JEE, ALBERT ARTHUR, L/Cpl., 18 Northd. Fus.
b., Croydon, 15 Mar., '95 ; *s.*, Mr. & Mrs. George Jee, 50 Dennet Rd., Croydon. *Educ.*, Mitcham Rd. Sch., Croydon. Married. Gas fitter. *Res.*, 50 Dennett Rd., Croydon. *Enl.*, 10 Apr., '16. *Fell*, Meulehouck, N. of Bailleul, 17 Apr., '18. *Buried*, Meulehouck.

JEFFERY, ALBERT CHARLES, Pte., 7 Norf. Regt.
b., 2 Lambeth Rd., Croydon, 18 Sept., '99 ; *s.*, Mr. & Mrs. Louis W. Jeffery, 2 Lambeth Rd., Croydon. *Educ.*, Christ Ch. Sch., Croydon. Single Shop asst. *Enl.*, 16 Oct., '17. *Fell*, France, 18 Sept , '18.

JEFFERY, PERCY, 9 Aust. I.F.
Educ., M. Whitgift Sch. Empl. by Nat. Bank of Australia. *Fell*, Dardanelles, '15.

JEFFREY, F. T., 492430, Pte., Lond. Regt.
Res., Norbury. *Fell*, '17.

JENKIN, T. R., Rflmn., 5 R.B.
Res., 8 Exeter Rd., Addis. *Fell*, nr. Cambrai, 27 Sept., '18.

JENKINS, EDWARD HENRY, Act.-Coy.Sgt.Maj., 7 R.W.S.Regt.
b., St. James, London, W., 14 Jul., '89 ; *s.*, Mr. & Mrs. H. Jenkins, 123 Edridge Rd., Croydon. *Educ.*, Kilburn Counc. Sch., and Wanstead Counc. Sch. Single. Commercial clerk. *Enl.*, 9 Sept., '14. *Fell*, Trones Wood, Somme, 13-14 Jul., '16.

JENNER. ARTHUR PHILIP, Cpl., 6 R.W.S. Regt.
b., Kenley, 7 Jan., '93 ; *e.s.*, Philip & Sarah Jenner, 24 Kemble Rd., Croydon. *Educ.*, Par. Ch. Sch., Croydon. Single. Stockman. *Res.*, 1 Waddon Court Rd., Croydon. *Enl.*, in 2/4 R.W.S. Regt., 15 Aug., '16. *Fell*, Arras, 9 Apr., '17.

JENNER, FRANK ALFRED, Rflmn., 53 R.B.
b., Croydon, 12 Aug., '00 ; *s.*, Philip & Sarah Jenner, 24 Kemble Rd., Croydon. *Educ.*, Par. Ch. Sch., Croydon. Single. Jeweller's asst. *Enl.*, 12 Sept., '18. *D.* of pneumonia following influenza, Wellingborough Hosp., 19 Oct., '18.

JESSOP, F. E., 4246, L/Sgt., Lond. Regt.
Res., T. Heath. *Fell*, '16.

JEWELL, HAROLD WILLIAM, Pte., 2/4 R.W.S Regt.
b., Croydon, 21 Nov., '95 ; *s.*, Sgt. William & Elizabeth M. Jewell, 12 St. John's Gr., Croydon. *Educ.*, Brit. Sch., Croydon. Single. Draper's asst. *Enl.*, 15 Sept., '14. *Fell*, Gallipoli, 9 Aug., '15.

JEX, ERNEST WASHINGTON, Gnr., R.F.A.
b., Croydon, 22 Nov., '97 ; *s.*, W. & Mary Jex, 60 Waddon New Rd., Croydon. *Educ.*, Bynes Rd. Sch., Croydon. Single. Messenger lad. *Enl.*, Oct., '12. *Fell*, Ypres, 15 Oct., '16. (Plate II., 3).

JIGGINS, WILLIAM, Pte., R.W.S. Regt.
Married. *Res.*, 44 Princess Rd., Croydon. *Fell*, France, 1 Jul., '16.

THE CROYDON ROLL OF HONOUR

JINKS, W. H., 2870, Pte., R. Fus.
Res., Croydon. *Fell,* '17.

JINMAN, EWART, R.A.F.
b., '99. *Res.*, 2 Barclay Rd., Croydon. *Fell,* 14 Aug., '18.

JOHNSON, -, Cpl., R.W.S. Regt.
Married. *Res.*, 2 Cecil Rd., T. Heath. *Fell,* 20 Nov., '17.

JOHNSON, ARTHUR CHAPLIN, Sgt., 6 Australian I.F.
b., Great Shelford, Cambs., 20 Mar., '82 ; *s.*, Mr. & Mrs. Johnson, 3 Vincent Rd., Dorking. *Educ.*, Par. Ch. Sch., Croydon. Single. Empl. by Melbourne Harbour Trust. *Res.*, Melbourne. Served 12 years in R.M.A. *Enl.*, Aug., '14. *Fell,* Lone Pine, Gallipoli, 18 Aug., '15.

JOHNSON, FREDERICK HENRY, *V.C.*, Maj., R.E.
b., '90. *Educ.*, M. Whitgift Sch, Croydon, St. Duncan's, Catford, & Battersea Polytechnic ; B.Sc., Lond. (1st cl. Hon.), '14. Gained V.C. when 2/Lt. for leading several charges against a German redoubt, Hill 70, after he had been wounded, Loos, 25 Sept., '15. *D.*, Dec., '17.

JOHNSON, G., Pte., 1 Welsh Regt.
Fell, 17 Feb., '15.

JOHNSON, GEORGE ROBERT, Sgt., Aust. I.F.
Educ., M. Whitgift Sch.

JOHNSON, J. A., Leading Stoker, R.N.
Married ; 3 children. *Res.*, 3 Wandle Rd., Croydon. Lost with H.M.S. " Cressy," sunk by submarine in N. Sea, 22 Sept., '14.

JOHNSON, JOHN, Cpl., 3 Coy., Australian Field Engineers.
b., Croydon, 4 Apr., '81 ; *s.*, John & Mary Johnson, 4 Burdett Rd., Croydon. *Educ.*, Sydenham Rd. Sch., Croydon. Single. Brass finisher. *Res.*, Perth, W. Aust. Served 12 years in R.E. ; Queen's & King's S.A. Meds., 4 bars. *Re-enlisted,* Sept., '14. *Fell,* Gaba Tepe, Gallipoli, 14 May, '15. (Plate X., 3).

JOHNSON, R. G., Sgt., Aust. I.F.
Educ., M. Whitgift Sch., Croydon. *Fell,* '16.

JOHNSTON, GEORGE E., Pte., 1 Welsh Regt.
s., Mr. & Mrs. Johnston, 91 Nova Rd., Croydon. Member of Croydon Boy Scouts. *Fell,* 17 Feb., '15.

JOHNSTON, WALTER HENRY, Pte., 2 R.W.S. Regt.
b., 34 Dover Rd., Newtown, U. Norwood. *Educ.*, Rockmount Rd. Sch., U. Norwood. Married. Labourer. *Res.*, 92 Queen's Rd., Crown Hill, U. Norwood. Served in S.A. War (med., 8 clasps), India, etc. *Re-enlisted,* 5 Oct., '14. *Fell,* Festubert, 16 May, '15.

JOHNSTONE, WILLIAM, C.Q.M.S., 5 E. Sur. Regt.
b., Yorkshire, 9 May, '77. *Educ.*, Hammersmith. Married. Sorter, G.P.O., Lond. *Res.*, 66 Oakley Rd., S. Norwood. *Enl.*, Aug., '14 ; went to India, Oct., '14 ; joined Indian Exped. Force in May, '15 ; captured at Kut, Dec., '15 ; released, Oct., '18. *D.* of influenza at Constantinople, 13 Nov., '18, while on his journey home.

JONAS, W. P., 25332, Rflmn., R.B.
Res., Norbury. *Fell,* '17.

JONES, ARCHIBALD FRANCIS, Pte., 1/22 Lond. Regt.
b., T. Heath, 12 May, '97 ; *s.*, Henry Joseph & Emma Ann Jones, 127 Holmesdale Rd., S. Norwood. *Educ.*, Whitehorse Rd. Sch., T. Heath. Single. Warehouseman. *Enl.*, in R.W.S. Regt., 13 May, '14. *Fell,* France, 7 Oct., '16.

JONES, ARTHUR EDWARD, L/Cpl., 6 D.C.L.I.
    b., Sydenham, 8 Mar., '89 ; *s.*, Henry Joseph & Emma Ann Jones, 127 Holmesdale Rd., S. Norwood. *Educ.*, Whitehorse Rd. Sch., T. Heath. Single. Clerk. *Enl.*, 25 Aug., '14. *Fell*, Hooge, Belgium, 30 Jul., '15.

JONES, C., 46720, Pte., M.G.C.
    Res., S. Norwood. *Fell*, '17.

JONES, CHARLES WILLIAM, R.W.S Regt.
    b., '90 ; *s.*, Mr. & Mrs. Jones, Caterham Valley. Married. *Res.*, Croydon. *Fell*, 11 Oct., '18.

JONES, ERNEST DAVID, R.B.
    y.s., Mr. & Mrs. Bowen Jones, 24 Headcorn Rd., T. Heath. *Fell*, '18.

JONES, ERNEST SAMUEL, Trooper, 20 Hussars.
    b., 59 High St., Croydon, 3 Apr., '86 ; 3rd *s.*, Mr. & Mrs. G. J. Jones, 7 Chatsworth Rd., Croydon. *Educ.*, Modern Sch., Croydon. Married. Hosier. *Res.*, Chatsworth Rd., Croydon. *Enl.*, 9 Sept., '14. , *Fell*, Hangard Wood, Somme, 23 Mar., '18. (Plate XVI., 5).

JONES, G. F., 3442, Pte., Ox. & Bucks. L.I.
    Res., T. Heath. *Fell*, '16.

JONES, HERBERT VICTOR, Cpl., 1 D.C.L.I.
    b., Sydenham, 16 Aug., '91 ; *s.*, Henry Joseph & Emma Ann Jones, 127 Holmesdale Rd., S. Norwood. *Educ.*, Whitehorse Rd. Sch., T. Heath. Single. Grocer's asst. *Enl.*, 21 Oct., '10. *Fell*, France, 8 May, '17.

JONES, J. C., 651397, Pte., Lond. Regt.
    Res., W. Norwood. *Fell*, '17.

JONES, JESSE WILMOT.
    b., '54. Surveyor. *Res.*, 39 Morland Rd., Croydon. *D.* of shock during Zeppelin raid, Oct., '15.

JONES, L., 2/Lt., R.W.Fus.
    Educ., High Sch., Croydon. *Fell*, '16.

JONES, PERCIVAL HALLEY-, Capt., E. Sur. Regt.
    Educ., Univ. of Wales ; B.A. with hons. in hist., '07 ; M.A., '09 ; master at City of Norwich Sch., and later at M. Whitgift Sch., Croydon. *Joined*, Inns of Court O.T.C., '14 ; M.C., bestowed by the King, Jul.,'17. *Fell*, Chipilly Ridge, nr. Albert, 8-9 Aug.,'18.

JONES, STANLEY FOX GORE-, 2/Lt., Wilts. Regt.
    b., '93. *Fell*, 7 Jun., '17.

JONES, SYDNEY EDWARD, Pte., Northants. Regt.
    b., Old Town, Croydon, 9 May, '79 ; *s.*, Mrs. Jones, 91 Albert Rd., Addis. *Educ.*, M. Whitgift Sch. Married. Horsekeeper. *Enl.*, 9 Mar., '17. *D.* of gas poisoning at Stockport, Manchester, 27 Mar., '19.

JONES, VICTOR, Signaller.
    b., '99 ; *s.*, Mr. & Mrs. Jones, St. Mark's Rd., Mitcham. *Educ.*, Tavistock Gr. Sch., Croydon. *Enl.*, Sept., '14. *Fell*, 29 Sept.,'18.

JOPLING, STANLEY, Bdr., R.F.A.
    b., '92 ; *s.*, Mr. & Mrs. Jopling, 1 Quadrant Rd., T. Heath. *Enl.*, 8 Aug., '14 ; served in France, Sept., '14-Jan., '16 ; transf. to R.F.A. & trained in England ; further 14 months in France. *D.* of pneumonia, France, 15 Jul., '18.

JORDAN, W., 5925, Cpl., R.W.S. Regt.
    Res., T. Heath. Called up on Res., 5 Aug., '14. *Fell*, '17.

JUDD, PERCY, Pte., Wilts. Regt.
    b., 62 Napier Rd., 29 Dec., '95 ; *s.*, Harry & Alice Judd, 119 Bynes Rd., Croydon. *Educ.*, Brighton Rd. Sch., Croydon. Single. Motor driver. *Res.*, Haywards Heath. *Enl.*, '14. *Fell*, Hooge, 16 Jun., '15.

THE CROYDON ROLL OF HONOUR

KEAL, BERTRAM J., Pte., Middlesex Regt.
 s., Mr. & Mrs. Keal, 73 Queen's Rd., Croydon. *Educ.*, Sydenham Rd. Sch., Croydon. *Enl.*, Mar., '16. *Fell*, 26 Sept., '18.

KEAR, WALTER NELSON, Pte., 14 Welsh Regt.
 b., Addis., 10 Jan., '91. *Educ.*, Woodside Sch., Croydon. Married. Bacon stove hand. *Res.*, 4 Church Path, Croydon. *Enl.*, 28 Feb., '16. *D.*, 3 Jun., '19, after discharge from Army, at Croydon Boro. Hosp., Waddon, of pulmonary tuberculosis caused by gas poisoning.

KEARNS, JAMES, Pte., 2 R.W.S. Regt.
 b., Kingstown, co. Dublin, 17 Jan., '80. *Educ.*, Ireland. Married. Labourer. *Res.*, 60 Leighton St. E., Croydon. *Enl.*, 20 Sept., '14. *Fell*, France, 16 May, '15.

KEEFE, HAROLD JOHN, Pte., 12 E. Sur. Regt.
 b., Peckham, 30 Dec., '95 ; *s.*, Mr. & Mrs. Keefe, 28 Exeter Rd., Addis. *Educ.*, Woodside Sch., Croydon. Single. Carpenter. *Enl.*, 11 Dec., '15. *Fell*, Somme, 15 Sept., '16.

KEELING, WILLIAM JOHN, 1st Cl. Stoker, R.N.
 b., Addis., 15 Dec., '90 ; *s.*, Mrs. Sophia Keeling, 21 Union Rd., Croydon. *Educ.*, Princess Rd. Sch., Croydon. Single. Chauffeur. *Lost* on submarine E20, in Sea of Marmora, 5 Nov., '15.

KEEN, NORMAN, Pte., 1/5 Gordon H.
 b., Rickmansworth, 30 Sept., '99 ; *y.s.*, William & Annie Keen, 46 Grant Rd., Addis. *Educ.*, Oval Rd. Sch., Croydon. Single. Clerk. *Enl.*, in Lond. Scottish, Nov., '17. *Fell*, S.S.W. of Soissons, 28 Jul., '18. *Buried*, Buzancy Cem., 'A' Row, Grave 17. (Plate XXIII., 1).

KEEP, J., 41729, Driver, R.F.A.
 Fell, '16.

KEEP, W., 37770, Pte., R.W.S. Regt.
 Res., Croydon. *Fell*, '17.

KEIN, C. T., Pte., R.W.S. Regt.
 Fell, '17.

KELLY, J., Stoker, R.N.
 b., '93. *Res.*, 33 Donald Rd., Croydon. *Drowned*, 10 Apr., '17.

KEMBE, R., 10977, Pte., R.W.S. Regt.
 Fell, '16.

KEMBER, L. H. E., Pte., R.A.M.C.
 b., '94 ; 2nd *s.*, Henry & Ellen Kember, 161 Oval Rd., Croydon. Empl. by Messrs. Sainsbury. Served 2 years in Egypt. *Fell*, France, 23 Jul., '18.

KEMBER, PERCY, Pte., 10 Essex Regt.
 b., 84 Gloucester Rd., Croydon, 23 Aug., '99 ; *s.*, Mr. & Mrs. Kember, 22a Mitcham Rd., Croydon. *Educ.*, St. James' Sch., Croydon. Single. Empl. by Messrs. Hall & Co., Croydon, as coal porter. *Res.*, 2 Evans Yard, High St., Sutton. *Enl.*, 30 Oct., '17 ; *w. & missing*, 9 Aug., '18.

KENDALL, NORMAN BERNARD, Pte., R. Fus.
 b., "Penwortham," Birdhurst Rd., Croydon, 26 Mar., '94 ; *s.*, late Joseph, & Amelia Kendall. *Educ.*, Cliftonville Coll., Margate. Single. *Enl.*, '14. *Fell*, Beaumont Hamel, 13 Nov., '16. *Buried*, Mailly Maillet Wood, nr. Albert.

KENNETT, A., Cpl., E. Sur. Regt.
 Res., Croydon. *Fell*, '17.

KENSHOLE, F., Officers' Steward, R.N.
 b., 19 Jul., '95. *Educ.*, High Sch., Dovercourt. Master at Tavistock Gr. Sch., Croydon. *Joined*, Nov., '15. *D.*, in hosp., Sept., '16.

KENT, J. S., 722177, Pte., Lond. Regt.
 Res., Tooting. *Fell*, '17.

THE GLORIOUS DEAD

KENT, PERCY, 18080, Signaller, R.W.S. Regt.
    b., Cheam, Surrey, 26 Sept., '84 ; *s.*, Mr. & Mrs. Kent, 25 Duppas Hill Lane, Croydon. *Educ.*, Par. Ch. Sch., Croydon. Married ; 2 sons. Empl. for 19½ years in P.O. Sorting Office, E. Croydon. *Res.*, 42 Rymer Rd., Croydon. *Enl.*, 28 Jul., '16. *Missing*, presumed killed, France, 23 Mar., '18. (Plate XVI., 2).

KERNICK, C. R. H., 512522, Pte., Lond. Regt.
    Res., S. Norwood. *D.*, '17.

KERRY, ALFRED THOMAS PENFOUND, Rflmn., 13 K.R.R.C.
    b., 48 Surrey Lane, Battersea, 31 Aug., '97 ; *s.*, Mr. & Mrs. A.E. Kerry, 17 Whitehorse Lane, S. Norwood. *Educ.*, Brit. Sch., Croydon. Single. Grocer's asst. *Res.*, 39 Saxon Rd., Selhurst. *Enl.*, Nov., '15. *D.*, 20 Feb., '17, at 6 C.C.S., France, of wounds recd. same day.

KEYS, WILLIAM, Pte., 15 Btn., 1 Can. Div.
    b., 12 Bourne St., Croydon, 27 Apr., '94 ; *y.s.*, Mr. & Mrs. W. Keys, 7 Bourne St., Croydon. *Educ.*, Brit. Sch., Croydon. Single. Storekeeper's asst. *Res.*, 1247 Cannon St., Hamilton, Canada. *Enl.*, Aug., '14. *D.*, 9 Aug., '18, at 5 C.C.S., France, of wounds recd. same day.

KIDD, CLAUDE BERNARD, Capt., Cheshire Regt.
    b., '96 ; *s.*, Charles & Amy Howard Kidd, Castlemaine Av., Croydon. *Educ.*, Dulwich Coll. M.C. *Fell*, '18.

KILBY, FREDERICK, Gnr., R.G.A.
    b., '92 ; 3rd *s.*, Mr. & Mrs. Kilby, 3 Hampton Rd., Croydon. *Educ.*, Sydenham Rd. Sch., Croydon. Empl. by Messrs. Lyons, Cherry Orchard Rd., Croydon. *Enl.*, Oct., '15. *Fell*, 20 Oct.,'17.

KILBY, RICHARD, Seaman, R.N.
    b., '89 ; *s.*, Mr. & Mrs. Kilby, 3 Hampton Rd., Croydon. *Educ.*, Sydenham Rd. Sch., Croydon. Empl. at a laundry. *Fell*, Battle of Jutland, 31 May, '16.

KILLICK, MAURICE JOHN, P.O., R.N.
    b., '77. *Lost* with H.M.S. " Queen Mary," sunk during Battle of Jutland, 31 May, '16.

KILTY, WILLIAM, Cpl.
    b., '95. *Res.*, St. James' Rd., Croydon. Served 8 years in Gibraltar, Malta, S. Afr., etc. *Fell*, 7 Nov., '15.

KIMPTON, N. H., 2/Lt., R.F.A. (attd. T.M.B.)
    b., '97 ; 2nd *s.*, Mr. & Mrs. A. G. Kimpton, " Glengarry," Stanthorpe Rd., Streatham. *Educ.*, Whitgift G. Sch. *Enl.*, as pte. in L.R.B., '14 ; served in France from Jan., '15, but was invalided to England & subsequently discharged ; *Re-enlisted* in O.T.C. for R.H.A., May, '16 ; commis., Sept., '16. *D.* of wounds recd. at Boesinghe, 14 Jul., '17.

KINDER, CHARLES EDWARD, Sgt., R.B.
    b., Croydon, '87 ; *s.*, Mr. & Mrs. C. E. Kinder, 150 Melfort Rd., T. Heath. *Educ.*, Par. Ch. Sch., Croydon. Empl. as telegraph messenger. *Enl.*, '06 ; served 7 years in India. *Fell*, France, 11 Jan., '18.

KING, EDWARD HARRY, Pte., R. Suss. Regt.
    b., 4 Oct., '89 ; *s.*, Mr. & Mrs. King, High St., Petworth. Married ; 1 child. Empl. by Motor Union Insurance Co., St. James' St. *Res.*, 75 Grange Pk. Rd., T. Heath, & later 25 Foxley Gardens, Purley. *Enl.*, 1 Jan., '17. *Fell*, 1 Aug., '17.

KING, FRANK JAMES, Pte., 20 Can. Inf. (R. Grenadiers).
    b., 43 Derby Rd., Croydon, 1 Oct., '94 ; *s.*, William & Alice Mary King. *Educ.*, Par. Ch. Sch., Croydon. Single. Clerk while in England, farmer in Canada. *Res.*, Ontario. *Enl.*, 22 Dec., '15. *D.*, 10 May, '17, at 30 C.C.S., of wounds recd. at Arleux Loop Trench, Vimy, 8 May, '17. *Buried*, Aubigny.

KING, GEORGE FREDERICK HAMILTON, Bdr., R.G.A.
  b., " Close House," Houghton, Castle Ward, Stamfordham, Northumberland, 28 Feb., '79 ; s., George Sims & Grace Simpson King, Houghton. *Educ.*, Peckham. Married. Banker's clerk. *Res.*, 16 Alexandra Rd., Addis. Memb. of Croydon Dolphin Swimming Club. *Enl.*, 1 Aug., '16. *Fell*, France, 3-4 Nov., '18. *Buried*, St. Souplet, nr. Le Cateau.

KING, JAMES WILLIAM, 4688, Rflmn., L.R.B. (5 Lond. Regt.)
  Married. *Res.*, 9 Southcote Rd., S. Norwood. *Enl.*, 25 Apr., '16; went to France, 28 Aug., '16. *Fell*, Les Boeufs, Somme, 8 Oct.,'16.

KINGLEY, T. M., Pte., Manchr. Regt.
  b., '96. Porter at Mitcham Junct. *Res.*, 60 Tamworth Rd., Croydon. *Fell*, '17.

KINGSBURY, H. G., 54805, Pte., R. Fus.
  Res., T. Heath. *D.* of wounds, '17.

KINGSHOT, GEORGE, Gnr., 64 Bde., 12 Div., R.F.A.
  b., '95. *Res.*, 36 Woodside Green, S. Norwood. *Fell*, France, Oct., '15.

KINGSLAND, FREDERICK GEORGE, A.M., R.F.C.
  b., '89 ; s., Mr. & Mrs. F. C. Kingsland, Wellbrock Rd., Farnborough. *Educ.*, Abp. Tenison's Sch., Croydon. Business career. *Res.*, 143 St. Peter's St., Croydon. *Enl.*, in R.A.S.C., Apr., '15 ; transf. to R.F.C., Jul., '17. *Killed* while flying, France, 18 Jan., '18.

KINGSMAN, RICHARD GEORGE, Pte., E. Sur. Regt.
  b., Wimbledon, 4 Oct., '73. *Educ.*, Curtain Rd. Sch., Shoreditch. Married. Carman. *Res.*, Elis David Rd., Croydon. *Enl.*, 2 Feb., '15. *Fell*, Pont le Nieppe, 20 Aug., '15.

KINGSTON, JOHN SEABROOK, Pte., 6 Australian I.F.
  b., 8 Warwick St., Regent St., Lond., '94 ; s., Mr. & Mrs. Kingston, 55 Broughton Rd., T. Heath. *Educ.*, St. Leonard's Sch., Streatham, & Winterbourne Rd. Sch., Croydon. Single. Motor mechanic. *Res.*, Australia. *Fell*, Dardanelles, 11 Aug., '15.

KINNEAR, ANGUS MACPHERSON.
  b., Wandsworth, 17 Jul., '83 ; s., Mr. & Mrs. A. M. Kinnear, 65 Dalmeny Av., Norbury. *Educ.*, Emmanuel Sch., Wandsworth Common, & G. Sch., Margate. Single. Marine engineer. *Lost*, with S.S. " Narragansett," torpedoed off English Coast, 16 Mar., '16.

KINNEAR, GEORGE ROBERTSON, Gnr., R.N.
  b., Lavender Hill, 7 Feb., '85 ; s., Mr. & Mrs. A. M. Kinnear, 65 Dalmeny Av , Norbury. *Educ.*, Wandsworth. Married. Mechanician. Served in S.A. War. *Joined*, Mar., '00. *Lost* with H.M.S. " Queen Mary," Battle of Jutland, 30 May, '15.

KIRBY, R., 18249, Rflmn., K.R.R.C.
  Res., Norbury. *D.* of wounds, '17.

KIRBY, W., 40391, Pte., E. Yorks. Regt.
  Res., S. Norwood. *Fell*, '17.

KIRSCH, CHARLES FREDERICK, Pte., Lancs. Fus.
  b., Portsmouth, 22 Dec., '88. *Educ.*, Christ Ch. Sch., Croydon. Married. Traveller. *Res.*, 14 Mayday Rd., Croydon. *Enl.*, 7 May, '16. *Fell*, France, 1 Oct., '18. (Plate XVI., 4).

KITT, SIDNEY A., Cpl., R.W.S. Regt.
  Married ; 4 children. Confectioner. *Res.*, 15 Surrey St., Croydon. *Enl.*, Sept., '14 ; served at Suvla Bay, Egypt, Jerusalem ; *w.*, Jerusalem, '17. *D.*, 3 Aug., '18, of wounds recd., 27 Jul., '18.

KNELL, EDWARD WARREN HARCOURT, Pte., Civil Service Rif. (15 Lond. Regt.)
  b., Clapham, 7 Aug., '94 ; s., Mr. & Mrs. Warren Knell, "Hurst," Glossop Rd., Sanderstead. *Educ.*, Whitgift G. Sch. Single. Clerk, Anglo-Mexican Oil Co. *Enl.*, 7 Aug., '14. *D.*, 14 Oct.,'16, at Rouen, of wounds recd. at Eaucourt L'Abbaye, France, 7 Oct., '16. (Plate XVI., 1).
KNIGHT, ALFRED THOMAS, Sgt., 2 R.W.S. Regt.
  b., Croydon, 8 Jun., '82. *Educ.*, Par. Ch. Sch., Croydon. Married. Printer. *Res.*, 47 Cranmer Rd., Croydon. *Enl.*, 6 Feb., '15. *Fell*, Delville Wood, Somme, 1 Sept., '16.
KNIGHT, GERALD HOWARD, Pte., 2 R.W.S. Regt.
  b., Croydon, 18 Nov., '97 ; s., Mr. & Mrs. Knight, 30 Crowther Rd., S. Norwood. *Educ.*, Birchanger Rd. Sch., S. Norwood. Single. Clerk. *Enl.*, Jun., '14 ; w. & missing, believed killed, Festubert, 16 May, '15.
KNIGHT, JAMES, L/Cpl., R. Fus.
  b., '87. Traveller for Messrs. Watson & Co. *Enl.*, Feb., '16. *Fell*, 29 Apr., '17.
KNIGHT, N. Q., Sgt., Lond. Regt.
  Sec. of Selhurst United Football Club. *Res.*, 9 Dagnall Pk., S. Norwood. M.M., and bar. *Fell*, 2 Sept., '18.
KNIGHT, OSCAR WILFRED, Pte., Lond. Scottish (14 Lond. Regt.).
  b., U. Norwood, 16 Jul., '89 ; s., Mr. & Mrs. W. F. Knight, "The Mount," Duppas Hill, Croydon. *Educ.*, Devonshire House Sch., Bexhill, & Bradfield Coll., Berks. Single. Served 2 years in Berks. Vols., & 5 years in Lond. Scottish before war ; mobilised 8 Aug., '14. *Fell*, Zillebeke, 10 Nov., '14.
KNIGHT, STEPHEN JOHN ROBERT, Pte., 3/4 R.W.S. Regt.
  b., Selhurst New Rd., 15 Sept., '97 ; s., Stephen & Sarah Knight, 8 Selhurst New Rd., S. Norwood. *Educ.*, Sydenham Rd. Sch., Croydon. Single. Engineer's asst. *Enl.*, 10 Oct., '14. *D.*, 30 May, '16, at Reigate, of wounds recd. the same day through accident while firing a trench mortar.
KNIGHT, W., 434, Pte., R.W. Kent Regt.
  Res., E. Croydon. *Fell*, '17.
KNIGHT, W. G., Lond. Regt.
  b., '97 ; s., Mr. & Mrs. Knight, T. Heath. *D.* of wounds recd. in Palestine, 22 Feb., '18.
KNIGHT, WALTER, Pte., 1 R.W.S. Regt.
  b., 25 Thornton Rd., T. Heath, 29 Sept., '94 ; s., Mr. & Mrs. Knight, 68 Winterbourne Rd., T. Heath. *Educ.*, Ecclesbourne and Winterbourne Rd. Schs., T. Heath. Single. Laundryman. *Enl.* as drummer, 12 Jan., '12. *Fell*, Ypres, 29 Oct., '14.
KNOWLER, HAROLD, Pte., 11 Suff. Regt.
  b., '99 ; adopted " son " of Mr. & Mrs. Plowman, 5 Bridle Path, Beddington. *D.*, 27 Oct., '18, of wounds recd. 4 days prev.
KNOX, J. L. (Larry), 2/Lt., R. Suss. Regt.
  2nd s., Mr. & Mrs. John Knox, formerly of Holmesdale Rd., S. Norwood. Married Jennie, y. daughter of Mr. & Mrs. John Feaver, formerly of Whitworth Rd., S. Norwood. *Fell*, Cambrai, 20 Nov., '17.
KRAUSS, A., 8254, Pte., R. Fus.
  b., '97. *Educ.*, Boro. Sec. Sch., Croydon. Empl. by L.B.& S.C.R. *Res.*, Croydon. *Fell*, nr. La Bassée Canal, 5 Jul., '16.
KURN, J. C., Pte., R.A.S.C.
  Empl. by Croydon Corp. Tramways. *Fell*, '16.

KURTEN, GASTON P., 2/Lt. (Act.-Maj.), R.G.A.
  b., '89; e.s., Mr. & Mrs. R. Kurten, "Beverley Lodge," Brigstock Rd., T. Heath. *Educ.*, Whitgift G. Sch., '98-07; gained classical scholarship, Pembroke Coll., Oxford, '07; 1st class Hon. in Philosophy, King's Coll., Lond., '11; B.A.; entered Civil Service, '12; Private Sec. to Under Sec. for Ireland, '14. *Commis.* in R.A.S.C., '16; Act.-Capt., '17; ment. in desp., Nov., '17. *Fell*, France, 24 Apr., '18.

LAINE, CHARLES JANION, 2/Lt., M.G.C.
  b., 3 Sept., '76; s., Mr. & Mrs. Thomas Hamelin Laine, "Fermain," Lewin Rd., Streatham. *Educ.*, Whitgift G. Sch., '91-92.

LAING, JAMES ALEXANDER, 2/Lt.
  b., '92. *Res.*, T. Heath. *Joined*, 26 Oct., '14; w., France., '16. *Fell*, 14 Oct., '18.

LAING, JAMES GORDON, Maj., Lond. Regt. (attd. M.G.C.)
  b., '85; s., Mr. & Mrs. Robert A. Laing, "Shirley Hyrst," Croydon. Married. *Res.*, Croydon. *Fell*, 3 Oct., '18.

LAKE, FREDERICK, L/Cpl., 1 E. Sur. Regt.
  b., '88; s., late Mr., & Mrs. Alfred Lake, Croydon. Married; 2 children. *Fell*, 20 Oct., '18.

LAMBERT, F. A., Coy.Sgt.Maj., R.Fus.
  Res., 54 Beechwood Av., T. Heath. *Missing*, 23 Mar., '18.

LAMBERT, F. W. M., 2/Lt., S. Staff. Regt.
  b., '92; s., Mr. & Mrs. W. H. Lambert, 20 Katharine St., Croydon. When war broke out was in S.E. Mounted Bde. (Terr. A.S.C.). *Commis.*, '16; w. twice, and gassed '18; taken pris., 23 Mar., '18, at Cambrai; returned to England, Dec., '18. *D.*, at 20 Katharine St., Croydon, 25 Feb., '19, of pneumonia.

LAMPORT, THOMAS, L/Cpl., K.S.L.I.
  b., 120 Leighton St. E., Croydon, 30 Jun., '89; s., Maria Lamport, 37 Albion St., Croydon. *Educ.*, Mitcham Rd. Sch., Croydon. Single. General labourer. *Res.*, 105 Priory Rd., Croydon. *Enl.*, 8 Oct., '07; w. once. *Fell*, France, 26 Feb., '16.

LANDER, JOHN HERBERT, Pte., Artists Rif. (28 Lond. Regt.)
  b., Reigate, 15 Jul., '78; s., late Mr., & Mrs. Lander, 3 Beech House Rd., Croydon. *Educ.*, Whitgift G. Sch. Married. Bank clerk. *Res.*, Wallington. *Enl.*, 21 Feb., '17. *D.* of septic poisoning, 20 Mar., '17, at 1 Lond. Gen. Hosp., Camberwell.

LANDPORT, WILLIAM, 4052, Pte., 1 Hants. Regt.
  b., 4 West St. Lane, Carshalton, 23 Jul., '95; s., William & Amy Landport, 103 Wentworth Rd., Croydon. *Educ.*, Mitcham Rd. Sch., Croydon. Single. Van boy. *Enl.*, May, '14. *Fell*, France, 3 May, '15.

LANDYMORE, FREDERICK, Pte., E. Sur. Regt.
  b., '95; y.s., Mr. & Mrs. M. Landymore, 5 Leighton St. E., Croydon. *Educ.*, Mitcham Rd. Sch., Croydon. *Enl.*, 14 Aug., '14; went to France, 1 May, '15; w., Hulluch, Mar., '16; awarded M.M., for work at Monchy, '17 (bestowed on Mrs. Landymore by Mayor of Croydon and Lt.-Col. Thompson, at Town Hall, Croydon, Mar., '18). *Fell*, Cambrai, 20 Nov., '17.

LANE, F. M., 17615, L/Cpl., Coldstream Gds.
  Res., S. Norwood. *Fell*, '16.

LANE, MAURICE, Gnr., R.F.A.
  b., '97; 6th s., Mr. & Mrs. Alfred Lane, 105 Marlow Rd., Anerley. *Educ.*, Stanley Tech. Sch., S. Norwood. *Res.*, 28 Dagnall Pk., S. Norwood. *D.*, 23 Apr., '17, of wounds recd., 21 Apr., '17.

LANE, W., Rflmn., R.B.
  Empl. by Croydon Corp., Roads Dept.

THE GLORIOUS DEAD

LANGDALE, EDWARD GEORGE, Capt., 5 Leicester Regt.
 b., Notting Hill, 27 Jan., '83 ; s., the late Frederick William Langdale (Boro. Treasurer, 1893-1912), and Ada Maria Langdale, 39 Heathfield Rd., Croydon. *Educ.*, Elmhurst Sch., Croydon, Eastbourne Coll., where he was capt. of cricket eleven, and Merton Coll., Oxford (Hons. in Hist.). Married, 6 Aug., '14 ; 1 daughter. Asst. master, Oakham Sch., and prev. at King Edward VII. Sch., Sheffield. *Commis.* in 5 Leicester Rgt., 5 Aug., '14 ; went to France, 22 Feb., '15 ; w., Sept., '15. Ment. in despatches, 30 Nov., '15. *Fell*, France, 13 Oct., '15. (Plate XXXVI, 5).

LANGFORD, JOHN JOSEPH, 2/Lt., 18 K.R.R.C.
 b., Burham, Kent, 11 Feb., '94 ; s., John & Sarah Langford, 50 Canterbury Rd., Croydon. *Educ.*, Churcher's Coll., Petersfield, Boro. Sec. Sch., Croydon, and King's Coll., Lond. Single. *Joined* Lond. Univ. O.T.C., Aug., '14 ; transf. to Artists Rif., Aug., '15 ; 18 K.R.R.C., Dec., '15. *Fell*, nr. Flers, 15 Sept., '16. (Plate XVI., 3).

LANGFORD, WALLACE GEORGE, 2/Lt., 18 K.R.R.C.
 b., Barham, Kent, 19 Aug., '15 ; s., John & Sarah Langford, 50 Canterbury Rd., Croydon. *Educ.*, Churcher's Coll., Petersfield, Boro. Sec. Sch., Croydon, and King's Coll., Lond. Single. *Joined* Lond. Univ. O.T.C., Aug., '14 ; transf. to Artists Rif., Aug., '15 ; 18 K.R.R.C., Dec., '15. *D.*, 22 Jun., '16, at 2 C.C.S., nr. Bailleul, of wounds recd. at Ploegsteert, 25 Jun., '16. (Plate XVI., 6).

LANGLEY, H. W., Pte., Suff. Regt.
 b., '99 ; s., Mr. & Mrs. Langley, 82 Pawson's Rd., Croydon. Single. Empl. by Patent Steam Carpet Beating Co., Croydon. *Fell*, 4 Apr., '18.

LANGRIDGE, A. W., 60985, Pte., R. Fus.
 Res., Croydon. *Fell*, '17.

LANGRIDGE, W. C., Rflmn., Lond. Regt.
 b., '97 ; s., Mr. & Mrs. C. Langridge, Orpington, Kent. *Educ.*, Bynes Rd. Sch., Croydon. Empl. by Messrs. Mason, art printers, St. James' Rd., Croydon. *Enl.*, May, '15. *Fell*, 23 Jul., '17.

LANNING, PERCIVAL HERBERT HENRY, 21 Can. M.G.C.
 b., '89 ; s., Mr. & Mrs. L. E. Lanning, 66 George St., Croydon. *Fell*, 27 Nov., '15.

LARKIN, REGINALD HARRY, Rflmn., Lond. Regt.
 4th s., Mr. & Mrs. F. J. Larkin, " Jesmond Dene," S. Croydon. *Fell*, 1 Jul., '16.

LARKING, RONALD GUY, Capt., R.E.
 b., '91 ; y.s., late Richard James Larking, of Melbourne, Australia, and Mrs. Larking, 121 Victoria St., S.W. *Educ.*, Melbourne, and King's Coll., Camb., where he was in the rowing eight and football team ; broke record for combined Pub. Sch. "Mile," '09, and held it until '16 ; represented Camb. at boxing (middle weight), '11 ; elected Pres. of Univ. Boxing and Fencing Club, '12; B.A., '14 ; M.A., '17 ; a Freemason. *Enl.* as cpl. (desp. rider) in R.E., Aug., '14 ; *served* in France from Sept., '14 ; *commis.*, Sept., '14 ; awarded M.C., while attd. to A.I.F. as signal officer, at Pozieres, '16, and gained bar at Messines, '17. *Killed* in motor bicycle accident abroad, '18.

LATHAM, CLIFFORD, L/Cpl., 8 Middlesex Yeom.
 Res., Croydon. *D.* of wounds recd., 26 Oct., '17.

LATHAM, HARRY, L/Cpl. (Piper), Lond. Scottish (14 Lond. Regt.)
 b. about '78 ; s., late Mr., & Mrs. Alfred Latham, Croydon. Formerly engaged as sanitary engineer, Katharine St., Croydon. *Enl.*, '00. *Fell*, France, Nov., '14.

LATREILLE, ERNEST GEORGE, Pte., 1/23 Lond. Regt.
    b., Croydon, 16 Mar., '94 ; *s.*, Mr. & Mrs. G. S. Latreille, 3 St. Augustine's Av., S. Croydon. *Educ.*, Purley. Single. *Res.*, Croydon. *Enl.*, 8 Sept., '14. *Fell*, France, 25-26 May, '15.

LATTER, ALLEN, Pte., 12 E. Sur. Regt.
    b., Handcroft Rd., Croydon, 5 Dec., '80 ; *s*, Mr. & Mrs. Latter, 9 Campbell Rd., Croydon. *Educ.*, Mitcham Rd. Sch., Croydon; Married. Blacksmith's mate. *Res.*, 4 Mitcham Rd., Croydon. *Enl.*, 25 Sept., '14. *Fell*, France, 5 Apr., '17.

LAWN, WALTER HERBERT, L/Cpl., M.G.C.
    b., '91. Empl. by "Croydon Advertiser." *Res.*, 146 Whitehorse Rd., Croydon. *Enl.*, in 4 R.W.S. Regt. *D.*, in India, 29 Oct., '18, of influenza.

LAWRENCE, ROBERT REGINALD, Lt., R.N.V.R.
    b., '92 ; *s.*, Mrs. Julia Lawrence, Purley. *Res.*, 18 Havelock Rd., Croydon. Memb. of R.N.V.R. before war ; *mobilised*, Aug., '14 ; ment. in desp., '16, for work while in command of H.M. Motor Launch 506, in the Mediterranean. *D.* of pneumonia at Taranto, Italy, 1 Feb., '19.

LAWTON, PETER, Pte., 1 Irish Gds.
    b., '93. *W.*, '14. *Fell*, '15.

LEACH, E. L., 2436, Cpl., R.E.
    Res., T. Heath. *Fell*, '16.

LEANEY, FREDERICK GEORGE, Pte., Glo'ster Regt.
    5*th s.*, Mr. & Mrs. T. H. Leaney, 4 Alexandra Rd., Croydon. *Educ.*, Woodside Sch., Croydon. *Enl.* before war ; was serving in China in '14 ; *w.*, Ypres, 6 May, '15 ; *w.* and gassed, Loos, 13 Jun., '16. *Fell*, Salonica, 8 Mar., '18.

LEANING, R. W., 2/Lt., 9 King's L/pool. Regt.
    b., '99 ; *e.s.*, Mr. & Mrs. Leaning, Spencer Rd., Croydon. *Educ.*, Whitgift G. Sch., where he was cpl.-bugler in O.T.C. *Enl.* in Artists Rif., Dec., '15 ; *commis.*, Sept., '17. *Fell.* France, 31 May, '18.

LEAREY, JOHN THOMAS, 9607, Pte., 1 & 2 E. Sur. Regt.
    b., Deptford, 15 Mar., '89 ; *s.*, Mr. & Mrs. William Learey, 63 Priory Rd., Croydon. *Educ.*, Creek Rd. Sch., Deptford. Single. General labourer. *Res.*, Dryden Rd., Croydon. *Enl.*, in Spec. Res., 26 Mar., '08 ; transf. to Reg. Forces, 25 Jun., '08. *Fell*, St. Eloi, 14 Feb., '15.

LEATCHFORD, A., 8073, Pte., R.W.S. Regt.
    Res., T. Heath. *Fell*, '17.

LEBISH, FRANK ROLAND, 2/Lt., R.F.A.
    b., '97 ; *y.s.*, Mr. & Mrs. George Lebish, Court Rd., W. Norwood. *Educ.*, Dulwich Coll. ; intermediate B.A. *Joined*, Inns of Court, O.T.C., Sept., '15 ; went to R. Mil. Acad., Woolwich, Sept., '16; commis., 7 Jun., '17. *Fell*, France, 25 Jul., '17.

LEE, HEDLEY GEORGE.
    s., late Mr. & Mrs. John Rogers Lee. *Res.*, 18 Oakfield Rd., Croydon. *Fell*, 30 Apr., '18.

LEE, JAMES FRANK LEWIS, L/Cpl., R.W.S. Regt.
    b., '95 ; *s.*, late Lt. James Victor Lee, R.A.O.C., formerly of 45 Greenside Rd., Croydon. Empl. by Messrs. T. Smith & Sons, Church St., Croydon. *Res.*, 62 Mersham Rd., T. Heath. *Enl.*, 6 Jan., '15. *Fell*, 15 Jul., '16.

LEE, JAMES VICTOR, Lt., R.A.O.C.
    Res., 45 Greenside Rd., Croydon.

LEE, PERCY WILLIAM, 2/Lt., K. Shropshire L.I.
    b., '88. Single. Clerk, L.B. & S.C.R. *Res.*, "Springwell," Inglis Rd., Croydon. *Enl.* in O.T.C., '15. *Fell*, Arras, 9 Apr., '17.

XVII.

1. Pte. J. H. HEGARTY, Machine Gun Corps
2. Capt. G. H. LEWIS, D.F.C., R.F.C.
3. Signaller E. J. S. HULETT, Machine Gun Corps
4. 2/Lt. J. C. LISTER, 17 Bde., R.F.A.
5. Lt. F. A. MATTHEWS, 10 R. Suss. Regt. (attd. R.F.C.)
6. 2/Lt. H. S. S. de JASTRZEBSKI, 24 Lond. Regt.

XVIII.

1. 2/Lt. E. J. Trubshawe, R.E.
2. Lt. E. L. Lewis, R.F.C.
3. 2/Lt. H. A. Link, 1 H.A.C.
4. Pte. J. Hall, 6 R.W.S. Regt.
5. Lt. A. T. Libby, 12 E. Sur. Regt.
6. Capt. H. C. Willders-Lewis, R.W.S. Regt.

LEECH, F. C., Pte., Middlesex Regt.
Res., T. Heath. *Fell*, '17.

LEECH, ERNEST JOHN, Rflmn., 1 L.R.B. (5 Lond. Regt.)
b., Croydon, 4 Dec., '91 ; *s.*, Mr. & Mrs. J. T. Leech, 44 Tanfield Rd., Croydon. *Educ.*, Abp. Tenison's & Brit. Schs., Croydon. Single. Accountant's clerk. *Enl.*, 15 May, '16. *Fell*, Laventie, France, 20 Jan., '17. (Plate XIX., 1).

LEGG, GEOFFREY HAROLD BLACKWELL, L/Cpl., R. Suss. Regt.
b., Paddington Green, 18 Aug., '94. *Educ.*, Campbell St. Sch., Edgware Rd., Lond. Single. Stock-keeper. *Res.*, 164 Livingstone Rd., T. Heath. *Enl.*, 9 Nov., '14 ; *w.*, Thiepval, 3 Sept., '16. *Fell*, Sharia, Palestine, 6 Nov., '17.

LENNARD, PERCY CHARLES, Civil Serv. Rif. (15 Lond. Regt.)
b., Addis., 12 Jul., '94 ; *s.*, Mr. & Mrs. F. W. Lennard, 64 Heathfield Rd., Croydon. *Educ.*, M. Whitgift Sch. Single. Civil Service clerk. *Enl.*, 3 Sept., '14. *D.*, St. Omer, 29 Dec., '15, of wounds recd., Hulluch, 20 Dec., '15.

LENNEY, ALFRED, Pte., 4 R.W.S. Regt.
b., S. Croydon, 5 Jan., — ; *s.*, Mr. & Mrs. Alfred Lenney, 26 Dominion Rd., Addis. *Educ.*, St. Peter's Sch., Croydon. Married. Labourer, empl. by Croydon Corp. Rds. Dept. *Enl.*, Sept., '14 ; *served* in India and Persian Gulf. *D.* of wounds recd., Mesopotamia, 22 Dec., '15.

LEPPARD, FRANK WILLIAM, Pte., 17 R. Fus.
b., '98 ; *y.s.*, Mr. & Mrs. Leppard, 132 Church St., Croydon. Empl. at " Croydon Advertiser " Office. *Enl.*, May, '15. *Fell*, 29 Sept., '18.

LETTO, HENRY GEORGE, Pte., 1/7 Middlesex Regt.
b., St. Heliers, Jersey, 3 Dec., '77 ; *s.*, Adolphus, & late Louisa Letto, 169 Victoria St., Lond., S.W.1. *Educ.*, Wesleyan Sch., St. Heliers, Jersey. Married. Outfitter's asst. *Res.*, 140 Pemdevon Rd., Croydon. *Enl.*, 11 Aug., '16. *D.*, 1 May, '18, at 2 Western Gen. Hosp., Grecian St., Broughton, Manchester, of gas poisoning and wounds recd. nr. Arras, 28 Mar., '18.

LETTS, RICHARD, Pte., 2 R.W.S. Regt.
b., S. Norwood, 2 Feb., —. *Educ.*, S. Norwood. Married. Labourer. *Res.*, 32 Coventry Rd., S. Norwood. *Enl.*, 2 Oct., '14. *Fell*, France, 30 Sept., '17.

LETTS, SIDNEY HERBERT, A.B. Seaman, R.N.
b., Addington Rd., 13 Jan., '96 ; *s.*, Alice Wynne, 20 Exeter Rd., Addis. *Educ.*, Davidson Rd. Sch., Croydon. Single. *Joined* training ship " Arethusa," 13 May, '13 ; *joined* R.N. about 18 months later. *Lost* with H.M.S. "Indefatigable," Battle of Jutland, 31 May, '16. (Plate XV., 5).

LEVY, WILLIAM GEORGE, Pte., R.A.M.C. (82 Gen. Hosp.)
b., '99 ; *s.*, W. G. & Catherine J. Levy, Wintons Garage, Fairfield Rd., Croydon. *Enl.*, Sept., '15 ; served in Egypt, France, and Salonica. *D.*, of cerebro-spinal meningitis at 67 Gen. Hosp., Macedonia, Greece, 23 May, '18. *Buried*, Karaburnum Brit. Cem., nr. Salonica.

LEWCOCK, WILLIAM JOHN, Pte., 6 Lond. Regt.
b., U. Norwood, 3 Jul., '89 ; *s.*, Mr. & Mrs. W. J. Lewcock, 16 South Vale, Central Hill, U. Norwood. *Educ.*, Rockmount Rd. Sch., U. Norwood. Married. Warehouseman. *Enl.*, Aug., '14. *Fell*, Bullecourt, France, 21 May, '17.

Lewin, Edmund George, 1704, Pte., 17 R. Fus.
 b., Croydon, 2 Nov., '93 ; s., William George & Emma Elizabeth Lewin, 162 Dennett Rd., Croydon. *Educ.*, Christ Ch. Sch., Croydon. Single. Grocer's asst. *Enl.*, 7 Jun., '15. *Fell*, Somme, 27 Jul., '16.

Lewin, S. P., 29358, Rflmn., K.R.R.C.
 Res., S. Norwood. *D.* of wounds, '17.

Lewis, A. A., 34826, Pte., Welsh Regt.
 Res., Croydon. *Fell*, '17.

Lewis, Edmund Llewelyn, Lt., R.F.C.
 b., Birmingham, 5 Oct., '95 ; s., Mr. & Mrs. Hugh Lewis, " St. David's," Templewood Av., Hampstead. *Educ.*, Whitgift G. Sch., Marlborough Coll., King's Coll., Lond. Univ., and in Germany and Switzerland. Single. Empl. at Lloyd's. *Res.*, " Mayfield," Croydon. *Enl.*, as pte. in 1/7 Essex Regt., Sept. '14 ; *commis.* as 2/Lt. in 1/7 Essex Regt., 24 Sept., '14 ; went to France, Jul., '15 ; seconded to R.F.C. (Squadrons 32 & 24), Jun., '16 ; *w.* in single-handed fight with six German machines. *Fell* in fight with five German machines, one of which he brought down, Beaulencourt, Somme, 26 Dec., '16. (Plate XVIII., 2).

Lewis, Edward John, Rflmn., 8 Lond. Regt.
 b., Surrey, 28 Apr., '78. Married. Civil servant. *Res.*, 80 Malvern Rd., T. Heath. *Enl.*, 29 May, '17. *Fell*, Passchendaele, 30 Oct., '17.

Lewis, F. H. W., 24022, Pte., D.C.L.I.
 Res., T. Heath. *Fell*, '17.

Lewis, Henry Charles Willders-, Capt., R.W.S. Regt.
 b., 31 Jul., '96 ; s., late Henry & Nora Willders-Lewis, Anerley. *Educ.*, High Sch., Croydon ; matriculated, Lond. Univ. ; memb. of Sur. County Cricket Club. *Enl.* in U.P.S. Batt., R. Fus. ; served in France, Nov., '15-17 ; *commis.*, Sept., '16 ; Capt., '17. *Fell*, 31 Jul., '17. (Plate XVIII., 6).

Lewis, Thomas Charles Victor, R.W.S. Regt.
 b., 11 Nov., '95 ; s., Mr. & Mrs. Thomas Edward Willson Lewis 126 George St., Croydon. *Educ.*, Whitgift G. Sch., '05-13. *D.* of pneumonia, Egypt, 24 Dec., '16.

Lewsey, G. F., L/Cpl., 2/4 R.W.S. Regt.
 s., Mr. & Mrs. Lewsey, 31 Leslie Pk. Rd., Croydon. *D.* of wounds recd. at Suvla Bay, 29 Aug., '15.

Libby, Alfred Thomas, Lt., 12 E. Sur. Regt.
 b., Chislehurst, Kent, Feb., '79 ; s., late John Henry & Elizabeth Libby, Truro, Cornwall. *Educ.*, Truro. Single. Compositor, empl. by " Transvaal Leader," Johannesburg. *Res.*, Croydon, at time of enlistment. Served in Boer War ; 2 med. *Enl.*, in an O.T.C., Aug., '15 ; *commis.* early in '16 ; *w.*, France, Feb., '17. *Fell*, Passchendaele, 20 Sept., '17. (Plate XVIII., 5).

Libby, Frank Thomas, Sgt., L.R.B.
 b., Thames Ditton, 6 Mar., '93 ; s., John & Emily Libby, 51 Broughton Rd., T. Heath. *Educ.*, M. Whitgift Sch., Croydon. Single. Civil servant (Board of Trade). *Res.*, Croydon. *Enl.*, Apr., '15 ; M.M. for conspicuous bravery, Passchendaele, 20 Sept., '17. *D.*, 19 Apr., '18, at Mil. Hosp., Etaples, of wounds recd. nr. Mailly-Maillet, 2 Apr., '18. (Plate XX., 4).

Libby, Harry George, Cpl., Q.W. Rif. (16 Lond. Regt.)
 b., Croydon, 26 Sept., '94 ; s., John & Emily Libby, 51 Broughton Rd., T. Heath. *Educ.*, M. Whitgift Sch. Single. Civil servant (Board of Trade). *Res.*, Croydon. *Enl.*, Apr., '15. *Fell*, Ypres, 18 Jan., '16.

LIDDEL, D., 11995, Pte., E. Kent Regt.
  Res., Croydon. *Fell*, '17.
LINDLEY, ERNEST W., 2/Lt., Manchr. Regt. (attd. R.F.C.)
  b., 13 Oct., '96 ; *s.*, Mr. & Mrs. Edward Thomas Lindley, 126 Selhurst Rd., S. Norwood. *Educ.*, Whitgift G. Sch. *D.* while pris. of war in German Hosp., '17.
LINDSELL, C. J., Coy. Sgt. Maj., 17 Lancers.
  Empl. by Croydon Corp., Boro. Engineer's Dept. *Fell*, '16.
LINEAMAN, F., Pte., R.A.S.C. (M.T.)
  D., 14 Nov., '18, of broncho pneumonia, at 61 Gen. Hosp., Salonica.
LINK, HORACE ARTHUR, 2/Lt., 1 H.A.C.
  b., Croydon, 29 Jun., '91 ; *s.*, Mr. & Mrs. Charles W. Link, " Eversley," Chichester Rd., Croydon. *Educ.*, Glenhurst Sch., S. Croydon, and Mill Hill Sch. Single. Empl. with Messrs. J. D. Link & Son, provision merchants, W. Smithfield. *Joined*, Sept., '14. *Fell*, nr. Bully Grenay, France, Sept., '16. (Plate XVIII., 3).
LINTOTT, GERALD, Cpl., 2 L.R.B.
  b., 27 Oliver Gr., S. Norwood, 22 Jun., '88 ; *s.*, Herbert & Fanny Louisa Lintott, 70 Waddon Rd., Croydon. *Educ.*, Elmhurst Sch., S. Croydon. Single. Clerk. *Enl.*, 7 Sept., '14. *D.*, 9 Jun., '15, of acute septicaemia, 1 Eastern Gen. Hosp., Cambridge.
LISNEY, GEORGE, Sgt., R.W.S. Regt.
  b., 18 Tamworth Place, Croydon, 26 May, '82 ; *s.*, Frederick & Charlotte Lisney, 18 Tamworth Place, Croydon. *Educ.*, Mitcham Rd. Sch., Croydon. Single. Slater and tiler. *Enl.*, 4 Aug., '14 ; went to France, '14 ; *w.*, 12 May, '17. *Fell*, Cambrai, 20 Nov., '17.
LISNEY, HAMILTON P., L/Cpl., 5 Ox. & Bucks. L.I.
  b., 19 Sept., '89 ; *s.*, Frederick & Charlotte Lisney, 18 Tamworth Place, Croydon. *Educ.*, Brit. Sch., Croydon. Single. Grocer's manager. *Res.*, Datchet, Bucks. *Enl.*, 15 Sept., '14. *Fell*, Loos, 25 Sept., '15.
LISTER, JOHN CURTIS, 2/Lt., 92 Bty., 17 Bde., R.F.A.
  b., Sydenham, 19 May, '94 ; *y.s.*, George & Harriet Lister, Pampisford House, S. Croydon. *Educ.*, King's Coll., Wimbledon Single. Tea buyer. *Enl.*, in 9 E. Sur. Regt., Dec., '14. *Fell*, nr. Arras, 19 May, '17. (Plate XVII., 4).
LITOLFF, ALEXANDER DAVID, L/Cpl., K.R.R.C.
  b., 4 Drummond Rd., Croydon, 10 Jan., '97 ; *s.*, David James & late Eliza Litolff, " Pembury," Chelsham Rd., Croydon. *Educ.*, Abp. Tenison's Sch., Croydon, and Boro. Sec. Sch., Croydon. Student teacher, Dering Pl. Sch., Croydon ; entered Goldsmiths' Coll., Sept., '15. Single. *D.* of gas poisoning, Ypres, 8-9 Aug., '16. *Buried*, Ferme Olliver Cem., Elverdinghe, nr. Ypres.
LITTLE, A., 201836, L/Cpl., R.W.S. Regt.
  Res., Addis. *Fell*, '17.
LITTLE, WILLIAM ALFRED, Pte., 3/4 R.W.S. Regt.
  b., 58 Apsley Rd., S Norwood, 4 Oct., '95. *Educ.*, Woodside Sch., Croydon. Married. Railway porter. *Res.*, 52 Apsley Rd., S. Norwood. *Enl.*, 1 Mar., '17. *Fell*, France, 4 Oct., '17
LITTLECHILD, GEORGE, Pte., 2 R.W.S. Regt.
  b., '88. Married. *Res.*, 57 Leighton St. E., Croydon. *Enl.*, 25 Dec., '10 ; served at Gibraltar, Bermuda and S. Africa, before war. *Fell*, Ypres, 7 Nov., '14.

LIVINGSTONE, DAVID, 1235, Pte., 22 R. Fus.
    b., Chelsea, 22 Aug., '96; s., Alfred & Mary Livingstone, 20 Aschurch Rd., Croydon. *Educ.*, Cooks Ground Sch., Chelsea. Single. Ticket writer. *Res.*, 27 Bredon Rd., Croydon. *Enl.*, 9 Nov., '14. *Fell*, France, 19 Jun., '16.
LLOYD, ALBERT EDWARD, 9281, Pte., 1 R. Warwick. Regt.
    b., S. Croydon. *Educ.*, Abp. Tenison's and Brighton Rd. Schs., Croydon. Married. General labourer. *Res.*, 92 Paulet Rd., Camberwell. Served in S.A. War, and in India and Egypt; *Re-joined*, 17 Nov., '14. *Fell*, 25 Apr., '15.
LLOYD, DENIS. *Educ.*, High Sch., Croydon. *Enl.*, '14. *Missing*, '18.
LLOYD, EDWARD STANLEY, Lt., R.F.A.
    b., '86; 2nd s., Mr. & Mrs. Lloyd, " Ventura," Addis. Rd., Croydon. *Res.*, 28-29 Wood St., Lond. M.C. *D.* of broncho-pneumonia, France, 23 Nov., '18.
LLOYD, LYNDSEY, 2/Lt., Hants. Regt.
    b., Huddersfield, 4 Aug., '98; *e.s.*, late F. C. Lloyd (Town Clerk of Croydon), and Mrs. Lloyd, 20 Colson Rd., Croydon. *Educ.*, Whitgift G. Sch. Single. *Enl.* as pte. in R.A.M.C., 2 Feb., '15; *commis.* in Hants. Regt., 1 Mar., '17. *Fell*, Langemarck Stn., nr. Ypres, 9 Oct., '17. (Plate XXXVI., 2).
LOCK, ROBERT WILLIAM, G17089, Pte., 4 Middlesex Regt.
    b., Croydon, 17 Aug., '97; s., Mr. & Mrs. Edward Lock, 52 Wentworth Rd., Croydon. *Educ.*, Boston Rd. Sch., Croydon. Single. Labourer. *Res.*, 17 Wentworth Rd., Croydon. *D.* of wounds in 1 Can. Gen. Hosp., Etaples, 9 Apr., '18.
LOCKTON, GEORGE WOODHAMS, Capt., R.G.A.
    b., T. Heath, 17 Jun., '92; s., George Upton & Edith Caroline Lockton, 166 Melfort Rd., T. Heath. *Educ.*, M. Whitgift Sch. Single. Bank clerk. *D.*, 21 Oct., '17, at 1 Aust. C.C.S., Bailleul, of wounds recd. at Spoil Bank, Hollebeke, nr. Ypres, same day.
LONG, A. W. E., 2/Lt., R.W.S. Regt.
    Fell, '16.
LONG, ALBERT EDWARD, 6890, Pte., 1 E. Kent Regt.
    b., 48 Addington Rd., Croydon, 27 Mar., '90; s., Mr. & Mrs. Henry Long, 4 Grafton Rd., Croydon. *Educ.*, Mitcham Rd. Sch., Croydon. Single. Shop asst. *Enl.*, Sept., '14. *Fell*, France, 19 Apr., '16. *Buried*, La Brique Cem.
LONG, FRANCIS WILLIAM, 2/Lt., R.F.A.
    b., Ulverston, Lancs., 9 Sept., '95; s., Mr. & Mrs. G. Long, 5 Liverpool Rd., T. Heath. *Educ.*, Ampleforth Coll., Yorks. Single. *Res.*, T. Heath. *Gazetted*, 2/Lt., 23 Dec., '14. *D.*, 28 Jun., '16, while pris. of war at Iseghem Hosp., Belgium. of wounds recd., 2 Jun., '16.
LONGBOTTOM, CHARLES DAVID, 9644, Pte., 12 E. Sur. Regt.
    b., T. Heath, 25 Nov., '97; s., Mr. & Mrs. C. W. Longbottom, 73 Clarendon Rd., Croydon. *Educ.*, Mitcham Rd. Sch., Croydon. Single. Driver. *Enl.*, about Mar., '15. *Fell*, nr. Messines Ridge, 21 Sept., '17.
LONGMAN, LESLIE LIONEL, Rflmn., Q.V. Rif. (9 Lond. Regt.)
    b., 138 Moffat Rd., T. Heath, 1 Feb., '99; 2nd s., Harry James & Rose Longman, 138 Moffat Rd., T. Heath. *Educ.*, M. Whitgift Sch. Single. Clerk. *Enl.*, 1 Feb., '17. *D.*, 25 Aug., '18, at 55 C.C.S., France, of wounds recd. on the Somme same day. (Plate XIX., 5).
LOOMES, J., 19879, Rflmn., K.R.R.C.
    Fell, '16.
LOUT, GEORGE, King's L/pool Regt.

THE GLORIOUS DEAD

LOUVEL, THEODORE, Pte., 1/7 R. Warwick. Regt.
b., 6 Holland Rd., S. Norwood, 25 May, '98 ; *s.*, Theodore George & Emmeline Dorothy Louvel, 187 Portland Rd., S. Norwood. *Educ.*, Birchanger Rd. Sch., S. Norwood. Single. Lift attendant. *Enl.*, 8 Jan., '17 ; went to France, 12 Jun., '17. *Fell*, nr. Ypres, 21 Aug., '17.

LOVATT, STANLEY WALTER, L/Cpl.
y.s., Mr. & Mrs. Lovatt, 2 Crowther Rd., S. Norwood. *Fell*, 28 Apr., '17.

LOVELL, WILLIAM LESLIE, 2/Lt., R.W. Kent Regt. (attd. R.F.C.)
b., Bromley, '96 ; *s.*, Edgar & Maud Lovell, " The Gables," Cheyne Walk, Croydon. *Educ.*, Clare House Sch., Beckenham ; went to Sandhurst, Apr., '16 ; *gazetted*, '16. *Fell*, France, 27 Jul., '17.

LOVER, ARTHUR CHARLES WALTER, Pte., 8 Sherwood For. (Notts. and Derby. Regt.)
b., 5 Sussex Rd., Croydon, 26 Sept., '85 ; *y.s.*, Walter & Louisa Lover, 3 Waverley Av., Netley Abbey, Hants., (late of Croydon). *Educ.*, Princess Rd. Sch., Croydon. Single. Dental mechanic. *Res.*, Mansfield, Notts. *Enl.*, 3 Mar., '16. *D.*, 16 Jun., '18, at 1 Can. C.C.S., France, of wounds recd. prev. day. *Buried*, Pernes Mil. Cem.

LOVETT, JOHN, Pte., Lancs. Fus.
b., '95 ; *s.*, late Mr., & Mrs. Lovett, Ely Rd., Croydon. *Enl.*, '14. *Fell*, '16.

LOW, GEORGE, 1 King's L/pool Regt.
b., Aberdeen, 17 Apr., '88 ; *e.s.*, Alexander & Elspet Low, 17 Bensham Manor Rd., T. Heath. *Educ.*, Boston Rd. Sch., Croydon, and Aberdeen. Single. Plumber. *Enl.*, Jun., '16. *Fell*, nr. Arras, 11 Aug., '18.

LOWE, JOHN, Pte., R.A.S.C.
b., Fawley, nr. Southampton, '86 ; *s.*, Mr. & Mrs. G. Lowe, Fawley. *Educ.*, Fawley. Married. Chauffeur. *Res.*, 45 Churchill Rd., Croydon. *Enl.*, Apr., '15. *D.* of diphtheria at 14 Stat. Hosp., Wimereux, nr. Boulogne, 25 Jun., '16.

LUCAS, ALBERT EDWARD, Pte., R.F.C.
b., Hackney, 29 Jul., '89 ; *s.*, Edward (late Sgt., 2nd Drag. Gds.) and Catharine Lucas, Union Bank Chambers, Katharine St., Croydon. *Educ.*, Whitgift G. Sch. Married Winifred, daughter of Mr. Jackson, of Brighton. Clerk. *Res.*, 10 Genoa Rd., Anerley. *Enl.*, 25 Nov., '16. *D.* of meningitis, Windlesham Mil. Hosp., Surrey, 6 Mar., '17. (Plate XX., 2).

LUCK, WILL,
Res., Croydon. *D.* of wounds, 17 Sept., '18.

LUXTON, J., Cpl., Suff. Regt.
b., '96 ; *e.s.*, Mr. & Mrs. Luxton, 1 Parker Rd., Croydon. *Enl.*, in R.W.S. Regt., Sept., '14 ; served in France, Jul., '16-Nov., '17. *Fell*, 19 Nov., '17.

MABBOTT, ALFRED L.
Educ., M. Whitgift Sch. *Fell*, Somme, 1 Jul., '16.

MABEY, JOHN HUME, Capt., Lond. Regt.
b., '81 ; *y.s.*, late Counc. and Mrs. Mabey, of Croydon. *Educ.*, Whitgift G. Sch. Married a daughter of Counc. Bishop, of Croydon. *Res.*, Pollards Hill N., Norbury. *Enl.*, in Artists Rif., '14 : served in France, Salonica, & Palestine. *D.*, 18 Nov., '17, of wounds recd., Palestine, 7 Nov., '17.

MCCABE, ALBERT PETER, Sgt., 2 R.W.S. Regt.
Nephew of late Maj. McCabe. *Enl.*, '05. *Fell*, France, 16 May, '15.

MACALDIN, THOMAS GRAHAM, Sgt., 31 Can. Inf.
b., 2 St. Helen's Rd., Norbury, 5 Mar., '94 ; *s.*, Mr. & Mrs. Macaldin, 9 Tamworth Villas, Mitcham Common. *Educ.*, Streatham Sch. Single. Farmer. *Res.*, Chigwell, Alberta, Canada. *Enl.*, Nov., '14. *Fell*, Courcelette, Somme, 26 Sept., '16.

MACCALL, HENRY DOBREE, Capt., 33 Punjab Regt.
b., '82. First appointed to Border Regt. from the Militia, '02 ; Lt., Apr., '04 ; transf. to Indian Army, Aug.,'05 ; Capt., Nov., '10 ; served in S.A. War, Queen's Med., 5 clasps. *Fell*, Flanders, 25 Sept., '15.

McCARNEY, JOSEPH DUNCAN, R.N.
Lost with H.M.S. " Hogue," torpedoed in N. Sea, 22 Sept., '14.

McCARTHY, THOMAS, Pte., 6 R.W.S. Regt.
b., 5 Pump Pail, Croydon, 23 Oct., '96 ; *s.*, Timothy & Mary McCarthy, 8 Donald Rd., Croydon. *Educ.*, St. Mary's Sch., Croydon. Single. Lead-light worker. *Res.*, 8 Donald Rd., Croydon. *Enl.*, 9 Sept., '14. *Fell*, Somme, 3 Jul., '16.

McCHLERY, W. D., Sgt., R.W.S. Regt.
e.s., Mr. & Mrs. McChlery, 32 Buxton Rd., T. Heath. *Fell*, 13 Oct., '17.

McCLURG, J. B., 464, R. Fus.
Res., Croydon. *Fell*, '17.

McCOLVIN, NORMAN, Pte., 8 Border Regt.
b., Heaton, Newcastle-on-Tyne, 5 Apr., '92 ; *e.s.*, John Andrew & Isabel McColvin, 38 Lebanon Rd., Croydon. *Educ.*, Whitley Bay, Northumberland, Brixton, Portland Rd. Sch., S. Norwood, and Lond. Sch. of Economics. Single. Senior asst. librarian, Croydon Public Libraries. *Enl.*, in 24 Middlesex Regt., 17 Nov., '15 ; served in France with 2 Border Regt., Dec., '16-Oct., '17 ; *w.*, The Mound, Polygon Wood, Ypres, 4 Oct., '17 ; returned to France, spring, '18 ; *w.*, between Rheims and Soissons 27 May, '17, and taken prisoner. *D.* of wounds at Prisoners of War Hosp., at Neuhammer, Queis, Germany, 21 Aug., '18. (Plate I., I).

McCULLOCH, KENNETH LIONEL NEVILL, 2/Lt., 16 Middlesex Regt.
b., Croydon, 23 Sept., '95 ; *e.s.*, late Lionel W. B. & Bertha McCulloch, 340 Lond. Rd., Croydon. *Educ.*, Royal St. Anne's, Redhill, and City of Lond. Sch. Single. Clerk in Anglo-Austrian Bank. *Enl.* as pte. in 16 Middlesex Regt. (Pub. Sch. Btn.), 1 Sept., '14 ; *commis.*, in 6 Middlesex, 5 Apr., '15 ; *w.*, Somme, Oct., '16. *Fell*, Arras, 31 May, '17. (Plate XIX., 3).

McGILL, BENJAMIN, Ox. & Bucks. L.I.
Res., Croydon. Was in India when war broke out, serving later at Dardanelles and in Mesopotamia. Taken prisoner with Gen. Townshend's forces. *D.* a few weeks after in a Turkish Hosp., through hardship and starvation.

McGILL, VICTOR, Sgt., Lond. Regt.
b., '97 ; *s.*, late Mr. J., & Mrs. McGill, Dartnell Rd., Croydon. *D.* of wounds recd., 12 Jun., '17.

McGILVRAY, DONALD, Cpl., Singapore Volunteer Rif.

McGREGOR, MARCUS, 2/Lt., 2 Cheshire Regt.
b., '73 ; *s.*, Mr. & Mrs. Joseph McGregor, " Glengyle," Victoria Rd., U. Norwood. *Educ.*, Dulwich Coll. *Joined*, 27 Sept., '14. *Fell*, France, between 1-4 Oct., '15.

McGREGOR, RONALD, 2/Lt., 2 Cheshire Regt.
b., '89 ; *s.*, Mr. & Mrs. Joseph McGregor, " Glengyle," Victoria Rd., U. Norwood. *Fell*, Flanders, 25 May, '15.

THE GLORIOUS DEAD

McGroarty, Roland Dryden, Cyclist Scout.
b., '89 ; *s.*, Mr. & Mrs. McGroarty, Whitworth Rd., S. Norwood. *Educ.*, S. Norwood Coll. Engineer ; graduate of Inst. of Mech. Engineers ; engaged in Brit. E. Africa on railway construction work. *D.* while pris. of war, of wounds recd. at Tsaro, Brit. E. Africa, 7 Sept., '14.

McGuinness, Richard Ernest, Sgt., 1 E. Sur. Regt.
b., Croydon, 1 Aug., '92 ; *s.*, Charles E. & .T. McGuinness, 23 Rolleston Rd., Croydon. *Educ.*, Bynes Rd. Sch., Croydon. Single. Skin dresser. *Enl.*, 10 Jun., '12 ; served with original Exped. Force. *Fell*, Loos, 23 Sept., '15.

McGuire, Reginald Arthur, 492713, L/Cpl., 2/13 Lond. Regt.
b., Bristol, 5 May, '88 ; *s.*, late Samuel & Emily McGuire, 67 Richmond Rd., St. Andrew's, Bristol. *Educ.*, Bristol G. Sch. Single. Civil servant, 2nd div. clerk (Companies' dept., Board of Trade). *Res.*, "Ethelhurst," Downs Court Rd., Purley, '10-15 ; connected with Christ Church, Purley. Memb. of Sanderstead Cricket Club ; deputy organist, Christ Ch., Purley. *Enl.*, 29 Nov., '15, in L.R.B. *Fell*, Lake Doiran, Balkans, 12 Apr., '17. (Plate XX., 1).

Mack, T., 47637, Cpl., R.F.A.
Res., Croydon. *Fell*, '16.

McKay, William Alexander, Act.-C.Q.M.S., 1 E. Yorks. Regt.
b., 2 Cairo Rd., Pitlake Bdge., Croydon, 11 Jul., '91 ; *s.*, Alexander & Emily McKay, 74 Derby Rd., Croydon. *Educ.*, Brit. Sch., Croydon. Married. Apprentice in electricity works. *Res.*, 53 Southsea Rd., Croydon. *Enl.*, Nov., '07. *Fell*, France, 29 Aug., '15.

Mackmin, Alec Lawrence, T164, Driver, R.A.S.C. (attd. Suss. Yeom.)
b., Cadbury, Somerset, 16 Jan., '92 ; *y.s.*, Mr. & Mrs. A. Mackmin, Av. Mans., Elms Av., Eastbourne. *Educ.*, Trinity Sch., Eastbourne. Single. Electrician. *Res.*, 73 Malvern Rd., T. Heath. *Enl.*, 5 Aug., '14 ; *w.*, Gallipoli, 5 Jan., '16. *D.*, 7 Jan., '16, on Hosp. Ship "Assaye," Alexandria. *Buried*, 8 Jan., Chatby Mil. Cem., Alexandria.

McLaren, Reg. S., Sgt., 6 R.W.S. Regt.
Married. *D.*, 8 Dec., '17, of wounds recd. at Cambrai, 30 Nov., '17.

Maclean, Alan Charles, Pte., Lond. Scottish (14 Lond. Regt.)
b., Grove Pk., Denmark Hill, 8 Jun., '94 ; *s.*, Alan Walter & Kate Maclean, "Heatherseat," Cavendish Rd., Sutton. *Educ.*, Whitgift G. Sch. (Rev. Mason's House). Single. Clerk on Stock Exchange. *Enl.*, 4 Aug., '14. *D.*, Nov., '15, while pris. of war, of wounds recd. at Messines, 1 Nov., '14.

McLean, Daniel, 37550, Pte., E. Sur. Regt.
Res., 14 Kynaston Rd., T. Heath. Missing between 22-27 Mar., '18.

MacMasters, E. W., A.B. Seaman, R.N.
Married. *Res.*, 10 St. Saviour's Rd., Croydon. Lost his life on H.M.S. "Natal," 30 Dec., '15.

McMinn, Hugh Bell, Major, D.A.D.R.T.
b., '85 ; *y.s.*, late Robert Inglis McMinn, & Mrs. McMinn, "Midholm," Birdhurst Rd., Croydon. B.A., Oxon. *D.* in a Mil. Hosp. abroad, after a short illness, 29 Jul., '18.

McQuaigue, Arthur Charles, Pte., Gren. Gds.
b., S. Norwood, '98 ; *s.*, Mr. & Mrs. McQuaigue, Harrington Rd., S. Norwood. *Educ.*, Birchanger Rd. Sch., S. Norwood. *Enl.*, '16. *Fell*, France, 25 Aug., '18.

MacSorley, 2/Lt., 5 Northd. Fus.
    s., Mr. & Mrs. MacSorley, Mersham Rd., T. Heath. Served in
    army for 20 years, partly in India and through S.A. War ; was
    Coy.Sgt.Maj. in H.L.I. ; *commis.*, about Feb., '17. *Fell*,
    Apr., '17.
McSweeny, Felix J., 2/Lt., 19 Middlesex Regt.
    b., 16 Mar., '90. Single. Teacher. *Res.*, Balham. *Joined*,
    2/Lt., Jul., '15. *Fell*, Vierstrate, 30 Jul., '17.
McWhannell, J., 2/Lt., Wilts. Regt.
    b., '80. Married. *Res.*, Waddon Marsh Lane, Croydon. *D.*
    of wounds recd. in France, 3 Jul., '16.
Madder, Robert, Lt., 5 Glo'ster. Regt. (M.G. Sect.)
    b., Tooting Graveney, 11 Dec., '87 ; *s.*, Mr. & Mrs. Alan George
    Madder, Westcroft Farm House, Carshalton. *Educ.*, Whitgift
    G. Sch., '03-04. Single. Clerk. *Res.*, Carshalton. *Enl.*,
    as pte. in L.R.B., 4 Sept., '14. *Fell*, Somme, 20 Jul., '16.
Mahoney, William John, 43042, Pte., 54 M.G.C.
    b., Brixton, 22 Jul., '94. *Educ.*, St. Mary's (R.C.) Sch., Croydon.
    Single. Chemist's asst. *Res.*, 18 Hastings Rd., Addis. *Enl.*,
    in 2/4 R.W.S. Regt, 23 Mar., '18 ; *w.*, Gallipoli, 18 Aug., '15.
    Fell, Failloeul, France, 23 Mar., '18.
Maile, E. F., 393093, Pte., Lond. Regt.
    Res., S. Norwood. *Fell*, '17.
Major, Henry A.B. Seaman, R.N.V.R. (" Howe " Btn.)
    b., 85 Blackwall Bldgs., Whitechapel, 15 Oct., '95 ; *s.*, Mr. & Mrs.
    Major, 18 'B' Block, Peabody Bldgs., Hackney Rd., N.E. *Educ.*,
    Rockmount Rd. Sch., U. Norwood. Single. Seaman, Mercan-
    tile Marine. *Joined*, 16 Oct., '10. *D.*, 4 Sept., '15, at Bombay
    Presidency Gen. Hosp., Alexandria, from dysentery and wounds
    recd. in action, 12 May, '15. (Plate XX., 6).
Malcher, James Denis, Signaller, 7 R. Suss. Regt.
    b., 27 George St., Hertford ; *s.*, Denis & Ethel Marian Malcher,
    59 Edward Rd., Croydon. *Educ.*, Davidson Rd. Sch., Croydon.
    Single. Booking clerk, L.B. & S.C.R. Memb. of No. 51 (Croydon)
    Div., St. John Ambulance Bde. *Enl.*, 9 Nov., '15. *Fell*,
    Aveluy Wood, N. of Albert, 1 Aug., '16.
Mallet, Thomas Messervy, 2nd Offr., Mercantile Marine.
    b., Chatham, 3 Sept., '92 : *s.*, Mrs. Julia Mallet, 20 Whitehorse
    Rd., Croydon. *Educ.*, Brighton Sec. Sch., York Place, and
    School-ship " Conway," Liverpool. Single. 2nd Offr., " Duchess
    of Cornwall." *Joined*, before war, as apprentice. *Lost* with his
    ship, torpedoed between England and Le Havre, 11 Apr., '17.
Mallinson, John Frank.
    b., '95 ; *s.*, Mr. & Mrs. Mallinson, 3 Farquharson Rd., Croydon.
    Accidentally killed, in France, 3 Oct., '17.
Maltby, Albert Edward, Cpl., Can. Inf.
    b., '95 ; *y.s.*, late Mr. (of 10 Hussars) and Mrs. Maltby, 8 Frant
    Rd., T. Heath. *Educ.*, St. Mary's (R.C.) Sch., Croydon. *Res.*,
    Canada. *Enl.*, '14 ; discharged owing to results of an accident.
    Re-enlisted, '15. *Fell*, France, Oct., '17.
Maltby, Reginald, Pte., Can. Inf.
    b., Aldershot Barracks, '87 ; *e.s.*, late Mr. (of 10 Hussars) and
    Mrs. Maltby, 8 Frant Rd., T. Heath. Married ; 3 children.
    Res., Canada. *Fell*, France, Aug., '17.
Maltby, Walter, Pte., R. Fus.
    b., '91 ; 2nd *s.*, late Mr. (of 10 Hussars) and Mrs. Maltby, 8
    Frant Rd., T. Heath. *Educ.*, St. Mary's (R.C.) Sch., Croydon.
    Empl. for 10 yrs. as asst., Messrs. Watson, tobacconists, George
    St., Croydon. *Enl.*, Apr., '16. *D.*, of injuries inflicted by a
    bomb dropped by enemy air-craft, 14 Oct., '17.

THE GLORIOUS DEAD

MANN, ALEXANDER CHARLES DOUGLAS, Pte., 13 Canterbury Regt., N.Z. Exp. Force.
b., '93 ; *s.*, late Q.M. Sgt. George Mann, 38 Mansfield Rd., Croydon. Went to New Zealand early in '14. *Enl.*, 12 Aug., '14 ; *w.* twice at Dardanelles. *D.* at sea on the Hosp. ship, "Valdiva," 12 Aug., '15.

MANN, G. W., Capt., Act.-Major, M.G.C. (Heavy Branch).
e.s., late Q.M. Sgt. George Mann, 38 Mansfield Rd., Croydon. *Educ.*, Abp. Tenison's Sch., Croydon. Married. *Enl.*, in R. Scots, '14 ; twice ment. in desp. *Fell*, France, Aug., '17.

MANN, GEORGE CYRIL STANLEY, L/Cpl., 8 E. Sur. Regt.
b., Clapham Common, 15 Sept., '97 ; *s.*, Samuel Edward & Emma Louisa Mann, "Keston," Alton Rd., Waddon. *Educ.*, M. Whitgift Sch., Croydon. Single. Bank clerk. *Enl.*, 13 May, '16. *Fell*, Ypres, 9 Aug., '17.

MANSFIELD, HARRY, Pte., 6 Lond. Regt.
b., London. *Educ.*, Bensham Man. Rd. Preparatory Sch., and Dr. Simpson's Sch., S. Norwood. Single. *Res.*, "Glenagle," Cotford Rd., T. Heath. *Enl.*, May, '15. *Fell*, Hill 60, nr. Ypres, 22 Oct., '16.

MANTON, JOHN MAURICE, Pte., 1/4 R.W.S. Regt. (attd. 2 Norf. Regt.)
b., Livingstone Rd., T. Heath, 13 Jul., '93 ; *s.*, Mr. & Mrs. Manton, 49 Broadway Av., Croydon. *Educ.*, Sydenham Rd. Sch., Croydon. Single. House decorator. *Enl.*, 21 Sept., '14. *D.* of dysentery, Mesopotamia, 24 Aug., '15.

MARCH, THOMAS H., Pte., 2 R.W.S. Regt.
b., 4 Queen St., Croydon, 2 Jan., '95 ; *s.*, Mr. & Mrs. J. March, 1 Magdala Rd., Croydon. *Educ.*, Bynes Rd. Sch., Croydon. Single. Labourer. *Enl.*, Apr., '14. *Fell*, Bullecourt, 11 May, '17.

MARCHANT, GEORGE H. E., Sgt., Can. Exp. Forces.
b., '92. *Res.*, S. Norwood. *D.* of wounds, 17 Sept., '16.

MARKS, A. W., 14651, Sgt., Dorset Regt.
Res., T. Heath. *D.* of wounds, '17.

MARLOW, WILLIAM, Pte., R.W.S. Regt.
b., Croydon, 18 Jan., '83 ; *s.*, Mr. & late Mrs. Marlow, 23 Pound Lane, Epsom. *Educ.*, St. Andrew's Sch., and Brit. Sch., Croydon. Married. Lead glazier. *Res.*, 104 Old Town, Croydon. *Enl.*, in 1/4 R.W.S. Regt., Mar., '09 ; served in India ; ret. home time expired, and was sent to France, Oct., '16. *D.* at 5 C.C.S., France, of acute bronchitis and pneumonia, 26 Feb., '17.

MARR, JAMES NEIL THOMSON, Cpl., 32 Lab. Coy., R.A.S.C.
b., '84. *Educ.*, Ashe's Sch. Married ; 3 children. *Res.*, 57 Broughton Rd., T. Heath. Freemason. *D.* at West Bridgford Hosp., nr. Nottingham, 3 Nov., '16.

MARSH, ARTHUR, Pte., Australian I.F.
b., '92 ; *s.*, Mr. & Mrs. Marsh, 22 Hastings Rd., Addis. *Educ.*, Woodside and Oval Rd. Schs., Croydon. For 5 yrs. empl. at Messrs. Smith's bookstall at E. Croydon Stn. ; afterwards steward on R.M.S. "Dunottar Castle," and R.M.S. "Osterley." *Enl.*, at Sydney, Feb., '15 ; *w.*, Gallipoli, '15. *Fell*, France, 27 Mar., '18.

MARSH, CHARLES RICHARD, 3419, Pte., 1 Middlesex Regt.
b., 18 Dec., '85 ; *s.*, Mr. & Mrs. Marsh, "Crabble Farm," nr. Dover. *Educ.*, Dover. Married. Medical dispenser. *Res.*, "Crabble," 4 Compton Rd., Addis. *Enl.*, 5 Jun., '16. *Fell*, Arras, 23 Apr., '17.

MARSHALL, C. H., Lt.
School teacher, Winterbourne Rd. Boys' Sch., T. Heath. *Fell*, 2 Apr., '18.

MARSHALL, D. S., L/Cpl., Q.W. Rif. (16 Lond. Regt.)

MARSHALL, HARRY, Driver, R.F.A.
b., Croydon, 2 Nov., '95 ; *s.*, Henry & Eliza Marshall, 5 Albion St., W. Croydon. *Educ.*, Mitcham Rd. Sch., Croydon. Single. *Enl.*, Aug., '13. *Fell*, Battle of the Aisne, 15 Sept., '14.

MARSHALL, HENRY, 2/Lt., R.W.S. Regt.
b., Lond., 26 Jan., '92 ; 2nd *s.*, late Mr., & Mrs. Charles Marshall, "Daylesford," Norbury. Single. Estate agent. *Enl.*, Aug., '14 ; went to India, Oct., '14 ; ret. to Eng. for commis., Nov., '15. *Fell*, Amiens, 1 Aug., '18.

MARSHALL, STANLEY S., L/Cpl., Gordon H.
b., '99 ; *y.s.*, Mr. & Mrs. Albert Marshall, 49 Mansfield Rd., Croydon. *Educ.*, Abp. Tenison's Sch., Croydon. *Enl.*, in Lond. Scottish, Apr., '17. *D.*, 18 Aug., '18, of wounds recd. in France.

MARTIN, ALBERT HENRY, 1st Class Stoker, R.N.
e.s., Mr. & Mrs. A. J. Martin, "Beechhurst," Grange Rd., S. Norwood. *Educ.*, Ingram Rd. Sch., Croydon. *Joined*, 19 Sept., '13. *D.* while on active service, Oct., '18.

MARTIN, FRANCIS HENRY, Pte., R.W.S. Regt.
b., Eagle Hill, Norwood, 18 Sept., '76. *Educ.*, Rockmount Rd. Sch., U. Norwood. Married. Lather and painter. *Res.*, 7 Naseby Rd., U. Norwood. *Enl.*, 19 Nov., '15 ; *w.*, Somme, Jul., '16. *D.* of wounds, 12 Oct., '18.

MARTIN, GEORGE, Pte., 16 Can. Scottish (Medical Sect.).
b., 25 Sept., '85 ; *s.*, Mr. & Mrs. Martin, 45 Stanger Rd., S. Norwood. *Educ.*, Skerry's Coll., Croydon. Single. Engineer. *Res.*, London, Ontario. *Enl.*, Feb., '15. *Fell*, France, 12 Sept., '17.

MARTIN, HARRY EDWARD, 2/Lt., R.F.C.
b., Kilburn, 15 Feb., '93 ; *s.*, Mr. & Mrs. A. A. Martin, 67 Lr. Addis. Rd., Croydon. *Educ.*, Oval Rd. Sch., Croydon. Single. Partner in Martin Bros., builders, Croydon. *Res.*, in Croydon since '97. Trained at Hendon ; gained pilot's certif., 21 Jun., '16 ; obtained his wings, Sept., '16 ; went to France, 28 Oct., '16. *Fell*, nr. Arras, 16 Nov., '16. *Buried* at Aubigny Communal Cem. (Plate XIX., 2).

MARTIN, JAMES HUBERT, 2nd A.M., R.F.C.
b., Swanscombe, Kent, 27 Dec., '92 ; *s.*, Mr. & Mrs. Martin, 389 Thornton Rd., Croydon. *Educ.*, Galley Hill Sch., Swanscombe, Kent. Single. Electrician. *Res.*, 1 Cecil Rd., Croydon. *Enl.*, 1 Nov., '15. *D.* of injuries recd. in accident while flying at Gosport, 11 Mar., '16.

MARTIN, JOHN STANLEY, Pte., R.W. Kent Regt.
b., Redhill, 4 Jun., '90 ; *s.*, George & Eliza Martin, 31 Cresswell Rd., S. Norwood. *Educ.*, Woodside Sch., and Portland Rd. Sch., S. Norwood. Single. Milk carrier. *Enl.*, 3 Jun., '15. *Fell*, Somme, 15 Sept., '16.

MARTIN, ROBERT SOMERVILLE, Sgt., Winnipeg Grenadiers.
b., Scotland, '80. Married, Gertrude, daughter of Mr. & Mrs. Usher, 116 Sydenham Rd. N., Croydon. *Res.*, Anerley, and later in Canada. *D.*, '18, at Winnipeg, Manitoba, of wounds recd. in France. *Buried*, at Brookside Cem., Winnipeg.

THE GLORIOUS DEAD

MARTIN, STANLEY, Drummer, Lancs. Fus.
    b., '99 ; y.s., Mr. & Mrs. Martin, " Retreat House," T. Heath. *Educ.*, Whitehorse Rd. Sch., T. Heath. *Enl.*, Oct., '15. *Fell*, 14 Oct., '18.

MARTIN, STANLEY CURLEY JAMES, 2/Lt., Hants. Regt.
    b., 2 Dec., '83 ; s., Daniel & Amelia Martin, 6 Sunny Bank, S. Norwood. *Educ.*, Whitgift G. Sch., '97-98.

MARTIN, W. H., L/Cpl., Argyll & Sutherland H.
    y.s., Mr. & Mrs. G. H. Martin, 103 Selsdon Rd., Croydon. *Educ.*, Brighton Rd. Sch., Croydon. Single. Booking clerk, S. Croydon and Forest Hill Stns. *Enl.*, 8 Nov., '15 ; went to France, Apr., '16 ; gassed, 7 Jul., '18. *Fell*, 23 Aug., '18.

MARTIN, W. J., Pte.
    b., '97 ; s., Mr. & Mrs. Martin, 9 Rymer Rd., Addis. Empl. by Mr. Boxall, greengrocer, Cherry Orchard Rd., Croydon. *Enl.*, '15 ; served in Egypt, '16-Jul., '18. *Fell*, France, Aug., '18.

MARTIN, WALTER PERCIVAL, 2/Lt., Leicester Regt.
    b., 4 Jun., '90 ; s., Mr. & Mrs. Walter Joseph Martin, 69 Waddon Rd., Croydon. *Educ.*, Whitgift G. Sch., '01-06.

MARTIN, WILLIAM HAROLD, 2/Lt., Lond. Regt.
    b., '90 ; s., Mr. & Mrs. Herbert Martin, U. Norwood. *Educ.*, Dulwich Coll., and Wadham Coll., Oxford. *Joined*, Oct., '14.

MARTINS, JOHN, Pte., R.W. Fus.
    b., Norwich, '85. *Educ.*, Norwich. Married ; 1 child. Empl. as attendant at Croydon Infirmary for 7 yrs. *Res.*, 289 Bensham Lane, T. Heath. *Enl.*, 19 May, '16. *Fell*, N.W. of Albert, 22 Apr., '18.

MARTYR, FRANK ROBERT, Pte.
    b., Woodside, '92. *Educ.*, M. Whitgift Sch. Empl. at Lond. and S. Western Bank. *Res.*, 85 Woodside Green, S. Norwood. *Enl.*, Oct., '15 ; served in France, May, '16-Aug., '17. *Fell*, Messines, 6 Aug., '17.

MASH, ARTHUR, Pte., Aust.I.F.

MASH, W., 12062, Rflmn., R.B.
    Fell, '16.

MASLIN, CHARLES, Coy.Q.M.Sgt., 2/4 Lond. Regt. (R. Fus.)
    b., '82. Married. *Res.*, 90 St. Saviour's Rd., Croydon. *Enl.*, '14 ; served in Gallipoli, from where he was invalided home, 15 Dec., '16. *D.* at Grange Mil. Hosp., Southport, 8 Jan., '16.

MASSEY, HUGH ALEXANDER, Lt., R.N.D. ("Howe" Btn.)
    b., 2 Mar., '85 ; s., Mr. & Mrs. Hugh Holland Massey, Whitley. *Educ.*, Whitgift G. Sch., '93-99. *Fell*, Gallipoli.

MATES, THOMAS ST. GEORGE, R.W.S. Regt.
    b., Victory Place, U. Norwood ; s., Mr. & Mrs. Mates, 59 Ridsdale Rd., Anerley. *Educ.*, Rockmount Rd. Sch., U. Norwood. Married. Shoe maker. *Res.*, 30 Eagle Hill, U. Norwood. Previously served 13 yrs. in army. *Enl.*, 4 Aug., '14. *D.*, 6 Nov., '14, in a German pris. of war hosp., of wounds recd. at Ypres.

MATHERS, CHARLES, 2722, Pte., 2/4 R.W.S. Regt.
    b., Ware, Hertford., 23 Nov., '68. Married. Painter. *Res.*, 15 Fountain Rd., T. Heath. *Enl.*, 3 Oct., '14. *Fell*, Dardanelles, 28 Aug., '15.

MATHEWS, FREDERICK JOHN, 43623, Pte., 17 Middlesex Regt.
    b., Lond., 1 Mar., '91 ; s., William & Lillah Mathews, 15 Balfour Rd., S. Norwood. *Educ.*, Aldgate Ward Schs., & Sir John Cass Sch. Single. Clerk. *Enl.*, 13 Mar., '16. *Fell*, Beaumont Hamel, 13 Nov., '16.

MATTHEWS, F., 43623, Pte., Middlesex Regt.
Res., Norwood. *Fell*, '17.
MATTHEWS, F. R., Lt., E. Sur. Regt.
Educ., Whitgift G. Sch., Croydon. *Missing*, '18.
MATTHEWS, FRANK ARTHUR, Lt., 10 R. Suss Regt., attd. R.F.C.
b., Bexhill, Suss., 11 Nov., '93 ; s., Mr. & Mrs. Matthews, 312 Brighton Rd., S. Croydon. *Educ.*, Holmwood Sch., Bexhill. Single. Actor (with Sir F. R. Benson's Coy.). *Enl.*, 5 Sept., '14, in R. Berks. Regt.; sgt., Dec., '14 ; commis., Jan., '16 ; served for 1 yr. in Egypt ; attd. to R.F.C., and gained his wings, Dec., '16 ; went to France, Mar., '17. *Fell*, 24 Apr., '17, while on bombing raid over German lines, nr. St. Quentin. (Plate XVII., 5).
MATTHEWS, W., Pte., R.W.S. Regt.
Educ., Abp. Tenison's Sch., Croydon. *Enl.*, Aug., '14 ; served abroad, May, '15-Oct., '17. *Fell*, 11 Oct., '17.
MATTHEWS, WILLIAM, Pte., Northd. Fus.
s., Mr. & Mrs. J. Matthews, Avington Grove, Penge. Married, L. R., daughter of Mr. & Mrs. Baldwin, of Anerley. *Res.*, Hebburn, Newcastle-on-Tyne. *Fell*, 3 May, '17.
MATTHEWS, WILLIAM HENRY, L/Sgt., 1 Gren. Gds.
b., S. Norwood, 25 Mar., '94 ; s., Mr. & Mrs. Matthews, 13 Albert Rd., S. Norwood. *Educ.*, Birchanger Rd. Sch., S. Norwood. Single. Memb. of St. Mark's, S. Norwood, C.L.B. *Enl.*, '13. *Fell*, Givenchy, 16 Jun., '15.
MAUD, A. J., 25553, Pte., E. Sur. Regt.
Res., W. Croydon. *Fell*, '17.
MAUNSELL, WILFRID INNOCENT, Capt., Scottish Rif.
b., '84 ; s., Surgeon-Gen. T. Maunsell, C.B., 29 Broughton Rd., T. Heath. *Joined* Lancs. Fus., '02 ; transf. to Scottish Rif., '08 ; company commdr., Feb., '13. *Fell*, France, 8 Feb., '15.
MAWSON, W. F., 4527, Pte., Lond. Regt.
Fell, '16.
MAY, HAROLD GOSTWYCK, 2/Lt., 1 Dorset Regt.
b., Croydon, 16 May, '87 ; y.s., Mr. & Mrs. R. C. May, "Sherborne," Woodside Green, S. Norwood. *Educ.*. Sherborne Sch., where he was capt. of cricket team ; represented sch. in Publ. Schs. Boxing at Aldershot, etc. ; took his degree at Trinity Coll., Dublin. Single. Schoolmaster at Kelly's Coll., Llandovery, Clifton and Sherborne, to which he returned as a master in Sept., '14. *Joined* as 2/Lt., Nov., '14. *D.*, 27 Mar., '15, at 7 Gen. Hosp., Boulogne, of wounds recd. at St. Eloi, 14 Mar., '15.
MAYES, WALTER HENRY, Gnr., R.F.A.
b., 3 Seymour Place, S. Norwood, 17 Apr., '89 ; s., late Mr., & Mrs. Mayes, 20 Cresswell Rd., S. Norwood. *Educ.*, Birchanger Rd. Sch., S. Norwood. Single. Clerk. *Enl.*, 17 Mar., '15. *Fell*, France, 3 Jun., '18.
MAYO, A. G., S/307259, Pte., R.A.S.C.
Res., S. Norwood. *D.* of wounds, '17.
MAZZEY, JOHN, Driver, R.F.A.
b., Clewer, nr. Windsor ; s., Mr. & Mrs. Mazzey, 90 High St., Caterham. *Educ.*, Godstone and Caterham Counc. Schs. Single. Engineer. *Res.*, 38 Farningham Rd., Caterham Valley. *Enl.*, 5 Jan., '15. *D.* at Mil. Hosp., Southsea, of pneumonia, 31 Jan., '15.
MEADES, HARRY EDWARD, L/Cpl., 2/4 R.W.S. Regt.
b., Swanley, Kent, 29 Oct., '96 ; s., Ernest & Elizabeth Meades, 120 Church St., Croydon. *Educ.*, Mitcham Rd. Sch., Croydon. Single. Compositor. *Enl.*, 10 Aug., '14. *Fell*, Dardanelles, 23 Aug., '15.

THE GLORIOUS DEAD

MEDHURST, E., 52497, Pte., R.W.S. Regt.
Res., S. Norwood. *Fell*, '17.

MEECH, EDGAR FREDERICK, Pioneer, R.E.
b., Brixton, 7 Feb., '97 ; *s.*, Frederick & Frances Meech, 26 Kilmartin Av., Norbury. *Educ.*, Streatham Mod. Sch. Single. Analytical chemist. *Enl.*, 25 Mar., '16. *D.*, 1 Apr., '17, at 19 C.C.S., of wounds recd. 28 Mar., '17.

MELBOURNE, R., 153250, Pte., 43 Btn., Can. Inf.
Formerly res. in Croydon, being empl. as turncock.

MERCER, C. J., L/Cpl., L.R.B. (5 Lond. Regt.)
b., '95 ; *e.s.*, Mr. & Mrs. W. J. Mercer, Milton Rd., Croydon. Empl. by Messrs. Curwen, Wood St., E.C. *Enl.*, Aug., '15 ; served 15 months in France. *Fell*, 27 Mar., '18.

MERCER, WALTER CHARLES, Coy.Sgt.Maj., 17 R. Fus.
b., '91. Empl. by Messrs. Allder, North End, Croydon. *Res.*, S. Norwood. Goal-keeper for S. Norwood Wednesday Football Club, and memb. of S. Norwood Wednesday Cricket Club. *Enl.*, 8 Dec., '14. *D.*, 8 Apr., '18, of wounds recd. in France 2 days prev.

MERRIMAN, ARTHUR PRESTON, Pte., Manchr. Regt.
b., Penge, 26 Jan., '95 ; *s.*, Henry & C. Merriman, 62 Donald Rd., Croydon. *Educ.*, Boston Rd. Sch., Croydon. Married. Baker. *Res.*, 60 Howbury Rd., Nunhead. *Enl.*, in E. Sur. Regt., 19 Jan., '16. *Fell*, Sanctuary Wood, nr. Ypres, 3 Jul., '17.

MERRIMAN, HENRY JOHN, Pte., R.W.S. Regt.
b., Penge, 14 Sept., '90 ; *s.*, Henry & C. Merriman, 62 Donald Rd., Croydon. *Educ.*, Boston Rd. Sch., Croydon. Single. Shop asst. *Res.*, W. Croydon. *Enl.*, 1 Oct., '06. *Fell*, Zonnebeke, 21 Oct., '14.

MESSENGER, HERBERT SYDNEY.
2nd *s.*, Sydney & Sophia Messenger, Lodge Rd., Croydon. Married, Haddie, daughter of Mr. Novell. *Res.*, Brockley. *D.* of wounds recd. in France, 29 Jul., '18.

METCALFE, W. C., 2/Lt., E. Sur. Regt.
Fell, '16.

MEYERS, EDWIN J., L/Cpl., R. Fus.
b., Australia, '97 ; *s.*, Mr. & Mrs. H. W. Meyers, 52 Temple Rd., Croydon. *Educ.*, M. Whitgift Sch. *Enl.*, Aug., '14. *D.* of wounds, '16.

MEYRICK, GEOFFREY JAMES, Pte., Gordon H.
b., Lond., 18 Apr., '99 ; *s.*, James Frederick Battram & Wilhelmina Meyrick, 71 Gonville Rd., T. Heath. *Educ.*, M. Whitgift Sch. Single. Bank clerk. *Enl.*, in Lond. Scottish, 1 May, '17. *Fell*, Bois de Rheims, 23 Jul., '18.

MIDDLETON, AUBREY FRANCIS, Rflmn., Kensingtons (13 Lond. Regt.).
b., '97. *Res.*, S. Norwood. *Fell*, 29 Aug., '18.

MIDDLETON, LEONARD W., 2/Lt., R.F.C.
Educ., Whitgift G. Sch. *Enl.*, in R.E., as despatch rider, '14 ; served in France, Oct., '14-Nov., '17 ; transf. to R.F.C., '16. *Fell*, France, 8 Nov., '17.

MILES, BERNARD C., 8 Suff. Regt.
Empl. as maintenance attendant, Croydon Gas Coy. *Missing*, 12 Oct., '17.

MILES, CHARLES TALBOT, Rflmn., L.R.B. (2/5 Lond. Regt.)
b., Alexandra Rd., Addis., 28 Dec., '96 ; *s.*, Walter Talbot & Sophie J. Miles, 399 Whitehorse Rd., T. Heath. *Educ.*, Croydon. Single. Junior clerk, Messrs. Pearson & Son, Billiter St., E.C. *Enl.*, 19 Apr., '15 ; went to France, 10 Nov., '15 ; invalided to England with trench feet, Mar., '16 ; returned to France, 13 Feb., '17 ; *w.*, 17 Jun., '17. *Fell*, Wurst Farm, Ypres, 20 Sept., '17.

MILES, GEORGE HENRY, Pte., E. Sur. Regt.
  b., Earlsheaton, Yorks., 28 Sept., '93 ; s., Mr. & Mrs. Richard Miles, 31 Cuthbert Rd., W. Croydon. *Educ.*, Mitcham Rd. Sch., Croydon. Single. Printer. *Enl.*, 1 Feb., '15. *Fell*, Ypres, 4 Jan., '18.

MILES, HERBERT.
  b., Earlsheaton, 13 Sept., '91 ; s., Mr. & Mrs. Miles, 31 Cuthbert Rd., Croydon. *Educ.*, Mitcham Rd. Sch., Croydon. Single. Labourer. *Enl.*, 17 Aug., '12. *Fell*, Delville Wood, Somme, 18 Aug., '16.

MILES, HERBERT TALBOT. 2/Lt., R.F.A.
  b., Croydon, 3 Aug., '89 ; s., late Mr. Miles, & Mrs. H. Fuller, 16 Alexandra Rd., Leyton. *Educ.*, Reedham Sch., Purley. Single. Accountant. *Res.*, Leyton. *Enl.*, as pte. in A.P.C., 21 Oct., '14 ; commis. in Yeom., 18 Oct., '15 ; transf. to R.F.A. *Fell*, Bapaume, 16 Apr., '17.

MILES, W. G., Pte., Lond. Regt.
  b., '97 ; e.s., Mr. & Mrs. Miles, 15 Frith Rd., Croydon. *Educ.*, Welcome Hall, Croydon. *Enl.*, in E. Sur. Regt., 14. *Fell*, 7 Oct., '16.

MILLARD, A. G., 2/Lt., E. Sur. Regt.
  b., '91 ; s., Mr. & Mrs. Millard, Langdale House, T. Heath. *Educ.*, Eton Choir Sch. (while there acting as asst. organist to Dr. C. H. Lloyd) and R. Coll. of Mus. ; later organist to Par. Ch., Farnham, and music master at Marlborough Coll., and Felstead Sch. ; F.R.C.O., and A.R.C.M. ; hon. memb. of Royal Albert Inst., Windsor ; memb. of Windsor Orchestral Soc., and first hon. conductor, Amateur Operatic Soc. *Enl.*, in Artists Rif. O.T.C., Jan., '16 ; commis., Dec., '16. *Fell*, 7 Aug., '17.

MILLEN, WILLIAM GEORGE, Cpl., Wilts. Regt.
  5th s., late Mr. G. A. & Mrs. Millen, 82 Sumner Rd., Croydon. *Educ.*, M. Whitgift Sch., and Oxford County Sch. Married. Empl. on " Croydon Advertiser," and managing editor of " The Brick and Pottery Trades Journal." *Res.*, " St. Aubyn's," Royston Rd., Penge. *Enl.*, Sept., '14. *Fell*, Neuville Vitasse, 9 Apr., '17.

MILLER, CLEMENT FRANCIS, 2/Lt., 46 Signals, Engineers, Ind. Army Res.
  s., Mr. & Mrs. S. A. Miller, 45 Richmond Rd., T. Heath. *Enl.* in R.W.S. Regt. (Territorial), 23 Apr., '12 ; commis. in I.A.R., 15 Jan., '18. *D.* of pneumonia, King George's Hosp., Poona, India, 5 Oct., '18.

MILLER, E., 10730, Pte., R.W.S. Regt.
  Res., W. Croydon. *Fell*, '17.

MILLER, MISS JANE SOPHIA MARY ANN.
  b., '65. Dressmaker's asst. *Res.*, 51 Oval Rd., Croydon. *Killed* during air-raid, Oct., '15.

MILLER, JOHN, 33315, Pte., Middlesex Regt.
  Married. *Res.*, 9 Elm Rd., T. Heath. *Fell*, France, 13 Jul., '17.

MILLIAM, MATTHEW MARK, 9625, Pte., R.W.S. Regt.
  b., '82 ; s., late Mr., & Mrs. Milliam, 26 Purley Rd., Croydon. *Educ.*, Bynes Rd. Sch., Croydon. Empl. by Mr. Knight, builder. *Enl.*, Sept., '15. *Fell*, 18 Aug., '17.

MILLIGAN, ERIC EDGAR, Rflmn., 17 K.R.R.C.
  b., Croydon, Jan., '99 ; s., Mr. & Mrs. John Milligan, 177 Sydenham Rd. N., Croydon. *Educ.*, Brit. Sch., Croydon. Single. Pawnbroker's asst. *Enl.*, 29 May, '15. *Fell*, Thiepval, Somme, 3 Sept., '16.

THE GLORIOUS DEAD

MILLIGAN, HAMILTON HERRIES, Officers' Cook, 2nd Class., R.N.
b., Croydon, 5 Nov., '89 ; 2nd *s.*, Mr. & Mrs. John Milligan, 177 Sydenham Rd. N., Croydon. *Educ.*, Brit. Sch., Croydon. Married. Chef and roast-cook. *Joined*, 8 Feb., '16. *Lost* on H.M.S. " Mary Rose " (T.B.D.), sunk in North Sea, 17 Oct.,'17.

MILLS, JOHN, Pte., 7 R.W.S. Regt.
b., '88 ; *s.*, Mr. & Mrs. Mills, 92 Leighton St. East, Croydon. Empl. by Croydon Corporation as boatman at Wandle Park. *Fell*, France, 25 Aug.,' 15.

MILSTEAD, WILLIAM WALTER, Pte., 7 R. Suss. Regt.
b., T. Heath, 23 Feb., '89 (?). *Educ.*, Beulah Rd. Sch., Croydon. Married ; 1 child. Baker, empl. by Mrs. Graham, Norbury Rd., T. Heath. *Res.*, 46 Mersham Rd., T. Heath. *Fell*, France, 3 May, '17.

MIRIAM, LEONARD, Rflmn., L.R.B. (5 Lond. Regt.)
b., '99 ; *s.*, Mr. & Mrs. Miriam, 18 Mayo Rd., Croydon. Empl. by Messrs. Cook & Son, St. Paul's Churchyard, Lond., E.C. *Enl.*, Jun., '17. *Fell*, 18 Aug., '18.

MITCHELL, ERIK HARRISON, Capt., att. R.F.C.
b., 5 Jul., '94. *Educ.*, Whitgift G. Sch., '04. Ment. in desp., M.C.

MITCHELL, FRANK O., Pte., R.W.S. Regt.
b., '92. Empl. by Messrs. Heath & Co., sign writers, Croydon. *Res.*, Parchmore Rd., T. Heath. *Enl.*, Nov., '15. *Fell*, 17 Sept., '16.

MITCHELL, HAROLD DAVID, Bdr., R.F.A.
b., 31 Thornton Rd., T. Heath, 1 Mar., '98 ; *s.*, Mr. & Mrs. Mitchell, 31 Thornton Rd., T. Heath. *Educ.*, Winterbourne Rd. Sch., T. Heath. Single. Milkman. *Enl.*, 13 May, '16. *Fell*, France, 21 Mar., '18. (Plate XIX., 4).

MITCHELL, HERBERT THOMAS, Pte., 9 R. Suss. Regt.
b., 88 Old Town, Croydon, 26 Feb., '91 ; *s.*, William James & Elizabeth Ann Mitchell, 54 Pawson's Rd., Croydon. *Educ.*, Princess Rd. Sch., Croydon. Single. Empl. by L.B. & S.C.R., at Rowfant Stn. *Res.*, Crawley, Suss. *Enl.*, 1 Sept., '14. *Fell*, Ypres, 13 Feb., '16.

MITCHELL, J. M., 263037, Pte., Seaforth H.
Res., S. Norwood. *Fell*,'17.

MITCHELL, JAMES, Driver, R.A.S.C.
b., Croydon, 3 Oct., '83 ; *s.*, Mr. & Mrs. W. Mitchell, 10 Boston Rd., W. Croydon. *Educ.*, Boston Rd. Sch., Croydon. Married. Labourer. *Enl.*, 8 May, '08 ; served in France from Aug., '14. *D.* of heart disease and tuberculosis, 7 Apr., '20.

MITCHELL, JAMES HILL, 2902, Sgt., 2/4 R.W.S. Regt.
b., 71 Villa St., Walworth, 29 Nov., '77 ; *s.*, Mr. & Mrs. Mitchell, 15 Siddons Rd., Croydon. *Educ.*, Brit. Sch., Croydon. Single. Wireman. *Enl.*, 9 Oct., '14. *D.*, 5 Dec., '15, of wounds recd. at Suvla Bay, 2 Dec., '15.

MITCHELL, JESSE ARTHUR, Pte., 1/5 Seaforth H.
b., 2 St. John's Rd., S. Norwood, 28 Feb., '82 ; *s.*, George & Fanny E. Mitchell, 186 Holmesdale Rd., S. Norwood. *Educ.*, Birchanger Rd. Sch., S. Norwood. Single. Motorman, Croydon Corp. Tramways. *Enl.*, 15 May, '16. *Fell*, Belgium, 5 Jul., '17. (Plate XV., 2).

MITCHELL, JOHN, L/Cpl., 5 Seaforth H.
s., late Harry William Mitchell, of S. Norwood. Married a daughter of W. Rowlinson, of Letchworth, Herts ; 4 children. Baker. *Res.*, 110 Stanley Rd., Croydon. *Enl.*, 29 May, '16. *Fell*, 27 Jul., '18. *Buried*, Jouchery, nr. Rheims.

MITCHELL, JOHN LEISHMAN, 2/Lt., R. Irish Rif.
  b., '97; y.s., Mr. & Mrs. Adam Mitchell, "Hurley House," Belvedere Rd., U. Norwood. *Educ.*, Alleyn Coll., Dulwich. *Enl.*, in Artists Rif., Oct., '15; commis., 10 Jul., '16; went to France, 4 Feb., '17, with 2/11 Lond. Regt. *D.*, Jun., '17, of wounds recd. in France, 24 May, '17.
MITCHELL, W., 17847, Pte., R.W. Kent Regt.
  Res., Norwood. *Fell*, '17.
MOAT, CHARLES WALTER, Rflmn., 1 R.B.
  b., T. Heath, 10 Aug., '93; s., late Henry Ernest, & Mary Ann Moat, 37 Penrith Rd., T. Heath. *Educ.*, All Saints' Ch. Sch., U. Norwood. Single. Motor driver. *Enl.*, 18 Feb., '15. *Missing*, presumed fallen, Le Transloy, 18 Oct., '16.
MOLTON, G., 20190, Pte., Essex Regt.
  Res., Addis. *Fell*, '16.
MOLYNEUX, N. W., 20934, Pte., E. Kent Regt.
  Res., Croydon. *Fell*, '17.
MONCKTON, ALFRED EDWARD, Sapper, R.E.
  s., Mr. & Mrs. Monckton, 244 Bensham Lane, T. Heath. *Missing*, '18.
MONTAGUE, EDWARD ARCHIBALD WILLIAM, 11260, Pte., R. Suss. Regt.
  b., Melbourne, Australia, 11 Jun., '92; s., Edward & Susanna Montague, 92 Portland Rd., S. Norwood. *Educ.*, St. Augustine's Upper Grade Sch., Kilburn. Single. Ship's steward. Served on H.M.S. "Engadine" as officers' steward, 13 Aug., '14-16 Dec., '15. *Enl.*, 1 Apr., '16. *Fell*, Somme, 9 Sept., '16.
MONTAGUE, JOHN GEORGE, A.B Seaman, R.N.D.
  b., Selhurst New Rd., 3 May, '97; s., Mr. & Mrs. E. Montague, 180 Gloucester Rd., Croydon. *Educ.*, Sydenham Rd. Sch., Croydon. Single. Wireman. *Enl.*, Aug., '15. *D.*, 26 Apr., '17, at 1 Can. C.C.S., France, of wounds recd. nr. Arras, 24 Apr., '17.
MOODY, FREDERIC ARTHUR, 208514, Pte., 4 Norf. Regt.
  b., Walham Green, Fulham, 26 Oct., '92; s., late Mr., & Mrs. A Moody, 143 Northwood Rd., T. Heath. *Educ.*, All Saints' Sch. Fulham. Single. Gas engineer. Memb. of C.L.B., and V.T.C until enlistment. *Enl.*, 29 Sept., '16. *Fell*, Cambrai, 20 Nov., '17
MOOJEN, WALTER LENS, Pte., R. Fus. (U.P.S.)
  b., 12 Feb., '95; s., Mr. & Mrs. Walter Moojen, 6 Pollard's Hill N., Norbury. *Educ.*, Whitgift G. Sch., '04-11.
MOON, J. F., 130830, Sapper, R.E.
  Res., S. Norwood. *D.* of wounds, '16.
MOON, RICHARD JOHN, L/Cpl., 1/19 Lond. Regt.
  b., 88 Stepney Green, 14 Jun., '80; s., Richard & Fanny Moon, 102 Mansfield Rd., Hampstead. *Educ.*, Princess Rd. Sch., Regent's Park. Married. Bookseller's clerk. *Res.*, 33 Ferndale Rd., S. Norwood. Served with 17 Middlesex Regt. (Volunteers), 21 Oct., '03-31 Mar., '08. *Enl.*, 22 May, '15. *D.* of wounds recd., 23 May, '16. *Buried*, Barlin Cem., nr. Vimy Ridge.
MOORE, HENRY GLANVILLE ALLEN, Col., 6 E. Yorks. Regt.
  b., Nov., '65; s., Rev. & Mrs. Henry Dawson Moore, "Clydesdale," North Park, Croydon. Served in Nile Exped. (Khartoum). *Fell*, Dardanelles, '15.
MOORE, LESLIE, Trooper, R. Bucks. Hussars.
  b., Albert Rd., Addis., 14 Oct., '96; y.s., Mr. & Mrs. Moore, 6 Albert Rd., Addis. *Educ.*, Oval Rd. Sch., Croydon. Single. Empl. at Valuation Dept., Somerset House. *Enl.*, Sept., '14; w., Gallipoli, '15, and W. Egypt, '16. *D.* of wounds recd. at Gaza, 29 Apr., '17.

XIX.

1. Rflmn. E. J. LEECH, 1 Lond. Rif. B.
2. 2/Lt. H. E. MARTIN, R.F.C.
3. 2/Lt. K. L. N. McCULLOCH, 16 Middlesex Regt.
4. Bdr. H. D. MITCHELL, R.F.A.
5. Rflmn. L. L. LONGMAN, Q. Vict. Rif. (9 Lond. Regt.)
6. 2/Lt. L. H. MULKERN, Machine Gun Corps

XX.

1. L/Cpl. R. A. McGuire, 2/13 Lond. Regt.
2. Pte. A. E. Lucas, R.F.C.
3. Sgt. J. S. Mugford, Machine Gun Corps
4. Sgt. F. T. Libby, Lond. Rif. B.
5. Lt. K. Morfey, 16 Rajputs (Ind. Army)
6. Seaman H. Major, R.N.V.R

THE GLORIOUS DEAD

MOORE, R. J., Act.-Sgt., R.W.S. Regt.
Res., Croydon. *Fell*, '16.
MOORE, SIDNEY HERBERT, Pte., E. Kent Regt.
b., '86 ; *4th s.*, Mr. & Mrs. Moore, 6 Albert Rd., Addis. *Educ.*, Oval Rd. Sch., Croydon. Married. Fruiterer. *Res.*, 136 Cherry Orch. Rd., Croydon. *Enl.*, Mar., '16. *Fell*, France, 27 Aug., '18.
MORANT, GERALD A., Capt., W. Yorks. Regt.
b., '96 ; *y.s.*, late Mr. & Mrs. McKay Morant, " The Glade," Farquhar Rd., U. Norwood. *Educ.*, Whitgift G. Sch. Married. M.C. *Fell*, 15 Apr., '18.
MORDEN, W. H., Sgt., M.G.C.
b., '82. Married. Manager, Messrs. Wm. Glaisher, Ltd., booksellers, George St., Croydon. *Res.*, 89 Ashburton Av., Croydon. *Served* in S. African War. *D.* of influenza and pneumonia, Le Havre, 4 Mar., '19.
MORETON, ROBERT, Pte., 12 Suff. Regt.
b., 107 Biggin Hill, 7 Jun., '96 ; *s.*, Mr. & Mrs. Moreton, 22 Queen's Rd., U. Norwood. *Educ.*, Rockmount Rd. Sch., U. Norwood. Single. Grocer's asst. *Enl.*, Sept., '15. *D.* of wounds, France, 27 Jul., '16.
MORFEY, KENNETH, Lt., 16 Rajputs (attd. 97 Inf.)
b., '95 ; *y.s.*, Cyrus & Edith Morfey, 3 Altyre Rd., Croydon. *Educ.*, Laleham Sch., Margate. Single. Asst. to his father (merchant). *Enl.*, in H.A.C., 5 Aug., '14 ; went to France, Sept., '14 ; *w.*, Ypres, Jun., '15 ; ret. to Sandhurst, Sept., '15, passing exam. for Indian Army ; *commis.*, 7 Apr., '16 ; went to India, 5 Oct., '16 ; posted to 16 Rajputs, 7 Nov., 16 ; *served* in Mesopotamia, '17-18. *D.* after an operation for appendicitis, Baghdad, 20 May, '18. (Plate XX., 5).
MORGAN, D. H., Pte., Lond. Regt.
Educ., Whitgift G. Sch., '01-05. *Fell*, '16.
MORGAN, HENRY EDWARD ALFRED, Chief P.O., R.N.
s., Mr. & Mrs. H. A. Morgan, Belmont Rd., S. Norwood. Held Royal Humane Soc. Cert. for saving life from drowning. *Fell* in Battle of Jutland, 31 May, '16.
MORGAN, W., R.N.V.R.
Educ., High Sch., Croydon. *Fell*, Dardanelles, '16.
MORGAN, W. G., 6476, Pte., Lond. Regt.
Empl. by Pub. Health Dept., Croydon Corp. *Res.*, Croydon. *Fell*, '16.
MORLEY, H., 1052, Pte., R.W.S. Regt.
Fell, '16.
MORRIS, ALBERT E., Gnr., R.F.A.
b., 20 Apr., '95 ; *y.s.*, Mr. & Mrs. S. T. Morris, 43 Lond. Rd., Croydon. *Enl.*, 1 Jun., '15 ; *served* in France, 27 Nov., '15-Jul., '17. *Fell*, 5 Jul., '17.
MORRIS, LIONEL BERTRAM FRANK, 2/Lt., R.F.C.
b., Lond., 26 Dec., '96 ; *s.*, Mr. & Mrs. Alfred Frank Morris, " Merle Bank," Rotherfield Rd., Carshalton. *Educ.*, Whitgift G. Sch., '10-13. Single. *Joined* Inns of Court O.T.C., May, '15 ; brought down over German lines, 17 Sept., '16. *D.* at a German Hosp., nr. Cambrai, same day.
MORRIS, WILFRID STANLEY, Pte., 6 K.S.L.I.
b., Brockley, 5 Jun., '90 ; *e.s.*, William H. & Clara Morris, 21 Northampton Rd., Croydon. *Educ.*, M. Whitgift Sch. Single. Tailor's cutter. *Res.*, Shrewsbury, Salop. *Enl.*, Aug., '14 ; taken pris. nr. Ham, about 24 Mar., '18. *D.* of pneumonia at Giessen, Germany, 31 Jul., '18.

w

THE CROYDON ROLL OF HONOUR

MORRISH, HAROLD, A.B. Seaman, R.N.
    b., Oldfield Rd., Stoke Newington, 18 Nov., '88; *s.*, T. S. & late Celia Morrish, 38 Cranbrook Rd., T. Heath. *Educ.*, Oldfield Rd. Sch., Stoke Newington. Single. *Joined* 27 Sept., '02. Lost with H.M.S. "Bulwark," destroyed by internal explosion, Sheerness, 6 Nov., '14.

MORTER, ALAN GORDON, Artists Rif. O.T.C.
    b., '87; 2nd *s.*, Mr. & Mrs. James Morter, Norwood and Lingfield. *D.*, 7 Mar., '17.

MORTIMER, C., Pte.
    b., '93. Married. *Res.*, 93 Lr. Addis. Rd., Croydon. *Fell*, 26 Apr., '18.

MORTIMER, CHARLES, Pte., R.W.S. Regt.
    b., 21 Keen's Rd., Croydon; *s.*, Mr. & Mrs. Alfred Mortimer, 21 Keen's Rd., Croydon. *Educ.*, St. Andrew's Sch., Croydon. Married. Printer. Mobilised with Territorials, 4 Aug., '14; went to India; ret., time expired May, '16; went to Egypt with 3/4 R.W.S. Regt., Jan., '17; *w.*, Gaza, 4 Nov., '17. *Fell*, nr. Jerusalem, 26 Apr., '18.

MORTON, HORACE, Pte., 19 Middlesex Regt.
    b., Dulwich, 28 Sept., '86. *Educ.*, Dulwich Hamlet and Whitechapel Foundation Sch. Married. Clerk. *Res.*, 119 Mayall Rd., Herne Hill. *Enl.*, 13 Feb., '15. *Fell*, France, 31 Jul., '17.

MORTON, W. A., Pte., R. Fus.
    Res., Croydon. *Fell*, '17.

MOSCROP, ERNEST ARTHUR, Pte., Manchr. Regt.
    b., '96; *s.*, Mr. & Mrs. Moscrop, 39 Moffatt Rd., T. Heath. *Educ.*, Beulah Rd. Sch., T. Heath. Empl. by Messrs. Weldon and Co., Mitcham Rd., Croydon. *Enl.*, 8 Mar., '17. *Fell*, France, 31 Jul., '17.

MOSS, EDMUND CHARLES, 22341, Pte., R.W.S. Regt.
    Married. *Res.*, 250 Bensham Lane, T. Heath. *Enl.*, Nov., '14. *Fell*, May, '17.

MOTT, EDWARD CHARLES, Pte., 4 R. Fus.
    b., Croydon, 3 Mar., '00; *s.*, James & Jane Mott, 67 Clarendon Rd., Croydon. *Educ.*, Mitcham Rd. Sch., Croydon. Single. Baker's asst. *Enl.* in R.W.S. Regt., May, '15; discharged as under age, 2 Sept., '15. Re-enlisted, Sept., '16. *Fell*, Belgium, 27 Sept., '17.

MOTT, FRANK, Pte., 1/4 R.W.S. Regt.
    b., Croydon, 9 Apr., '92; *s.*, Mr. & Mrs. James Mott, 67 Clarendon Rd., Croydon. *Educ.*, Mitcham Rd. Sch., Croydon. Married. Milk roundsman. *Res.*, 61 Lancing Rd., Croydon. *Enl.*, 2 Sept., '14. *D.* of pneumonia, Mil. Gen. Hosp., Ferozepore, India, 4 Nov., '18.

MOTT, JAMES GEORGE, Pte., 2 Notts. & Derby. Regt.
    b., Croydon, 7 Apr., '84; *s.*, James & Jane Mott, 67 Clarendon Rd., Croydon. *Educ.*, Mitcham Rd. Sch., Croydon. Single. Railway goods clerk. *Enl.*, Aug., '17. *D.*, 7 Dec., '17, at 6 Gen. Hosp., Rouen, of wounds recd. in France, 2 Dec., '17.

MOTT, P. M., 82315, Act.-Bdr., R.G.A.
    Empl. by Croydon Gas Coy. *Res.*, Croydon. *Enl.*, May, '16 *Fell*, 8 Oct., '17.

MOULDER, HARRY, Coy. Sgt. Maj., 1/4 R.W.S. Regt.
    b., '81. *D.*, Nowshira, India, 20 Nov., '16.

MOWLE, J. H., Lab. Coy.
    Res., W. Norwood. *Fell*, '17.

THE GLORIOUS DEAD

MUGFORD, JACK HERBERT, Gnr., R.G.A. (103 Anti-Aircraft Sect.).
  b., Acton Green, Chiswick, 28 Dec., '94; s., Mr. & Mrs. Mugford, 44 Stanger Rd., S. Norwood. *Educ.*, Birchanger Rd. Sch., S. Norwood. Single. Ledger clerk. *Enl.*, Dec., '16; *served* in Egypt from May, '17. D. at Cairo, Egypt, of cerebro-spinal meningitis, 3 Jul., '18. (Plate XV., 1).

MUGFORD, THOMAS GEORGE, Lt., 1/35 Sikhs (Ind. Army).
  b., Chiswick, 19 Jan.,'92; s., Mr. & Mrs.Mugford, 44 Stanger Rd., S. Norwood. *Educ.*, Birchanger Rd. Sch., S. Norwood. Clerk. Single. *Mobilised* with 4 R.W.S. Regt., 4 Aug., '14; proceeded to India, Oct., '14; commis., May, '17. *Fell*, Somerset Hill, Khyber Pass, Afghanistan, 17 May, '19. Buried in Brit. Cem., Sandi-Kotal, Khyber, 19 May, '19.

MULKERN, LIONEL HENRY, 2/Lt., M.G.C.
  b., Sutton, 1 Sept., '84. *Educ.*, Sutton G. Sch. Married. Empl. on Stock Exchange. *Res.*, "Eversdene," Bishop's Pk. Rd., Norbury. *Enl.*, in 9 Lond. Regt., 22 May., '02; Sur. Yeom., 21 Feb., '11; M.G.C., 25 Jun., '17; Territorial Efficiency Med. *Fell*, France, 26 Sept., '17. (Plate XIX., 6).

MURRELL, F., 6196, Pte., Lond. Regt.
  Fell, '16.

MURRELL, THOMAS GEORGE, Pte., 2/5 Notts. & Derby. Regt.
  b., 2 Albion St., 15 Mar., '99; s., Mr. & Mrs. R. Murrell, 65 Donald Rd., Croydon. *Educ.*, Mitcham Rd. Sch., Croydon. Single. Carman. *Res.*, 97 Handcroft Rd., Croydon. *Enl.* in 3 R.W.S. Regt. D., 19 Apr., '18, at 36 C.C.S., France, of wounds recd. prev. day.

MUSGROVE, ALBERT, Cpl., R.A.S.C. (M.T.)
  b., '92. *Educ.*, Sydenham Rd. Sch., Croydon. Married; 1 child. Empl. by Mr. Ward, photographer, W. Croydon. *Res.*, 28 Arundel Rd., Croydon. *Enl.*, Jun., '16. D. of wounds, 18 Oct., '18.

MUSK, HERBERT ERNEST, Pte., 23 R. Fus.
  b., Battersea, 14 Mar., '82; s., Philip & Martha Sarah Musk, "Rothesay," Graham Rd., Mitcham. *Educ.*, Mantua and Shillington St. Schs., Battersea. Married; 4 children. Postman. *Res.*, 80 Tylecroft Rd., Norbury. *Enl.*, 22 Jun., '16. *Fell*, France, 10 Mar., '17.

MUSTO, H. W., 24 R. Fus.
  Cashier. empl. at Farrow's Bank, Croydon. *Enl.*, in 2/5 E. Sur. Regt., 29 Feb., '16. *Fell*, 7 Feb., '17.

MUSTOE, H. G., 121240, Cpl., R.F.A.
  Res., W. Norwood. *Fell*, '17.

NAISH, CYRIL FREDERICK ROBERT, Pte., L.R.B. (5 Lond. Regt.).
  Educ., M. Whitgift Sch. *Fell*, Aug., '18.

NAPIER, HENRY ROBERT, L/Cpl., R.E.
  b., Hither Green, 9 Jan., '85; s., Mr. & Mrs. E. Napier, 11 Helder St., Croydon. *Educ.*, Bynes Rd. Sch., Croydon. Married. Plate-layer, empl. by S.E. & C.R. *Res.*, 40 Upland Rd., Croydon. *Enl.*, 20 Nov., '14; *served* in France, Jan., '15-10 Jun., '18. D. at Christchurch Hosp., Hants., of cancer and ulcer in the chest, 13 Jun., '18.

NASH, EDWARD HORACE BUTTERWORTH, L/Cpl., 1 Dorset Regt.
  b., Devonshire Rd., Forest Hill, 2 Sept., '95; e.s., Horace & Olive A. Nash, 26 Eridge Rd., T. Heath. *Educ.*, Winterbourne Rd. Sch., T. Heath. Single. Shop asst. *Enl.*, Aug., '14; trench feet, Jan., '15. *Fell*, Passchendaele, nr. Ypres, 4 Dec., '17.

NATUSCH, R. W., 2/Lt., R.F.A.
    Educ., Whitgift G. Sch., '10-15. *Fell,* '17.
NEAL, C., 26943, Act.-Sgt., Northd. Fus.
    Res., S. Croydon. *D.*, '17.
NEAL, REUBEN, 6901, L/Sgt., 2 R.W.S. Reg'.
    b., 38 Love Lane, S. Norwood, 10 Sept., '95 ; *s.*, William & Harriet Neal, 32 Love Lane, S. Norwood. *Educ.*, Woodside Sch., S. Norwood. Single. Engineer (fitter). *Enl.*, 28 Aug., '14 ; *served* in France, 7 Nov., '14-14 Mar., '17. *Fell*, France, 14 Mar., '17.
NEALON, JOHN HENRY, Pte., 4 R. Fus.
    b., Dalston, 26 Jul., '98 ; *s.*, Mr. & Mrs. Nealon, 63 Gonville Rd., T. Heath. *Educ.*, M. Whitgift Sch. Single. Shipping clerk, Lloyd's Exchange. *Enl.*, 1 Sept., '16. *D.*, 5 May, '18, at 22 C.C.S., Bethune, of wounds recd., 3 May, '18. (Plate XXII., 2).
NEATE, CHARLES VICTOR, Gnr., R.F.A.
    b., Anerley, 3 Sept., '91 ; *s.*, William Henry & Sarah Weaver Neate, 54 Station Rd., Anerley. *Educ.*, Oakfield Rd. Sch., Anerley. Married. Wood engraver. *Enl.*, 5 Oct., '15 ; invalided home with frost-bitten feet, Jan., '17 ; ret. to France, Jun., '17. *Fell*, nr. Rheims, 27 May, '18.
NEILL, DONALD, 1642, Act.-Sgt., Black Watch.
    s., Mr. & Mrs. Albert A. Neill, 27 Richmond Rd., T. Heath. *W.*, nr. Zonnebeke, 29 Oct., '14 *Fell*, nr. Kut-el-Amara, Mesopotamia, 22 Apr., '16.
NEILL, EDWARD CHARLES, 425, Cpl., Black Watch.
    s., Mr. & Mrs. Albert A. Neill, 27 Richmond Rd., T. Heath. *Fell*, nr. Soissons, 15 Sept., '14.
NELKI, A. M., Rflmn., L.R.B.
    b., '96 ; *s.*, Insp. Nelki, of S. Norwood Spec. Constab. *Res.*, S. Norwood. *Enl.*, about Dec., '14. *Fell*, France, 18 May, '17.
NELSON, J., 4306, Pte., Lond. Regt.
    Res., S. Norwood. *Fell*, '16.
NEVARD, A. H., Pte., Lond. Regt.
    Empl. by L.B. & S.C.R. *Res.*, 45a Mersham Rd., T. Heath. *D.* of wounds, 25 Sept., '16.
NEW, A. W., Essex Regt.
    b., '95 *Educ.*, Whitgift G. Sch. Held a commis. in Territorials before war ; acted as transport offr. with his btn. at Gallipoli, from Jul., '15-Dec., '15. *Accidentally killed*, Ypres, 14 May, '18.
NEW, HEDLEY BRUCE, Lt., Essex Regt. (attd. R.F.C.)
    b., '93. *Educ.*, Whitgift G. Sch., and Crystal Pal. Sch. of Engineering. Civil engineer and surveyor. *Joined*, Aug., '14 ; *served* at Gallipoli ; transf. to R.F.C., '16. *Fell*, France, 31 Nov., '17.
NEW, STANLEY CHARLES, L/Cpl., Can. Forces.
    b., '90 ; *s.*, Mr. & Mrs. C. New, S. Croydon. Empl. by Messrs. Quelch & Sons, boot and shoe manuf., Croydon. *D.*, 1 Nov., '16, of wounds recd., 13 Sept., '16.
NEWBURY, HAROLD, 30285, Cpl., 4 Gren. Gds.
    b., Devonport, 4 Aug., '98 ; *s.*, Walter J. S. & Mary Jane Newbury, 24 Carew Rd., T. Heath. *Educ.*, Plymouth Sec. Sch., & Skerry's Coll., Croydon. Single. Civil Serv. clerk (Board of Trade). *Enl.* in R. Horse Gds., May, '16. *Fell*, nr. Hazebrouck, 13 Apr., '18.

THE GLORIOUS DEAD 357

NEWCOMBE, HAROLD VICTOR, Pte., 7 E. Kent Regt.
    b., 71 Coningham Rd., Shepherd's Bush, 27 Mar., '97 ; *s.*, Mr. & Mrs. Newcombe, 21 Belgrave Rd., S. Norwood. *Educ.*, Birchanger Rd. Sch., S. Norwood, and Whitgift Sch. Single. Ledger clerk. *Res.*, 53 Enmore Rd., S. Norwood. *Enl.*, 5 Sept., '14 ; went to France, 25 Jul., '15. *Fell*, between Montauban and Carnoy Craters, Somme, 1 Jul., '16. (Plate XXII., 1).

NEWELL, S. J., Gnr., R.F.A.
    b., '91. *Res.*, 25 Watcombe Rd., S. Norwood. *Fell*, 19 Apr., '17.

NEWLYN, LESLIE, L/Cpl., R.W.S. Regt.
    b., '92 ; *s.*, Mr. & Mrs. Newlyn, Home Farm Dairy, Chelsham Rd., S. Croydon. *Fell*, 11 May, '17.

NEWNHAM, E., L/Cpl., R.W.S. Regt.
    Res., W. Croydon. *Fell*, '17.

NICHOLASS, HENRY JOHN, Driver, R.F.A.
    b., 294 Parchmore Rd., T. Heath, 2 Apr., '97 ; *s.*, Mr. & Mrs. H. J. Nicholass, 296 Parchmore Rd., T. Heath. *Educ.*, Beulah Rd. Sch., T. Heath. Single. Clerk. *Enl.*, 1 Apr., '16. *Fell*, France, 3 Aug., '17. (Plate XXIII., 5).

NICHOLLS, FREDERICK ALBERT, Gnr., R.G.A.
    Married ; 6 children. Greengrocer. *Res.*, 115 Parchmore Rd., T. Heath. *Enl.*, Mar., '17 ; *w.*, France, Aug., '17 ; in hosp. at Leicester for 10 mths. ; discharged, 10 Jul., '18. *D.* of wounds and pneumonia, at Croydon Hosp., 10 Sept., '18.

NICHOLS, ALEXANDER, 2 R.W.S. Regt.
    s., L. & A. Nichols, 7 Broadway Av., Croydon. *Fell*, Festubert, 16 May, '15.

NICHOLS, DUDLEY MATTHEW, Lt., R.A.F.
    b., '99 ; *y.s.*, Mr. & Mrs. Nichols, of Addis. *Educ.*, Bedford House Sch., Addis. Single. Empl. by Mr. E. E. Clark, solicitor, Eastcheap ; wrote much poetry, etc., published by Messrs. G. Newnes, and Messrs. Raphael Tuck. *Killed* at a flying sch. in England, Sept., '18.

NICHOLS, H., Gnr., R.G.A.

NICHOLSON, BERNARD GEORGE MAURICE, Lt., Northd. Fus.
    y.s., Mr. & Mrs. Nicholson, Norwood. *D.* in hosp., at Lincoln,'18.

NICKLESS, F., Pte., R.Fus.
    Single. Empl. by Croydon Corp., Roads Dept. *Res.*, 87 Albany Rd., Reading. *Enl.*, 15 Oct., '14 ; *w. & missing*, France, 8 Oct., '16.

NIGHTINGALE, BERT GEORGE, Pte., Yorks. Regt.
    b., Sutton, 26 Oct., '81 ; *s.*, Mr. & Mrs. George Nightingale, 65 Warwick Rd., Sutton. *Educ.*, Sutton Counc. Sch. Married. Warehouseman. *Res.*, 16 Kynaston Rd., T. Heath. *Enl.*, 20 Jul., '16. *Fell*, France, 6 May, '18.

NIGHTINGALE SIDNEY, Pte., Q.W. Rif. (16 Lond. Regt.)
    b., Tunbridge Wells, 26 Feb., '91 ; *s.*, Mr. & Mrs. Nightingale, 5 The Exchange, Purley. *Educ.*, Abp. Tenison's Sch., Croydon. Single. Partner in his father's business. *Enl.*, 26 Feb., '16. *Fell*, Ashecourt, France, 8 Apr., '17.

NIGHTINGALE, STUART D., L/Cpl., 2/4 R.W.S. Regt.
    b., '99 ; *s.*, Mr. & Mrs. Nightingale, 66 Torridge Rd., T. Heath. *Educ.*, Winterbourne Rd. Sch., T. Heath, where he was several yrs. memb. of winning team in inter-sch. relay race at Crystal Pal. Single. Junr. asst., Croydon Public Libraries. *Enl.*, Jan., '15 ; *served* at Suvla Bay ; invalided home with dysentery ; sent to Egypt, '16 ; participated in capture of Beersheba, Hebron, Bethlehem and Jerusalem ; proceeded to France, Jul., '18. *Fell*, France, 1 Aug., '18.

NIGHY, JOSHUA, Pte., R.W.S. Regt.
s., Mr. & Mrs. Nighy, 96 Old Town, Croydon. *Fell*, 1 Jul., '16.
NIMMO, STUART HENRY, Capt., 8 R.S. Fus.
b., Dunoon, Argyllshire, 18 Aug., '97 ; *s*., Mr. & Mrs. Charles Stuart Nimmo, 33 The Crescent, Croydon. *Educ*., Hillhead High Sch., Glasgow, where he was a cadet. Single. Shipbroker's clerk. *Res*., Glasgow. *Joined* as 2/Lt., Sept., '15. *Fell*, Doiran Front, Salonica, 19 Sept., '18.
NOAKES, STUART BERTRAM, Capt.
b., '75; *4th s*., Mr. & Mrs. Wickham Noakes, Selsdon Pk., Croydon. *Lost* with the transport " Aragon," torpedoed in the Mediterranean nr. Alexandria, 30 Dec., '17.
NOAKES, WILLIAM JAMES.
s., Mr. & Mrs. Noakes, 195 Bensham Lane, T. Heath. *Fell*, 7 Oct., '17.
NOBLE, J. S., 2/Lt., R. Berks. Regt.
b., '99. *Educ*., Whitgift G. Sch., Croydon. *D*. of wounds, 30 Mar., '18.
NOLAN, CHARLES DOUGLAS, 841951, Rflmn., Lond. Irish Rif. (18 Lond. Regt.).
b., Godalming, 27 Nov., '95 ; *y.s*., Michael James & Emily Nolan, 84 Harrington Rd., S. Norwood. *Educ*., Portland Rd. Sch., S. Norwood. Single. Grocer's asst. *Enl*., 27 Oct., '15. *Fell* nr. Albert, 24 Aug., '18.
NORMAN, A. G., Pte., Ox. & Bucks. L.I.
s., Mr. & Mrs. Norman, 12 Mitcham Rd., Croydon. *Res*., Croydon. Was in the Res. when war broke out ; *w*., Oct., '14. *Fell*, Jul., '16.
NORMAN, ARTHUR JAMES, Sgt., 14 R.W.S. Regt.
b., Croydon, '89. *Educ*., Mitcham Rd. Sch., Croydon. Married. Empl. as tram conductor by S. Met. Tramways. *Res*., 2 Park Cottages, Morden. *Enl*., 4 Aug., '14. *Fell*, France, 12 Apr., '18.
NOYCE, F. C., Pte.
b., 21 Dec., '96 ; *3rd s*., Mr. & Mrs. A. J. Noyce, 101 Parson's Mead, Croydon. *Enl*., 21 Dec., '14. *D*., 16 Oct., '16, of wounds inflicted by bomb dropped from enemy aircraft, 2 days prev.
NUNN, B. A., Sgt., Welsh Regt.
Res., S. Norwood. *Fell*, '17.
NYE, A. H., R.W.S. Regt.
Fell, '16.
NYE, R. T., Pte., R. Fus.
b., '00 ; *s*., Mr. & Mrs. James T. Nye, Victory Hotel, Croydon. *Educ*., Shirley Ch. Sch. Empl. by Messrs. Cashman, and by Mr. Baldwin, butchers. *Enl*., in Middlesex Regt., 9 Feb., '18. *D*. of wounds recd. in France, 24 Aug., '18.
NYREN, D. R., 2/Lt., R. Fus.
Educ., Whitgift G. Sch. *Fell*, '18.
OAKES, F. W., Sgt., R.E. (Signal Serv.)
b., '94 ; *s*., Mr. & Mrs. Oakes, 136 Holmesdale Rd., S. Norwood. Empl. as sorting clerk and telegraphist, Croydon Post Office, Dec., '10-15. *Enl*., Apr., '15. *D*., 25 Jul., '17, at Egginton Hall Hosp., Derby, of gas poisoning contracted at Ypres. *Buried*, Queen's Rd. Cemetery, Croydon.
OBORNE, GEORGE EDWARD, Pte., 1 Middlesex Regt.
b., 97 Honeywell Rd., Wandsworth ; *2nd s*., Mr. & Mrs. J. W. Oborne, 4 Charnwood Rd., S. Norwood. *Educ*., Whitehorse Rd. Sch., T. Heath. Single. Apprentice to compositor. *Enl*., 6 Mar., '15. *Fell*, 16 Apr., '16.

THE GLORIOUS DEAD

O'CONNOR, W. P., 302115, Cpl., Lond. Regt.
  Res., T. Heath. *Fell*, '17.
O'DONNELL, J., 29295, L/Cpl., M.G.C.
  Res., Croydon. *Fell*, '17.
OLDFIELD, BERNARD STEWART, Pte., 1/5 Manchr. Regt.
  b., '88 ; *y.s.*, Mr. & Mrs. Oldfield, 59 Hunter Rd., T. Heath.
  D. of wounds recd. in France, 21 Oct., '18.
OLDHAM, CYRIL, Pte., L.R.B. (1/5 Lond. Regt.).
  Educ., M. Whitgift Sch. *Fell*, 9 Oct., '16.
OLIVIER, JASPER GEORGE, 2/Lt., 7 D.C.L.I.
  b., 26 Apr., '96 ; *e.s.*, Henry Eden Olivier (Vicar, St. James' Ch.)
  & Gertrude Olivier. *Educ.*, St. Anselm's Sch., Croydon, Rossall,
  and Worcester Coll., Oxford (History Exhibitioner). *Gazetted*
  to 9 E. Lancs. about Dec., '14 ; transf. to D.C.L.I. *Fell* nr.
  Lesboeufs, France, 16 Sept., '16.
OLIVIER, ROBERT HAROLD, Capt. & Adjt., 4 Leicester Regt.
  b., '79. *Gazetted* to D.C.L.I., Nov., '99 ; Lt., '01 ; Capt., '09 ;
  Adjt., 4 Leicester Regt., '09 ; served in S. African War as Station
  Staff Offr. at Paardeburg, Poplar Grove and Dreinfontein (Queen's
  Med., 4 clasps, and King's Med., 2 clasps) ; Nandi, '05-06. *Fell*,
  Belgium, 17 Sept., '14.
OLLEY, C. W., Pte., R. Berks. Regt.
  b., Croydon, 3 Jun., '00 ; *s.*, Mr. & Mrs. E. T. Olley, 2B John
  St., Coventry Rd., S. Norwood. *Enl.* in R.E. *Missing*, 5 Apr., '18.
ORD, JAMES WILLIAM, Pte., 16 Middlesex Regt.
  b., '96 ; *s.*, Mr. & Mrs. Wm. O. Ord, 13 Lebanon Rd., Croydon.
  Educ., Boro. Sec. Sch., Croydon. Single. Junr. asst., Boro.
  Engineer's Dept., Croydon Corp. (empl. at Russell Hill Water-
  works). *Enl.*, Aug., '15 ; served in France, Apr.-Jul., '16.
  Fell, Beaumont Hamel, 1 Jul., '16. (Plate XXXVI., 3).
ORGAN, ALBERT OSWALD, Pte., 1 R.W.S. Regt.
  b., New Rd., Battersea, 12 Jun., '83 ; *s.*, Oswald & Elizabeth
  Organ, 53 Russell Rd., Croydon *Educ.*, Sleaford St. Sch.,
  Battersea Park. Married. Carman. *Res.*, Zion Rd., T. Heath.
  Enl., Oct., '14. *D.* of wounds recd. at Loos, 25 Sept., '15.
OSBORNE, C., 23009, Pte., Essex Regt.
  Res., W. Croydon. *D.*, '17.
OSBORNE, FREDERICK CHARLES, 7220, Pte., Lond. Scottish (14 Lond. Regt.)
  b., Cherry Orchard Rd., Croydon, 10 Jan., '96 ; *s.*, late Mr., &
  Mrs. Mark Osborne, 88 Cross Rd., Croydon. *Educ.*, Oval Rd.
  Sch., Croydon. Single. Engraver. *Res.*, 88 Cross Rd.,
  Croydon. *Enl.*, 15 Mar., '16. *Fell*, Arras, 28 Mar., '17.
OSEMAN, CHARLES EMBLEM.
  Married. Labourer, empl. by Croydon Corp., Rds. Dept.
  Res., 20 Addison Rd., S. Norwood. *D.* of wounds recd., 25
  Sept., '14.
OUTTRIM, CHARLES E., Pte., R.W.S. Regt.
  y.s., Mr. & Mrs. W. Outtrim, " Guildford Villa," 174 Selsdon
  Rd., Croydon. *Enl.*, 30 Oct., '15. *D.* at Stat. Hosp., Rawal
  Pindi, India, of malaria, 17 Jun., '17.
OVETT, H. T., 60871, Pte., R. Fus.
  Res., Croydon. *Fell*, '17.
PADBURY, HENRY RAYMOND, L/Cpl., R. Innis. Fus.
  s., Mr. & Mrs. Padbury, 29 Tanfield Rd., Croydon. *Enl.* about '06 ;
  served in Ireland, Malta, Crete, China and India ; *w.*, '14. *Fell*,
  Richebourg, 16 May, '15.
PAGE, G. W., Pte., R.W.S. Regt.
  Fell, '16.

PAGE, L. R., Sgt., E. Kent Regt.
  b., '95. D., 14 Aug., '17, of wounds recd. 9 Aug., '17.
PAGE, R. W., Rflmn., R. Irish Rif.
  b., '79. Married ; 1 son. Empl. as representative of Messrs. Hall & Co., coal merchants, Whitehorse Rd., Croydon. *Res.*, 88 Rymer Rd., Addis. *Enl.* in R.A.S.C., Oct., '16. *Fell*, 7 Aug., '17.
PAGE, W., Pte., 3/5 E. Sur. Regt.
  Empl. by Croydon Corp., Rds. Dept. *Fell*, '18.
PAICE, STANLEY CECIL, 2/Lt., R.A.F.
  b., 47 Croydon Grove, Croydon, 7 Apr., '88 ; *s.*, George & Eunice Mary Paice, 7 Third Av.,Queen's Pk.,W.(late of 4 Warrington Rd., Croydon). *Educ.*, Par. Ch. Sch., Croydon, & M. Whitgift Sch. Single. Motor mechanic. *Res.*, La Vegas, New Mexico, U.S. *Enl.* in Can. R.H.A., 11 Nov., '15, rising to rank of cpl., act.-sgt. *Killed* in accident while flying at Upavon, Wilts., 4 Jun., '18.
PAIGE, ALFRED HENRY, Pte., 1/20 Lond. Regt.
  b., 8 Junction Cottages, Croydon, 20 Sept., '96 ; *s.*, Alfred Edward & Elizabeth Paige, 12 Russell Rd., Croydon. *Educ.*, Sydenham Rd. Sch., Croydon. Single. Porter. *Enl.*, in R. Fus., 3 Mar., '16. *Fell*, High Wood, Somme, 15 Sept., '16.
PAINE, HARRY, 2/Lt., Sher. For. (Notts. & Derby. Regt.)
  b., '97 ; *4th s.*, Mr. & Mrs. J. H. Paine, 83 London Rd., Croydon. *Enl.*, '14. *Fell*, 29 Sept., '18.
PAINE, JAMES HORACE, Pte., Lond. Regt.
  b., '98 ; *3rd s.*, Mr. & Mrs. George Cuthbert Paine, "Beechwood," Parkstone (late of Norwood). *Fell*, 30 Dec., '17.
PAINE, WALTER LIONEL, Capt. & Adjt., 10 K.O.R.L. Regt.
  b., '81 ; *s.*, Mr. & Mrs. Paine, " Cotswold," Farquhar Rd., U. Norwood. *Educ.*, Oundle G. Sch., & Sydney Sussex Sch. Single. M.A., Camb. ; house master at Oundle G. Sch.; asst. master, Whitgift Sch. ; secretary, " Reform of Latin Teaching Association." *Enl.* as pte. in Gren. Gds., Aug., '14. *Fell*, Gallipoli, 4 Jun., '15.
PALMER, ALEXANDER THOMAS HERBERT, Pte., 6 R.W.S. Regt.
  b., Chelsea, 1 Jul., '97 ; *s.*, Thomas & Helena Charlotte Palmer, 36 Windmill Grove, Croydon. *Educ.*, Oval Rd., & Brit. Schs., Croydon. Single. Reporter, " Croydon Times." *Enl.*, 18 Jun., '15. *D.*, 10 Apr., '17, of wounds recd. nr. Arras, 4 Apr., '17. *Buried*, Duisans Brit. Cem., nr. Arras.
PALMER, W. C., Rflmn., K.R.R.C.
  Married ; 1 child. Clerk, Croydon Gas Coy., Apr., '99-16. *Res.*, 36 Raymead Av., T. Heath. *Enl.*, Jun., '16 ; served in France and Italy. *D.* of wounds, 30 Mar., '18.
PALMER, WALTER MONTAGUE, Pte., 3 R. Fus.
  b., Bromley-by-Bow, 11 Feb., '96 ; *s.*, Mr. & Mrs. H. Palmer, 108 Holmesdale Rd., S. Norwood. *Educ.*, Ecclesbourne Rd. Sch., T. Heath. Single. Butcher's asst. *Res.*, 295 Whitehorse Rd., Croydon. *Enl.*, 18 Jan., '14. *Fell*, Loos, 27 Sept., '15.
PALSER, ERNEST MANICORN, L/Cpl.
  Fell, 1 Jul., '16.
PANTING, ARNOLD CLEMENT, 2/Lt., 9 R.W.S.Regt. (attd. R. Munster Fus.)
  b., Brixton, 30 Apr., '90 ; *s.*, Mr. & Mrs. J. Harwood Panting, " The Shack," Melrose Av., Norbury. *Educ.*, Alleyn's Coll., Dulwich. Single. Journalist on editorial staff of Amalgamated Press. *Enl.* in an O.T.C., 19 Oct., '14 ; served in Egypt and Balkans. *Killed* while on reconnaissance work with R.F.C., Stavros, Salonica, 13 Jan., '17.

THE GLORIOUS DEAD

PARADIN, W., 17810, Pte., Essex Regt.
  Fell, '16.
PARHAM, F. L., Sapper, R.E.
  Married. *Res.*, 86 Grant Rd., Croydon. *D.* of pneumonia, Mesopotamia, 12 Oct., '18.
PARISH, S., Cpl., 4 R.W.S. Regt.
  Empl. by Croydon Corp., Electricity Dept. *Fell*, '16.
PARKER, Cpl., R. Irish Rif.
  b. about '98 ; *s.*, Mr. & Mrs. Parker, Forest Hill. Empl. as cinema operator, Electric Pal., Croydon. *Res.*, Cassland Rd., T. Heath. *Accidentally killed* by premature explosion of a bomb at Co. Down Training Camp, Ireland, Dec., '17.
PARKER, EDWARD, Pte., M.G.C.
  b., '96 ; *2nd s.*, Mr. & Mrs. Parker, late of 46 Cobden Rd., S. Norwood. *Educ.*, Birchanger Rd. Sch., S. Norwood. *Enl.*, Apr., '17 ; transf. to Wilts. Regt., Oct., '17, and to M.G.C., Feb., '18.
PARKER, G. A., Pte.
  b., Croydon, '86. *Educ.*, Boston Rd. Sch., Croydon. Married ; 2 children. Empl. by L.B. & S.C.R. *Res.*, 2 Cecil Rd., Croydon. *Enl.*, Mar., '17. *Fell*, Passchendaele, 10 Oct., '17.
PARKER, G. S., 14216, Sapper, R.E.
  Res., T. Heath. *Fell*, '17.
PARKER, GEORGE, Pte., 6 R.W.S. Regt.
  Empl. by Messrs. Streeter Bros., and Messrs. Smith, Wilkinson & Sons. *Res.*, 38 Mitcham Rd., Croydon. *Enl.*, Aug., '14. *Fell*, France, 14 Mar., '16.
PARKER, JAMES GEORGE, Pte., 6 R.W.S. Regt.
  b., Croydon, 30 May, '87. *Educ.*, Whitehorse Rd. Sch., T. Heath. Married. Paperhanger. *Res.*, 9 Talbot Rd., T. Heath. *Enl.*, 27 Aug., '14. *Fell*, Armentières, 23 Sept., '15.
PARKER, ROBERT, Pte.
  b., '91. *Educ.*, Boston Rd. Sch., Croydon. Married ; 1 daughter. Empl. by L.B. & S.C.R. *Enl.*, Mar., '17 ; *w.*, Cambrai, Nov., '17. *Fell*, France, 23 Aug., '18.
PARKER, W. H., Capt., Lond. Regt.
  Educ., Whitgift G. Sch., Croydon. *Fell*, '17.
PARR, EDWIN, L/Cpl., R.W. Kent Regt.
  b., '93 ; *s.*, Mr. & Mrs. Parr, 56 Tanfield Rd., Croydon. Married; 2 children. Empl. by Mr. Cooper, hairdresser. *Res.*, 66 Southbridge Rd., Croydon. *Enl.*, Apr., '16. *Fell*, Somme, 7 Oct., '16.
PARROTT, J. T., 111882, Gnr., R.G.A.
  Res., Croydon. *Fell*, '17.
PARSONS, E. D.
  Formerly Res. Med. Offr. at Croydon Boro. Hosp. *Res.*, at Wimbledon. *D.* of typhoid, contracted in France. (Plate I., 4).
PARSONS, ALBERT VICTOR, 14667, Sgt., 1 Beds. Regt.
  b., '86 ; *s.*, Mr. & Mrs. Parsons, 1 Leighton St. E., Croydon. *Educ.*, Mitcham Rd. Sch., Croydon. *Enl.*, '15 ; *w.*, twice. *Fell*, nr. Arras, 23 Apr., '17.
PARSONS, E. H., Sgt., Can. E.F.
  b., '87. *Res.*, Vancouver, late of Croydon. *Fell*, France, 29 Sept., '16.
PARSONS, HAROLD COPE, Cpl., Q.V. Rif. (9 Lond. Regt.)
  b., T. Heath, 3 Dec., '88 ; *s.*, Mr. & Mrs. George Keble Parsons, 53 The Beeches, Carshalton. *Educ.*, M. Whitgift Sch. Married. Clerk. *Res.*, " The Glen," Heathview Rd., T. Heath. *Enl.*, 10 Nov., '14. *Fell*, nr. Albert, 24 Jun., '18 ; *buried*, Bavelincourt Cem., nr. Corbie-sur-Somme. (Plate XXII., 3).

PARSONS, J. E., 11552, Rflmn., R.B.
    Res., W. Croydon. *Fell*, '16.
PASCALL, THOMAS OSBORNE, Pte., R. Fus.
    b., 21 Feb., '95 ; *s.*, Mr. & Mrs. Thomas George Pascall, Boro. Green, Kent, formerly of Woodside Green, S. Norwood. *Educ.*, Whitgift G. Sch., Croydon. *Fell*, France, 2 Jan., '16.
PATCHING, HENRY JOHN, Rflmn., L.R.B. (5 Lond. Regt.)
    b., Brighton, 5 Apr., '95. *Educ.*, St. Saviour's Sch., Croydon. Single. Clerk. *Res.*, 16 Arundel Rd., Croydon. *Enl.*, 15 Feb., '15. *D.* of cerebro-spinal meningitis, at 7 Gen. Hosp., St. Omer, 11 Feb., '17.
PATEMAN, HENRY LEWIS, 2/Lt., R.F.C.
    b., 26 Jan., '97 ; *s.*, Mr. Lewis, Res. Eng., Croydon Gas Coy., Waddon Marsh Lane, Croydon. *Educ.*, Boro. Sec. Sch., Croydon. *Enl.*, Jun., '15, as 2nd a.m. ; 2nd cl. pilot's certif., 1 May, '16 ; 1st cl., 23 May, '16 ; sgt., Jul., '16 ; commis., Nov., '16 ; Croix de Guerre (French). *Fell*, '17.
PATIENCE, F. C., Pte., R.W.S. Regt.
    b., '93. *Educ.*, Princess Rd. Sch., Croydon. Married ; 1 child. Stoker, Croydon Cement Works. *Res.*, 47 Leighton St., Croydon. *Enl.*, Jun., '16 ; taken pris., 18 Nov., '16. *D.* while pris. of war, Dec., '16.
PAUL, W., Capt. & Adjt., W. Yorks. Regt.
    b., '75 ; *e.s.*, Mr. & Mrs. W. Paul, 39 South End, Croydon. *Res.* in India before war. M.C. *D.* of wounds, 1 Dec., '17.
PAULLEY, GEORGE HENRY, Sgt., R.G.A.
    b., 53 Brigstock Rd., T. Heath, 22 Oct., '90 ; *s.*, William & Ellen Paulley, 53 Brigstock Rd., T. Heath. *Educ.*, Ecclesbourne Rd. Sch., T. Heath. Single. Police constable. *Enl.* in R.F.A., 150 Bty., Feb., '06.; on reserve, Feb., '12-Aug., '14, during which time he served with Met. Police Force, attd. " C " Div., Vine St. *Rejoined*, 5 Aug., '14 ; served from Aug., '14-Mar., '17. *D.* of cerebro-spinal meningitis, St. Pol, 18 Mar., '17.
PAYNE, CHRISTOPHER CHARLES, Pte., 2 R. Suss. Regt.
    b., Worth, Sussex, 1 May, '98 ; *s.*, George & Fanny Payne, 41 Strathmore Rd., Croydon. *Educ.*, Tavistock Rd. Sch., Croydon. Single. Railway employee. *Enl.*, 16 Feb., '17. *Fell*, nr. St. Quentin, 18 Sept., '18. (Plate XXI., 1).
PAYNE, HAROLD GEORGE, Pte., D.L.I.
    b., Croydon, 20 Jan., '87 ; *s.*, Arthur & Emma Payne, 20 Mayo Rd., Croydon. *Educ.*, Whitehorse Rd. Sch., T. Heath. Married. Gasfitter. *Enl.*, 28 May, '16. *Fell*, France, 29 Mar., '18.
PAYNE, WILLIAM HENRY, L/Cpl., 1 R.W.S. Regt.
    b., 8 Leslie Grove, Croydon, 10 Jun., '97 ; *s.*, Mr. & Mrs. Payne, 8 Leslie Grove, Croydon. *Educ.*, Oval Rd. Sch., Croydon. Single. Signal box lad. *Fell*, Mons, 31 Oct., '14.
PAYNTER, G., Cpl., 11 E. Sur. Regt.
    Empl. by Croydon Corp., Roads Dept. *Res.*, 41 Selhurst Rd., S. Norwood. *Enl.*, about Dec., '16. *Fell*, France, 9 Sept., '17.
PEACOCK, THOMAS GORDON, Capt. & Adjt., 8 R. Berks. Regt.
    b., '93 ; *e.s.*, Mr. & Mrs. Thomas Peacock, late of Hadleigh Mount, Croydon. *Fell*, '15.
PEACOCK, WALTER JAMES, Pte., Middlesex Regt.
    b., Brixton, 3 Oct., '96 ; *s.*, Mr. & Mrs. Walter Hugh Peacock, 430 Lr. Addis. Rd., Croydon. Single Clerk. *Enl.*, as 2nd a.m., in R.F.C., Aug., '15. *Fell*, Flanders, 21 Mar., 18 ; *buried*, Nine Elms Cem., Poperinghe.

THE GLORIOUS DEAD

PEARCE, A. A., Pte., R.W.S. Regt.
b., '95. Single. Empl. as fitter's mate by Croydon Gas Coy., from 16 May, '12. *Enl.*, May, '15. *Fell*, 21 Sept., '18.

PEARCE, GEORGE, Rflmn., 1 R.B.
Married ; 6 children. *Res.*, 144 Gloucester Rd., Croydon. *Enl.*, '99 ; served in S.A. War ; recalled to colours, 4 Aug., '14 ; *w.* & buried by shell nr. Armentières, Oct., '14, and as a result lost his eyesight ; inmate of St. Dunstan's Hosp. and Convalescent Home at Torquay. *D.*, Nov., '17. *Buried*, Queen's Rd. Cem., Croydon.

PEARCE, LESLIE CHALLINGSWORTH, Sgt., 12 Lond. Regt.
b., Croydon, 18 Aug., '82 ; *5th s.*, late George & Annie Pearce, "Florence House," Whitehorse Rd., Croydon. Single. Commercial traveller. *Res.*, "Florence House," Whitehorse Rd., Croydon. *Enl.*, 6 Feb., '15. *D.*, 10 Aug., '18, at 41 C.C.S., France, of wounds recd., at Morlancourt, 9 Aug., '18.

PEARCE, REGINALD CHALLINGSWORTH, Cpl., 12 Lond. Regt.
b., Croydon, 31 Jul., '84 ; *6th s.*, late George & Annie Pearce, "Florence House," Whitehorse Rd., Croydon. Single. Private secretary. *Res.*, "Florence House," Whitehorse Rd., Croydon. *Enl.*, 6 Feb., '15. *Fell*, Villers-Bretonneaux, 13 Apr., '18.

PEARLESS, R. F., Middlesex Regt
Res., T. Heath. *Fell*, '16.

PEARMAN, H., R.W.S. Regt.
Fell, '16.

PEARSE, CYRIL NORMAN, Pte., L.R.B. (5 Lond. Regt.)
b., Anerley, 3 Sept., '88 ; *s.*, Mr. & Mrs. L. F. Pearse, 8 Eldon Pk., S. Norwood. *Educ.*, High Sch., S. Norwood. Single. Accountant's clerk. *Enl.*, Aug., '14. *Fell*, Ploegsteert, nr. Ypres, 27 Nov., '14.

PEARSE, PHYLLIS ADA, A/Sister, Q.A.I.M.N.S.
b., Anerley, 22 Dec., '86 ; daughter of Mr. & Mrs. L. F. Pearse, 8 Eldon Pk., S. Norwood. *Educ.*, Sydenham High Sch. Single. Nurse ; first entered nursing service at The Yarrow Home, Broadstairs ; St. Bartholomew's Hosp., Lond., for 3 years ; then in Q.A.I.M.N.S., Tidworth Hosp. ; served at 10 Gen. Hosp., Rouen. *D.* of acute neurasthenia at 2 Gen. Hosp., Le Havre, 29 Apr., '15.

PEARSON, CLAUDE STANLEY.
b., '88 ; *y.s.*, Mr. & Mrs. E. T. Pearson, 70 Church St., Croydon. Married Gladys (*née*) Woodhouse, of T. Heath. A.I.M.E., M.I.M.M. *D.* of heart failure, Nigeria, W. Africa, 15 Nov., '18.

PEARSON, RALPH VERNON, 242109, Pte., Lincoln Regt.
b., Croydon, 11 Nov., '97 ; *s.*, Mr. & Mrs. Charles Pearson, 47 Lansdowne Rd., Croydon. *Educ.*, Oval Rd. Sch., Croydon. Single. Estate agent's clerk. *Enl.*, 4 Sept., '16. *Fell*, France, 26 Sept., '17. (Plate XXV., 6).

PEAT, JOHN, 201171, Pte., 8 R.W.S. Regt.
b., 3 Ellis David Pl., '96 ; *s.*, Mr. & Mrs. E. Peat, 8 Mitcham Rd., Croydon. *Educ.*, Par. Ch. Sch., Croydon. Single. Cabinet maker's apprentice. *Enl.*, 29 Aug., '15. *Missing, presumed killed*, 1 Aug., '17.

PEGG, HALLAM WILLIAM, 2/Lt., 8 E. Sur. Regt.
b., T. Heath, 8 Dec., '96 ; *s.*, Mr. & Mrs. H. Carter Pegg, Alnwick House, T. Heath. *Educ.*, Whitgift G. Sch., to Dec., '14. Single. Commis., 21 Dec., '14. *D.* on amb. train, 4 Jul., '16, of wounds recd. at Montauban, Somme, 1 Jul., '16. *Buried*. Abbeville.

PEIRCE, EDWARD, 9903, Sgt., Ox. & Bucks. L.I.
  b., Brixton; s., Mr. & Mrs. Peirce, 11 Alexandra Rd., Addis
  Educ., Keston, Kent. Single. Gardener. Res., Wallingford.
  Enl., 25 Aug., '14. D. of diabetes, Camiers, France, 25 Apr., '17.
PELLING, LENNARD, L/Cpl., Tank C.
  b., '85; y.s., Mr. & Mrs. Pelling, 118 Handcroft Rd., Croydon.
  Empl. by Messrs. Beringer & Strohmenger, North End, Croydon.
  Res., "Sussex Villas," Croydon Grove, Croydon. Enl., '16.
  Fell, 17 Apr., '18.
PELLING, W. S., Sgt., Can. E.F.
  y.s., Mr. & Mrs. A. Pelling, 7 Seneca Rd., T. Heath. Went to
  Canada, '12. Served in Can. Militia. Enl., Oct., '14. Fell,
  6 Jun., '16.
PENDRIGH, ALEXANDER CONRAD CUTHBERTSON, 2/Lt., 6 (attd. 2) DevonRgt.
  b., Greenwich, 5 Nov., '97; s., David Croll & Vally Pendrigh,
  1 Fell Rd., Croydon. Educ., Whitgift G. Sch., where he was
  Coy.Sgt.Maj. in O.T.C.; winner of several shooting contests;
  good at all branches of athletics, etc., and capt. of his House.
  Enl. in Inns of Court O.T.C., 1 Nov., '15; gazetted to Devon
  Regt., Aug., '16; went to France, 3 Jan., '17. D., 17 Aug., '17,
  at 8 Gen. Hosp., Rouen, of wounds recd. at Ypres, 31 Jul., '17.
  (Plate XXI., 2).
PENDRY, GEORGE FREDERIC, 1st Class Stoker, R.N.
  b., 82 Wilford Rd., Croydon, 4 Mar., '93; s., I. J. & R. Pendry,
  113 Windmill Rd., Croydon. Educ., Princess Rd. Sch., Croydon.
  Single. Empl. at Fremlin's Brewery, Croydon. Res., 17 Tait
  Rd., Croydon. Joined, 14 Mar., '11. Lost with H.M.S.
  "Amphion," 6 Aug., '14.
PENMAN, ARNOLD, Coy.Q.M.Sgt., 116 Can. Regt.
  b., Ashton-under-Lyne, 2 Jun., '79; s., Rev. & Mrs. George
  Penman, 29 Leander Rd., T. Heath. Educ., Kent Coll., Canter-
  bury. Married. Draper. Res., Orillia, Ontario, Canada.
  Enl., Mar., '16. Fell, France, 31 Dec., '17.
PENMAN, GEOFFREY EVANS, Lt., M.G.C.
  b., '98; s., Mr. Edgar Penman (Secty. Brit. Home for Incurables,
  Streatham) & Mrs. Penman. Educ., Epsom Coll., & member of
  coll. O.T.C. Commis. in R.W.S. Regt., '14; went to France,
  May '16; transf. to M.G.C., Sept., '16. Fell, France, 9 May, '17.
PENNY, J. H., 64208, Cpl., R.H.A.
  b., '90; s., Mr. & Mrs. Penny, 10 Donald Rd., Croydon. Educ.,
  Brit. Sch., Croydon. Enl., about '07. Fell, France, 24 Apr., '17.
PENTELOW, G. N. E., Coy.Sgt.Maj., 6 Staff. Regt.
  Educ., Whitgift G. Sch., Croydon. D., 7 Oct., '17, of wounds
  inflicted by aeroplane bomb, about 30 Sept., '17.
PERKINS, ALBERT, L/Cpl., Worcester Regt.
  b., '86; 7th s., Mr. & Mrs. Perkins, 18 Chelsham Rd., Croydon.
  Educ., Bynes Rd. Sch., Croydon. Enl., '15. Fell, France,
  between 11 & 17 Apr., '18.
PERKINS, JAMES PHILIP, L/Cpl., R. Suss. Regt.
  b., '97. Empl. by "Croydon Times." Res., 95 Stanley Rd.,
  Croydon. Enl., 1 Sept., '16; went to France, Jan., '17;
  M.M., Cambrai, '17. Fell, Oct., '18.
PERKINS, WILLIAM EWART.
  Married. Fell, Suvla Bay, 9 Aug., '15.
PERRIN, T. F., Capt., R.E.
  s., Mr. & Mrs. Thomas Perrin, Morden Coll., Blackheath,
  formerly Cheltonville, Addis., Croydon. Educ., Whitgift G. Sch.
  D., 24 Jul., '17.

THE GLORIOUS DEAD

PERRY, ARTHUR, Drummer, R.W.S. Regt.
s., Mr. & Mrs. Perry, Oval Rd., Croydon. Empl. by " Croydon Advertiser." *Enl.*, Aug., '14. *Fell*, 24 Aug., '16.

PERRY, CHARLES STANLEY, 10103, Pte., 2 Scottish Rif.
b., Ryde, Isle of Wight ; *s.*, Mr. & Mrs. Perry, 25 Woodland Rd., T. Heath. *Educ.*, Lenham, Kent, & Lond. Single. Hairdresser. *Res.*, Norbury. *Fell*, Champagne, France, 24 Nov., '14.

PERRY, KENNETH GEORGE, 2/Lt., R. Suss. Regt.
b., 21 Oct., '83 ; *s.*, Mr. & Mrs. Charles Archibald Perry, Chipstead and " Hazelglen," Horley. *Educ.*, Whitgift G. Sch., '95-99. Married. Railway surveyor. *D.* of wounds, 1 Nov., '16.

PERRY, T. W., Pte., E. Kent Regt.
Res., 12 Crunden Rd., Croydon. *W. & missing*, 21 Mar., '18.

PERRY, WILLIAM ARTHUR, L/Cpl., 4 R.W.S. Regt.
b., Wellington, Salop, 18 Dec., '96 ; *s.*, Mr. & Mrs. H. Perry, 81 The Drive, T. Heath. *Educ.*, Mitcham Rd. Sch., Croydon. Single. Oilman's asst. *Res.*, 2 Euston Rd., Croydon. *Enl.*, 19 Nov., '14. *Reported missing*, presumed fallen, 3 Aug., –.

PERRYMAN, A., 2424, Pte., Middlesex Regt.
Res., Croydon. *Fell*, '17.

PESTELL, CLIFFORD LESLIE, Engineer Sub-Lt., R.N.
b., 17 Jul., '88 ; *s.*, Mr. & Mrs. Henry Pestell. *Educ.*, Lancaster Coll., Herne Hill, & Beccles, Suffolk. Engineer ; served as apprentice with Messrs. Ruston, Proctor & Co., Lincoln ; later held appointments with L.S.W.Ry., Grand Trunk Ry. of Can., and Can. Pacific Ry. *Enl.* in R.A.S.C. (M.T.), Jan., '15 ; served in France, Sept., '15-17 ; obtained appointment under Admiralty, 25 Jun., '16. *Lost* in the North Sea, 20 Jun., '17.

PESTRIDGE, FREDERICK, Pte., 7 R.W.S. Regt.
b., '86 ; 3rd *s.*, Mr. & Mrs. G. T. Pestridge, 34 Trafford Rd., T. Heath. *Enl.*, 21 Oct., '15 ; served in France 2 years 8 months. *Fell*, Morlancourt, 8 Aug., '18.

PETERS, RICHARD, 22601, Pte., 8 E. Sur. Regt.
b., Tamworth Rd., Croydon, 22 Feb., '82. *Educ.*, Brit. Sch., Croydon. Married ; 1 child. Decorator., empl. by Mr. C. Lewin, builder, then of Bensham Lane, Croydon. *Res.*, 87 Parson's Mead, Croydon. *Enl.*, 19 Jun., '16. *Fell*, France, 22 Sept., '18. *Buried*, Villers Faucon.

PETERS, WALTER STANLEY, Pte., Civil Serv. Rif. (15 Lond. Regt.)
b., '98 ; *y.s.*, Mr. & Mrs. Walter Peters, 10 Zermatt Rd.,T. Heath. *Educ.*, M. Whitgift Sch. Clerk at Scotland Yard. *Enl.*, '17. *Fell*, 8 Aug., '18.

PETO, JOSEPH, Act.-Sgt., R.G.A.
b., '90. Married ; 2 children. Empl. by L.B. & S.C.Ry. *Res.*, 13a Henderson Rd., Croydon. *Enl.*, 9 Nov., '14 ; served in France, Jan., '16-Apr., '18. *D.* of wounds, France, 30 Apr., '18.

PETRIE, ARTHUR H., 2/Lt., E. Sur. Regt. (attd. Trench Mortar Bty.)
b., '97 ; *e.s.*, Major James & Mrs. Petrie, Addiscombe. *Educ.*, Haywards Heath, Brighton G. Sch., & Whitgift G. Sch., where he was memb. of O.T.C. to '14. *Gazetted*, 26 Jan., '15 ; served in France, 18 Nov., '15-Jul., '17 ; ment. in desp., May, '17. *Fell*, France, 31 Jul., '17.

PETTIFER, SIDNEY, Pte., R.A.S.C.
b., '83 ; *s.*, Mr. & Mrs. Pettifer, 4 Wyche Grove, Croydon. *Educ.*, Bynes Rd. Sch., Croydon. Married ; 2 children. Clerk. *Enl.*, Nov., '16 ; discharged, '17. *D.* of illness incurred on service, 1 Apr., '18.

PFUNDT, BARRY, Pte., Hauraki Regt., N.Z. Forces.
  b., Wallington, 30 Aug., '87; s., Rudolf & Isabel Pfundt, "Rollodene," 13 Birdhurst Rd., Croydon. *Educ.*, at Croydon. Single. Engineer, Waihi Gold Mining Coy. *Res.*, Waihi, N.Z. *Enl.*, '14. *Fell*, Anzac, Gallipoli, 25 Apr., '15. (Plate XXVII., 6).

PHARE, DUDLEY GERSHAM, Lt., K.S.L.I.
  b., Crouch End, 18 Oct., '88; s., George & Edith Annie Phare, 4 Ashburton Rd., Croydon. *Educ.*, Private Sch., & St. Olave's G. Sch., Tooley St., E.C., '03-04. Single. Chartered accountant (A.C.A.). *Joined* as 2/Lt., Sept., '15; served in R.A.S.C. *Fell*, Henin-sur-Cojeuil, 28 Mar., '18.

PHILLIPS, BERT E., Sgt., R.W.S. Regt.
  b., '89. *Educ.*, Abp. Tenison's Sch., Croydon; memb. of St Peter's C.L.B. *Res.*, 17 Haling Rd., Croydon. *Enl.*, '08; went to India, '14; ret. to Eng., time expired, '16; *re-enlisted* and went to France, '17; D.C.M. *Fell*, 6 Apr., '18.

PHILLIPS, HERBERT CHARLES, Pte., 6 R.W.S. Regt.
  b., Copthorne, Surrey, 6 Oct., '87; s., Charles & Elizabeth Phillips, 25 Totton Rd., T. Heath. *Educ.*, Tenison's Sch., and Beulah Rd. Sch., T. Heath. Single. Gardener. *Enl.*, Aug., '14. *Fell*, Armentières, 23 Sept., '15.

PHILLIPS, PERCY THOMAS, Pte., 8 R.W.S. Regt.
  b., Helder St., Croydon, 19 Apr., '94; s., Charles & Elizabeth Phillips, 25 Totton Rd., T. Heath. *Educ.*, Beulah Rd. Sch., T. Heath. Single. *Enl.*, 30 Apr., '16. *D.* from gas poisoning, Ypres, 30 Apr., '16.

PICKERING, A. E., Cpl., R.E.
  Married; 1 daughter. Empl. by Messrs. Collins, Old Broad St. *Res.*, Worthing, formerly Lincoln Rd., S. Norwood. *D.* of influenza, France, '18.

PICKERING, WALTER, Sgt., 1 R.W.S. Regt.
  b., Bridlington, Yorks., 7 Apr., '95. Single. Hairdresser. *Res.*, S. Croydon. *Enl.*, 15 Nov., '15; M.M. *Fell*, '17.

PICKFORD, A. J. ERNEST, Pte.
  b., '96; *e.s.*, Arthur & Emily Pickford, 206 Livingstone Rd., T. Heath. *D.* of wounds, France, 25 Aug., '18.

PIERCE, SIDNEY, Pte.
  Educ., Abp. Tenison's Sch., Croydon. *Fell*, Somme, 15 Sept., '16.

PIGE, HERBERT JOSEPH, Cpl., Lond. Regt.
  Fell, '16.

PIGGOTT, CHARLES W.
  b., '81; s., Mr. & Mrs. Piggott, 53 Kingswood Rd., Penge. Married. *Res.*, Wickham Market, Suffolk. *Fell*, Cambrai, 30 Nov., '17.

PIGGOTT, HAROLD EDGAR, 1 Essex Regt.
  b., S. Norwood; s., Mr. & Mrs. G. P. Piggott, 12 Norwich Rd., T. Heath. *Educ.*, Whitehorse Rd. Sch., T. Heath. Single. Fitter. *Res.*, 12 Norwich Rd., T. Heath. *Fell*, nr. Poperinghe, 16 Mar., '18.

PIGGOTT, JOHN A., R.E.
  b., '87; *y.s.*, Mr. & Mrs. Piggott, 53 Kingswood Rd., Penge. Married. *Res.*, 6 Venner Rd., Sydenham. *D.* of pneumonia, France, 6 Dec., '18.

PIGGOTT, SAMUEL, 325172, Pte., W. Yorks. Regt.
  s., Mr. & Mrs. Piggott, 12 Norwich Rd., T. Heath. *Fell*, Cambrai, 11 Oct., '18.

PIGHTLING, JAMES, 55773, Pte., 19 Can. Btn.
  Res., 14 Church Rd., Croydon. *Fell*, 22 Jan., '16.

THE GLORIOUS DEAD 367

PILCHER, J. W., Gnr., R.F.A.
  Married. Empl. at T. Heath Model Laundry. *Res.*, 126 Beulah Rd., T. Heath. *Enl.*, 27 May, '15. *Fell*, 22 Sept., '17.
PINK, H. A., 1402, Pte., R.W.S. Regt.
  Res., Croydon. *Fell*, '16.
PINK, J. W.
  b., '82. Married. Empl. as lamplighter by Croydon Gas Coy since Nov., '11. *Enl.*, May, '18. *Fell*, France, 24 Oct., '18.
PIPER, H. H., Pte., 2 Suff. Regt.
  b., '93. *Educ.*, Whitehorse Rd. Sch., Croydon. Empl. by Mr. Ramsdale, dairyman, Whitehorse Lane, S. Norwood. *Res.*, 10 Swain Rd., T. Heath. *Enl.* in R.W.S. Regt. *Fell*, 2 Mar., '16.
PIPER, LESLIE B., Rflmn., Lond. Regt.
  b., '99 ; *s.*, Mr. & Mrs. Piper, 38 Alexandra Rd., Addis. *Educ.*, Croydon Mod. Sch., & Clark's Coll. *Enl.*, Dec., '16. *D.* of wounds, 8 Apr., '18.
PITMAN, THOMAS STUART, Lt., 6 York & Lancs. Regt.
  b., Streatham, 10 Jul., '91 ; *s.*, Mr. & Mrs. Guilbert Pitman, 34 Coombe Rd., Croydon. *Educ.*, Whitgift G. Sch., & Queen's Coll., Oxford. Single. Scholar ; scholarship to Queen's Coll., Oxford, '09 ; B.A. with hons., '14 ; memb. of Oxf. Univ. O.T.C. for 4 years. *Enl.*, 1 Oct., '14. *Fell*, Poel Cappelle, Belgium, 26 Sept., '17. (Plate XXI., 3).
PITTAM, H. T., Gnr., R.F.A.
  s., Mr. & Mrs. Pittam, 228 Gloucester Rd., Croydon. *Educ.*, Whitehorse Rd. Sch., T. Heath. Empl. at Home & Colonial Stores, Whitehorse Rd. *Fell*, 4 Dec., '17.
PITTMAN, CECIL FREDERICK, Lt., R.F.C.
  b., '91 ; *e.s.*, Mr. & Mrs. Frederick John Pittman, " Beechcroft," St. Augustine's Av., Croydon. B.Sc. *Killed* while flying in England, 20 Jul., '17. *Buried*, Bandon Hill Cem.
PLANTEROSE, E. A., Observer Sub-Lt., R.N.A.S.
  s., Mr. & Mrs. G. Planterose, 8 East Drive, Brighton. *Educ.*, Whitgift G. Sch., Croydon. *Fell*, '17.
PLAYFAIR, L., Lt., 1 R. Scots (attd. R.F.C.)
  Educ., High Sch., Croydon. *Fell*, '15.
PLAYSTEAD, LIONEL HENRY WILLIAM, 320922, L/Sgt., 2/6 Lond. Regt.
  Res., Croydon. *Fell*, '17.
PLISTED, C., 26128, Pte., K.S.L.I.
  Res., W. Croydon. *Fell*, 20 Sept., '17.
PLOWMAN, ARTHUR ERNEST, Pte., 13 R. Fus.
  b., Wallington, 15 Apr., '98 ; *s.*, Mr. & Mrs. A. J. Plowman, 4 Ainsworth Rd., Croydon. *Educ.*, Welcome Hall, Croydon. Single. Apprentice to printer's machine minder. *Enl.*, 1 Sept., '16. *Missing*, Gavrelle, France, 29 Apr., '17.
PLUMRIDGE, CHARLES FREDERICK, Pte., 8 R.W.S. Regt.
  b., Slough, 3 Jan., '84. *Educ.*, Croydon. Married. Plumber. *Res.*, 58 Woodside Rd., S. Norwood. *Enl.*, 27 Jun., '17. *Missing*, France, 21 Mar., '18.
POFFLEY, W. A., Pte., R.W.S. Regt.
  b., '98 ; *y.s.*, Mr. & Mrs. Poffley, 8 Salisbury Rd., Woodside. *Enl.*, 4 May, '15. *D.* of wounds, 1 Jul., '16.
POLGE, WILLIAM EDWIN, 2/Lt., 7 Lond. Regt.
  b., S. Norwood, 2 Nov., '92 ; 3rd *s.*, Henry & Ella Polge, 7 Dornton Rd., Croydon. *Educ.*, High Sch., Croydon. Single. Banker's clerk. *Joined*, Sept., '14. *Fell*, Glencorse Wood, nr. Ypres, 16 Aug., '17.

POLHILL, HERBERT WILLIAM, Gnr., Australian Trench Mortar Bty.
b., Croydon, '88 ; *s.*, Mr. & Mrs. Arthur Polhill, 14 St. John's Gr., Croydon. *Educ.*, Brit. Sch., Croydon. *D.* of wounds at Liverpool Camp, Australia, 23 Aug., '17.

POLHILL, WILLIAM HENRY, Cpl., 13 Aust.I.F.
b., Croydon, 15 Nov., '90 ; *s.*, Mr. & Mrs. Arthur Polhill, 14 St. John's Gr., Croydon. *Educ.*, Brit. Sch., Croydon. Single. Seedsman. *Res.*, Australia. *Enl.*, '15. *D.*, 12 Apr., '17, of wounds recd. prev. day. *Buried* at Australian Mil. Cem., Bapaume.

POLS, HENRY JAMES, A.B. Seaman, R.N.
b., '95 ; *s.*, Mr. & Mrs. W. A. Pols, 90 Sutherland Rd., Croydon. Telegraph messenger. Served on H.M.S. " Impregnable " and " Berwick." *Lost* on H.M.S. " Bulwark," destroyed by internal explosion at Sheerness, 26 Nov., '14.

POOLE, CHARLES, Sgt., 4 K.R.R.C.
b., Croydon, 20 Mar., '86 ; *s.*, Charles & Ann Poole, 29 Union Rd., Croydon. *Educ.*, Sydenham Rd. Sch., Croydon. Single. *Enl.*, 26 Feb., '07. *Fell*, St. Eloi, 2 Mar., '15. (Plate XXI., 4).

POOLE, GEORGE EDDY, Cpl., L.R.B. (5 Lond. Regt.)
b., '94 ; *v.s.*, Mr. & Mrs. Poole, 20 Dagnall Pk., S. Norwood. *Educ.*, Christ Ch. Higher Grade Sch., Southport. Married. Empl. by Messrs. Duncan McNeill, tea growers, Old Broad St. *Fell*, Flanders, 10 Jan., '16.

POOLE, LIONEL ANTHONY, Pte., 99 Coy., M.G.C.
b., T. Heath, 30 Sept., '84 ; *s.*, Mr. & Mrs. Richard F. Poole, 124 Bensham Manor Rd., T. Heath. *Educ.*, Mr. A. C. Dent's Sch., Bensham Manor Rd., T. Heath. Married ; 1 child. Salesman to wholesale stationer. *Res.*, 23 Norman Rd., T. Heath. *Enl.*, 21 Jul., '16. *Fell*, France, 3 May, '17.

POORE, W., Rflmn.
b., '84. *Educ.*, Willesden G. Sch. Married, Amy, daughter of Mr. Frank Saunders, of Egerton Rd., S. Norwood. Empl. by Pearl Insurance Coy. *Fell*, Messines, 7 Jun., '17.

PORTER, CHARLES HENRY, Gnr., R.F.A.
b., Kentish Town, 12 Jul., '92 ; *s.*, Mr. & Mrs. Porter, 40 Purley Rd., Croydon. *Educ.*, Brighton Rd. Sch., Croydon. Single. Insurance agent. *Res.*, 36 Purley Rd., Croydon. *Enl.*, 18 Nov., '10. *Fell*, Vendresse, 8 Oct., –.

PORTER, EDWARD J., Lt., Lond. Regt.
b., '84 ; 4*th s.*, Mr. & Mrs. S. Porter, Chancellor Rd., Southend-on-Sea. Graduate in 1st cl. hon. (science) Lond. & Camb. Univ. ; science master at Kingsbridge G. Sch., Devon, and Manchester G. Sch., & for 18 mths. prev. to enlistment was senior physics master, Whitgift G. Sch. *Gazetted* to Lond. Regt., Jan., '16. *D.*, 22 Sept., '16, while pris. of war in a German Hosp., nr. Ypres, of wounds recd., 16 Sept., '16.

PORTER, GEORGE EDWARD, Gnr., R.F.A.
b., Cresswell Rd., S. Norwood, 30 Dec., '94 ; *s.*, Mr. & Mrs. C. Porter, 60 Harrington Rd., S. Norwood. *Educ.*, Birchanger Rd. Sch., S. Norwood. Single. Pastrycook. *Enl.*, 25 May, '15. *Fell*, France, 11 Jul., '17.

PORTER, WILLIAM REGINALD, Pte., 8 E. Sur. Regt.
b., Alexandra Rd., Croydon, 22 May, '98 ; *s.*, Mr. & Mrs. William Porter, Warlingham. *Educ.*, Whitgift G. Sch., '09-14, where he was memb. of O.T.C. Single. Warehouseman. *Res.*, Warlingham. *Enl.*, in 16 Middlesex Regt., Aug., '15. *Fell*, Thiepval, 29 Sept., '16.

XXI.

1. Pte. C. C. PAYNE, 2 R. Suss. Regt.
2. 2/Lt. A. C. C. PFNDRIGH, Devon. Regt.
3. Lt. T. S. PITMAN, 6 York & Lancs. Regt.
4. Sgt. C. POOLE, 4 King's R.R.C.
5. L/Cpl. E. C. L. READ, 8 Norf. Regt.
6. Pte. T. M. RICHARDSON, 5 Notts. & Derby. Regt.

XXII.

1. Pte. H. V. Newcombe, 7 E. Kent Regt.
2. Pte. J. H. Nealon, 4 R. Fus.
3. Cpl. H. C. Parsons, Q.Vict. Rif.
4. Pte. S. C. Riddick, H.A.C.
5. Pte. J. Read, S.Wales Borderers
6. Pte. H. E. Randall, Machine Gun Corps

THE GLORIOUS DEAD

POTTER, HERBERT FOREMAN, Cpl., R.E.
 b., '99 ; 3rd s., W. & M. Potter, 68 Oakley Rd., S. Norwood.
 D., 2 Nov., '16, at Aylesbury Mil. Hosp., of injuries recd. in a motor car accident while engaged on mil. duties.

POTTS, F., 532082, Pte., Lond. Regt.
 Res., T. Heath. Fell, '17.

POTTS, LEONARD, 19850, Pte., R.W. Kent Regt.
 s., Mr. & Mrs. Potts, 11 Sylverdale Rd., Croydon. Formerly in 21 Lancers. Missing, 23 Mar., '18.

POTTS, WALTER, Pte., R.W.S. Regt.
 b., 36 Keen's Rd., Croydon, 12 May, '95 ; s., Mr. & Mrs. Potts, 36 Keen's Rd., Croydon. Educ., Dering Pl. Sch., Croydon. Single. Compositor. Enl., 19 Oct., '14. Fell, Belgium, 1 Oct., '18.

POULTER, D., R.E.
 Educ., Whitgift G. Sch., Croydon, '06-09. Served as desp. rider. Fell, '17.

POWELL, ARTHUR TREVANION, 2/4 Cameron H.
 b., Dulwich, 11 Dec., '91 ; s., A. E. M. & Elizabeth Annie Powell, 28 Maberley Rd., U. Norwood. Educ., Alleyn's Sch., Dulwich. Single. Banking clerk (Thos. Cook & Son). Enl., in R. Bucks. Hussars, 18 Apr., '15 ; commis., 27 Aug., '15. Fell, Vimy Ridge, 22 Jul., '16.

POWELL, A. W., 2/Lt., R.W.S. Regt.
 Fell, '16.

POWELL, OWEN LEONARD, 32831, Rflmn., K.R.R.C.
 b., Herne Hill, 29 Sept., '85 ; s., Mr. & Mrs. Powell, 50 Tremadoc Rd., Clapham, S.W. Educ., Christ Ch. Sch., Brixton. Married. Commercial traveller. Res., 17 Norton Gardens, Norbury. Enl., 5 Jun., '16. Fell, France, 7 Oct., '16.

POWELL, PATRICK J. G., Lt., R.F.C.

POWELL, WILLIAM, Sgt., 1 Gordon H.
 b., Basingstoke, 9 Jul., '65. Educ., G. Sch., Basingstoke. Married. Gasfitter. Res., 56 Mersham Rd., T. Heath. Served in Malta and Ceylon as schoolmaster in Gordon H., prior to '89 ; served in S.A. War. Re-enlisted, 25 Sept., '14. D., Crescent War Hosp., Croydon, 3 Oct., '18.

POWNEY, J. T., Maj., R.E.
 Married. Res., St. Augustine's Av., Croydon. Accidentally killed, Le Havre, Dec., '14.

POZON, G., Cpl , 4 R. Fus.
 s., Mr. & Mrs. Pozon, 81 Askew Terr., Shepherd's Bush. Single. Res., Whitehorse Rd., Croydon. Served through S.A. War with the same regt. Fell, '15.

PRAGNELL, GEORGE, Capt., Gen. Staff Offr.
 s., late Sir George & Lady Pragnell. D.S.O. Fell, Jul., '17.

PREDDY, HERBERT VICTOR, Pte., 9 E. Sur. Regt.
 b., 18 Armills Rd., Gibson's Hill, U. Norwood, 7 Oct., '91 ; s., Mr. & Mrs. H. Joseph Preddy, U. Norwood. Educ., Rockmount Rd. Sch., U. Norwood. Single. Printer. Enl., 9 Feb., '16. Fell, Guillemont, 16 Aug., '16.

PREEDY, J. C., 2053, Pte., R.W.S. Regt.
 D. while pris. of war in Turkish hands.

PRETIOUS, ALFRED GREENAWAY, Pte., 2/4 R.W.S. Regt.
 b., Norfolk Terr., Bayswater, W., 16 Mar., '67. Educ., Colfe G. Sch., & Abp. Tenison's Sch., Leicester Sq., W. Married. Insurance clerk. Res., 32 Carew Rd., T. Heath. Enl., Nov., '14. Killed at Purley, 29 Apr., '15.

PRETIOUS, D., L/Cpl., R. Fus.
Fell, Ypres, about Jul., '17.
PREVETT, ALBERT CHARLES, Pte., 8 E. Sur. Regt.
b., 13 Bishop's Rd., Croydon, 3 Feb., '98 ; *s.*, Mr. & Mrs. A. R. Prevett, 43 Addington Rd., Croydon. *Educ.*, Christ Ch. Sch., Croydon. Single. Empl. at Crowley's Brewery. *Enl.*, 24 Jan., '16 ; *w.*, Somme, Sept., '16. *Fell*, Poelcappelle, 12 Oct., '17.
PRICE, ARTHUR E., Pte., R.W.S. Regt.
b., '93 ; 3rd *s.*, late Mr., & Mrs. Price, 196 Oval Rd., Croydon. *Fell*, 1 Aug., '17.
PRICE, E. L., Pte., Lond. Regt.
b., '98. *Educ.*, St. Saviour's Sch., Croydon. Empl. at Woolwich Arsenal. *Res.*, 28 St. Saviour's Rd., Croydon. *Enl.* in R. Suss. Regt., 7 Dec., '16 ; served in France with R.W.S. Regt. ; *w.*, Oct., '17 ; transf. to Lond. Regt., Apr., '18. *Fell*, France, 22 Aug., '18.
PRICE, GRAHAM, Pilot, R.F.C.
e.s., Mr. & Mrs. James Price, Sydenham (res. in Croydon until '07). *Fell*, 9 Mar., '16.
PRICE, J. W. J., 2/Lt., Northd. Fus.
b., '87 ; *s.*, late Mr., & Mrs. Price, 196 Oval Rd., Croydon. *Enl.* as pte. in Hants. Regt., '14 ; served in India until Aug., '16 ; commis. in Northd. Fus., Dec., '16. *D.* of wounds, 22 Apr., '17.
PRIDDY, SIDNEY RANDALL.
b., '95 ; *s.*, Robert & Annie Priddy, S. Norwood. *D.* of wounds, 18 Mar., '16.
PROCTOR, F., 2739, Pte., Tank C.
Res., T. Heath. *Fell*, '17.
PRYCE, S. T., 13349, Rflmn., R.B.
Res., Shirley. *Fell*, '16.
PRYKE, ALBERT EDWARD, Pte., 13 E. Sur. Regt.
b., E. Battersea, 4 Jun., '95 ; *s.*, late Mr., & Mrs. H. J. Pryke, 5 Harrington Rd., S. Norwood. *Educ.*, Portland Rd. Sch., S. Norwood. Single. Fitter's mate. *Enl.* in 4 R.W.S. Regt., Dec., '16. *Fell*, France, 24 Apr., '17.
PRYKE, WILLIAM ZECHARIAH, 240246, Pte., 1/5 Seaforth H.
b., 21 Lambeth Rd., Croydon, 30 Jul., '93 ; *s.*, Zechariah & Alice Pryke, 134 Bensham Lane, T. Heath. *Educ.*, Christ Ch. Sch., Croydon. Single. Shop asst. *Res.*, 51 Theobald Rd., Croydon. *Enl.*, 7 Sept., '14 ; served in France for 23 months. *Fell*, Arras, 9 Apr., '17. *Buried*, Rochincourt, nr. Arras.
PUDDEPHAT, REGINALD F. J., Pte., 16 Middlesex Regt.
b., Leavesden, Herts., 25 Dec., '97 *s.*, Joseph & Sarah A. Puddephat, 6 Beddington Terr., Mitcham Rd., Croydon. *Educ.*, New Town, Sutton, & Boston Rd., Croydon. Single. Electrical engineer. *Enl.*, 15 May, '15. *Fell*, Somme, 1 Jul., '16.
PULHAM, ROBIN, Gnr., 63 Bde., R.F.A.
Res., 39 Livingstone Rd., T. Heath. *Fell*, France, 31 Jul., '15.
PUNT, ALBERT EDWARD, Pte., 2 Devon Regt.
b., T. Heath, 17 May, '97 ; *s.*, Mr. & Mrs. Walter Punt, 71 Windmill Rd., Croydon. *Educ.*, Boston Rd. Sch., Croydon. Single. Baker's roundsman. *Enl.*, Nov., '15 ; taken pris., 24 Apr., '18 ; found dead by British troops, 14 Jul., '18. *Buried*, Peronne.
PURKISS, HENRY WILLIAM, Driver, R.A.S.C.
b., Gloucester Rd., Croydon, 20 May, '80 ; *s.*, Benjamin & Charlotte Purkiss, 29 Princess Rd., Croydon. *Educ.*, Princess Rd. Sch., Croydon. Married. Driver *Res.*, 61 Johnson Rd., W. Croydon. *Enl.*, 11 Nov., '14. *Fell*, La Neuville, Corbie, 30 Nov., '16.

THE GLORIOUS DEAD

PURNELL, FREDERICK DAVID, A.B. Seaman, R.N.
    b., '79.   Empl. by Croydon Corp., as attendant at S. Norwood
    Baths.   Res., 62 Carmichael Rd., S. Norwood.   Served for 12
    years in R.N., and was on reserve when war broke out. *Lost* on
    H.M.S. " Hawke," torpedoed, Oct., '14.
PURVES, THOMAS WARREN, Lt., Middlesex Regt.
    b., '97 ; y.s., Mr. & Mrs. P. W. Purves, " Lilburn," Plough Lane,
    Purley.   *Educ.*, West House Sch., Edgbaston, Glasgow Acad.,
    and Whitgift G. Sch., Croydon.   *Enl.*, as pte. in Lond. Scottish,
    '14 ; w., France, Nov., '14 ; commis., Aug., '15.   *Fell*, 7 Jun., '17.
PURVEY, H. A., S. Staffs. Regt.
    Res., Croydon.   *Fell*, '17.
QUINTON, WILLIAM CHARLES, Pte., Can. E.F.
    b., '94 ; s., Mrs. Hellard, 9 Frant Rd., T. Heath.   *Educ.*, Princess
    Rd. Sch., Croydon.   Formerly empl. by Messrs. Joyce, dairymen.
    Res., Canada, from '13.   *Enl.* in Can. E.F., landing in France,
    Jul., '16.   *Fell*, 25 Oct., '16.
RACINE, E. GUY, 2/Lt.
    b., '96 ; s., Mr. & Mrs. Ernest Racine, W. Croydon.   *Fell*,
    9 Apr., '17.
RACKETT, HAROLD GORDON, R.E.
    b., '91 ; 5th s., late W. H., & E. Rackett, S. Norwood.   Served
    in army 4 years.   *D.*, St. Albans, Herts., 30 Oct., '18.
RADFORD, P. P., 10769, Pte., R.W.S. Regt.
    Res., S. Norwood.   *D.* of wounds, France, 16 Nov., '16.
RADFORD, V. P. U., 10769, Pte., R.W.S. Regt.
    Res., S. Norwood.   *Fell*, '16.
RADLEY, CHRISTOPHER SEPTIMUS, Pte., 1 Sur. Rif. (21 Lond. Regt.)
    b., 23 Jan., '84 ; s., late William, & Sarah Jane Radley.   *Educ*,
    Whitgift G. Sch., Croydon, '97-00.   *D.* of pneumonia,8 Sept.,'14.
RANDALL, HENRY E., Pte., M.G.C.
    b., '93 ; e.s., Henry & Clara Randall, 119 Penshurst Rd., T. Heath.
    Fell, France, 2 Dec., '17.   (Plate XXII., 6).
RANGER, P. J., 50866, Pte., N. Staffs. Regt.
    Res., T. Heath.   *D.* of wounds, '17.
RANSFORD, LIONEL BOLTON, Flight Sub-Lt., R.N.A.S.
    b., U. Norwood, 3 May, '99 ; s., Robert Bolton Ransford, M.A.,
    J.P., & Mrs. Ransford, 16 Mowbray Rd., U. Norwood.   *Educ.*,
    Dulwich Coll., where he was sgt. in O.T.C.   *Joined* R.N.A.S.,
    Jun., '17 ; flight sub-lt., Nov., '17 ; appointed to 5 Squad., at
    Dunkirk, whence he took part in many bombing raids on
    Zeebrugge, etc.   *Fell*, 18 Mar., '18, in aerial combat, nr. St.
    Quentin.
RAPHAEL, JOHN EDWARD, Lt., Gen. Staff Offr.
    b., '82 ; s., late Albert, & Harriet Raphael, Lewin Rd., Streatham
    and Wildhatch, Hendon.   *Educ.*, Merchant Taylor's Sch., and
    Oxf. Univ. ; studied law ; memb., and later capt. of Sur. County
    Cricket Club ; capt. of Old Merchant Taylor's Rugby Club ;
    played Rugby football for Eng. against Wales, Scotland, Ireland,
    N. Zealand & France ; pres. of Oxf. Palmerston Club, '04-05 ;
    contested Croydon in the Liberal interest in Mar., '09, when he
    was defeated by Sir Robert Trotter Hermon-Hodge, Bart., the
    Unionist candidate.   *Joined* an O.T.C. in Aug., '14 ; gazetted
    to Duke of Wellington's Regt., afterwards transferring to K.R.R.C.;
    appointed to G. Staff as A.D.C. to G.O.C., 41 Div.   *D.*, 11 Jun.,
    '17, of wounds recd. 7 Jun., '17.

RATTEE, WALTER EDWARD, Sgt., 6 Lond. Regt.
    b., Felixstowe, 20 Jan., '96 ; *s.*, Daniel Edward & Lucy Rattee, 94 Bensham Manor Rd., T. Heath. *Educ.*, Eastward Ho. Coll., Felixstowe. Single. Draper's asst., empl. by Messrs. Marshall and Snelgrove, Oxford St., W. *Res.*, Lond. Before war was memb. of K.R.R. Cadet C. *Enl.*, Aug., '14 ; went to France, Mar., '15 ; *w.*, Festubert, May, '15 ; gassed, Loos, Sept., '15. *Fell*, High Wood, Somme, 15 Sept., '16.

RAWLINGS, F., 16113, Pte., S.W.B.
    Res., W. Croydon. *Fell*, '17.

RAWLINGS, F., 2092, Pte., Lond. Regt.
    Fell, '16.

RAY, W. W., Coy.Sgt.Maj., Princess Patricia's Can. L.I
    b., '88 ; *s.*, Mr. & Mrs. W. Ray, 6 Addis. Av., Croydon. Married. *Fell*, 16 Sept., '16.

RAYNER, C., 2747, Pte., Argyll & Sutherland H.
    Res., W. Croydon. *Fell*, '16.

RAYNER, EDWARD, Surgeon, R.N.
    b., Hampstead, '86 ; *e.s.*, late Edward Rayner, of " Beechlands," Wadhurst, Sussex, & Mrs. Rayner, Queen's Hotel, U. Norwood. *Educ.*, Heddon Court, & S.E. Coll., Ramsgate ; entered Pembroke Coll., Camb., '05 ; 1st cl. in Natural Science Tripos, '08 ; recd. his med. educ. at Camb., & St. Thomas' Hosp., Lond. ; M.R.C.S., Eng., & L.R.C.P., Lond., '12 ; M.B. & B.Sc., Cantab., '12 ; acted as house surgeon and casualty officer at St. Thomas' while working for his F.R.C.S., which he obtained, '13. Served at Gallipoli with R.N.D. (Engineers) ; appointed surgeon to H.M.S. " Vanguard," autumn, '16. *Killed* on H.M.S. " Vanguard," destroyed by internal explosion, 9 Jul., '17.

RAYNER, ERNEST WALTER, 65344, Pte., 4 R. Fus.
    b., 50 Limes Rd., Croydon, 3 Sept., '88 ; *s.*, late Col. & Mrs. Robert Rayner, 50 Limes Rd., Croydon. *Educ.*, Sydenham Rd. Sch., Croydon. Married : 1 child. Press prover. *Res.*, 9 Croydon Grove, Croydon. *Enl.*, Aug., '16. *D.* of wounds recd. in France, 29 Sept., '17.

RAYNER, FREDERICK WILLIAM, Pte., 1 R.W.S. Regt.
    b., Croydon, 25 Aug., '86 ; *e.s.*, Frederick & Alice Rayner, 16 Alpha Rd., Croydon. *Educ.*, Plassy Rd. Sch., Catford, & Woodside Sch., Croydon. Single. Moulder in brass foundry. *Res.*, Stratford, Ontario, Canada. *Enl.*, '04 ; pris. of war from 31 Oct., '14 to Nov., '18. *D.* of pneumonia while on his way home on board H.M. Hosp. Ship " Formosa," at Copenhagen, 1 Jan., '19.

RAYNER, HAROLD LESLIE, 2/Lt.
    s., late Edward Rayner, of " Beechlands," Wadhurst, Sussex, and Mrs. Rayner, Queen's Hotel, U. Norwood. *Fell*, 1 Jul., '16.

RAYNER, R. S., 25467, Pte., Lancs. Fus
    Res., Croydon. *Fell*, '16.

RAZZELL, A., Pte., R.W.S. Regt.
    b., Gloucester Rd., Croydon, 12 Feb., '86 ; *s.*, Mr. & Mrs. W. Razzell, 279 Whitehorse Rd., Croydon. *Educ.*, National Sch. Married. Coal porter. *Res.*, 231 Gloucester Rd., Croydon. Served in S.A. War. *Enl.*, 4 Aug., '14 ; participated in battle of Mons ; *w.* on the Aisne, '14 ; ret. to France, Mar., '16. *Fell*, Ypres, 31 Mar., '16.

XXIII.

1. Pte. N. KEEN, 1/5 Gordon H.
2. Pte. T. G. ROFFEY, 17 Middlesex Regt.
3. Pte. A. W. STEVENS, 1/4 R.W.S. Regt.
4. Pte. E. B. SHAW, 9 R. Fus.
5. Driver H. J. NICHOLASS, R.F.A.
6. 2/Lt. F. W. ROBARTS, Lond. Scottish

XXIV.

1. Rflmn. A. J. RUDDLE, Lond. Regt.
2. Signaller H. J. SMITH, Queen's Westm. Rif.
3. Sgt. F. F. ROTHEN, Queen's Westm. Rif.
4. Trooper E. J. SAUNDERS, M.M., Sur. Yeom.
5. 2/Lt. E. G. ROUTLEY, M.C., R. Fus.
6. Capt. A. E. RYAN, M.C., R.W.S. Regt.

THE GLORIOUS DEAD

READ, EDWIN CYRIL LAFFAN, L/Cpl., 8 Norf. Regt.
Educ., L.C.C. Sch., Eardley Rd., Streatham. Single. Tailor. *Res.*, 2 Bulkeley Rd., Norbury. *Enl.*, 1 Sept., '14. *Fell*, Somme, 1 Jul., '16. (Plate XXI., 5).

READ, JAMES PATRICK, Gnr., R.G.A.
b., 9 Palmerston Rd., Croydon, 14 Nov., '89 ; *s.*, Mr. & Mrs. Read, 9 Palmerston Rd., Croydon. *Educ.*, Whitehorse Rd. Sch., Croydon. Married. Greengrocer. *Res.*, 25 Queen's Rd., Croydon. *Enl.*, 14 Sept., '16. *Fell*, France, 5 Nov., '17.

READ, JOHN, Pte., S.W.B.
b., 9 Palmerston Rd., Croydon, 10 Oct., '87 ; *s.*, Mr. & Mrs. Read, 9 Palmerston Rd., Croydon. *Educ.*, Whitehorse Rd. Sch., Croydon. Married. Fruiterer and greengrocer. *Res.*, 12 Northbrook Rd., Croydon. *Enl.*, 24 Oct., '16. *Fell*, France, 31 Aug., '18. (Plate XXII., 5).

REDMAN, FREDERICK WILLIAM, Sgt., 1 R.W.S. Regt.
b., 24 Pridham Rd., Croydon, 14 Mar., '92 ; *s.*, Charles & Esther Redman, 4 Garnet Rd., T. Heath. *Educ.*, Whitehorse Rd. Sch., Croydon. Single. Cleaner, empl. at Whitehorse Rd. Sch. *Enl.*, 3 Dec., '11 ; fought at Mons and Aisne, where he was *w.*, 23 Oct., '14 ; returned to France, 15 Jan., '15. *Fell*, Somme, 15 Jul., '16.

REDPATH, ROBERT, 683145, Pte., Lond. Regt.
b., 29 Sidney Rd., S. Norwood, 26 Sept., '96 ; *s.*, Mr. & Mrs. Redpath, 29 Sidney Rd., S. Norwood. *Educ.*, Birchanger Rd. Sch., S. Norwood. Single. Butcher's asst. *Enl.*, 12 Oct., '14. *Fell*, Messines, 7 Jun., '17.

REED, GEORGE F. B., 148713, Gnr., R.G.A.
Empl. as fitter's mate by Croydon Gas Coy. *Res.*, Croydon. *Fell*, '17.

REED, GEORGE HENRY, Cpl., 2 H.L.I.
b., Croydon, 16 Dec., '90 ; *s.*, Mr. & Mrs. Reed, 9 Bute Rd., Croydon. *Educ.*, Mitcham Rd. Sch., Croydon. Single. Empl. in telegraph office. *Enl.*, Jan., '10 ; *w.*, France, Nov., '14. *D.* at Bethune, 16 May, '15, of wounds recd. at Festubert, the same day. *Buried*, Bethune Cem.

REED, WILLIAM, Pte., R. Suss. Regt.
b., Caterham, 28 Apr., - ; *s.*, Mr. & Mrs. Reed, 224 Bensham Lane, T. Heath. *Educ.*, Croydon. Single. Farm labourer. *Res.*, Lewes. *D.*, 6 Jul., '17, of wounds recd. at Coxyde, 5 Jul.,'17.

REES, W., Pte., E. Sur. Regt.
b., '88. Married ; 4 children. Empl. by Messrs. Marshall, Murray & Co., dairymen, 55 Union Rd., Croydon. *Res.*, 11 Adelaide St., Croydon. *Fell*, 10 Apr., '17.

REEVE, JOHN STANLEY, Lt., H.A.C.
b., Mar., '97 ; *s.*, Mr. & Mrs. J. Reeve, 99 S. Norwood Hill. *Educ.*, Whitgift G. Sch., & Palmer's Coll., Grays. *Enl.* as pte. in H.A.C., Jan., '15 ; later promoted sgt. ; gazetted, Jan., '17 ; went to France, Mar., '17 ; *w.*, Bullecourt, May, '17 ; *re-joined* his btn. in Italy, May, '18. *Fell*, Italy, 29 Jun., '18. (Plate XXVI., 1).

REEVES, E. F., Pte.
Married ; 1 son. *Res.*, 6 Ann's Place, Croydon. *Fell*, Arras, 3 May, '17.

REEVES, VICTOR FREDERICK, Pte., 2/10 Lond. Regt.
b., 6 Frith Rd., Croydon, 3 Dec., '00 ; *s.*, Mr. & Mrs. Fred. Reeves, 82 Waddon New Rd., Croydon. *Educ.*, Par. Ch. Sch., Croydon. Married. *Res.*, 82 Waddon New Rd., Croydon. *Enl.*, 14 Jan., '17. *Fell*, France, 24 Aug., '18.

REID, ERIC BRUCE, Capt., N. Staff. Regt.
Res., 37 Alexandra Rd., S. Norwood. Fell, Armentières, 21 Oct., '14.

REID, JAMES ARCHIBALD JOHN, 2/Lt., Cambridgeshire Regt.
b., 6 Mar., '82 ; s., Mr. & Mrs. James Reid, 3 Cherry Orch. Rd., Croydon. Educ., M. Whitgift Sch., & Whitgift G. Sch., '96-98. Enl. as pte. in 16 Middlesex Regt., Sept., '14. D., 16 Oct., '16, in France, of wounds recd. the prev. day.

REPTON, ARTHUR GERALD, Cpl., 7 E. Sur. Regt.
b., Bolney, Sussex, 3 Feb., '95 ; s., Mr. & Mrs. Repton, 70 Richmond Rd., T. Heath. Educ., Ecclesbourne Rd. Sch., T. Heath. Single. Clerk. Enl., 3 Feb., '15 ; served in France, 21 Jun.-9 Nov., '15. D. of wounds recd. at Givenchy, 9 Nov., '15. (Plate XXV., 4).

REVELL, JOHN HENRY, R.N.
b., 21 Dec., '96 ; s., Mr. & Mrs. Revell, 10 Laurier Rd., E. Croydon. Educ., Woking & Mitcham. Single. Empl. by Messrs Allder, North End, Croydon. Joined, Sept., '13. Lost, with H.M.S. " Queen Mary," sunk in Battle of Jutland, 31 May, '16

REVENE, HOWARD, Lt., R.G.A.
s., Mr. & Mrs. Frederic Revene, 7 High St., S. Norwood, and " Southella," St. Saviour's Rd., Croydon. D. from syncope, Basra, 25 Aug., '17.

REW, DOUGLAS JOLLAND, 2/Lt., Essex Regt.
3rd s., late Maj. H. G., & Mrs. Rew, 22 Queen's Rd., S. Norwood. Enl. in Artists Rif. O.T.C. ; served in France with 13 Essex Regt. until w., '16 ; ret. to France, Apr., '17. Fell, 28 Jun., '17.

REYNOLDS, G., 323358, Pte., Lond. Regt.
Res., S. Croydon. Fell, '17.

REYNOLDS, R. L., 703336, L/Cpl., Lond. Regt.
Res., Tooting. Fell, '17.

RHODES, A. E., Pte., M.G.C.
b., '95. Educ., Par. Ch. Sch., Croydon. Res., 37 Zion Rd., T. Heath. Fell, 28 Aug., '16.

RHODES, DAVID ROBERT, Pte., Lond. Regt.
b., Worth, Sussex, 25 Apr., '91 ; y.s., James, & late Emily Rhodes, 119 Whitehorse Rd., Croydon. Educ., Oval Rd. Sch., Croydon. Empl. by Mr. Alfred Bullock. Enl. in E. Sur. Regt., 9 Feb., '16. Fell, 22 Aug., '18.

RHODES, JAMES CHARLES, Rflmn., K.R.R.C.
Memb. of St. Mark's, S. Norwood, C.L.B. Res., 53 Sidney Rd., S. Norwood. Enl., 23 Feb., '17. Fell, 18 Nov., '17.

RHODES, W., M2/184228, Pte., R.A.S.C.
Res., S. Croydon. D. of wounds, '17.

RICHARDS, GEORGE WILLIAM, 200954, Signaller, 3/4 R.W.S. Regt.
s., Mr. George Richards, Stationmaster, Wimbledon (L.B. & S.C.R.) Stn., & Mrs. Richards. Res., Waddon Stn. Enl., Sept., '14. Fell, Meteren, Belgium, 14 Apr., '18.

RICHARDSON, B. G., Gnr., R.F.A.
b., '82 ; s., Mr. & Mrs. H. Richardson, late of Tanfield Rd., Croydon. Married ; 2 children. Empl. by Messrs. J. Pascall, Blackfriars. Enl., 6 Feb., '18. D. of wounds at Rouen, 27 Oct., '18.

RICHARDSON, BERTRAM FRANK, Rflmn., 13 R.B.
b., Forest Hill, 8 Jul., '97 ; s. Walter & Marian Richardson, 58 Heath Rd., T. Heath. Educ., Katherine Rd. Sch., Forest Hill. Single. Clerk at Messrs. Methuen's, publishers. Res., 58 Heath Rd., T. Heath. Enl., 28 Aug., '14. Fell, Somme, 10 Jul., '16.

THE GLORIOUS DEAD

RICHARDSON, F., 53261, Pte., R. Fus.
Res., E. Croydon. *D.* of wounds, '17.

RICHARDSON, HARRY THOMAS, Lt., 5 Northd. Fus.
s., Mr. & Mrs. John Richardson, Gosforth. *Enl.*, 11 Sept., '14; went to France, Apr., '15; *w.*, 1 May, '15; removed to hosp. at Boulogne and Oxford. *D.*, 23 Aug., '15.

RICHARDSON, HECTOR LAWRENCE, Rflmn., 9 R.B.
b., Leeds, 27 Jan., '94; *s.*, Charles Frederick & Bertha Richardson, 29 Preston Rd., Beulah Hill, U. Norwood. *Educ.*, St. George's Sec. Sch., Lond., E.C. Single. Chauffeur. *Enl.*, 4 Jan., '15; M.M. for bravery in field, awarded 8 Sept., '16. *D.*, 20 Aug., '16, at Amiens, of wounds recd. 15 Aug., '16.

RICHARDSON, PERCY FREDERICK.
s., Mr. & Mrs. E. H. Richardson, Addis. *Fell*, France, 21 May, '17.

RICHARDSON, PERCY LEWIS, Pte., 5 Lond. Regt.
b., Forest Hill, 21 Sept., '99; *s.*, Walter & Marian Richardson, 58 Heath Rd., T. Heath. *Educ.*, Whitehorse Rd. Sch., T. Heath. Single. Empl. at Lond. Bdge. *Enl.*, 9 Mar., '15. *Fell*, Somme, 1 Jul., '16.

RICHARDSON, THOMAS CHARLES, Maj., R.E.
b., Croydon, '84; *s.*, Mr. & Mrs. Richardson, " St. David's," Clifton Park Rd., Clifton, Bristol. *Educ.*, High Sch., Croydon, and Monkton Combe Sch. Single. Civil engineer (A.M.I.C.E.) *Res.*, Birmingham. *Joined* as sub-lt., '09; twice ment. in despat.; M.C. *D.* of gas poisoning, Albert, Feb., '16.

RICHARDSON, THOMAS MARTIN, Pte., 5 Notts. & Derby. Regt. (Sherwood For.).
b., Penge, 3 Nov., '83; *s.*, late Robert Henry, & Alice Olivia Richardson, 1 Blenheim Pk. Rd., Croydon. *Educ.*, The Skinners' Coy. Publ. Sch., Tunbridge Wells. Single. Musician. *Enl.*, 25 Mar., '16. *Fell*, France, 26 Jun., '17. (Plate XXI., 6).

RICHENS, ALBERT EDWARD, Pte., 13 Middlesex Regt.
b., Sydenham, 16 Apr., '98; *s.*, Albert Edward & Eliza Harriet Richens, 140 Harrington Rd., S. Norwood. *Educ.*, Portland Rd. Sch., S. Norwood. Single. Milk carrier. *Enl.*, 6 Sept., '16. *Fell*, Messines, 11 Jun., '17.

RICHMOND, PERCY STUART, Pte., 5 Yorks. Regt.
b., Lond., 6 Mar., '91; *s.*, Mr. & Mrs. Richmond, 389 Whitehorse Rd., T. Heath. *Educ.*, Whitehorse Rd. Sch., T. Heath. Single. Warehouseman. Goalkeeper for Holy Trinity Football Club. *Enl.*, 1 Apr., '16. *Fell*, France, 23 Apr., '17.

RICHMOND, SIDNEY WILLIAM, Pte., Lond. Regt.
b., Croydon, 2 Nov., '89; *s.*, William & Emily Richmond, 70 Lond. Rd., Croydon. *Educ.*, Whitehorse Rd. Sch., T. Heath. Married. Railway employee, engineer's dept. *Enl.*, 11 Dec.,'15; *w.*, France, Nov., '17. *Fell*, France, 28 Sept., '18. (Plate XXVIII., 4).

RIDDICK, STANLEY CHARLES, Pte., H.A.C.
b., Nunhead, 2 May, '97; *s.*, Harry & Mabel Riddick, " Trevena," 73 Brigstock Rd., T. Heath. *Educ.*, Boro. Sec. Sch., Croydon. Single. Bank clerk. *Res.*, 336 Bensham Lane, T. Heath. *Enl.*, May, '15. *Fell*, Beaumont Hamel, 13 Nov., '16. (Plate XXII., 4).

RIDLEY, A. E., Pte., E. Sur. Regt.
b., '98. *Educ.*, Whitehorse Rd. Sch., T. Heath. Postman. *Res.*, 353 Whitehorse Rd., Croydon. *Enl.*, Jul., '15. *Fell*, France, 1 Jan., '17.

RIDLEY, BERT, Sapper, R.E.
 b., '93. Married ; 1 child. *Res.*, 9 Anthony Rd., Woodside.
 Fell, 3 Jan., '18.
RIDLEY, G. W., L/Cpl., M.G.C.
 b., '92 ; *s.*, Mr. & Mrs. Ridley, 26 Anthony Rd., Woodside.
 Served 3 years. *D.* of gas poisoning at Bermondsey Mil. Hosp.,
 22 Sept., '18.
RILEY, ALFRED VALENTINE COLE, P.O., R.N.
 b., Caterham, '87 ; *s.*, Mr. & Mrs. Alf. Riley, 3 Cedar Rd.,
 Croydon. *Educ.*, Caterham Valley Counc. Sch. At one time
 in service of Orient Line ; later joined an American line, and for
 4 years before war was with R.M.S.P. Co. In Dec., '14, his ship
 was taken over by the Admiralty as an aux. cruiser, and he continued in the service, becoming a p.o. *Killed* in engagement
 between H.M.S. " Alcantara " and the German raider " Greif,"
 29 Feb., '16.
RILEY, W., 9449, L/Sgt., E. Yorks. Regt.
 Fell, '16.
RITCHINGS, ARTHUR WILLIAM, 2/Lt.
 e.s., Mr. & Mrs. A. E. Ritchings, 14 Estcourt Rd., S. Norwood.
 Enl., Nov., '14 ; M.M., Messines, 7 Jun., '17. *Fell*, 27 Sept., '17.
RIVERS, TOM LANGLEY, Cpl., 169 Can. Inf.
 b., The Drive, T. Heath, 29 Sept., '85 ; *s.*, Mr. & Mrs. Tom Rivers,
 614 Woodbine Av., Toronto, Canada. *Educ.*, Whitehorse Rd.
 Sch., Croydon. Married. *Res.*, 213 Chisholm Av., Toronto,
 Canada. *Enl.*, 25 Jan., '16. *Fell*, Passchendaele, 28 Oct., '17.
ROAF, ARTHUR BOX, Pte., 2 Hants. Regt.
 b., Gloucester Rd., Croydon, 12 Jan., '94 ; *y.s.*, Mr. & Mrs. T.
 Roaf, 43 Sidney Rd., S. Norwood. *Educ.*, Birchanger Rd. Sch.,
 S. Norwood. Single. Labourer. *Enl.*, 3 Sept., '14. *D.* at
 2 Can. Gen. Hosp., Le Tréport, France, of wounds recd. at
 Cambrai, 7 Dec., '17.
ROBARTS, FRANCIS WATSON, 2/Lt., 14 Lond. Regt. (Lond. Scottish).
 b., Woodford, Essex, 5 Mar., '82 ; *s.*, Nathaniel Francis & Margaret
 Elizabeth Robarts, 23 Oliver Grove, S. Norwood. *Educ.*,
 Whitgift G. Sch. Single. Chemical merchant, partner in the
 firm of Bryce Robarts & Co., 43-45 Gt. Tower St., Lond., E.C.
 Memb. of Sur. County Cricket Club, and R.A.C. ; formerly
 Hon. Sec. of Addis. Cricket Club, & Norwood Cricket Club ;
 Sec. to the Church Committee of St. Andrew's Presbyterian Ch.,
 U. Norwood ; superintendent of New Town Sunday Sch.,
 U. Norwood. *Enl.* as pte., Sept., '14. *Fell*, nr. Loos, 13 Oct., '15.
 (Plate XXIII., 6).
ROBERSON, FRANK H. L., 2/Lt., R.W.S. Regt.
 b., '83. Married Grace Dorothy (*née* Gatfield). *Res.*, Streatham
 and Croydon. *D.*, 12 Aug., '17, of wounds recd. 2 days prev.
ROBERTS, FRANK MARSHALL, Sgt., 7 R.W.S. Regt.
 b., U. Norwood, 24 May, '80 ; *s.*, Mr. & Mrs. George Roberts,
 Nottingham. *Educ.* at a private sch. in U. Norwood. Married.
 Insurance clerk. *Res.*, 48 Lebanon Rd., Croydon. Hon. Sec.
 Croydon Nat. Hist. & Sci. Soc. at time of enlistment. *Enl.*,
 Sept., '14. *Fell*, Inverness Copse, Ypres, 10 Aug., '17.
ROBERTS, JOHN, Pte., 8 R. Fus.
 b., Finsbury Park, 24 Jun., '82 ; *s.*, Mr. & Mrs. Roberts, 53
 Donald Rd., Croydon. *Educ.*, Kenley Sch. Married. General
 labourer. *Res.*, Hillside Cottages, Kenley. *Enl.*, 26 Dec., '00 ;
 called up on reserve, 5 Aug., '14. *Fell*, France, 7 Jul., '16.

ROBINSON, FREDERICK, Driver, R.G.A.
Married. Empl. by L.B. & S.C.R. *D.* of pneumonia, Italy, 9 Oct., '18.

ROBINSON, LEONARD HERBERT FRANK, Lt., 7 E. Sur. Regt.
b., 25 Aug., '91 ; *s.*, Mr. & Mrs. Henry Bartlett Robinson, late of 12 Dingwall Rd., Croydon. *Educ.*, Whitgift G. Sch., '06-10, Camb. Univ. to '13, and Ely Theological Coll. *D.* of wounds recd. at Hohenzollern Redoubt, France, 18 Mar., '16.

ROBINSON, N. J., Pte., 2/4 R.W.S. Regt.
Fell, Dardanelles, 9 Aug., '15.

ROBINSON, ROBERT, 8 R.W.S. Regt.
s., Mr. & Mrs. Robinson, 15 Lansdowne Rd., Purley. *Fell*, France, 27 Sept., '15.

ROCKALL, FREDERICK ROBERT GEORGE, Pte., 11 R. Fus.
b., Highbury, 21 Sept., '82 ; *s* , Frederick James & Clara Rockall, 37 Richmond St., Plaistow. *Educ.*, St. Paul's, Canonbury. Married. Cellarman. *Res.*, 18 Gilsland Rd., T. Heath. *Enl.*, 19 Jun., '16. *Fell*, E. of Combles, 30 Aug., '18.

RODD, ALBERT FRANK, Rflmn., 20 K.R.R.C.
b., 1 Raleigh Rd., Penge, 18 Jun., '98 ; *s.*, Mr. & Mrs. A. Rodd, 4 New Cottages, Middle Park Farm, Eltham. *Educ.*, Melvin Rd. Sch., Penge. Single. Gardener. *Res.*, 39 Raleigh Rd., Penge. *Enl.*, 15 Nov., '15. *D.*, 24 Mar., '17, at 45 Field Amb., France, of wounds recd. 19 Mar., '17.

RODWELL, ERNEST SAMUEL, Bdr., R.F.A.
b., '82. Empl. by Brit. Cement Works. *Res.*, Pitlake Bdge., Croydon. *Enl.*, Aug., '14. *Fell*, 23 Sept., '16.

ROFFEY, CHARLES ALFRED, Pte., H.A.C.
b., '89 ; *e.s.*, Mr. & Mrs. A. J. Roffey, 55 Church Rd., Croydon. *Educ.*, M. Whitgift Sch., Croydon. Empl. by Union of Lond. and Smiths' Bank, Princes St., E.C. *Fell*, Passchendaele, 9 Oct,'17.

ROFFEY, FRANK ALLEN, Pte., 13 Australian I.F.
b., '97 ; *y.s.*, Mr. & Mrs. A. J. Roffey, 55 Church Rd., Croydon. *Educ.*, M. Whitgift Sch., Croydon. On leaving sch. he was apprenticed to Central Motor Co., Ltd; left Eng. for N.S. Wales, 30 Jul., '14, for tuition on Gov. Experimental Farm, at Cowra. *Enl.*, Jan., '15. *Fell*, Suvla Bay, 10 Aug., '15.

ROFFEY, THOMAS GEORGE, Pte., 17 Middlesex Regt.
b., Devonshire Rd., Croydon, 10 Dec., '97 ; *s.*, Mr. & Mrs. George Roffey, 9 Russell Rd., Croydon. *Educ.*, Princess Rd. Sch., Croydon. Single. Labourer, empl. by L.B. & S.C.R. *Enl.*, 1 Sept., '16. *Missing*, Oppy, nr. Arras, 28 Apr., '17. (Plate XXIII., 2).

ROFFEY, W. H., Pte., 3 E. Sur. Regt.
b., '78. *Educ.*, St. Andrew's Sch., Croydon. Married. Postman. *Res* , 79 Rymer Rd., Croydon. Served through S.A War. *Enl.*, 3 Dec., '14. *Fell* nr. Festubert, 16 May, '15.

ROGERS, ALFRED JOSEPH, Driver, R.A.S.C.
b., 25 Jun., '80. *Educ.*, Par. Ch. Sch., Croydon. Married ; 2 children. Empl. for 24 years by Messrs. Waghorn Bros., jewellers, Croydon. *Enl.*, Apr., '17. *D.* of pneumonia, 14 May, '17.

ROGERS, F., 24344, Pte., E. Sur. Regt.
Res., T. Heath. *Fell*, '17.

ROMSFORD.
Res., 16 Mowbray Rd.

THE CROYDON ROLL OF HONOUR

RONCA, EDWARD HENRY, 2/Lt., E. Kent Regt.
b., '82. *Educ.*, King's Coll., London. Married. Civil servant. *Res.*, 26 Linton Av., T. Heath. *Enl.*, '15. *Fell*, France, 17 Oct., '18. (Plate XXIX., 3).

ROOM, F. A., Pte., M.G.C.
Married ; 3 children. Carpenter, empl. by L.B. & S.C.R. *Res.*, 27 Old Town, Croydon. *Enl.*, in R.E., 8 Mar., '17. *Fell*, France, 4 Aug., '18.

ROOME, PHILIP WILLIAM, Fleet Paymaster, R.N.
b., 28 Jun., '72 ; *s.*, Henry & Phœbe Roome, 114 Breakespeare Rd., Brockley. *Educ.*, Whitgift G. Sch., '85-87, & Mercer's Sch. *Joined* R.N. as asst. clerk, Dec., '88. *Killed* in action in North Sea on H.M.S. " Aboukir," 22 Sept., '14.

ROOTS, W. J., 3994, Pte., Lond. Regt.
Res., T. Heath. *Fell*, '16.

ROPE, J. A., 2/Lt., R.W.S. Regt.
Fell, '16.

ROSE, DOUGLAS JOHN, 6 Lond. Regt.
b., '98 ; *s.*, Mr. & Mrs. Rose, 19 Brafferton Rd., Croydon. Empl. by Mr. French, baker, Croydon. *Enl.* in 3/4 R.W.S. Regt., '14. *Fell*, Ypres, 22 Oct., '16.

ROSE, L. A., R.W.S. Regt.
Fell, '16.

ROSE, PHILIP VIVIAN.
Solicitor. *D.* of wounds recd. at Loos, Sept., '15.

ROSIER, W., Driver, R.E.
Married. Labourer, empl. by Croydon Corp., Roads Dept. *Res.*, 67 Lancing Rd., Croydon. *Enl.*, 30 Oct., '15. *D.* at Aldershot of cerebro-spinal meningitis, 21 Jan., '16.

ROSS, THOMAS HESKETH, S.A. Inf.
b., '89. *Res.*, T. Heath. Served in German S.W. Afr., Egypt, and France. M.C. *Fell*, France.

ROTHEN, FRANCIS FREDERICK, Sgt., 1 Q.W. Rif. (16 Lond. Regt.)
b., Stamford Bridge, Worcester, 28 Jan., '85 ; *s.*, late John, and Elizabeth Rothen, 5 Elliott House, Elliott Rd., T. Heath. *Educ.*, Royal G. Sch., Worcester, & St. Mark's Coll., Chelsea ; B.Sc., Lond. Single. Asst. master, Boro. Sec. Sch. for Boys, Croydon. *Enl.*, 3 Nov., '15. *Fell*, Arras, 14 Apr., '17. Buried in French Cem., nr. Heninel. (Plate XXIV., 3).

ROUTE, S. W., 23669, Pte., D.C.L.I.
Res., T. Heath. *Fell*, '16.

ROUTLEY, ERNEST GEORGE, 2/Lt., 6 E. Kent Regt.
b., Clapham Park, 3 Apr., '92 ; *s.*, Mr. & Mrs. Routley, 139 Melfort Rd., T. Heath *Educ.*, M. Whitgift Sch., Croydon. Single. Bank clerk. *Enl.* as pte. in 10 R. Fus., 19 Aug., '14 ; commis. in E. Kent Regt., Aug., '15 ; went to France, Feb., '16 ; M.C. for conspicuous gallantry when on a reconnoitring patrol, Aug., '16, bestowed 20 May, '17, at Woolwich. *Fell*, Geudecourt, between Bapaume and Combles, 7 Oct., '16. (Plate XXIV., 5).

ROWE, ARTHUR WILLIAM, Pte., 1 R.W.S. Regt.
b., Pridham Rd., T. Heath, 11 Apr., '87 ; *s.*, Mr. & Mrs. H. Rowe, 8 Nursery Rd., T. Heath. *Educ.*, Whitehorse Rd. Sch., T. Heath. Married. Coal porter. *Res.*, 157 Whitehorse Rd., T. Heath. *Enl.*, 11 Nov., '14. *D.*, 18 Jun., '16, at West Riding C.C.S., France, of wounds recd. at Armentières the prev. day.

ROWLAND, B. A., 15312, Pte., Coldstream Gds.
Res., S. Croydon. *Fell*, '16.

RUDDLE, ARTHUR JAMES, Rflmn., 2/17 Lond. Regt.
b., Clapham, 15 Jun., '96 ; 2nd *s.*, James Mills & Mary Ruddle, 16 Arundel Rd., Croydon. *Educ.*, St. Saviour's, & Brit. Schs., Croydon. Single. Shipbroker's clerk. *Enl.*, in L.R.B., Dec., '14 ; went to France, Sept., '15, returning with cynovitis, Nov., '15 ; returned to France, Jul., '16, and from there was drafted to Salonica and Egypt ; served at Jerusalem, Jericho, etc. *D.* of dysentery, 74 C.C.S., Syria, 2 Jun., '18. (Plate XXIV., 1).

RUDDOCK, E. H. M., Capt., 13 Worcester Regt.
Married. House agent, in empl. of Messrs. Dickins and Sons, George St., Croydon. *Res.*, Croydon. Served in S.A. War. *Joined* as Lt., Aug., '14. *Fell*, Dardanelles, '15.

RUDKIN, W. S., Pte., 4 R.W.S. Regt.
Empl. by Croydon Corp., Tramways Dept.

RUFFELL, CLIFFORD WILLIAM, Pte., 58 Can. Regt.
b., Albion St., Lewisham, 28 Jul., '98. *Educ.*, Mitcham Rd. Sch., and Nat. Children's Home. Single. Farm hand. *Res.*, Ontario, Canada. *Fell*, Passchendaele, 26 Oct., '17. (Plate XXVII., 5).

RUMSEY, CHARLES EDWIN, Pte., Middlesex Regt.
b., '98 ; *s.*, Mr. & Mrs. Rumsey, Windmill Rd., Croydon. *Educ.*, Boston Rd. Sch., T. Heath. Single. Empl. by L.B. & S.C.R. *Enl.*, 26 Feb., '17. *Fell*, France, 7 Jun., '17.

RUSSELL, A. E., 14866, Rflmn., R.B.
Res., E. Croydon. *Fell*, '16.

RUSSELL, CHARLES FRANK, Trooper, 1 Life Gds.
b., Norwood, 10 Apr., '92 ; *s.*, David & Phyllis Russell, 116 Queen's Rd., U. Norwood. *Educ.*, Rockmount Rd. Sch., U. Norwood. Single. *Enl.*, 6 Sept., '11. *Fell*, Belgium, 13 May, '15.

RUSSELL, F., 533676, Pte., Lond. Regt.
Res., Mitcham. *Fell*, '17.

RUSSELL, FREDERICK ALFRED, Pte., Middlesex Regt.
b., 2 Leeds Cottages, Church St., Croydon, '84. *Educ.*, Bynes Rd. Sch., Croydon, and St. John's Sch., Croydon. Single. Painter and paperhanger. *Res.*, 12 Sanderstead Rd., Croydon. Served with Middlesex Regt. for 5 years from 22 Jun., '03. *Re-joined*, Aug., '14 ; taken pris. at Mons ; released, Jun., '16, after 22 months imprisonment, suffering from paralysis and tuberculosis ; admitted to Grosvenor Sanatorium, 19 Jul., '16 ; transf. to Warlingham Mental Asylum, Mar., '17. *D.*, 12 Sept., '17. *Buried*, Queen's Rd. Cem., Croydon.

RUSSELL, WILLIAM, Lt.
s., late Mr., & Mrs. Edward Russell, Croydon. *Educ.*, Charterhouse and Oxford Univ. *Joined*, '14 ; *w.*, end of '15. *Fell*, '17.

RUTTER, FRANK LIONEL, 2/Lt., R.W.S. Regt.
b., '95. *Fell*, France, 14 Jul., '16.

RUXTON, PERCY JAMES, Pte., Middlesex Regt.
b., Croydon, 5 Feb., '96 ; *s.*, David F. & Eleanor Ruxton, 23 Beaconsfield Rd., Croydon. *Educ.*, Brit. Sch., Croydon. Single. Electrical engineer. *Res.*, 13 Grosvenor Rd., S. Norwood. *Enl.*, 24 Aug., '15. *Fell*, Les Bœufs, France, 28 Oct., '16.

RYAN, ALFRED ERIC, Capt., R.W.S. Regt.
b., Forest Hill, 27 Sept., '97 ; *s.*, A. E. & Grace Ryan, 17 Croham Pk. Av., Croydon. *Educ.*, Whitgift G. Sch., Croydon, Mill Hill, and R.M.C., Sandhurst. *Gazetted*, 25 Aug., '16 ; M.C., Jan., '17 ; ment. in desp., Dec., '17 ; twice *w.* in '17. *D.* of wounds recd., 23 Mar., '18. (Plate XXIV., 6).

THE CROYDON ROLL OF HONOUR

RYAN, MICHAEL, Pte., 1 E. Kent Regt.
 b., Lond., 25 Aug., '80. Married. Postman. Res., 196 Holmesdale Rd., S. Norwood. For 8 yrs. with 4 R.W.S. Regt.; served in S.A. War (King's & Queen's Medals, bars for Transvaal, Driefontein, Paardeburg, Kimberley). Enl., 4 Aug., '14. Fell, Loos, 9 Apr., '17.

RYCRAFT, WILLIAM RAYNER, Pte., 9 E. Sur. Regt.
 Married. Memb. of Croydon Fire Bde. Res., 5 St. John's Rd., S. Norwood. Fell, Trones Wood, 21 Mar., '18.

SACH, HERBERT E., Pte., 1/24 Lond. Regt.
 b., '87; s., Mr. & Mrs. E. C. Sach, Whitehorse Lane, S. Norwood. Married; 1 child. Stationer. Res., High St., S. Norwood. Fell, 22 Aug., '18.

SADLER, ALFRED JOHN, Pte., R.W. Kent Regt.
 b., '86; e.s., Mr. & Mrs. Sadler, 37 Churchill Rd., Croydon. D. of illness, Mesopotamia, '17.

SADLER, F. W., Pte., R.W.S. Regt.
 s., Mr. & Mrs. Sadler, Gloucester Rd., Croydon. Empl. at Messrs. Brown's Mills. Fell, '16.

SADLER, W. D., 2/Lt., E. Sur. Regt.
 b., '93; 3rd s., Mr. & Mrs. E. W. Sadler, " Bella Vista," New Church Rd., Hove. Educ., High Sch., Croydon. Fell, 4 Aug., '17.

SALTER EDWARD, Pte., Lond. Regt.
 b., '80; e.s., Mr. & Mrs. Edward Salter, Southampton. Empl. as clerk by Mr. R. Dickenson, army contractor. Res., 24 Canterbury Rd., Croydon. Memb. of N. End Brotherhood. Enl., '15. Fell, 24 Aug., '18.

SAMSON, B. T., Cpl., R.F.A.
 b., '96; e.s., Mr. & Mrs. Samson, 18 Adelaide St., Croydon. Empl. by Messrs. Marshall, Murray & Co., dairymen, Brixton. Enl., Sept., '14. Fell, 2 May, '17.

SANDERS, H. W., 2/Lt., Middlesex Regt.
 Educ., Whitgift G. Sch., Croydon. Missing, '17.

SAUNDERS, A. C., Pte., 11 R.W.S. Regt.
 b., '92; s., Mr. & Mrs. Saunders, 25 Priory Rd., Croydon. Empl. by Messrs. Chapman, Tamworth Rd., Croydon. D. of wounds, at 3 Aust. C.C.S., 22 Jul., '18.

SAUNDERS, ALFRED GEORGE, Gnr., R.F.A.
 b., Croydon, 2 Jun., '81. Educ., Mitcham Rd. Sch., Croydon. Married. Carman, empl. by Messrs. Carter Paterson. Res., 38 Hathaway Rd., Croydon. Enl., Sept., '14. D., 15 May, '15, at Boulogne, of wounds recd. in France, 1 May, '15.

SAUNDERS, CAREY, Rflmn., 12 Lond. Regt.
 b., Croydon, 5 Jun., '90; s., Mr. & Mrs. Percy Saunders, 19 Coombe Rd., Croydon. Educ., M. Whitgift Sch., Boro. Sec. Sch., Croydon, & Strand Sch., Lond. Single. Civil servant. Enl., 7 Sept., '14. Fell, nr. Ypres, 8 May, '15.

SAUNDERS, J., 1st Cl. P.O., R.N.
 Empl. by Croydon Corp., Electricity Dept. Fell, '16.

SAUNDERS, L. H. C., 201845, Gnr., R.F.A.
 Res., E. Croydon. Fell, '17.

SAVAGE, REGINALD ALEXANDER, Act.-Bdr., R.F.A.
 b., 30 Temple St., Southwark; s., Mr. & Mrs. Savage, 48 Burlington Rd., T. Heath. Educ., Beulah Rd. Sch., T. Heath. Single. Fitter's mate. Enl., Mar., '15. Fell, Somme, 16 Jul., '16.

SAVILLE, B. C., 86391, Bdr., 162 Siege Bty., R.G.A.
 Married. Res., Croydon. Fell, Zillebeke, 29 Sept., '17.

XXV.

1. Pte. E. E. PERFECT, D.C.M., 2 R.W.S. Regt.
2. Pte. L. SIMPSON, Glo'ster: Regt.
3. Stoker W. L. SHIRLEY, R.N.
4. Cpl. A. G. REPTON, 7 E. Sur. Regt.
5. Gnr. W. J. SLYFIELD, R.F.A.
6. Pte. R. V. PEARSON, Lincoln. Regt.

XXVI.

1. Lt. J. S. REEVE, H.A.C.
2. Capt. Rev. C. H. SCHOOLING, C.F.
3. Pte. E. S. SHAW, Lond. Scottish
4. 2/Lt. S. G. SMITH, Machine Gun Corps
5. 2/Lt. A. G. SEVERS, R.F.C.
6. Pte. F. R. SMITH, 23 Lond. Regt.

THE GLORIOUS DEAD 381

SAW, WILLIAM GEORGE, Pte., 7 R.W.S. Regt.
b., Beddington, 31 Jul., '93 ; *s.*, Mr. & Mrs. Albert Saw, 3 Richmond Rd., Beddington. *Educ.*, Beddington & Par. Ch. Sch., Croydon. Single. Empl. by Croydon Corp., Roads Dept. *Enl.*, 7 Sept., '14. *D.*, 3 Jul., '16, of wounds recd. in France, 1 Jul., '16.

SAWORD, RALPH, 2/Lt., R. Fus.
b., 20 May, '90 ; *s.*, Mr. & Mrs. Frederick C. E. Saword, 100 Frant Rd., T. Heath. *Educ.*, Whitgift G. Sch., Croydon. *Fell*, '17.

SAWYER, GEORGE, 3057, Pte., 2/4 R.W.S. Regt.
b., Meadow Stile, Croydon, 25 Nov., '97 ; *s.*, Mr. & Mrs. Sawyer, 82 Southbridge Rd., Croydon. *Educ.*, Par. Ch. Sch., Croydon. Single. Butcher. *Enl.*, 19 Oct., '14. *Fell*, Suvla Bay, 9 Aug., '15.

SAWYER, HERBERT, 2/Lt., Suff. Regt.
b., 25 Mar., '89 ; *s.*, Mr. & Mrs. Joseph Sawyer, "The Tower," Kenley. *Educ.*, Whitgift G. Sch., '04-06.

SAWYER, J., 41804, Trooper, Hussars.
Res., W. Croydon. *D.*, '17.

SAXBY, CLEMENT PERCIVAL GEORGE, L/Cpl., 1 R.W.S. Regt.
b., 119 Northcote Rd., Croydon, 31 Mar., '95 ; *s.*, Frederick George & Bertha Annie Saxby, 91 Northcote Rd., Croydon. *Educ.*, Sydenham Rd. Sch., Croydon. Single. Grocer's asst. *Enl.* in 16 Lancers, 20 May, '12. *D.*, 8 Nov., '16, at 11 Stat. Hosp., Rouen, of wounds recd., 3-4 Nov., '16. (Plate XXVII., 3).

SAY, CECIL A., Pte., 8 N. Staff. Regt.
Married. *Res.*, "Hillcrest," St. Mary's Rd., S. Norwood. *Fell*, France, 3 Jan., '18.

SAYER, JAMES HERBERT, 2/Lt., R.F.C.
b., 11 Feb., '98 ; *e.s.*, Mr. & Mrs. Charles Joseph Sayer, Wallington. *Educ.*, Whitgift G. Sch., '10-16, where he was sgt. in the O.T.C. *Commis.*, Jun., '16. *Fell*, 3 Apr., '17.

SAYERS, F. C., 608599, Pte., Lond. Regt.
Res., Croydon. *D.* of wounds, 26 Aug., '18.

SCHOFIELD, REGINALD GEORGE HORNBY, 15 Australian I.F.
s., Mr. & Mrs. Schofield, 65 Belvedere Rd., U. Norwood. *Fell*, Dardanelles, 26 Apr., '15.

SCHOLEY, GERALD PERCIVAL, Cpl., H.A.C.
b., Clapham, 3 Mar., '91 ; *s.*, Mr. & Mrs. Scholey, 295 Lond. Rd., T. Heath. *Educ.*, High Sch., Croydon. Single. Bank clerk. *Enl.*, Jan., '15. *D.* of erysipelas, at Paisley, Scotland, Sept., '16.

SCHOLEY, NORMAN VICTOR, Bdr., R.G.A.
b., Clapham, 1 Jun., '92 ; *s.*, Mr. & Mrs. Scholey, 295 Lond. Rd., T. Heath. *Educ.*, Wyncott House Sch., & T. Heath Sch. Single. *Enl.*, '08. *Fell*, Hill 60, nr. Ypres, May, '15.

SCHOOLING, REV. CECIL HERBERT, Capt., C.F.
b., '85 ; *y.s.*, Mr. & Mrs. F. Schooling, "Holly Dene," Beckenham Lane, Bromley. Sen. Curate at Par. Ch., Croydon. B.A., Trin. Coll., Camb., '06 ; M.A., '10 ; ordained deacon, '07, and priest, '08 ; curate at All Saints', Wakefield, '07-10 ; Secty., Ruri-decanal Conference. *D.*, 21 Jun., '17, of wounds recd. prev. day. (Plate XXVI., 2).

SCOT, FREDERICK, R. Fus.
Married. *Accidentally killed*, France, '15.

SCOTT, ARTHUR, Sapper, R.E.
   b., Birmingham, 13 Mar., '95 ; s., Alfred & Frances C. Scott, 157 High St., Croydon. *Educ.*, Dering Pl. Sch., Croydon. Single. Fitter. Memb. of St. Peter's, Croydon, C.L.B. *Enl.*, 5 May, '13. *Fell*, France, 17 Nov., '15.

SCOTT, FREDERICK THOMAS, Cpl., 2/20 Lond. Regt.
   b., 48 Bensham Grove, T. Heath, 26 Aug., '94 ; s., Mr. & Mrs. F. J. Scott, 48 Bensham Grove, T. Heath. *Educ.*, Beulah Rd. Sch., T. Heath, Boro. Sec. Sch., Croydon, & Goldsmiths' Coll., Lond. Single. Student. *Enl.*, in Territorials before war. *Fell*, France, 13 Aug., '16.

SCOTT, STUART HARRY, Lt., R.A.F.
   b., Riddlesdown, Kenley, 14 Sept., '00 ; s., Donald James and Lilian K. Scott, 95 Mayfield Rd., Sanderstead. *Educ.*, Whitgift G. Sch. Single. Student. *Joined* as cadet, 25 Jul., '16. *Fell* while flying nr. Amiens, 29 Sept., '18. *Buried* behind enemy lines where he fell.

SCOTT, THOMAS GEORGE, Bdr., 223 Bde., R.F.A.
   b., Camberwell, 1 Jan., '94 ; s., James & Jane Scott, 69 Croydon Grove, Croydon. *Educ.*, Boston Rd. Sch., Croydon. Single. Pawnbroker's salesman. *Enl.*, 23 Nov., '14. *D.*, 22 Mar., '18, at 48 C.C.S., France, of wounds recd. at Edge Hill, nr. Combles, 21 Mar., '18.

SCRIVENER, A. E., Sgt., Som.L.I.
   b., '85 ; 4*th* s., late Mr., & Mrs. W. J. Scrivener, 34 Newark Rd., Croydon. Married ; children. *Enl.* about '03, in R.G.A., transf. to Som.L.I. *Called up* on reserve, Aug., '14. *D.* at 34 Newark Rd., Croydon, 7 Apr., '17.

SCUTT, GILBERT ARTHUR, Gnr., R.F.A. (attd. Trench Mortar Bty.)
   b., '97 ; s., Mrs. Mary Biggs, 5 Bourne St., Croydon. *D.* of gas poisoning and wounds, France, 14 Aug., '17.

SEABROOK, H. DAN, 76170, Gnr., R.H.A.
   b., '95 ; s., H. D. & A. M. Seabrook, 63 Alderton Rd., Addis. *Educ.*, Woodside Sch., & M. Whitgift Sch., Croydon. Served 2 years and 8 months in France. *Fell*, Vimy Ridge, 12 Apr., '17.

SEAGER, E. J., Rflmn., Lond. Regt.
   b., '97 ; s., Mr. & Mrs. Seager, 9 Roberts' Yard, Croydon. *Educ.*, Par. Ch. Sch., Croydon. *Fell*, 23 Nov., '17.

SEAGER, SAMUEL WILLIAM, Pte., R.W.S. Regt.
   b., Penge, 28 Jun., '80 ; s., Mr. & Mrs. Seager, 155 Maple Rd., Penge. *Educ.*, St. John's Sch., Penge. Married ; 3 children. Printer. *Res.*, 80 Canterbury Rd., Croydon. *Enl.*, Oct., '14. *Fell*, Suvla Bay, 9 Aug., '15.

SEARLE, B. WHITMORE-, 2/Lt., 4 S. Staff. Regt.
   Educ., High Sch., Croydon. *D.* of enteritis, '15.

SEARLE, HARRY CAREW, A.B. Seaman, R.N.A.S. (A.A.C.)
   b., Dulwich, 30 Jun., '88 ; s., Mr. & Mrs. Searle, 143 Langdale Rd., T. Heath. *Educ.*, St. John's Sch., Dulwich. Single. Accountant. *Enl.*, 29 May, '15. *D.* of trench fever, Mudros, Isle of Lemnos, 30 Jun., '16.

SELBY, GEORGE.
   b., '99. *Fell*, 13 Jul., '16.

SELBY, J. F., L/Cpl., R. Fus.
   Married ; 1 child. Empl. by Croydon Corp. Tramways. *Res.*, 63 Ecclesbourne Rd., T. Heath. *Enl.*, Nov., '14 ; served at Malta, Egypt, Dardanelles, & France ; *w.*, at Trones Wood, Jul., '16, and at Cambrai, Nov., '17. *Fell*, France, 28 Mar., '18.

THE GLORIOUS DEAD

SELBY, WILLIAM, *V.C.,* Lt.-Col.
  b., 16 Jun., '69. *Educ.,* Whitgift G. Sch., '79-85, & St. Bartholomew's Hosp. ; Principal, St. George's Medical Coll., Lucknow, India, & Hon. Surg. to the Viceroy ; M.R.C.S., Eng., '92 ; L.R.C.P., Lond. & F.R.C.S., '05. Served in N.W. Frontier Campaign, Tirah & Chitral, '97-98, gaining V.C. in '97, & ment. in despat., '98 ; awarded D.S.O. during this war. *Accidentally killed,* '16.

SELWAY, –, Rflmn., 3 K.R.R.C.
  Res., 140 Pawson's Rd., Croydon. *Enl.,* 1 Sept., '14. *Fell,* France, 16 Aug., '15.

SERRES, CHARLES HERBERT, Cpl., 23 Lond. Regt.
  b., Osgathorpe, Leicestershire ; *s.,* Mr. & Mrs. Serres, 73 Stretton Rd., Croydon. *Educ.,* Ashby Grammar Sch., Leicestershire, and M. Whitgift Sch. Married. Bank clerk. *Res.,* 75 Clyde Rd., Addis. *Enl.,* Sept., '14 ; discharged, 17 Sept., '17. *D.* of nephritis at the Nursing Home, 3 Tavistock Place, Croydon, 12 Jan., '18.

SEVERS, ALFRED GEORGE, 2/Lt., R.F.C.
  b., 5 Jul., '93 ; *s.,* Mr. & Mrs. Severs, 11 Vincent Rd., Croydon. *Educ.,* M. Whitgift Sch., Croydon. Civil servant (National Insur. Dept.). Joined Civil Serv. Cadets, '12. *Joined* Inns of Court O.T.C., '15 ; gazetted to 15 Middlesex Regt. ; transf. to R.F.C., being sent to France when qualified as an observer, Dec., '16. *Fell,* France, 28 Mar., '17. (Plate XXVI., 5).

SEWARD, EDWIN MARK, R.F.A.

SHAKESPEARE, FREDERICK EDRIDGE, Pte., Argyll & Sutherland H.
  b., 9 Jun., '92 ; *y.s.,* Mr. & Mrs. J. B. Shakespeare, 67 George St., Croydon. *Educ.,* M. Whitgift Sch., Croydon. Memb. of Legion of Frontiersmen. *Enl.,* Aug., '14 ; went to France, Jun., '15 ; *w.,* '16. *Fell,* 26 Mar., '18.

SHARKER, J. F., 228227, Pte., R. Fus.
  Res., T. Heath. *Fell,* '17.

SHARMAN, W., Sapper, R.E.
  b., '84. Married ; 5 children. *Enl.,* Oct., '14 ; went to Egypt, 17 Mar., '15 ; *w.,* Suvla Bay, 2 Jul., '15 ; after short time in hosp. at Bristol & elsewhere, was sent to France, 24 Feb., '16 ; invalided home with diabetes, 7 Aug., '16 ; discharged from army, Feb., '17. *D.* at his home, 29 Dec., '17.

SHARP, G. E., 30118, Pte., E. Sur. Regt.
  Res., T. Heath. *Fell,* '17.

SHARP, HARRY, Sapper, R.E. (Signal Serv.).
  b., '95. Empl. at Croydon Post Office, '10-15. *Enl.,* Apr., '15. *D.,* Gen. Hosp., Camiers, France, 11 Aug., '17.

SHARPE, W. D. C., Pte., S. Staff. Regt.
  Res., 135 Whitehorse Rd., Croydon. *Missing,* 21 Mar., '18.

SHARPLES, CHARLES EDWARD, L/Cpl., E. Sur. Regt.
  b., 12 Northumberland St., Marylebone, 28 Sept., '91 ; *s.,* Mr. & Mrs. Bacon, Upper Green, Mitcham. *Educ.,* Whitehorse Rd. Sch., Croydon. Married. Foreman at Docks, Lond. Bridge. *Res.,* Fountain Rd., Tooting. *Enl.,* early in '16. *Fell,* France (probably nr. Bullecourt), 3 May, '17.

SHARPLESS, W., 18233, Pte., E. Sur. Regt.
  Res., Croydon. *Fell,* '16.

SHARPS, ROBERT, 2/Lt., M.G.C.
  b., Winchelsea, Suss., 25 Jul., '94. *Educ.,* Christ Ch. Sch., Croydon. Single. Printer. *Res.,* 61 Benson Rd., Waddon. *Enl.* in R. Fus., 3 Jun., '15. *D.,* 18 Apr., '18, of wounds recd. at Baquerolles Farm, Merville-Robecq Rd., France, 17 Apr., '18.

SHAW, EDWARD STUART, Pte., Lond. Scottish (14 Lond. Regt.)
    b., Croydon, 29 Mar., '96 ; s., late Edward John, & Margaret
    Stuart Shaw, 66 Croham Rd., Croydon. *Educ.*, Elmhurst Sch.,
    and Whitgift G. Sch., Croydon. Single. Insurance clerk,
    Royal Insurance Co., Ltd., Lombard St., E.C. *Enl.*, 11 Nov., '15.
    Fell, Gommecourt, France, 1 Jul., '16. *Buried*, Hebuterne.
    (Plate XXVI., 3).
SHAW, EDWIN BRUCE, Pte., 9 R. Fus.
    b., Croydon, 23 Mar., '00 ; s., Samuel B. & Minian Alice Shaw,
    21 St. John's Grove, Croydon. *Educ.*, Dering Pl. Sch., Croydon,
    Boro. Sec. Sch., Croydon, & King's Coll., Lond. Single.
    Teacher. *Enl.*, 29 Jan., '16. *Fell*, France, 5 Aug., '16. (Plate
    XXIII., 4).
SHEARS, J. S., 1378, Cpl., R.W.S. Regt.
    b., '92. *Res.*, 53 Albert Rd., Addis. *Fell*, France, 1 Jul., '16.
SHELDRICK, THOMAS EDWARD, Pte., 12 E. Sur. Regt.
    b., 21 Sainsbury Rd., Gipsy Hill, U. Norwood, 6 Oct., '81 ;
    s., Mr. & Mrs. Sheldrick, 21 Sainsbury Rd., U. Norwood.
    Educ., Woodland Rd. Sch., U. Norwood. Married. Plasterer.
    Res., 36 Queen's Rd., U. Norwood. *Enl.*, 23 Jun., '16. *Fell*,
    Ypres, 25 Apr., '18. *Buried*, Vlamertinge, W. of Ypres.
SHELLEY, FREDERICK CHARLES, Pte., 6 R.W.S. Regt.
    b., 40 Fawcett Rd., Croydon, 13 Nov., '95 ; s., Mr. & Mrs.
    Shelley, 40 Fawcett Rd., Croydon. *Educ.*, Par. Ch. Sch.,
    Croydon. Single. Engineer's apprentice. *Enl.*, 3 Sept., '14.
    Fell, Hohenzollern Redoubt, France, 13 Oct., '15.
SHEPPARD, W. J., 1866, Rflmn., 2 R.B.
    b., Winchester ; s., Mr. & Mrs. Sheppard, 8 Pridham Rd. E.,
    T. Heath. *Educ.*, Whitehorse Rd. Sch., Croydon. *Res.*, T. Heath.
    Enl., '07 ; served in India, '08-Oct., '14 ; landed in France, 5 Nov.,
    '14. *Fell*, Neuve Chapelle, 10 Mar., '15.
SHERBORN, GEOFFREY ROBERT, Pte., E. Sur. Regt.
    b., T. Heath, 26 Feb., '97 ; s., Sidney N., & Helen Sherborn,
    31 Beulah Rd., T. Heath. *Educ.*, Mr. Davies' Sch., T. Heath.
    Single. Apprentice to Messrs. Kennard Bros., drapers, Croydon.
    Memb. of 8 Croydon Boy Scouts. *Enl.* as trooper in Sur. Yeom.,
    17 Mar., '15 ; transf. to E. Sur. Regt. in France, in '16. *D.*,
    8 Jun., '17, at 46 C.C.S., France, of wounds recd. nr. Voormezeele
    same day. *Buried*, Mendingham Cem., Proven.
SHERLOCK, A. H., Pte.
    e.s., late Mr. & Mrs. H. Sherlock, Woodside. *D.*, Rouen,
    20 Sept., '18.
SHERMAN, GEORGE WILLIAM, 5403, L/Cpl., R.W.S.Regt.(attd. 72 T.M.B.)
    b., Jarvis Rd., Croydon, 2 Oct., '92 ; s., George & Annie Sherman,
    5 Bartlett St., Croydon. *Educ.*, Abp. Tenison's Sch., Croydon.
    Single. Shopman. Memb. of St. Peter's, Croydon, C.L.B.
    Enl., 16 Apr., '15. *Fell*, France, 10 Apr., '17.
SHERSBY, W. H., 2894, L/Cpl., Lond. Regt.
    Res., S. Norwood. *Fell*, '16.
SHERWOOD. FRANCIS COLIN, Lt., R.N.A.S.
    b., Streatham, 13 Jun., '99 ; s., Mr. & Mrs. Sherwood, 7 Pollard's
    Hill W., Norbury. *Educ.*, " Cheltonia " & Mod. Schs., Streat-
    ham. Single. *Enl.*, May, '17. *D.* of heart failure following
    influenza and pneumonia, Brooklands Hosp., Hull.
SHEWARD, ERNEST WILLIAM, 1 Essex Regt.
    b., Stourport, Worcestershire ; s., Mr. & Mrs. Sheward, 36
    Brindley St., Newtown, Stourport. *Educ.*, Stourport. Married.
    Grocer & provision merchant. *Res.*, 2 Clifton Terr., Parish
    Lane, Penge. *Enl.*, 1 Jun., '16. *Fell*, nr. Ypres, 31 Jan., '18.

XXVII.

1. W. G. Steer, R.N.
2. 2/Lt. Harold Taylor, M.C., R.A F.
3. L/Cpl. C. P. G. Saxby, 1 R.W.S. Regt.
4. L/Cpl. R. H. Treffry, Queen's Westm. Rif.
5. Pte. C. W. Ruffell, 58 Can. Regt.
6. Pte. B. Pfundt, N.Z. Forces

XXVIII.

1. Rflmn. L. S. STEVENS, Lond. Irish Rif.
2. Pte. T. C. S. SIMMONDS, R.W.S. Regt.
3. Pte. A. TOMKINS, E. Sur. Regt.
4. Pte. S. W. RICHMOND, Lond. Regt.
5. Pte. B. T. TREFFRY, R.W.S. Regt.
6. Pte. E. V. TYLER, M.M., R.W.S. Regt.

THE GLORIOUS DEAD

SHIPPEY, GEORGE EDWARD, Rflmn., 2/6 Lond. Regt.
b., Lr. Sydenham, 3 May, '92 ; *s.*, Mr. & Mrs. Shippey, 15 Walter's Rd., Selhurst Rd., S. Norwood. *Educ.*, Portland Rd. Sch., S. Norwood. Single. Electrotyper and stereotyper. *Enl.*, 6 Sept., '14. *D.*, 21 May, '17, at 45 C.C.S., of wounds recd. at Bullecourt, same day.

SHIPTON, CUTHBERT, L/Cpl., Princess Patricia's Can. L.I.
b., '94 ; 4*th s.*, Mr. & Mrs. George Walter Shipton, Round Hill, Nova Scotia. *Educ.*, Guelph Univ., and by his uncle, Mr. Arthur E. P. Voules, Birdhurst Lodge, Croydon ; B.Sc. *D.* of cerebrospinal meningitis, 7 Gen. Hosp., France, 16 Jan., '16.

SHIRLEY, WILLIAM LEONARD, H20753, 1st Cl. Stoker, R.N.
b., Beckenham, May, '96 ; *s.*, Mr. & Mrs. Charles Edward Shirley, 2 Drover's Rd., Croydon. *Educ.*, Abp. Tenison's Sch., Croydon. Single. *Res.*, 5 Haling Rd., Croydon. *Enl.*, 29 Sept., '13 : served on board H.M.S. " Doon," '14-17. *Killed* during air-raid at Chatham Naval Barracks, 3 Sept., '17. (Plate XXV., 3).

SHORT, T. W., Pte., Cambs. Regt.
b., '86. Married. Empl. by Messrs. Harrison & Barber, Croydon. *Res.*, 64 Mitcham Rd., Croydon. *Enl.*, Jun., '16 ; M.M., Jul., '17. *Fell*, 26 Sept., '17.

SHORTER, ARTHUR.
b., '98 ; *s.*, William & Barbara Shorter, Mansfield Rd., Croydon. *Fell*, 7 Nov., '17.

SHRUBB, GEORGE, Pte., R.W.S. Regt.
b., Croydon, 23 Apr., '84 (or '85) ; *s.*, Mr. & Mrs. Shrubb, 53 Priory Rd., Croydon. *Educ.*, Croydon (or Mitcham). Single. Stoker. Served in R.N. before the war. *Enl.*, in R.W.S. Regt., '14. *Fell*, 16 Feb., '15.

SILCOCK, JOHN COOKE, L/Cpl., 11 R.W. Kent Regt.
b., Church Rd., Croydon, 27 Jul., '93 ; *y.s.*, John Cooke & Mary Ann Silcock, 25 Harrison's Rise, Croydon. *Educ.*, Par. Ch. Sch., Croydon. Married. Milk carrier. *Res.*, 25 Harrison's Rise, Croydon. *Enl.*, 6 Feb., '15. *Fell*, nr. Zillebeke, 20 Sept., '17.

SILCOTT, CHRISTIAN PHILIP, Can. D.A.C.
b., '94 ; *y.s.*, Mr. & Mrs. Silcott, 46 Kidderminster Rd., Croydon. *D.*, 22 Oct., '18, at Eastbourne, of wounds recd. in France, 27 Sept., '18.

SILVER, HARRY, Pte., 4 R.W.S. Regt.
b., '94 ; *s.*, Mr. & Mrs. Silver, 18 Bridport Rd., T. Heath. Single. Empl. by Croydon Corp., Roads Dept. *D.* of gastritis, Lucknow, India, 20 May, '15.

SIMKINS, FREDERICK JOHN, Trooper, 1 M.G. Gds.
b., '98 ; *s.*, James & Hannah Bella Allenby-Simkins, 144 Frant Rd., T. Heath. *Educ.*, T. Heath Sch. (Mr. J. D. Davies). *Enl.*, in Life Gds., May '16 ; served in France, 6 Dec., '17 to May, '18. *Killed* during an enemy air-raid, France, 19 May, '18.

SIMMONDS, ALFRED H., Driver, 57 Bty., R.F.A.
b., Brighton, 12 Dec., '92 ; *s.*, William & Edith Simmonds, 69 The Drive, T. Heath. *Educ.*, Ecclesbourne Rd. Sch., Croydon. Single. Learning motor trimming. *Enl.*, 19 Oct., '10. *Fell*, Hooge Chateau, nr. Ypres, 1 Nov., '14.

SIMMONDS, ERNEST EDWARD, Sgt., R.E.
b., Benson Rd., Croydon, 14 Nov., '89 ; *s.*, Mr. & Mrs. Simmonds, " Wandle House," Waddon New Rd., Croydon. *Educ.*, Brit. Sch., Croydon. Single. Builder. *Enl.*, Nov., '14 ; D.C.M., Sept., '16. *Fell*, 31 May, '18. *Buried*, La Kreule Cem., nr. Hazebrouck.

SIMMONDS, GUY BLOXAM, 2/Lt., M.G.C.
b., 22 Apr., '87 ; *2nd s.*, Mr. & Mrs. William Henry Simmonds, formerly " Lansdowne," Spencer Rd., Croydon, now of Hobart, Tasmania. *Educ.*, Whitgift G. Sch., '98-02. Empl. on Stock Exchange. *Enl.* as pte. in Middlesex Regt., '14 ; served in France as sgt. ; commis., '16. *Accidentally killed* on a railway, France, 29 Dec., '16.

SIMMONDS, THOMAS CHARLES STURTON, Pte., 11 R.W.S. Regt.
b., Clay Hill, Bushey, Watford, 19 Dec., '91 ; *s.*, Mr. & Mrs. Simmonds, 10 Benskin Rd., Watford. *Educ.*, Victoria Sch., Watford. Married. Conductor, Croydon Corp. Tramways. *Res.*, 8 Colvin Rd., T. Heath. *Enl.*, 27 Oct., '15. *Fell*, Spoilbank, Zillebeke, 11 Dec., '16. (Plate XXVIII., 2).

SIMMONS, D., 273060, Pte., 18 D.L.I.
b., '85 ; *s.*, Mr. & Mrs. A. Simmons, 198 Northwood Rd., T. Heath. *Fell*, France, 2 Jul., '18.

SIMMONS, ERIC WARR, 2/Lt., 6 York & Lancs. Regt.
b., Croydon, 6 Apr., '93 ; *s.*, Thomas Frederick & Agnes Simmons, 5 Heathfield Rd., Croydon. *Educ.*, Whitgift G. Sch., Croydon, and Univ. Coll., Lond., where he studied geology ; B.Sc., 1st cl. hon., '14 ; elected Fellow, Geological Soc., '15 ; demonstrator in geology, Univ. Coll. Memb. of Lond. Univ. O.T.C. *Missing*, Suvla Bay, 12 Aug., '15.

SIMPKINS, C., 2332, Pte., R.W. Kent Regt.
Res., S. Norwood. *Fell*, '16.

SIMPSON, ARTHUR JOHN, Pte., M.G.C.
b., Croydon, 5 Aug., '98 ; *s.*, J. W. & E. J. Simpson, 9 Tudor Rd., S. Norwood. *Educ.*, Par. Ch. Sch., Croydon. Single. Storekeeper (electrical branch), L.B. & S.C.R. *Res.*, 8 Cranmer Rd., Croydon. *Enl.*, 13 Aug., '17. *D.*, 25 Mar., '18, at 36 C.C.S., France, of wounds recd. at Ypres, 24 Mar., '18.

SIMPSON, FRANK, Cpl., 1 Middlesex Regt.
b., S. Norwood, 18 Sept., '89 ; *s.*, William & Sarah Ann Simpson, 90 Crowther Rd., S. Norwood. *Educ.*, Birchanger Rd. Sch., S. Norwood. Married. Clerk. *Res.*, 90 Crowther Rd., S. Norwood. *Enl.*, 17 May, '16. *Fell*, Passchendaele, 3 Apr.,'18.

SIMPSON, GEORGE, Rflmn., R.B.
b., 16 Naseby Rd., U. Norwood, 16 Aug., '88 ; *s.*, Mr. & Mrs. Simpson, 9 Eagle Hill, U. Norwood. *Educ.*, Rockmount Rd. Sch., U. Norwood. Married. Carman. *Res.*, 25 Eagle Hill, U. Norwood. *Enl.*, 3 Sept., '14. *Fell*, nr. Poperinghe, 18 Oct., '17.

SIMPSON, LEONARD, Pte., Glo'ster. Regt.
b., 35 Dover Rd., U. Norwood, 28 May, '99 ; *s.*, Mr. & Mrs. E. Simpson, 9 Eagle Hill, U. Norwood. *Educ.*, Rockmount Rd. Sch., U. Norwood. Single. Newsagent's asst. *Enl.*, 28 May, '17. *Fell*, France, 9 Jul., '18. (Plate XXV., 2).

SIMPSON, W. A., Sub-Lt., R.N.V.R.
b., '90. Empl. by Lacy Hulbert & Co., Croydon. *Res.*, " Torwood," Alton Rd., Croydon. *Joined*,'15 ; *w.*, France,'17. *Fell*, 23 Mar., '18.

SIMPSON, WILLIAM, L/Cpl., 3 R.W.S. Regt.
Educ., Gordon Boys' Home, Croydon. *Fell*, 1 Jul., '16.

SIMS, ERNEST VICTOR, Gnr., R.F.A.
b., Whitehorse Rd., Croydon, 23 Jun., '93 ; *s.*, Mr. & Mrs. Thomas Sims, 144 Canterbury Rd., Croydon. *Educ.*, Boston Rd. Sch., Croydon. Single. Painter. *Enl.*, 4 Aug., '14. *Fell*, France, 11 Dec., '16.

THE GLORIOUS DEAD

SINCLAIR, LESLIE J. HARTNELL-, 2/Lt., 3 E. Sur. Regt.
    b., '95 ; *s.*, Mr. & Mrs. Charles Hartnell-Sinclair, " Memphis," Addis. *Fell*, France, 26 Sept., '15.
SINGLETON, E. J., 552796, Pte., Lond. Regt.
    Res., T. Heath. *Fell*, '17.
SKEDDON, LLOYD, Lt., Can. E.F. (attd. R.A.F.)
    s., Mr, & Mrs. Skeddon, Canada, late Croydon. *Fell*, France, '18.
SKEDDON, MATHEW, Can. Engineers.
    b., '69 ; *e.s.*, Mr. & Mrs. Skeddon, Canada, late Croydon. *Fell*,'18.
SKELTON, J., 6995, Pte., R.W.S. Regt.
    Res., T. Heath. *Fell*, '17.
SKILTON, WILLIAM GEORGE, Signaller, L.R.B. (5 Lond. Regt.)
    b., 111 Holmesdale Rd., S. Norwood, 2 Nov., '97 ; *s.*, William Robert & Lucy Skilton, 14 Bungalow Rd., S. Norwood. *Educ.*, Whitehorse Rd. Sch., T. Heath. Single. Clerk. *Enl.*, 12 May, '16. *D.*, 16 Aug., '17, at 32 C.C.S., France, of wounds recd. at Polygon Wood, Ypres, same day.
SKINNER, E. H. G., 12879, Rflmn., K.R.R.C.
    Res., W. Croydon. *Fell*, '17.
SKINNER, EDWARD WALTER, Rflmn., L.R.B. (5 Lond. Regt.)
    b., West Norwood, 5 Oct., '93 ; *s.*, Edward & Emily Jane Skinner, 310 Lr. Addis. Rd., Croydon. *Educ.*, Tiffins' G. Sch., Kingston-on-Thames. Single. Clerk. *Enl.*, in 8 Lond. Irish Rif., 22 Dec., '15 ; transf. to 1/5 Lond. Regt. (L.R.B.), 5 May, '16 ; sent to France, 14 Jul., '16. *Missing*, Les Bœufs, France, 8 Oct., '16.
SKINNER, FRANCIS GEORGE, Pte., E. Sur. Regt.
    b., '98 ; *s.*, Mr. & Mrs. Skinner, 4 Lion Rd., Croydon. *Educ.*, Princess Rd. Sch., Croydon. Single. Empl. by Messrs. Whitbread, & Messrs. Blackwell, Lansdowne Rd., Croydon. *D.* of wounds, 15 May, '18.
SKITTERAL, B. T., Sgt., R.W.S. Regt.
    Married ; 1 son. *Res.*, S. Norwood. *Enl.* in W. Yorks. Regt., '95, serving in S.A. War. Re-enlisted 18 Oct., '14 ; served in France, Apr., '16-Nov., '17, & in Italy, Nov., '17-Apr., '18, when he returned to France ; D.C.M., Jun., '17, & M.M. *Fell*, France, 10 Aug., '18.
SKOTTOWE, C. M., 2/Lt., S. Lancs. Regt.
    b., '98 ; *s.*, Mr. & Mrs. Skottowe, " Strathfield," Brighton Rd., Purley. *Educ.*, Forest Sch., & Sandhurst. *Gazetted*, Jan., '16 ; went to France, Sept., '16. *Missing*, France, 21 Oct., '16.
SKUSE, EDWARD JAMES, L/Cpl., 3/4 R.W.S. Regt.
    b., 35 Warren Rd., Addis, 4 Sept., '95 ; *s.*, Mr. & Mrs. E. J. Skuse, 35 Warren Rd., Addis. *Educ.*, Oval Rd. Sch., Croydon. Single. Empl. by Westminster Gas Co. Teacher at St. Matthew's Sunday Sch., Croydon. *Enl.*, 4 Jun., '15. *Fell*, Polygon Wood, Ypres. 4 Oct., '17. (Plate XXIX., 6).
SKUSE, WILLIAM HENRY, Rflmn., 1/17 Lond. Regt.
    b., 35 Warren Rd., Addis., '99 ; 2nd *s.*, Mr. & Mrs. Skuse, 35 Warren Rd., Addis. *Educ.*, Oval Rd. Sch., Croydon. Single. Empl. as fitter's asst., Westminster Gas Co. *Enl.*, 9 Jun., '17. *Fell*, Froyennes, Belgium, 8 Nov., '18. *Buried*, White Chateau, Froyennes. (Plate XXX., 6).
SLACK, JOHN, Pte., R.W.S. Regt.
    b., Croydon. *Educ.*, Bynes Rd. Sch., Croydon. Married ; 1 child. *Res.*, 127 Bynes Rd., Croydon. Served in S.A. War. *Enl.*, 5 Aug., '14. *Fell*, Mons. 30 Oct., '14.

SLADE, WILLIAM, Pte., R.E.
b., S. Norwood, 27 Mar., '87 ; s., Mr. & Mrs. Slade, 27 Apsley Rd., S. Norwood. *Educ.*, Birchanger Rd. Sch., S. Norwood. Married ; 1 daughter. Builder & decorator. *Res.*, 27 Apsley Rd., S. Norwood. *Enl.*, 21 Jun., '16 ; w., four times (once at Battle Wood, nr. Ypres, 30 Jul., '17) ; gassed. *D.*, Dover, of pneumonia contracted at Calais, 7 Feb., '19.

SLEEMAN, CHARLES, Cpl., Lancs. Fus.
b., 32 Handcroft Rd., Croydon, 12 Jan., '92 ; s., Mr. & Mrs. Sleeman, 6 Clarendon Rd., W. Croydon. *Educ.*, Brit. Sch., Croydon. Single. Shop asst. *Enl.*, 20 Oct., '14. *Fell*, 9 Jul., '16.

SLYFIELD, WILLIAM JOHN, Gnr., R.F.A.
b., 73 Beulah Hill, U. Norwood, 5 Jan., '95 ; s., Wm. George & Kate Slyfield, 66a Queen's Rd., U. Norwood. *Educ.*, Wesleyan Sch., Eden Rd., W. Norwood. Single. Gardener. *Enl.*, 12 Apr., '15. *D.*, 5 Nov., '17, at 10 Gen. Hosp., Rouen, of wounds recd. at Passchendaele, 29 Oct., '17. (Plate XXV., 5).

SMEE, ARTHUR JOSEPH, Lt., Wilts. Regt. (attd. R.A.F.)
b., S. Norwood, 4 Feb., '95 ; s., Joseph & Anne M. Smee, 7 Whitworth Rd., S. Norwood. *Educ.*, M. Whitgift Sch., Croydon, Strand Sch., & King's Coll., Lond. Single. Marine insurance clerk. *Enl.* as pte. in U.P.S. Bde., Sept., '14 ; served, France, Jun.-Sept., '16, where he was w. ; Macedonia, Jan.-Dec., '17, & Egypt, Jan.-Sept., '18. *Killed* in aeroplane accident at Shoreham, Sussex, 28 Oct., '18.

SMETHURST, CYRIL VALENTINE, L/Cpl., H.A.C.
b., 14 Feb., '80 ; s., Mr. & Mrs. George Smethurst, " Homestead," Lewis Rd., Streatham. *Educ.*, Whitgift G. Sch., '90–93. *Fell*, '17.

SMETHURST, FREDERICK HOWARD, 1st Cl. W.O., R.A.S.C.
b., " Homestead," Streatham Common, 23 May, '89 ; s., George & Sophia Matilda Smethurst, " Highfield," Tring, Herts. *Educ.*, M. Whitgift Sch. Married. Buyer of stores and engineer to G.W. Rly. of Brazil, & Gen. Manager, Rly. Accessories Co., Lond. *Res.*, 28 Egerton Gardens, Hendon, N.W. *Enl.*, Oct., '16. *D.* as the result of an accident whilst in the execution of his duty, 17 Aug., '-.

SMITH, –, L/Cpl., 10 R.Fus. (City of Lond.)
Fell, '16.

SMITH, A., Pte.
b., '96. Empl. by Croydon Corp. Tramways. *Enl.*, Aug., '14. *D.* of wounds, 19 Dec., '14.

SMITH, A.
Educ., Ecclesbourne Rd. Sch., Croydon. *D.* of wounds recd. at Mons, Oct., '14.

SMITH, ALFRED G., Sgt., R.W.S. Regt.
s., Mr. & Mrs. Smith, 4 Dickenson's Pl., Woodside. *Educ.*, Woodside Sch., Croydon. Single. Labourer. *Enl.*, 3 Mar., '13 ; went to France, Aug., '14 ; w., Oct., '14 ; ret. to France, Oct., '15. *D.*, 3 May, '16, of gas poisoning, contracted on 30 Apr., '16.

SMITH, A. H., 201949, Gnr., R.F.A.
Res., Croydon. *Fell*, '17.

SMITH, A. S., 15128, Gnr., R.F.A.
Res., S. Norwood. *Fell*, '17.

THE GLORIOUS DEAD

SMITH, ALBERT EDWARD GEORGE, 301437, L/Sgt., 13 Tank Corps.
    b., 28 Albion St., Croydon, 5 Nov., '92 ; *s.*, George William & Emily Phœbe Smith, 126 Handcroft Rd., Croydon. *Educ.* Mitcham Rd. Sch., Croydon. Married. Grocer's asst. *Res.*, 28 Albion St., Croydon. *Enl.*, 7 Nov., '14. *Fell*, Kemmel Hill (?), 25 Apr., '18.

SMITH, ALEC KENNETH, Pte., 13 Lond. Regt.
    b., '98 ; *y.s.*, Mr. & Mrs. F. Smith, 26 Crowther Rd., S. Norwood. *Fell*, Neuve Chapelle, 12 Mar., '15.

SMITH, ARTHUR, Pioneer, R.E.
    b., '95 ; *2nd s.*, Mr. & Mrs. Charles Smith, 54 Northbrook Rd., Croydon. *Educ.*, Sydenham Rd. Sch., Croydon. Single. Carman, empl. by Mr. Clifford, Mayo Rd., Croydon. *Enl.* as driver in R.F.A., 1 Sept., '14 ; went to France, 5 Jul., '15. *Accidentally killed*, 5 Oct., '17.

SMITH, ARTHUR DONALD THORNTON, Capt., K.R.R.C.
    b., '92 ; *y.s.*, Rev. & Mrs. E. Thornton Smith, of Bromley. *Educ.*, Whitgift G. Sch., Croydon, & Univ. Coll. Sch., Hampstead. *Joined* Inns of Court O.T.C., Nov., '15 ; commis., Aug., '16 ; went to France, 2 Oct., '16 ; D.S.O., May, '17. *Fell* nr. Langemarck, 16 Aug., '17.

SMITH, CHARLES ALFRED, Gnr., 70 Bde., R.F.A.
    b., Croydon, 30 Jun., '80 ; *e.s.*, late Mr., & Mrs. S. A. Smith, 50 Selhurst New Rd., S. Norwood. *Educ.*, St. James' Sch., Croydon. Single. Decorator. *Enl.*, Aug., '14. *Fell*, Albert, 27 Jan., '17.

SMITH, DOUGLAS BRADLEY, Pte., B Coy., 8 Platoon, 8 R. Fus.
    b., 15 Nov., '80 ; *s.*, Mr. & Mrs. Smith, 3 Woodstock Rd., Croydon. *Educ.*, Univ. Coll., Lond. Insurance secretary. *Res.*, Paris. *Enl.*, '15. *Missing*, between Le Sars & Guedecourt, 7 Oct., '16.

SMITH, E., 9100, Rflmn., K.R.R.C.
    Res., Croydon. *Fell*, '17.

SMITH, ERNEST HAMMOND, Cpl., S.W.B.
    b., Tadworth, 5 Nov., '89 ; *s.*, late E. W., & F. E. Smith, Tadworth, Surrey. *Educ.*, Reigate. Married. Clerk. *Res.*, 102 Oval Rd., Croydon. *Enl.*, 22 Jan., '16. *Fell*, Gouzeaucourt, France, 12 Sept., '18.

SMITH, FRANCIS LEONARD, Cpl., 6 R.W.S. Regt.
    b., Queen's St., Croydon, '94 ; *s.*, Mr. & Mrs. Ernest Smith, 5 Wandle Rd., Croydon. *Educ.*, St. Andrew's Sch., Croydon. Single. *Enl.*, 3 Sept., '14 ; *w.*, 3 times. *D.*, 25 Dec., '15, at Bethune, of wounds recd. at Givenchy, prev. day.

SMITH, FRANK RODWELL, Pte., 23 Lond. Regt.
    b., S. Hackney, Dec., '94 ; *s.*, Mr. & Mrs. Smith, 43 Park Lane, Wallington. *Educ.*, Upper Tooting High Sch. Single. Insurance clerk. *Res.*, 46 Alexandra Rd., Addis. *Enl.*, Sept.,'14. *Fell*, Givenchy, France, 29 May, '15. (Plate XXVI., 6).

SMITH, FRANK W. HOWARD, Lt., Lond. Regt.
    b., '83. Married. Master at Dering Pl. Counc. Sch., Croydon, from '06. *Res.*, 55 Temple Rd., Croydon. *Joined*, May, '15. *D.*, 4 Dec., '17, at Rouen, of gas poisoning, contracted at Bourlon Wood.

SMITH, FREDERICK CHARLES, Pte., E. Sur. Regt.
    b., Croydon, 4 Jan., '73 ; *s.*, Mr. & Mrs. Smith, 103 St. James' Rd., Croydon. *Educ.*, Brit. Sch., Croydon. Married. Sign writer. *Enl.*, 29 Sept., '14. *D.* at 5 C.C.S., France, 4 Feb., '16.

SMITH, FREDERICK GRANVILLE WALKER, 2/Lt., Lond. Regt.
    b., '85. *Educ.*, Whitgift G. Sch. Married. *D.*, in France, 21 Dec., '17, of wounds recd. 4 weeks prev. at Cambrai.

THE CROYDON ROLL OF HONOUR

SMITH, FREDERICK STANLEY, Cpl., R.A.S.C.
　　b., T. Heath, 18 Nov., '91 ; 2nd s., Charles William & Mary Smith, 49 Eridge Rd., T. Heath. *Educ.*, Sydenham Rd. Sch., Croydon. Married. Prudential Insurance agent. *Res.*, 16 York Rd., Brentford. *Enl.*, Apr., '15 ; served in France, May-Nov., '15 ; with M.E.F., Nov., '15-May, '16. *D.* of dysentery at the Can. Mil Hosp., Salonica, 16 May, '16.

SMITH, F. W., 204534, Pte., Lond. Regt.
　　Res., S. Norwood. *Fell,* '17.

SMITH, G., 2168, L/Cpl., Glo'ster. Regt.
　　Res., W. Croydon. *Fell,* '16.

SMITH, GEOFFREY HAROLD, 2/Lt., Northants. Regt.
　　b., May, '96. *Educ.*, Whitgift G. Sch. Associated with St. George's Mission Ch. *Enl.* in Artists Rif. O.T.C., '14. *Fell,* Jul., '17.

SMITH, GODFREY BRADLEY, Lt., R.A.M.C.
　　b., 29 Sept., '86 ; s., Mr. & Mrs. Smith, 3 Woodstock Rd., Croydon. *Educ.*, Univ. Coll. Sch., Bedford. Single. Doctor (M.R.C.S., L.R.C.P.). *Res.*, Croydon. *Joined,* '15. Lost with the " Arcadian," torpedoed in the Aegean Sea, 15 Apr., '17.

SMITH, H., Essex Regt.
　　Married. Fireman. Served 8 yrs. with Essex Regt., mostly in India. *D.* of wounds, '15.

SMITH, HAMLYN JAGO, 556987, Signaller, Q.W. Rif. (16 Lond. Regt.)
　　b., 26 Jul., '99 ; s., Mr. & Mrs. A. D. Smith, 14 Shrewsbury Rd., Redhill. *Educ.*, Bethany House, Goudhurst, Institute S. Louis, Brussels, & Whitgift G. Sch. Single. Clerk. *Res.*, Redhill, formerly at Croydon. *Enl.*, Aug., '17. *Fell* nr. Bapaume, 9 Aug., '18. (Plate XXIV., 2).

SMITH, HAROLD WILLIAM, L/Cpl., 1 H.A.C.
　　s., Mr. W. Smith, 34 Farnley Rd., S. Norwood. *Enl.*, Aug., '15. *Fell,* nr. Beaucourt Farm, Grandecourt, 8 Feb., '17. Buried, Queen's Cem., Bucquoy.

SMITH, JAMES, Gnr., R.F.A.
　　e.s., Mr. & Mrs. Smith, 18 Pawson's Rd., Croydon. *D.* in India, after 6 yrs. service abroad, 21 Apr., '16.

SMITH, JAMES, 206343, Rflmn., R.B.
　　b., '72. Married ; 5 children. *Res.*, 119 Boston Rd., Croydon. Memb. of Nat. Res., R.W.S. Regt. *D.* of cholera at Sialkot, India, 28 Aug., '17.

SMITH, JAMES FREDERICK, Pte., 2 Essex Regt.
　　b., Croydon, 11 May, '- ; 2nd s., Mr. & Mrs. George Smith, 23 Beulah Grove, Croydon. *Educ.*, Princess Rd. Sch., Croydon. Married ; 5 children. Labourer, empl. by Croydon Corp. *Res.*, 23 Beulah Grove, Croydon. *Enl.*, 15 Jun., '16. *D.*, 11 May, '17, at a C.C.S. in France, of wounds recd. same day.

SMITH, P., L/Cpl., Australian I.F.
　　Fell, '16.

SMITH, RICHARD H., 1054, Pte., 6 R.W.S. Regt.
　　b., '94. *Educ.*, Par. Ch. Sch., Croydon. *Enl.*, 9 Sept., '14. *Fell,* 4 Oct., '16.

SMITH, ROBERT VERNON, L/Cpl., 10 R. Fus.
　　b., about '92 ; s., Mr. & Mrs. M. P. Smith, 100 Oakfield Rd., Croydon. *Educ.*, Royal Brit. Sch., Slough. Empl. by Messrs. Newman, Smith & Newman, Newgate St., Lond., '06-09 ; and by Messrs. Rata, Turner & Atkinson, Old Bailey, Lond., '09-14. *Enl.*, Aug., '14 ; trained at Colchester, Andover & Windmill Hill Camp, Salisbury Plain ; left for France, 31 Jul., '15 ; L/cpl., Mar., '16. *Fell,* Pozieres, 15 Jul., '16.

THE GLORIOUS DEAD

SMITH, RUPERT CASTLE-, Pte., Aust.I.F.
  b., '91 ; 2nd *s.*, Mr. & Mrs. Pering Castle-Smith, 5 Park Hill Rise, Croydon. *Fell*, France, 11 Apr., '17.

SMITH, S. F., Lt., 1 Cheshire Regt.
  Educ., High Sch., Croydon. *Fell*, '16.

SMITH, S. G., Cpl., R.W.S. Regt.
  Res., 32 Pridham Rd. E., T. Heath. *Mobilised*, Aug., '14 ; served in India, Oct., '14-16 May, '16, when he ret., time expired ; *re-enlisted*, May, '16 ; went to France, 13 Jan., '17. *Fell*, 23 Apr., '17.

SMITH, SIDNEY GEORGE, 2/Lt., 200 M.G.C.
  b., S. Hackney ; *s.*, Mr. & Mrs. Smith, 43 Park Lane, Wallington. *Educ.*, Upper Tooting High Sch. Single. Insurance clerk. *Res.*, 46 Alexandra Rd., Addis. *Enl.* as pte., Aug., '14. *Fell*, France, 31 Mar., '18. (Plate XXVI., 4).

SMITH, W. A., L/Cpl., 2 R.W.S. Regt.
  b., '92 ; *s.*, Mr. & Mrs. Smith, 50 Selhurst New Rd., S. Norwood. *Educ.*, St. James' Sch., Croydon. Electrician. *Fell*, Loos, 25 Sept., '15.

SMITH, W. H., Driver, R.F.A.
  b., '96 ; *s.*, Mr. & Mrs. Smith, 18 Pawson's Rd., Croydon. *Enl.*, '14. *D.* of pneumonia, France, 25 Feb., '19.

SMITH, WILLIAM ALEXANDER, Pte., 1/4 R.W.S. Regt.
  b., Church St., Croydon, 18 Nov., '76 ; *s.*, James & Ellen Smith, 12 Leighton St. E., Croydon. *Educ.*, Mitcham Rd. Sch., Croydon. Single. Painter. Served in S.A. War. *Mobilised* with Territorials, 2 Aug., '14. *D.*, 17 Dec., '15, at Calaba Station Hosp., Bombay, of wounds recd. at Ctesiphon, 22-24 Nov., '15.

SMORTHWAITE, REGINALD, 6606, Rflmn., Q.W. Rif. (1/16 Lond. Regt.)
  Educ., Ecclesbourne Rd. Sch., Croydon., and M. Whitgift Sch. *Missing*, 18 Sept., '16.

SNELGROVE, HENRY JOHN, Rflmn., Lond. Regt.
  b., '97 ; *s.*, John & Ellen Snelgrove, 10 Thirsk Rd., S. Norwood. *Enl.* in R.W.S. Regt., Oct., '14 ; went to France with Lond. Regt., Aug., '16 ; *w.*, Jul., '17. *Fell*, 30 Nov., '17.

SNELGROVE, H. D. B., 2/Lt., R.F.C.
  Educ., Whitgift G. Sch. Chemist. *Res.*, America. *Enl.*, '16. *Missing*, presumed killed in an air fight, '17.

SOMERSCALES, E. C., Pte., Wilts. Regt.
  b., '71 ; *s.*, Mr. & Mrs. Somerscales, 58 Pemdevon Rd., Croydon. *D.* of fever in India, 25 Sept., '16.

SONGHURST, G., Pte., E. Sur. Regt.
  Married ; 4 children. *Res.*, 21 Salisbury Rd., Woodside. Went to France, Sept., '16 ; *w.*, Oct., '16 ; ret. to France, Sept., '17 ; saw service in Italy. *D.* of wounds, 21 Oct., '18.

SOPER, W. H., 201700, Pte., R.W.S. Regt.
  Res., S. Norwood. *Fell*, '17

SORRELL, W. P., 201683, Pte., 8 R.W.S. Regt.
  s., Mr. & Mrs. Sorrell, 7 Union Rd., Croydon. *Taken pris.*, 21 Mar., '18. Last heard of, 8 Oct., '18.

SOUTH, WILLIAM HARRY.
  e.s., Mr. & Mrs. South, 4 Mead Pl., Croydon. *D.* in France, 16 Jul., '18.

SPARK, FRANK EVANS, Rflmn., L.R.B. (5 Lond. Regt.)
  b., 4 Dec., '84 ; s., Mr. & Mrs. Francis John Spark. *Educ.*, Whitgift G. Sch., '95-02, and Barnet G. Sch. *Fell*, nr. Ypres, May, '15.
SPARKES, E., 12133, Pte., R.W. Kent Regt.
  Res., Croydon. *D.* of wounds, '17.
SPARKS, ERNEST, Pte., E. Kent Regt.
  y.s., Mr. & Mrs. George Sparks, late of S. Croydon. Married. *Res.*, 28 Warren Rd., Addis. *Enl.*, 16 Aug., '16. *D.*, 16 Jun.,'17, of wounds recd. prev. day.
SPARKS, F. E., Rflmn., L.R.B. (5 Lond. Regt.)
  Educ., Whitgift G. Sch., '95-98. *Fell*, Flanders, '15.
SPEARING, W., 12309, Pte., R. Fus.
  Res., Addis. *Fell*, '17.
SPENCER, FRANK SIDNEY, Pte., R.W.S. Regt.
  b., 24 Grange Pk., T. Heath, 27 Jan., '– ; s., Mr. & Mrs. Spencer, 55 Sidney Rd., S. Norwood. *Educ.*, Birchanger Rd. Sch., S. Norwood. Single. House decorator. *Enl.*, 26 Aug., '14. *D.*, 2 Sept., '15, at 21 Gen. Hosp., Alexandria, of wounds recd. at Dardanelles, 29 Aug., '15.
SPENCER, GEORGE DOUGLAS, Pte., Lancs. Fus.
  b., Islington, 7 Oct., '85 ; s., Mr. & Mrs. Spencer, Laud St., Croydon. Married. Billiard-cue maker. *Res.*, 134 Pemdevon Rd., Croydon. *Enl.*, 5 Jun., '16. *Fell*, Beaumont-Hamel, France, 23 Nov., '16.
SPENCER, RICHARD MARTIN, 2/Lt., 1 R. Warwick. Regt.
  b., Putney, '94 ; y s., late Ernest Nelson Spencer, formerly of Croydon and Hounslow, and Mrs. Fitzjames, 17 St. Martin's Rd., Knowle. *Educ.*, Elmhurst Sch., Croydon, & St. Paul's. *Joined*, '14. *Fell*, France, 22 Jan., '16.
SPENCER, SIDNEY CHARLES, 7489, Cpl., 11 R. Fus.
  b., T. Heath ; s., Mr. & Mrs. K. Spencer, 8 Boston Rd., Croydon. *Enl.*, 7 Sept., '14. *Fell*, 10 Aug., '17.
SPICE, T., 351606, Pte., Lond. Regt.
  Res., W. Croydon. *Fell*, '17.
SPICER, ROBERT WILLIAM, Capt., R.W.S. Regt.
  b., 25 Nov., '15 ; e.s., Mr. & Mrs. R. W. Spicer, "Chartleigh," S. Croydon. *Educ.*, Oxford House Sch., Croydon, St. Edmund's, Canterbury, & Whitgift G. Sch., '10-11, where he was memb. of O.T.C. *Enl.* in Artists Rif., proceeding to France with them, Oct., '14 ; gazetted to R.W.S., and promoted capt., Jul., '15. *Fell*, 26 Mar., '17.
SPICER, STANLEY THOMAS, Lt., S. Staff. Regt.
  b., Catford, 4 Apr., '90 ; s., Mr. & Mrs. Spicer, Sharnford, nr. Hinckley, Leicestershire. *Educ.*, M. Whitgift Sch. Single. Clerk in Colombo (Ceylon) offices of Cook's Tourist Agency. *Res.*, 29 Farnley Rd., S. Norwood. *Enl.* as rflmn. in R.B., Dec., '14 ; commis. in S. Staff. Regt., '15 ; went to France, Jan., '16. *D.*, 9 Aug., '16, of wounds recd. at Trones Wood, France, the prev. day.
SPURGIN, H. J., 3311, Pte., R. Suss. Regt.
  Fell, '16.
STABLES, L. T. D., Lt., Beds. Regt. (attd. Northants. Regt.)
  b., '91 ; 2nd s., Mr. W. W. G. Stables, M.R.C.S., 5 Auckland Rd., U. Norwood. *Educ.*, St. Olave's, Lond. Empl. in office of Publ. Trustee. *Enl.* in 25 Lond. Regt. (Cyclists) ; commis. (posted to 6 Beds. Regt.), 25 Oct., '16 ; w., Arras, 23 Apr., '17 ; ret. to France, 25 Sept., '18. *Fell*, 23 Oct., '18.

THE GLORIOUS DEAD

STACEY, ARTHUR HORRIS, Pte., R.W.S. Regt.
Res., 89 Queen's Rd., Croydon. *Enl.*, '15. *Fell*, 26 Apr., '15.
STACEY, GERALD ARTHUR, Maj., Lond. Regt.
b., '82 ; *s.*, Mr. & Mrs. Crosley, U. Norwood. D.S.O. *Fell*, 11 Oct., '16.
STACEY, JOHN HAROLD, Lt., R.F.C.
Educ., M. Whitgift Sch. *Fell*, Oct., '18.
STACEY, JOHN JAMES, 6252, Pte., Lond. Scottish (14 Lond. Regt.)
b., Caterham, 22 Nov., '87 ; *s.*, Mr. & Mrs. Stacey, 61 Beaconsfield Rd., Croydon. *Educ.*, Sydenham Rd. Sch., Croydon. Single. Writer and Grainer. *Enl.*, 9 Dec., '15. *D.*, 11 Jul., '16, at Etretat, France, of wounds recd. at Gommecourt Wood, 1 Jul., '16.
STAELMAN, PHARAILDA.
b., Belgium, '54. Widow. *Res.*, 163 St. James' Rd., Croydon. *D.* from shock during Zeppelin raid, Oct., '15.
STANLEY, FREDERICK EDWARD, Pte., 9 E. Sur. Regt.
b., Slough, Bucks., 10 Jul., '95 ; *s.*, Mr. & Mrs. Stanley, "Rylands," Gibson's Hill, U. Norwood. *Educ.*, Rockmount Rd. Sch., U. Norwood. Single. Grocer's asst. *Res.*, 66a Queen's Rd., U. Norwood. *Enl.*, 9 Sept., '14. *Fell*, Neuve Eglise, France, 14 Jul., '16. (Plate XXX., 4).
STANLEY, W., 6606, Pte., R.W.S. Regt.
Res., Croydon. *D.* of wounds.
STANNARD, C. H. STANLEY, Cpl., R. Fus.
b., '97 ; *s.*, Mr. & Mrs. Stannard, 61 Zion Rd., T. Heath. *Educ.*, Whitehorse Rd. Sch., T. Heath, & Boro. Sec. Sch., Croydon. Empl. by Westminster Gas Co. *Enl.*, May, '15 ; served in France, Jul., '15-Oct., '17. *Fell*, 4 Oct., '17.
STEADMAN, JAMES WILLIAM GILBERT, Musician, R.N.
b., Walmer, Kent, 8 Jul., '91 ; *s.*, Mr. & Mrs. Steadman, 89 Newlands Rd., Norbury. *Educ.*, Walmer, Kent. Single. *Joined*, '06 (?) *Lost* with H.M.S. " Queen Mary," 31 May, '16.
STEEL, DOUGLAS G., Capt., 3 Suff. Regt.
b., '95 ; *s.*, Mr. & Mrs. Steel, Lond. Rd., T. Heath. *Educ.*, Boro. Sec. Sch., Croydon. Single. Clerk. M.C. *Enl.* in Middlesex Regt., Sept., '14. *Fell*, '16.
STEELE, FRANK GEORGE, Pte., D.C.L.I.
b., Croydon, 27 Mar., '95 ; *s.*, Mr. & Mrs. Alfred Steele, 60 Arundel Rd., Croydon. *Educ.*, Boro. Sec. Sch., Croydon. Single. Clerk. *Enl.*, Aug., '14. *D.*, 6 Apr., '16, at 19 C.C.S., of wounds recd. prev. day.
STEELE, ROLLO PETER, Pte., E. Sur. Regt.
b., Fillebrooke Rd., Leytonstone, 22 Apr., '95 ; *s.*, Philip Richard & Ethel Gertrude Steele, 58 Croham Rd., Croydon. *Educ.*, St. Dunstan's Coll., Catford. Single. Clerk in Royal Exchange Assurance Corporation. *Res.*, Harcourt Mans., Croydon Rd., Anerley. *Enl.*, 21 Jan., '16. *Fell*, Bazentin-le-petit, France, 14 Jul., '16.
STEER, WILLIAM GEORGE, Sick Berth Steward, R.N.
b., W. Croydon, 2 Jun., '88 ; *s.*, Mr. & Mrs. J. H. Steer, 15 Stanley Grove, Croydon. *Educ.*, St. Saviour's Sch., Croydon. Single. *Joined*, 25 Jul., '06 ; with H.M.S. " Medina " on the Indian Coronation Tour, '11-12 ; served for 4½ yrs. at Bighi Hosp., Malta ; on H.M.S. " Latona," Sept., '14-Mar., '15. *Killed* by explosion on H.M.S. " Princess Irene," 27 May, '15. (Plate XXVII., 1).
STEMP, L. F., Capt., R.F.A.
Educ., Whitgift G. Sch. *Missing*, '18.

STEPAN, PERCY REGINALD, Pte., R. Fus.
  b., '93. Res., 5 Fairholme Mans., Croydon. Fell, 15 Jul., '16.
STEVENS, ARTHUR ERNEST, Sapper, Can. Engineers.
  b., Seaford, 22 May, '87 ; s., late Mr..& Mrs. Stevens, 24 Hathaway Rd., Croydon. Educ., Brit., & St. Saviour's Schs., Croydon. Married ; 2 children. Plumber. Res., Vancouver, B. C. Enl. about '15. Fell, France, 13 Jan., '18.
STEVENS, ARTHUR WILLIAM, Pte., 1/4 R.W.S. Regt.
  b., Lond., 11 May, '96 ; s., Arthur William & Caroline Stevens, 6 Eridge Rd., T. Heath. Educ., St. Thomas's Sch., Orchard St., Portman Sq., W. Single. Stockbroker's clerk. Enl., 12 Aug., '14. D., 10 Apr., '16, at Colaba Hosp., Bombay, of wounds recd. at Ctesiphon, 22-23 Nov., '15. (Plate XXIII., 3).
STEVENS, CHARLES H., 554401, Sapper, R.E.
  b., '86 ; s., Mr. & Mrs. Edward Stevens, 5 Epsom Rd., Croydon. Enl., Apr., '16. Fell, Monchy, nr. Arras, Oct., '17 ; buried, Monchy.
STEVENS, F. G., Lt., R.W.S. Regt.
  Res., 3 Parson's Mead, Croydon. Enl. as pte., 14 Sept., '14 ; went to France, Jun., '15 ; w., Festubert, Jan., '16 ; ret. to France as sgt., May, '16 ; commis., Sept., '16 : M.M., Somme, '16 (bestowed on mother by Mayor of Croydon & Col. Thompson, at Town Hall, Croydon, Apr., '18). Fell, Apr., '17.
STEVENS, G. H., 30032, Pte., Beds. Regt.
  Res., S. Norwood. Fell, '17.
STEVENS, H. H., Pte., Cameron H.
  b., '81. Married ; 2 children. Res., 9 Newhaven Rd., S. Norwood. Helped to start Croydon Common Football Club. Enl., May, '16. D. from exposure, France, 23 Dec., '17.
STEVENS, JAMES ALFRED, Pte., R.W.S. Regt.
  b., 5 Naseby Rd., U. Norwood, 10 Oct., '94 ; s., Mr. & Mrs. Stevens, 5 Naseby Rd., U. Norwood. Educ., Rockmount Rd. Sch., U. Norwood. Single. Labourer. Enl., 17 Apr., '16. Fell, France, 28 Sept., '16.
STEVENS, JOSEPH SAMUEL, Rflmn., Civil Serv. Rif. (15 Lond. Regt.)
  b., 132 Commercial Rd., Peckham ; s., Mr. & Mrs. Stevens, 3 Drover's Rd., Croydon. Educ., Par. Ch. Sch., Croydon. Single. Clerk. Enl., 1 Feb., '16. Fell, Ypres, 10 Apr., '18.
STEVENS, LEONARD S., Rflmn., Lond. Irish Rif. (18 Lond. Regt.)
  b., '96 ; s., Mr. & Mrs. Edward Stevens, 5 Epsom Rd., Croydon. Enl., Aug., '14. Fell, Festubert, 4 May, '15 ; buried, Festubert. (Plate XXVIII., 1).
STEVENS, SIDNEY FREDERICK, Sgt., 2 R. Fus.
  b., 124 Windmill Rd., Croydon, 23 Aug., '87 ; s., late George, & Matilda Stevens, 114 Windmill Rd., Croydon. Educ., Sydenham Rd. Sch., Croydon. Single. Painter. Enl. about '05 ; Delhi Durbar Med. Fell, France, 20 Sept., '16.
STEVENSON, GEORGE, L/Cpl., M.G.C.
  b., '93. Educ., Beulah Rd. Sch., T. Heath. Married ; 1 son. Res., 40 Northwood Rd., T. Heath. D. of wounds, 15 Sept., '17.
STEWARD, MORRIS, Pte., R.W.S. Regt.
  s., Mr. & Mrs. Steward, 14 Whitgift St., Croydon. Gardener, empl. by Mr. Frank Lloyd, Croydon. Enl., Aug., '14. D. of wounds, 6 Oct., '16.
STEWARD, REGINALD, L.R.B. (5 Lond. Regt.)
  Educ., High Sch., Croydon. D. of wounds, 23 Jul., '17.

THE GLORIOUS DEAD 395

STEWART, DOUGLAS ALEXANDER, 2/Lt., Cheshire Regt.
b., 2 Nov., '89 ; *s.*, Mr. & Mrs. Joseph Stewart, 13 Chepstow Rd., Croydon. *Educ.*, Whitgift G. Sch., '01-07. *Enl.* as pte. in Lond. Scottish before war ; D.C.M., awarded while cpl. in Lond. Scottish, Jul., '15 ; Russian medal of St. George, 4th cl. *Fell,* 9 Jul., '16.

STEWART, ERNEST GEORGE, A.B. Seaman, R.N.
b., Lond., 5 Sept., '96 ; *s.*, Mr. & Mrs. Stewart, Lakemba, nr. Sydney, N.S.W. *Educ.*, Portland Rd. Sch., S. Norwood. Single. Sailor. *Res.*, Australia. *Joined*, Sept., '12. *Lost* on H.M.S. " Egmont," 11 Nov., '17.

STEWART, GEORGE, Pte.
Late History Master, M. Whitgift Sch. *Fell,* Nov., '16.

STEWART, ROBERT, Pte., R. Fus.
b., 12 Lahore Rd., Croydon ; *s.*, Mr. & Mrs. Stewart, 85 Gloucester Rd., Croydon. *Educ.*, Nat. Sch., Croydon. Single. Carman. *Enl.*, 6 Mar., '15. *Fell*, Dardanelles, 29 Aug., '15.

STILL, WILLIAM GEORGE, Pte., 13 R. Suss. Regt.
b., 3 Victoria Place, Croydon, 31 Dec., '98 ; *s.*, late Mr., & Mrs. Still, 3 Victoria Pl., Croydon. *Educ.*, St. Andrew's Sch., Croydon. Single. Groundsman. *Enl.*, 22 Mar., '17. *Fell*, nr. Kemmel Hill, 26 Apr., '18.

STIMSON, JOHN WILLIAM, Cpl., R.F.A.
b., Croydon, 31 Oct., '90 ; *s.*, late Mr. Stimson, & Mrs. Elizabeth Weaver, 22 Cuthbert Rd., Croydon. *Educ.*, Mitcham Rd. Sch., Croydon. Single. Office boy. *Enl.*, 22 Jan., '09. *D.*, 2 Mar., '17, of wounds recd. in France prev. day.

STIRLING, JOHN HUNT, Lt., R.F.A.
b., '95 ; *s.*, Mr. & Mrs. John Stirling, " Grangehurst," S. Norwood. *D.* of wounds, 22 Aug., '17.

STOCKBRIDGE, E. A., 203058, Pte., Lond. Regt.
Fell, '17.

STOCKER, GERALD, Cpl., R.W.S. Regt.
2nd *s.*, Mr. & Mrs. Stocker, 67 Bensham Man. Rd., T. Heath. *Educ.*, Winterbourne Rd. Sch., T. Heath. Single. *Enl.*, Aug., '14 ; M.M., Messines, '17. *Fell*, 6 Jul., '17.

STOCKLEY, HARRY, Cpl., 73 Field Amb., R.A.M.C.
b., '93. *Educ.*, Boston Rd. Sch., T. Heath. Empl. by Mr. Newman, butcher, Lr. Addis. Rd., Croydon. *Res.*, 38 Dominion Rd., Croydon. *Fell,* France, 9 Oct., '18.

STONE, RICHARD, Pte., 7 R. Suss. Regt.
b., Stuart's Rd., Clapham, S.W., 13 Oct., '91 ; *s.*, Mr. & Mrs. Stone, 3 Cotford Rd., T. Heath. *Educ.*, Whitehorse Rd. Sch., T. Heath. Single. Gas collector. *Res.*, 3 Cotford Rd., T. Heath. *Enl.*, 14 Oct., '16 ; served in France 13 months. *D.*, 27 Nov., '18, at Crescent Mil. Hosp., Croydon, of pneumonia, contracted while on leave.

STONE, SIDNEY JOHN, A.B. Seaman, R.N.
b., 22 The Drive, T. Heath, 18 Aug., '97 ; *s.*, Mr. & Mrs. Stone, 3 Cotford Rd., T. Heath. *Educ.*, Whitehorse Rd. Sch., T. Heath. Single. Clerk. *Res.*, 3 Cotford Rd., T. Heath. *Joined*, Sept., '13. *Lost* with H.M.S. " Clan MacNaughton," off Irish Coast, 3 Feb., '15.

STONEHAM, REGINALD PERCY, Lt., 1 Notts. & Derby. Regt.
b., '91 ; *s.*, Mr. & Mrs. A. W. Stoneham, 73 Brigstock Rd., T. Heath. *Educ.*, M. Whitgift Sch. Single. Bank clerk (Bank of Bombay). D.C.M. *Fell*, Hill 60, Ypres, May, '15.

STONEMAN, GEORGE, R.W.S. Regt.
 b., '91 ; s., late Mr. Stoneman, & Mrs. Caroline Fox, 70 Bynes Rd., Croydon. Empl. at S. Croydon Stn. D. of wounds, 14 Jul., '17.

STRAHAN, W. E., 9062, Pte., 2 R.W.S. Regt.
 b., '88. Res., Croydon. Enl., '06; served at Gibraltar, Bermuda, and S. Africa; w., France, Oct., '14. Fell, Festubert 16 May, '15.

STRAKER, FRANK, 2/Lt., R.F.A.
 b., '98 ; s., Mr. & Mrs. Straker, 5 Park Lane Mans., Park Lane, Croydon. Fell, '16.

STREET, SIDNEY, Cpl., 1/19 Lond. Regt.
 b., Furze Rd., T. Heath, 16 Jun., '87 ; 2nd s., Mr. & Mrs. Street, 5 Lucerne Rd., T. Heath. Educ., Beulah Rd. Sch., T. Heath. Married ; 1 son. Tobacconist. Res., 82 Burlington Rd., T. Heath. Enl. in R.W.S. Regt, 13 Sept., '14. Fell, France, 22 Aug., '18.

STREETER, ALFRED W., Sgt., R.E.
 b., '66. Single. Res., 98a Cherry Orchard Rd., Croydon. M.M. Fell, '17.

STREETER, GEORGE, Pte., E. Sur. Regt.
 b., '96. Res., 59 Exeter Rd., Croydon. W., France, Apr., '15. Fell, 23 Jul., '16.

STREETER, JEREMIAH EMERY, Pte., 4 Middlesex Regt.
 b., 60 Napier Rd., Croydon. Educ., Bynes Rd. Sch., Croydon. Married. Plate layer. Res., 63 Bynes Rd., Croydon. Enl., 7 Aug., '01. Fell, Fleurbaix, 10 Nov., '14.

STREETER, WILLIAM, Pte., E. Sur. Regt.
 s., Mr. & Mrs. Streeter, 59 Exeter Rd., Croydon. Fell, Aug., '14.

STREETER, WILLIAM ROBERT, 46229, Driver, R.F.A.
 b., Croydon, 4 Sept., '92 ; s., Mr. & Mrs. S. J. Streeter, 26 Napier Rd., Croydon. Educ., Bynes Rd. Sch., Croydon. Single. Groundsman, Shirley Golf Links. Enl., 8 Oct., '15 ; served in Italy and France. Fell, France, 13 Nov., '18.

STRETT, W. E., R.W.S. Regt.
 Res., S. Croydon. Fell, '17.

STRUDWICK, G., 19921, Gnr., R.H.A.
 Res., Croydon. Fell, '16.

STRUDWICK, WILLIAM MAURICE. 44844, Pte., 2 Lincoln Regt.
 b., 2 Pump Pail, Croydon, 24 Feb., '99 ; s., Mr. & Mrs. Strudwick, 125 Old Town, Croydon. Educ., St. Andrew's Sch., Croydon. Single. Waiter. Enl., 5 Jan., '17. Fell, France, 17 Apr., '18.

STUART, J. H., 203491, Rflmn., R.B.
 Res., S. Norwood. Fell, '16.

STUBBS, EDWARD WOODHOUSE, L/Cpl., 32 Div., R.A.M.C.
 b., Norwich, '87 ; s., Mr. & Mrs. J. Woodhouse Stubbs, Marlborough Rd., Croydon. Educ., Sunderland Boys' High Sch., Ilkley Gram. Sch., Newcastle-on-Tyne Gram. Sch., & Norwich Middle Sch. Single. Architect, A.R.I.B.A. Enl., Aug., '15. Fell, Bethune, 7 Aug., '16, while rescuing civilians from houses that were being demolished by shell fire.

STUBBS, REGINALD ARTHUR, 2/Lt., R. Mun. Fus. (attd. R.F.C.)
 Chorister and Server, Holy Innocents' Ch., S. Norwood ; undergraduate, Keble Coll., Oxford ; studying for Holy Orders. Enl., in U.P.S. Corps as pte. Fell, France, 8 Jun., '16.

STUDHAM, A. E., R.W.S. Regt.
 b., '85 ; s., Mr. & Mrs. J. Studham, Croydon. Educ., Par. Ch. Sch., Croydon. Married. Fell, 5 Apr., '18.

THE GLORIOUS DEAD

STURGES, MONTAGUE E., Pte., Lond. Regt.
 b., Anerley, '98 ; *s.*, Rev. M. C. & Mrs. Sturges, Anerley. *Educ.*, Anerley Coll., & Whitgift G. Sch. Empl. in merchant's office in City. *Enl.*, '15. *Fell*, '17.

STURROCK, WILLIAM HENRY JAMES, Pte., Australian I.F.
 b., 14 Ivy Lane, Brockley, 3 Jan., '96 ; *s.*, Mr. & Mrs. James B. Sturrock, "Trentham," 45 Woodside Av., S. Norwood. *Educ.*, Portland Rd. Sch., S. Norwood. Single. Farmer. *Res.*, Gippsland, Victoria, Aust. *Enl.*, Mar., '15 ; served in Gallipoli, Soudan, Egypt, &'France. *Killed* in explosion of the Town Hall at Bapaume, 25 Mar., '17.

STYLES, FRANCIS FREDERICK, Pte., 2/4 R.W.S. Regt.
 b., 14 Walter's Rd., S. Norwood, 28 Sept., '86 ; *s.*, William John & Louisa Styles, 19 Cresswell Rd., S. Norwood. *Educ.*, Birchanger Rd. Sch., S. Norwood. Single. Empl. by Croydon Corp. *Enl.*, 13 Oct., '14. *Fell*, Palestine, 27 Dec., '17.

SUDLOW, F., Pte., Australian I.F.
 Educ., High Sch., Croydon. *Fell*, '16.

SULLIVAN, C., Driver, R.F.A.
 b., '97 ; *s.*, Mr. & Mrs. Sullivan, 84 Addington Rd., Croydon. Empl. by Messrs. Packham & Co. *Enl.*, '14. *Fell*, nr. Amiens, 29 Mar., '18.

SUMMERFORD, F., 63211, Pte., Lab. Corps.
 Res., S. Norwood. *Fell*, '17.

SURKITT, W. A., Pte., R.W. Kent Regt.
 s., Mr. & Mrs. S. Surkitt, 34 Sussex Rd., Croydon. *Enl.*, 6 Sept., '14 ; went to France, Jun., '16 ; *w.*, 10 Aug., '16 ; retd. to France, 12 Dec., '16 ; went to Italy Nov., '17, where he was *w.* ; gassed at Messines, '18. *Fell*, France, 25 Oct., '18.

SURRY, NORMAN F., Lt., K.R.R.C.
 Married. *Res.*, 22 Freemason's Rd., Croydon. *Fell*, 12 Oct.,'18.

SUTCLIFFE, JOHN, Pte., 10 Can. Inf.
 b., '82 ; *s.*, Mr. & Mrs. J. Sutcliffe, 4 Oakfield Rd., Croydon. *Fell*, Loos, 15 Aug., '17.

SUTCLIFFE, ROBERT WILLIAM, Pte., 17 R. Fus.
 s., Mr. & Mrs. J. Sutcliffe, 4 Oakfield Rd., Croydon. *Fell*, Delville Wood, Somme, 27 Jul., '16.

SUTTON, C. A., 1200, Driver, R.F.A.
 Res., Croydon. *Fell*, '17.

SUTTON, R. C. J., Pte., R.W.S. Regt.
 b., '79. Married. Empl. by Croydon Corp. for 14 yrs. *Res.*, 67 Farnley Rd., S. Norwood. *Fell*, 12 May, '17.

SWALE, F. ALAN, Lt., Can. Divnl. Sig. Coy.
 b., '93 ; *s.*, Mr. & Mrs. Swale, "Brudenell," Altyre Rd., Croydon. *Educ.*, Whitgift G. Sch. *Fell*, 24 Apr., '15.

SWALLOW, LEONARD, Sgt., H.A.C.
 b., '93 ; *s.*, Rev. & Mrs. Swallow, late of T. Heath. *Fell*, '16.

SWALLOW, R., Gnr., R.H.A.
 Res., T. Heath. *Fell*, '16.

SWANSBY, S. E., Pte., R.W.S. Regt.
 b., '94 ; *s.*, Mr. & Mrs. Swansby, 13 Rymer Rd., Croydon. Empl. by Messrs. Hall & Co. *Res.*, 41 Lancing Rd., Croydon. *Enl.*, 16 Oct., '14 ; went to France, Sept., '15. *Fell*, 31 Jul., '17.

SWANSTON, JOHN TAYLOR, Coy.Sgt.Maj., Lond. Scottish (14 Lond. Regt.)
 b., Tunbridge Wells, 19 Nov., '79 ; *s.*, Mr. & Mrs. Swanston, "Shiplake," Moreton Rd., Croydon. *Educ.*, Moore Park G. Sch., Fulham. Single. Hemp merchant. Served for 18 yrs. with Lond. Scottish. *Fell*, Givenchy, 21 Dec., '14.

SWINNERTON, WILLIAM, Bdr., Anti-Aircraft Bde., R.M.A.
    b., Amsterdam, Holland, 20 Apr., '92 ; *s.*, late John, & Hermina Swinnerton. *Educ.*, Woodside Sch., & Boro. Sec. Sch., Croydon. Single. *Res.*, 39 Grange Rd., S. Norwood. *Enl.*, '10. *Fell*, Ypres, 15 May, '15.

SYDENHAM, JOHN, R.N.
    Educ., Shirley Sch., Wickham Rd., Croydon. *Joined* Oct., '09. *Lost* on H.M.S. " Amphion," 6 Aug., '14.

SYKES, WALTER ERNEST, Lt., 5 R. W. Kent Regt.
    b., Calcutta ; *s.*, Mr. & Mrs. Sykes, 26 Moreton Rd., Croydon. *Educ.*, Paradise House Sch., Stoke Newington. Married. Chartered patent agent. *Res.*, Mecklenburgh Sq., Lond., W.C. Served in Territorials several yrs. before war ; mobilised as Lt., 4 Aug., '14 ; went to India, Nov., '14 ; was later transf. to France. *Fell*, nr. Cambrai, 20 Nov., '17.

TAGG, A. E., Cpl.
    b., '84 ; *s.*, Mr. & Mrs. Henry Tagg, 16 Gloucester Rd., Croydon. Married ; 4 children. Empl. by Mr. Gryspeerdt, Lansdowne Rd., Croydon. *Res.*, 86 Strathmore Rd., Croydon. Served in S.A. War ; re-joined Aug., '14 ; went to France, 22 Aug., '14 ; *w.*, '17.; retd. to France, 22 Aug., '17. *Fell*, 27 Aug., '18.

TAGG, ALBERT SIDNEY, 1st Cl. Stoker, R.N.
    b., Croydon, 27 Jan., '89 ; *s.*, Mr. & Mrs. Tagg, 16 Gloucester Rd., Croydon. *Educ.*, St. James' Sch., Croydon. Single. School cleaner. Joined R.N., Jul., '08. *Lost*, with H.M.S. " Black Prince," Battle of Jutland, 31 May, '16.

TAGG, HAROLD ARTHUR, 2/Lt., Middlesex Regt.
    b., 10 Jan., '90 ; *s.*, Mr. & Mrs. James Tagg, 70 Oakfield Rd., Croydon. *Educ.*, Whitgift G. Sch., '03-07. Ment. in despat. *Fell*, Flanders, Nov., '14.

TANT, C., 1265, Rflmn., R.B.
    Res., Croydon. *Fell*, '16.

TAPSELL, A., Sgt., E. Kent Regt.
    b., '86 ; *s.*, late Mr., & Mrs. Tapsell, Clifton Rd., S. Norwood. *Enl.*, Aug., '14 ; went to France, Jul., '15. *Fell*, '17.

TARLTON, F. J., 13805, L/Sgt., R.E.
    Res., Croydon.

TARRANT, HARRY, Cpl., 6 R.W.S. Regt.
    b., Warlingham, 8 Aug., '94 ; *s.*, Mr. & Mrs. James Tarrant, 183 Bynes Rd., Croydon. *Educ.*, Brighton Rd. Sch., Croydon. Single. Gardener. *Res.*, 31 Purley Rd., Croydon. *Enl.*, 22 Aug., '14. *D.*, 26 Oct., '18, at 20 C.C.S., France, of wounds recd. prev. day ; *buried*, Prémont.

TARRANT, J., Sgt., 1 Essex Regt.
    b., Woldingham, 16 Jan., '90 ; 2nd *s.*, Mr. & Mrs. James Tarrant, 183 Bynes Rd., Croydon. *Educ.*, Brighton Rd. Sch., Croydon. Married. Gardener. *Res.*, 24 Crunden Rd., Croydon. *Enl.*, Aug., '06 ; served in India & Africa ; retd. home, '14 ; served and was *w.* at Gallipoli, May, '15 ; retd. to France. *D.* of wounds recd. in France, 30 Nov., '17.

TARRY, WILLIAM THOMAS, 62893, Pte., 9 R. Fus.
    b., Edinburgh, 30 Jan., '98 ; *s.*, William Ivens & Jane Tarry, 23 Grace Rd., Croydon. *Educ.*, Par. Ch. Sch., Croydon. Single. Empl. by " Croydon Guardian." *Enl.*, 24 Aug., '15. *D.* of tetanus in enemy hospital at Contalmaison, France, 2 Apr.,'18.

TAYLOR, ALBERT ARTHUR, Bandsman, 1 E. Sur. Regt.
    b., Battersea, 2 Oct., '82 ; *s.*, Mr. & Mrs. Taylor, 50 Newark Rd., Croydon. *Educ.*, Royal Duke of York Sch., Chelsea. Single. Musician. *Enl.*, 2 Oct., '97. *D.*, 27 Sept., '14, at 10 Gen. Hosp., St. Nazaire, of wounds recd. at the Battle of the Aisne, 24 Sept.,'14.

TAYLOR, ARTHUR, Driver, 72 Bde., R.F.A.
b., Croydon, 22 Dec., '84 ; *s.*, Mr. & Mrs. Taylor, 73 Gloucester Rd., Croydon. *Educ.*, Sydenham Rd. Sch., Croydon. Married. Carman. *Res.*, 3 Milton Rd., Croydon. *Enl.*, 5 Sept., '14. *D.*, 31 Aug., '18, at 43 C.C.S., of wounds recd. at St. Leger, 28 Aug., '18.

TAYLOR, E., 6754, Cpl., Wilts. Regt.
Res., S. Norwood. *D.* of wounds, '17.

TAYLOR, EDWARD JOHN, A.B. Seaman, R.N.
b., Deal, Kent, 19 Feb., '97 ; *s.*, late Mr., & Mrs. Taylor, 53 Strathmore Rd., Croydon. *Educ.*, Woodside & Davidson Rd. Schs., Croydon. Single. Van boy. Joined R.N., 11 Sept., '12 ; served on H.M.S. " Queen Elizabeth." *D.*, of enteric fever, City Hosp., Edinburgh, 27 Nov., '17.

TAYLOR, FRANK ALLAN, Gnr., R.G.A.
Married ; 2 children. *Fell*, '17.

TAYLOR, FREDERICK HENRY, Pte., R.W.S. Regt.
b., S. Norwood, 8 Aug., '97 ; *s.*, William & Eliza Taylor, 21 Harrington Rd., S. Norwood. *Educ.*, Birchanger Rd. Sch., S. Norwood. Single. Clerk. *Enl.*, 2 Nov., '15. *Fell*, La Bassée, 9 Aug., '16.

TAYLOR, GEORGE, Pte., 7 R. Suss. Regt.
b., S. Norwood, 16 Jan., '00. *Educ.*, Birchanger Rd. Sch., S. Norwood. Single. Draper's asst. *Res.*, 21 Harrington Rd., S. Norwood. *Enl.*, 23 Feb., '18. *D.*, 18 Oct., '18, at Northern Gen. Hosp., Sheffield, of wounds recd. at Cambrai, 18 Sept., '18. *Buried*, Queen's Rd. Cem., Croydon.

TAYLOR, SIDNEY HERBERT, Pte., R. Fus.
b., '87 ; *4th s.*, Mr. & Mrs. Mark Taylor. Married ; 1 child. *Res.*, Eridge Rd., T. Heath. Sec. of Waddon Park Football Team. *Fell*, Ypres, 26 Oct., '17.

TEAGUE, CHARLES MIDDLEMORE, L/Cpl., 1 Lond. Scottish (14 Lond. Rgt.)
b., Crediton, Devon, 16 Dec., '88 ; *s.*, Rev. John Jessop Teague (*Morice Gerard*), formerly Vicar of Woodside, now of 97 York Mansions, S.W., and Elizabeth Teague. *Educ*, All Hallows, Honiton. Single. Journalist. *Res.*, Royal Cres., Holland Park, W. *Enl.*, Sept., '14. *Fell*, Hulluch, nr. Loos, 15 Oct., '15.

TEAGUE, JOHN COCKBURN JESSOP, Capt., R.M.L.I.
b., Streatham Hill, S.W., 20 Feb., '82 ; *s.*, Rev. John Jessop Teague (*Morice Gerard*), formerly Vicar of Woodside, now of 97 York Mansions, S.W., and Elizabeth Teague. *Educ.*, All Hallows, Honiton. Single. Barrister-at-law. *Res.*, Exminster Vicarage, Devon. *Joined* R.M.L.I., '00 ; re-joined, Aug., '14. *Fell*, Gallipoli, 4 May, '15.

TEE, A. G., L/Sgt., R.W.S. Regt.
s., Mr. & Mrs. Tee, Worthing. Empl. at E. Croydon Railway Goods Office. *D.*, 5 Nov., '17.

TEGETMEIER, ALAN, Pte., 2/13 Lond. Regt.
b., Clapham, Nov., '91 ; *s.*, Mr. & Mrs. Charles G. Tegetmeier, " Normanhurst," Brighton Rd., Purley. *Educ.*, Dulwich Coll. Single. Secty. to a Public Company. *Enl.*, Sept., '14. *Fell*, Ain-Karim, Palestine, 8 Dec., '17. (Plate XXXI., 3).

TERRY, WILLIAM JOHN, Pte., 2 R.W.S. Regt.
b., New Town, U. Norwood, 8 Jan., '93 ; *s.*, William & Charlotte Terry, 17 Crystal Terr., New Town, U. Norwood. *Educ.*, Rockmount Rd., & Salter's Hill Schs., U. Norwood. Single. Errand boy. *Res.*, 55 Eagle Hill, New Town, U. Norwood. *Enl.*, 13 Sept., '10. *Fell*, Ypres, 21 Oct., '14.

TESTER, SYDNEY FREDERICK, Pte., R.A.S.C. (M.T.)
  b., Oxted, 6 Sept., '86. *Educ.*, Oxted Nat. Sch. Married.
  Gardener. *Res.*, 113 Edridge Rd., Croydon. *Enl.*, 14 May, '17.
  D., 24 Mar., '18, at High Rough Mil. Hosp., Haslemere, of acute
  pneumonia.
THACKER, HERBERT LANE, 2/Lt., R.A.S.C.
  b., 5 Mar., '06 ; *s.*, late Herbert, & Mrs. Thacker, " Liliesleaf,"
  Woodcote Valley Rd., Purley. *Enl.* as pte. in M.G.C.:
  served with Tank Corps ; M.M., & M.C. Drowned in torpedoed
  transport, '17.
THAIRS, MAURICE, Rflmn., 2/17 Lond. Regt.
  b., Gladstone Rd., Croydon, 3 May, '97 ; *6th s.*, Mr. & Mrs.
  Thairs, 107 Old Town, Croydon. *Educ.*, St. Mary's Sch.,
  Croydon. Single. Baker. *Res.*, Whitechapel Rd. *Enl.*,
  1 Jul., '15 ; served at Salonica & Egypt. *Fell*, France, 17 Aug.,'18.
THAKE, H. T. J., 5710, 1st A.M., R.F.C.
  Res., S. Norwood. *Fell*, '16.
THALER, SYDNEY OSCAR, Rflmn., K.R.R.C.
  b., '90 ; *s.*, Mr. & Mrs. Thaler, Station Rd., Croydon. *Enl.*,
  Nov., '15. *Fell*, 15 Sept., '16.
THIRKETTLE, JAMES W. H., Sgt., R.E.
  b., '00. *Res.*, 6 Eldon Pk., S. Norwood. Memb. of St. Mark's
  S. Norwood, C.L.B. *Enl.*, '15. *D.* of pneumonia at Bedford
  Mil. Hosp., 10 Nov., '18.
THOMAS, A. J., Sapper, R.E.
  e.s., Mr. & Mrs. Thomas, 27 St. James's Rd., Croydon. *Educ.*,
  St. James's Sch., Croydon. Married ; 5 children. *Enl.*, '14.
  Fell, 14 Apr., '18.
THOMAS, ALBERT EDWARD, Cpl., 2 Seaforth H.
  b., Bermondsey, 3 Aug., '95 : *s.*, Mr. & Mrs. Thomas, 163
  Portland Rd., S. Norwood. *Educ.*, Portland Rd. Sch., S Nor-
  wood. Single. Engineer's draughtsman. *Enl.*, 26 May, '15.
  Fell, nr. Fampoux, 11 Apr., '17.
THOMAS, LEONARD ELYSTAN OWEN, Pte., Civ. Serv. Rif. (15 Lond. Regt.)
  b., 8 Mar., '94 : *s.*, Mr. & Mrs. Leonard W. Thomas, 119 High St.,
  Croydon. *Educ.*, Whitgift G. Sch., '04-09, Strand Sch., & King's
  Coll., Lond. *Fell*, France, 7 Oct., '17.
THOMAS, R. A., L/Cpl , K.R.R.C.
  b., '90. Married. Empl. by Messrs. Roffey & Clark, Croydon.
  Res., 31 St. John's Gr., Croydon. *Fell*, Somme, 15 Sept., '16.
THOMPSON, ALBERT, 7781, Pte., 2 R.W.S. Regt.
  b., 24 Sept., '84 ; *s.*, Mr. & Mrs. Thompson, 23 Grace Rd.,
  Croydon. *Educ.*, Princess Rd. Sch., Croydon. Married.
  General dealer. *Res.*, 42 Foster Rd., Croydon. *Enl.*, '03.
  Fell, Fleurbaix, France, 18 Dec., '14.
THOMPSON, LESLIE CHARLES DE COURCY, 1st A.M., R.N.A.S., Armoured
  Car Squadron
  b., Canonbury, 8 Jan., '87. *Educ.*, Summit, New Jersey, U.S.A.,
  and Clevedon, Somerset. Married. Managing clerk to firm
  of Eastern shippers. *Res.*, Croydon *Enl.*, Jun., '15. *D.*, 22
  Nov., '16, at Hammersmith Orthopædic Hosp., of injuries recd.
  while carrying out experiments at Wembley.
THOMPSON, ROBERT ARTHUR.
  b., '96. *Res.*, 57 Oval Rd., Croydon. *Killed* during Zeppelin
  raid, Oct., '15.
THOMSON, RICHARD A., Pte , 17 R. Fus.
  b., '97. *Fell*, 13 Nov., '16.

XXIX.

1. 2/Lt. B. WARNER, Lond. Rif. B.
2. Sgt. R. S. TONGE, 22 R. Fus.
3. 2/Lt. E. H. RONCA, E. Kent Regt.
4. Pte. F. WALTERS, 6 Lond. Regt.
5. Capt. E. S. UNDERHILL, 8 L.N. Lancs. Regt.
6. L./Cpl. E. J. SKUSE, 3/4 R.W.S. Regt.

XXX.

1. Pte. A. J. F. TRACEY, 15 Lond. Regt.
2. Pte. W. T. WAINWRIGHT, 12 Middlesex Regt.
3. Pte. C. TITMUSS, 7 R. Fus.
4. Pte. F. E. STANLEY, 9 E. Sur. Regt.
5. Rflmn. C. F. WALLIS, Artists Rif.
6. Rflmn. W. H. SKUSE, 1/17 Lond. Regt.

THE GLORIOUS DEAD

THOMSON, WALTER, Pte., 21 Montreal Regt. (Can. Scottish).
b., Cross Rd., Croydon, about '78 ; *s.*, late Mr., & Mrs. Thomson, Mount Pleasant Cottages, Mitcham Rd., Croydon. *Educ.,* Oval Rd. Sch., Croydon. Married. Decorator. *Res.,* Montreal. *Enl.,* Sept., '14. *Fell,* Hill 60, nr. Ypres.

THOMPSON, WILLIAM FRANK, Signaller, 2/5 E. Lancs. Regt.
b., 17 Frith Rd., Croydon, 17 Jan., '98 ; *s.,* Mr. & Mrs .Richard Thompson, 37 Gladstone Rd., W. Croydon. *Educ.,* Oval Rd. Sch., Croydon. Single. Printer. *Enl.,* 3 Oct., '16, in 2/5 E. Sur. Regt. *Missing,* 21-31 Mar., '18.

THOMPSON, WILLIAM HENRY, Pte., 3/4 R.W.S Regt.
b., 7 Russell Rd., Croydon, 25 Jun., '97; *s.,* Mr. & Mrs Thompson, 7 Russell Rd., Croydon. *Educ.,* Tavistock Grove Sch., Croydon. Single. Plumber's labourer. *Enl.,* 8 Jun., '15. *Fell,* nr. St. Eloi, 15 Dec., '16.

THORN, EDWARD J., Sapper, R.E.
Educ., Abp. Tenison's Sch., Croydon. *Enl.,* Apr., '16. *D.* of pneumonia, Rouen, 27 Oct., '18.

THORN, THOMAS, Pte., D.L.I.
b., New Town, U. Norwood, 14 Sept., '85. *Educ.,* Rockmount Rd. Sch., U. Norwood. Single. Railway porter. *Res.,* 14 Bradford Rd., Sydenham. *Enl.,* 4 Aug., '14. *Fell,* France, 21 Sept., '14.

THORNTON, DOUGLAS SAVILLE, 2/Lt., Sherwood For.
Fell, '16.

THORPE, R., 14302, Cpl., Beds. Regt.
Res., T. Heath. *Fell,* '16.

THURGOOD, JOHN, Cpl., R.W.S. Regt.
b., 31 Albion St., Croydon, 27 Feb., '91 ; *s.,* Mr. & Mrs. Thurgood, 19 Mitcham Rd., Croydon. *Educ.,* Mitcham Rd. Sch., Croydon. Single. Engine room asst. (ice works). *Res.,* 19 Cambridge Terr., Mitcham Rd., Croydon. *Enl.,* 3 Sept., '14. *Fell,* France, 16 May, '15.

TIDY, CHARLES, Pte., Lancs. Fus.
s., late Thomas Henry, & Mrs. Tidy. Married ; 3 children. Wellknown local footballer. *Fell,* Passchendaele, 10 Oct., '17.

TIDY, FREDERICK E., R.W.S. Regt.
s., Mr. & Mrs. F. Tidy, 114 Sutherland Rd., Croydon. *Fell,* 23 Apr., '17.

TIDY, J., 17381, Pte., D.C.L.I.
Res., S. Croydon. *Fell,* '16.

TIDY, THOMAS WILLIAM, Pte., Coldstream Gds.
s., Mr. & Mrs. Tidy, Carmichael Rd., S. Norwood. *Fell,* Landrecies, 25 Aug., '14.

TIDY, W. HENRY, Pte., R. Scots Fus.
b., '87 ; *s.,* Mr. & Mrs. Tidy, 114 Sutherland Rd., Croydon. *Fell,* Ypres, 31 Oct., '14.

TILBURY, HENRY ALEXANDER PHILBY, Rflmn., Post Off. Rif. (8 Lond. Regt.)
b., Acton, 6 Jan., '89 ; *s.,* Mr. & Mrs. H. W. Tilbury, 10 Aylett Rd., S. Norwood. *Educ.,* E. Grinstead. Single. Postman. *Res.,* 17 Notson Rd., S. Norwood. Served for 4 yrs. with R.W.S. Territorials. *Re-enlisted* in 8 Lond. Regt., Sept., '14 ; *w ,* Festubert. *Fell,* Vimy, 21 May, '16.

TITMUSS, CHARLES, Pte., 7 R. Fus.
b., '96 ; *s.,* J. & A. Titmuss, 123 Southbridge Rd., Croydon. Ticket collector at T. Heath Stn. *Res.,* Croydon. *Fell,* 13 Nov., '16. (Plate XXX., 3).

TITMUSS, WILLIAM GEORGE, R.N.
  b., St. Peter's St., Croydon, 10 Jul., '93 ; *s.*, Walter George & Elizabeth Titmuss, 18 Helder St., S. Croydon. Single. Shop asst. *Lost*, with H.M.S. " Formidable," 1 Jan., '15.
TODD, JAMES WILLIAM, 2/Lt., R.F.C.
  b., May, '98 ; *e.s.*, Mr. & Mrs. E. J. Todd, 18 Wellington Rd., Croydon. *Educ.*, Latimer Sch., Hammersmith. Single. Clerk empl. by L.C.C. *Enl.* as pte. in Artists Rif., Jan., '17 ; commis. in R.F.C., May, '17. *D.*, 28 Sept., '17, of injuries recd. in accident while flying nr. Narborough. Norfolk. *Buried*, Mitcham Rd. Cem., Croydon.
TOFIELD, W. J. H., Rflmn., 1 R.B.
  b., '00 ; *e.s.*, Mr. & Mrs. William Tofield, 247 Whitehorse Rd., T. Heath. *Enl.* end of '17 ; went to France about Apr., '18. *Fell*, 7 Jun., '18.
TOLLEMACHE, J. E., 2/Lt., R.W.S. Regt.
  Fell, '16.
TOMKINS, ALBERT, Pte., E. Sur. Regt.
  b., 44 Eagle Hill, U. Norwood, 10 Jul., '91 ; *s.*, Mr. & Mrs. E. Tomkins, 10 Crystal Terr., U. Norwood. *Educ.*, Rockmount Rd. Sch., U. Norwood. Single. Carman. *Res.*, 6 Dover Rd., U. Norwood. *Enl.*, 10 Aug., '14. *Fell*, France, 14 May, '15. (Plate XXVIII., 3).
TOMKINS, VIGOR, Capt., 7 E. Sur. Regt.
  b., 18 Nov., '93 ; *s.*, Mr. & Mrs. Samuel John Tomkins, " Bedford," Manor Rd., Wallington. *Educ.*, Whitgift G. Sch., '08-11. Engineering student, Lond. Univ. *Joined*, Aug., '14. *Fell*, France, 13 Oct., '15.
TONGE, REGINALD SEVERN, Sgt., 22 R. Fus.
  b., S. Norwood., 8 Nov., '78 ; *s.*, late Mr., & Mrs. Julia Tonge, Raby Lodge, S. Norwood. *Educ.*, Selhurst Pk. Coll., S. Norwood. Single. Clerk. *Res.*, Bloomsbury, W.C. Served in S.A. War with R.W.S. Regt. (Med. with 3 bars) ; later joined S.A. Mounted Constabulary. *Re-joined*, Aug., '14, went to France, '15. *D.* of wounds recd. at Albert, 17 Feb., '17. (Plate XXIX., 2).
TOPE, A. F., 3855, Pte., Lond. Regt.
  Res., T. Heath. *Fell*, '16.
TOPP, CHARLES FREDERICK.
  Married. *Res.*, 3 Duppas Terr. Parade, Old Town, Croydon. *D.* of fever, E. Afr., 3 Feb., '19.
TOURLE, EDGAR, 60977, Pte., 7 R. Fus.
  s., Mr. & Mrs. Tourle, 94 Fairholme Rd., Croydon. *Fell*, Arras, 23 Apr., '17. (Plate XXXI., 1).
TOWERSEY, T. W., 1386, Sgt., R.W.S. Regt.
  Fell, 1 Jul., '16.
TOWNEND, CLIVE HAMILTON, Rflmn., L.R.B. (5 Lond. Regt.)
  b., Croydon, 14 Oct., '89 ; *s.*, Frank & May Townend, " Harefield," Croham Rd., Croydon. *Educ.*, Elmhurst Sch., Croydon, and Abbottsholme, Rochester. Single. Colonial broker. *Enl.*, Sept., '14. *D.*, 23 Jun., '15, at Charing Cross Hosp., Lond., of wounds recd. at Ypres, 3 May, '15. (Plate XXXV., 4).
TOWNSEND, J., 1305, Pte., R.W.S. Regt.
  Fell, '16.
TRACEY, ALBERT JAMES F., Pte., 15 Lond. Regt.
  s., Mr. & Mrs. Tracey, 24 Belmont Rd., S. Norwood. *Educ.*, M. Whitgift Sch., and S. Norwood Sch. Civil servant. *Fell*, 25 May, '15. (Plate XXX., 1).

TRACEY, C. J., 121814, Pte., R.A.S.C.
Res., W. Croydon. *Fell*, '16.
TREDINNICK, W. P., 4293, Pte., Lond. Regt.
Res., S. Croydon. *Fell*, '16.
TREFFRY, BASIL THOMAS, Pte., R.W.S. Regt.
b., Peckham, 25 Aug., '93 ; *s.*, Mr. & Mrs. T. A. Treffry, 16 Bensham Manor Rd., T. Heath. *Educ.*, Thornton Heath Sch. Single. Commercial clerk. *Enl.*, 9 Sept., '11. *Fell*, Langemarck, 31 Oct., '14. (Plate XXVIII., 5).
TREFFRY, RICHARD HAROLD, L/Cpl., Q.W. Rif. (16 Lond. Regt.)
b., T. Heath, 14 Mar., '98 ; *s.*, Mr. & Mrs. T. A. Treffry, 16 Bensham Manor Rd., T. Heath. *Educ.*, Thornton Heath Sch. Single. Bank clerk. *Enl.*, 16 May, '16. *Fell*, Langemarck, France, 16 Aug., '17. (Plate XXVII., 4).
TREHERNE, EDWARD ALLAN, Pte., 7 R.W.S. Regt.
b., Croydon, 8 Apr., '88 ; *s.*, late Mr. & Mrs. Treherne, 35 Fairholme Rd., Croydon. *Educ.*, St. Saviour's Sch., Croydon. Single. Commercial traveller. *Enl.*, 2 Mar., '16. *Fell* nr. Albert, 3 Nov., '16.
TREMEARINE, CECIL FRANCIS SHIRLEY, Pte., S.A. Inf.
Fell, 12 Oct., '16.
TRIBE, G. H., 24374, Pte., 9 E. Sur. Regt.
Res., 72 Grant Rd., Croydon. Pris. of war in Germany (Güstrow) ; not heard from since 19 Aug., '18.
TRINDER, CECIL MONTAGUE, Pte., H.L.I.
b., '97 ; *s.*, Mr. & Mrs. Trinder, 6 Frant Rd., T. Heath. *Enl.*, 25 Jan., '15. *Fell*, France, 25 Sept., '15.
TRINDLER, GEORGE, Pte., 1 R. Scots.
b., Abingdon, 8 Mar., '67. *Educ.*, National Sch., Abingdon. Married. Leather dresser. *Res.*, 26 Cuthbert Rd., Croydon. *Enl.*, 3 Oct., '14. *D.* of wounds at Boulogne, 6 May, '15.
TRIPTREE, A. G., 7914, Pte., E. Kent Regt.
Res., Croydon. *Fell*, '17.
TROWER, A. H., 1919, Pte., R.W.S. Regt.
Res., Sutton. *Fell*, '16.
TROWNSON, GRAHAM FRANCIS JAMES, Midshipman, R.N.
b., 11 Jul., '97 ; *s.*, Mr. & Mrs. Francis Thomas Trownson, 122 Birchanger Rd., S. Norwood. *Educ.*, Whitgift G. Sch., '09-11. *Lost* with H.M.S. " Good Hope," sunk off Chili, 1 Nov., '14.
TRUBSHAWE, C. H., 7405, Pte., H.A.C.
Res., Croydon. *Fell*, '17.
TRUBSHAWE, ERIC JAMES, 2/Lt., 62 (W. Riding, Yorks.) Div., R.E.
b., Richmond, Surrey, 8 Aug., '97 ; *s.*, Mr. & Mrs. V. Trubshawe, 21 Fairfield Rd., Croydon. *Educ.*, Bedales Sch. ; matriculated Lond. Univ., '15. Single. *Joined* Inns of Court O.T.C., 22 Apr., '15. *Fell*, Hebuterne, France, 2 Feb., '17. (Plate XVIII., 1).
TRUSS, GEORGE MARQUAND, 2/Lt., Scots Gds.
s., Mr. & Mrs. Geo. M. Truss, Fox Hill, U. Norwood. *Educ.*, Dulwich Coll. *Fell*, 25 Sept., '16.
TUCK, CHARLES ERNEST, Cpl., 8 E. Kent Regt.
b., '85. Empl. at Messrs. Hall's cement works for 7 yrs. Served in S.A. War. *D.* of wounds recd. at Hill 70, 25 Oct., '15.
TUCKER, FREDERICK CLAUDE, L/Cpl., R.W.S. Regt.
b., Seaforth, Liverpool,'93 ; *s.*, Mr. & Mrs. Tucker, 24 Albert Rd., S. Norwood. *Educ.*, Woodville Sch., Formby, and Birchanger Rd. Sch., S. Norwood. Single. Empl. in wine and spirit trade. *Enl.*, 9 Sept., '14. *Fell*, nr. Guillemont, Somme, 12 Aug., '16.

THE CROYDON ROLL OF HONOUR

TUCKER, REGINALD, Rflmn., Q.W. Rif. (16 Lond. Regt.)
  b., 13 Sept., '91 ; *s.*, Mr. & Mrs. John Leach Tucker, "Avonrath," Park Hill, Carshalton. *Educ.*, Whitgift Sch., '05-08. *Fell*, Flanders, 4 Dec., '14.

TULLETT, H., 14959, L/Cpl., E. Sur. Regt.
  Res., W. Croydon. *Fell*, '16.

TULLEY, J. R., Flight Sub-Lt., R.N.A.S.
  Educ., Whitgift G. Sch., Croydon. *Fell*, '17.

TURNER, ARTHUR, L/Cpl., 16 Middlesex Regt.
  Married ; 3 children. Empl. by Croydon Corp., Roads Dept. *Res.*, 37 Russell Rd., Croydon. *Enl.*, 9 Jun., '16. *Fell*, 1 Dec., '17.

TURNER, ERNEST HENRY, Pte., 1 E. Sur. Regt.
  b., Croydon, 15 Jul., '83 ; *s.*, Richard & Florence Turner, 71 Selhurst New Rd., S. Norwood. *Educ.*, Princess Rd. Sch., Croydon. Single. Painter. Served in India for 9 yrs. before war ; re-joined, Aug., '14. *Fell*, Hill 60, nr. Ypres, 12 Apr., '15.

TURNER, FREDERICK WALTER, Pte., 2/4 R.W.S. Regt.
  b., Arthur Square, Lond., 15 Aug., '98 ; *s.*, Mr. & Mrs. Turner, 34 Derby Rd., Croydon. *Educ.*, Par. Ch. Sch., Croydon. Single. Printer. *Enl.*, Oct., '14. *Fell*, Suvla Bay, Dardanelles, 9 Aug., '15.

TURNER, GEORGE JAMES, 201309, Pte., 3/4 R.W.S. Regt.
  b., Landells Rd., E. Dulwich, 15 Nov., '97 ; *s.*, Alfred James & Annie Elizabeth Turner, 78 Strathmore Rd., Croydon. *Educ.*, Sydenham Rd., Woodside, and Davidson Rd. Schs., Croydon. Single. Coal carter's boy. *Res.*, 26 Fullerton Rd., Addis. *Enl.*, in 2/4 R.W.S. Regt., 4 Nov., '14. *Fell*, nr. Peronne, 5 Jan., '18. *Buried*, Heudicourt.

TURNER, HARRY, Cpl., 2 R.W.S. Regt.
  b., Elm Rd., Croydon, 16 Apr., '84 ; *s.*, George Edward & Mary Ann Turner, 8 Talbot Rd., T. Heath. *Educ.*, Whitehorse Rd. Sch., T. Heath. Single. House decorator. *Enl.*, 2 Oct., '14 *Fell*, France, 2 Apr., '17.

TURNER, HERBERT, Rflmn., 6 Lond. Regt.
  b., 11 Talbot Rd., T. Heath, 30 Oct., '00 ; *s.*, George & Mary Ann Turner, 8 Talbot Rd., T. Heath. *Educ.*, Whitehorse Rd. Sch., T. Heath. Single. Grocer's asst. *Enl.*, 22 Oct., '17. *D.* of wounds in France, on or after 31 Aug., '18.

TURNER, J. H., Lt., R.W. Kent Regt.
  b., '93. Married e. daughter of Mr. & Mrs. Russell, " St. Abbs," S. Norwood. *Enl.* in W. Kent Yeom., '14 ; gazetted to R.W Kent Regt. ; served in France and Italy ; *w.*, Aug., '18. *D.* of wounds recd. in France, 21 Sept., '18.

TURNER, STANLEY, Pte., R.W.S. Regt.
  b., Croydon, 31 Dec., '90 ; *s.*, Mr. & Mrs. Turner, 31 Windmill Rd., Croydon. *Educ.*, Sydenham Rd. Sch., Croydon. Married. Ticket and show card writer. *Res.*, Howley Rd., Croydon. *Fell*, France, 12 May, '16.

TURNER, STANLEY THOMAS, Signaller, 16 K.R.R.C.
  b., Islington, 24 Jan., '97 ; *s.*, Frederick & Elizabeth Turner, 12 Seymour Place, S. Norwood. *Educ.*, Portland Rd. Sch., S. Norwood. Single. Grocer's asst. *Enl.*, 1 Jul., '15. *Fell*, France, 23 Apr., '17.

TURNER, THOMAS ALFORD, Lt., R.F.A.
  b., 10 Aug., '78 ; *s.*, Mr. & Mrs. Alfred William Turner, " Cambridge House," Canning Rd., Croydon. *Educ.*, Whitgift G. Sch., '93-96. *Fell*, '17.

XXXI.

1. Pte. E. TOURLÉ, 7 R. Fus.
2. Pte. S. E. WILKINS, Artists Rif.
3. Pte. A. TEGETMEIER, 2/13 Lond. Regt.
4. A.B. Seaman F. C. H. VOLZE, R.N.
5. Act.-Capt. J. G. WOOD, 2/5 S. Lancs. Regt
6. Signaller A. TAYLOR, M.M., R.H.A.

XXXII.

1. A. E. Williams, O.B.E., D.C.M., 2/17 Lond. Regt.
2. Lt. E. C. Hooton, R. Warwick. Regt.
3. Rflmn. H. R. Waterman, Queen's Westm. Rif.
4. Cpl. F. Halliday, M.M., 9 E. Sur. Regt.
5. Pte. F. W. G. Warren, 2/4 R.W.S. Regt.
6. Cpl. F. A. Wortley, 13 Aust. Imp. Forces

THE GLORIOUS DEAD

TURNER, THOMAS FREDERICK, Pte., R. Suss. Regt.
b., 110 Waddon New Rd., 21 Nov., '99 ; *2nd s.*, Mr. & Mrs. T. Turner, 2 Latimer Rd., Croydon. *Educ.*, Par. Ch. Sch., Croydon. Empl. by Messrs. Baines & Sons, dairymen. *Enl.* in R.F.A., 23 Nov., '17 ; went to France, being transf. to R. Suss. Regt., 13 Jun., '18. *D.* of wounds recd., 8 Aug., '18.

TURNER, WILLIAM ARTHUR FARNBOROUGH, Cpl., Gordon H.
b., '99 ; *e.s.*, Mr. & Mrs. Arthur Turner, 23 Beulah Cres., T.Heath. *Educ.*, St. Saviour's, & Beulah Rd. Schs., Croydon. *Enl.*, 27 Dec., '16 ; serving for 9 mths. with Q.W. Rif. ; went to France, 19 Feb., '18 ; *w. & gassed*, 28 Mar., '18 ; retd. to France, 14 Sept., '18. *Fell*, 13 Oct., '18.

TURNER, WILLIAM HENRY, Gnr., R.G.A.
b., Tunbridge Wells, 3 May, '90 ; *s.*, Frederick & Elizabeth Turner, 12 Seymour Place, S. Norwood. *Educ.*, St. Mark's Sch., City Rd., Lond., E.C. Single. Butcher. *Enl.*, 8 Oct.,14. *Fell*, Balkans, 24 Apr., '17.

TURRELL, A., 17670, Rflmn., R.B.
Res., Croydon. *Fell*, '17.

TURTLE, CLIFFORD LOUIS, 5833, Rflmn., Q.W. Rif. (2/16 Lond. Regt.)
b., Sheffield, 18 Apr., '91 ; *s.*, L. H. & Kate Turtle, " Homefield," Stafford Rd., Croydon. *Educ.*, Dulwich Coll. Single. Manager of tool and cutlery branch of L. H. Turtle, Ltd. *Enl.*, Feb., '16. *Fell*, Leuze Wood, nr. Combles, 10 Sept., '16. (Plate XXXVI., 1).

TUZO, JOHN ATKINSON, Capt., R. Suss. Regt.
b., '75 ; *s.*, late Henry Tuzo, M.D., & Mrs. Tuzo, Warlingham. *Educ.*, Whitgift G. Sch. *D.*, E. Africa, 8 Apr., '18.

TWENTYMAN, JOSEPH EDWARD, Pte., 17 R. Fus.
b., 102 Denmark St., Camberwell, '98. *Educ.*, Warner Rd. Sch., Camberwell. Single. Butcher. *Res.*, 49 Whitehorse Rd., Croydon. *Enl.*, 24 Jun., '15. *Fell*, Delville Wood, Somme, 27 Jul., '16.

TWORT, THOMAS WALTER, Pte., 2 R. Warwick. Regt.
b., '91 ; *s.*, Mr. & Mrs. W. Twort, 23 Benson Rd., Croydon. *D.* of wounds at Boulogne, 14 Nov., '14.

TYLER, EDWARD VICTOR, Pte., R.W.S. Regt.
b., Brockley, 7 Dec., '91 ; *s.*, Mr. & Mrs. M. Forrest, 32 Holland Rd., S. Norwood. Single. Groundsman on Golf Links. *Enl.*, 3 Sept., '14 ; M.M., Jul., '16. *D.*, 31 May, '17, at Lewisham Mil. Hosp., 23 Apr., '17. (Plate XXVIII., 6).

TYRRELL, JAMES WALTER, Driver, R.F.A.
b., '93 ; *s.*, Mr. & Mrs. Tyrrell, 24 Sandown Rd., S. Norwood. *Enl.*, 9 Sept., '14. *D.* of gas poisoning, 4 Aug., '17.

TYSON, WILLIAM, Pte., R.W. Kent Regt.
b., 16 Dec., '84. *Educ.*, Camberwell. Married. Omnibus conductor. *Res.*, 5 Newhaven Rd., S. Norwood, and Lambeth. *Enl.*, 5 Sept., '14 ; *w.*, Jan., '15, May, '15, & 17 Mar., '16. *Fell*, Somme, 25 Sept., '16.

UFFINDELL, HENRY LESTER, Pte., R. Warwick. Regt.
b., Gt. Alice St., City, 27 Dec., '86 ; *s.*, Mr. & Mrs. J. E. Uffindell, 79 Mitcham Rd., Croydon. *Educ.*, Brit. Sch., Croydon. Married. Asst. *Res.*, 2 High St., Purley. *Fell*, Ypres, 27 Aug., '17.

UFFINDELL, WILLIAM CHARLES, Pte., Beds. Regt.
b., Cock Tavern, Camberwell Green, 17 Jun., '80 ; *s.*, Mr. & Mrs. J. E. Uffindell, 79 Mitcham Rd., Croydon. *Educ.*, Brit. Sch., Croydon. Married. Manager. *Res.*, 129 Bensham Lane, Croydon. *Fell*, Ypres, 24 Aug., '17.

UNDERHILL, EDWARD SAMUEL, Capt., 8 L.N.L. Regt.
b., Croydon, 1 Jul., '95 ; s., Capt. Joseph Underhill (R.A.S.C.) & Mrs. Edith Sophia Underhill, " Egremont," Warlingham. *Educ.*, Whitgift G. Sch. Single. Student. *Enl.* as pte. in U.P.S. Bde. ; commis., 22 Sept., '14. *Fell*, Stuff Redoubt, nr. Thiepval, 12 Oct., '16. *Buried*, Ovillers Mil. Cem. (Plate XXIX., 5).

UNDERHILL, WILLIAM SAMUEL, Pte., Suff. Regt.
b., Pond House, Lower Clapton, 25 Feb., '81. *Educ.*, " Limes " Sch., Croydon, & Mill Hill Sch. Married. Memb. of, and authorized clerk on Stock Exchange. *Res.*, 16 Dornton Rd., Croydon. *Enl.*, 3 Jan., '16. *D.*, 25 Dec., '16., of septic poisoning at 3 C.C.S., Puchevillers, France.

UPTON, GAIS, Pte., R. Suss. Regt.
Married. Empl. by Messrs. Brown & Co., flour millers. *Res.*, Siddons Rd., Croydon. Memb. of Nat. Res. ; served in India and Africa. *Fell*, 18 Jun., '16.

UPTON, GEORGE, L/Cpl., 4 R. Irish Drag. Gds.
b., Northbrook Rd., Croydon, 10 Apr., '91 ; s., Mr. & Mrs. A. Upton, 4 Lahore Rd., Croydon. *Educ.*, Sydenham Rd. Sch., Croydon. Single. Carman, empl. by Messrs. Pickford. *Enl.*, 21 Oct., '11. *Fell*, Mons, 4 Sept., '14.

UTTON, KENNETH PIERRE, Pte., 2/4 R.W.S. Regt.
b., Hornsey, 27 Jul., '96 ; s., Mr. & Mrs. A. Pierre Utton, 71 Parchmore Rd., T. Heath. *Educ.*, Ecclesbourne Rd. Sch., and Boro. Sec. Sch., Croydon. Single. Clerk. *Enl.*, Oct., '14. *Fell*, Gallipoli, 18 Aug., '15.

VAUGHAN, CHARLES HENRY, 69692, Gnr., R.F.A. (attd. T.M.B.)
b., 179 Gloucester Rd., Croydon ; s., Mr. & Mrs. William Henry Vaughan, 157a Gloucester Rd., Croydon. *Educ.*, Sydenham Rd. Sch., Croydon. Single. Labourer. *Enl.*, 8 Feb., '15. *Fell*, N.E. of Ypres, Feb., '18.

VEDAST, ANGELO, Pte.
b., Italy, '00 ; s., Mr. & Mrs. Vedast, 15 Cherry Orch. Rd., Croydon. Motor engineer. *D.* of wounds recd. nr. Soissons, 3 Jun., '18.

VERDEN, GEORGE, A.B. Seaman, " Drake " Btn., 63 (R.N.) Div.
b., Croydon, '98 ; s., Mr. & Mrs. Verden, Thorpe Lane, Caywood Selby, Yorks. *Educ.*, Davidson Rd. Sch., Croydon. Single. *Res.*, Croydon. *Enl.*, '15. *D.* in Germany while pris. of war, 25 Mar., '18.

VERNER, GUY LANCELOT, 2/Lt., M.G.C.
b., '86 ; s., Mr. & Mrs. Ernest Verner, Shirley Glen, 23 Sunny Bank, S. Norwood. *Educ.*, King's Coll., Bruton. Manager of rubber plantation in Negri Sembilan. Commis. in 9 Suff. Regt., Dec., '14 ; transf. to M.G.C. *D.*, 27 Aug., '16, of wounds recd., Trones Wood, 26 Jul., '16.

VERNON, EDWARD JOSEPH, Pte., Civ. Serv. Rif. (1/15 Lond. Regt.)
b., 11 Carmichael Rd., S. Norwood, 20 Jul., '98 ; s., Joseph Benjamin & Elizabeth Vernon, 8 Oakley Rd., S. Norwood. *Educ.*, Birchanger Rd. Sch., S. Norwood. Single Clerk. *Enl.*, 17 Feb., '17. *Fell*, Cambrai, 30 Nov., '17.

VERRELL, FRANK, Sgt., R.E.
Empl. by Croydon Corp., at Mental Hosp. *D.* of wounds.

VERYARD, ALBERT T., Capt., Trench Mortar Bty.
b., '85. *Educ.*, Abp. Tenison's Sch., Croydon. *Fell*, France 28 Jun., '17.

VEYSEY, STANLEY, 2/Lt., R.G.A.
  b., Addis., 25 Apr., '90 ; s., Mr. & Mrs. Veysey, 39 Lr. Addis. Rd., Croydon. *Educ.*, M. Whitgift Sch., Croydon, Boro. Sec. Sch., Croydon, and Goldsmiths' Coll., S.E. Single. Asst. master, Ware St. Mary's Sch., Herts. ; represented Goldsmiths' Coll. at cricket, rugby & tennis. *Enl.* as pte. in 20 Lond. Regt., Aug., '14; served in France until Oct., '16, when he ret. to take up commis. ; ret. to France, Mar., '17. *Fell*, Flanders, 20 Sept., '17.

VIGUS, H., 19361, Pte., R.W. Kent Regt.
  b., '91. Married. Tobacconist and newsagent. *Res.*, West St., Croydon. *D.* of wounds, Jul., '17.

VINCENT, C. L., Lt., Can. Inf.
  s., Mr. & Mrs. J. Vincent, 5a Selhurst Rd., S. Norwood. *Res.*, Ontario. *Fell*, 22 Sept., '16.

VINCENT, STANLEY, Lt., R.A.S.C.
  Married ; 1 son. *Res.*, 231 Lond. Rd., T. Heath, & Sanderstead. Chief Insp. of Sanderstead Sub-Div., Special Constabulary, Aug., '14 ; joined Red Cross Amb., Sept., '15. *Enl.* in O.T.C., 1 Jan., '17 ; commis., 4 Mar., '17 ; appointed to Siege Bty. Column in France, Jun., '17 ; ret. to England with wounds and nerve strain ; appointed Comdg. Offr., No. 4 M.T. Examination Area, Leeds. *D.* of heart failure, Mar., '18.

VINE, A. J., 159592, Gnr., R.G.A.
  Res., Croydon. *Fell*, '17.

VINING, ERNEST GEORGE, Rflmn., Q.V.Rif. (9 Lond. Regt.)
  b., Croydon, 12 Jun., '89 ; s., late Thomas Isaac, & Elizabeth Maria Vining, 4 Bedford Pl., Bedford Pk., Croydon. *Educ.*, "Bestreben," and M. Whitgift Sch., Croydon. Single. Stationer's traveller. *Enl.*, 5 Aug., '14 ; went to France, 4 Nov., '14. *D.*, 9 Jun., '15, at Springburn Red Cross Hosp., Glasgow, of wounds recd. at Ypres, 29 Apr., '15.

VINTEN, T., 3421, Pte., R.W.S. Regt.
  Res., E. Croydon. *D.* of wounds, '16.

VIVYAN, ROBERT, E. Sur. Regt.
  Fell, '16.

VOICE, F. B., 51861, Pte., R. Fus.
  Res., T. Heath. *D.* of wounds, '17.

VOLLER, HERBERT EDWARD, Pte., R.A.S.C.
  Married. *Res.*, 26 Pawson's Rd., Croydon. *Fell*, 10 May, '17.

VOLZE, FREDERICK CHARLES HEDGES, A.B. Seaman, R.N.
  b., 29 Windmill Rd., Croydon, 9 Sept., '94 ; s., Mr. & Mrs. Volze, 79 Limes Rd., Croydon. *Educ.*, Sydenham Rd. Sch., Croydon. Single. Carpenter's asst. *Joined*, 5 Sept., '10. *Lost* with Submarine E30, 22 Nov., '16. (Plate XXXI., 4).

VORLEY, WILLIAM KENNETH, Pte., R.F.A.
  b., 23 Oct., '95 ; s., Mr. & Mrs. Henry Alfred Vorley, 23 Temple Rd., Croydon. *Educ.*, Whitgift G. Sch., '06-11. *D.* after an operation at Millbank Mil. Hosp., 30 Nov., '16.

WACHER, J. S., 2/Lt., R. W. Kent Regt.
  Fell, Sept., '16.

WADE, G. E. A., Lt., R.B.
  b., '94 ; e.s., Mr. & Mrs. G. E. A. Wade, " Lismore," Wellesley Rd., Croydon. *Enl.* as pte. in Artists Rif. *W. & missing*, France, 3 Apr., '17.

WADEY, –, Pte., R.W. Kent Regt.
  Fell, 14 Sept., '16.

WAGHORN, LIONEL, Pte., 1/22 R.W. Kent Regt.
b., Croydon, 19 Feb., '93 ; *s.*, William & Sarah Waghorn, 259 Lond. Rd., T. Heath. *Educ.*, M. Whitgift Sch., Croydon. Jeweller's asst. *Enl.*, 26 Sept., '16. *D.*, 55 C.C.S., Dernancourt, France, 2 Sept., '18.

WAINWRIGHT, WILLIAM THOMAS, Pte., 12 Middlesex Regt.
b., S. Norwood, 23 Aug., '97 ; *s.*, George & Annie Wainwright, 63a Portland Rd., S. Norwood. *Educ.*, M. Whitgift Sch. Joiner. *Enl.*, Sept., '15, in 3 Lond. Yeom. *Fell*, Cherisy, 3 May, '17. (Plate XXX., 2).

WAKEFORD, H. L., 37985, Gnr., R.G.A.
s., late Henry, & Mrs. Wakeford, 10 Clarendon Rd., Croydon. Served 3 yrs. in S. China, and came to England, 5 Nov., '16 ; went to France at end of Feb. following. *Fell*, 7 Jul., '17.

WAKERELL, LEONARD, Pte., Welsh Regt.
b., '81 ; *y.s.*, Mr. & Mrs. Wakerell, S. Croydon. *Educ.*, Bynes Rd. Sch., Croydon, & Abp. Tenison's Sch., Croydon. Driver, Croydon Corp. Tramways. Married. *Enl.*, 3 Nov., '15. *Fell*, France, 23 Aug., '18.

WALES, H., 1384, Pte., R.W.S. Regt.
Res., Croydon. *Fell*, Nov., '16.

WALKER, ALFRED JOHN, Pte., 2/5 Sherwood For. (Notts. & Derby. Regt.)
b., Ely Rd., Croydon, 24 Jul., '86. *Educ.*, Sydenham Rd. Sch., Croydon. Married. Painter. *Res.*, 41 Sidney Rd., S. Norwood. *Enl.*, 24 Aug., '16 ; gassed, 4 Oct., '17. *Fell*, west of Kemmel, Belgium, 16 Apr., '18.

WALKER, CHARLES JOSEPH, Pte., R. Suss. Regt.
Empl. by Croydon Corp., at Mental Hosp. *D.* of wounds.

WALKER, HERBERT AUGUSTUS, Pte., L.R.B. (5 Lond. Regt.)
b., Croydon, 25 Jun., '– ; *s.*, Mr. & Mrs. Walker, 21 Greenside Rd., Croydon. *Educ.*, Croydon. Married. Draper. *Res.*, Leigh-on-Sea, Essex. *Enl.*, May, '15. *Fell*, France, 17 Jun., '17.

WALKER, J., 71004, Cpl., R.F.A.
Fell, Aug., '17.

WALLACE, A. J., Armourer's mate, R.N.
b., '95 ; *s.*, Mr. & Mrs. Alfred Wallace, 3 Sussex Rd., S. Croydon. *Enl.*, '12. *Lost* with H.M.S. "Vanguard," destroyed by internal explosion, Scapa Flow, '17.

WALLACE, JAMES ROBERT, Pte., M.G.C.
b., '90 ; *e.s.*, James & Caroline Wallace, 85 Ferry Rd., Cardiff. *Educ.*, Par. Ch. Sch., Croydon, *Enl.* in 11 Hussars, '08. Served in India, '09-14, France, '14-16, Mesopotamia (in M.G.C.), '16-18. *Drowned*, while crossing Tigris, 28 Oct., '18.

WALLER, CHARLES DAVID, Rflmn., Q.W. Rif. (16 Lond. Regt.)
b., 20 Dec., '93 ; *s.*, Mr. & Mrs. David Waller, "Ferndene," 10 Warrington Rd., Croydon. *Educ.*, Whitgift G. Sch. Master builder. *Enl.*, 28 Aug., '14. *Fell*, Gommecourt, France, 1 Jul., '16.

WALLIS, CHARLES FREDERICK, Rflmn., Artists Rif. (28 Lond. Regt.)
b., "Rembrandt Lodge," Spencer Rd., Croydon, 30 Dec., '91 ; *s.*, Mr. & Mrs. Walter Wallis, "Rembrandt Lodge," 20 Spencer Rd., Croydon. *Educ.*, Elmhurst Sch., Croydon, Croydon Sch. of Art, & Royal Academy Schs., Lond. Single. Art student. *Enl.*, Nov., '15. *D.* of wounds recd. at Bullecourt, France, 29 Aug., '18. Buried nr. Bullecourt. (Plate XXX., 5).

WALLIS, G., 632957, Lond. Regt.
Res., Mitcham. *Fell*, Aug., '17.

WALLIS, J., 7023, Cpl., K.R.R.C.
Res., Croydon. *Fell*, Jul., '17.

THE GLORIOUS DEAD

WALLIS, R., Pte., 1 Artists Rif.
b., '78. Married; 3 children. *Res.*, 25 Selhurst New Rd., S. Norwood. *Enl.* in S.W.B., May, '15. *D.* of wounds, France, 30 Sept., '18.

WALTER, BENJAMIN, 2 Worcester Regt.
Educ., Shirley Sch., Wickham Rd., Croydon. *Enl.*, Dec., '05. *Fell*, 11 Dec., '14.

WALTER, BERT.
b., '97. *Fell*, 8 Aug., '16.

WALTER, DAISY ALICE.
b., '92. *Res.*, 73 Stretton Rd., Croydon. *Killed* during Zeppelin raid, Oct., '15.

WALTER, ELIZA H.
b., '63. *Res.*, 73 Stretton Rd., Croydon. *Killed* during Zeppelin raid, Oct., '15.

WALTER, SIDNEY AMOR.
b., '00. *Res.*, 73 Stretton Rd., Croydon. *Killed* during Zeppelin raid, Oct., '15.

WALTER, FREDERICK CHARLES, Bdr., R.F.A.
b., Gloucester Rd., Croydon, 13 Oct., 92; *s.*, Mr. & Mrs. Walter, 7 Selhurst New Rd., S. Norwood. *Educ.*, Sydenham Rd. Sch., Croydon. Carman. *W.* in France. *Accidentally drowned* in Mesopotamia, 4 Mar., '17. (Plate II., 2).

WALTER, J. B., L/Cpl., R. Berks. Regt.
Fell, Sept., '16.

WALTER, JOSEPH STANLEY, Capt., 7 R.W.S. Regt.
b., W. Norwood, 10 Sept., '89; *s.*, Mr. & Mrs. Walter, 139 Albert Rd., Croydon. *Educ.*, Whitgift G. Sch., Croydon. Single. Traveller. *Res.*, Albert Rd., Croydon. *Enl.* as pte. in Inns of Court O.T.C., 10 Sept., '14; went to France, Jul., '15; taken prisoner, 19 Nov., '16. M.C., 20 Oct., '16. *Killed* while attempting to escape from the pris. of war camp at Bad Colberg, Germany. (Plate XXXV., 5).

WALTERS, FREDERICK, Pte., 6 Lond. Regt.
b., Croydon, 22 Sept., '97; *s.*, Mr. & Mrs. W. Walters, 51 Waddon New Rd., Croydon. *Educ.*, Brit. Sch., Croydon. Film manufacturer. *Enl.*, Mar., '15. *Fell*, France, 5 Oct., '16. (Plate XXIX., 4).

WALTERS, W. G., 9124, L/Cpl., R. Suss. Regt.
Res., Croydon. *Fell*, Oct., '16.

WALTON, E. W., 25610, E. Sur. Regt.
Res., Sutton. *Fell*, Jul., '17.

WALTON, F., 15912, Pte., E. Sur. Regt.
Res., S. Croydon. *Fell*, Jul., '16.

WALTON, LEONARD, L/Cpl., Gren. Gds.
b., '92; *s.*, Mr. & Mrs. Walton, Wentworth Rd., Croydon. *Enl.*, '12 (?). *Drowned* by overturning of canal barge during embarkation, 2 Feb., '18.

WALTON, WILLIAM JOHN, Rflmn., R.B.
b., Frith Rd., Croydon, 29 Nov., —. *Educ.*, Mitcham Rd. Sch., Croydon. Married. Labourer. *Res.*, 26 Cromwell Rd., Croydon. *Enl.*, 30 Apr., '15. *Fell*, France, 3 Sept., '16.

WARD, ALAN DUDLEY WALTER, 2/Lt., R.W.S. Regt.
b., '95; *s.*, Mr. & Mrs. F. W. Ward, "Homelea," Coombe Rd., Croydon; grandson of founder of "Croydon Advertiser." *Educ.*, privately. Journalist on staff of "Croydon Advertiser." *Enl.* in Inns of Court O.T.C., Sept., '14; commis., Jan., '15; *w.*, Somme, Jul., '16. *D.* of trench fever, Rouen, 23 Jul., '17.

WARD, J., Pte., R.W.S. Regt.
Married. *Res.*, Priory Rd., Croydon. *Enl.*, '15. *Fell*, 1 Jul., '16.

WARD, JOHN ROBERT, Pte.
b., Addis., 24 Aug., '93 ; *s.*, George & Charlotte Ward. *Educ.*, Sydenham Rd. Sch., Croydon, & St. Peter's Sch., Croydon. Railway porter. Married. *Res.*, 36 Sussex Rd., Croydon. *Enl.* about 14 Aug., '14. *D.* of wounds at 1 C.C.S., France, 27 Jan., '15.

WARD, RICHARD, Shoeing Smith, R.F.A.
b., '87. Married ; 4 children. *Res.*, 5 Union St., Croydon. Knocked down by taxi-cab in Rouen, 27 Oct., '18, and *died* the following day.

WARD, SYDNEY HERBERT, Sgt., 1 Border Regt.
b., Croydon, 24 May, '86 ; *s.*, Mr. & Mrs. J. Ward, 90 Tamworth Rd., Croydon. *Educ.*, Par. Ch. Sch., Croydon. Carman. *Res.*, Waddon New Rd., Croydon. *Enl.*, 27 Nov., '06. *Fell*, Dardanelles, 26 Aug., '15.

WARD, W., Cpl., R.W.S. Regt.
Fell, Dec., '16.

WAREHAM, HAROLD, P.O., R.N.A.S., Armoured Car Div.
b., S. Norwood, 17 Dec., '83 ; *s.*, Mr. & Mrs. Frederick W. Wareham, 268 Portland Rd., S. Norwood. *Educ.*, St. Michael's Sch., Woodside. Violinist. *Res.*, 26 Blackhorse Lane, Addis. *Enl.*, 18 Nov., '14. *D.* of dysentery, St. George's Mil. Hosp., Malta, 1 Oct., '15.

WAREHAM, STANLEY B., Cpl., Can. F.A.
b., 1 Nov., '86 ; *s.*, Mr. & Mrs. Fred. W. Wareham, 268 Portland Rd., S. Norwood. *Educ.*, St. Michael's Sch., Woodside. Single. Clerk. *Res.*, Toronto. *Enl.*, Aug., '14. M.M. *Fell*, N. Russia, 14 Nov., '18.

WARNER, A. H., 2849, Pte., Lond. Regt.
Res., Selhurst. *Fell*, Sept., '16.

WARNER, ARCHIBALD, 2/Lt., L.R.B. (5 Lond. Regt.)
b., Waddon, 13 Feb., '84 ; *s.*, John, & late Alice Warner, Waddon House, Croydon. *Educ.*, "The Limes," Croydon., Whitgift G. Sch., Croydon, Leighton Pk Sch., Reading, & Queen's Coll., Camb. Married. Solicitor. *Res.*, "Penarth," Carshalton. *Enl.* as pte. in Artists Rif., 4 Jun., '15. *Fell*, Gommecourt, France, 1 Jul., '16. (Plate XXXV., 1).

WARNER, BERT W., A.B. Seaman, R.N.
Educ., Caterham Hill Council Sch. *Lost* with H.M.S. "Bulwark," destroyed by internal explosion, Sheerness, 26 Oct., '14.

WARNER, BERTRAM, 2/Lt., L.R.B. (5 Lond. Regt.)
b., Waddon, 19 Apr., '88 ; *s.*, John, & late Alice Warner, Waddon House, Croydon. *Educ.*, "The Limes," Croydon, & Reading Sch., Reading. Agriculturist. *Res.*, Sedgeberrow, nr. Evesham. *Enl.* as pte. in 8 Worcester Regt., 8 Aug., '14 ; commis., Sept., '16 *Fell* nr. Arras, 12 Apr., '17. (Plate XXIX., 1).

WARNER, EVAN, Sgt., L.R.B. (5 Lond. Regt.)
b., Waddon, 25 Nov., '80 ; *s.*, John, & late Alice Warner, Waddon House, Croydon. *Educ.*, "The Limes," Croydon, & Whitgift G Sch., Croydon. Manager for wharfingers. *Enl.*, 3 Mar., '04. *Fell*, Flanders, 11 Dec., '14. (Plate XXXIII., 5).

WARNER, FREDERICK LEONARD, 6020, Pte., 25 Middlesex Regt.
b., 98 Holmesdale Rd., S. Norwood, 23 Apr., '75 ; 3rd *s.*, Alfred, and late Jessie Keturah Warner, 30 Princess Rd., S. Norwood. *Educ.*, Brit. Sch., Croydon. Single. Optician. *Res.*, 30 Princess Rd., S. Norwood. *Enl.* in R. Fus., Mar., '16. *Fell*, Le Transloy, Oct., '16. *Buried* by 5 Scottish Rif.

THE GLORIOUS DEAD

WARNER, HENRY JAMES, 2/Lt., 6 Northants. Regt.
b., Derby Rd., Croydon, 9 Sept., '86 ; *s.*, Mr. & Mrs. William J. Warner, 80 Oakfield Rd., Croydon. *Educ.*, Whitgift G. Sch., Croydon. Single. Commercial clerk. *Res.*, 35 Oakfield Rd., Croydon. *Enl.* as pte. in Artists Rif., 29 Nov., '15. *Fell*, nr. Cherisy, France, 3 Jun., '17.

WARREN, A., 4578, Pte., K.R.R.C.
Res., Croydon. *Fell*, Sept., '16.

WARREN, E., R. Suss. Regt.
Res., T. Heath. *Fell*, Sept., '17.

WARREN, E., 22486, E. Sur. Regt.
Res., Croydon. *Fell*, Sept., '17.

WARREN, FREDERICK WILLIAM GERALD, Pte., 2/4 R.W.S. Regt.
b., Sandy, Bedfordshire, 30 Jun., '98 ; *s.*, Fred & Alice Warren, 4 Fernham Rd., T. Heath. *Educ.*, Par. Ch. Sch., Croydon, and Winterbourne Rd. Sch., T. Heath. Stencil cutter. *Enl.*, 17 May, '15. *Fell*, White Hill, Zambia, Palestine, 21 Dec., '17. *Buried*, Mt. of Olives Cem., Jerusalem. (Plate XXXII., 5).

WARRENDER, A. R., Stoker, R.N.
Empl. by Croydon Corp., at Mental Hosp. *Lost*, with H.M.S. " Cressy," 22 Sept., '14.

WARRENS, ERIC KENELM, L/Cpl., 16 Middlesex Regt.
b., Sydenham, 30 Nov., '97 ; *s.*, H. L. & A. G. Warrens, 1 Addis. Grove, Croydon. *Educ.*, Whitgift G. Sch., Croydon. Single. Clerk. *Enl.*, 5 Jan., '15. *D.*, 6 Jul., '16, on 26 Amb. Train, of wounds recd. at Beaumont Hamel, Somme, 1 Jul., '16. *Buried* at Etretat, 8 Jul., '16.

WARWICK, H., 46841, Gnr., R.F.A.
Res., Shirley. *Fell*, Jul., '16.

WASHINGTON, WILLIAM JOHN, Pte., R.W. Kent Regt.
b., Clapham, 22 Feb., '91. *Educ.*, Kingswood Rd., Brixton Hill. Married. Solicitor's clerk. *Res.*, 44 Mersham Rd., T. Heath. *Enl.*, 12 Apr., '16. *Fell*, France, 7 Oct., '-.

WATERMAN, GUY, Rflmn., Q.W. Rif. (16 Lond. Regt.)
b., 125 Moffatt Rd., T. Heath, 24 Mar., '93 ; *e.s.*, Horace & Janet Waterman, 27 Grange Pk. Rd., T. Heath. *Educ.*, Beulah Rd. Sch., T. Heath. Married, Ethel, *d.* of Mr. & Mrs. Knight, 19 Parchmore Rd., T. Heath. Boot salesman. *Enl.*, 5 Jul., '15. *Fell*, St. Jean, France, 11 Sept., '17. (Plate XXXV., 2).

WATERMAN, HORACE RAYMOND, Rflmn., Q.W. Rif. (16 Lond. Regt.)
b., 125 Moffatt Rd., T. Heath, 7 Apr., '94 ; *y.s.*, Horace & Janet Waterman, 27 Grange Pk. Rd., T. Heath. *Educ.*, Beulah Rd. Sch., T. Heath, and Stanley Tech. Trade Sch., S. Norwood. Artist. *Enl.*, 5 Dec., '15. *Fell* nr. Vimy Ridge, 23 Sept., '16. (Plate XXXII., 3).

WATSON, H. C., L/Cpl., R.W.Kent Regt.
Married. Empl. by Croydon Corp. *Res.*, 15 Boston Rd., Croydon. *Enl.*, 21 Dec., '14. *Fell*, 22 Jul., '16.

WATSON, KEITH RUSSELL, Cpl., 7 R. Fus.
b., Waltham Cross, Herts., 7 Sept., '98 ; *s.*, Rev. & Mrs. F. Russell Watson, Wesley Manse, Derby Rd., Woodford. *Educ.*, Kingswood Sch., Bath. Single. Empl. by Messrs. Hollington Bros., wholesale clothiers. *Res.*, 8 Elgin Rd., Croydon. *Enl.*, Dec., '15. *Fell*, nr. Cambrai, 29 Sept., '18.

WATSON, WILLIAM GEORGE, 2/4 R.W.S. Regt.
b., Camden Town, '86 ; *s.*, Mr. & Mrs. Watson, 66 Parson's Mead, Croydon. *Educ.*, Brit. Sch., Croydon. Married. Coachman. *Res.*, 17 Mint Walk, Croydon. *Enl.*, Apr., '15. *Missing*, Dardanelles, 9 Aug., '16.

WATT, GEORGE HERBERT, Master, Mercantile Marine.
WATT, JOHN FRANK, Sgt., Beds. Regt.
  s., Mr. & Mrs. Watt, 45 Oakfield Rd., Croydon. Married.
  Fell, Beaumont Hamel, France, 13 Nov., '16.
WATTS, AUGUSTINE CUTHBERT, 301796, Rflmn., L.R.B. (5 Lond. Regt.)
  b., Croydon, 21 Oct., '97; s., Albert L. & Mary Watts, 12
  Mansfield Rd., Croydon. *Educ.*, Coloma House, Croydon, and
  Modern Sch., Croydon. Commercial clerk. *Enl.*, 1 Sept., '15.
  Fell, probably at Les Bœufs, France, 8 Oct., '16.
WAYTE, SAMUEL WILFRID, 2/Lt., 103 Bde., R.F.A.
  b., Croydon, '95; s., Dr. & Mrs. Wayte, Park Lane, Croydon.
  Educ., King's Sch., Canterbury. Single. *Joined* Inns of Court
  O.T.C., '16; commis., '17; M.C., Sept., '17; w. *D.*, Oct., '17,
  at 2 C.C.S., Bailleul, of wounds recd. nr. Ypres.
WEALD, LEONARD J., Pte., D.L.I.
  b., '85. Married. Butcher. *Res.*, 14 Gilsland Rd., T. Heath.
  Enl., 17 Aug., '16. *Fell*, 26 Jun., '17.
WEATHERLEY, G. F., 1143, R. Fus.
  Fell, Jul., '16.
WEBB, JAMES, Sgt.
  Fell, Festubert, 16 May, '15.
WEBB, LOUIS VICTOR, Lt., 1/1 Gurkha Rif.
  b., 21 Lr. Addis. Rd., Croydon, 24 Jul., '94; e.s., Mr. & Mrs.
  Webb, 21 Lr. Addis. Rd., Croydon. *Educ.*, Coloma House,
  Croydon, & St. Joseph's Coll., W. Norwood. Commercial
  traveller. *Enl.* as pte. in R.W.S. Regt., Aug., '14. *D.*, 10 Jan.,
  '17, of wounds recd. in Mesopotamia prev. day.
WEBB, SIDNEY E., 798, L/Cpl., R.F.A.
  s., Mr. & Mrs. Webb, 28 Pridham Rd. E., T. Heath. *Educ.*,
  Whitehorse Rd. Sch., T. Heath. Cinematograph operator.
  D. in hosp. in France, from jaundice, 22 Aug., '17.
WEBB, THOMAS HENRY, Pte., R.W. Kent Regt.
  b., Croydon, 10 Jan., '93; s., Mr. & Mrs. Webb, 75 Rymer Rd.,
  Addis. *Educ.*, Oval Rd. Sch., Croydon. Single. Motor
  body builder. *Enl.*, Sept., '14. *Fell*, France, 3 Jul., '16.
WEBSTER, C., 25640, Pte., E. Sur. Regt.
  Res., T. Heath. *Fell*, Dec., '16.
WEITZMANN, CECIL GOTHET, 2/Lt., S. Staff. Regt.
  s., Mr. & Mrs. G. H. Weitzmann, "Miraflor," U. Norwood.
  Commis., 25 Sept., '15. *Fell*, France, Sept., '15.
WELLER, JOHN CHARLES, Pte., 4 Beds. Regt.
  b., '99; s., Mr. & Mrs. Weller, 175 Gloucester Rd., Croydon.
  Educ., Tavistock Rd. Sch., Croydon. *Enl.* when 16 yrs. of age,
  and claimed by parents. Re-joined at age of 18. *Fell*, France,
  9 Nov., '18.
WELLS, WALTER ARTHUR, Pte., 17 R. Fus.
  b., 30 Mar., '86, Southbridge Pl., Croydon; s., Mr. & Mrs.
  Wells, 65 Exeter Rd., Addis. *Educ.*, St. Andrew's
  Sch., Croydon. Married. Waiter. *Res.*, 61 Edward Rd.,
  Addis. *Enl.*, 8 Jun., '15. *D.* of wounds, France, 2 Aug., '15.
WELLS, WALTER JOHN, Pte., 18 Lancs. Fus.
  b., 24 Jun., '99; e.s., Mr. & Mrs. Wells, Sibthorpe Rd., Mitcham.
  Educ., Upper Mitcham Sch. *Enl.*, 24 Jun., '17. *Fell*, 1 Jun., '18.
WELLSON, D., 612149, Gnr., R.H.A.
  Res., S. Croydon. *Fell*, Jun., '17.
WELSBY, SYDNEY J., L/Cpl., R.B.
  b., '85; s., Mr. & Mrs. Welsby, 135 St. Peter's St., Croydon.
  Educ., Abp. Tenison's Sch., Croydon. Married; 1 son.
  Res., 108 Fairholme Rd., Croydon. *Fell*, 24 Aug., '18.

XXXIII.

1. Pte. F. WHITE, 13 R. Fus.
2. Rflmn. H. H. WILLSHER, King's R.R.C.
3. Rflmn. H. E. WILLIAMS, Lond. Rif. B.
4. Sgt. J. H. WORTLEY, D.C.M., Lond. Rif. B.
5. Sgt. E. WARNER, Lond. Rif. B.
6. 2/Lt. L. G. WEST, Lond. Rif. B.

XXXIV.

1. Capt. H. T. WHYBROW, Motor Machine Gun Corps
2. Driver A. E. WILLS, 311 Bde., R.F.A.
3. 2/Lt. P. J. WILLIAMS, R. Berks. Regt.
4. L/Cpl. E. T. WHITE, 17 R. Fus.
5. Trooper A. J. WHEATLAND, Sur. Yeom.
6. L/Cpl. E. J. H. WHITE, D.C.M., Machine Gun Corps

THE GLORIOUS DEAD

WENHAM, A., 16252, E. Sur. Regt.
Fell, Nov., '16.
WEST, ALBERT, Sadler, R.F.A.
b., S. Norwood, Aug., '96 ; *s.*, Mr. & Mrs. A. M. West, 90 Watcombe Rd., S. Norwood. *Educ.*, Birchanger Rd. Sch., S. Norwood. Single. Boot finisher. *Res.*, 63 Apsley Rd., S. Norwood. *Enl.*, Jun., '15. *Fell*, Ypres, 12 Jul., '17.
WEST, CHARLES A., 1480, Pte., 7 R.W.S. Regt.
Educ., Ingram Rd. Sch., T. Heath. *Fell*, 11 Oct., '15.
WEST, GEORGE FREDERICK, Pte., R. Fus.
b., 15 Tamworth Pl., 17 Jul., '94 ; *s.*, Mr. & Mrs. H. West, 22 Southsea Rd., Croydon. *Educ.*, Mitcham Rd. Sch., Croydon. Wharfman. *Res.*, 22 Southsea Rd., Croydon. *Enl.*, 1 Apr., '16. *Fell*, Arras, 9 Apr., '17.
WEST, J., Rflmn., L.R.B. (5 Lond. Regt.)
b., '97 ; *y.s.*, Mr. & Mrs. West, 5 Cameron Rd., Croydon. *Educ.*, Modern Sch., Croydon. Insurance clerk. *Enl.*, Apr., '15 ; *w.*, Gaudecourt, France, Jul., '16. *Fell*, 9 Oct., '16.
WEST, LESLIE GOWER, 2/Lt., L.R.B. (5 Lond. Regt.)
b., Sutton, 12 Oct., '98 ; *s.*, Mr. & Mrs. R. H. West, " Haslemere," 109 Brigstock Rd., T. Heath. *Educ.*, T. Heath High Sch., and at Bapaume, Pas-de-Calais. Clerk. *Enl.* as pte., 3 Mar., '17. *Fell*, S. of Antoine, France, 24 Oct., '18. (Plate XXXIII , 6).
WEST, WILLIAM, Seaman, R.N.
b., '96 ; *2nd s.* Mr. & Mrs. Albert West, 118 Livingstone Rd., T. Heath. Empl. at offices of " Norwood News." *Lost* when H.M.S. " Champagne " was torpedoed, about 16 Oct., '17.
WEST, WILLIAM, 2/Lt., 9 Sher. For.
b., " Sherwood," Dingwall Av., Croydon, 6 Feb., '95 ; *s.*, William West, Councillor, County Boro. of Croydon, & Lillian West, daughter of William Spowage, of Sherwood Rise, Nottingham. *Educ.*, Whitgift G. Sch., '04-14, where he won Eastty Cup, '13-14 ; played football for sch., '10-14 ; capt. of his House ; sgt. in Sch. O.T.C., and shot in the Bisley team for the Ashburton '11-12-14, winning Banks' Cup, '14. *Commis.*, 26 Sept., '14 ; trained at Belton Pk., Grantham, & Frensham ; left Eng. with 11 Div., 1 Jul., '15, for Mediterranean E.F., in Gallipoli ; *w.*, Achi Baba, 26 Jul., '15 ; re-joined btn., 1 Aug., '15 ; took part in Suvla Bay landing, 6-7 Aug., '15, landing with his btn. on beach, S. of Lala Baba. *Fell*, nr. Biyuk Anafarta, 9 Aug., '15. *Buried*, Azmac Dere Cem., Suvla. (Plate I., 3).
WESTALL, W. H., 30383, Sgt., 61 M.G.C.
s., Mr. & Mrs. Westall, Keeper's Cottage, Selsdon Pk., Croydon. *Fell*, Mar., '18.
WESTBROOK, JOHN MERVYN, Rflmn., attd. R. Irish Rif.
b., Croydon, 11 May, '97 ; *s.*, Mr. & Mrs. John Westbrook, 7 Warrington Rd., Croydon. *Educ.*, M. Whitgift Sch. Bank clerk. *Enl.* in 1 L.R.B., May, '16. *Fell*, Ypres, 10 Mar., '17.
WESTON, FREDERIC GEORGE, Coy.Sgt.Maj., Q.W. Rif. (16 Lond. Regt.)
b., Whickham, co. Durham, 8 Jun., '85 ; *3rd s.*, John & Mary Weston, Whitley Bay, Northumberland. *Educ.*, Gateshead, Liverpool Univ., & Goldsmith's Coll., Lond. Univ. Married ; 2 children. Schoolmaster. *Res.*, 2 Beechwood Av., T. Heath. Territorial since '05. Ment. in despat. *Fell*, nr. Bullecourt, 28 Aug., '18.
WESTRUP, LEONARD, 200599, Pte., 1/4 R.W.S. Regt.
b., '90 ; *s.*, Mr. & Mrs. Westrup, 32 Oval Rd., Croydon. *Enl.*, Aug., '14 ; served Persian Gulf, and India, Oct., '14-Nov., '18. *D.* from influenza & pneumonia, 11 Nov., '18. *Buried*, Dalhousie.

THE CROYDON ROLL OF HONOUR

WHEAT, FREDERICK, Armourer Sgt., R.A.O.C.
b., Nottingham, 7 Mar., '76 ; *s.*, late John & Lucy Wheat; Nottingham. *Educ.*, Nottingham. Married. Adding machine mechanic. *Res.*, 59 Albert Rd., S. Norwood. *Enl.*, 16 Aug., '16, attd. first, Glasgow Yeom., & later 9 M.G. Squadron, 1 Can. Div. *Killed* by bomb from aeroplane, nr. Le Cateau, 8 Oct., '18. *Buried*, Prospect Hill Brit. Cem., Gouy.

WHEATLAND, ALBERT JOSEPH, 40078, Trooper, Sur. Yeom.
b., '93 ; *y.s.*, late Edmund, & Mrs. Wheatland, 11 Rolleston Rd., Croydon. *Educ.*, Brighton Rd. Sch., Croydon. Empl. at Streatham Garage. *Enl.*, 30 Oct., '15 ; attd., R.W.S. Regt. *Fell*, France, 7 Jun., '17. (Plate XXXIV., 5).

WHEATLEY, J. A., 207033, R.W.S. Regt.
Res., T. Heath. *Fell*, Oct., '17.

WHEELER, JOHN, Pte.
b., High St., Sidcup, Kent, 21 Aug., '92 ; *s.*, Mr. & Mrs. John J. Wheeler, 95 Norbury Crescent, Norbury. *Educ.*, Oval Rd. Sch., Croydon. Grocer. *Res.*, 3 Welford's Parade, London Rd., Norbury. *Enl.*, 1 Jul., '16. *Fell* nr. Fresnoy Wood, N.E. of Arras, 8 May, '17.

WHIBLEY, RICHARD EDWARD ELLIS, Sur. Yeom.
b., '97. *D.* in hosp., Chatham, Dec., '15, from wounds.

WHICKER, FREDERICK PAUL, Lt., Lond. Regt.
b., Sydenham, '98 ; *e.s*, Mr. & Mrs. J. Whicker, of Union ot Lond. & Smith's Bank, S. Norwood Branch. *Educ.*, Sydenham High Sch., & St. Dunstan's Coll., Catford. Bank clerk. *Enl.*, Inns of Court O.T.C., 20 Sept., '15 ; commis., 9 Jul., '16. *Fell*, 5 Apr., '18.

WHISSON, WILLIAM HENRY, Lt., Middlesex Regt.
b., 19 Mar., '96 ; *e.s.*, Mr. & Mrs. W. H. Whisson, 25 Arundel Rd., Croydon. *Educ.*, M. Whitgift Sch., Croydon. *Enl.*, Apr., '13, in Lond. Scottish, going to France, 15 Sept., '14 ; *w.*, Messines, 31 Oct., '14 ; commis., Aug., '15 ; ret. to front, 24 Oct., '16 ; M.C. *D.* of wounds, in 41 C.C.S., 6 May, '17.

WHITAKER, GEORGE, Act.-Capt., Lond. Regt.
b., '92 ; *s.*, Mr. & Mrs. George Whitaker, 2 Albemarle Mans., Kingsway, Hove, formerly of "Ravenswood," Croydon. *Educ.*, Whitgift G. Sch. *Fell*, 20 Sept., '17.

WHITBREAD, WILLIAM, Pte., S.W.B.
b., '87 ; *e.s.*, Mr. & Mrs. S. Whitbread, 16 Wentworth Rd., Croydon. *Educ.*, Boston Rd. Sch., Croydon. Married ; 1 son. *Served* some yrs. in Territorials. *Enl.*, in R.E., 1 Jun., '16. *Fell*, 10 Nov., '17.

WHITE, ARTHUR BRYAN, Capt., 1 L.R.B. (5 Lond. Regt.)
b., '89 ; *y.s.*, Mr. & Mrs. Will White, "Glenthorne," Birdhirst Rise, Croydon. *Educ.*, St. Paul's Sch., & International Coll., Geneva. Accountant. *Enl.* (Territorials) '06 ; went to France as sgt., 4 Nov., '14 ; commis., Feb., '15 ; *w.* twice ; ment. in despat., Apr., '17. *Fell*, 16 Aug., '17.

WHITE, CECIL JAMES LAWRENCE, 302258, Rflmn., L.R.B. (5 Lond. Regt.)
b., 55 Finsbury Pk. Rd., 9 Jun., '83. *Educ.*, City of Lond. Sch., Victoria Embankment. Married. Underwriter's clerk. *Res.*, Apsley House, Surbiton Crescent, Surrey. Freeman of City of Lond. *Enl.*, 29 Nov., '15. *Fell*, Metz-en-Couture, 23 Mar., '18. *Buried*, Metz Sugar Refinery.

WHITE, ERNEST TOMAS " JACK," L/Cpl., 17 R. Fus.
b., Ancaster Rd., Elmers End, Beckenham, 3 Sept., '95 ; *s.*, Ernest & Alice White, "Ivydene," 10 Windermere Rd., Addis. *Educ.*, St. James's Ch. Sch., Elmers End. Dairyman. *Enl.*, 8 Dec., '14. *Fell*, France, 27 Jul., '17. (Plate XXXIV., 4).

THE GLORIOUS DEAD

WHITE, FREDERICK, Pte., 13 R. Fus.
    b., 40 Beulah Grove, Croydon, Apr., '84 ; s., late Mr. White, & Mrs. Orr, 38 Beulah Grove, Croydon. *Educ.*, Sydenham Rd. Sch., Croydon. Married. Stage manager. *Res.*, 38 Beulah Grove, Croydon. *Fell*, 10-11 Apr., '17. Buried nr. Orange Hill, E.S.E. of Arras and S.W. of Hampoux. (Plate XXXIII., 1).

WHITE, GEORGE, Cpl., 2 Drag. Gds.
    b., '88. Married. *Res.*, 82 Beulah Grove, Croydon. *Enl.*, about '08. *Fell*, 30 Mar., '18.

WHITE, WALTER WILLIAM, Coy.Sgt.Maj., 9 E. Sur. Regt.
    b., Tooting, 8 Jul., '73. Married. Warehouseman. *Res*, 27 Beauchamp Rd., U. Norwood. Served at Relief of Chitral,'95, Punjab and Tirah, '97-98, and S.A. War. *Re-enlisted*, 11 Sept., '14 ; M.M., May, '16. *Fell*, Delville Wood, Somme, 1 Sept., '16.

WHITE, WILFRED APPLETON, 2/Lt., K.R.R.C.
    b., '99 ; s., Mr. & Mrs. Wilfred White, 10 Brambledown Rd., Wallington. *Educ.*, Whitgift G. Sch., & Exeter Coll., Oxford. *Enl.*, Nov., '17. *Fell*, 3 Oct., '18.

WHITE, WILLIAM, Pte., 60 M.G.C.
    b., Catford, 23 Nov.,'97 ; s., Mr. & Mrs. W.White, 9 Trafford Rd., T. Heath. *Educ.*, Winterbourne Rd. Sch., Croydon. Clerk. *Enl.* in 3/4 R.W.S. Regt., 3 Jun., '15. *Fell*, Ypres, 14 Aug., '17.

WHITEHEAD, ERIC WILFRED, 2/Lt., R.A.F.
    b., Eastbourne, 2 Oct., '98 ; s., Mr. & Mrs. Whitehead, Shettlestone, 5 Thornhill Rd., Croydon. *Educ.*, Whitgift G. Sch. *Res.*, " Sunnyside," Lodge Rd., Croydon. *Enl.* as bugler in Artists Rif., Sept., '14 ; commis., Nov., '17. *Killed* in a landing accident, while training at Salisbury, 16 Feb., '18.

WHITELEY, ERNEST JAMES, 21730, Trooper, Suss. Yeom.
    b., U. Holloway, 26 Feb., '84 ; *e.s.*, Mr. & Mrs. James Whiteley, " Fairlight Glen," Brighton Rd., Croydon. *Educ.*, Abp. Tenison's Sch., Croydon. Commercial clerk. *Enl.*, 13 Jul.,'15; attd. 10 R.W.S. Regt. *Fell*, France, 18 Aug., '17.

WHITHEAR, ALBERT FREDERICK, Pte., 1/19 Lond. Regt.
    b., 7 Dec., '99 ; s., Mr. & Mrs. Whithear, 30 Grange Pk. Rd., T. Heath. *Educ.*, Ecclesbourne Rd. Sch., T. Heath. Married. Milk carrier. *Res.*, 26 Thirsk Rd., S. Norwood. *Enl.*, 12 Mar., '17. *Fell*, 1 Sept., '18.

WHITING, CHARLES WILLIAM, 21907, Pte., 1 E. Sur. Regt.
    b., 27 Aug., '-. Married. Cigar salesman. *Res.*, 59 Ferndale Rd., S. Norwood. *Enl.*, 2 Jun., '16. *D.*, 4 May, of wounds recd., France, 4 days prev.

WHITNEY, J. F., Pte., Lond. Regt.
    s., Mr. & Mrs. Whitney, 61 Jarvis Rd., Croydon. *Fell*, France, Aug., '17.

WHITTEN, F. R., Capt., R.E.
    e.s., Mr. & Mrs. G. J. Whitten, 28 Braxted Pk., Streatham. Married. Empl. in Federated Malay States Civil Service. *Res.*, 32 Ederline Av., Norbury. M.C. *D.* of wounds, 18 Apr., '18.

WHITTLE, CHARLES, Pte., Welsh Regt.

WHITTLE, F. W., Pte., Welsh Regt.

WHYATT, A., 3497, R.W. Kent Regt.
    Res., S. Norwood. *D.* of wounds, Jun., '17.

THE CROYDON ROLL OF HONOUR

WHYBROW, HARRY THOMSON, Capt., Motor M.G.C.
  b., "The Almonds" (now "Sherbourne"), Woodside Green, 25 Mar., '79; *s.*, Mr. & Mrs. Francis Whybrow, Bosham, Sussex *Educ.*, Whitgift G. Sch. Married; 2 children. Accountant. *Res.*, Bulawayo. He was a big game hunter, writer on wild animals of Africa, and served on recruiting staff in Ireland. Commis., Nov., '14. *D.*, 21 Mar., '16, of wounds received in battle of Soko Nasia. (Plate XXXIV., 1).

WHYBROW, THOMAS WILKINS, Pte., 17 R. Fus.
  b., 79 Addison Rd., S. Norwood, 9 Nov., '79; *e.s.*, Mr. & Mrs. Mary Ann Whybrow, 24 Queen's Rd., Croydon. *Educ.*, Boston Rd. Sch., Croydon. Single. Empl. by Brit. Wood Heel Co. *Enl.*, 4 Jun., '15. *Fell*, France, 21 Mar., '18.

WHYTE, E. T., 1233, L/Cpl., R. Fus.
  Res., Addis. *Fell*, Sept., '17.

WICKER, FREDERICK, Lt., Lond. Regt. (Queen's).
  Res., S. Norwood. *Fell*, 5 Apr., '18.

WICKS, A. H., Pte., R.A.M.C.
  e.s., Mr. & Mrs. H. Wicks, 28 Edward Rd., Addis. *Educ.*, Ingram Rd. Sch., T. Heath. *Enl.*, 13 Feb., '13; attd. to 2 Seaforth H., Aug., '14; served in France, Aug., '14-May, '18. *D.* of wounds, 4 Can. C.C.S., 13 May, '18.

WICKS, HERBERT HARTLEY, Pte., 16 Middlesex Regt.
  b., Dulwich, S.E., 28 Aug., '96; *s.*, Mr. & Mrs. A. E. Wicks, 248 Whitehorse Rd., Croydon. *Educ.*, Askes Hatcham Boys' Sch., New Cross, S.E. Bank clerk. *Enl.*, Jun., '15. *Fell*, Glencorse Wood, nr. Hooge, 16 Aug., '17.

WILD, JACK, 13404, Pte., R.W.S. Regt.
  b., '95; *s.*, Mr. & Mrs. C. Wild, 8 Lr. Drayton Pl., Croydon. Married. *Res.*, S. Norwood. *Fell*, 18 Nov., '16.

WILD, LIONEL TUDOR, Capt., Somerset L.I.
  b., '88; 2nd *s.*, Mr. & Mrs. A. S. Wild, 21 Canning Rd., Addis. *Educ.*, St. Winifred's, Kenley, & Reading Sch. Motor engineer. As sgt. in Sur. Yeom. was mobilised at outbreak of war; commis., Feb., '15; served in France, Jul., '15-Nov., '17. *Fell*, 30 Nov., '17, in attempt to save remnant of his coy. during German counter attack, nr. Cambrai. *Buried* by enemy, nr. Masnieres.

WILD, W. S., Pte., S.A. Inf.
  2nd *s.*, Mr. & Mrs. William Wild, Addis. *Fell*, 17 Oct., '18.

WILD, WILLIAM GEORGE, Pte., Drag. Gds.
  s., Mr. & Mrs. E. Wild, Addis. *Fell*, 26 Aug., '18.

WILKINS, FRANK, Sgt., H.L.I.
  b., 1 Jun., '95; *s.*, Mr. & Mrs. Charles England Wilkins, 54 Blenheim Cres., Croydon. *Educ.*, Whitgift G. Sch. *Fell*, France, '15.

WILKINS, HERBERT JOHN, L/Cpl., 2 R.W S. Regt.
  b., Bletchingley, 10 Oct., '93. *Educ.*, Gloucester Rd. Sch., Croydon. Single. Printer. *Res.*, Pawsons Rd., Croydon. *Enl.*, 2 Sept., '14. *D.* of wounds, France, 4 Jun., '16.

WILKINS, HOWARD MORRIS, Sgt., City of Lond. Yeom.
  b., 18 Sept., '– ; *s.*, Mr. & Mrs. Edward Howard Wilkins, "Richmond Lodge," Sydenham Rd., Croydon. *Educ.*, Whitgift G. Sch. Ment. in despat. *Fell*, Gallipoli, '15.

WILKINS, SIDNEY ERNEST, Pte., Artists Rif. (1/28 Lond. Regt.)
  b., Dover, 31 Dec., '96; *s.*, A. J. & C. A. Wilkins, 58 Penshurst Rd., T. Heath. *Educ.*, Mod. Sch., Croydon. Clerk. *Enl.*, 8 Jan., '17. *Fell*, Passchendaele, 29 Oct., '17. (Plate XXXI., 2).

THE GLORIOUS DEAD

WILKINS, W. J., 66296, Pte., N. Fus.
  s., B. & G. Wilkins, 21 Grenaby Rd., Croydon. *Educ.*, Boro. Sec. Sch., Croydon. Clerk. *Missing*, 11 Apr., '18 (last seen going to dressing stn., wounded).
WILKINSON, –, Pte., R.W.S. Regt.
  b., '95. Empl. by Croydon Corp. Tramways. *Res.*, 1 Grafton Rd., Croydon. *Fell*, Dardanelles, 9 Aug., '15.
WILKINSON, CHARLES EDWARD GARNETT, Sgt., 10 R. Fus.
  b., U. Paurstone, Dorset, 24 Mar., '85 ; s., Mr. & Mrs. F. E. Wilkinson, Westbury, St. Paul's Rd., T. Heath. *Educ.*, Holme Sch., S. Norwood. Accountant. *Res.*, Valparaiso, Chili. *D.*, Boulogne, 10 Stat. Hosp., 16 Jul., '16, of wounds recd. nr. Pozieres.
WILKINSON, JOHN ALFRED, L/Cpl., R.E. (Lab. Coy.)
  b., Lond., 28 Mar., '75. *Educ.*, Lond. Married. Labourer. *Res.*, 4 Portland Cottages, Beddington Lane. *Enl.*, 23 Aug., '15. *D.* of bronchial pneumonia, at 11 C.C.S., France, 5 Apr., '17.
WILKINSON, JOHN H., Sgt., Leinster Regt. (R. Can. Regt.)
  Res., 27 Hathaway Rd., Croydon. Twice ment. in despat. ; served 4½ yrs. *D.* of pneumonia, Bramshott Hosp., Surrey, 18 Mar., '19.
WILKINSON, P., Pte., Middlesex Regt.
  s., Mr. & Mrs. Wilkinson, 59 Tankerton Terr., Mitcham Rd., Croydon. *Educ.*, Boston Rd. Sch., Croydon. Twice w. in eight mths. *Fell*, 7 Nov., '18.
WILLEY, SYDNEY FRANK, 2142, L/Cpl., 8 R.W.S. Regt.
  b., Croydon, 19 Aug., '95 ; s., Frank & Eva L. Willey, 50 Wandle Rd., Croydon. *Educ.*, Par. Ch. Sch., Croydon. Butcher. *Enl.*, Sept., '14. *D.* on Somme, from concussion, 26 Oct., '16.
WILLIAMS, CHARLES, Pte.
  Postman, attd. to E. Croydon Office. *Res.*, 11 Fernham Rd , Croydon. Territorial before war. *D.* in hosp., Feb., '17.
WILLIAMS, FREDERICK JOHN, Pte., 6 Hauraki Inf.
  s., Mr. & Mrs. Williams, 46 High St., Croydon. *Educ.*, Rain's Sch., Pitman's, and King's Coll., Lond. Stationer. *Fell* Dardanelles, 28 Apr., '15.
WILLIAMS, H. W., Despatch-Rider, R.E.
  s., late Mr. Williams, & Mrs. Bennett, River-view Gr., Chiswick. *Educ.*, Whitgift G. Sch., '05-09. *Fell*, '17.
WILLIAMS, HAROLD ERNEST, Rflmn., L.R.B. (5 Lond. Regt.)
  b., N. Lond., 3 Nov., '91 ; 2nd s., Mr. & Mrs. E. Williams, 10 Bingham Rd., Croydon. *Educ.*, Whitgift G. Sch., & East Lond. Coll. ; B.Sc. (Lond.), hons. in physics. Clerk in operative dept., Royal Mint. *Enl.*, Jun., '15. *Fell* in advance on Menin road, Ypres, 20 Sept., '17. (Plate XXXIII., 3).
WILLIAMS, J., Pte., E. Sur. Regt.
  Conductor, Croydon Corp. Tramways. *D.*, Western Heights Mil. Hosp., Dover, Jun., '16.
WILLIAMS, PERCY JOHN, 2/Lt., R. Berks. Regt.
  b., S. Croydon, Dec., '94 ; y.s., Mr. & Mrs. E. Williams, 10 Bingham Rd., Croydon. *Educ.*, M. Whitgift Sch., Whitgift G. Sch., & Corpus Christi Coll., Oxford. At grammar sch. he won a succession of prizes, including three Eastty medals and his scholarship to Oxford ; going to the Univ. in 1913, took a first in class. moderations ; was proxime accessit for the Hertford Scholarship, and won Chancellor's prize for Latin essay on Oliver Cromwell. *Enl.*, Inns of Court O.T.C., Jun., '15 ; commis., Oct., '16. *D.* in hosp. at Salonica, from wounds, Apr., '17 (Plate XXXIV., 3).

WILLIAMS, MONTGOMERY, Capt., R.M.A.
    b., '85 ; *s.*, Maj. & Mrs. Plunkett Williams, U. Norwood. *Educ.*, Dulwich Coll., & Naval Coll., Greenwich. Married. *D.*, 23 Aug., '16, from injury recd. prev. day. Twice ment. in despat.
WILLIAMS, W. HUTTON, Capt., 3 E. Sur. Regt.
    b., '75 ; *s.*, Mr. & Mrs. Williams, " Inglewood," Teddington. *Fell*, nr. Festubert, 17 May, '15.
WILLIAMSON, EDGAR ROWE, Lt., Lond. Regt.
    b., Argentine Republ., '95 ; *s.*, Mr. & Mrs. Rowe Williamson, 33 Vincent Rd., Croydon. *Educ.*, Repton. *Enl.* as pte. soon after outbreak of war ; commis. in his own regt., Feb., '15 ; M.C., 1 Jul., '16. *Fell*, 10 Sept., '16.
WILLMETT, H. E., Pte., R.W.S. Regt.
    b., '91. *Educ.*, Sydenham Rd. Sch., Croydon. *Res.*, 40 Broadway Av., Croydon. *Enl.*, 2 Mar., '16. *Fell*, Mar., '17.
WILLS, ALBERT ERNEST, 233526, Driver, 311 Bde., R.F.A.
    b., Bridlington, 18 Sept., '78. *Educ.*, Alderman Newton's Sch., Leicester, & Bishop Feild Coll., St. John's, Newfoundland. Married. Grocer & provision merchant : businesses, 217 Whitehorse Lane, & Queen's Rd., U. Norwood. *Res.*, 217 Whitehorse Lane, S. Norwood. *Enl.*, 20 Apr., '17 ; *w.*, Ypres, 5 Nov., '17. *D.* of wounds, 11 Nov., '17, at 18 Chicago (U.S.A.) Gen. Hosp., Camiers. Buried, Brit. Mil. Cem., Etaples. (Plate XXXIV., 2).
WILLS, CHARLES ALBERT, R.N.
    Married. *Res.*, 115 Norwood Rd. *Drowned* in action, 7 Sept.,'17.
WILLS, J. H., Pte., 1/1 Can. Regt.
    s., Mr. & Mrs. A. Wills, Church St., Croydon. *Educ.*, Sutton. *D.*, 28 May, '15, of wounds recd. at Festubert.
WILLSHER, HAROLD HENRY, Rflmn., 16 K.R.R.C.
    b., Holloway, 15 Mar., '98 ; *s.*, Mr. & Mrs. H. Willsher, 1 Cedar Villas, Cedar Rd., Croydon. *Educ.*, Abp. Tenison's Sch., S. Croydon. Clerk. *Enl* , 22 Jun., '16. *D.*, 19 Oct., '18, while pris. of war at Giessen, Germany. (Plate XXXIII., 2).
WILLSMORE, RICHARD JOHN, Pte., 7 E. Sur. Regt.
    b., 109 Queen's Rd., U. Norwood, 21 Jun., '95 ; *s.*, W. J. & Alice Willsmore, 225 Knight's Hill, W. Norwood. *Educ.*, Rockmount Rd. Sch., U. Norwood. Garage cleaner. *Res.*, 50 Queen's Rd., U. Norwood. *Enl.*, 13 Oct., '15. *Fell*, Arras, 9 Apr., '17.
WILLSON, CHARLES DOUGLAS, Gnr., Notts. Bty., R.H.A.
    b., 15 Lansdowne Rd., Croydon, 21 Apr., '90 ; *e.s.*, Charles E. & Bona Willson. *Educ.*, Avonhurst College, Burgess Hill, Suss. Single. Commercial Traveller. *Enl.* at Croydon. *Fell*, 4 May, '17, killed by bomb while in hosp., at Deir-el-Bela, nr. Gaza, Palestine.
WILMOT, WILLIAM JOHN, Pte., E. Sur. Regt.
    5th *s.*, Mr. & Mrs. C. W. Wilmot, Southall. Married ; 2 children. Butcher. *Res.*, 3 Tanfield Rd., Croydon. *Fell*, 3 May, '17.
WILSON, ALBERT ALFRED, Sgt., 23 Middlesex Regt.
    b., Battersea, 9 Jul., '81 ; *s.*, late William & Emma Wilson. *Educ.*, Battersea. Married. Labourer. Served in R.N. '99-01. *Enl.*, in Army, 10 Oct., '02. *Fell*, nr. Vlamertinghe, 27 Apr., '18 ; buried, Brandhoek New Mil. Cem., No. 3.
WILSON, C. W. " Neil," 2/Lt., R.F.A.
    e.s., Mr. & Mrs. W. Wilson, 21 Chisholm Rd., Croydon. *Educ.*, Whitgift G. Sch. Married. *Res.*, 15 Lansdown Rd., Lee. Mobilised, Aug., '14, as trooper in W. Kent Yeom., and served in Egypt and Gallipoli ; as officer in R.F.A., served in France and Italy. *D.* of pneumonia, 25 Nov., '18, at a C.C.S. in France.

XXXV.

1. 2/Lt. A. WARNER, Lond. Rif. B.
2. Rflmn. G. WATERMAN, Queen's Westm. Rif.
3. Rflmn. H. G. YOUNG, Lond. Rif. B.
4. Rflmn. C. H. TOWNEND, Lond. Rif. B.
5. Capt. J. S. WALTER, M.C., 7 R.W.S. Regt.
6. Capt. G. H. SAXE-WYNDHAM, M.C., 8 R.W.S. Regt.

XXXVI.

1. Rflmn. C. L. TURTLE, Queen's Westm. Rif.
2. 2/Lt. L. LLOYD, Hants. Regt.
3. Pte. J. W. ORD, 16 Middlesex Regt.
4. 2/Lt. H. P. N. DIXON, Northd. Fus.
5. Capt. E. G. LANGDALE, 5 Leicester Regt.
6. 2/Lt. G. P. ALLEN, 3/4 R.W.S. Regt.

THE GLORIOUS DEAD

WILSON, CHARLES WILFRID, Lt., S. Lancs. Regt.
  b., 12 Nov., '75 ; s., Rev. J. P. & Mrs. Wilson, " Hawthorns," Campbell Rd., Croydon. *Educ.*, M. Whitgift Sch., & Whitgift G. Sch.
WILSON, F., Pte., R.W. Kent Regt.
  b., '89. Married ; 2 children. *Res.*, 23 Moffat Rd., T. Heath. *Fell*, 14 Jun., '17.
WILSON, F., 25437, Pte., 18 Manchr. Regt.
WILSON, JAMES WILLIAM, Northd. Fus.
  b., 18 Nov., '98. *Res.*, 47 Addington Rd., Croydon. *Enl.* in A.C.C., Jun., '15 ; transf. to Northd. Fus. and went to France, Dec., '16. *Fell*, 21 Mar., '18.
WILSON, WALTER, Pte., 17 " Empire " Btn., R. Fus.
  b., '95 ; y.s., Mr. & Mrs. Edward Wilson, Wellesley Rd., Croydon. *D.*, 26 Dec., '15, of wounds recd. in Flanders prev. day.
WILSON, WILLIAM STANLEY, Pte., R.Fus.
  b., 1 Dec., '96 ; s., Mr. & Mrs. William Herbert Wilson, " Sunnybank," Duppas Hill Rd., Waddon. *Educ.*, Whitgift G. Sch., '09-10.
WILTSHIRE, E G., Pte.
  Married. Empl. by Croydon Gas Co. *Res.*, 5 Selhurst Pl., S. Norwood. *Enl.*, Apr., '16. *Fell*, 18 Sept., '18.
WINCHESTER, VICTOR CHRISTOPHER, Rflmn., L.R.B. (5 Lond. Regt.)
  b., Plumstead, 24 Dec., '94 ; s., Mr. & Mrs. J. A. Winchester, 30 Wiltshire Rd., T. Heath. *Educ.*, Plumstead, and Beulah and Winterbourne Rd. Schs., T. Heath. Builder's asst. *Enl.*, 3 Feb., '16 ; served in France from 1 Apr., '16 ; w., 7 Jun, '17 & Dec., '17. *Fell*, France, 14 Apr., '18.
WINDIBANK, JACK, 50955, Pte., 17 Middlesex Regt.
  b., 25 Middle St., Southsea, 24 Nov., '97 ; s., Henry & Emma Windibank, 29 Pemdevon Rd., Croydon. *Educ.*, Christ Ch. and Mitcham Rd. Schs., Croydon, & West Jesmond Sch., Newcastle-on-Tyne. Single. Electrician. *Enl.*, 31 Aug., '16 ; w., and taken pris. at Oppy Wood, 28 Apr., '17. *D.* of wounds while prisoner in the German C.C.S., Rue de St. Lazarre, Douai, 29 Apr., '17.
WINDSOR, ARTHUR, Pte., 7 R.W.S. Regt.
  b., Croydon, 31 Jan., '88 ; s., late Mr. Henry John, & Mrs. Windsor, 21 Nicholson Rd., Croydon. *Educ.*, Croydon. Married, 3 Oct., '14, Ellen Mabel Fisher. Draper. *Res.*, 21 Nicholson Rd., Croydon. *Enl.*, 4 Sept., '14 ; w., 31 Apr., '16 ; retd. to line, Aug., '16. *Fell*, 6 Oct., '16.
WINDSOR, HARRY, Pte., R. Fus.
  b., '92 ; s., Mr. & Mrs. Henry Windsor, 134 Dennett Rd., Croydon. *Res.*, Croydon. *Enl.*, Sept., '14. *Fell*, 6 Aug., '16.
WING, ARTHUR, A.B. Seaman, R.N.
  b., Upper Shirley, 14 Jul., '96 ; s., Mrs. Ellen Wing, 29 Boulogne Rd., Croydon. *Educ.*, Whitehorse Rd. Sch., T. Heath. Single. Butcher. Joined R.N., 11 Sept., '12. *Lost*, with H.M.S. " Queen Mary," sunk in Battle of Jutland, 31 May, '16.
WINSTONE, HENRY THOMAS, Pte., Gordon H.
  b., '99 ; s., George & Mary A. Winstone, Crowther Rd., S. Norwood. *Educ.*, M. Whitgift Sch. *Enl.*, May, '17, in Lond. Scottish. *Fell*, 27 Aug., '18.
WINSTONE, WILLIAM ERNEST, Pte., 13 Middlesex Regt.
  b., New Southgate, 26 Mar., '80 ; s., George & Mary A. Winstone, New Southgate. *Educ.*, Amwell St. Married. Master packer. *Res.*, 61 Crowther Rd., S. Norwood. *Enl.*, 23 Jan., '17. *Fell*, E. of Ypres, 24 Aug., '17.

THE CROYDON ROLL OF HONOUR

WINTER, R. B., 2526, Pte., Lond. Regt.
Res., Croydon. *Fell*, Oct., '16.

WINTER, SIDNEY, Pte., R.W.S. Regt.
Empl. by Croydon Gas Coy., as maintenance attendant. *Enl.*, May, '16. *Fell*, Oct., '17.

WIEBY, W. J., 288021, L/Cpl., Seaforth H.
b., '80. Married. Empl. by Croydon Corp. *Res.*, 16 Crossland Rd., T. Heath. *Enl.*, May, '16. *Fell*, 31 Jul., '17.

WISE, C. W., 2/Lt., R.F.A.
Educ., Whitgift G. Sch., '01-04.

WISE, CHARLES, Pte., Middlesex Regt.
b., '87. *Educ.*, Sydenham Rd. Sch., Croydon. Married; 6 children. Empl. by Ellis & Co., High St., Croydon. *Res.*, 76 Leighton St. E., Croydon. *Enl.*, 17 Apr., '15 ; *w.*, 17 Apr., '17. *Fell*, 23 Jul., '18.

WITHALL, SYDNEY H., Pte., L.R.B. (5 Lond. Regt.)
b., 8 Jul., '95 ; *s.*, Mr. & Mrs. S. H. Withall, 128 Onslow Gardens, Wallington. *Educ.*, Whitgift G. Sch., '10-12. *Fell*, Dec., '16.

WOOD, A., 3240, Pte., R. Fus.
Res., Norwood. *Fell*, Sept., '17.

WOOD, F., Pte., 3/4 Suffolk Regt.
Empl. by Croydon Corp., Roads Dept. *Res.*, 375 Whitehorse Rd., Croydon. *Enl.*, 13 Oct., '14 ; *w.*, Oct., '16. *D.* of wounds, 22 Dec., '16.

WOOD, GEORGE WILLIAM, Cpl., R.F.A.
b., '97 ; *s.*, late G. W., & Mrs. Wood, 29 Elm Rd., T. Heath. *Enl.*, 8 Jan., '13. Was in retreat from Mons, and battle of Loos ; had previously been wounded. *Fell*, 22 Nov., '17.

WOOD, HENRY GEORGE WESTMORLAND, Capt., Worcester Regt.
b., '89 ; *3rd s.*, late Mr., & Mrs. T. P. Wood, " Carlisle Lodge," Howard Rd., S. Norwood. *Educ.*, Dulwich Coll., & Peterhouse, Cambridge ; B.A., '12. *Joined*, Worcester Regt. (Territorials) before war ; served in France & Italy, Mar., '15-Aug., '18 ; *w.*, Somme, '16 ; D.S.O., 15 Jun., '18. *Fell*, Italy, 3 Aug., '18.

WOOD, J. B., 29750, Rflmn., R.B.
Res., W. Croydon. *Fell*, Oct., '17.

WOOD, JOHN GOLDSMITH, Act.-Capt., 2/5 S. Lancs. Regt.
b., Balham, S.W., 20 Dec., '89. *Educ.*, St. Mary's Sch., Balham, and Battersea Poly. Bank clerk. *Res.*, 32 Kemble Rd., Waddon. Commis., Feb., '16. *Fell*, Thiepval, 8 Dec., '16, while attd. to 9 Lancs. Fus. (Plate XXXI., 5).

WOOD, THOMAS PERCIVAL, Lt., Ind. Army Res.
e.s., late Thomas, & Mrs. Wood, " The Birches," Howard Rd., Woodside. Principal, La Martinière Coll., Lucknow, India. *Fell*, France, 25 Sept., '15.

WOODALL, C. J., Rflmn., R.W.S. Regt.
e.s., Mr. & Mrs. W. Woodall, 100 Pawson's Rd., Croydon. *Fell*, 22 Oct., '16.

WOODALL, FRANK, Pte., Public Sch. Btn.
b., '97. *Educ.*, Abp. Tenison's Sch., Croydon. *Res.*, Purley. *Enl.*, Aug., '15 ; *w.*, Jul., '16. *Fell*, France, 13 Sept., '17.

WOODALL, G. W., 30120, L/Cpl., Somerset L. I.
b., '96 ; *3rd s.*, Mr. & Mrs. F. Woodall, 100 Pawson's Rd., Croydon. *D.* from wounds after one year & ten months' service at the front.

WOODARD, R. S., Rflmn., K.R.R.C.
Res., E. Croydon. *Fell*, '16.

THE GLORIOUS DEAD

WOODCOCK, WALTER STANLEY, Pte., 9 R. Fus.
b., Ealing, 14 Oct., '99 ; *s.*, Mr. & Mrs. Woodcock, 133 Oval Rd., Croydon. *Educ.*, Ealing, Lond., and Tattenhall, Cheshire. Printer. *Enl.*, 17 Jan., '18. *Fell*, France, 8 Aug., '18. *Buried*, Beacon Brit. Cem., Sailly Laurette, Corbie sur Somme.

WOODLEY, HARRY, 40950, L/Cpl., 11 Essex Regt.
b., 6 Elmers Rd., Woodside, S. Norwood, 15 Dec., '85 ; *s.*, Thomas & Alice Woodley, 183 Portland Rd., S. Norwood. *Educ.*, Birchanger Rd. Sch., S. Norwood. Single. Greengrocer. *Enl.*, 12 May, '16. *Fell*, nr. Ypres, 20 Jun., '18.

WOODRUFF, G. NORMAN C., Lt., 1 Sur. Rif. (21 Lond. Regt.)
b., '90 ; *e.s.*, Mr. & Mrs. George Woodruff, 23 Whitworth Rd., S. Norwood. *D.* in hosp., 2 Dec., '18.

WOODS, H. J., 3710, Pte., R. Suss. Regt.
Fell, Aug., '16.

WOODWARD, NORMAN LLEWELLYN.
b., '97. *Fell*, Salonica, 4 Mar., '17.

WOODWARDS, W. C., 10358, Pte., Yorks. Regt. *Fell*, Aug., '16.

WOOLLATT, C. H., Capt., R.W.S. Regt.
Fell, Sept., '17.

WORMALD, H., 2170, Sgt., R.W.S. Regt.
Res., Croydon. *Fell*, Nov., '16.

WORSTER, FRANK COPELAND, Capt., Worcester Regt.
b., '89. *Educ.*, Josephite Coll., Louvain, Whitgift G. Sch., '02-07, & St. John's Coll.,Oxford, where he took 1st cl. in Classical Moderations and in "Greats." Married. Master at St. Paul's Sch. *Res.*, 5 Heathfield Rd., Croydon. *W.*, Somme, '16. *D.* of wounds, Mar., '18.

WORTHINGTON, ERNEST, Sgt.Maj., Can. Inf.
b., Selhurst, '80 ; *s.*, late J. H., & Mrs. Worthington, Selhurst. *D.* of pneumonia, Vladivostock, Siberia, 6 Mar., '19.

WORTLEY, FRANK A., Cpl., 15 Australian I.F.
b., T. Heath, '81 ; *s.*, G. & A. F. Wortley, "Silwood," Pollard's Hill S., Norbury. *Educ.*, M. Whitgift Sch., Croydon. Sugar planter. Married. *Res.*, Queensland. *Enl.*, Jan., '16. *Fell*, Ypres-Menin Rd., 27 Sept., '17. (Plate XXXII., 6).

WOTTON, HAROLD, 21524, Pte., Cheshire Regt.
s., Mr. & Mrs. Wotton, 2 St. Mary's Rd., S. Norwood. *Fell*, Aug., '16.

WREN, FREDERICK.
Fell, '15.

WRIGHT, FRANK MONTAGUE, Pioneer, R.E.
b., Croydon, 8 Aug., '95 ; *s.*, Frank E. & Alice M. Wright, 6 Chatfield Rd., W. Croydon. *Educ.*, Brit. Sch., Croydon. Postal clerk, Sutton P.O. *Enl.*, 24 Jun., '16. *Fell*, France, 10 Mar., '17.

WRIGHT, GEORGE, Pte., R. Fus.
Res., 34 Grafton Rd., Croydon. *Fell*, Jun., '17.

WRIGHT, P. C., Pte., 12 E. Sur. Regt.
Res., 18 Cambridge Rd., T. Heath. Married ; 2 children. Porter, Addington War Hosp. *Enl.*, Mar., '16 ; came home in Mar., '17, with trench fever. *Fell*, 22 Oct., '18.

WRIGHT, SIDNEY FREDERICK, Sapper, R.E.
b., Kingsland, '85 ; *s.*, Mr. & Mrs. Frederick William Wright, 193 Shakespeare Rd., Herne Hill. *Educ.*, Hollydale Rd. Sch., Peckham, & Santley Rd. (L.C.C.) Sch., Brixton. Single. Fitter (S. Suburban Gas Coy.). *Res.*, 26 Penrith Rd., T. Heath. *Enl.*, Jan., '15. *D.* of dysentery, at 19 Gen. Hosp., Alexandria, 13 Nov., '18.

WRIGHT, WILLIAM GERALD, 2/Lt., Hants. Regt.
 b., '93 ; y.s., Mr. & Mrs. W. J. Wright, "Rycroft," Harold Rd., U. Norwood. *Educ.*, St. Olive's, Southwark, & Alleyn's Sch., Dulwich. *Enl.* as pte. ; commis., Autumn, '15. *Fell*, France, 7 Jun., '17.

WRIGLEY, R., Pte., R.W.S. Regt.
 Pris. of war, reported dead.

WYARD, JOHN ERNEST, Seaman, R.N.
 b., Kensington, 18 Oct., '92 ; s., Mr. & Mrs. S. M. Wyard, 21 Boswell Rd., T. Heath. *Educ.*, Beulah Rd. Sch., T. Heath. *Enl.*, Apr., '10. *Lost* on H.M.S. "Natal," destroyed by internal explosion, Cromarty Harbour, Scotland, 30 Dec., '15.

WYATT, HARRY.
 b., '99 ; 2nd s., Mr. & Mrs. Wyatt, 181 Whitehorse Rd., Croydon. *Educ.*, Sydenham Rd. Sch., Croydon. Audit clerk. *Enl.*, Mar., '17 ; w., & taken prisoner, Contalmaison, 26 Mar., '18. *D.* in enemy Field Amb., 28 Mar., '18. *Buried*, Guillemont.

WYETH, ALLAN FREDERICK, Pte., E. Sur. Regt.
 Educ., M. Whitgift Sch. *Fell*, 13 Oct., '15.

WYNNE, T., Cpl., R. Suss. Regt.
 Res., S. Norwood. *Fell*, Sept., '16.

YARROW, H. E. G., 2/Lt., K.O.S.B.
 Fell, '16.

YELLOP, P. A., 200049, Norfolk Regt.
 Res., E. Croydon. *Fell*, '17.

YEOLL, A., 12878, K.R.R.C.
 Res., W. Croydon. *Fell*, '17.

YEOMAN, ROLAND SOUNES, L/Cpl., 9 E. Sur. Regt.
 b., Aldershot, 13 Dec., '94. s., Mr. & Mrs. Yeoman, 174 Lr. Addis. Rd., Croydon. *Educ.*, Croydon. Single. Heraldic artist. *Enl.*, Feb., '16. *Fell*, Somme, 16 Aug., '16.

YEWEN, CHARLES THOMAS, Pte., R.W.S. Regt.
 b., '98. *Educ.*, Ecclesbourne Rd. Sch., T. Heath, & Stanley Tech. Trade Sch., S. Norwood. Electrical engineer. *Fell*, 25 Sept., '17.

YIELDING, VICTOR, Coy.Sgt.Maj., 2 Wilts. Regt.
 Married, '16, Violet, *d.* of Frank Ward. Clerk. *Enl.* in D.C.L.I. Sept., '14. *Fell*, St. Quentin, Mar., '18.

YOUNG, –-, Seaman, R.N.
 Res., Sandfield Rd., T. Heath. *Lost* with H.M.S. "Aboukir," sunk by submarine, N. Sea, 22 Sept., '14.

YOUNG, ALBERT EDWARD, Pte , 1 Norf. Regt.
 b., Finsbury, 26 Jul., '94 ; s., Mr. & Mrs. Young, 9 Mayday Rd., T. Heath. *Educ.*, Brit. Sch., Croydon. Single. Clerk. *Enl.*, Nov., '11. *D.*, at 3 C.C.S., France, of wounds recd. at Bayneux, 31 Aug., '18.

YOUNG, CHARLES H., Pte.
 Educ., M. Whitgift Sch. *Missing.*

YOUNG, CUTHBERT FREDERICK, L.R.B. (5 Lond. Regt.)
 b., 31 Mar., '91 ; s., Mr. & Mrs. Cuthbert T. Young. *Educ.*, Whitgift G. Sch. *Fell*, France, 5 Mar., '15.

YOUNG, DONALD, Sgt., Can. Inf.
 b., '94 ; e.s., late F. C. Young, & Mrs. Stapleton, 41 Morland Rd., Croydon. Reporter. *Fell*, Vimy Ridge, 9 Apr., '17.

YOUNG, EDWARD, Rflmn.
 Educ., High Sch., Croydon. *Fell*, 28 Mar., '18.

THE GLORIOUS DEAD

YOUNG, HAMISH GEORGE, Rflmn., L.R.B. (5 Lond. Regt.)
b., Beckenham, 30 Jan., '98; *e.s.*, Mr. & Mrs. J. B. Young, 15 Wellesley Gr., Croydon. *Educ.*, Woodford Sch., Croydon, and High Sch., Croydon. *Enl.*, 11 Jan., '16. *Fell*, Glencorse Wood, nr. Ypres, 16 Aug., '17. (Plate XXXV., 3).

YOUNG, MORRIS, 2/Lt., R.Fus.
b., '94; *s.*, Mr. & Mrs. E. Morris, 84 Wyatt Rd., Streatham Hill. *Fell*, 11 Aug., '16.

YOUNG, T. W., Pte., Australian I.F.
b., '00; *nephew* of Mr & Mrs. W. Young, Station Rd., S. Norwood, by whom he was brought up and educated; joined parents in Australia, '16. *W.* in France. *D.* of pneumonia, following operation.

YOUNGER, H. E., 106490, Gnr., R.F.A.
Res., Croydon. *Accidentally killed.*

ADDENDA.

CARTER, FRANK, Trooper, 2 Life Gds.
Empl. by Croydon Corp., at Mental Hosp.

COBBLEDICH, THOMAS, Pte., 15 Lond. Regt.
Empl. by Croydon Corp., at Mental Hosp.

GRAYSON, FREDERICK ARTHUR, L/Cpl., 5 Drag. Gds.
b., T. Heath, '88; *s.*, Mr. & Mrs. Grayson, 166 Moffat Rd., T. Heath. *Educ.*, Beulah Rd. Sch., T. Heath. Single. Empl. by Croydon Corp. Tramways. *Enl.*, 4 Aug., '14. *Fell*, Messines, 31 Oct., '14.

MCNAMARA, JOHN, L/Cpl., 3 E. Sur. Regt.
Res., 26 Alma Place, T. Heath. Single. Empl. by Croydon Corp. Tramways. *Enl.*, Oct., '14. *Fell*, Hill 60, 22 Apr., '15.

PHILLIPS, WILLIAM, G92252, 2/2 R. Fus.
s., late Mr. & Mrs. Phillips, of Croydon *Res.*, Croydon. *Enl.* in R.A.S.C. *Fell*, 29 Sept., '18.

RACKETT, H. H. D., R. Fus.
s., late Mr. & Mrs. Rackett, of S. Norwood.

WILKINSON, GEORGE, Pte., E. Sur. Regt.
b., Croydon, Jun., '95; *s.*, Mr. & Mrs. Wilkinson, 1 Grafton Rd., Croydon. *Educ.*, St. Andrew's Sch., Croydon. Single. Empl. by Croydon Corp. Tramways. *Enl.*, Aug., '14. *Fell*, Salonica, Jun., '15.

WOOLGAR, CHARLES ALFRED, Pte., 2 Border Regt.
b., Croydon, 12 Jan., '96; *s.*, Mr. & Mrs. Woolgar, 1 Dorothy Cottages, Willett Rd., T. Heath. *Educ.*, Winterbourne Rd. Sch., T. Heath. Single. Empl. by Croydon Corp. Tramways. *Enl.*, Aug., '12. *Fell*, France, 18 Dec., '14.

"So he passed over, and all the trumpets sounded for him on the other side."   *Bunyan: Pilgrim's Progress.*

II. Naval and Military Honours

"Whom the King delighteth to honour." *Esther VI.,* 11.

*ADAMS, JOHN RODWAY, Pte., R.N.V.R.—*Ment. in despatches.*
ADKINS, A. D., Coy. Sgt. Maj.—*D.C.M.,* 23 Aug., '18.
ALBON, HARRY, Lt.—*M.C.*
ALDERMAN, EDGAR, R.E.—*M.M.*
ALLEN, CLARENCE GEORGE, Lt.-Col., R.A.S.C.—*Ment. in despatches several times, M.C.*
ALLEN, I. R., Capt., R.A.S.C.—*Ment. in despatches.*
ALLEN, STANLEY J., Pte., M.G.C.—*M.M.,* 28 Apr., '17.
*ANDERSON, BASIL, Capt.—*M.C.*
ANDERSON, J., Cpl., Seaforth H.—*D.C.M., M.M. & bar.*
ANDERTON, T. W., 1474, Pte., R.W.S. Regt.—*M.M.*
ANDREWS, P., Capt., R.E.—*Ment. in despatches,* Feb., '18.
ANNISON, REGINALD C., Sgt., R.F.A.—*M.M.*
ANNS, KENNETH, 10 E. Sur. Regt.—*M.C.*
APPLEYARD, HARRY, Capt., R.A.S.C.—*Ment. in despatches (thrice), M.C.,* 1 Jan., '19.
ARNOLD, P., 2/Lt.,—*M.C.,* 24-25 Mar., '18.
ASHWORTH, J., Driver.—*M.M.*
ATKINS, JOHN R., Pte., Aust. I.F.—*D.C.M.*
*ATKINSON, LEWIS DE BURGH, Capt., R.Suss. Regt.—*Ment. in despatches,* Jan., '17.
AUNGIER, H., Pte., R. Suss. Regt.—*M.M. & bar.*
*AUSTIN, THOMAS CARNELLY MACDONALD, Capt., 4 S.W.B.—*Ment. in despatches,* Dec., '15.
BACON, D. C., Capt., 2/20 Lond. Regt.—*M.C.*
*BAILEY, JAMES ALFRED, Sgt., 11 R. Fus.—*M.M.,* 26 Sept., '16.
BAILEY, W., Pte., 2 Middlesex Regt.—*M.M.,* 21 Mar., '17.
BAKER, FRANCIS HOSIER, 2/Lt., Som. L.I.—*M.C.*
BAKER, GEORGE, Pte.—*M.M.*
BAKER, J., 6 R.W.S. Regt.—*M.M.,* 22 Aug., '15.
BAKER, W., Lond. Regt.—*D.C.M.*
BALDWIN, REUBEN, 2 Worcester Regt.—*D.C.M.*
BANNERMAN, RONALD ROBERT BRUCE, Capt., R.W.S. Regt.—*M.C.*
BARCLAY, WALTER E. B., Lt., R.N.V R.—*M.C.*
BARLOW, A., Pte., R.W.S. Regt.—*M.M.*
BARLOW, BILLY, R.W.S. Regt.—*M.M.,* 27 Dec., '17.
BARNES, C., L/Cpl.—*M.M.*
BARNES, D. A., Cpl., Cameron H.—*M.M.*
BARNES, FREDERICK JAMES, Signaller, R.H.A.—*D.C.M.,* 22 Aug., '18.
BARNFATHER, PERCY, Capt.—*M.C.*
*BARNHAM, JOHN WILLIAM JAMES, Sgt., 14 R.W. Kent Regt.—*M.M.,* 7 Jun., '17, & bar, 20 Sept., '17.
BARTLETT, CECIL EDWARD, Lt., K.S.L.I.—*Ment. in despatches.*
BASSETT, DOUGLAS, 2/Lt., R.F.A.—*Ment. in despatches.*
BATSTONE, FRANK OLIVER, Sgt., R. Can. H.A.—*M.M.,* Dec., '16.
BAXTER, JOHN F., Lt., K.O.Y.L.I.—*Ment. in despatches.*
*BEAUMONT, SIDNEY, 2/Lt., E. Lancs. Regt.—*M.C.*
BELL, C. D., Pte., R.A.S.C. (attd.) G.H.Q., R.F.C.—*M.S.M.,* '16.
*BELL, JOHN JOSEPH, Sgt., 13 Cheshire Regt.—*D.C.M.,* 4 Oct., '15.
BENNETT, ALFRED WHITMORE, Cpl., E. Sur. Regt.—*Ment. in despatches,* Sept., '16.
BENNETT, LOUISA, Sister, Brit. Red Cross Soc.—*R. Red Cross,* Jan., '18.
*BENTHAM, THOMAS, Lt., R.A.M.C.—*Ment. in despatches.*

* Fallen ; see entries under "The Glorious Dead."

NAVAL AND MILITARY HONOURS 425

BENTLEY, R., Capt., Hants. Regt.—*Croix de Guerre.*
BICKMORE, W. E., Sgt., R.F.A.—*M.M.*, 23 Dec., '17.
BISHOP, GEORGE, Lt., R.E.—*M.C.*, April, '18, *Croix de Guerre (Belgian).*
*BLACKMAN, WILFRED ERNEST ARTHUR, Capt., M.G.C.—*Ment. in despatches.*
BLENKINSON, ALFRED V., Lt., R.F.C.—*M.C.*
BOSTON, GEOFFREY G., Lt., L.R.B.—*D.C.M.*
BOWDEN, P. SIDNEY, Gnr., R.F.A.—*M.M.*, 28 Mar., '18.
BOWDITCH, D. A. H., Pte., R.A.M.C.—*M.M.*
BOYD, J. H., Lt.-Col., R.E.—*O.B.E.*
BRACHI, C. C., Capt., K.O.R.L.—*Ment. in despatches.*
BRADING, ROY, Capt. (Flight Cmdr.), R.A.F.—*D.F.C.*, & *bar.*
BRAIN, W., 1 Lancs. Fus.—*D.C.M.*
BREADING, GEORGE REMINGTON, Maj., R. Warwick. Regt.—*D.S.O., Ment. in despatches* (4 times).
BREENS, ARTHUR, Pte., Lond. Regt.—*M.M.*
*BRESSEY, SYDNEY HERBERT, 2/Lt., R.E.—*M.M.*, 31 May, '16.
BRIDGER, G. F., Gnr., R.H.A.—*M.M.*, Apr., '18.
BRIDGER, H. J.—*Russian Order of St. George (4th class)*, 17 Jul., '17.
BRIGHT, JOHN, L/Cpl., R.W.S. Regt.—*M.M.*, 26-27 Mar., '17.
BRISTOW, E., Driver, R.A.S.C.—*D.C.M.*
BROAD, G. L., Capt., R.E.—*M.C.*
*BROCK, FRANK A., Act.-Wing Cmdr., R.N.A.S.—*O.B.E.*, Jan., '18.
BROOK, A. F., K.R.R.C.—*Croix de Guerre.*
BROOK, ALBERT EDWARD, R.N.—*D.S.M.*, Apr., '18.
*BROWN, CHARLES ROYDON, Capt., Essex Regt.—*Ment. in despatches,* Jan., '16, *M.C.*, Jan., '16.
*BROWN, FRANCIS CLEMENT, Lt., Lond. Regt.—*Ment. in despatches,* '17.
*BROWN, JOHN GORDON, Capt., 10 R. Fus.—*Ment. in despatches, M.C.*, '16.
BROWN, JAMES, 2/Lt., M.G.C.—*M.M.*, 28 Aug., '16.
BROWN, ROBERT RUPERT HARRISON, 21 Bde., R.F.A.—*M.M.*, 16 Sept., '16.
BROWN, SIDNEY WILLOUGHBY, Sgt., Lond. Regt.—*Ment. in despatches.*
*BUCK, CYRIL ALFRED SPENCER, 2/Lt., 18 Lond. Regt.—*M.M., Somme,* Sept., '16.
BUCKLEY, HORACE HENRY CLEMENT, Lt., 7 K.O.S.B.—*Ment. in despatches,* Sept., '16.
*BURRY, C. H., Cpl., 22 Lond. Regt.—*M.M.*
CALVER, CLARENCE STUART, Lt., 7 E. Sur. Regt.—*M.C.*, 9 Aug., '17. (Plate VII., 1).
CARR, GRAHAM, Capt. & Adjt., Motor M.G.C.—*M.C.*, Jun., '16.
CARTER, A., L/Cpl., R. Fus.—*M.M.*
CHARMAN, ARTHUR E., Coy. Sgt. Maj., 1 Sur. Rif. (21 Lond. Regt.)— *M.C., D.C.M., M.M.*, 3 May, '16, & *Croix de Guerre.*
*CHEQUER, HERBERT HENRY, Drummer, 1 Beds. Regt.—*Ment. in despatches.*
CHUFFER, THOMAS STURLEY, Lt., 10 Can. Inf.—*M.C.*
CLARK, CHARLES CECIL, Cpl., 3/4 R.W.S. Regt.—*M.M.*, 6 Oct., '17.
CLARK, EDWIN PITT, Capt., M.G.C.—*M.C.*
CLARK, MARTIN HARRY, Lt., 96 Siege Battery, R.G.A.—*Ment. in despatches,* 8 Nov., '18, *M.B.E.*, '19.
COATMAN, H. E.—*M.C.*, 6 Sept., '18.
COBBOLD, E. A., Lt., Northants. Regt.—*M.C., M.M.*, '16.
COLCUTT, E. H.—*Ment. in despatches,* 7 Nov., '17.
*COLDHAM, J., Cpl., R.E.—*M.M.*, '18.
COLE, G., Sgt., R.E.—*M.M.*, Sept., '14.
COLE, W. H., Act.-Coy. Sgt. Maj., 16 Lond. Regt.—*M.S.M.*, 17 Jun., '18.

COLEMAN, CYRIL, R.B.—*M.M.*
*COLLINS, DENNIS, Bdr., R.F.A.—*M.M.*, '16.
*COMLEY, EDGAR C., I.t., R. Mun. Fus.—*M.C.*, Oct., '17.
COPPEN, ARTHUR.—*M.M.*
CORBETT, ROBERT WILLIAM, Sgt., Yorks. Regt.—*M.M.*, 19 Sept., '16, & bar.
*CORKE, GUY HAROLD, 2/Lt., Northd. Fus.—*Ment. in despatches*, 13 Jul., '16.
COUGHLAND, J., Sgt., 204 Coy., R.E.—*M.S.M.*
COWDREY, BASIL, Cpl , R.W.S. Regt.—*M.M.*
DAVIS, C. W., Staff Sgt. Maj., R.A.S.C.—*Medaille Militaire (French)*, & *M.S.M.*, 3 Jan., '19.
*DAVIS, HERBERT CHOPE, Squadron Q.M.S., M.G.C. (Cav.)—*M.M.*
DAVIS, HOWARD, Lt.-Cmdr., R.N.R.—*D.S.C.*
DAY, E. W., Q.M.S., R.E.—*D.C.M.*
*DAY, HAROLD, Cpl—*Croix de Guerre (Belgian)*, 1 Aug., '17.
DEACON, J. NISSEN, Capt., R.A.M.C.—*M.M.*
DENNIS, A. R.,—*M.M.*, Jan., '16, & bar, Sept., '17.
DIXON, W. A., Pte., Sur. Yeom.—*M.M.*
DOCKING, S. R., Maj.—*Croix de Guerre (Belgian)*.
DONALDSON, J. O., Coy. Sgt. Maj., R.W.S. Regt.—*D.C.M.*, 9 Apr., '17.
DONALDSON, JOHN MUIR, Capt., K.R.R.C.—*M.C.*, 15 Jul., '16. (Plate VIII., 1).
DOPSON, PERCY ALFRED, Gnr., R.F.A.—*M.M.*, 2 Aug., '17.
*DORÉ, D., Cpl., M.G.C.—*M.M.*, 23 May, '18.
DREWITT, JAMES JOHN, Cpl., R.F.A.—*M.M.*
DRIVER, -, 1st cl. P.O., R.N.—*D.S.M.*
DUDLEY, WILLIAM HENRY, L/Sgt.,Middlesex Regt.—*M.M.*, 23 Apr.,'17.
DUNN, GEOFFREY, 2/Lt., R.N.D.—*M.C.*, 18 Oct., '16.
DURDEN, E. J., L/Cpl., 11 R.W.S. Regt.—*Croix de Guerre (Belgian)*.
DUTFIELD, D., Capt., 2 R. Fus.—*Ment. in despatches.*
ECOTT, H. E.—*M.M.*, 7 Jun., '17.
EDWARDS, WILLIAM DAVID, Sgt., 12 R.B.—*M.M.*, Feb., '16. (Plate IX., 3.)
ELLIS, REGINALD VICTOR, Pte., E. Sur. Regt.—*M.M.*, 13 Jun., '17.
ELWELL, R. G., Surgeon, R.N.—*D.S.O.*
ENGLEBURTT, JOHN FRANCIS, 2/Lt., 17 Middlesex Regt.—*M.C.*, Jun.,'16.
ENTWISTLE, FRANK, Capt., Q.V.O. Guides (Ind. Army).—*D.S.O.*, 16 Sept., '18, *M.C.*, 1 Jan., '16.
ESDON, D., 2/Lt., E. Sur. Regt.—*D.C.M.*
EVATT, JOHN THOROLD, Brig.-Gen., 116 Inf. Bde.—*Ment. in despatches, D.S.O.*
EVERETT, PERCY WILLIAM, Rflmn., L.R.B.—*D.C.M.*
FELDON, C. H.—*Ment. in despatches.*
*FILLINGHAM, REGINALD JOHN, Maj., R.G.A.—*M.C.*, 14 Jul., '16, & bar, 16 Sept., '16.
FITSALL, E., Sgt., 19 Hussars.—*M.M.*, Jun., '17, & bar, 21 Mar., '18.
*FLACK, WILFRED G., Capt., Coldstream Gds.—*M.C. & bar.*
*FORRESTER, FRANK OLIVER, Lt., R.N.V.R.—*M.C.*
FOSS, BERNARD THEOBALD, Capt., 23 Middlesex Regt.—*M.C.*, 1 Jan.,'18.
FOSS, CHARLES CALVERLEY, G.S.O. 2, (Bde. Maj., 2 Can. Div.)—*V.C.*, '16, *D.S.O.*, 31 Oct., '14.
*FOSTER, GRAHAM EDWIN, 301666, Sgt., L.R.B.—*M.M.*, 20 May, '17.
FRASER, HARRY, Cpl., Can. Engineers.—*M.M.*
FRENCH, A. G., Pte.—*M.M.*
*FROST, ARTHUR BYFIELD, Lt., R.W.S. Regt.—*M.C.*, Oct., '17.
GAIN, R. S., Capt., 1/20 Lond. Regt.—*D.S.O.*
GALLAGHER, HENRY NOEL, Capt., R.A.S.C.—*Ment. in despatches*, Sept., '16.

NAVAL AND MILITARY HONOURS 427

*GAMBLING, W., Sgt., K.R.R.C.—*M.M.*
GARBUTT, JOHN RESTARICK, 2/Lt., 1 R.W.Kent Regt.—*M.C.*, 28 Jun.'18.
GARDINER, H. S., Sgt.—*M.M.*
GARDNER, R. G., R.N.A.S.—*D.S.C.*, Oct., '17.
GARNER, FRANCIS, Cpl., 17 R. Fus.—*M.M.*
*GEORGE, DAVID VICTOR, Pte., R.W.S. Regt.—*M.M.*, 24 Feb., '17.
GIDDINGS, H., Pte., R.W.S. Regt.—*M.M.*, Feb., '15.
*GILBERT, JOB, Sgt., R.F.A.—*Ment. in despatches,* 9 Apr., '17.
GLAZE, ALBERT, 201348, Sgt., 3/4 R.W.S. Regt.—*M.M.*, 4 Oct., '17.
GLAZEBROOK, FREDERICK THOMAS, Gnr., R.F.A.—*M.M.*, *Medaille Militaire (French).*
*GLIDDON, MAURICE, Lt., R.F.A.—*M.C.*
GOLD, REGINALD C., Lt., 3 E. Sur. Regt.—*M.C.*, Nov., '16.
GOLD, ROBERT J. S., Capt., 15 Lond. Regt.—*Chev. de l'Ordre de Merite Agricole.*
GOODBODY, CECIL MAURICE, Brevet Lt.-Col., R.A.M.C.—*Ment. in despatches* (twice).
GOSSLING, FRANK NEWBERY, Lt., R.E.—*Ment. in despatches, M.C.,* 16 Jun., '16.
GOULDEN, CHARLES HERBERT, 2/Lt., R. Artillery.—*M.C.*
GOWARD, A. J., Cpl.—*D.C.M., M.M.*
GOWARD, WILLIAM, M.G.C. (Heavy).—*M.M.*
GRAHAM, REGINALD PORTMAN, Lt., Cameron H.—*Ment. in despatches,* Sept., '16.
GRANT, D. J., 2/Lt., R.F.A.—*D.C.M.*
GRANT, W. H. GOSS, R.W.S. Regt.—*M.C.*, 23 Mar., '18.
GRAY, HAROLD V., Capt., Glo'ster Regt.—*M.C.*
*GRAY, OLIVER JOHN, 60272, Pte., R.A.M.C.—*Ment. in despatches,* 30 May, '17.
GREEN, A. W. C., Pte., E. Sur. Regt.—*Medaille Militaire & Diploma,*'16.
GREEN, HENRY, 2/Lt., 2/4 R.W.S. Regt.—*D.C.M.*
GREEN, STAFFORD HUGH, Capt. (G.S.O.).—*Ment. in despatches, D.S.O.*
*GREEN, WALTER CHARLES, 200601, Sgt., Tank C.—*D.C.M.,* Nov., '17 ; *Croix de Guerre (French),* May, '18.
GREGORY, LAURIE LESLIE, Gnr., R.F.A.—*M.M.*, Oct., '17.
GRETHER, E. F., Capt., R.A.M.C.—*Ment. in despatches.*
GUNSON, FRED C., Cpl.—*M.M.*, 30 Nov., '17.
HALL, ARTHUR REEVE, 2/Lt., Northd. Fus.—*Ment. in despatches.*
*HALL, CECIL ADRIAN, 22504, Pte., 1 R.W.S. Regt.—*M.M.*, Apr., '18.
HALL, R. M., 2/Lt., Cheshire Regt.—*Ment. in despatches,* May, '17.
*HALLIDAY, FRANCIS, 2487, Cpl., 9 E. Sur. Regt.—*M.M.*, 21 Jun., '16.
HAMMOND, S., Middlesex Regt.—*D.C.M.*
HAMMOND, WILLIAM GEORGE, Sgt., R.A.S.C.—*Ment. in despatches,* 16 Jul., '16.
*HANDSCROFT, -, Sgt., R.E.—*D.C.M.*
HARDY, E. A., L/Cpl., A.C.C.—*M.M.*, Apr., '18.
HARRISON, PAUL ADRIAN, 2/Lt., R.F.A.—*Ment. in despatches,* May, '17.
HART, G. B., Sgt., R.W.S. Regt.—*D.C.M.*, Sept., '16, *M.M.*, *Belgian Decoration Militaire.*
*HARVEST, GORDON LINDSAY, Lt., Lond. Regt.—*M.C.*, '17.
HAWKINS, HERBERT HARVEY BAINES, Capt., R.G.A.—*Ment. in despatches.*
*HAWKINS, KENNETH EDWARDS, Capt., R. Fus.—*M.C.*
HAY, JOHN STUART, Capt.—*Ment. in despatches.*
HAYCRAFT, STANLEY MUIRHEAD, Lt., R.E.—*M.C.*
HAYMAN, -, Sgt., Coldstream Gds.—*D.C.M.*
HERBERT, CHARLES GEORGE YOUNG, Lt., Gren. Gds.—*M.C.*, '17.
HERBERT, PHILIP HUME, Capt., R.F.A.—*M.C.*, '17.
HETTLER, BERNARD W., Capt., K.O.Y.L.I.—*M.C., Ment. in despatches.*
HEWITT, ARTHUR, Act.-Capt., Lond. Regt.—*M.C.*, 29-30 Sept., '16.

*Hewitt, G., Pte., 11 Essex Regt.—*M.M.*, *Croix de Guerre* (*French*), 28 May, '18.
Hewitt, Herbert Edwin, 21 Lond. Field Amb.—*M.S.M.*
*Hextall, Leonard John, Lt., Can. Inf.—*Ment. in despatches.*
*Hill, Reginald Gordon, Lt., R.A.M.C.—*M.C.*, '17.
Hill, William E., Capt., Middlesex Regt.—*M.C.*
Hilliker, W., Aust. Heavy Art.—*M.M.*
Hills, E., Pte., R.W.S. Regt.—*M.M.*, 13 Feb., '18.
Hocken, Charles, P.O., R.N.—*D.S.M.*, 14-15 Mar., '15.
Holder, E. P., 2/Lt., H.A.C.—*Ment. in despatches*, May, '17.
Holloway, W. S., Lt., R.F.A.—*M.C.*
Holman, R., Trench Mortar Bty.—*D.C.M.*
Holt, Walter James, 2/Lt., R.G.A.—*M.M.*, 21 Aug., '17.
*Hornsby, Ernest Richard.—*M.M.*
Houlder, H. F., Sgt., R.A.M.C.—*M.M.*
Howlett, H. E., Pte., R.W.S. Regt.—*M.M.*, 7 Jun., '17, & *bar*.
Hubbard, Harold, Coy. Sgt. Maj.—*M.M.*
Huggett, Percy, Pte., E. Sur. Regt.—*D.C.M.*, 15 Sept., '15.
Hughes, H. F., Lond. Regt.—*D.C.M.*
Hughes, Harold, Lt., 83 Bde., R.F.A.—*Ment. in despatches.*
Hulett, Frederick William John, Sgt., M.G.C.—*M.M.*, Jul., '16. (Plate XIV., 4).
Humphrey, Frank, Pte., 9 Corps Cyclists Btn.—*M.M.*
Hurley, Patrick, Leading Signalman, R.N.—*D.S.M.*, Apr., '18.
Hurst, A., L/Cpl., M.G.C.—*M.M.*
Hurst, Sidney, Sgt., R.W.S. Regt.—*Medaille Militaire* (*French*), Jul., '18.
Hutchings, George.—*M.M.*
*Ingrams, Frank Ridley, Capt., 9 E. Sur. Regt.—*Ment. in despatches*, '16, *M.C.*, Sept., '16.
*Innes, J. S. D'A., Lt., R.F.A.—*M.C.*
Insall, G. S. M., 2/Lt., R.F.C.—*V.C.*, 7 Nov., '15.
Ireson, F., R. Fus.—*M.M.*
Jackson, Elvin, Wilts. Regt.—*M.M.*, 18 Oct., '16.
Jackson, Tom E., 2/Lt., Trench Mortar Bty.—*M.C.*, May, '17.
Jarrett, Charles Bernard, Asst.-Paymaster, R.N.V.R.—*Ment. in despatches.*
Johnson, A. E., Sgt., R.W.S. Regt.—*D.C.M.*, Jan., '17, *M.M.*, 9 Oct., '17, & *bar*, 20 Nov., '17.
*Johnson, Frederick Henry, Maj., R.E.—*V.C.*, 25 Sept., '15.
Johnson, Harold, Capt., E. Lancs. Regt.—*M.C.*
Johnson, Reginald Sidney, Capt., D.L.I.—*M.C.*
Jones, G. T., Sgt., Suff. Regt.—*M.M.*
*Jones, Percival Halley –, Capt., E. Sur. Regt.—*M.C.*
Jordan, George, Pte., R.A.M.C.—*M.M.*
Jupp, A. H., Sapper, R.E.—*M.M.*, Mar., '18.
Keating, Harold Ledger, Lt., R.G.A.—*M.C.*
Keen, R., Pte.—*M.M.*
Kendall, William John C., 2/Lt., 12 L. Fus.—*M.C.*, 16 Sept., '17.
Kennedy, William Nicol Watson, Maj., R.A.M.C.—*O.B.E.*
Kerckhove, Herbert Vincent, Lt., 9 E. Sur. Regt.—*M.C.*, '18.
*Kidd, Claude Bernard, Capt., Cheshire Regt.—*M.C.*
Kirby, H. McK–., Capt., R.A.O.C.—*D.C.M.*
*Knight, N. Q., Sgt., Lond. Regt.—*M.M.*, & *bar*.
*Kurten, Gaston P., 2/Lt. (Act.-Maj.), R.G.A.—*Ment. in despatches*, Nov., '17.
Kurten, J. A., R.G.A.—*M.C.*
Kyngdom, Leslie Herbert, Col., Aust. Garr. Art.—*Ment. in despatches.*
Laing, Robert G., Pte., 2/3 Lond. Field Amb.—*M.M.*

NAVAL AND MILITARY HONOURS 429

*LANDYMORE, FREDERICK, Pte., E. Sur. Regt.—*M.M.*, '17.
*LANGDALE, EDWARD GEORGE, Capt., 5 Leicester Regt.—*Ment. in despatches.*
*LARKING, RONALD GUY, Capt., R.E.— *M.C.*, '16, & bar, '17.
*LAWRENCE, ROBERT REGINALD, Lt., R.N.V.R.—*Ment. in despatches,* '16.
LEDBETTER, WILLIAM, Sapper, R.E. (Sig. Serv.).—*M.M.*, '17.
LEE, –, Reg. Sgt. Maj., R.G.A.—*M.S.M., Croix de Guerre (Belgian).*
LEE, ARTHUR HERBERT, Lt., Lond. Electrical Engineers (R.E.).—*Ment. in despatches,* '18, *M.C.*, 19 Sept., '18.
LEE, JOHN HANSANT, 2/Lt. (Act.-Capt.), Yorks. Regt.—*M.C.*, 15-16 Jun., '17.
LEEDS, W. A., E. Sur. Regt.—*M.M.*
LEWIS, A. H., Sgt., R.G.A.—*M.M.*, 24 Apr., '18.
LEWIS, GWILYM H., Lt., Northants. Regt. (attd. R.A.F.).—*D.F.C.* (Plate XVII., 2).
*LIBBY, FRANK THOMAS, Sgt., L.R.B.—*M.M.*, 20 Sept., '17. (Plate XX., 4).
LINDSALL, LEO, Pte., Lond. Regt.—*M.M.*
LINSEY, FRED J., Driver, R.W.S. Regt.—*M.M.*
*LLOYD, EDWARD STANLEY, Lt., R.F.A.—*M.C.*
LONGBOTTOM, ERNEST, Cpl., R.F.A.—*M.M.*, 28 Mar., '18.
LONGHURST, C. R., Pioneer, R.E.—*M.S.M.*, Apr., '18.
LOVETT, ALFRED CROWDY, Brig.-Gen.—*Ment. in despatches, C.B.*, 8 Oct., '14.
LYNCH, ROBERT GREENWOOD KINGSTON-, R.E.—*M.M.*, Apr., '18.
MACDONALD, A., L/Cpl., 7 R.W. Kent Regt.—*M.M.*, 17 Jul., '17.
McGILL, PETER, M.G.C.—*Ment. in despatches* (twice), *D.C.M.*
McGUIRE, A., R.E. (23 Sig. Coy.).—*M.M.*
MACKMIN, HENRY AUGUSTUS, Sgt., R.E.—*Ment. in despatches*, Jan., '19.
MACKRIELL, E. S., Sgt.—*D.C.M.*
*MANN, G. W., Capt. (Act.-Maj.), M.G.C. (Heavy).—*Ment. in despatches* (twice).
MANNING, G., Lt.—*M.C.*
MARCH, G., M.G.C.—*Croix de Guerre.*
MARJORAM, ALBERT JOHN, Cpl., K.R.R.C.—*D.C.M.*
MARSHALL, MARY DEVAS, F.A.N.Y.—*M.M.*
MARTIN, G. W., R.F.A.—*M.M.*, Nov., '17.
MARTIN, HEREWARD KEITH, R.E. (Sig. Coy.).—*Ment. in despatches, Croix de Guerre (French)*, Apr., '18.
MATTHEWS, G., Sgt., Middlesex Regt.—*M.M.*, 23 May, '17.
MAY, J. H., Coy. Sgt. Maj.—*D.S.M.*, 20 Apr., '15.
MAYNARD, CHARLES CLARKSON MARTIN, Brig.-Gen., 19 Bde.—*Ment. in despatches* (twice).
MENZIES, JOHN, Capt., R.A.M.C.—*M.C.*
MICHELMERE, E., Maj., Can. Exp. Force.—*M.C.*
MIDDLETON, ROY, Capt., Civil Serv. Rif.—*M.C.*
MILLER, G. W., S4/242031, S/Sgt., R.A.S.C.—*M.S.M.*, 3 Jun., '19.
MILLIGAN, JOHN S., Coy. Sgt. Maj.—*Ment. in despatches*, '18.
MILLS, CHARLES WILLIAM, Pte., 2 R.W.S. Regt.—*D.C.M., Order of St. George (Russian).*
MILLS, GEORGE P., Lt.-Col., Beds. Regt.—*Ment. in despatches*, '16, *D.S.O.*, May, '17.
MITCHELL, C. F., 275094, Sgt., R.G.A.—*M.M.*
*MITCHELL, ERIK HARRISON, Capt , attd. R.F.C.—*Ment. in despatches, M.C.*
MOBBS, CHARLES JOSEPH TRYMAN, Sgt., R.E.—*D.C.M.*, Sept., '16.
MONTEMBAULT, MAX J. MARC, 2/Lt., R.F.C.—*M.C.*
MOORE, W., Pte.—*Ment. in despatches.*
*MORANT, GERALD A., Capt., W. Yorks. Regt.—*M.C.*

MORGAN, ARTHUR SIDNEY, R.W.S. Regt.—*M.M.*, Oct., '18.
MORGAN, S., L/Cpl., 9 D.L.I.—*M.M.*, *Croix de Guerre avec Palme (French)*, Jul., '18.
MORGAN, STANLEY HERBERT, Maj., R.E.—*Croix de Guerre (Belgian)*, Apr., '18, O.B.E., Jan., '19, *Ment. in despatches*, Mar., '19.
MORGAN, WILLIAM HENRY, Maj., R.E.—*D.S.O.*, '17, *Ment. in despatches*, Jan., Apr., Jun., Dec., '17, & Jan., '19.
MORRIS, HAROLD, Pte., Gordon H.—*M.M.*, Aug., '18.
MOSS, -, Coy. Sgt. Maj., R.E.—*M.S.M.*
MOSS, J. L., Pte.—*M.M.*, 26 Mar., '17.
MOTT, C. W., Sgt., R.F.A.—*M.M.*
MOUNSEY, ROLAND J., Flight Cmdr., R.F.C.—*Croix de Guerre (French)*.
MUGFORD, JAMES SEARLE, Sgt., 18 M.G.C.—*Ment. in despatches*, Jan., '19. (Plate XX., 3).
MUIR, -, R.F.A.—*M.M.*
MULLEY, REGINALD, Cpl., R. Fus.—*M.M.*, 25 Aug., '18.
MUNTON, H. MUNTON BAKER-, Lt., R.F.A.—*M.C.*
NEWBERRY, FRANK, L/Cpl., Som. L.I.—*D.C.M.*
NEWMAN, ARTHUR JOHN, L/Cpl., 2 E. Kent Regt.—*D.C.M.*, 6 Mar., '16.
NEWPORT, CHARLES JOHNSTON, Capt. (G.S.O.).—*Ment. in despatches*, Jan. & Sept., '16.
NORMAN, CHARLES, R. Suss. Regt.—*M.M.*, Aug., '17.
NOTTRIDGE, WALTER H., Lancs. Fus.—*M.M.*, '18.
OGDEN, GORDON, R.F.A.—*M.C.*
O'LEARY, JOHN HENRY, R.E. (Sig. Serv.).—*M.M.*, '18.
O'MARA, LAWRENCE JOSEPH, Pte., R.W.S. Regt.—*M.M.*
ONGLEY, J., Sgt., R.F.A.—*D.C.M.*, 26 Sept., '17.
OSWALD, K. A., Maj., (Act.-Lt.-Col.), R.W.S. Regt.—*D.S.O.*
OVERTON, W.—*D.C.M.*
PALMER, F., Bdr., R. Art.—*Croix de Guerre*.
*PATEMAN, HENRY LEWIS, 2/Lt., R.F.C.—*Croix de Guerre (French)*.
PATERSON, A. K.—*M.M.*
*PAUL, W., Capt. & Adj., W. Yorks. Regt.—*M.C.*
PEARCE, ARTHUR CHARLES, Cpl., R.E.—*M.M.*, 10 Apr., '17.
PEARCE, SIDNEY, Coy. Sgt. Maj., Wilts. Regt.—*D.C.M.*, *M.M.*
PEARSON, J. M., Capt., R.N.—*D.S.C.*, Apr., '17.
PECKHAM, H.—*M.M.*
PEIRCE, HAROLD ERNEST, Sgt., 11 R.W.S Regt.—*Ment. in despatches*, '17, *M.S.M.*
PENNELLS, SIDNEY GILBERT, Coy. Q. M. S., 7 R.W.S. Regt.—*Ment. in despatches*, 23 May, '18.
PERFECT, ERNEST EDWARD, Pte., 2 R.W.S. Regt.—*D.C.M.*, 20 Oct., '14. (Plate XXV., 1).
*PERKINS, JAMES PHILLIP, L/Cpl., R. Suss. Regt.—*M.M.*, '17.
PERRY, ERNEST MIDDLETON, Maj., A.V.C.—*Ment. in despatches*, Jan., '16.
*PETRIE, ARTHUR H., 2/Lt., E. Sur. Regt. (attd. T.M.B.).—*Ment. in despatches*, May, '17.
*PHILLIPS, BERT E., Sgt., R.W.S. Regt.—*D.C.M.*
PHILLIPS, PERCY PRICE, Maj., 5 N. Fus.—*Ment. in despatches*, Jun., '16.
*PICKERING, WALTER, Sgt., 1 R.W.S. Regt.—*M.M*
PIERCE, JOHN WALTER, R.W. Fus.—*M.M.*
PIKE, KENNETH TWYNEHAM, Lt., M.G.C.—*M.C.*
PINCHEN, S. H., Leading Gunlayer, R.N.A.S.—*D.S.M.*, *Croix de Guerre (French)*, 14 Apr., '17.
PLATT, ARTHUR THEODORE, Capt., Imp. Gen. Staff.—*Ment. in despatches*.
PLATT, PERCY FREDERICK, R.W.S. Regt.—*D.C.M.*
PLOWMAN, T.—*D.C.M.*
PLUMBRIDGE, -, L/Cpl., R.E.—*M.M.*
POLHILL, ARCHIBALD STANFORD, 2/Lt., Middlesex Regt.—*M.C.*, Sept. '18.

NAVAL AND MILITARY HONOURS 431

POLHILL, OWEN CHARLES, 2/Lt., R. Fus.—*M.C.*
POLLARD, CECIL, Sgt.—*M.M.*
POOLE, H., Bdr., R.F.A.—*M.S.M.*, *Italian Bronze Med.*, 2 May, '18.
*PRAGNALL, GEORGE, Capt. (Gen. Staff Offr.).—*D.S.O.*
PRATT, PERCY FREDERICK, Sgt., R.W.S. Regt.—*D.C.M.*, 1 Jul., '16.
PRICE, ERNEST STANLEY, Sgt., R.E.—*D.C.M.*, 22 Sept., '18, *M.M.*, '17, & bar.
PRING, BERNARD VINCENT, Capt., 2 K.O.Y.L.I.—*D.S.O.*, *M.C.*, & *bar*, *Ment. in despatches.*
PROUT, HAROLD, Lt., R.A.F.—*Air Force Cross.*
PROUT, REGINALD ADDENBROOKE, Maj., R.A.F.—*O.B.E.*, *M.C.*, *Chevalier du Legion d'Honneur.*
PRYER, H. J., Pte., R.W.S. Regt.—*M.M.*
PRYKE, CHARLES WALTER, Pte., R.W.S. Regt.—*M.M.*
RABY, NIGEL STEPHENS VANNECK, 2/Lt., R. Berks. Regt. (attd. 1 Nigeria Regt.).—*M.C.*, 16 Oct., '17.
RANDALL, D. E., Lond. Regt.—*M.M.*
RANDALL, W. E., 8161, Sgt., Wilts. Regt.—*M.M.*
RANDOLPH, HARRY B., Lt., R.F.A.—*Ment. in despatches*, May, '17.
RATTI, ROBERT J., A.P.C.—*M.M.*
RAVENSCROFT, E., Sgt., E. Kent. Regt—*M.M.*
RAVENSCROFT, F., E. Kent Regt.—*M.M.*
READ, W.—*M.C.*
REID, CHARLES H., Capt., 5 Drag. Gds.—*M.C.*
REID, F. C., R.W.S. Regt.—*M.M.*, 4 Oct., '17.
RICE, CECIL, Capt.—*Ment. in despatches*, Dec., '18.
RICH, E. J., Pte., Suff. Regt.—*M.M.*, 21 Oct., '16.
*RICHARDSON, HECTOR LAWRENCE, Rflmn., 9 R.B.—*M.M.*, 8 Sept., '16.
RICHARDSON, J. O., Pte., R.W.S. Regt.—*D.C.M.*
*RICHARDSON, THOMAS CHARLES, Maj., R.E.—*Ment. in despatches* (twice), *M.C.*
RING, MICHAEL HENRY, R.A.O.C.—*M.M.*
*RITCHINGS, ARTHUR WILLIAM, 2/Lt.—*M.M.*, 7 Jun., '17.
ROBERTS, NORMAN LATIMER, Lt., R F.A.—*M.C.*
RODGER, WILLIAM MALCOLM, Cpl., 2 Lond. Scottish.—*Croix de Guerre (Belgian).*
*ROSS, THOMAS HESKETH, S. Afr. Inf.—*M.C.*
*ROUTLEY, ERNEST GEORGE, 2/Lt., 6 E. Kent Regt.—*M.C.*, Aug., '16.
RUMSEY, W. M., Cpl., R.A.F.—*M.M.*
RUSSELL, EDWARD POWYS COLIN, Lt., Ind. Army—*D.C.M.*, Jan., '16.
RUTTER, H. A., Sgt., R.G.A.—*Croix de Guerre (Belgian).*
*RYAN, ALFRED ERIC, Capt., R.W.S. Regt.—*Ment. in despatches*, Dec., '17, *M.C.*, Jan., '17. (Plate XXIV., 6).
SAGEMAN, WILLIAM EDMUND, Coy. Sgt. Maj., 1 R.W.S. Regt.—*M.S.M.*, Jul., '19.
SAUNDERS, ERNEST JAMES, Trooper, Sur. Yeom.—*M.M.*, Apr., '17.
SCOTT, H. E.—*M.M.*
SECKER, WALTER.—*M.M.*
SEIGNE, L. J. R., 95869, Pte., 10 R. Fus. (attd. 1 Intelligence Corps Coy.).—*M.S.M.*, Jun., '19.
*SELBY, WILLIAM, Lt.-Col.—*V.C.* (in '97), *D.S.O.*
SELWAY, G. A., Aust. I.F.—*D.C.M.*
SHAXSON, ERIC, Lt., R.F.A.—*M.C.*
SHELLARD, REGGIE S., Cpl., 1 Sur. Rif.—*D.C.M.*
SHEPPARD, G. E., Cpl., R.A.S.C.—*M.M.*
*SHORT, T. W., Pte., Cambs. Regt.—*M.M.*, Jul., '17.
*SIMMONDS, ERNEST EDWARD, Sgt., R.E.—*D.C.M.*, Sept., '16.
SIMMONS, H. W., 13142, 4 S.W.B.—*D.C.M.*
SIMPSON, J. E., M.G.C.—*D.C.M.*

SINCLAIR, J. K., Cpl., R. Fus.—*M.M.*
SINEY, J. J., Sgt., M.G.C.—*Croix de Guerre (French)*, 10 Oct., '18.
SKINNER, H. E., Cpl., R.E.—*M.M.*
*SKITTERAL, B. T., Sgt., R.W.S. Regt.—*D.C.M.*, Jun., '17, *M.M.*
SMITH, A. E. Stanley, Lt.—*M.C.*
*SMITH, ARTHUR DONALD THORNTON, Capt., K.R.R.C.—*D.S.O*, May, '17.
SMITH, ARTHUR GEORGE, Cpl., R.W.S. Regt.—*M.M.*, Jun., '17.
SMITH, C. H., Sgt., R.W.S. Regt.—*M.M.*
SMITH, STANLEY, Lt.—*M.C.*
SMITH, W. A., R.E.—*M.M.*, 4 Sept., '18.
*STACEY, GERALD ARTHUR, Maj., Lond. Regt.—*D.S.O.*
*STEEL, DOUGLAS G., Capt., 3 Suff. Regt.—*M.C.*
*STEVENS, F. G., Lt., R.W.S. Regt.—*M.M.*, '16.
*STEWART, DOUGLAS ALEXANDER, 2/Lt., Cheshire Regt.—*D.C.M.*, Jul.,'15, *Russian Med. of St. George (4th class).*
STICKLEY, LAWRENCE ALFRED, Sgt., 18 Aust. I.F.—*M.M.*, 27 Jun., '16.
*STOCKER, GERALD, Cpl., R.W.S. Regt.—*M.M.*, '17.
*STONEHAM, REGINALD P., Lt., 1 Notts. & Derby. Regt.—*D.C.M.*
*STREETER, ALFRED W., Sgt., R.E.—*M.M.*
STREETER, JAMES CHARLES, Coy. Sgt. Maj., 2 Border Regt.—*D.C.M.*, 25 Sept., '15.
STUART, DOUGLAS, Capt., R.F.A.—*M.C.*
SYKES, BARTON VALENTINE, 1st cl. Wireless Operator, R.N.R.—*Russian Silver Med.*, Feb.-May, '15.
*TAGG, HAROLD ARTHUR, 2/Lt., Middlesex Regt.—*Ment. in despatches.*
TAYLOR, ALFRED, Signaller, 11 Bty., R.H.A.—*M.M.*, 14 May, '15. (Plate XXXI., 6).
TAYLOR, HAROLD, Lt., R.A.F.—*M.C.*, 16 Aug., '17. (Plate XXVII., 2).
TAYLOR, ROBERT ALLEN GRANT, Capt., 1 R. Scots Fus.—*Ment. in despatches*, Jan., '16.
TEDDER, ARTHUR W., Maj., R.F.C.—*Ment. in despatches, Italian Silver Med.*, Apr., '17.
*THACKER, HERBERT LANE, 2/Lt., R.A.S.C.—*M.M., M.C.*
THEEDON, GEORGE, Norf. Regt.—*D.C.M.*
THIES, W. H., Sgt.—*D.C.M.*
THORN, T. C.—*M.M.*
TITMAS, JOHN FRANCIS, Lt., R.F.C.—*Ment. in despatches.*
TOBITT, J. E., Pte., H.A.C.—*M.S.M.*, Siberia, 20 Jan., '20.
TONKIN, S., Cpl., H.A.C.—*M.M.*
TOOGOOD, H. W.—*M.M.*
TOTTERDELL, H. P., Sgt., R.E.—*M.S.M.*
TUCKEY, C., Sgt., R.E.—*M.S.M.*
TURNER, ALFRED EDWIN, Pte., 7 E. Sur. Regt.—*D.C.M.*
*TYLER, EDWARD VICTOR, Pte., R.W.S. Regt.—*M.M.*, Jul., '16. (Plate XXVIII., 6).
UFFINDELL, -, Cpl., Seaforth H.—*M.M.*
UNWIN, L. P., Act.-Sgt., R.A.M.C.—*M.S.M.*
UNWIN, PHILIP T. F., Capt., R.E.—*Ment. in despatches*, May, '17.
VAUCOUR, AUDRY MORRIS, 2/Lt., R.F.C.—*M.C.*
WAIGHT, ALBERT EDWARD, S/Sgt., R.A.M.C.—*M.S.M.* & bar.
WALKER, G. A., Pte., R.E.—*D.C.M.*
WALLIS, ARTHUR STANLEY, Sgt., 28 Lond. Regt.—*Ment. in despatches*, Jan., '16.
*WALTER, JOSEPH STANLEY, Capt., 7 R.W.S. Regt.—*M.C.*, 20 Oct., '16.
WARD, RUFUS, Sgt., M.G.C.—*Ment. in despatches (thrice)*, *D.C.M.*
*WAREHAM, STANLEY B., Cpl., Can. F. Art.—*M.M.*
WATERIDGE, W. S., L/Cpl., Tank C.—*M.M.*, 3 May, '17.
WAYTE, JOHN WOOLLASTON, Capt., R.A.M.C.—*M.C.*, Oct., '16.

NAVAL AND MILITARY HONOURS 433

*WAYTE, SAMUEL WILFRID, 2/Lt., R.F.A.—*M.C.*, Sep., '17.
WEST, ALFRED, 2/Lt., R.W.S. Regt.—*M.C.*, Jul., '16. (Plate I., 2).
*WESTON, FREDERIC GEORGE, Coy. Sgt. Maj., Q.W. Rif.—*Ment. in despatches.*
*WHISSON, WILLIAM HENRY, Lt., Middlesex Regt.—*M.C.*
*WHITE, ARTHUR BRYAN, Capt., 1 L.R.B.—*Ment. in despatches*, Apr., '17.
WHITE, D. T., Pte., Middlesex Regt.—*M.M.*, 21 Dec., '17.
WHITE, EDWARD JOHN HENRY, 16264, L/Cpl., M.G.C.—*D.C.M.* (Plate XXXIV., 6).
*WHITE, WALTER WILLIAM, Coy. Sgt. Maj., 9 E. Sur. Regt.—*M.M.*, May, '16.
WHITING, H. R., Act.-Sgt., R.E.—*M.S.M.*
*WHITTEN, F. R., Capt., R.E.—*M.C.*
WHITTLE, A., L/Cpl., 1 R.W.S. Regt.—*M.M.*, Jan., '18.
WIEBKIN, HENRY WILLIAM, Maj. (D.A.Q.M.G.).—*M.C.*, Feb., '17, *Croix de Guerre (Belgian)*, Mar., '18.
WILDING, HARRY, Sgt., M.G.C.—*M.M.*
WILKIE, JAMES, Lt., M.G.C.—*Ment. in despatches* (twice).
*WILKINS, HOWARD MORRIS, Sgt., City of Lond. Yeom.—*Ment. in despatches.*
*WILKINSON, JOHN H., Sgt., Leinster (R.Can.) Regt.—*Ment. in despatches* (twice).
WILLIAMS, ALFRED DALBY, Capt., R.G.A.—*Croix de Guerre (Belgian)*.
WILLIAMS, ALFRED EDWIN, Capt. & Q.M., 2/17 Lond. Regt.—*Ment. in despatches*, 18 Jan., '18, *D.C.M.* (in '02), *O.B.E.*, 3 Jun., '19. (Plate XXXII., 1).
WILLIAMS, F. J., Sapper, R.E.—*M.S.M.*
WILLIAMS, HAROLD, Lt., R.E.—*O.B.E.*
WILLIAMS, HERBERT OWEN, Pte., 2 R.W.S. Regt.—*D.C.M.*, May, '15.
*WILLIAMS, MONTGOMERY, Capt., R.M.A.—*Ment. in despatches* (twice).
WILLIAMS, S., Lond. Regt.—*Ment. in despatches.*
WILLIAMS, TOM GODWIN, Sgt., R.E.—*M.M.*
*WILLIAMSON, EDGAR ROWE, Lt., Lond. Regt.—*M.C.*, 1 Jul., '16.
WILSON, CYRIL EDWIN, Sgt., R.A.S.C.—*Serbian Silver Med.*
WOOD, HARRY WILLIAM, L/Cpl., R.W. Kent Regt.—*M.M.*, 7 Oct., '16.
*WOOD, HENRY GEORGE WESTMORELAND, Capt., Worcester. Regt.— *D.S.O.*, 15 Jun., '18.
WOOLNOUGH, GEORGE, Pte., R.W.S. Regt.—*M.M.*
WOOLNOUGH, THOMAS, Sgt., R.E.—*D.C.M.*
WORDLEY, ERIC, Capt., R.A.M.C.—*M.C.*
WORTLEY, JOHN HAROLD, Sgt., 1 L.R.B.—*D.C.M.*, 1 Jan., '17. (Plate XXXIII., 4).
WRIGHT, RICHARD, Capt., R.G.A.—*M.C.*
WYETH, F. J. S., Capt., 10 Essex Regt.—*M.C.*
WYNDHAM, GERALD HEREFORD SAXE-, Capt., 8 R.W.S. Regt. (attd. 72 T.M.B.).—*M.C.*, 2 Sept., '16. (Plate XXXV., 6).
WYNN, JOSEPH, Sgt. R. Fus.—*M.M.*
YEATES, F. E., Sgt., R.F.A.—*D.C.M.*
YOUNG, ARCHIBALD FORD, Maj., R.E.—*D.S.O. & bar, Order of the Nile.*

III. Returned Prisoners of War*

"I'll yield myself to prison willingly, or unto death, to do my country good."
Shakespeare : *2 Henry VI.*, *Act 4, Scene 9.*

ADAMS, H. H., Pte.,
  19 Eland Rd.
AITON, F. C., Pte.,
  74 Watcombe Rd., S.N.
ALEXANDER, G., Pte.,
  21 Dunbar Av., Norbury.
ALLERY, F., Pte.,
  3 Amersham Rd.
ANDERTON, J., Pte.,
  1 Waterworks Yard.
ATKINSON, P., Pte.,
  12 Talbot Rd., T. Heath.
BALLARD, B. E., Rflmn.,
  1 Lucerne Rd., T. Heath.
BANCE, H., Pte.,
  15 Selhurst New Rd.
BARHAM, Pte.,
  5 Neville Rd.
BARKER, STANLEY,
  24 Chatsworth Rd.
BARNES, W., Sgt.,
  133 Bensham Lane, T. Heath.
BATCHELOR, Pte.,
  55 Queen's Rd.
BEADLE, F. E., Rflmn.,
  35 Donald Rd.
BELAM, F. A., Pte.,
  61 Clarendon Rd.
BENNETT, G., Pte.,
  95 Waddon Rd.
BENSLEY, Cpl.,
  9 Woodville Rd.
BERNELL, G., Pte.,
  95 Waddon Rd.
BETTS, W., Pte.
BIDDLE, Pte.,
  73 Clifton Rd., S.N.
BIRCH, Pte.,
  7 Canterbury Rd.
BLAKESBY, H. J., Pte.,
  8 Milner Rd., T. Heath.
BLOOMFIELD, D., Pte.,
  80 Selsdon Rd.
BOOTH, E. T., Pte.,
  6 Pridham Rd., T. Heath.
BOWYER, Pte.,
  32 Sumner Rd.

BRIGGS, WILLIAM, Pte.,
  18 Wentworth Rd.
BROOK, A. E., Pte.,
  56 Silverleigh Rd., T. Heath.
BROOM, Pte.,
  32 Livingstone Rd.
BROUGHTON, A. J., Pte.,
  56 Oakley Rd., S.N.
BUNDLE, LEONARD, Pte.,
  122 Whitehorse Rd.
BURN, Pte.,
  46 Elgin Rd.
BUTCHER, Pte.,
  5 Wellesley Pde., Wellesley Rd.
BYSH, H., Pte.,
  4 Crossland Rd., T. Heath.
CAPEL, A. H., L/Cpl.,
  5 Palmerston Rd.
CARTER, F. W., Rflmn.,
  1 Notson Rd., S.N.
CATES, F., Cpl.,
  c/o Mrs. Cates, 73 Oval Rd.
CHILVER, F., Pte.,
  7 Roberts Yard.
CLARK, B., Pte.,
  54 Derby Rd.
CLIFFORD, J., Pte.,
  61 Cromwell Rd.
CLIVLOW, P., Pte.,
  186 Livingstone Rd., T. Heath.
COLLETT, A. A., Pte.,
  5 Bank Buildings,
    Brighton Rd., Purley.
COLLINS, W., Pte.,
  37 Dennett Rd.
COOMBER, W., Pte.,
  21 Oakwood Rd.
COWDY, A. J., Pte.,
  65 Lodge Rd.
DANIELS, Pte.,
  22 Whitehorse Rd.
DAVIS, H., Cpl.,
  25 Borough Hill.
DEAN, F., Pte.,
  59 Wellesley Rd.
DENIAL, F., Rflmn.,
  149 Moffatt Rd., T. Heath.

* The addresses were given at the time of capture as those of the next-of-kin.

RETURNED PRISONERS OF WAR

DOBINSON, V., Pte.,
  Alwyn Cottages, Shirley.
DONOVAN, P., Pte.,
  11 Hill St., Old Town.
DOWBELL, Pte.,
  230 Gloucester Rd.
DUDLEY, Pte.,
  163 Windmill Rd.
DUNLOP, J., Pte.,
  5 Belmont Rd., S.N.
EASTAUGH, R. W.,
  48 Sydenham Rd. North.
ECOTT, H., Cpl.,
  13 Percy Rd., S.N.
EDWARDS, F. W., Pte.,
  44 Bredon Rd.
EDWARDS, G., Pte.,
  188a Gloucester Rd.
EDWARDS, H. G., Pte.,
  19 Cassland Rd.
EDWARDS, Rev. J. A. L., C.F.,
  South Norwood.
ELPHINCH, W., Pte.
EMBERSON, Sgt.,
  102 Churchill Rd.
ENGLAND, A. G., Cpl.,
  42 Ritchie Rd.
FENTON, A., Pte.,
  35 Harrison's Rise.
FERRIER, A., Cpl.,
  116 Churchill Rd.
FIELD, T., Pte.,
  106 Moffatt Rd., T. Heath.
FILCE, H., junr., Pte.,
  90 Sumner Rd.
FINNIGAN, A. E., L/Cpl.,
  82 Clarendon Rd.
FLETCHER, E., Pte.,
  16 Burdett Rd.
FRANCIS, R., Pte.,
  10 Lahore Rd.
FRIDAY, A., Pte.
FROST, W., Pte.,
  31 Northbrook Rd.
GORE, E. D., Cpl.,
  62 Parsons Mead.
GOSS, T., Pte.,
  c/o Mrs. Foster, Tramways
      Depot, T. Heath.
GREEST, L., Cpl.,
  69 Warren Rd.
GREETHAM, Pte.,
  154 Mitcham Rd.
GRIFFIN, Pte.,
  47 Borough Hill.
GRIFFITHS, E. E. L.,
  63 Whitehorse Rd.
GUE, F. C., Pte.,
  77 Princess Rd.

HADFIELD, W. D., Pte.,
  3 Frant Rd., T. Heath.
HALL, F., Pte.,
  56 Holmesdale Rd., S.N.
HALL, F. J., Pte.,
  152 Holmesdale Rd., S.N.
HALL, H., Pte.,
  22 Priory Rd.
HARMER, Pte.,
  111 Frant Rd., T. Heath.
HARRINGTON, L., Pte.,
  12 Leighton St.
HARRISON, L/Cpl.,
  12 Northcote Rd.
HART, A. S., Pte.,
  85 Boston Rd.
HATFIELD, THOMAS A., Sgt.,
  4 Rose and Crown Cottages,
      Church St.
HATHAWAY, Pte.,
  Town Hall.
HAWKINS, H. E., Sgt.,
  Lyndhurst, Woodside.
HAYDON, A., Pte.,
  30 Donald Rd.
HEARD, H. C., Pte.,
  49 Johnson Rd.
HEATH, A. E., Pte.,
  15 Southsea Rd.
HENRY, M., Pte.,
  133 Morland Rd.
HERBERT, F., Pte.,
  7 Southsea Rd.
HEROLD, J., Pte.,
  20 Crescent Rd., S.N.
HODGES, J. E., Pte.,
  20 Albion Rd.
HOGSDEN, Pte.,
  2 Beddington Terrace,
      Mitcham Rd.
HOULDER., H. F., Sgt., M.M.,
  Cromwell House,
      Duppas Hill Terr.
HULFORD, Pte.,
  88 Waddon New Rd.
HUGGETT, L. A., Pte.,
  31 Cecil Rd.
HUNT, G., Pte.,
  56a Leighton St.
HUNT, J., Pte.,
  56a Leighton St.
HUNT, T. E., Pte.,
  21 Kitchener Rd., T. Heath.
INGHAMS, B. W., Pte.,
  107 Sutherland Rd.
JACKSON, E., Pte.,
  9 Burdett Rd.
JENNINGS, A. C., Pte.,
  46 Waddon New Rd.

436   THE CROYDON ROLL OF HONOUR

KEARN, G. A., Pte.,
  48 Beulah Grove.
KEEN, F. A., Sgt.,
  121 Lebanon Rd.
KEMP, H., Pte.,
  22 Tugela Rd.
KILLICK, C., Pte.,
  61 Donald Rd.
KING, A. G., Pte.,
  113 Old Town.
KING, E. A., Pte.,
  28 Old Town.
KING, F., Pte.,
  13 Thirsk Rd., T. Heath.
KIRBY, V. H., Pte.,
  12 Portland Mans., S.N.
KNIGHT, H., Pte.,
  35 Frith Rd.
KNIGHT, J., Pte.,
  1 Marian Villas,
      Sydenham Rd. N.
KNIGHT, Sgt.,
  53 Abbey Rd.
LAMBERT, Cpl.,
  158 Mitcham Rd.
LARCOMBE, Pte.,
  9 Lambeth Rd.
LEIGH, A. G., Pte.,
  36 Windmill Rd.
LICENCE, C., Pte.,
  62 Pawsons Rd.
LISNEY, J., Pte.,
  9 Westville Rd. [?]
LOCKETT, Pte.,
  65 Oakfield Rd.
MCKENZIE, Pte.,
  10 Winterbourne Terr., T.H.
MCKEOWN, W., Pte.,
  13 Clarendon Rd.
MAGER, Pte.,
  11 Church St.
MARLOW, R., Pte.,
  14 Tamworth Rd.
MASCAL, C., Pte.,
  16 Mayo Rd.
MASSON, G., Pte.,
  22 Tait Rd.
MATTHEWS, G., Pte.,
  43 Gloucester Rd.
MATTHEWS, T., Pte.,
  46 Sanderstead Rd.
MEAD, Pte.,
  12 Walters Rd.
MILLEN, Pte.,
  214 Albert Rd.
MILLS, Cpl.,
  29 Apsley Rd., S.N.
MILLS, F. T., L/Cpl.,
  Municipal House. Pitlake.

MILLS, W., Pte.,
  1 Beaconsfield Rd.
MONCKTON, Pte.,
  50 Jarvis Rd.
MORGAN, C., Pte.,
  95 Waddon Rd.
MORRIS, G., Pte.,
  93 Northwood Rd., T. Heath.
MORRIS, R., Pte.,
  39 Oakfield Rd.
MOTHERSOLE, LEO, Cpl.,
  1 Parson's Mead.
MOUETT, C., Pte.,
  Station Rd.
MUDD, C. F., Sapper,
  133 Alexandra Rd.
MUSTO, F. C., Rflmn.,
  73 Crowther Rd., S.N.
NELMES, A., Pte.,
  60 Strathmore Rd.
NEVIN, H., Pte.,
  159 St. James' Rd.
NORTON, J., Rflmn.,
  202 Gloucester Rd.
OAKLEY, Pte.,
  23 Wandle Rd.
OLIVER, D. C. M., 2/Lt.,
  The Orchards, S. Croydon.
PALMER, E. H., Pte.,
  103 Boston Rd.
PARTRIDGE, E. G., Pte.,
  37 Beechwood Av., T. Heath.
PATCHING, W., Pte.,
  27 Gloucester Rd.
PECKHAM, H. G., Pte.,
  31 Southbridge Rd.
PHIPPS, R. J., Pte.,
  58 Jesmond Rd.
POTTS, L. E., Pte.,
  11 Sylverdale Rd.
PREDDY, A. W. F., Pte.,
  28 Bensham Gr., T. Heath.
PULLEYN, Sgt.,
  54 Ashburton Av.
RANN, W., Pte.,
  26 Sunnybank, S.N.
REIGATE, W. J., L/Cpl.,
  28 Bredon Rd.
RICHES, ARTHUR, Pte.,
  177 St. James' Rd.
RICHES, C., Pte.,
  177 St. James' Rd.
ROBERTS, B., Cpl.,
  1 High St., S N.
SAMSON, W. C., Pte.,
  18 Adelaide St.
SANDFORD, W., Pte.
SAPPIN, Pte.,
  25 Totton Rd., T. Heath.

RETURNED PRISONERS OF WAR

SARTER, L/Cpl.,
9 Amberley Gr.
SEAGRAVE, A. J., Pte.
SEARLE, S., Rflmn.,
127 Northwood Rd.,T.Heath.
SEVERS, F., Pte.,
11 Vincent Rd.
SEVERS, H., Pte.,
11 Vincent Rd.
SHERRINGTON, W. J., Cpl.,
12 Eland Rd.
SHIRVILLE, Pte.,
45 Churchill Rd.
SIMMONDS, G., Pte.,
1 Sanderstead Rd.
SKELTON, A., Pte.,
22 Elm Rd., T. Heath.
SMITH, C. G., Pte.,
40 Alpha Rd.
SMITH, E., Pte.,
47 Sumner Rd.
SMITH, F., Pte.,
29 Totton Rd., T. Heath.
SMITH, H., Sgt.,
87 Dennett Rd.
SMITH, SYDNEY M., Pte.,
34 Cresswell Rd., S.N.
STANFORD, J., Pte.,
12 Alfred Rd., S.N.
STANLEY, P. F., Rflmn.,
22 Percy Rd., S.N.
SULLETT, T., Pte.,
29 Russell Rd.
SWAIN, H., Sgt.,
27 Nova Rd.
SWARFIELD, Sgt.,
18 Westbury Rd.
TANNER, Pte.,
62 London Rd.
TEMPLE, Pte.,
9 Prospect Place.
THOMAS, HAROLD, Pte.,
39 Beaconsfield Rd.

TINSLEY, J., Pte.,
75 Donald Rd.
TURNER, J. H., Pte.,
22 Talbot Rd., T. Heath.
UPTER, J., Sapper.
58 Selhurst New Rd., S.N.
VINCE, F., Pte.,
112 Waddon New Rd.
VINCENT, A. C., Pte.,
29 Station Rd., S.N.
WALLACE, Cpl.,
3 Sussex Rd.
WALTER, V. T., Pte.,
118 Wentworth Rd.
WALTON, Pte.,
3 Buxton Rd., T. Heath.
WASHINGTON, L. C., Pte.,
17 Howberry Rd., T. Heath
WATSON, N., Pte.,
36 Crowther Rd., S.N.
WATSON, W., Pte.
WELLAND, W., Pte.
WEST, C. A., Cpl.,
10 Mead Gr., Parson's Mead.
WEST, W., Pte.,
The Grove, Parson's Mead.
WHITE, Pte.,
65 Wentworth Rd.
WICKS, W., Pte.,
11 Lahore Rd.
WILD, J., Pte.,
43 Mitcham Rd.
WILDY, Sgt.,
49 Hampton Rd.
WINTER, F. W., Pte.,
58 Kynaston Rd., T. Heath.
WOODS, Pte.,
5 Lavering Rd. [?]
WRIGHT, S. H., Cpl.,
34 Grafton Rd.
WYNN, W., Pte.,
2 Priory Rd.

www.ingramcontent.com/pod-product-compliance
Lightning Source LLC
Chambersburg PA
CBHW021953160426
43197CB00007B/121